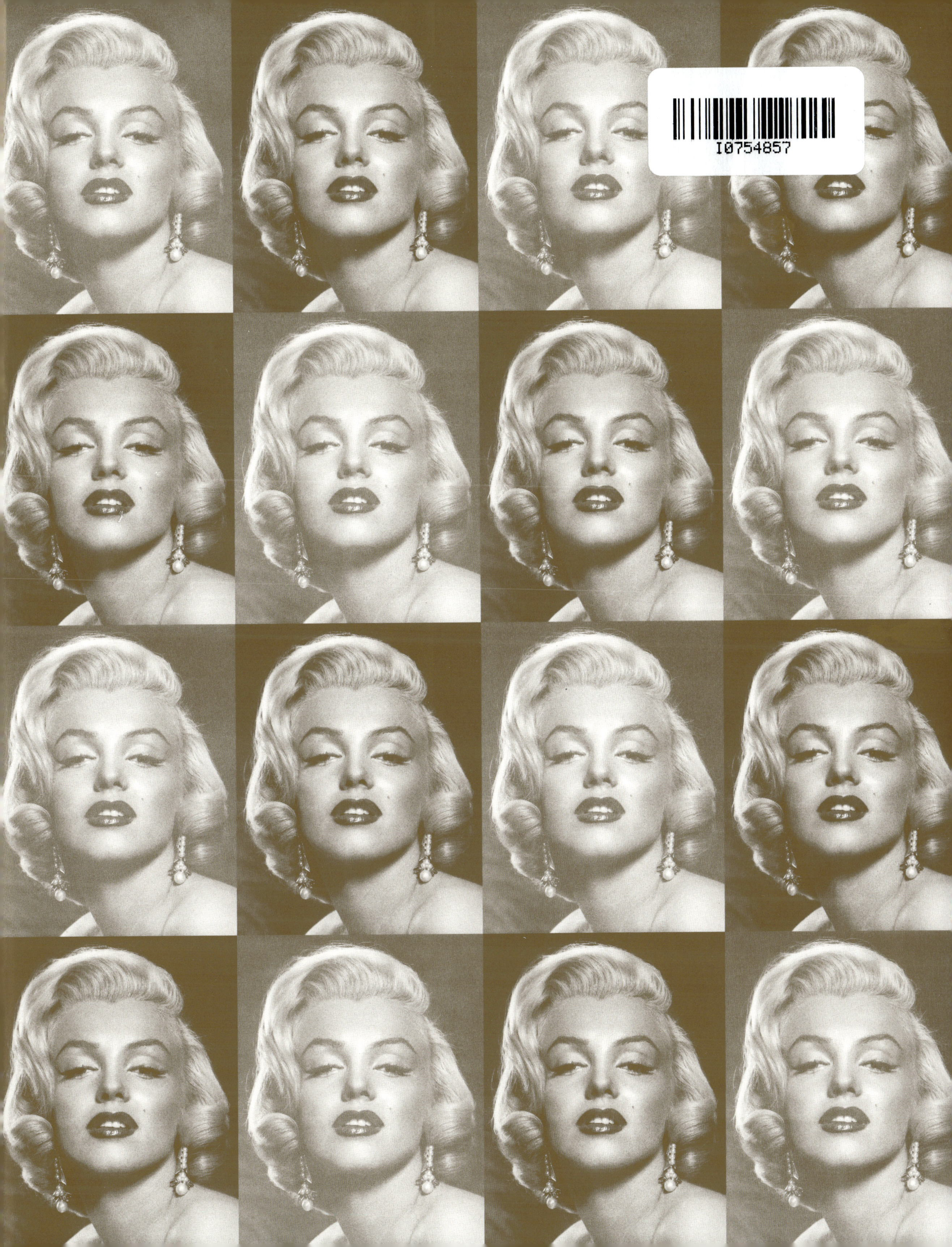

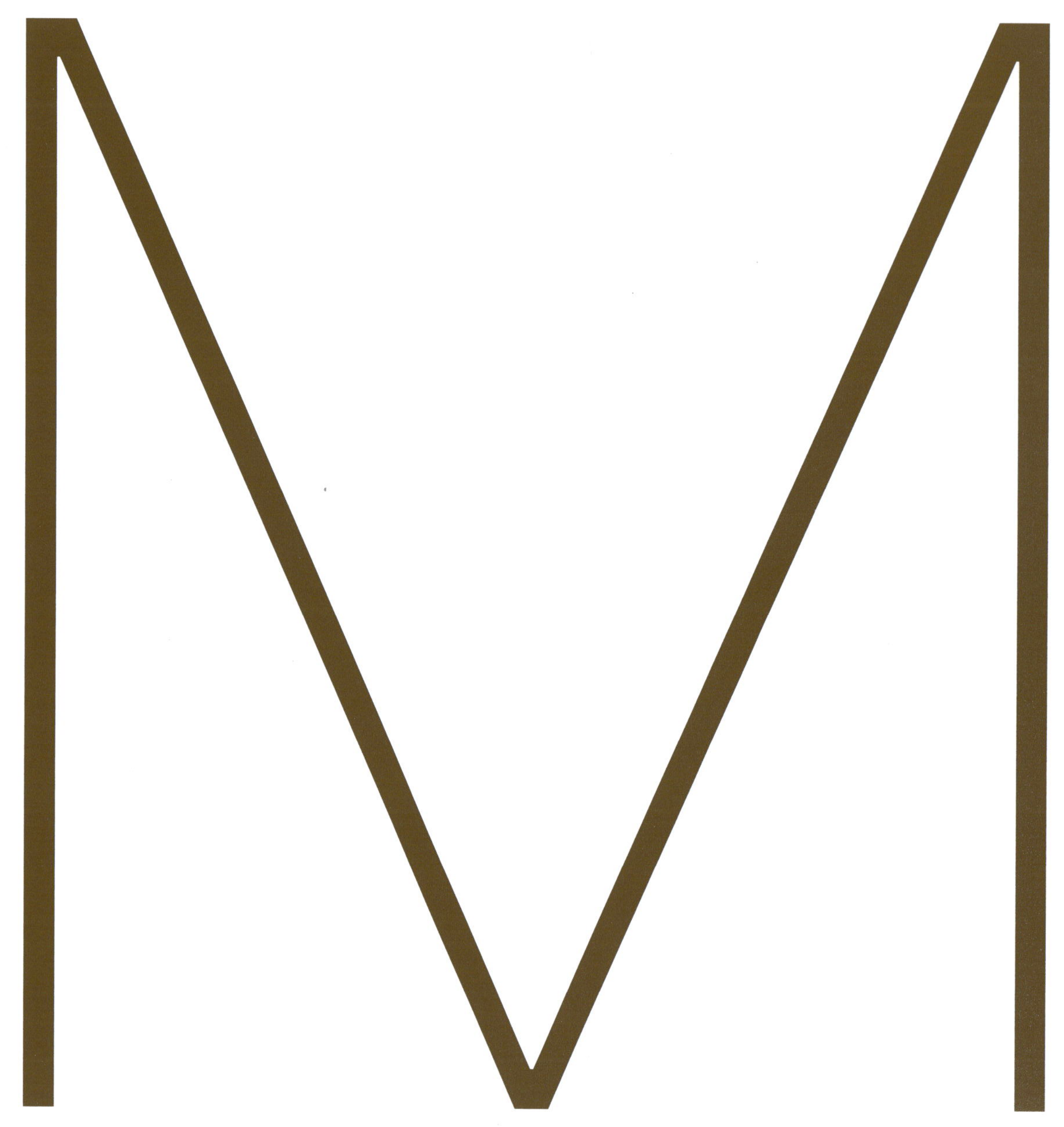

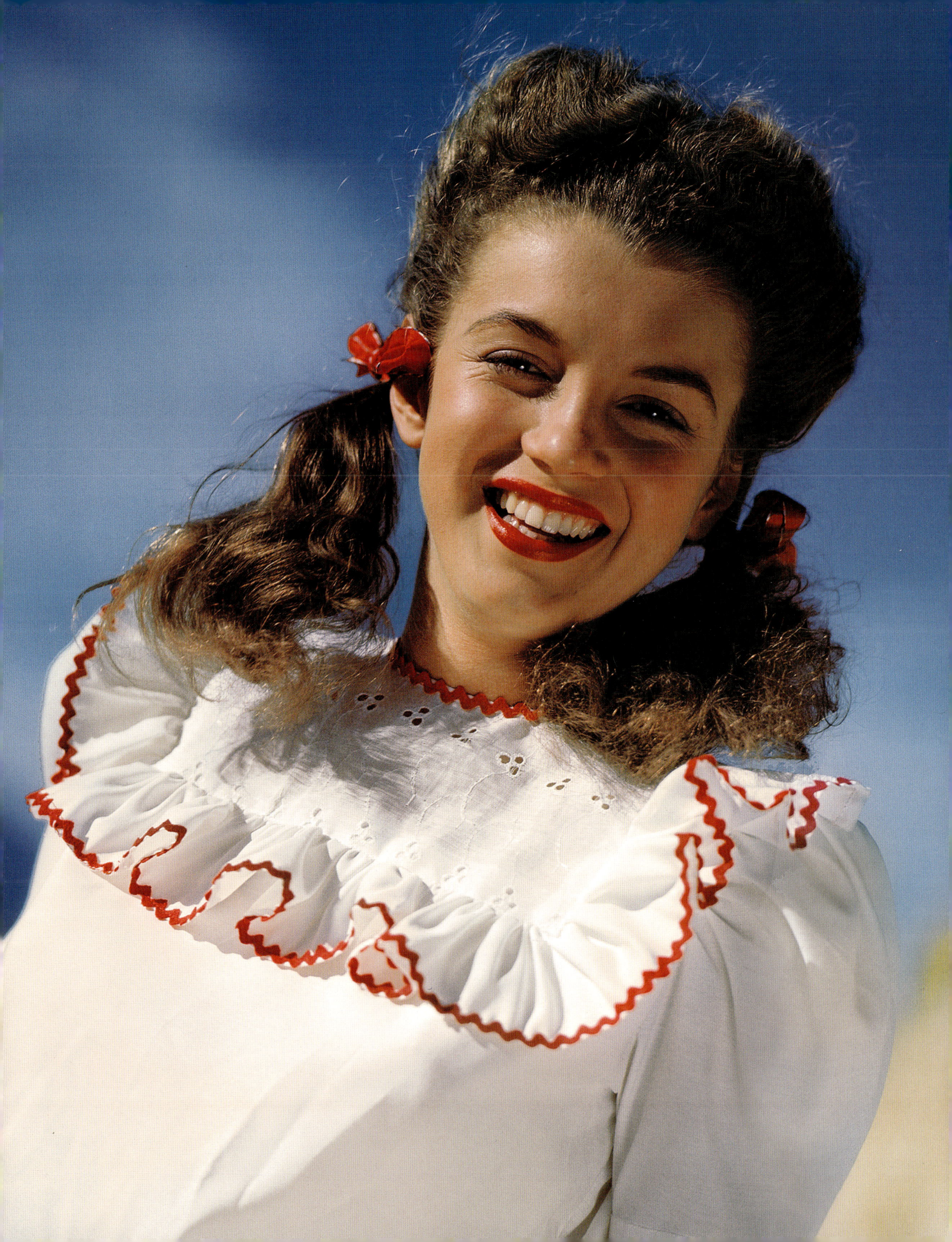

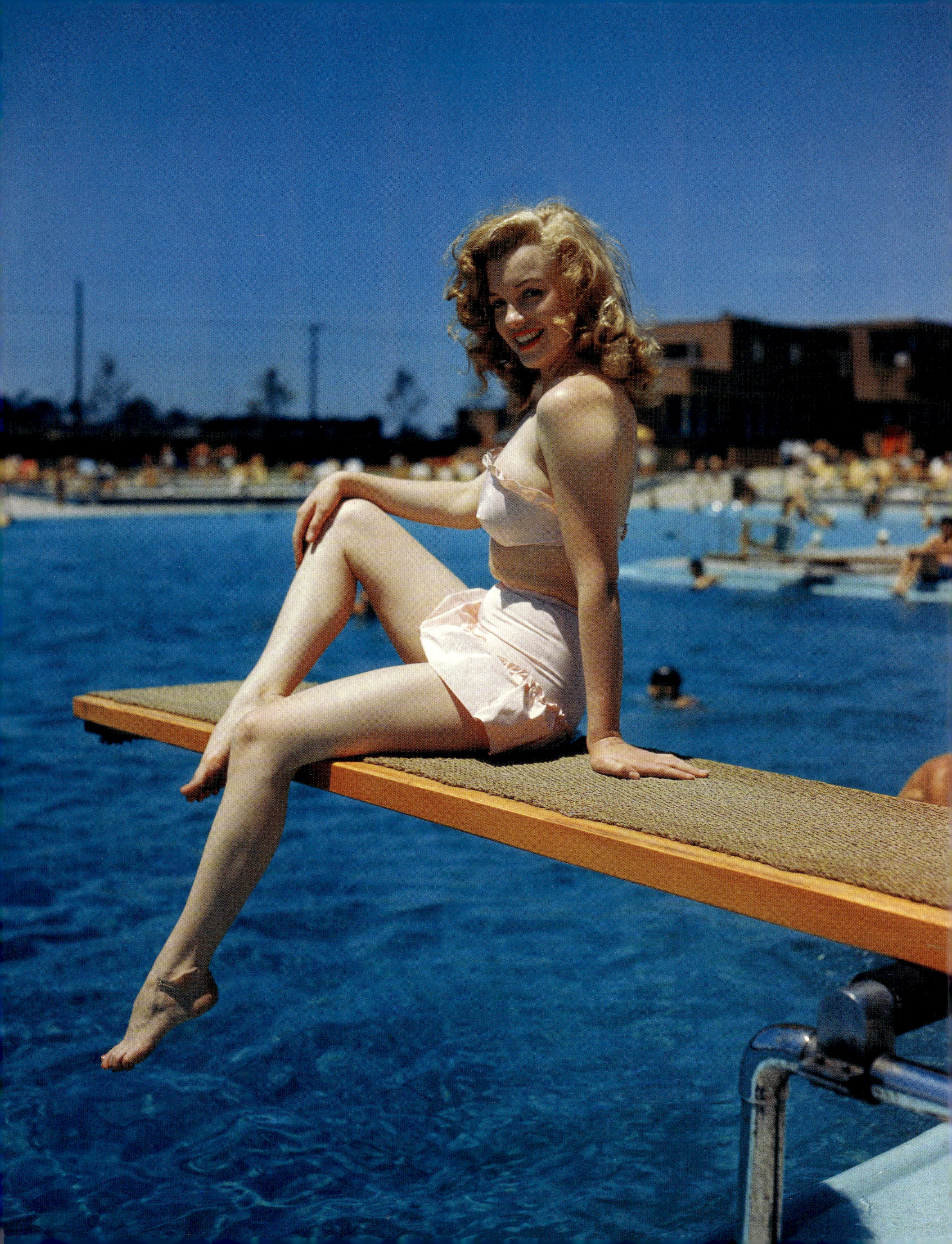

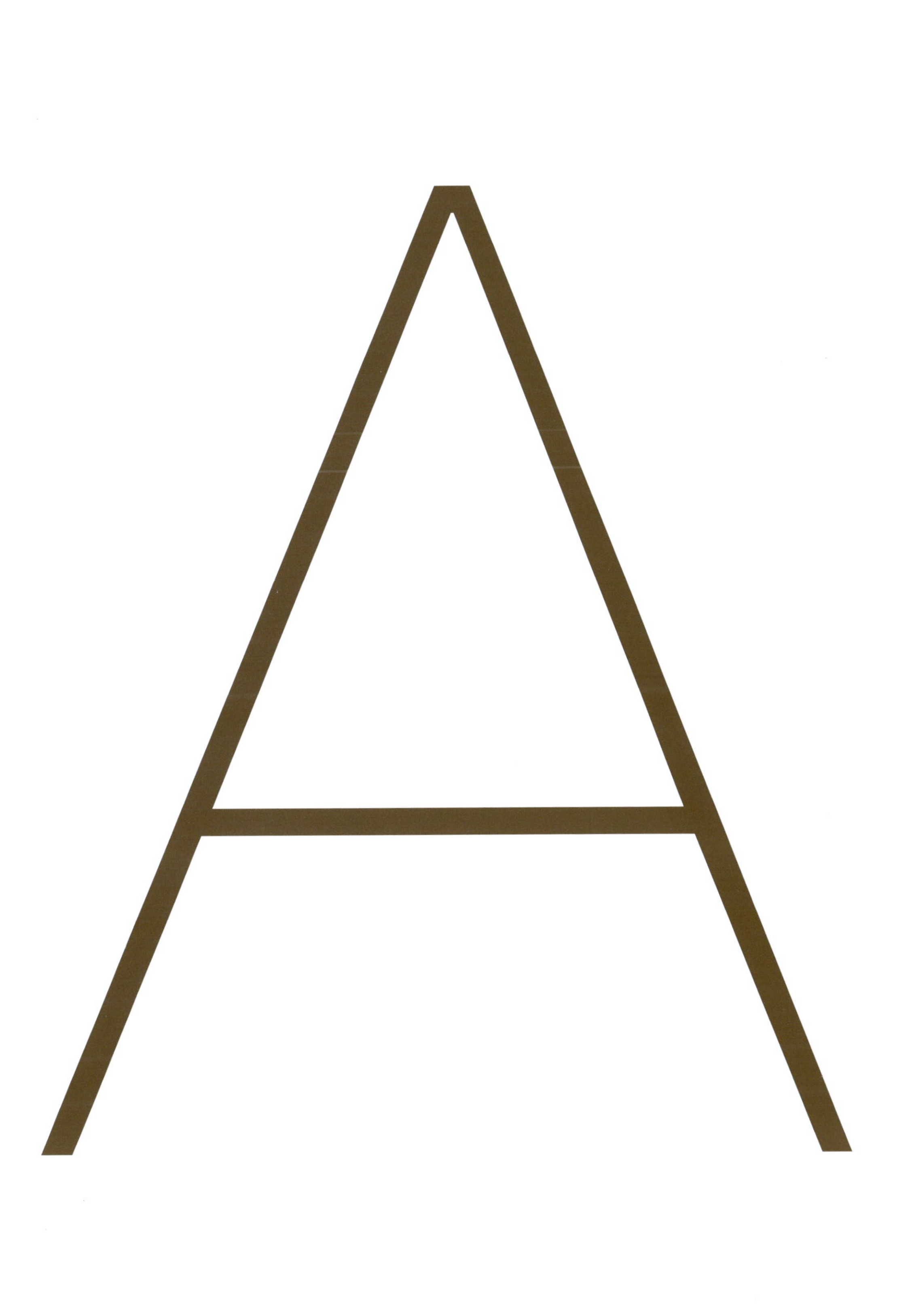

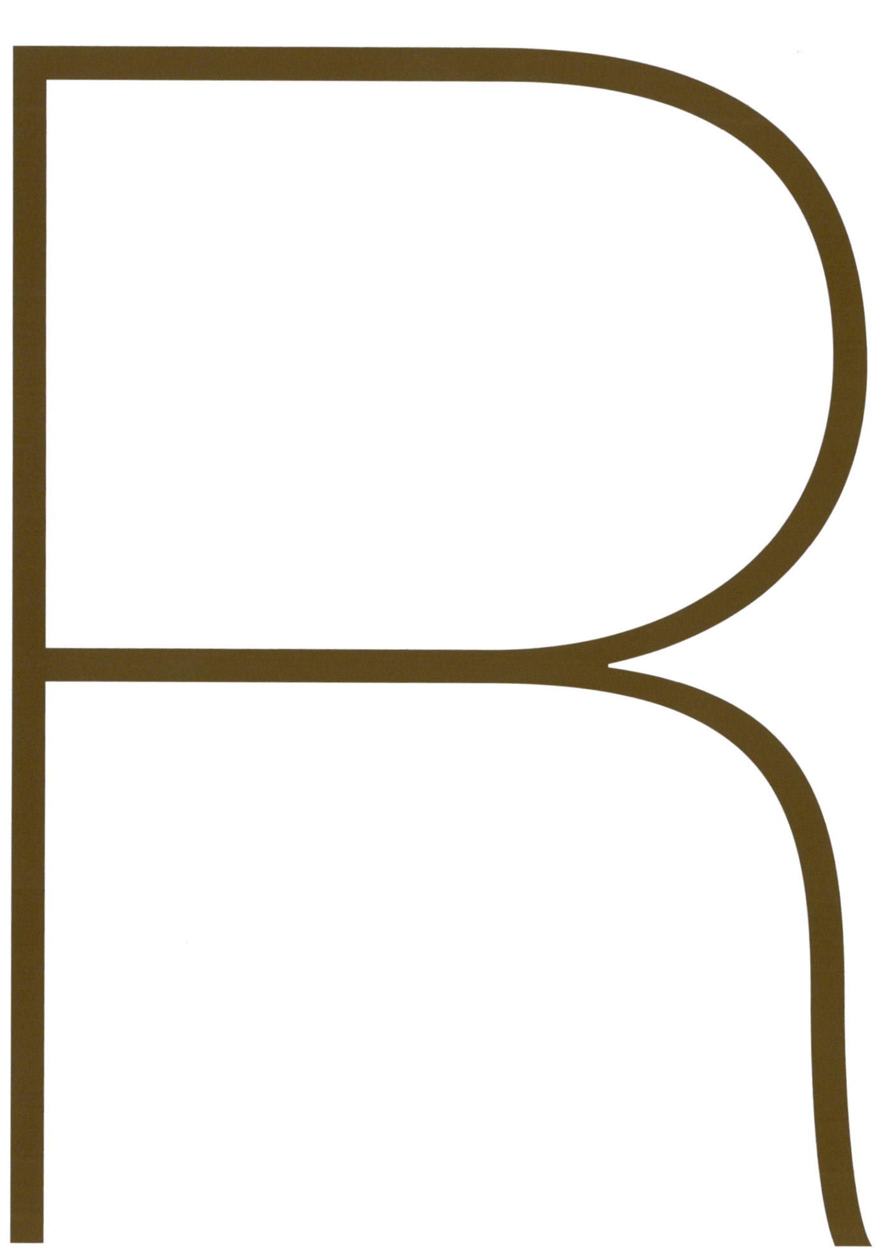

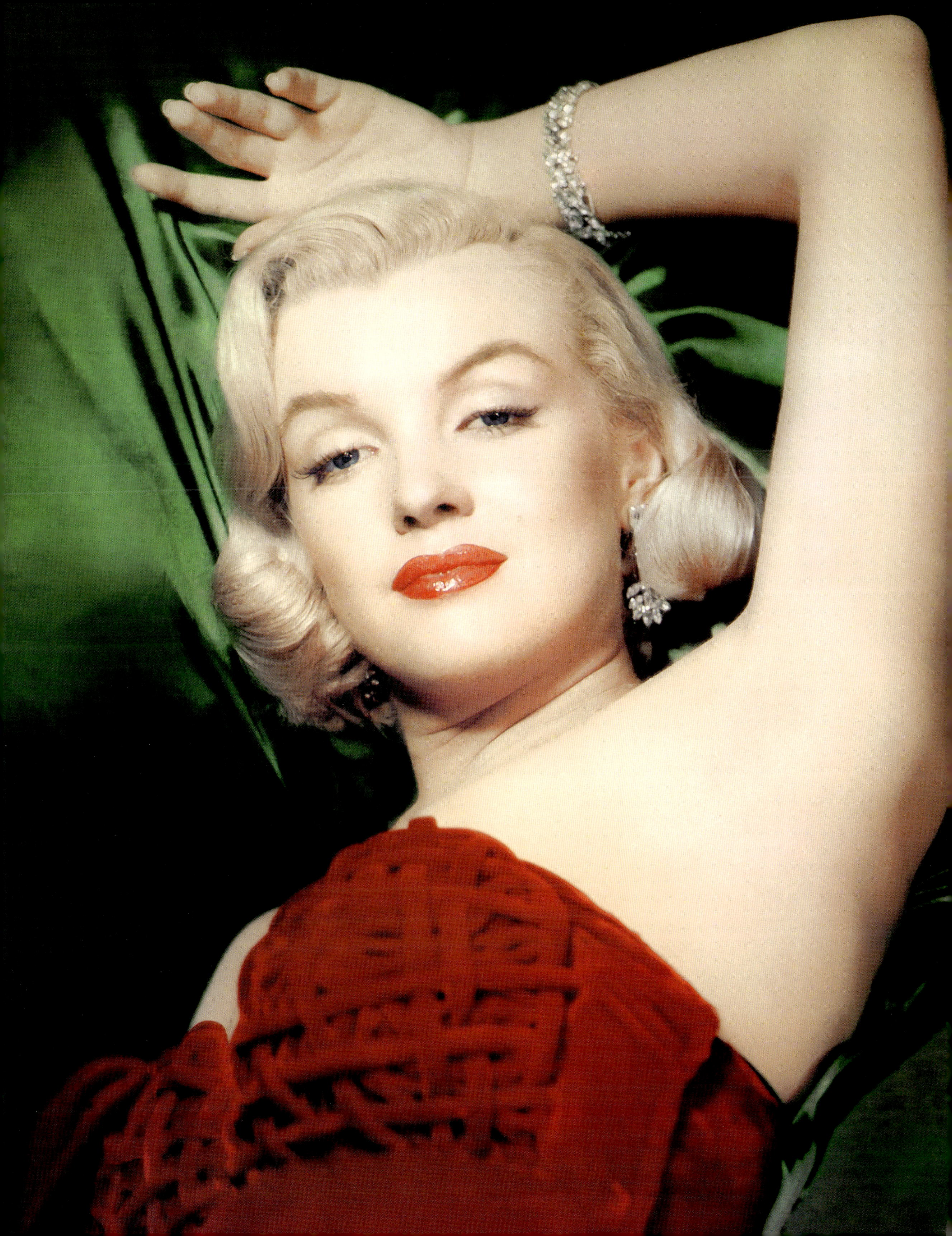

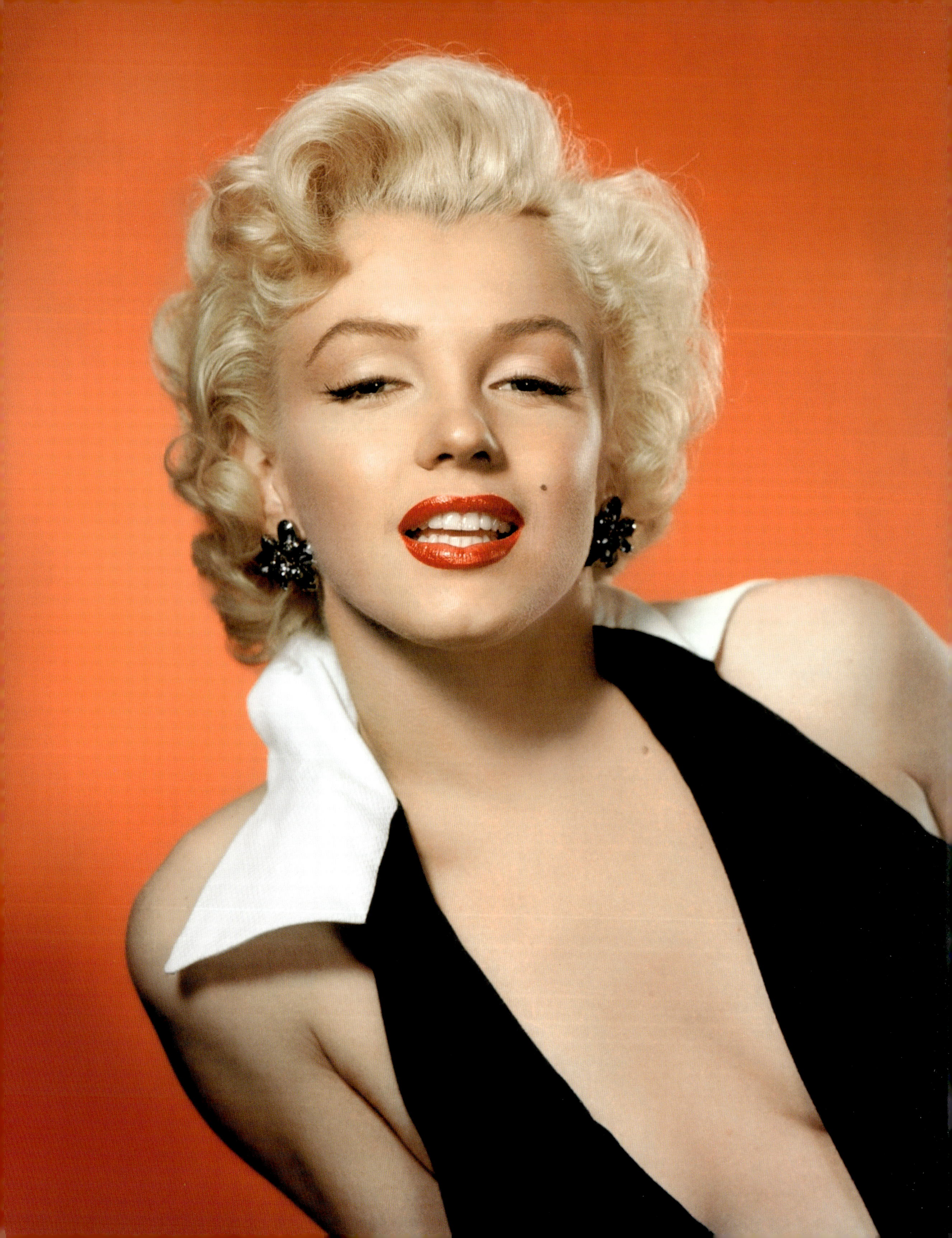

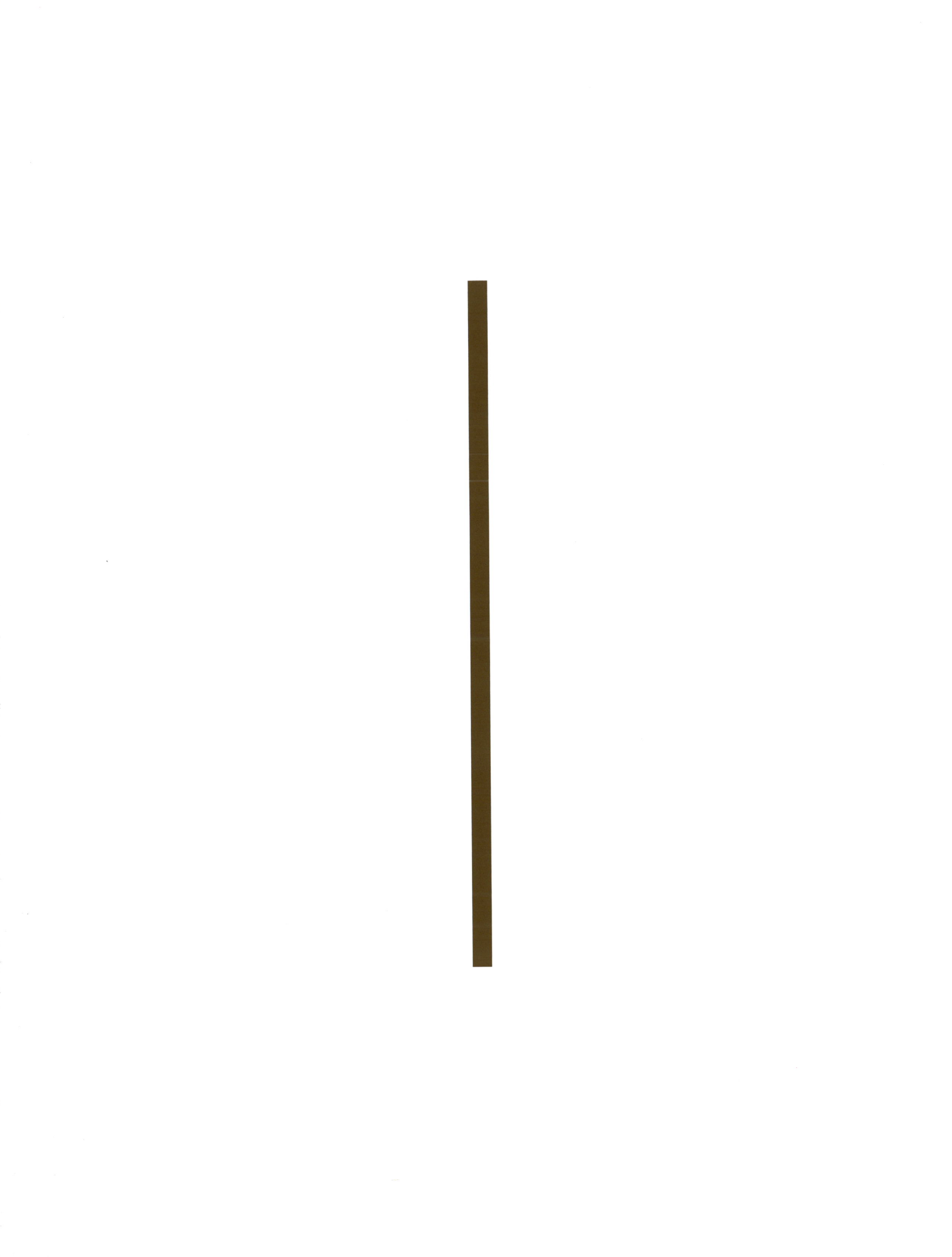

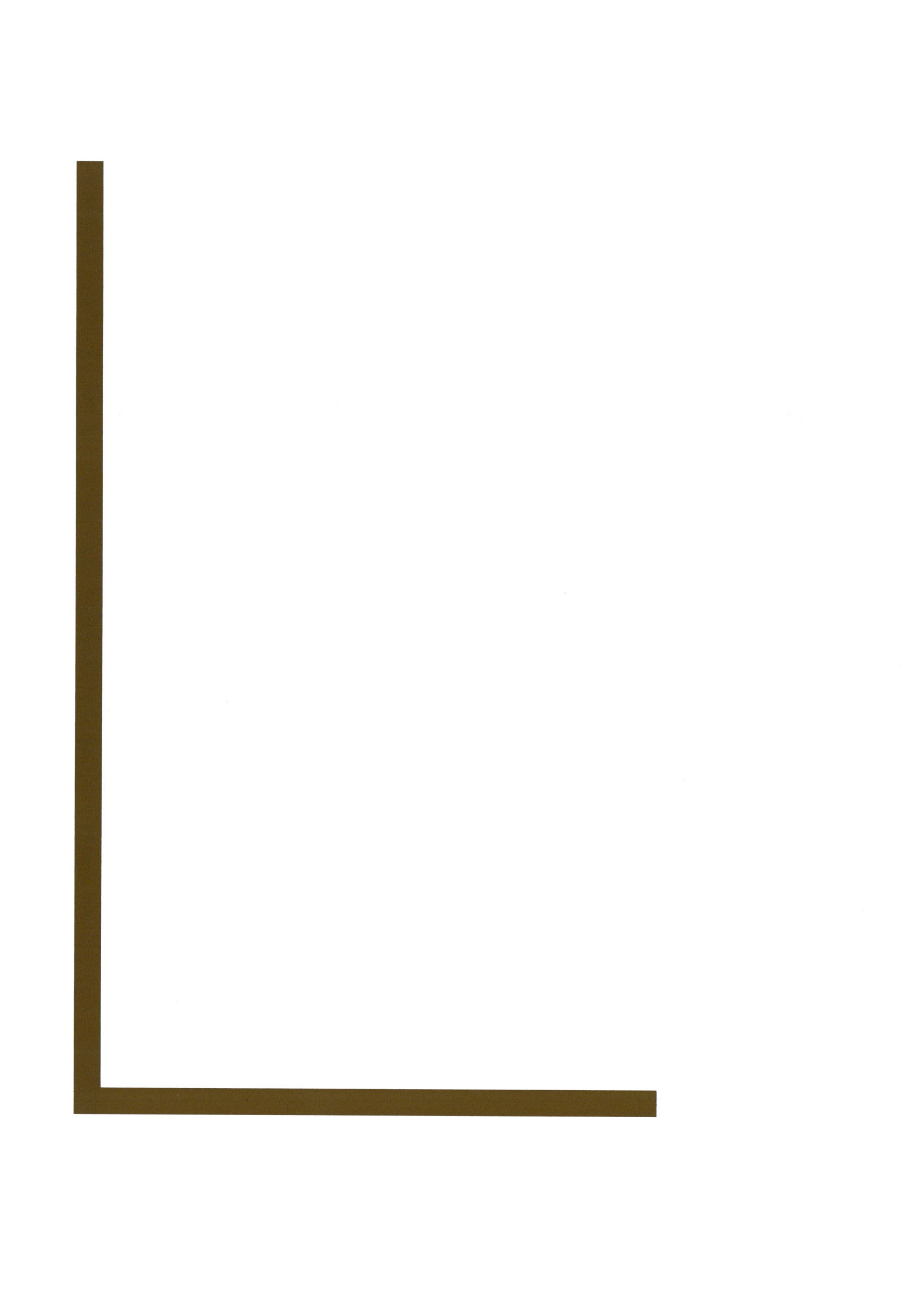

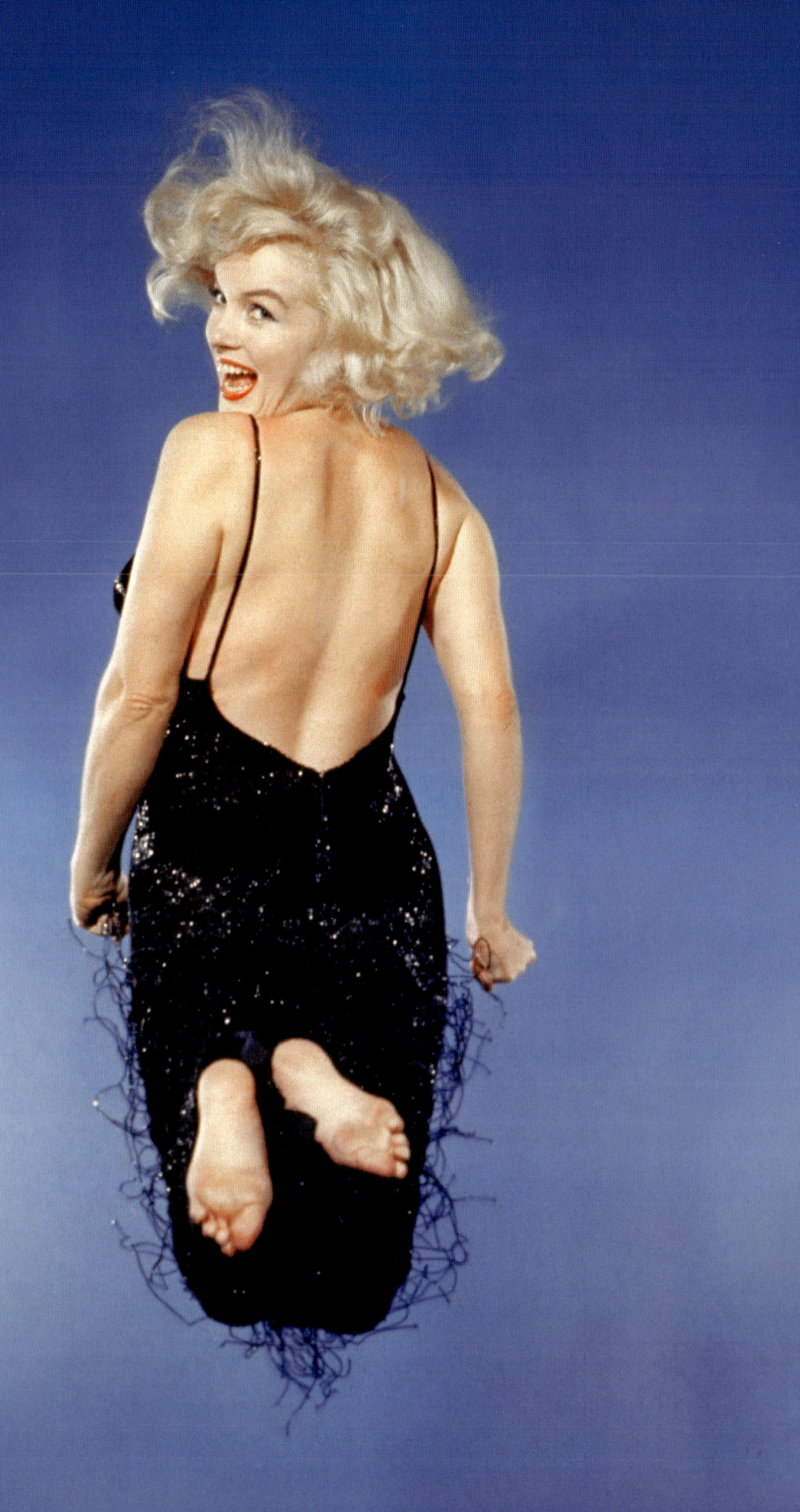

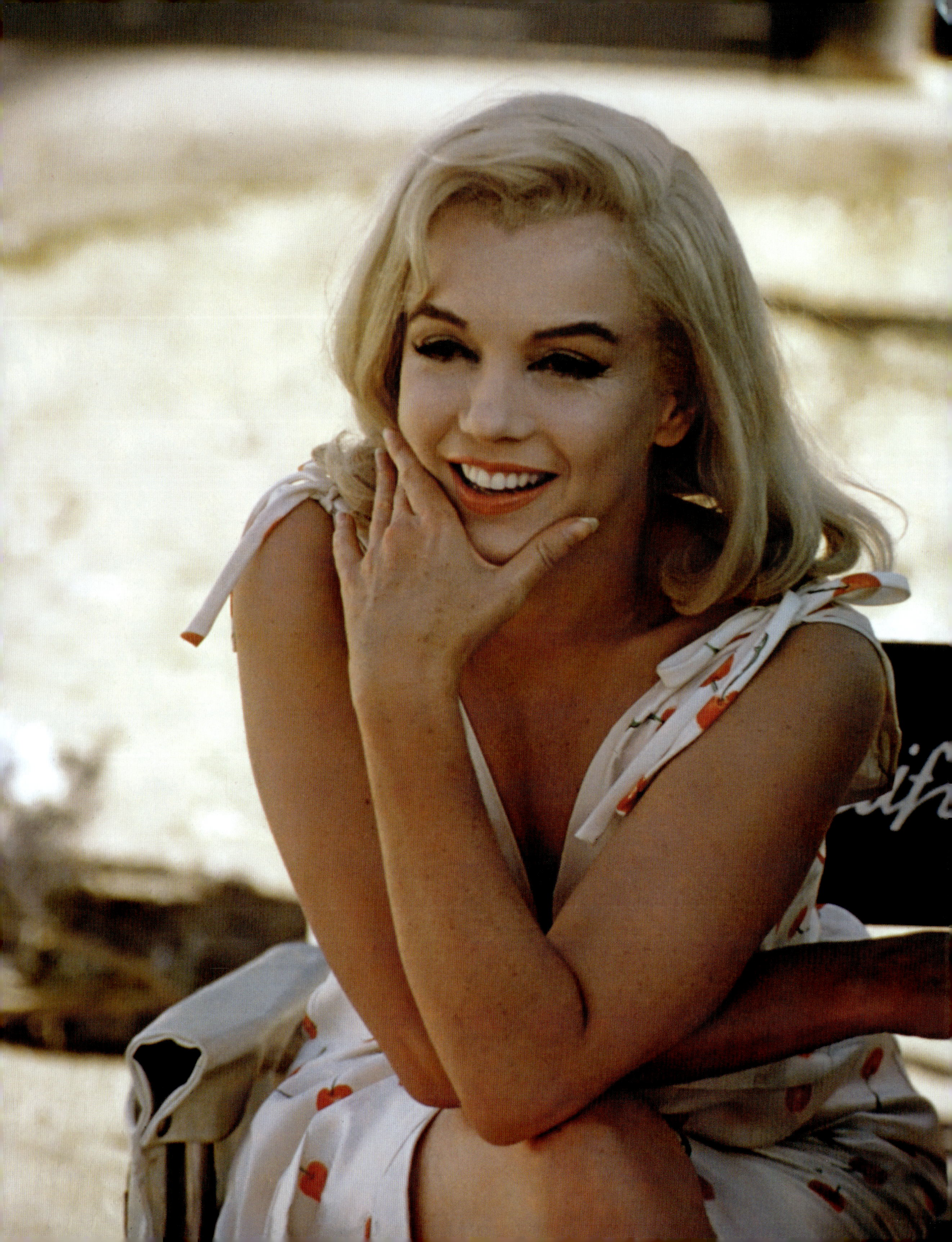

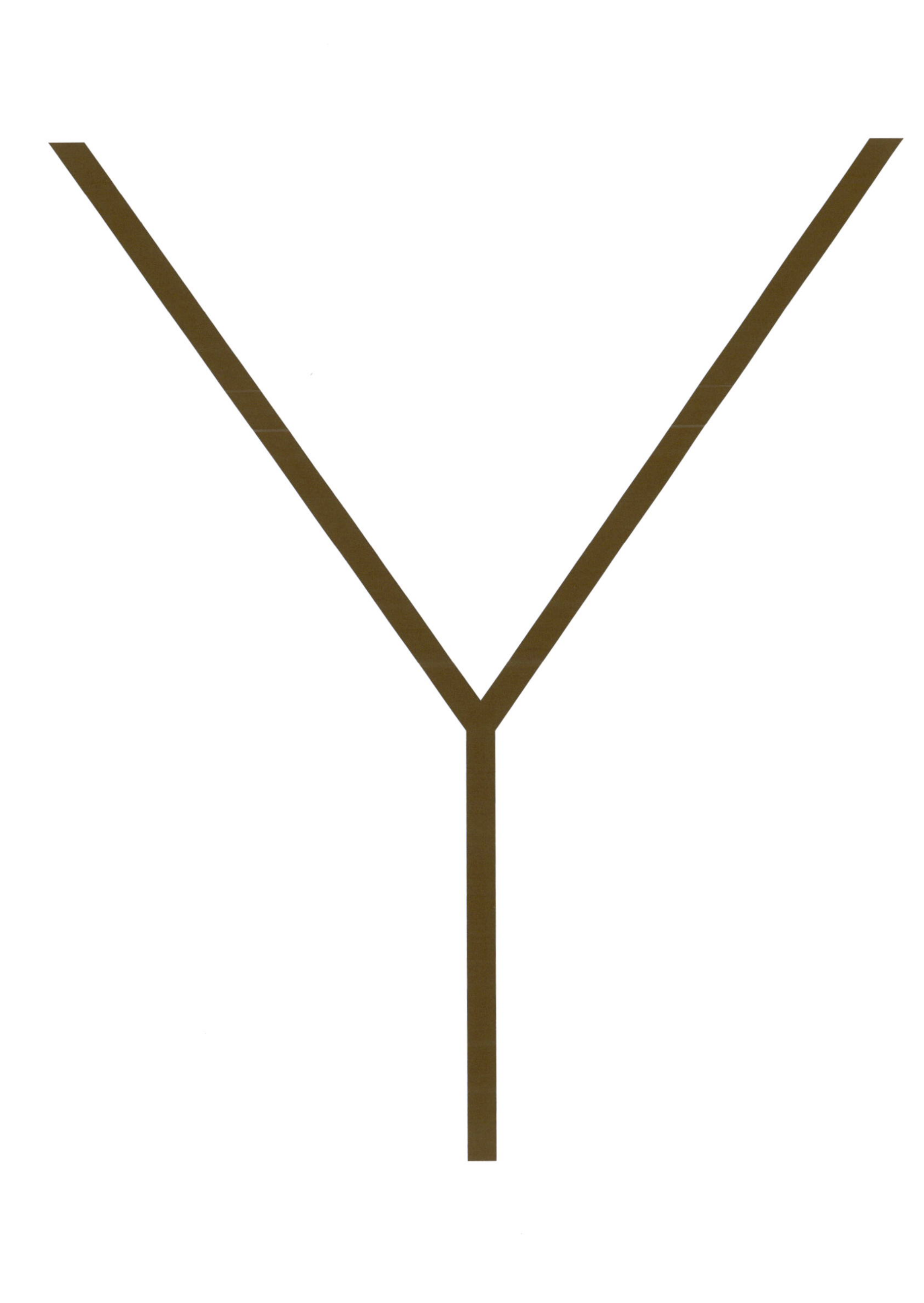

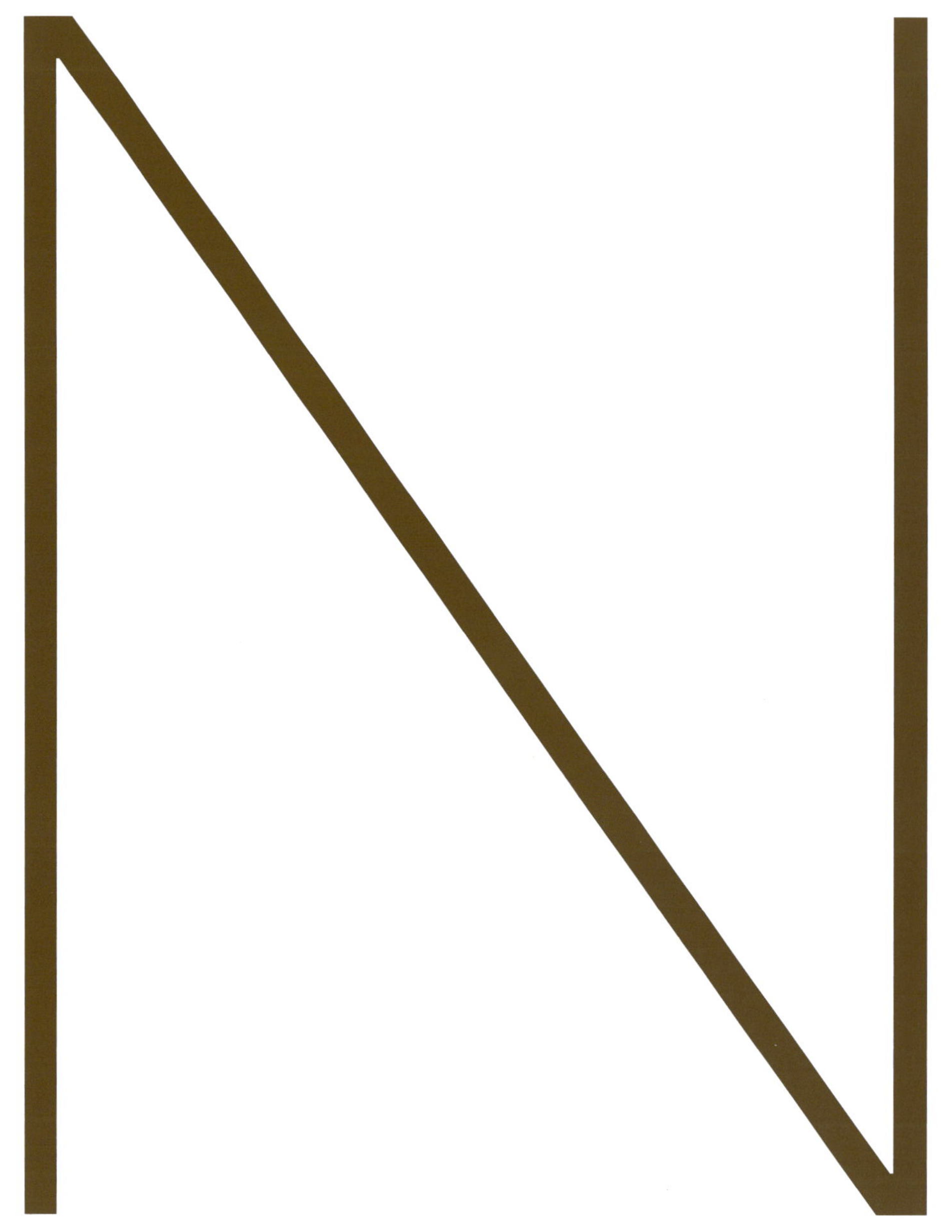

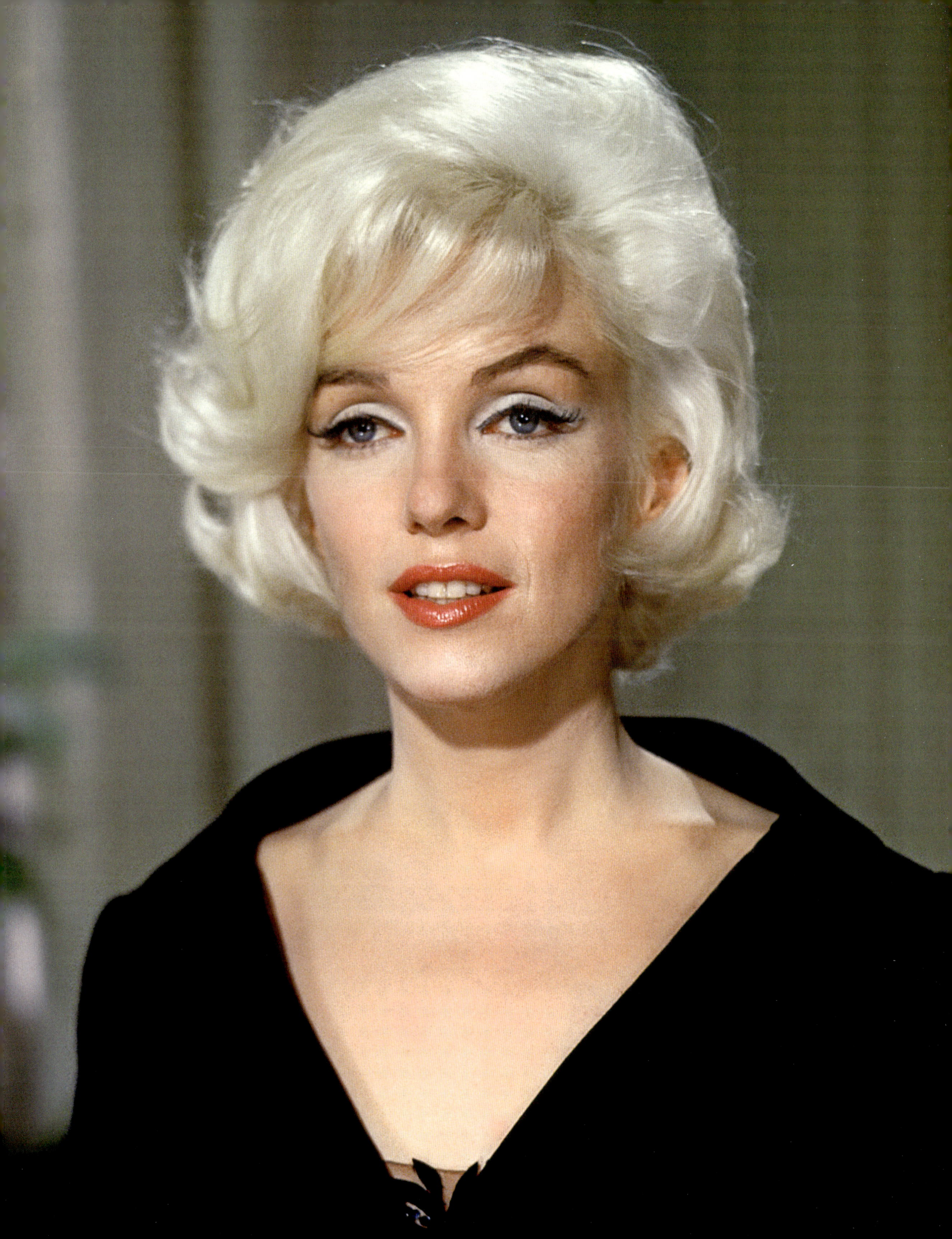

METAMO

MONROE

RPHOSIS

David Wills

and Stephen Schmidt

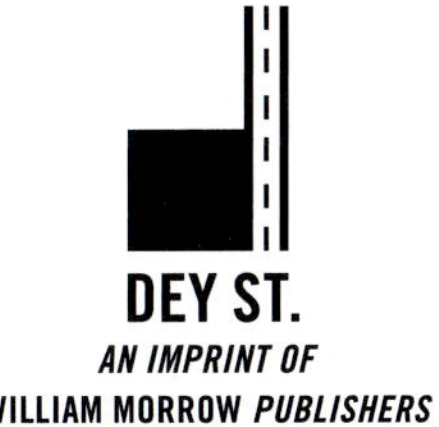

DEY ST.

AN IMPRINT OF

WILLIAM MORROW *PUBLISHERS*

Contents

INTRODUCTION XXI

CHRYSALIS 1

Norma Jeane 1942–1946

TRANSFIGURATION 31

Starlet 1947–1951

SIRIUS 71

Superstar 1952–1954

RENAISSANCE 161

The Independent Years 1955–1961

ICARUS 231

Goddess 1962

AFTERWORD 276

PHOTO CREDITS 286

ACKNOWLEDGMENTS & REFERENCES 289

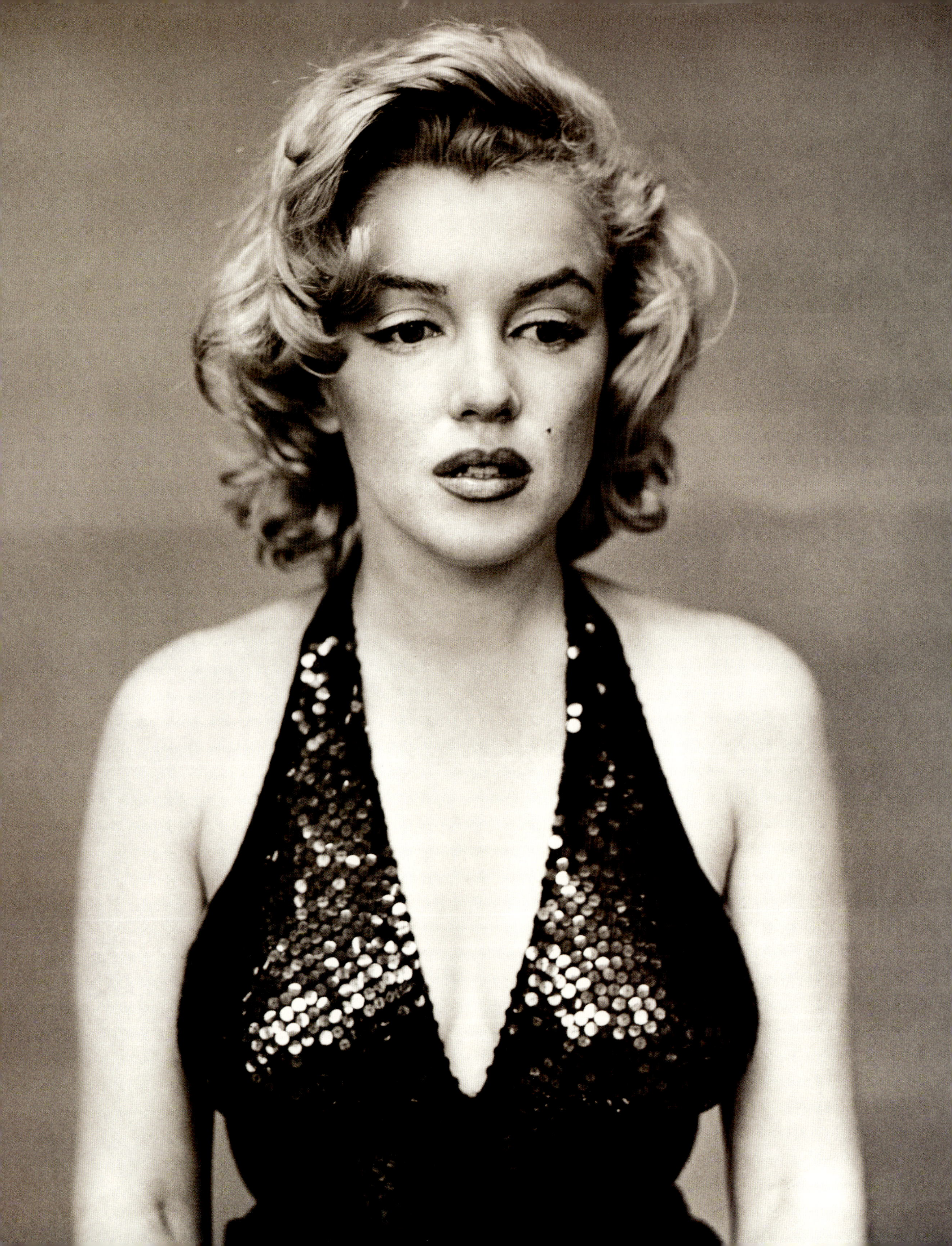

INTRODUCTION

History settles upon the earth in layers, each one shaped by those preceding and constantly rewritten by those that follow. Most is lost forever, but what survives, by virtue of strength or value, remains at the surface to inspire in present time.

Marilyn Monroe is an historical icon. The story of her life and legendary image have become reinforced to generations through constant exposure, marketing, and imitation. She is now indelible. However, with deification comes a loss of humanity. It is sometimes forgotten that behind the lacquered mask was a human being, a woman who worked and struggled and had doubts about her talent and self-worth.

In more than half a century of trying to analyze what made her so unique, critics and biographers have often overlooked that the primary reason for Marilyn's enduring popularity is her exceptional visual quality. As the definition of beauty constantly changes, the most alluring men and women are those who project an inner charisma from behind the face that is a perfect marriage of their time, their personality, and their art. Hollywood used to call it "star quality," "the It factor" or "that little something extra." What constitutes charisma is, however, a mystery, and trying to distill the essence of someone like Marilyn Monroe into a checklist of attributes or explainable formula is impossible.

She is, of course, a marvel of photogenicity, a genetic aligning of the planets, and the secret of her allure cannot be found in any one feature. Photogenicity suggests an alchemy that occurs as light is reflected off the planes of the face and is then captured on film. What the brain processes of a

Marilyn Monroe, actor, New York, May 6, 1957. Photograph by Richard Avedon.

face in person, in three dimensions, can differ markedly from what the camera imposes as reality, and therein lies the magic. It's also the reason screen tests were invented. Artists, scientists, and scholars generally agree that the photogenic face combines symmetry; defined bone structure; large, wide-set eyes; and a smaller nose with minimal projection so as not to cast obtrusive shadows on the face—but Hollywood is filled with exceptions to these rules. Not an example of the classic ideal, Marilyn's heart-shaped face framed very wide-set cornflower-blue eyes with a downturn at the outer corner of each lid; milky white skin; a slightly bulbous nose; and lips of average size with a bottom cleft. She didn't have a patrician bone structure or extraordinary features, and her facial symmetry was far from perfect. But collectively, on camera, the effect is mesmerizing.

We also know how much of Marilyn was maquillage, her deliberate glamorization beyond the natural by means of fashion, coiffure, and makeup to enhance and create the illusion of beauty. It is this creation, her "image," which could well be considered the pinnacle of her creative genius. She used her face as a blank canvas to create a gallery of looks and characters that are now legendary. Without makeup, most witnesses say she was unrecognizable and had the face of a child.

Her most dynamic physical feature was undoubtedly her mouth. In the thousands of photos she left behind, what perhaps first comes to mind is that billion-kilowatt smile. Throwing her head back and flashing those perfect teeth, she more than lights up the photograph, she consumes it. Also, rarely has a movie face exhibited so much variation of expression. Her features constantly in motion, she laughs, she wells with tears, she looks surprised, and most of all, she seduces. It's as if her beauty would vanish should she stay still or the camera turn away.

She emerges as spectacularly in the posed candids of news photographers and studio portraiture as she does on screen. Simone Signoret noted that Marilyn talked about her photo sessions with Richard Avedon with as much detail and enthusiasm as other stars described whole film productions. Indeed, few people have left such a photographic legacy. It is interesting to note that images of Norma Jeane are today far better preserved than those of Marilyn. Her modeling career launched at the height of mid-1940s Kodachrome, Norma Jeane had the benefit of being captured by perhaps the richest, clearest, most brilliant, and chemically dependable color film stock in history. With the popularization in the early 1950s of cheaper, faster, and smaller-format negative and transparency films, this standard of quality disappeared. Though saturated at the time, Marilyn's impression on the emulsion has deteriorated, faded, and turned to magenta over the decades. Through digital restoration, we are now able to breathe new life into these images, but it is not the same. A certain depth and authenticity of color are lost. Yet Norma Jeane remains unchanged.

As a work of art constantly in progress, Marilyn's face perfectly adapted to each passing decade: from the cherubic postwar pinup of the forties, to the atomic blonde bombshell of the fifties, to the refined platinum goddess of the sixties. Her personal and cinematic styles can be divided into five very distinct periods over twenty years, each one a reflection of both the fashion of the time and changes made of her own volition to advance or alter her career.

From 1942, the year of her first marriage at age sixteen, to 1946, was her "Norma Jeane" girl-next-door period, with long auburn hair, cotton sundresses, bare-midriff playsuits, pinafores, sweaters, cork wedges, and the occasional snood. In an era of post–World War II wholesomeness, the baby-faced teenager became very successful as a catalog and pinup model, her angelic features and pleasing figure appearing in and on the covers of countless men's magazines.

As the quintessential Hollywood starlet, by 1947 the newly named Marilyn Monroe embodied the legend of every pretty young girl who comes to Hollywood with dreams of becoming a star. Except this time, born and raised on the streets of Los Angeles, the girl didn't have to travel too far. No longer a regularly working model and not yet a movie star, Marilyn struggled as she and the studios labored to define her image. Columbia Pictures settled on a combination of Rita Hayworth and Betty Grable, dyeing her hair light blonde and styling it in a standard shoulder-length coiffure. In 1950, with the apparent assistance of minor cosmetic surgery to her nose and chin, and her hair cut into a sleek pageboy, the Monroe of popular culture began to take form. Well-received appearances in *The Asphalt Jungle* and *All About Eve* that same year considerably helped clear her path to future stardom.

Though by no means an overnight success, "Marilyn Monroe" finally exploded in 1952. For the next three years she dominated Hollywood and captivated audiences worldwide with her ultraglamorous poster image, for which she is today best remembered, in classic films like *Gentlemen Prefer Blondes*, *How to Marry a Millionaire*, and *The Seven Year Itch*. With the help of makeup artist Whitey Snyder, Marilyn disguised flaws and highlighted features to craft her ultimate incarnation. Firmly housed at Twentieth Century-Fox, she radiated in the fashions of its top designer, William Travilla, who created a series of mostly halter and pleated gowns engineered to simultaneously skim and reveal the body while giving the illusion of stature. She alights from limousines amid the blinding flashbulbs of the newsmen; she sings "Diamonds Are a Girl's Best Friend"; she signs autographs; she puts her handprints in cement at Grauman's Chinese Theatre; she sings for the troops in Korea; she stands over a subway grate with her skirt billowing high above her waist; she waves to fans. Every captured moment is now part of our popular history, part of the fairy tale, and has found its way onto a thousand calendars, coffee mugs, T-shirts, and mouse pads.

The years 1955 to 1961 saw a toned-down Marilyn: her Actors Studio look, precipitated by the need to be seen as a more serious actress. She was much heavier during this time, as witnessed in *Some Like It Hot* and *The Misfits*, and favored simple skirts, slacks, and blouses from Jax, Ferragamo shoes, and Ceil Chapman cocktail dresses in black, white, or beige to complement her pale complexion, which now featured a softer and more natural makeup. Norman Norell was her preferred designer for shimmering yet sophisticated evening wear. Though a time of renaissance in her life, this period of theatrical and intellectual growth was seen by many as quashing and confusing a fragile talent that should have been left spontaneous and instinctual.

By 1962, the metamorphosis was complete. Now paler, blonder, thinner, and more refined in Pucci prints and Jean Louis suits, her image retains little trace of the Norma Jeane of twenty years earlier. In the silent costume tests taken for her last film, *Something's Got to Give*, she seems to float ethereally across the room like a beautiful ghost. She is absolutely breathtaking in these sequences; never was star quality so potently evident. Her features and body transformed by an extreme weight loss, she appears touchingly evanescent at this time, like a goddess possessed of a beauty so delicate it could evaporate at any moment. How devastating it must have been for someone like Marilyn Monroe to look in the mirror and see the first signs of middle age. She left the earth right at that Icarus moment, when the structure of her wings would have begun to melt had she flown any closer toward the sun. She seemed to have a knowledge of this and it shows in her eyes—there is an absence, a surrendering.

As one of the most admired and influential style icons of the twentieth century—a crown shared only with Audrey Hepburn—Marilyn made at least one major contribution to fashion and style: she loosened things up. In contrast to the structured forties, and despite the complexity of her appearance, there was a casualness about her that always suggested she just rolled out of bed, threw on a dress, and showed up. A random lock of hair bouncing over her eye, a fallen shoulder strap, or the absence of nylons and undergarments—nothing she did ever seemed contrived, though of course it was. Bardot took nonchalant abandon to the next level a few years later, but it was Monroe who helped catapult society into the dawn of the sexual revolution. As a reflection of this change, fashion became less structured, more casual, more sensual.

The big debate has always been whether or not she was a great actress, or even a good one. Like so many movie stars, Marilyn essentially played variations on a signature character. Her performances were charisma-driven. That said, nobody could do what she did, and there are definite moments of acting genius in her films. Her fractured sex appeal, unthreatening to both men and women, allowed her to extract sympathy from an audience like no one else before or since. In her best roles she seems always to look at the world with a child's wonderment. When you see Marilyn on the screen you feel protective of her—and this undoubtedly contributed to the worldwide outpouring of grief when she suddenly died.

It must be conceded that Marilyn's screen image did contribute enormously to her personal unhappiness, her low self-esteem, and ultimately how she conducted her relationships with others. Overpromoted by the studio, overexposed by the newspapers and fan magazines, she was rammed down the public's throat from day one as a "celluloid aphrodisiac." The disconnect between her public and private personas wreaked havoc on what was already a borderline personality. Even as she was accomplishing her goal of becoming a movie star—the greatest of movie stars—she succumbed to the actor's prison of having to establish herself as a "type," and was therefore never given the encouragement or opportunity to portray or be anything else. Certainly not by her studio, which was making a fortune off the well-worn formula. The seeds were sown early, and while she came to detest the limitations of her stereotype, she ultimately depended on it.

In a life of mixed success and sorrow, Marilyn achieved so much in such a short time, and made such a significant impact, that in death she continues to intrigue and delight the world. It is unfair that she be seen as a tragic figure. Indeed, she must have been incredibly shrewd. Consider the journey of a little girl who began her life in orphanages and foster homes, only to become the most famous woman in the world. Her lack of self-worth belied an extraordinary drive and ambition that fought its way through years of initial rejection when Hollywood wasn't interested. She didn't reach success until twenty-six, quite an advanced age for a female star, then or now.

What has to be admired most about Marilyn is that she was a hard worker, whether as a factory laborer, a model, or a motion picture actress. She supported herself from the age of sixteen till the day she died twenty years later. Forced to sit at the back of the bus even as her own star power was driving it, Marilyn constantly strove for self-improvement, stood up for what she believed in, challenged the studio for better roles, fought for—and won—director and cinematographer approval, and started her own production company at a time when actresses rarely did so. With no interest in material possessions—clothes, jewelry, homes, or the accoutrements of success—she gave much of her money to friends in need and children's charities.

The day Marilyn died, the South African government arrested Nelson Mandela and charged him with incitement to rebellion. The decade unrolled an avalanche of change that marked the birth of contemporary culture. In 1962, the term *personal computer* was first mentioned by the media; The Beatles, The Rolling Stones, and Bob Dylan emerged as new voices in music; John Glenn became the first man to orbit Earth; Anthony Burgess's *A Clockwork Orange* was published; record numbers of women were using the contraceptive pill; Andy Warhol debuted his Campbell's soup can silkscreens; and the first Kmart department store opened in Garden City, Michigan. American cinema was changing to reflect more independent visions and a new breed of actor, not tied to any traditional studio system, became stars at a time when youth was at its most marketable. The sexual revolution progressing, titillation was replaced with graphic sex and it would not be long before the idea of a billowing skirt would be viewed as the relic of an unliberated era. Where a Marilyn Monroe fast approaching forty would have fit in this new world is uncertain. Without the benefit of reinvention, her screen persona was so vividly ingrained in audience perception, her type so specific, that she would probably have never progressed to character or older leading lady roles. Identity and self-worth would have to come from other sources.

In a world where everything is now an imitation, a retro fabrication to be adapted, used, and discarded by today's media and youth culture, Marilyn has survived, and her image and influence are seen everywhere. Such immortality may have been at the expense of her happiness, but she was ultimately able to achieve her dreams.

One wonders if Norma Jeane, poised above Earth in some celestial existence, had had the benefit of foresight, a way of seeing the life that lay ahead, would she have wanted to change her destiny for another, to forgo fame and the joy she was to bring millions in favor of a simple life.

When asked years later about his famous delivery on June 1, 1926, Dr. Herman M. Beerman stated, "She looked like any other baby I delivered. She was the same as the rest." As all lives are created equal, the road ahead could have led her to many destinations—a mother, a secretary, a teacher, a social worker, a businesswoman, an ambassador.

Norma Jeane would have chosen Marilyn.

David Wills

Los Angeles, 2011

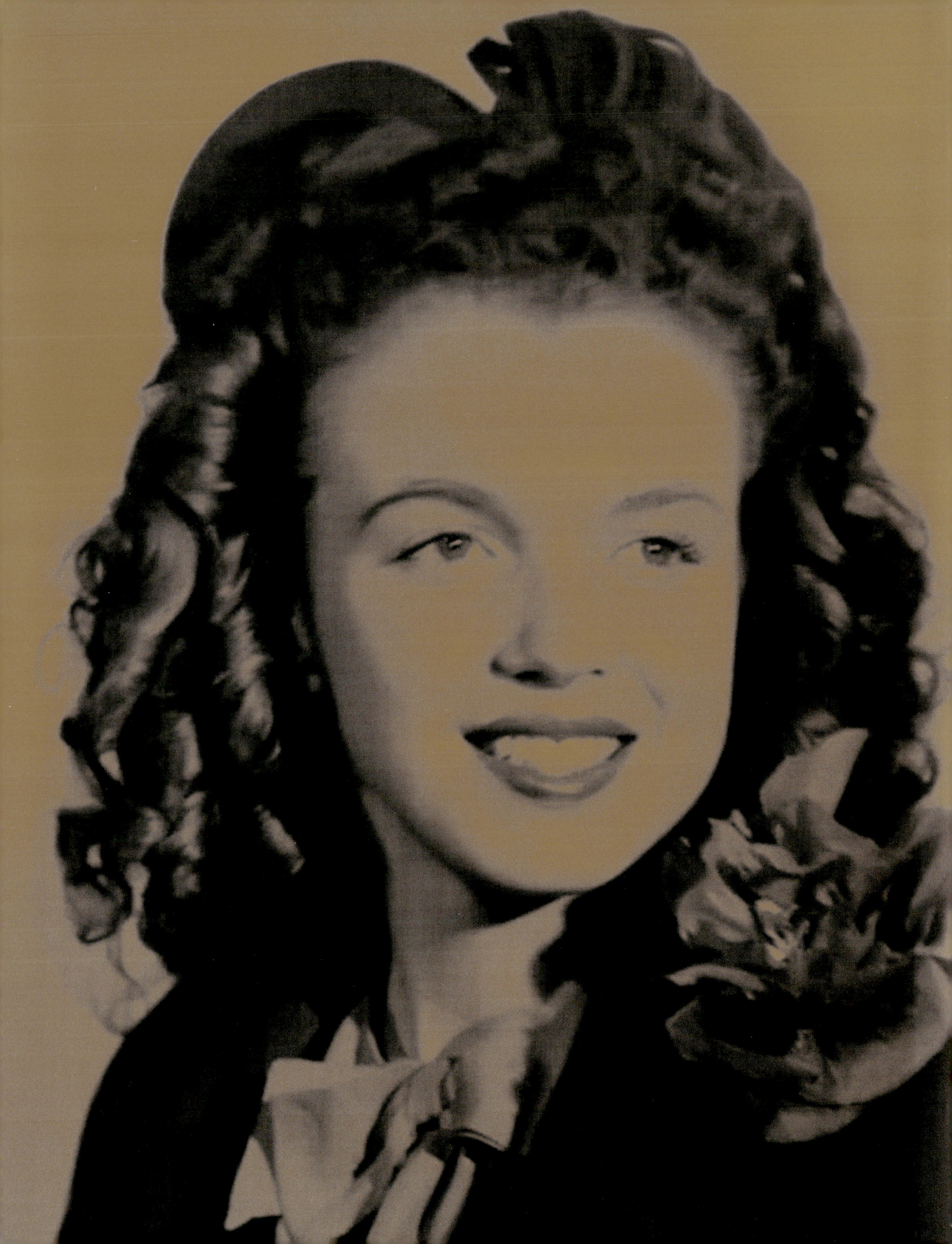

CHRYSALIS

Norma Jeane 1942–1946

The Road goes ever on and on
Down from the door where it began.
Now far ahead the Road has gone,
And I must follow, if I can,
Pursuing it with eager feet,
Until it joins some larger way
Where many paths and errands meet.
And whither then? I cannot say.

J. R. R. TOLKIEN

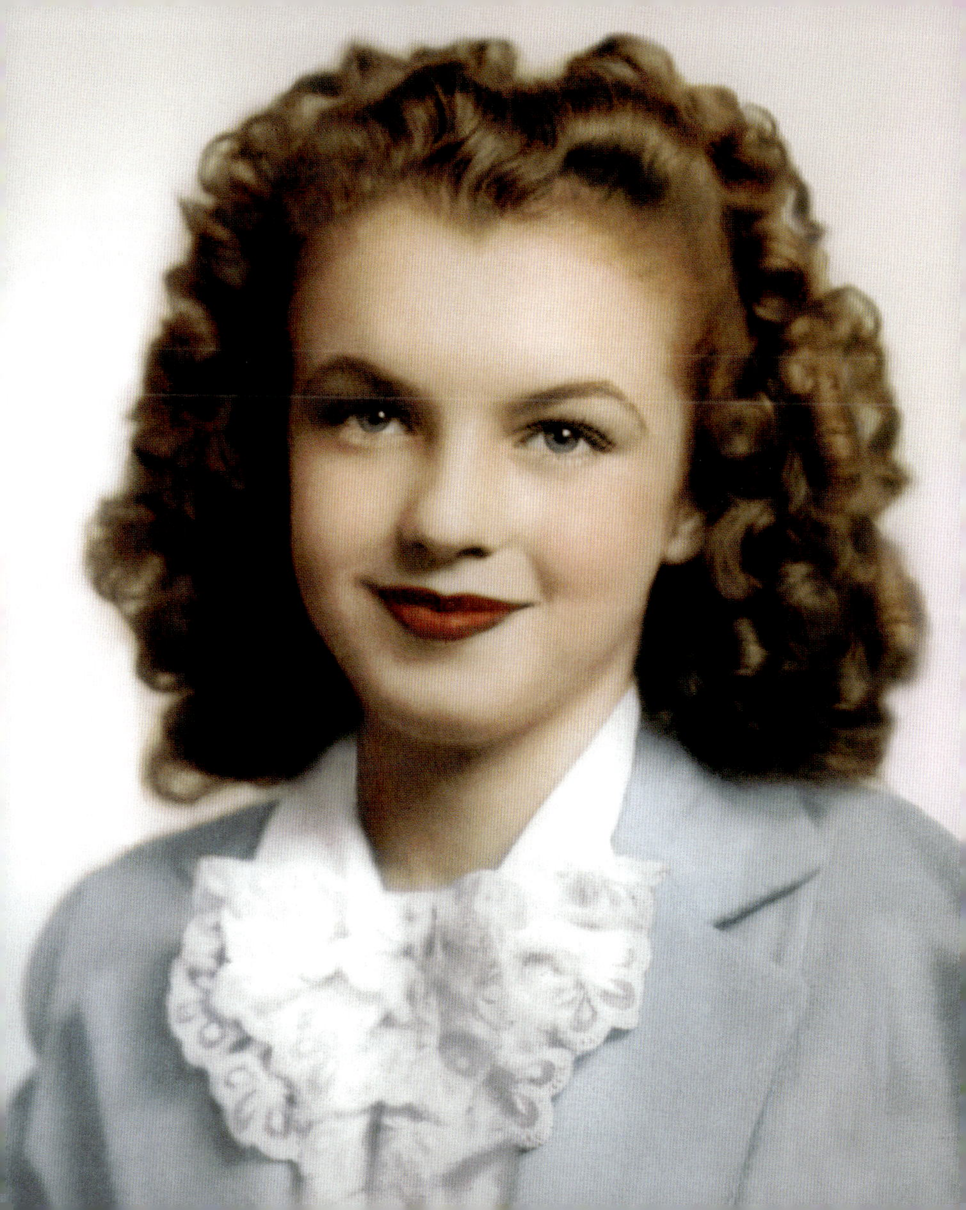

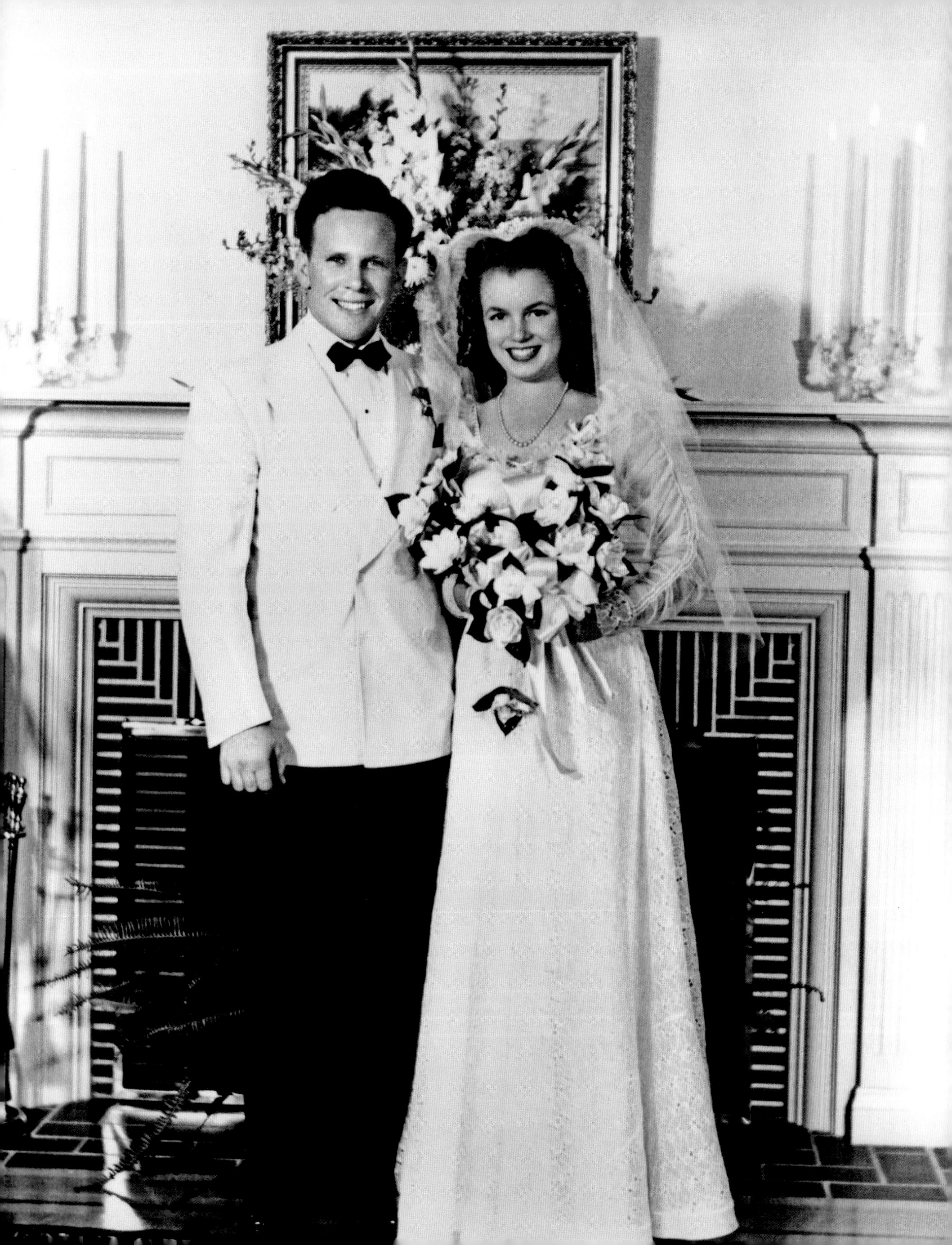

"Norma Jeane was always a butterfly. She was beautiful all of her life, within and without. During our courtship and marriage I never stopped loving to be with her, to stare at her, to laugh with and love her. We had a wonderful, joyful marriage. But in the end, it was not enough for Norma Jeane. Like all beautiful butterflies, she had to fly away."

JIM DOUGHERTY

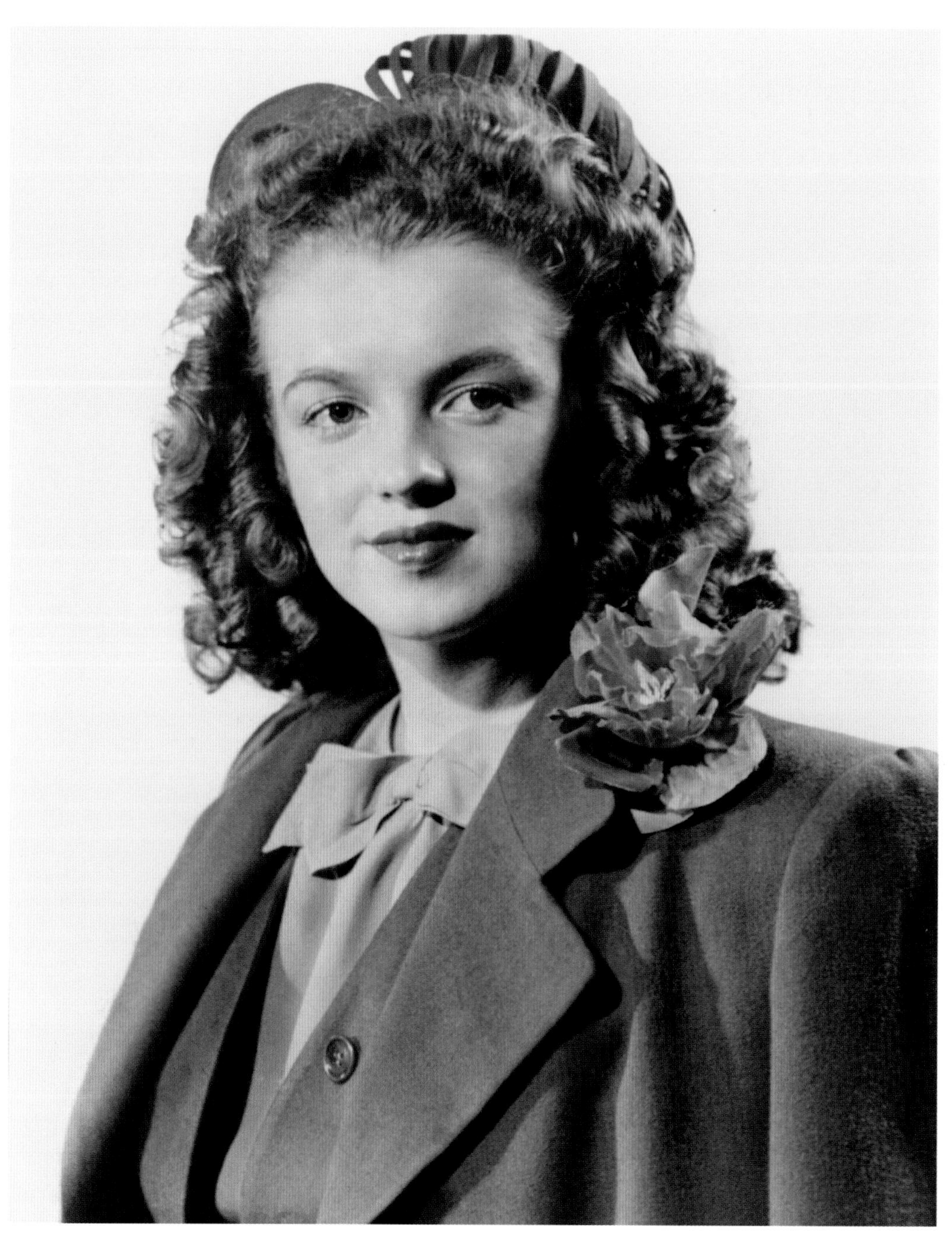

"No one ever told me I was pretty when I was a little girl. All little girls should be told they are pretty, even if they aren't."

MARILYN MONROE

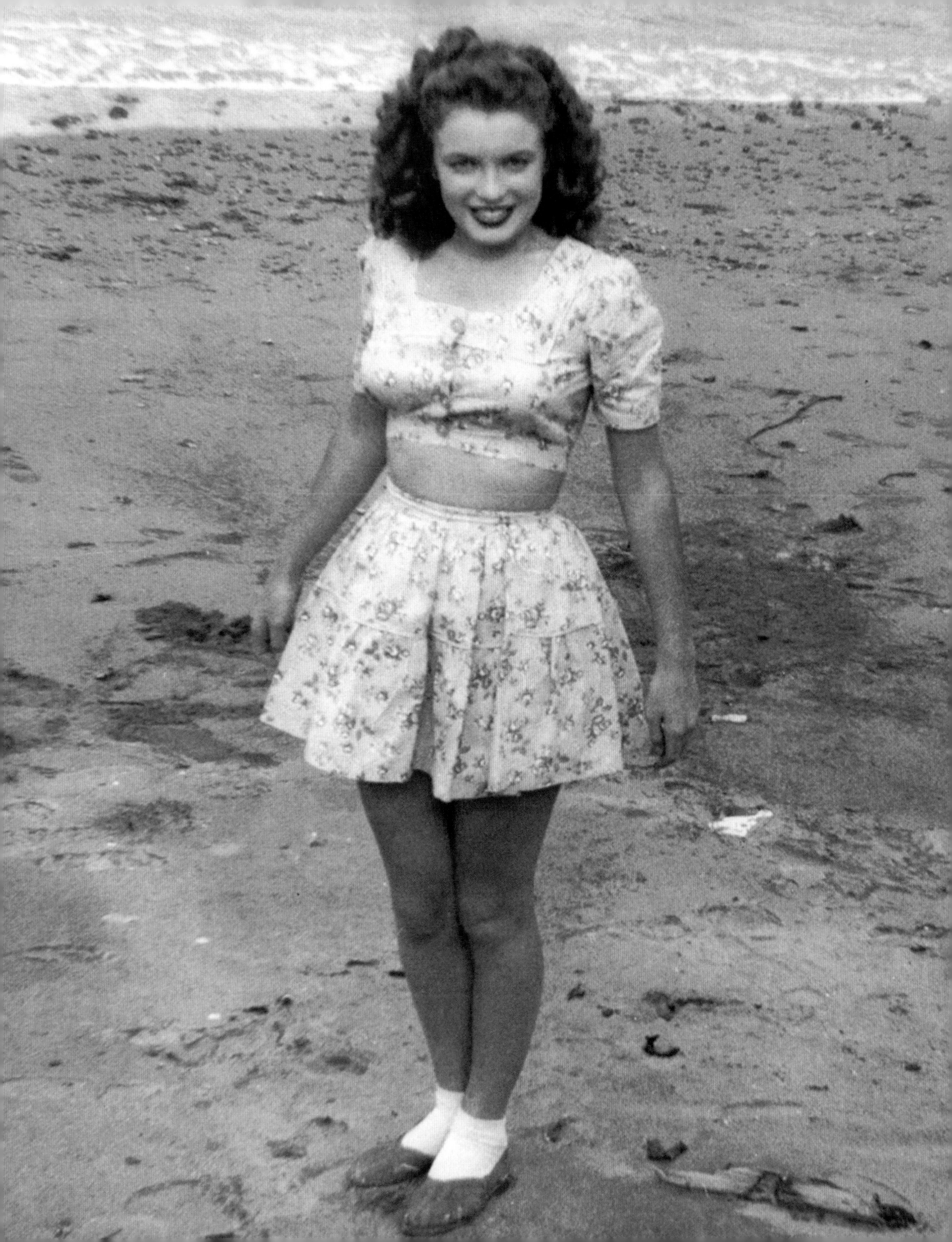

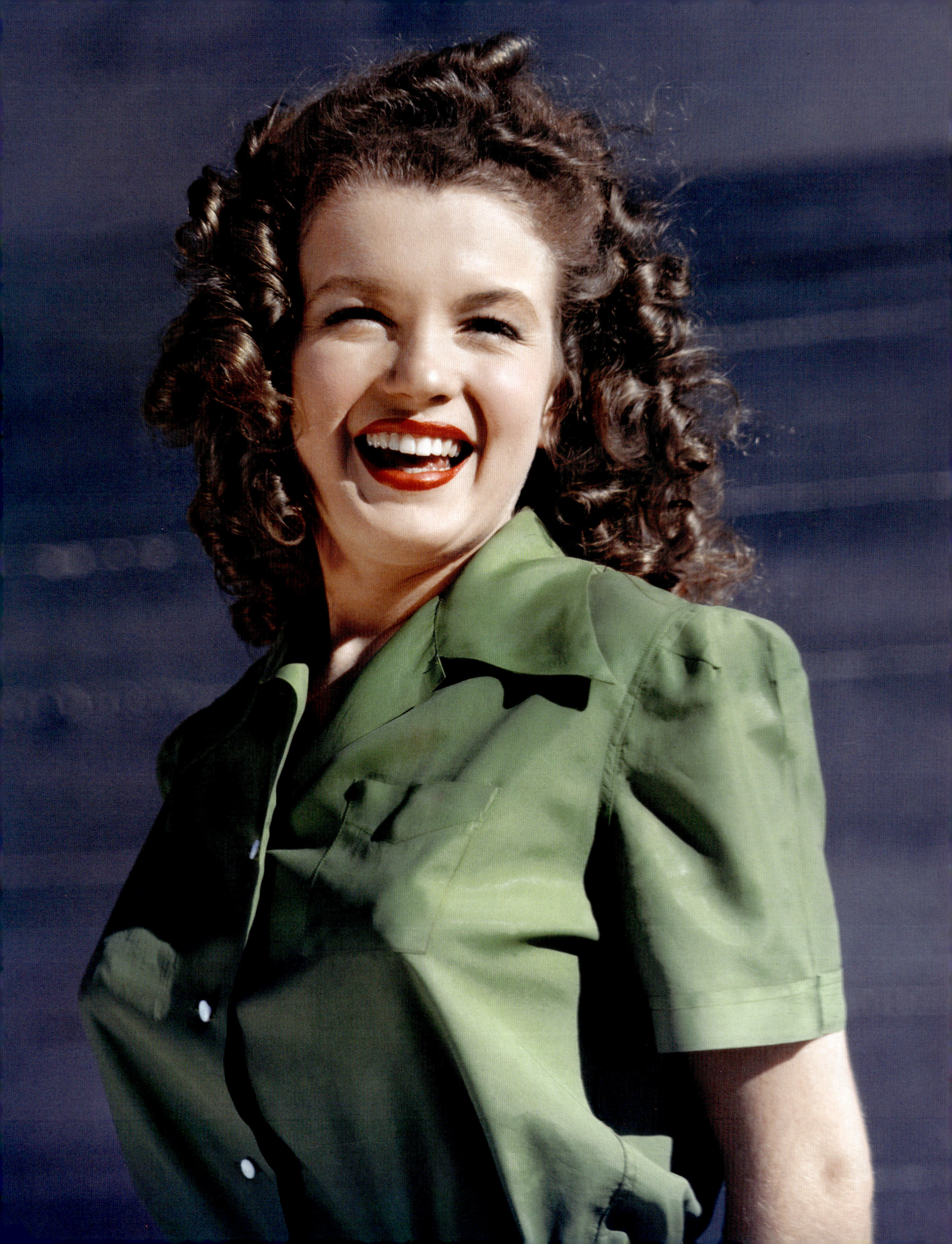

"It was the Radioplane Company, and I first had a job inspecting parachutes. That was before I worked in the 'dope' room, the hardest work I've ever done. The fuselage and various parts of the ships were made of cloth at that time—they use metal now—and we used to paint the cloth with a stiffening preparation. It wasn't sprayed on; it was worked in with brushes, and it was very tiring and difficult . . . very hard to take for eight hours a day. It was actually a twelve-hour day for the other workers, but I only did eight because I was underage."

MARILYN MONROE

NORMA JEAN 1945

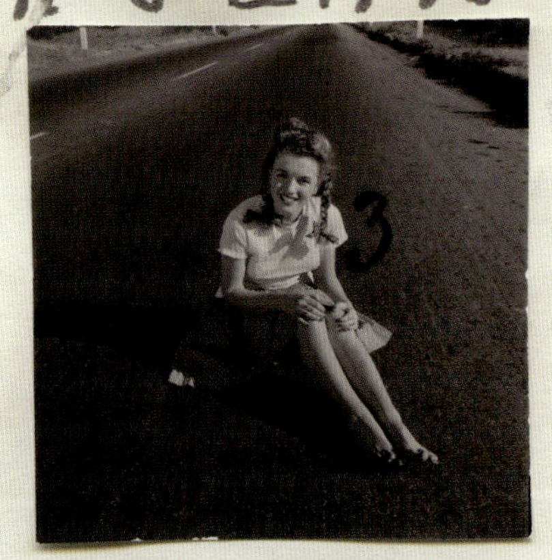

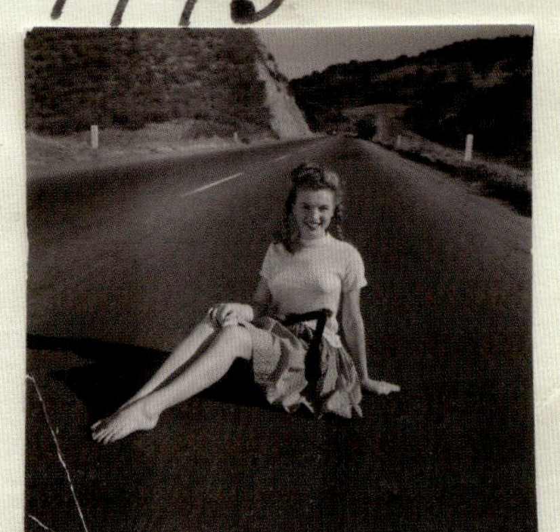

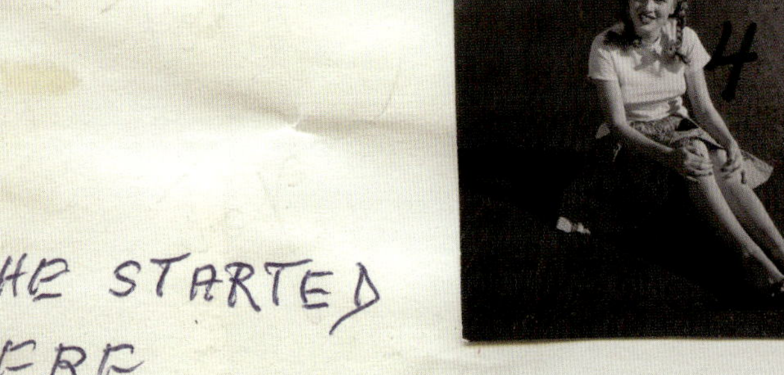

SHE STARTED HERE

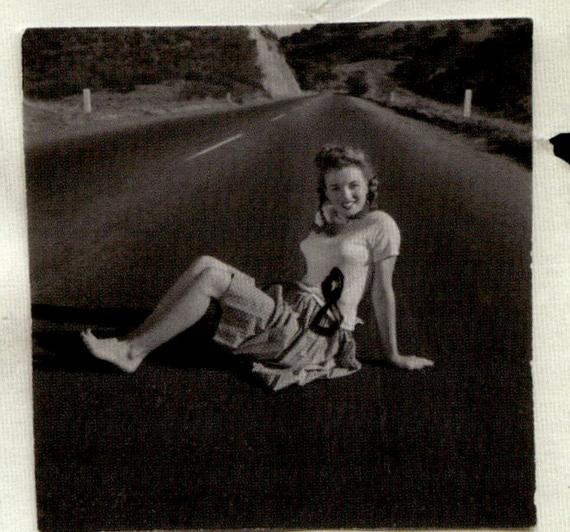

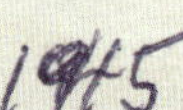

1945

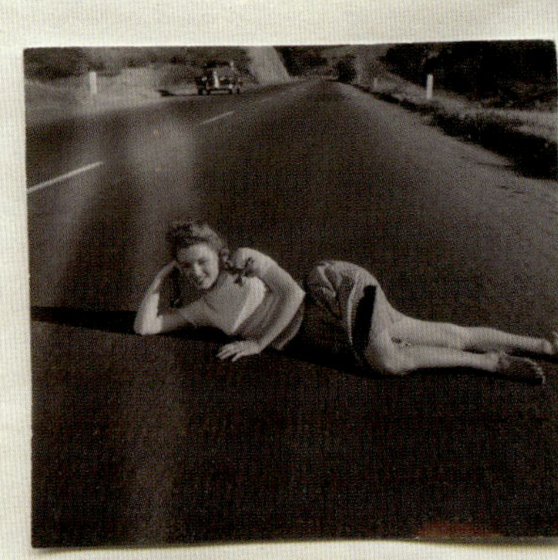

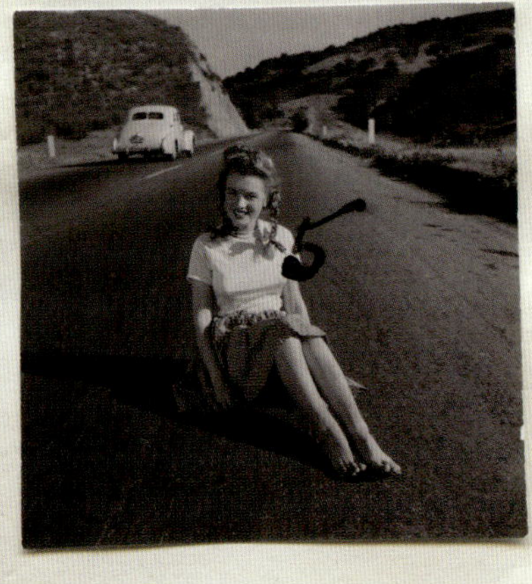

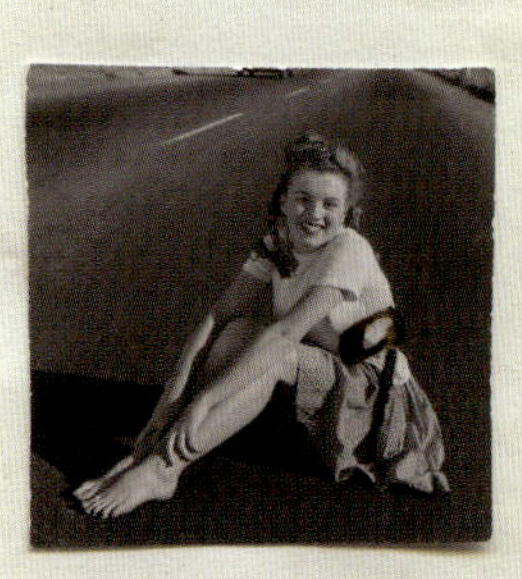

L

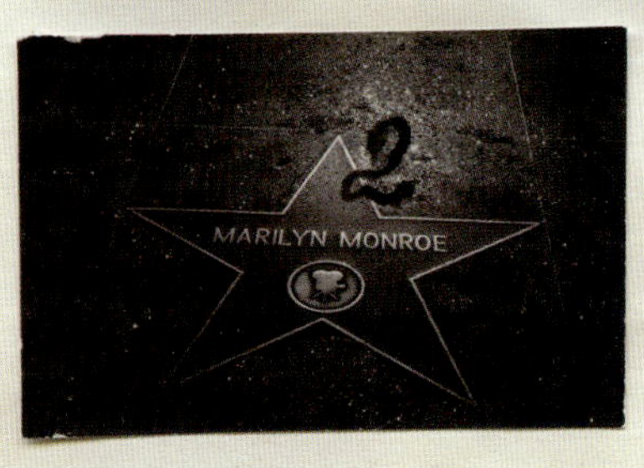

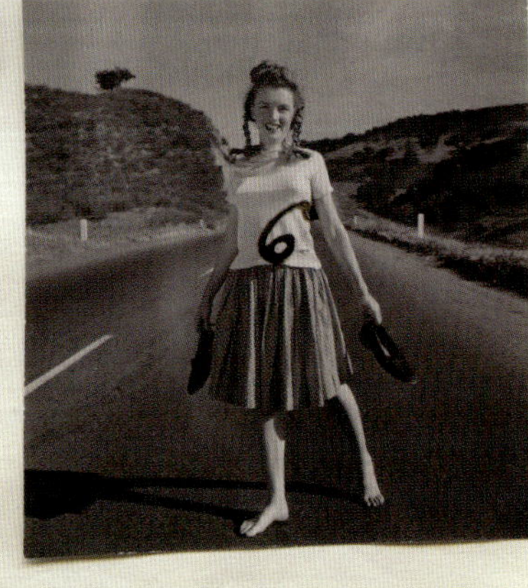

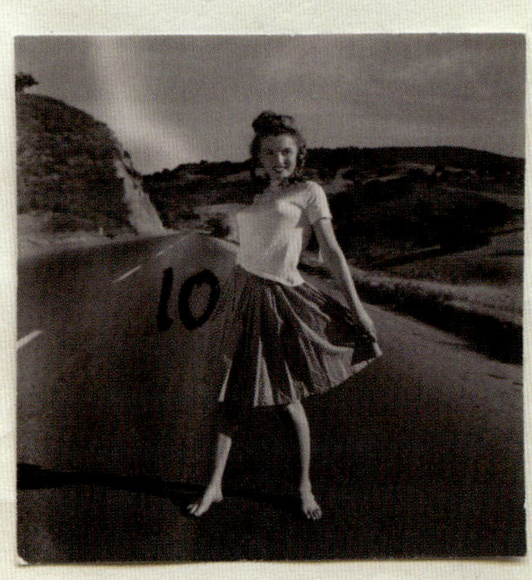

AND HER NAME BECAME A LEGEND...

ANDRE DE DIENE

1

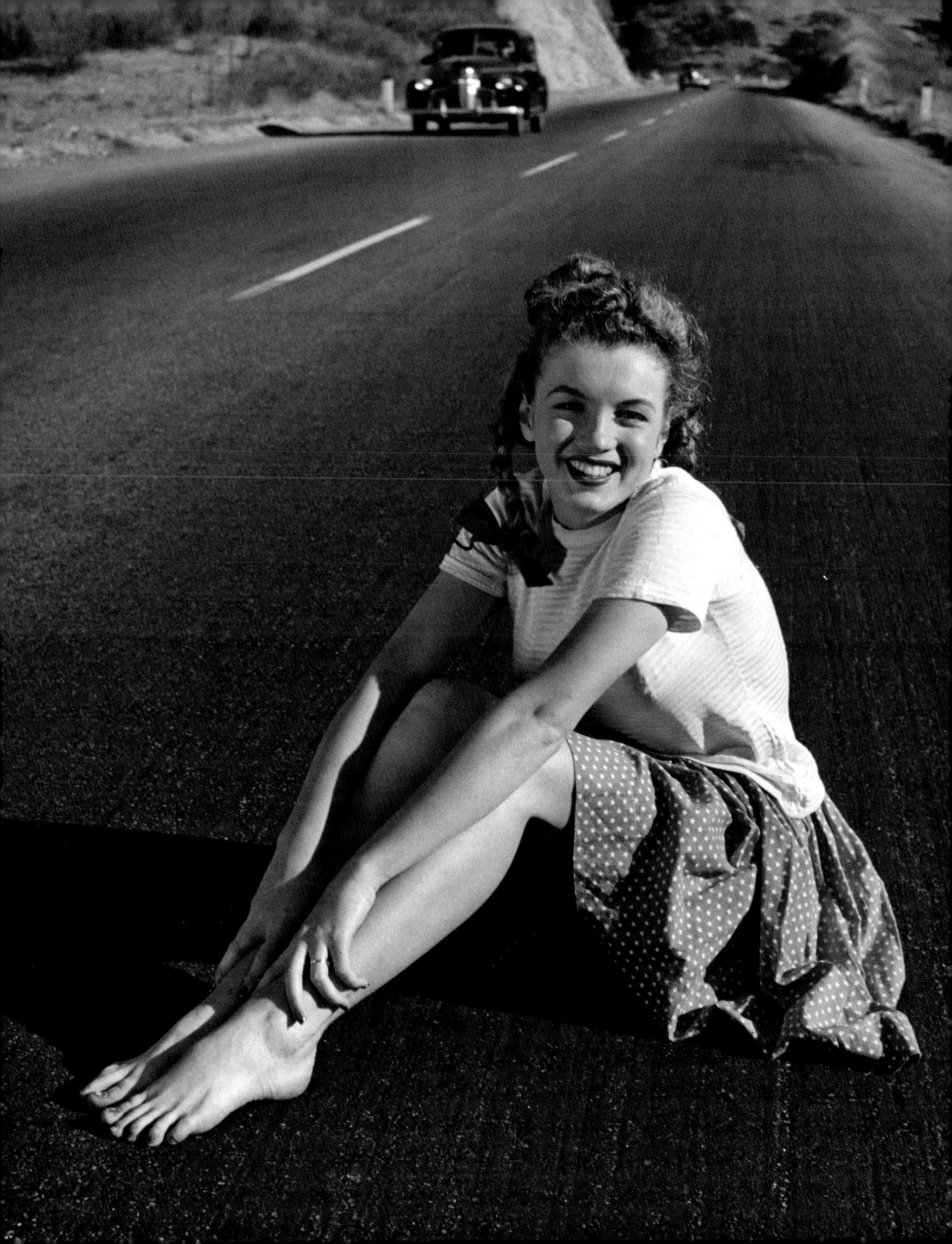

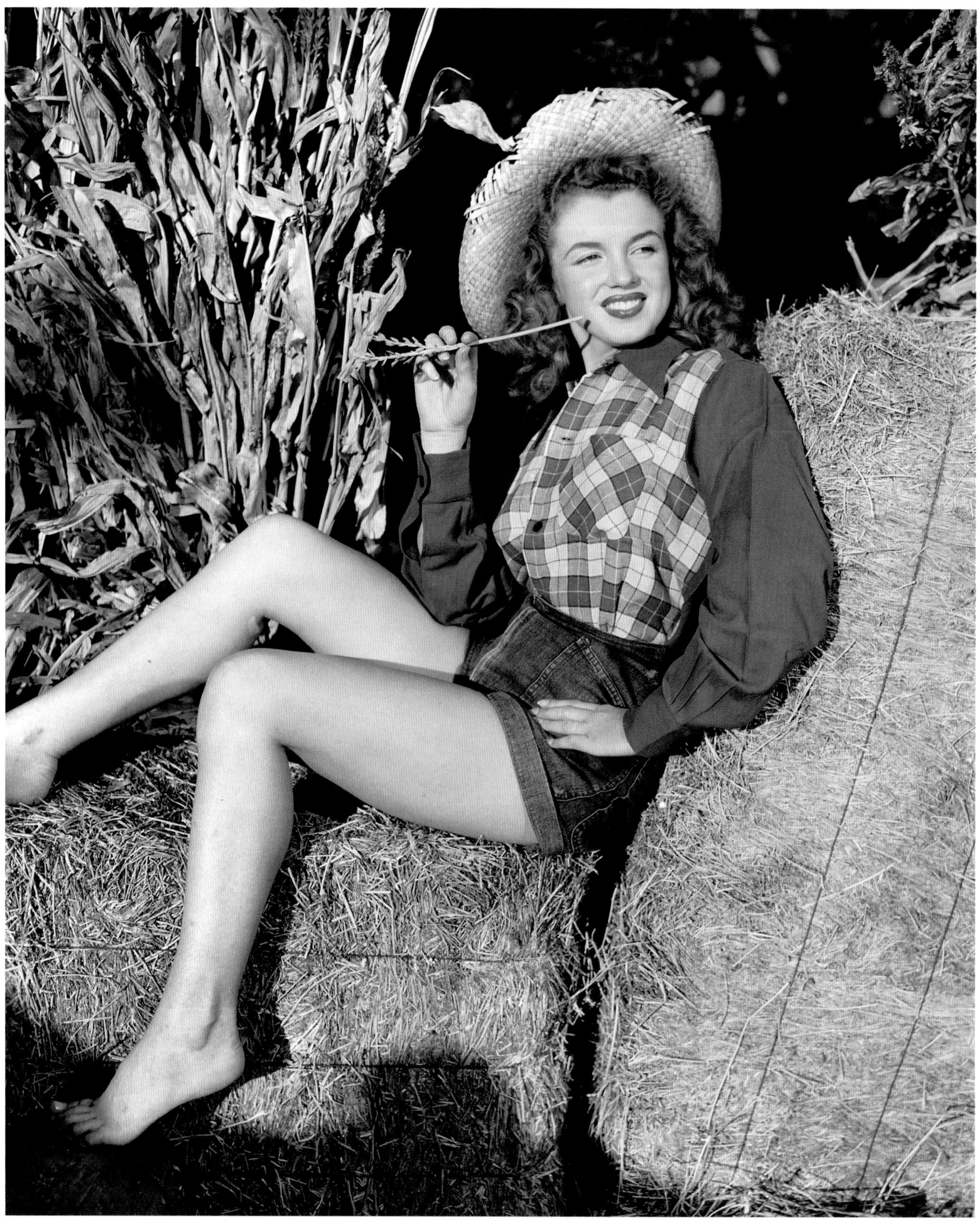

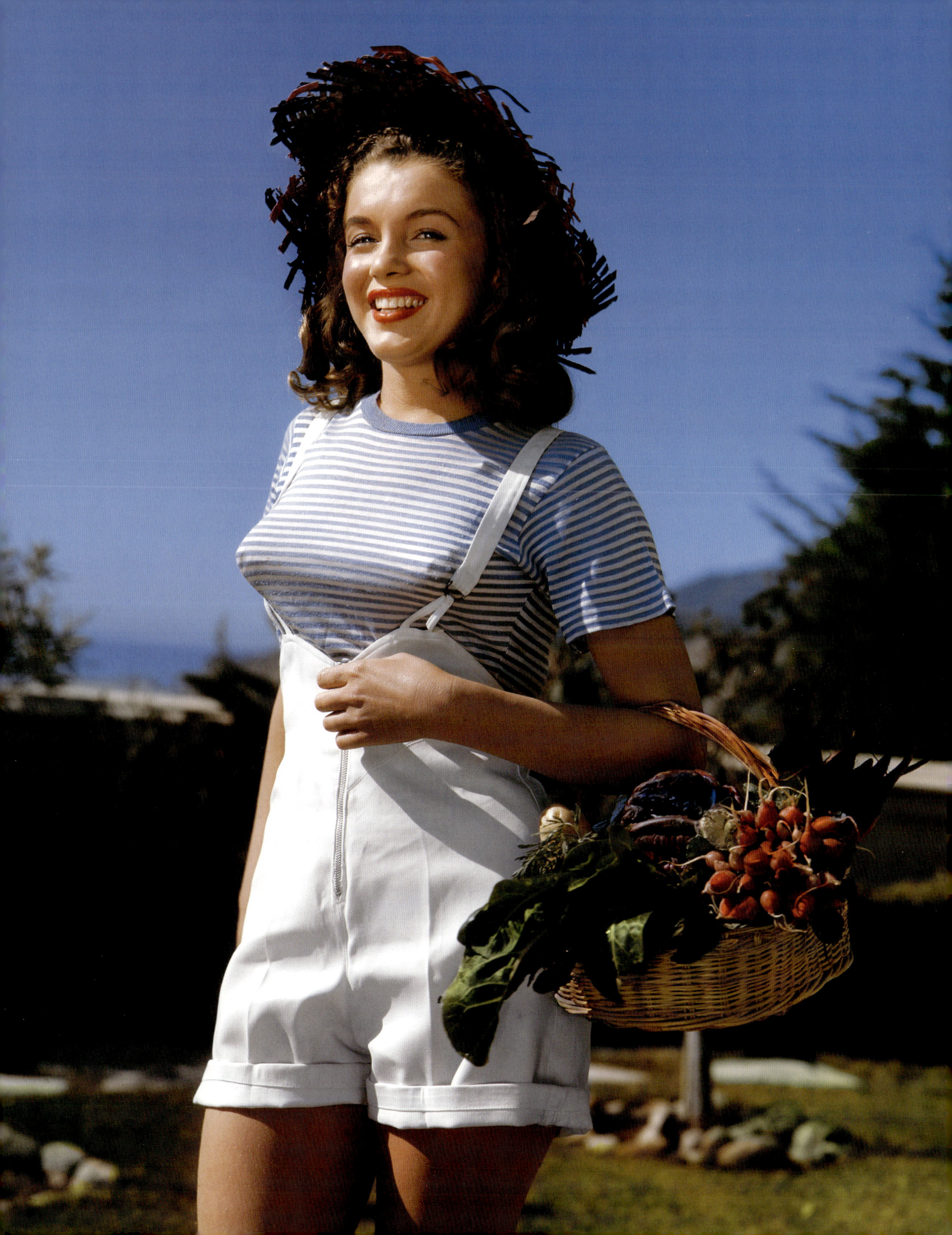

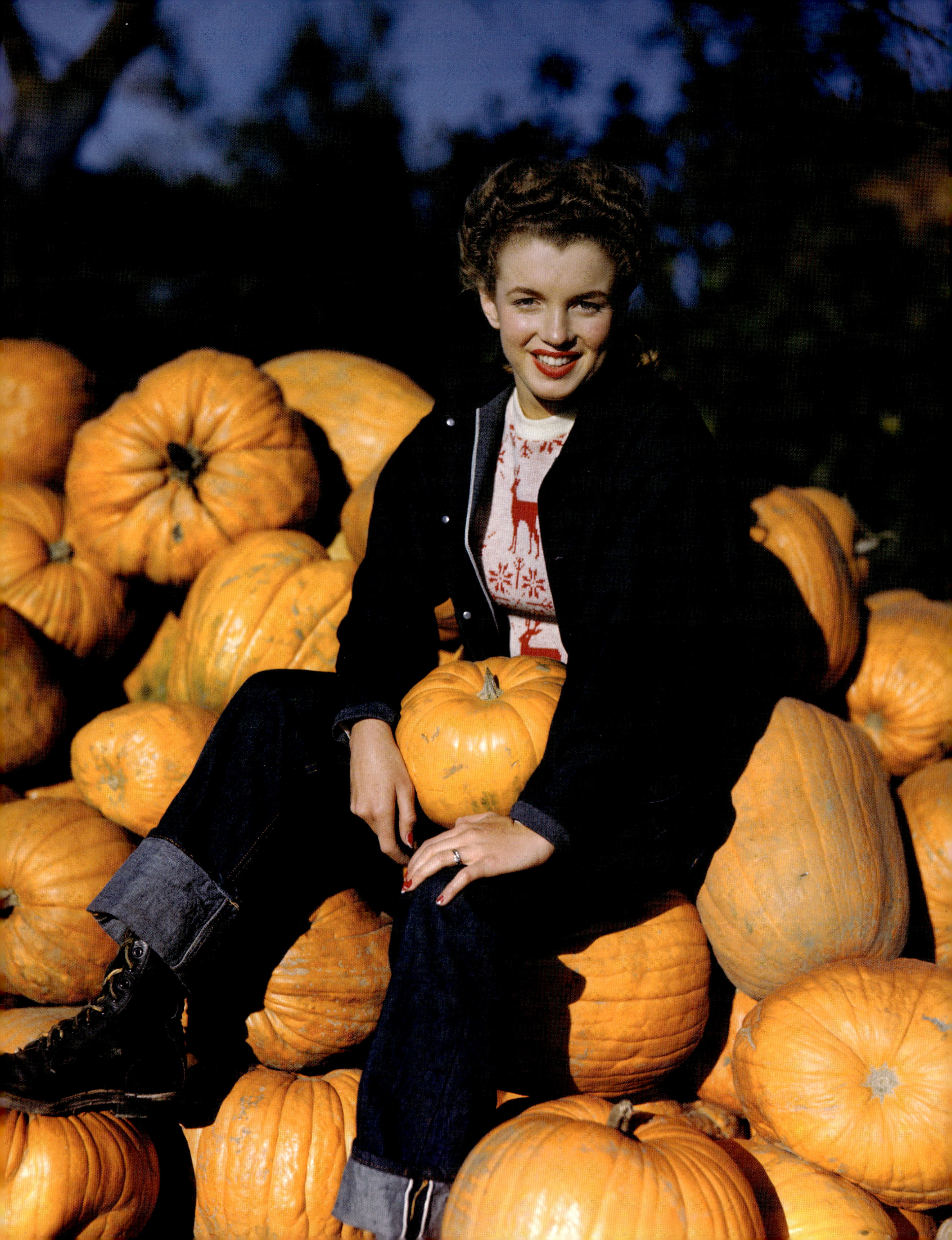

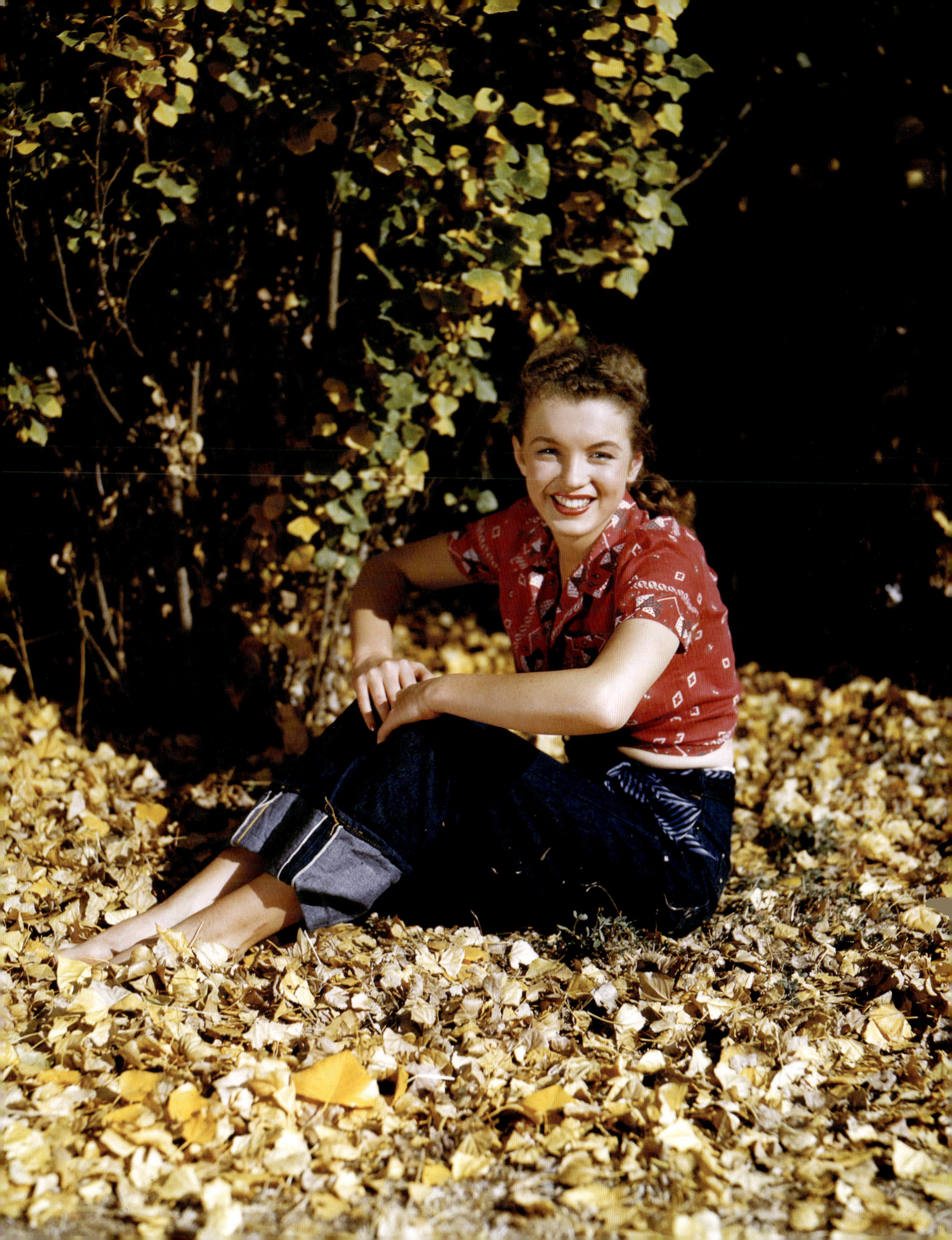

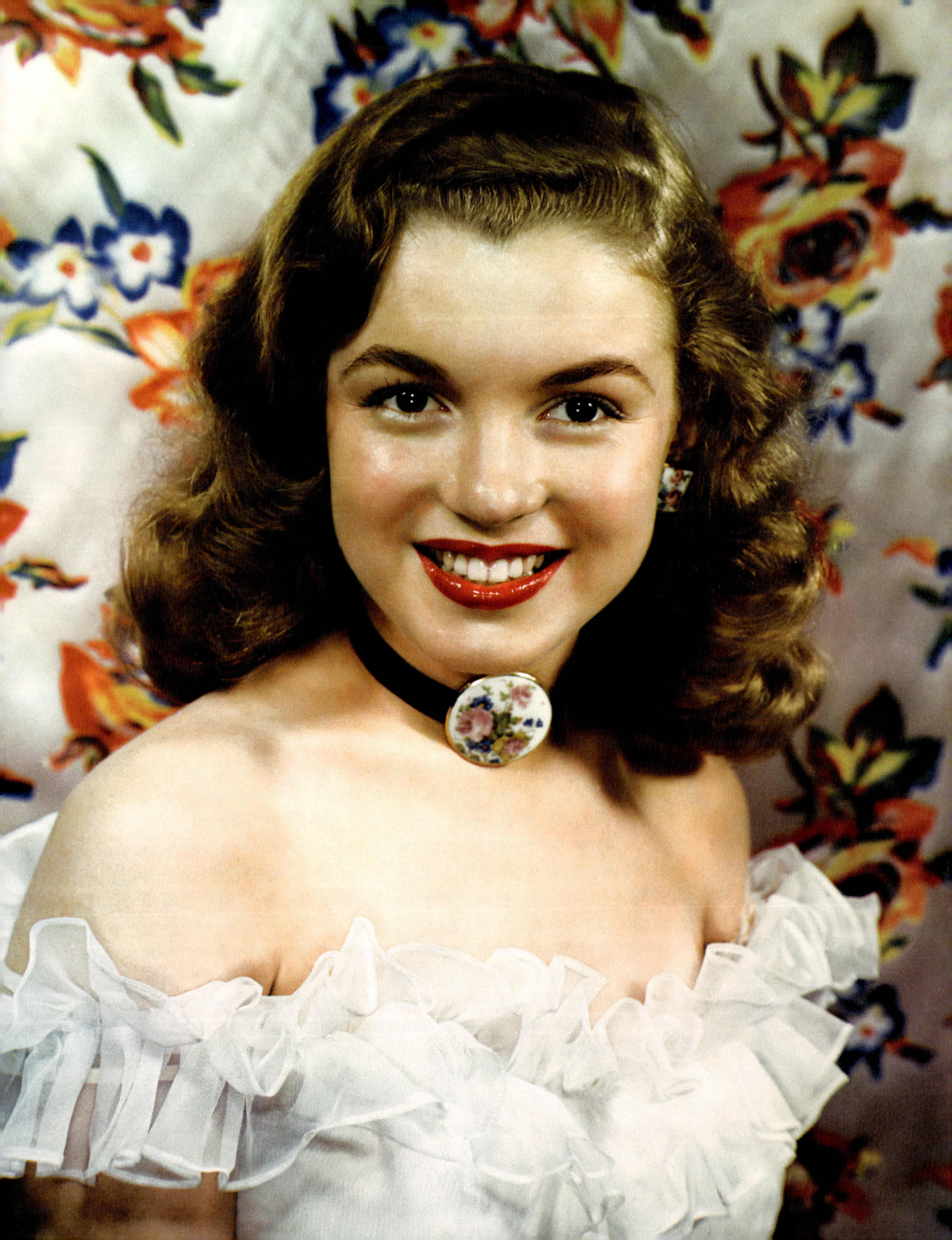

She was a clean-cut, American, wholesome girl—too plump, but beautiful in a way. We tried to teach her how to pose, how to handle her body. She always tried to lower her smile because she smiled too high, and it made her nose look a little long. At first she knew nothing about carriage, posture, walking, sitting, or posing. She started out with less than any girl I ever knew, but she worked the hardest. . . . She wanted to learn, wanted to be somebody, more than anybody I ever saw before in my life."

EMMELINE SNIVELY (Head of the Blue Book Modeling Agency)

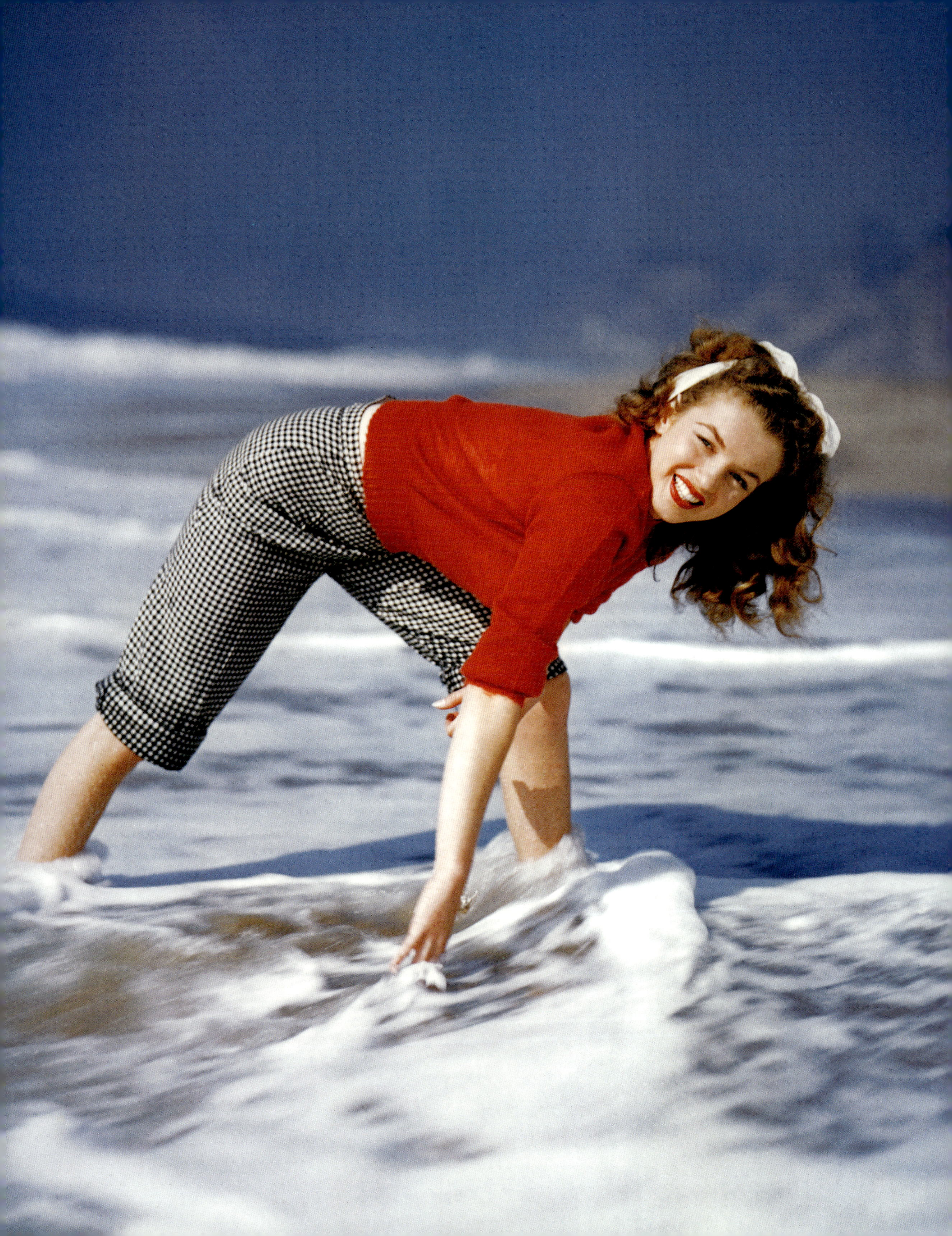

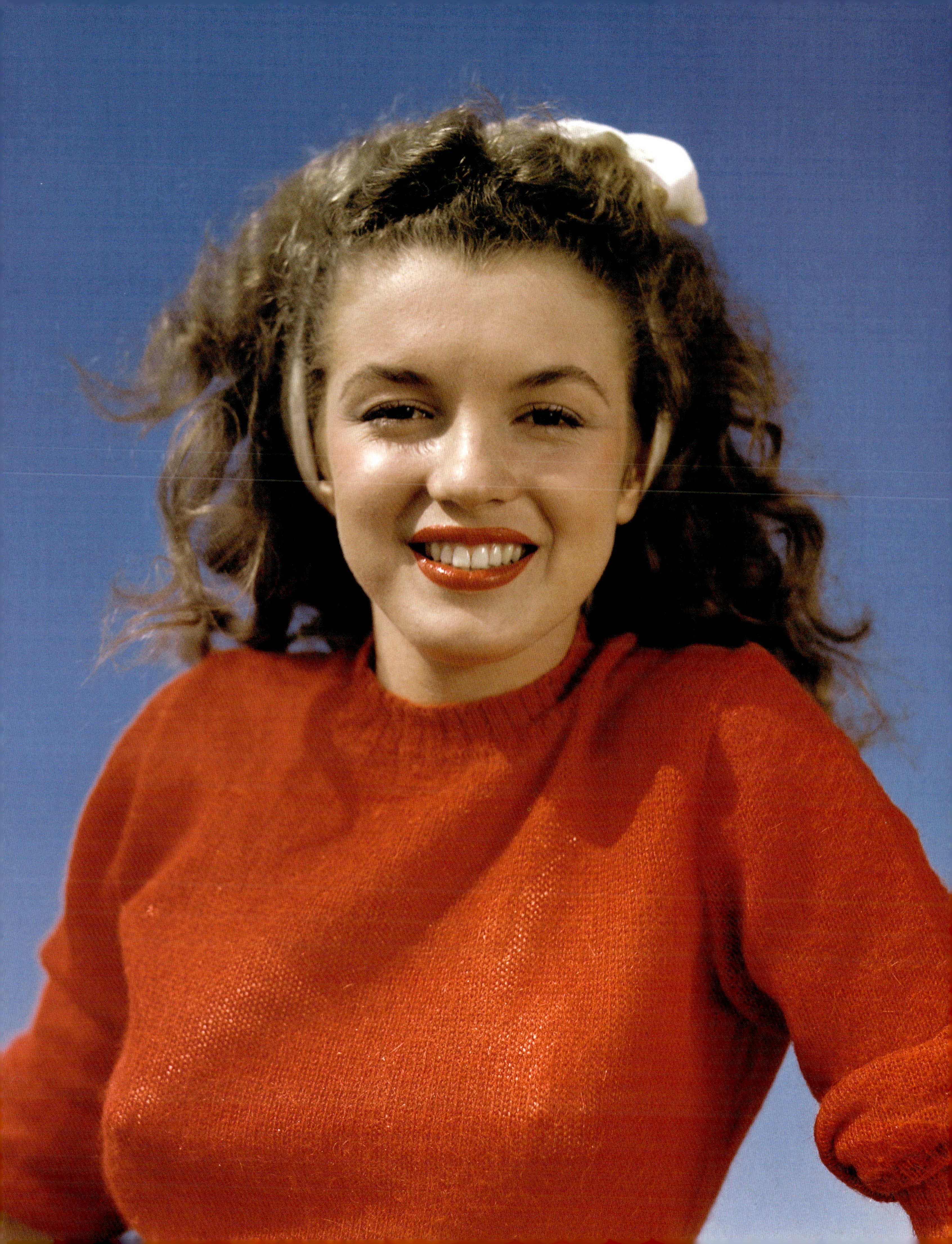

"Of all the many photographs my father was to take of Marilyn throughout her career, his first sitting with her always remained his favorite. Taken at his studio on the Sunset Strip in 1946, he wrote in his journal, 'I have never seen a model, beginner or pro, who is so at ease before the camera. Norma Jeane seems to have a sixth sense between the optical interplay of subject and camera. Concentration, projection, and synchronization are second nature to her.' Capturing the young Norma Jeane's fresh-faced wholesomeness, my father was so impressed that he presented a color portfolio of these images to Ben Lyon, the head of talent at Twentieth Century-Fox, and urged him to give her a color screen test which led to her first motion picture contract. At that time my father knew her as few did, becoming a close friend, confidant, and father figure. Later, as the world came to know her as Marilyn Monroe, to him she always remained Norma Jeane."

SUSAN BERNARD (Daughter of Bruno Bernard / Bernard of Hollywood)

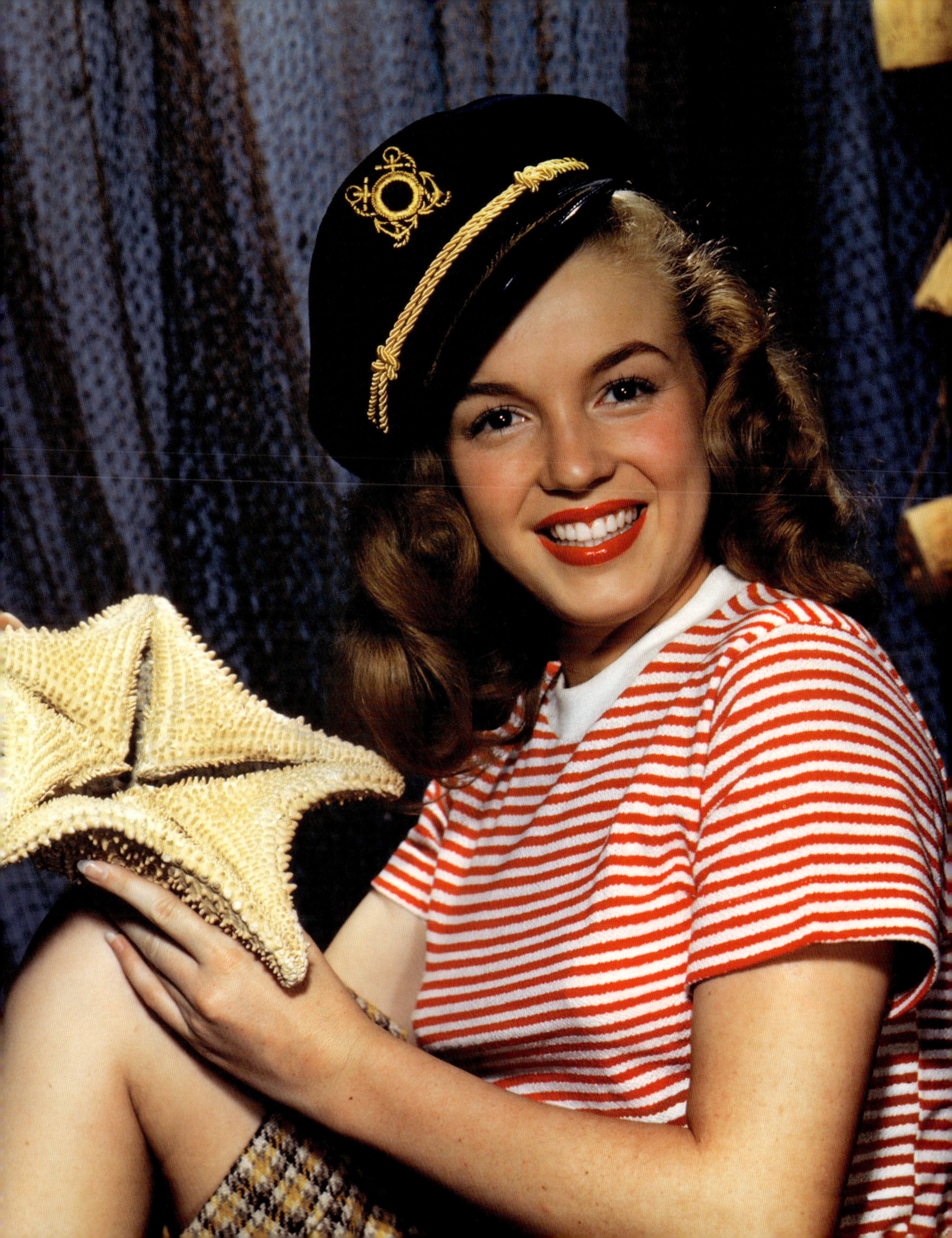

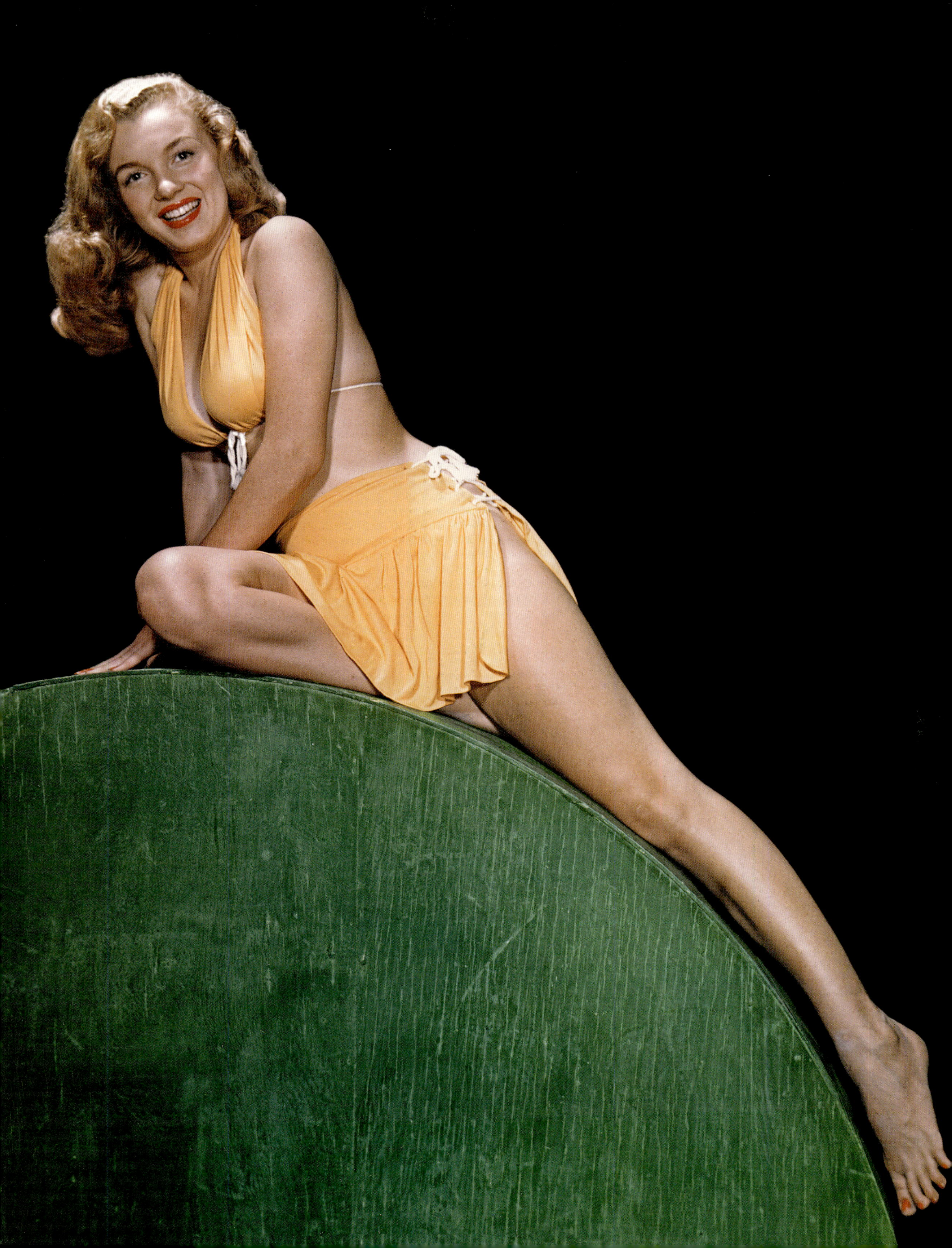

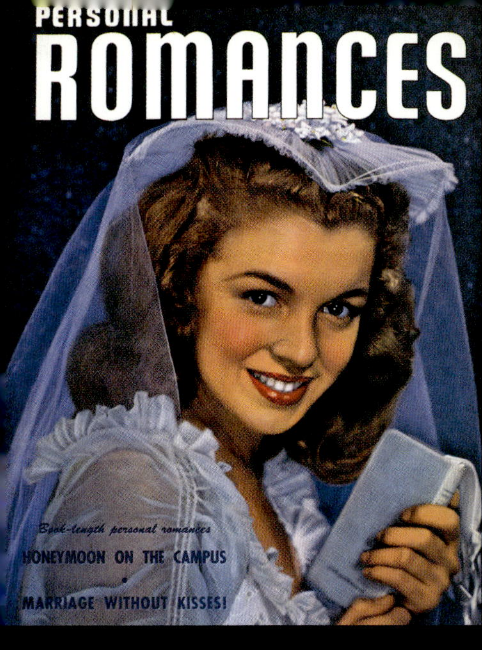
PERSONAL
ROMANCES
Book-length personal romances
HONEYMOON ON THE CAMPUS
MARRIAGE WITHOUT KISSES!

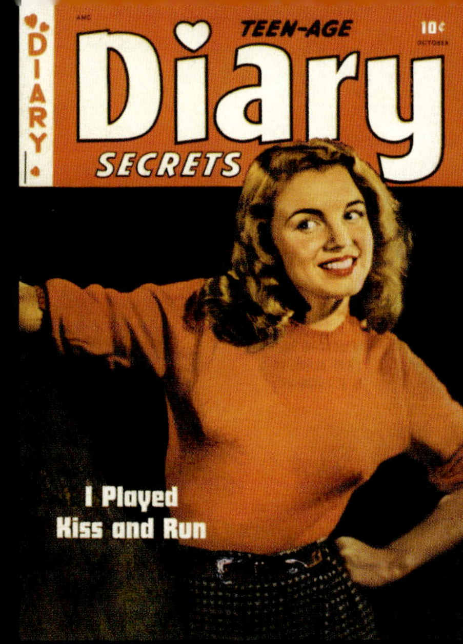
DIARY
TEEN-AGE
Diary
SECRETS
10¢
I Played
Kiss and Run

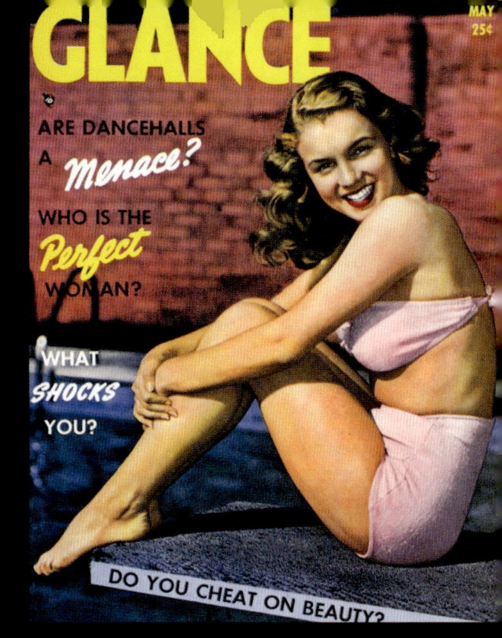
GLANCE
MAY
25¢
ARE DANCEHALLS
A Menace?
WHO IS THE
Perfect
WOMAN?
WHAT
SHOCKS
YOU?
DO YOU CHEAT ON BEAUTY?

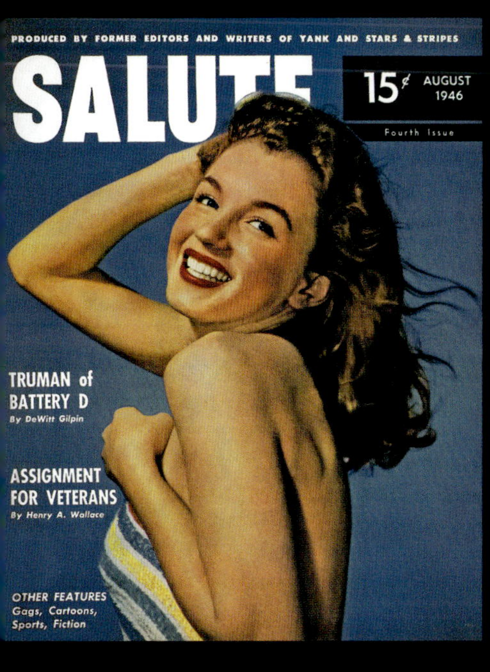
PRODUCED BY FORMER EDITORS AND WRITERS OF YANK AND STARS & STRIPES
SALUTE
15¢ AUGUST 1946
Fourth Issue
TRUMAN of BATTERY D
By DeWitt Gilpin
ASSIGNMENT FOR VETERANS
By Henry A. Wallace
OTHER FEATURES
Gags, Cartoons, Sports, Fiction

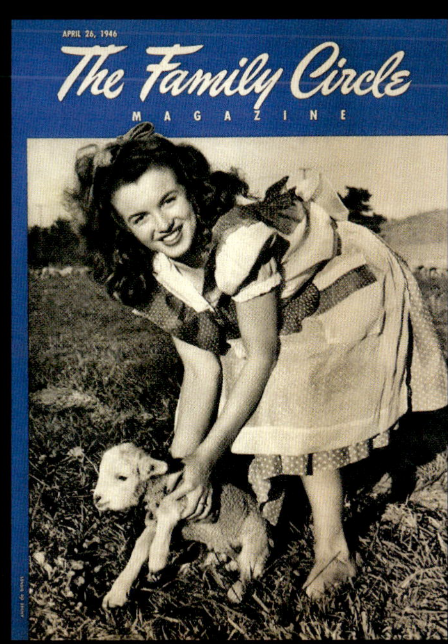
APRIL 26, 1946
The Family Circle
MAGAZINE

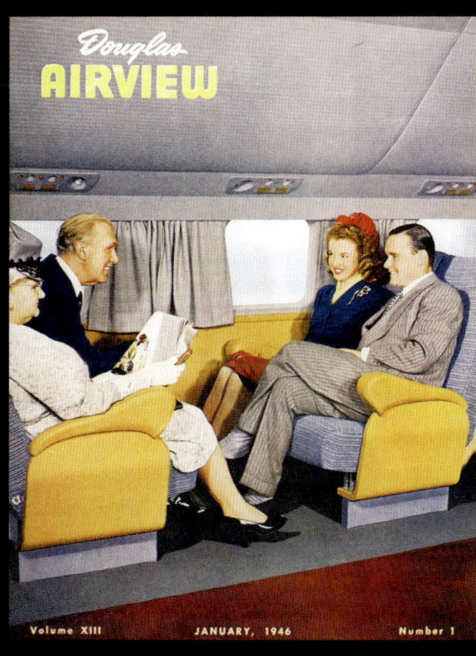
Douglas
AIRVIEW
Volume XIII
JANUARY, 1946
Number 1

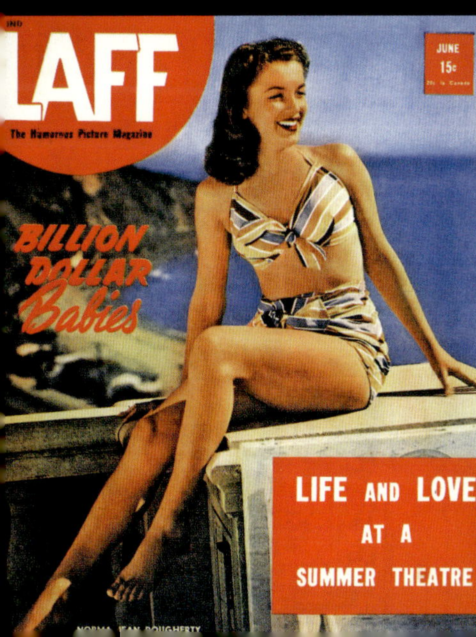
LAFF
The Humorous Picture Magazine
JUNE
15¢
BILLION DOLLAR Babies
LIFE AND LOVE
AT A
SUMMER THEATRE
NORMA JEAN DOUGHERTY

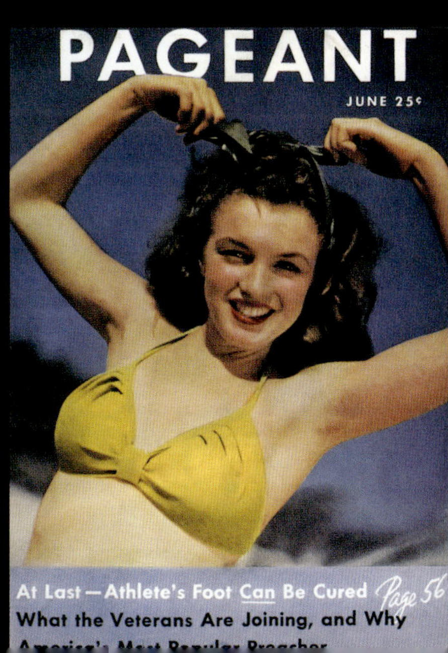
PAGEANT
JUNE 25¢
At Last—Athlete's Foot Can Be Cured Page 56
What the Veterans Are Joining, and Why

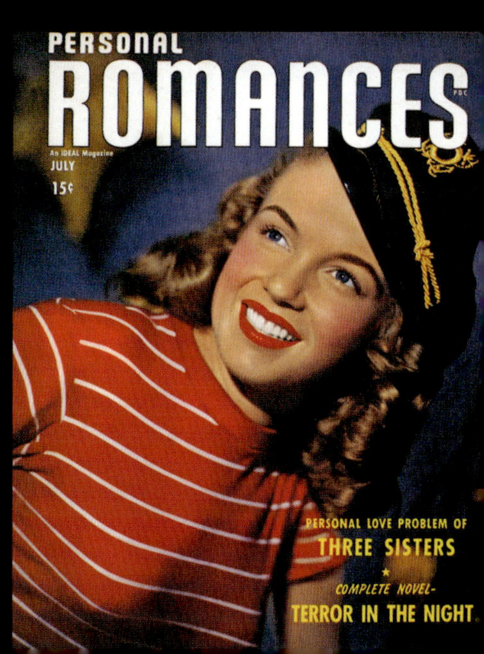
PERSONAL
ROMANCES
An IDEAL Magazine
JULY
15¢
PERSONAL LOVE PROBLEM OF
THREE SISTERS
COMPLETE NOVEL—
TERROR IN THE NIGHT

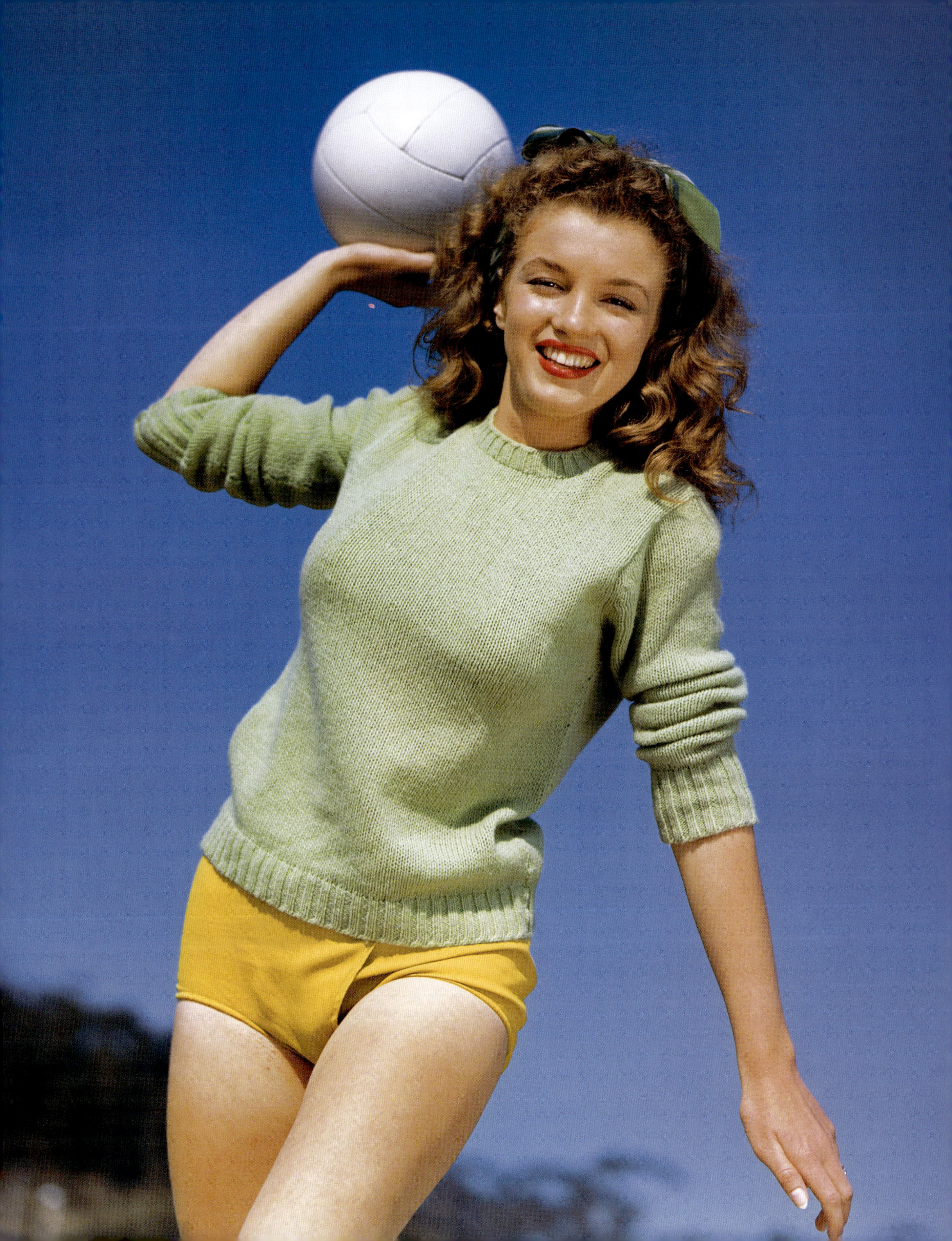

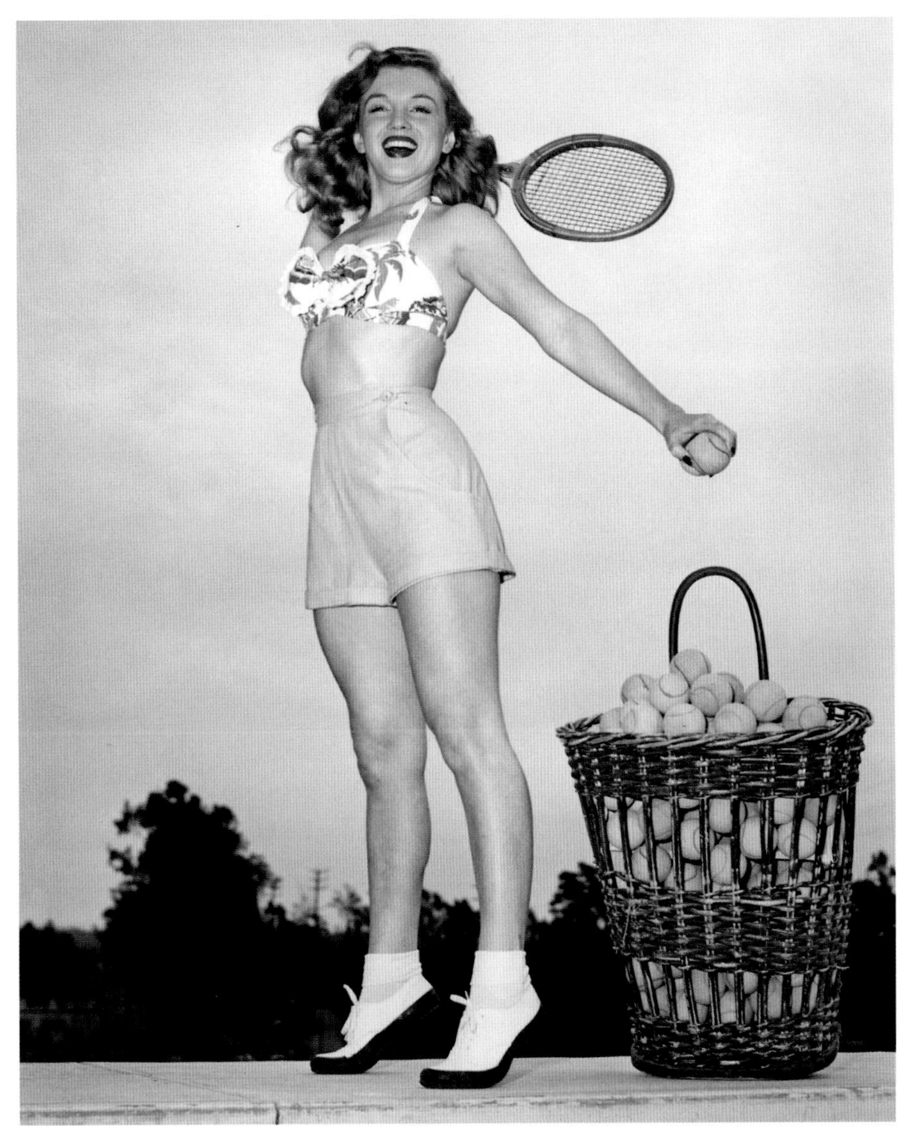

"[Norma Jeane was] very serious, very ambitious, and always pleasant to be with. There was only one problem for her. She did so many covers that for a while she was considered overexposed—the magazine and advertising people had seen so much of her that after a year she couldn't get much work."

LYDIA BODRERO REED (Blue Book Agency model, 1945–1946)

"I asked her where she lived, and when she said at the Studio Club, I was impressed because I knew that a girl who looked like that could have the biggest house in Beverly Hills, she could have whatever she wanted because men would give it to her. Therefore, if she lived at the Studio Club it was because she had character."

BEN LYON (Head of Talent at Twentieth Century-Fox)

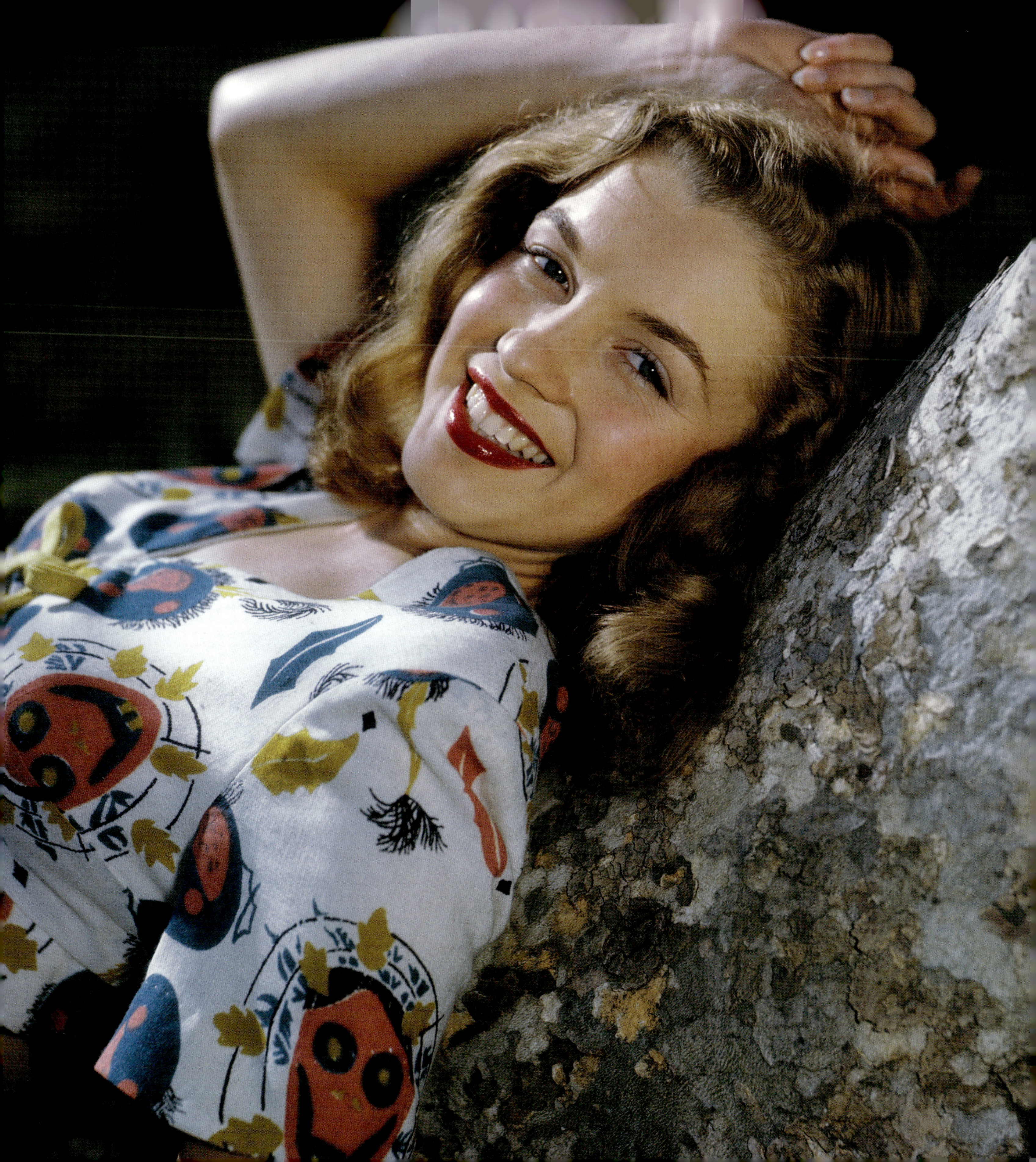

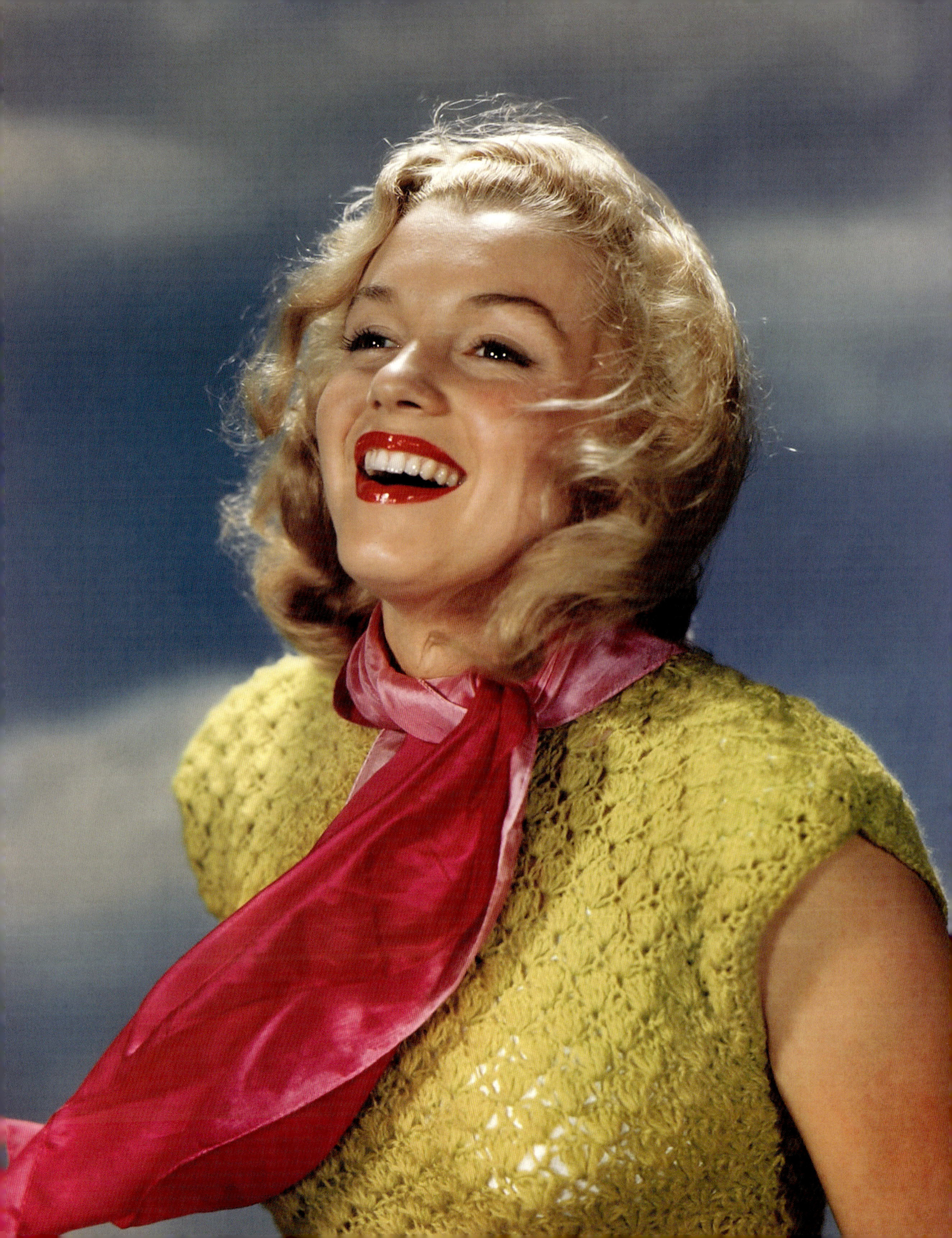

"I used to think as I looked out on the Hollywood night, there must be thousands of girls sitting alone like me, dreaming of becoming a movie star. But I'm not going to worry about them. I'm dreaming the hardest."

MARILYN MONROE

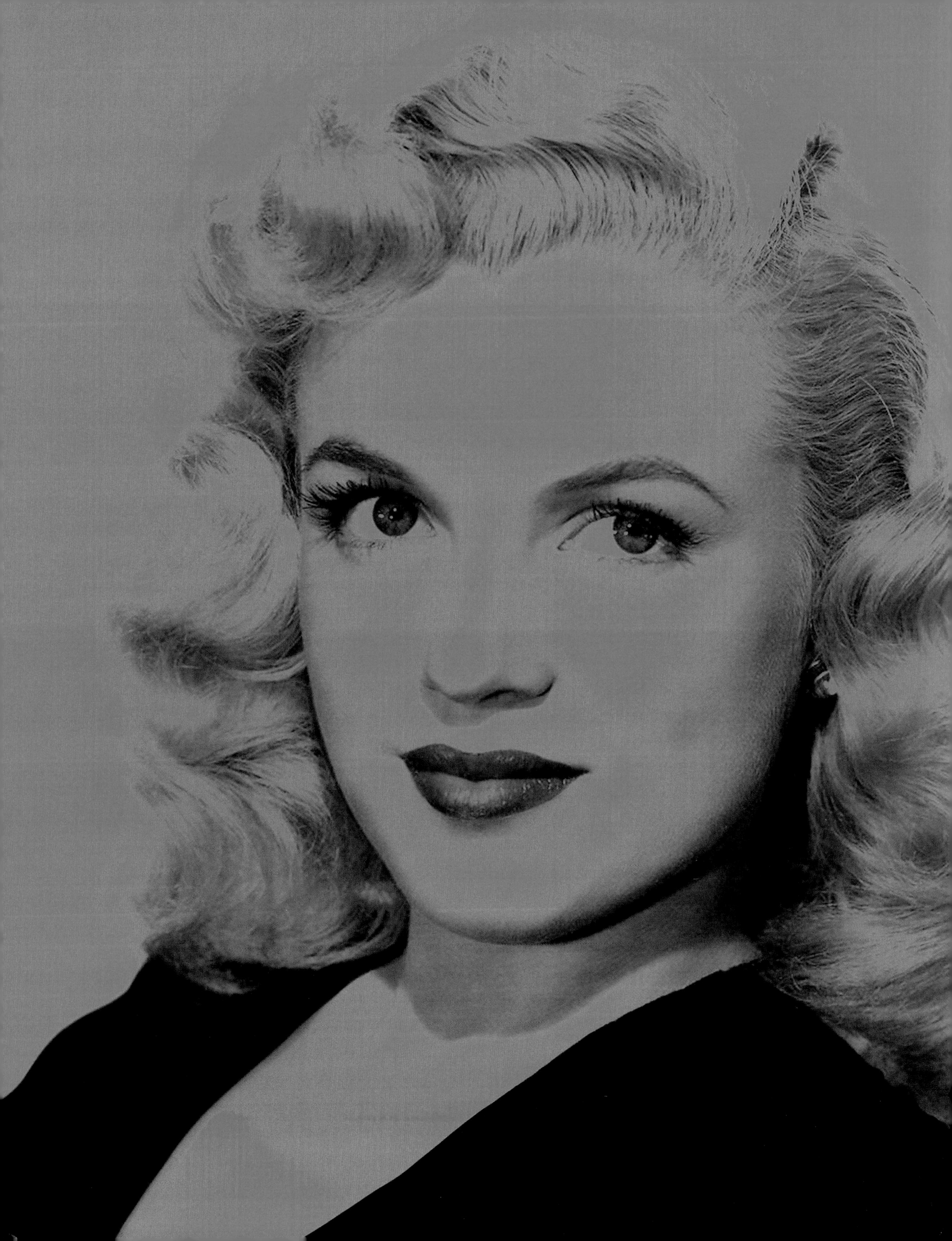

TRANSFIGURATION

Starlet 1947–1951

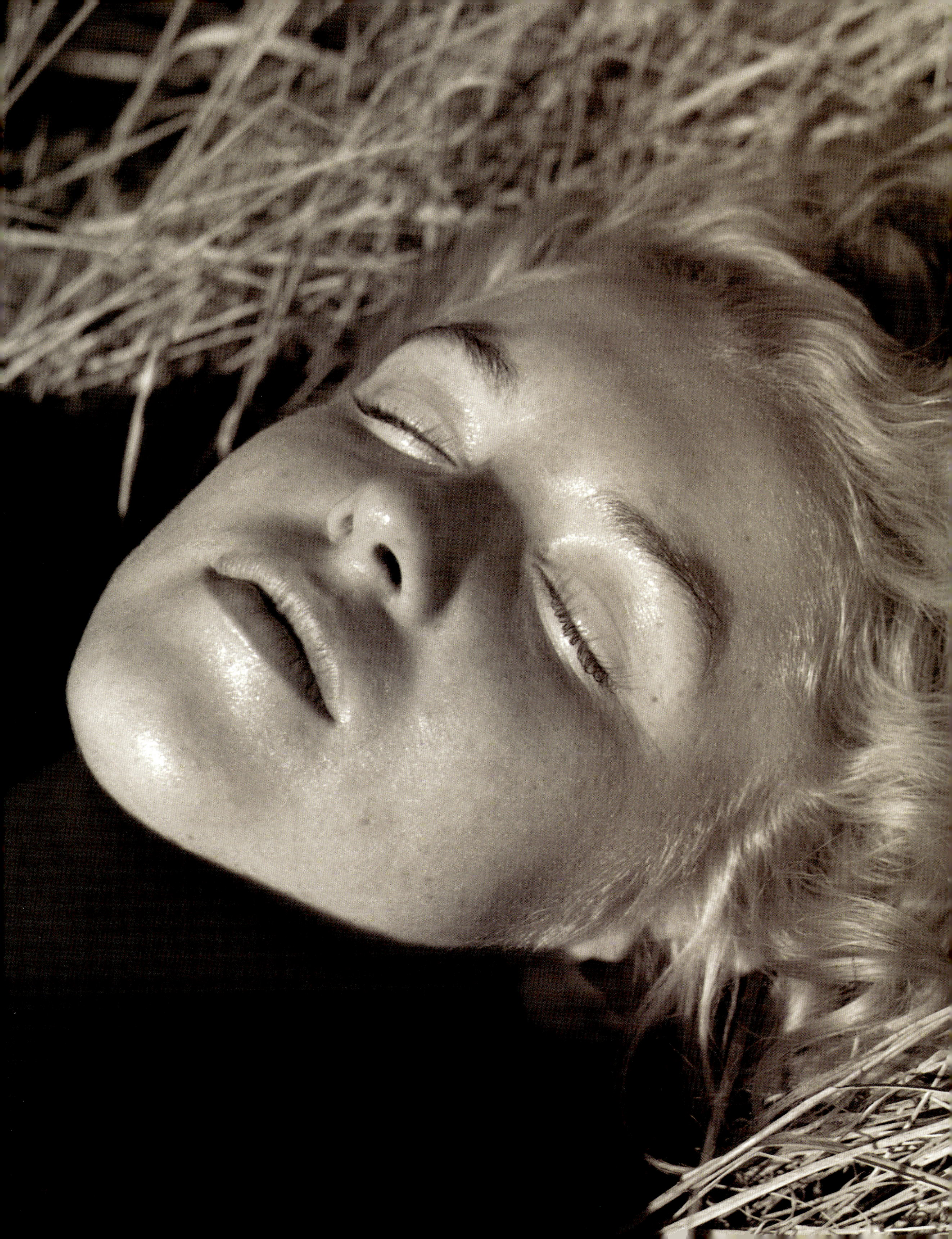

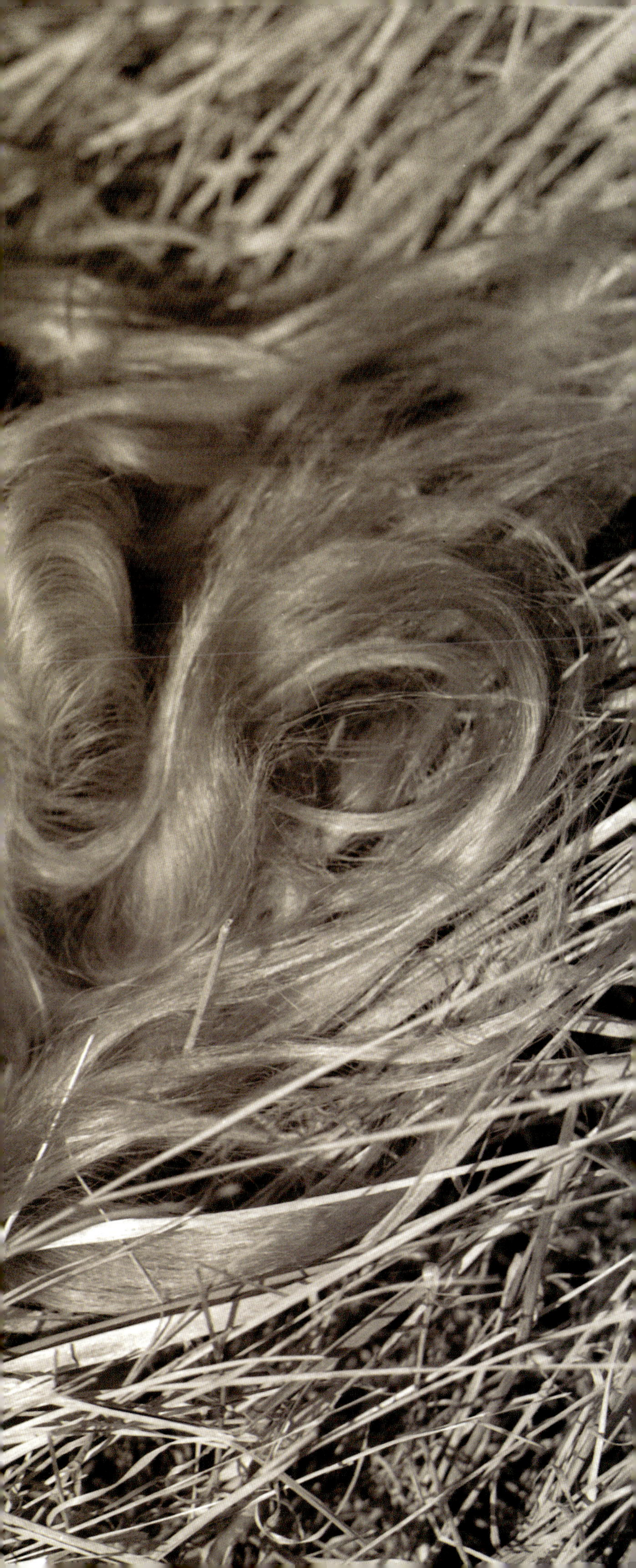

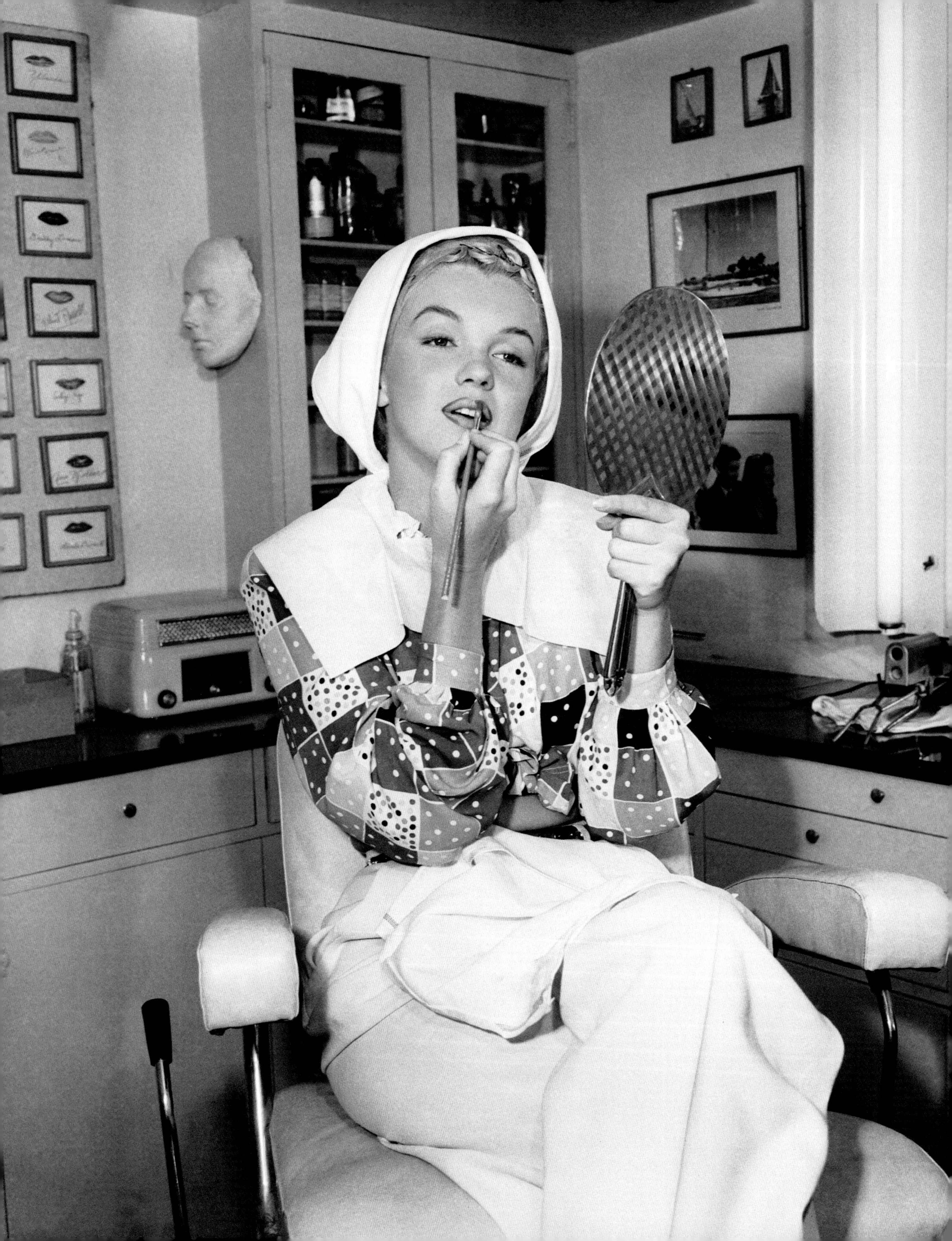

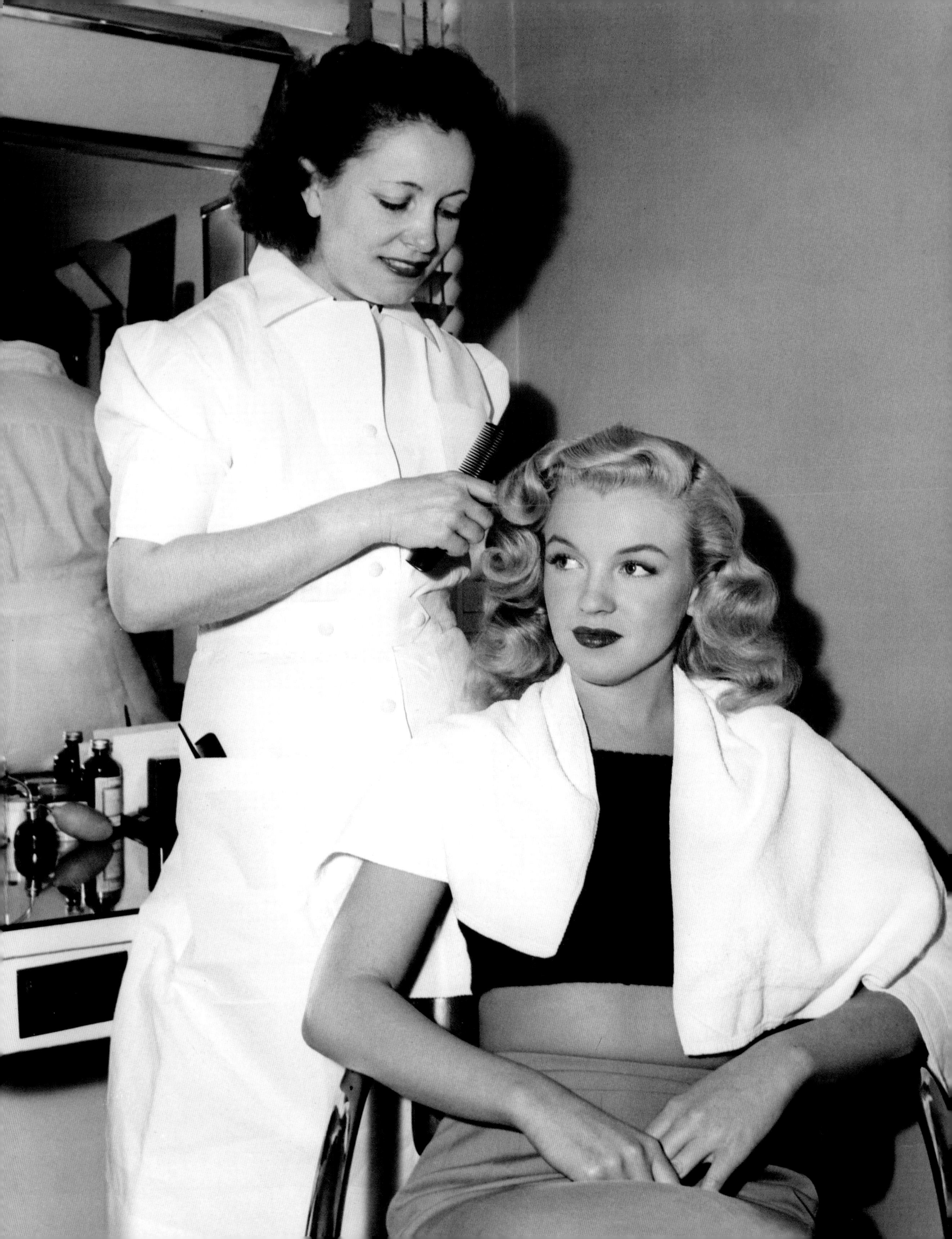

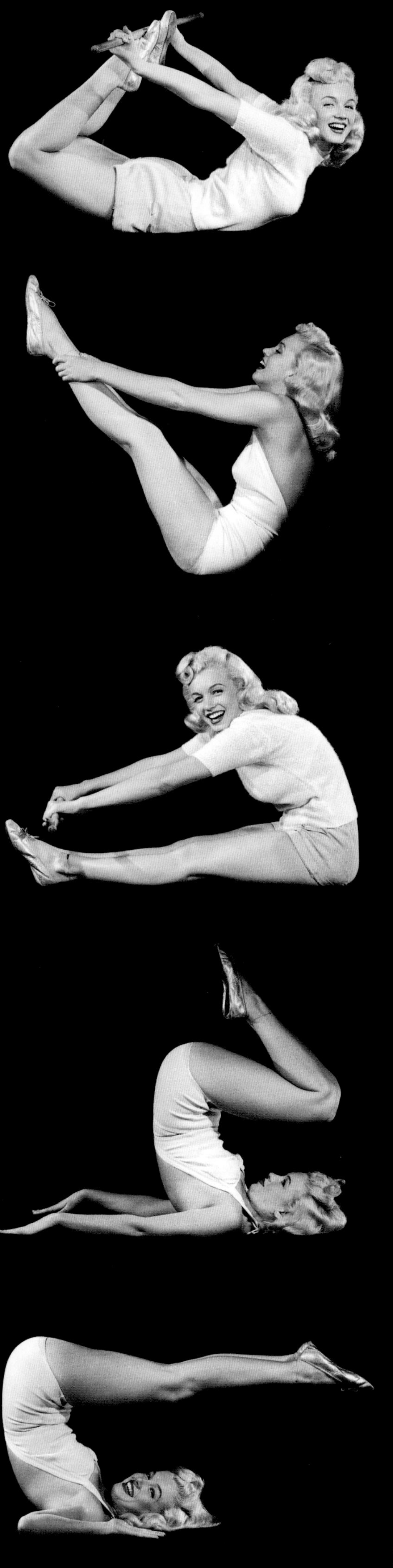

"When she saw a camera, any camera, she lit up and was totally different. The moment the shot was over, she fell back into her not very interesting position."

LASZLO WILLINGER (Photographer)

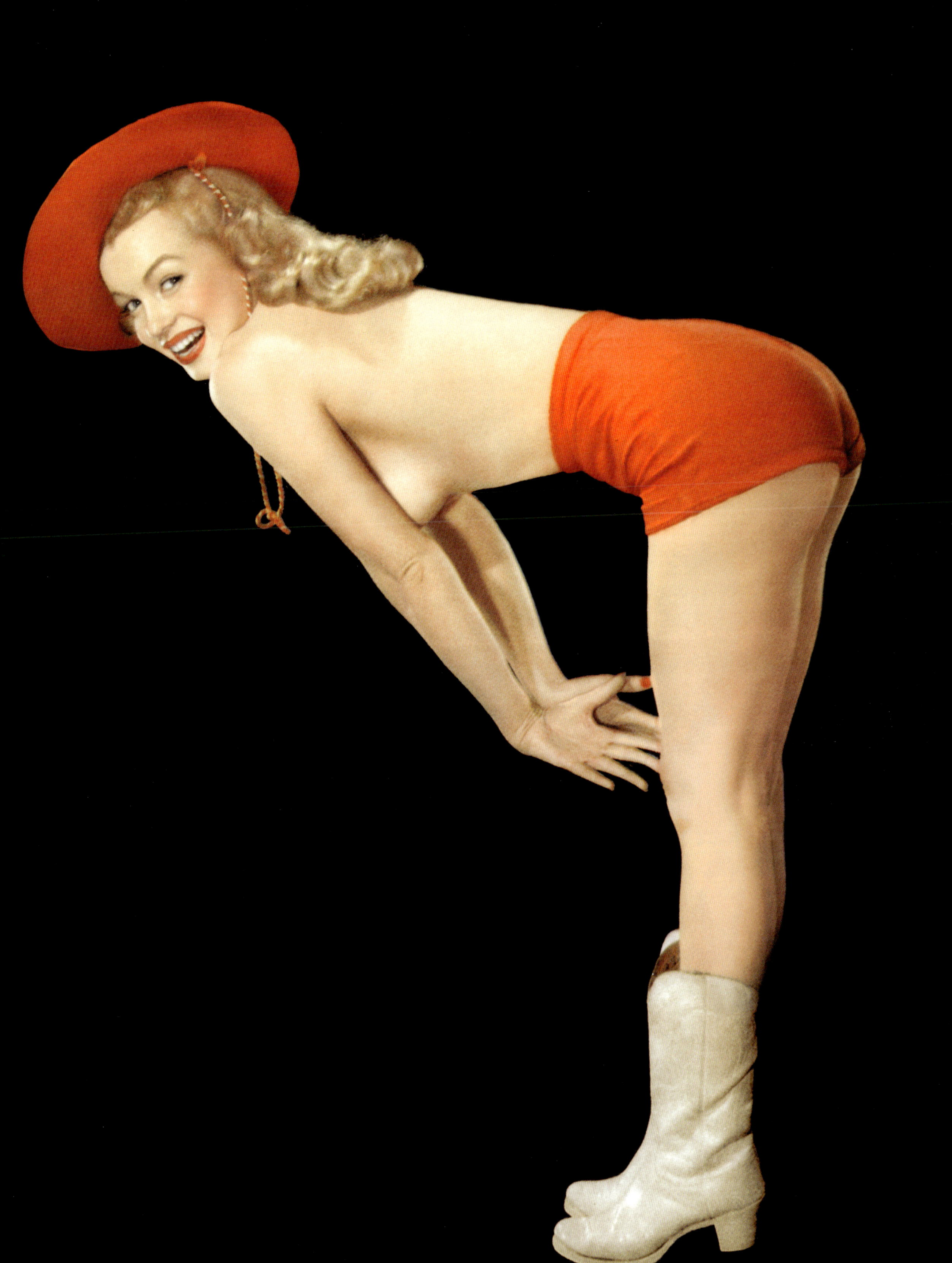

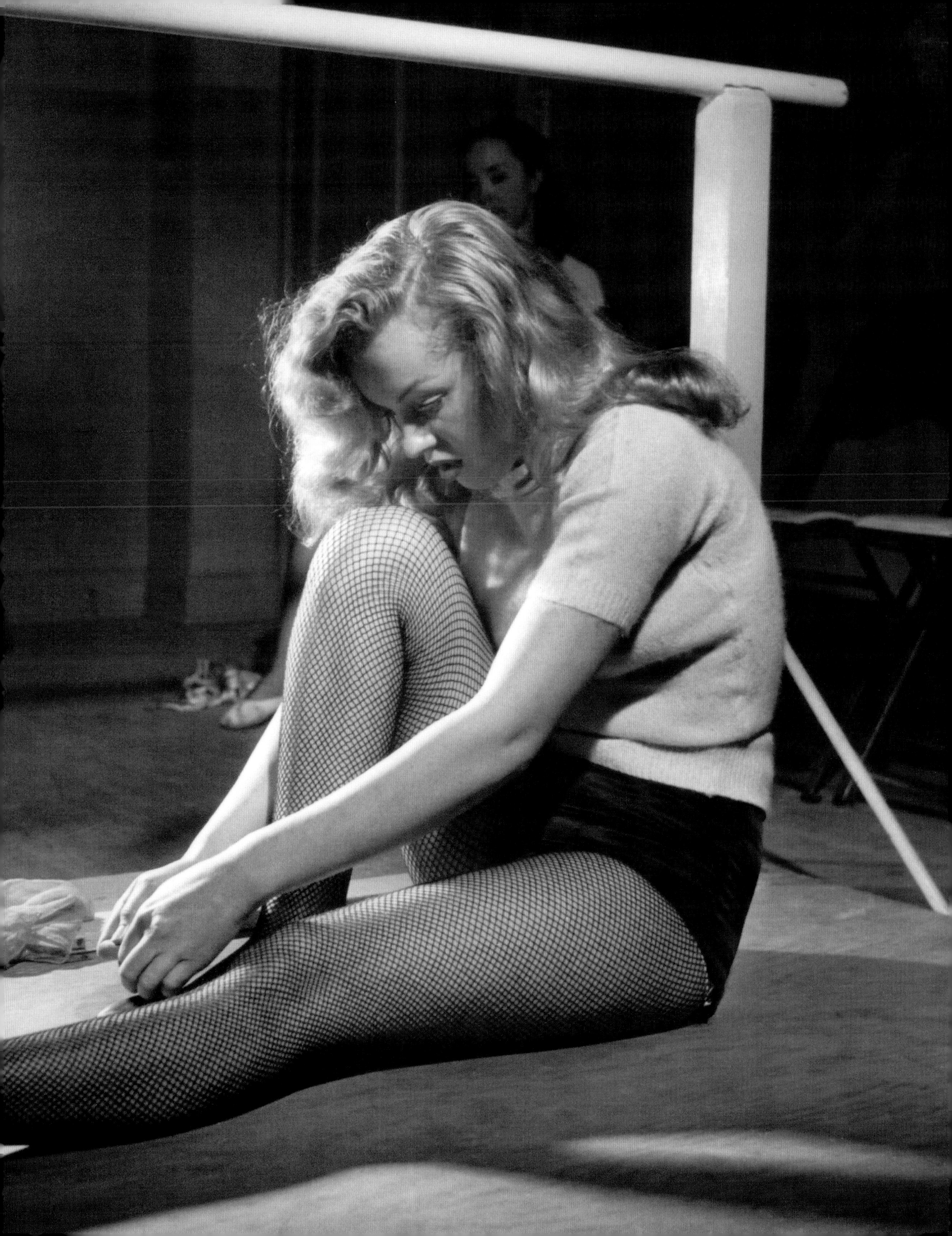

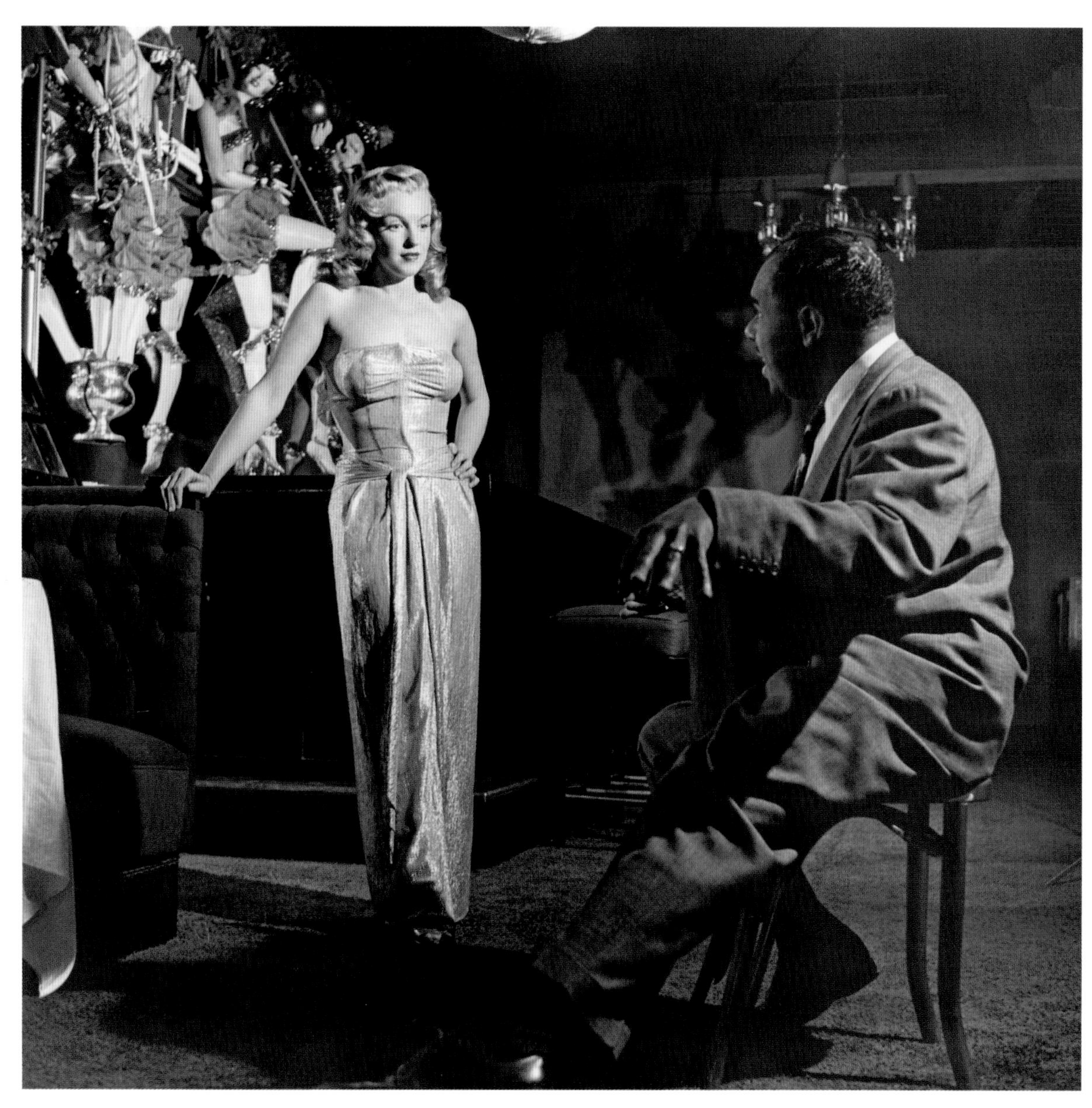

"She was always seeking advice. Marilyn was wiser than she pretended to be. . . . She appeared kind and soft and helpless. Almost everyone wanted to help her. Marilyn's supposed helplessness was her greatest strength."

SIDNEY SKOLSKY (Hollywood Columnist)

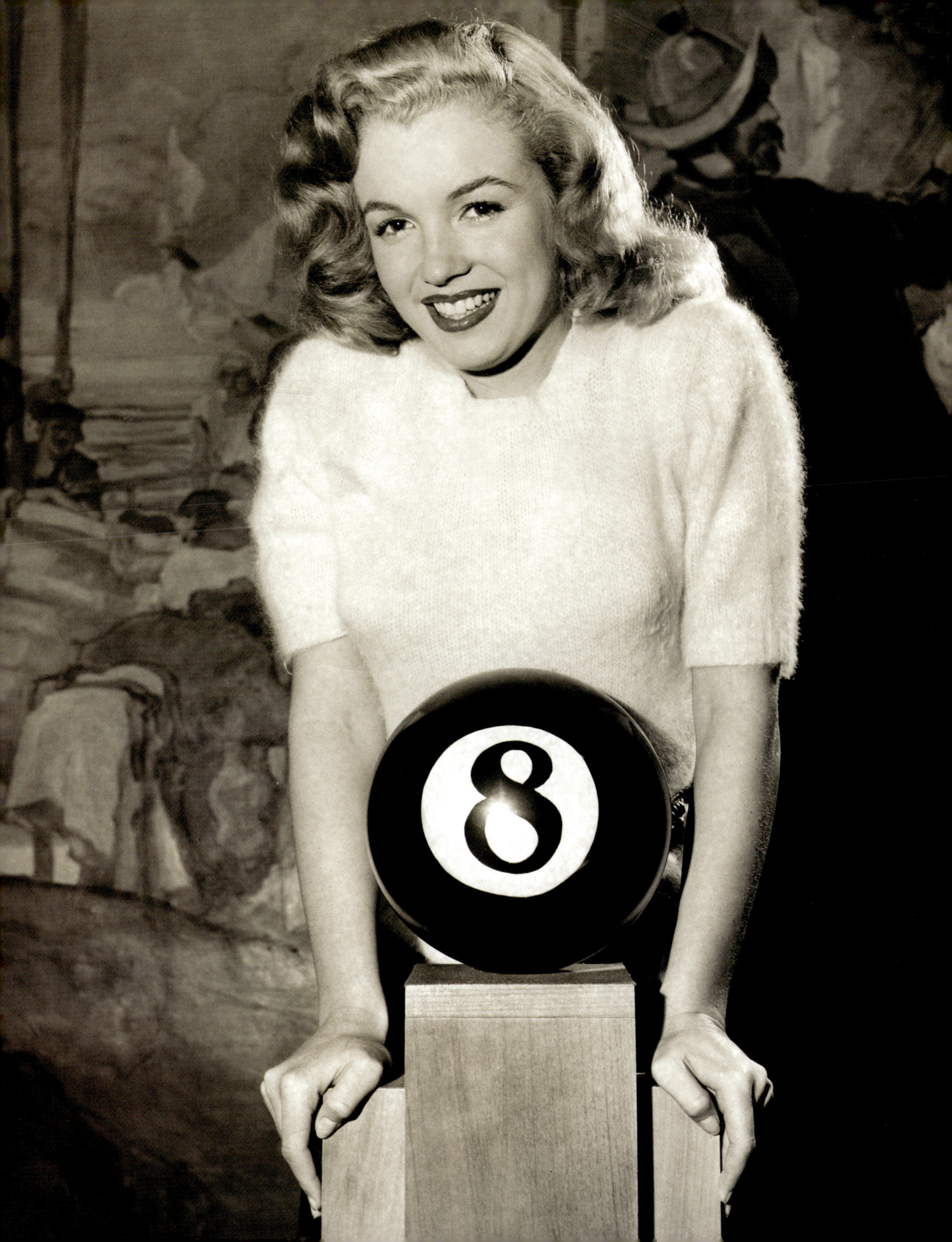
8

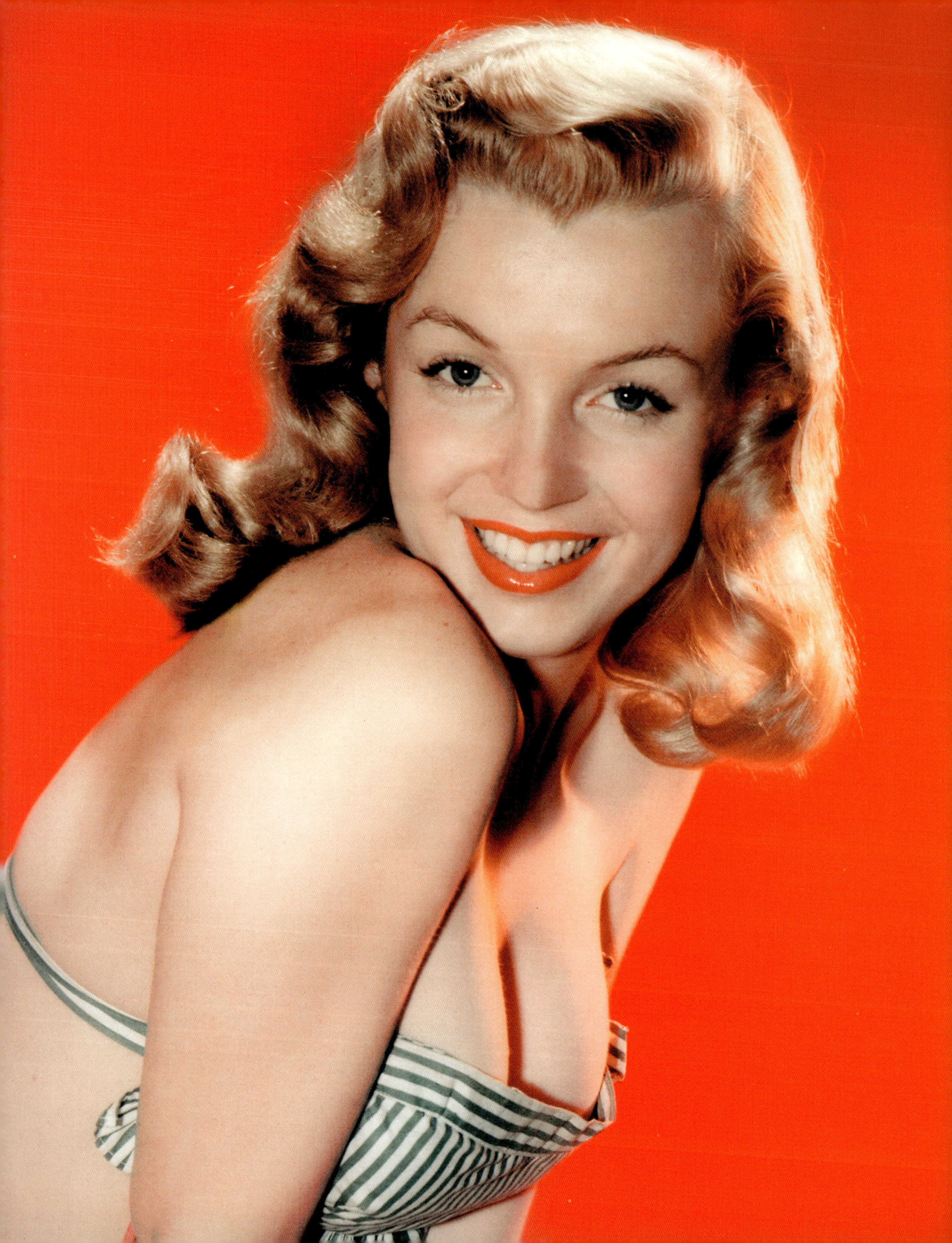

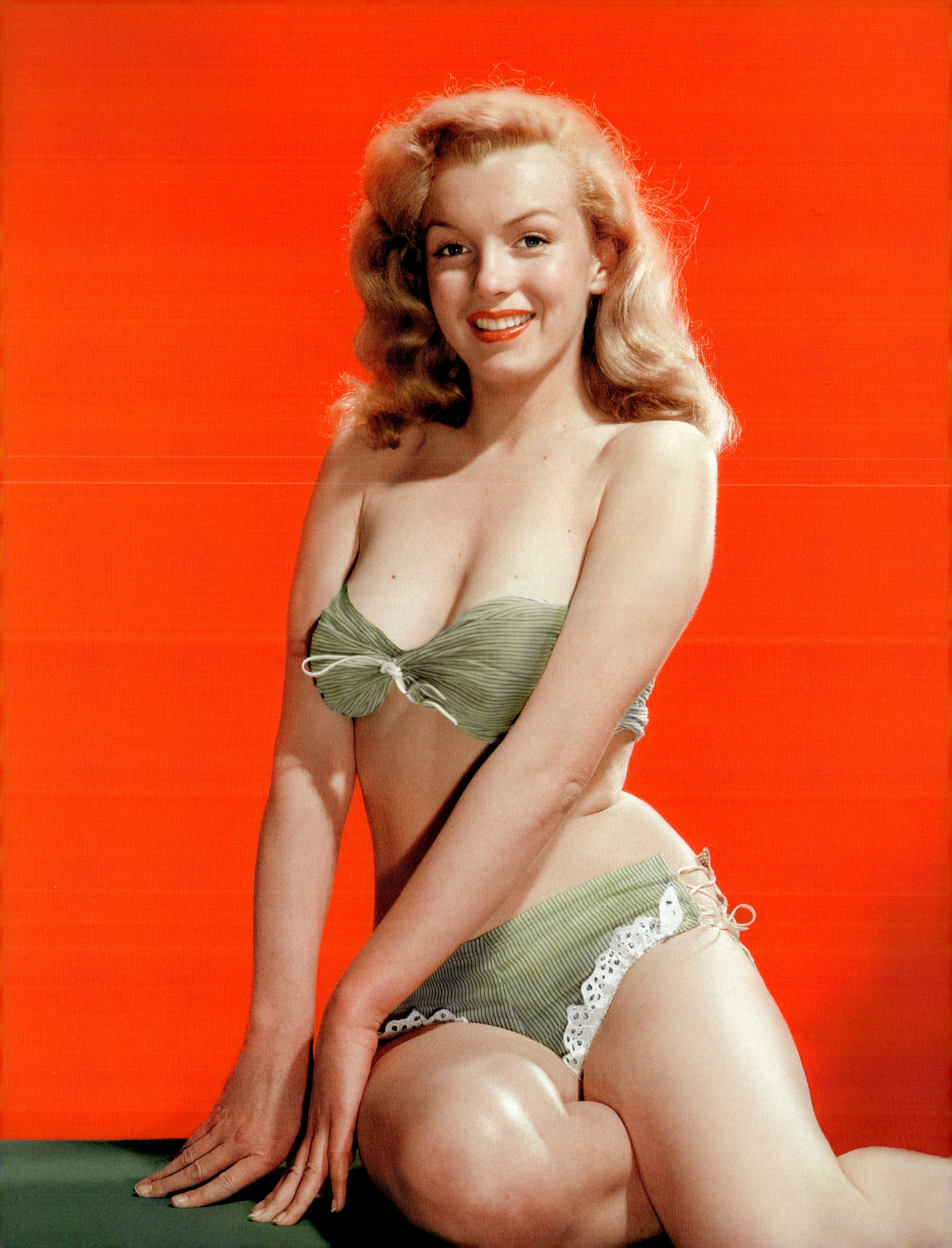

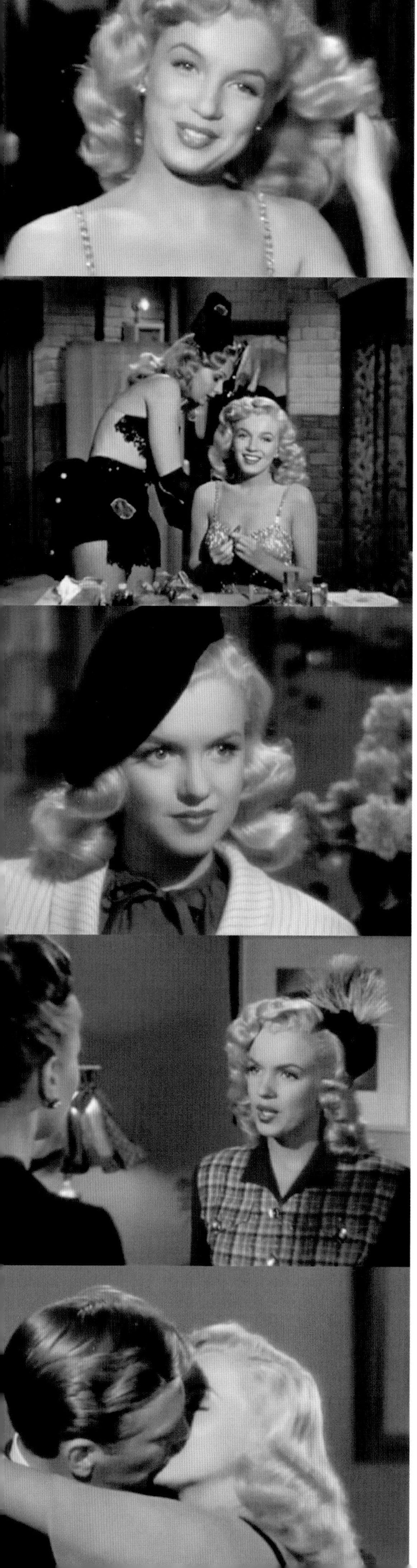

"I got a cold chill. This girl had something I hadn't seen since silent pictures. She had a kind of fantastic beauty like Gloria Swanson, when a movie star had to look beautiful, and she got sex on a piece of film like Jean Harlow."

LEON SHAMROY (Cinematographer)

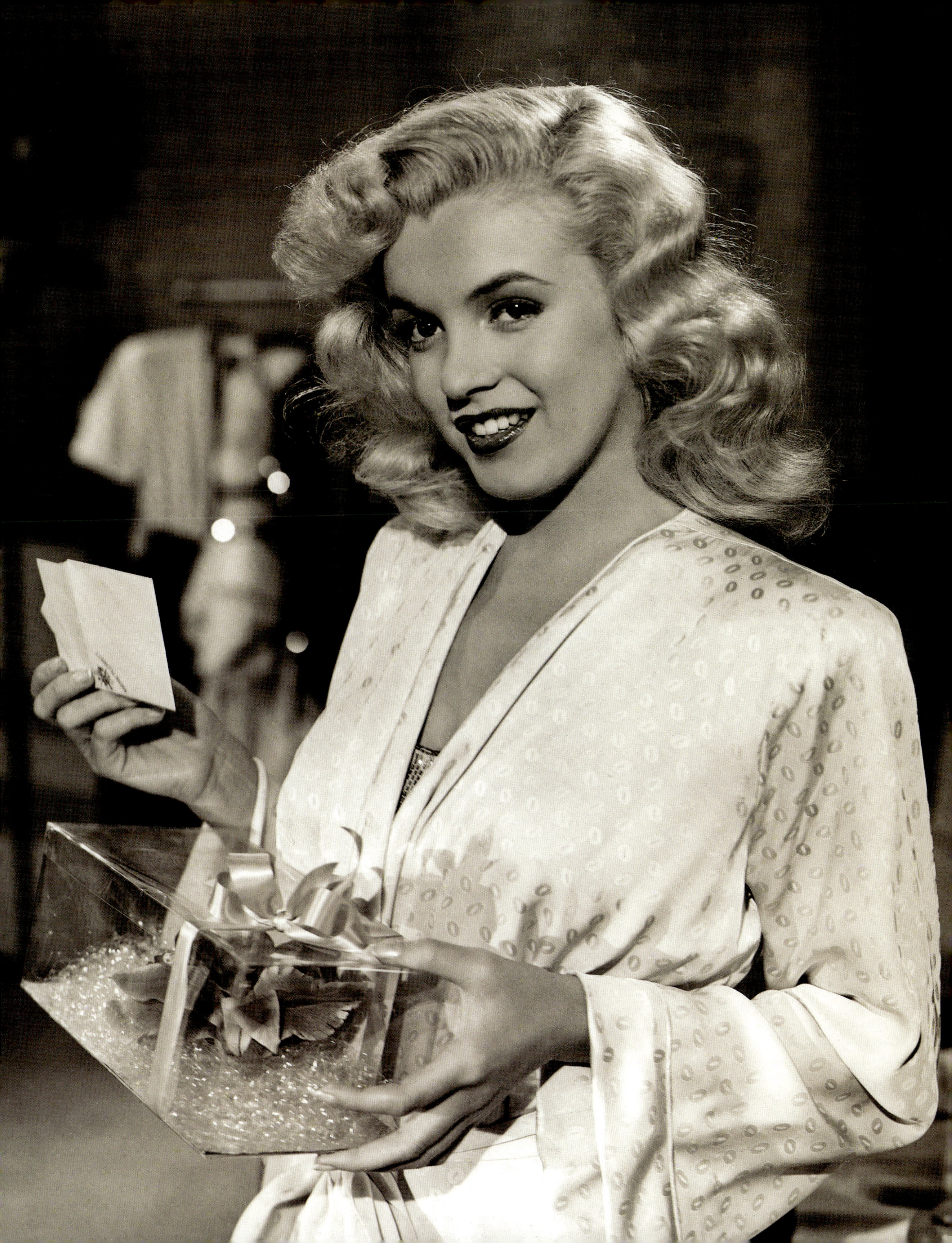

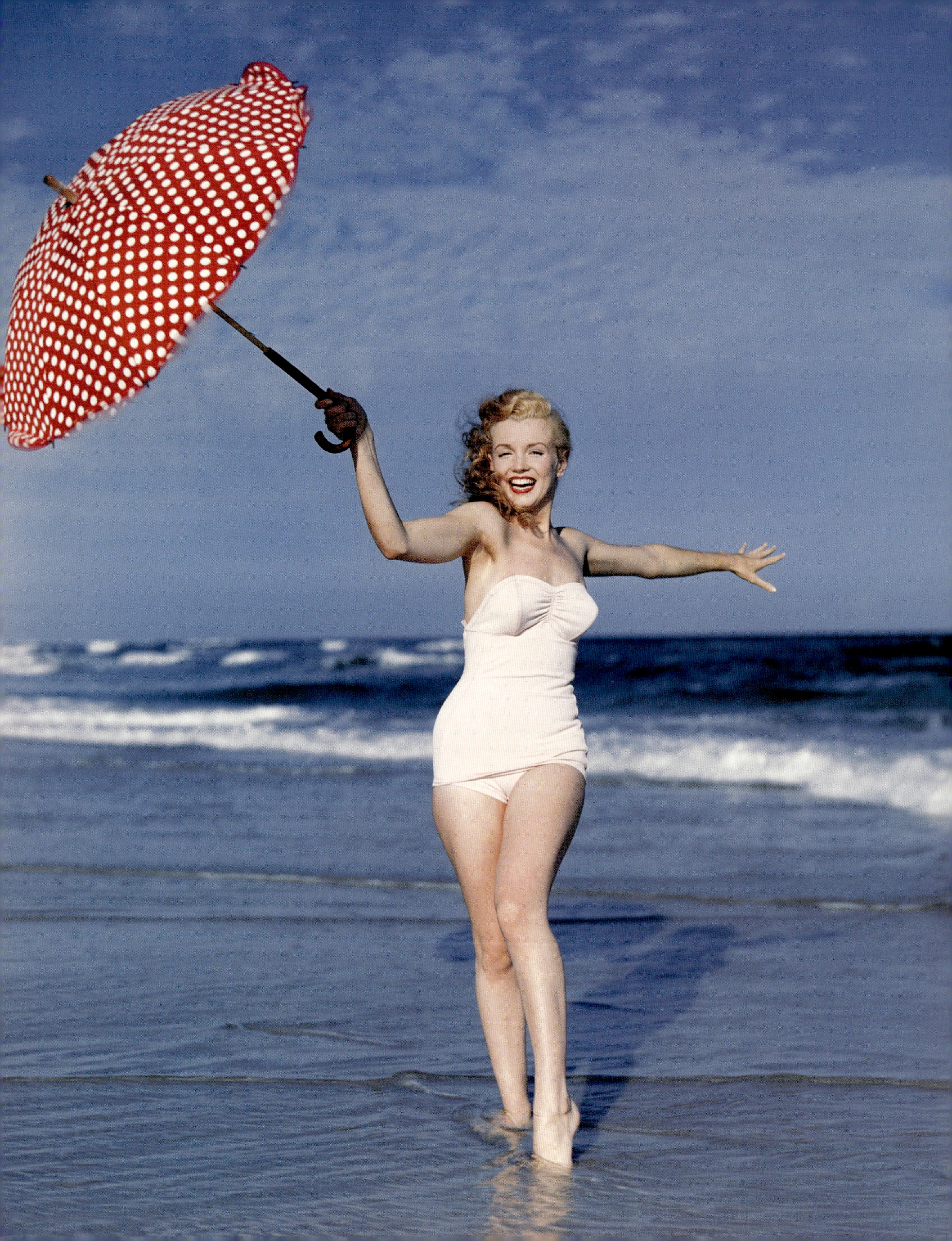

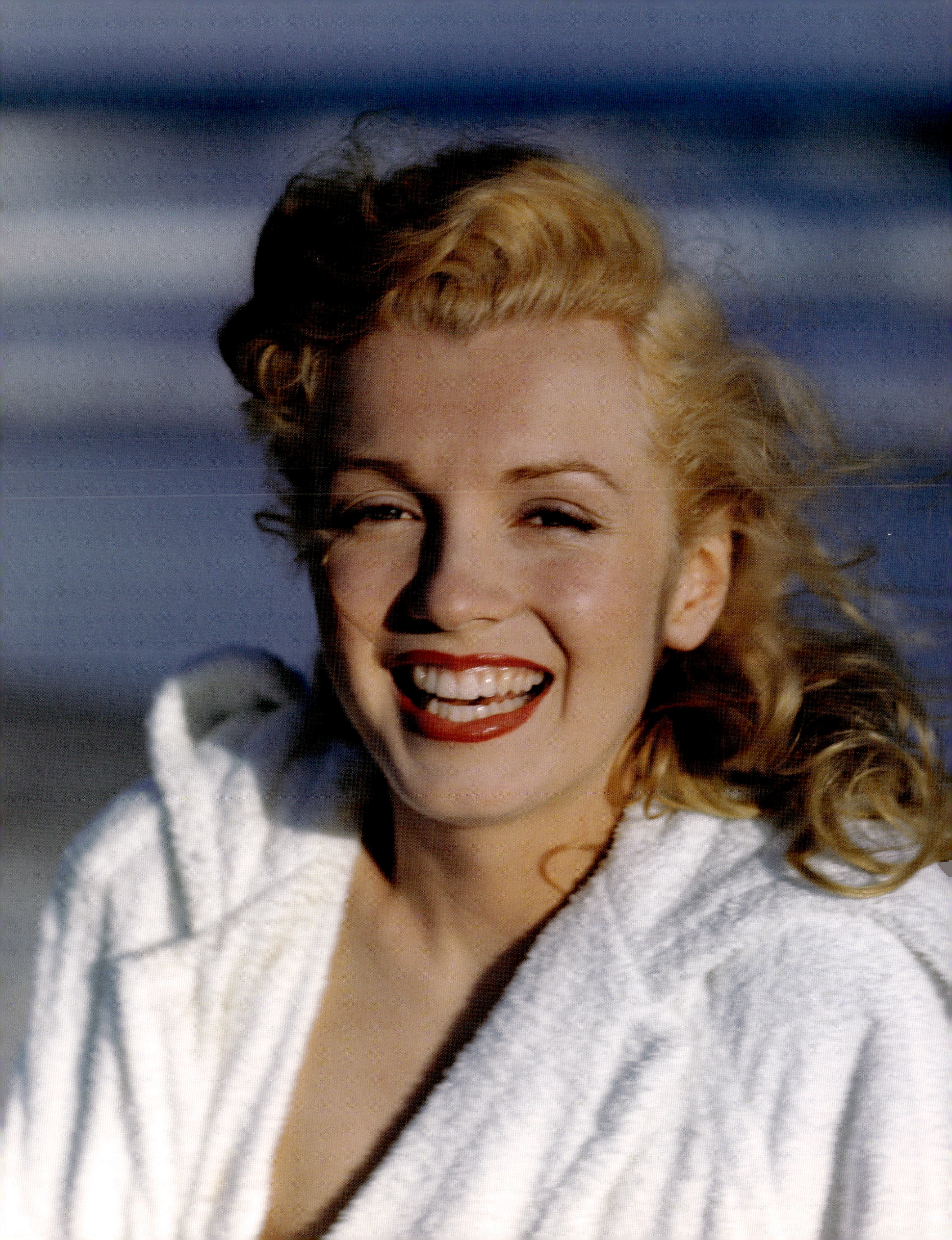

“She seemed to have a kind of unconscious glow about her physical self that was innocent, like a child. When she posed nude, it was ‘Gee, I am kind of, you know, sort of dishy,’ like she enjoyed it without being egotistical.”

ELIZABETH TAYLOR

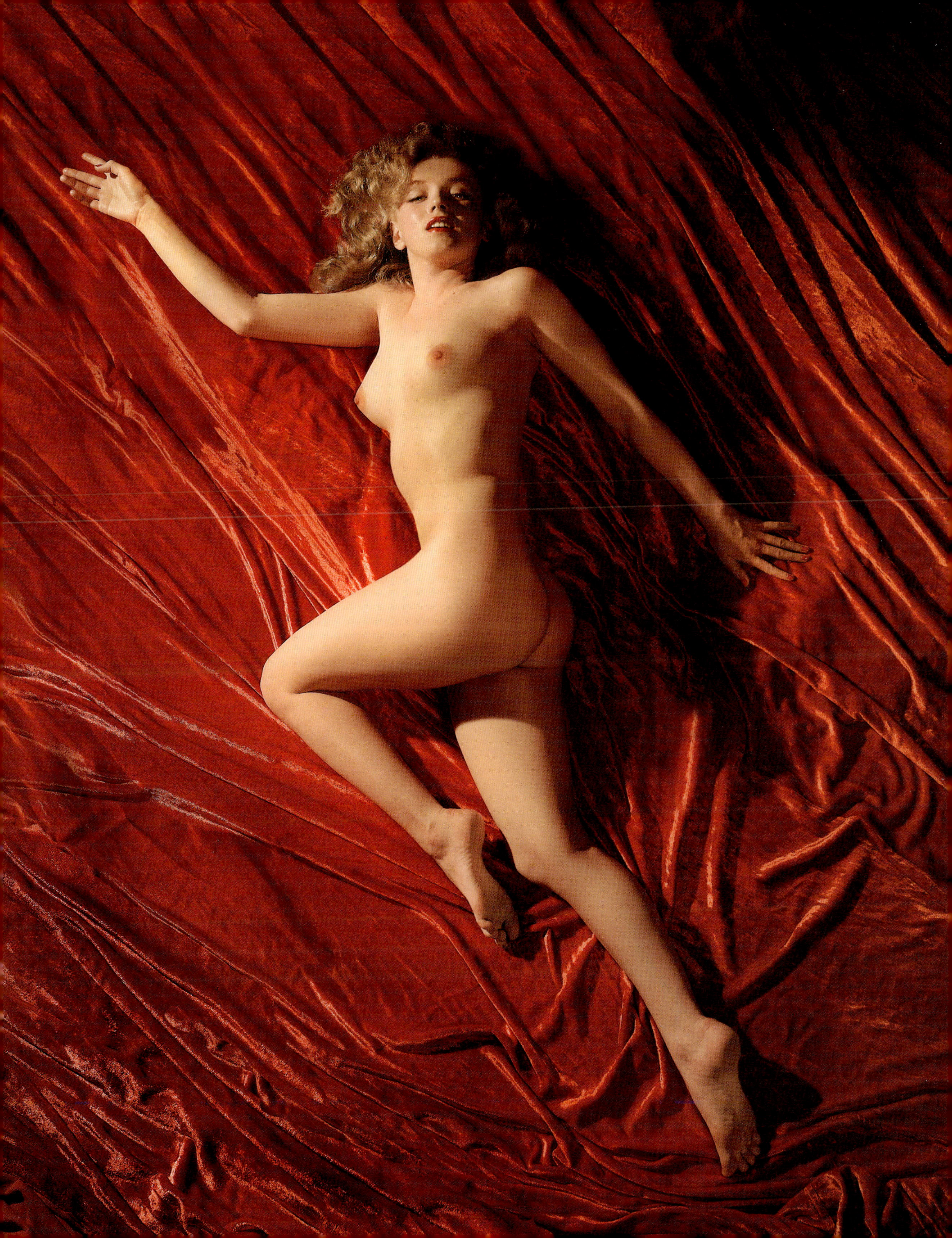

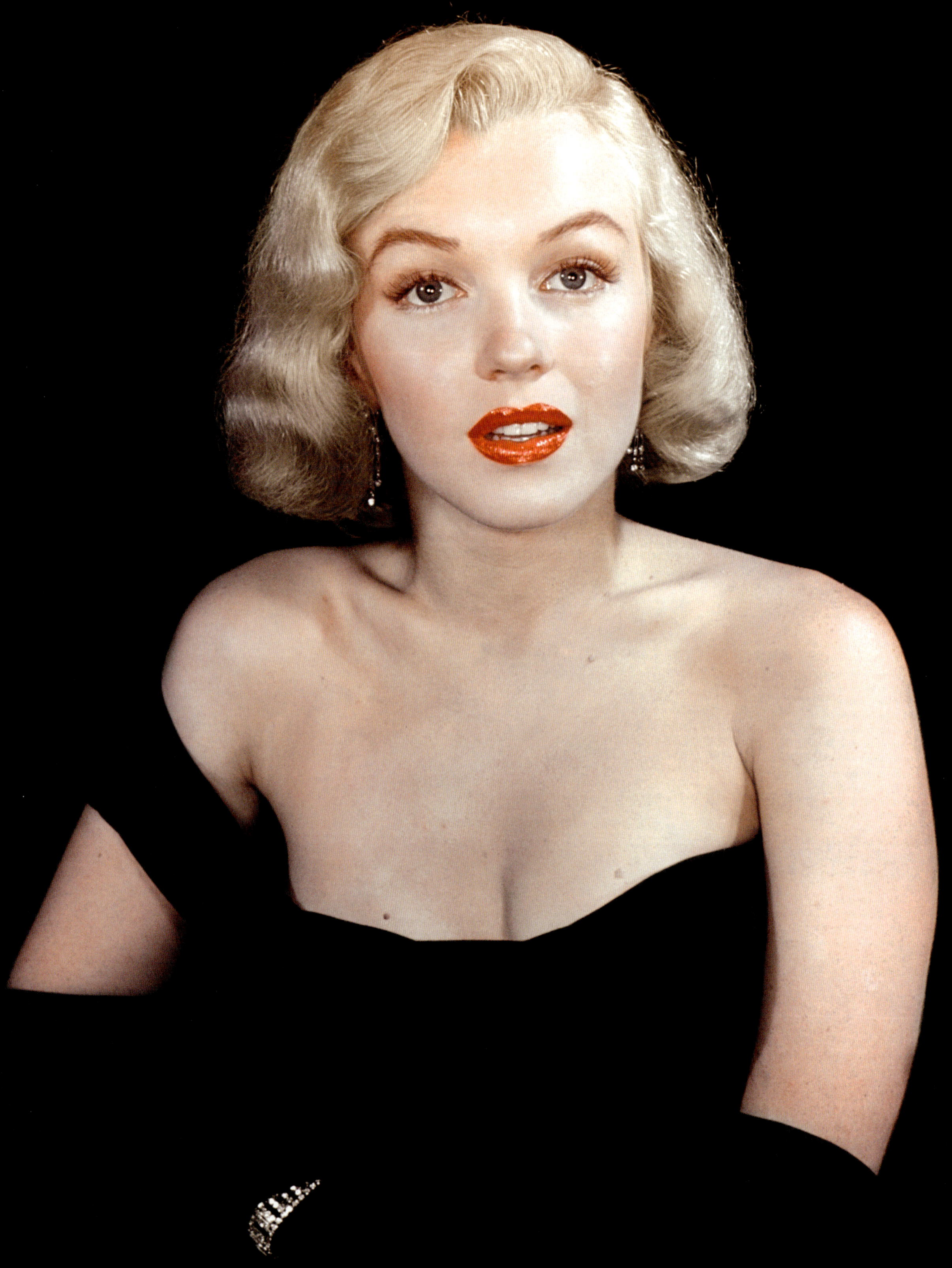

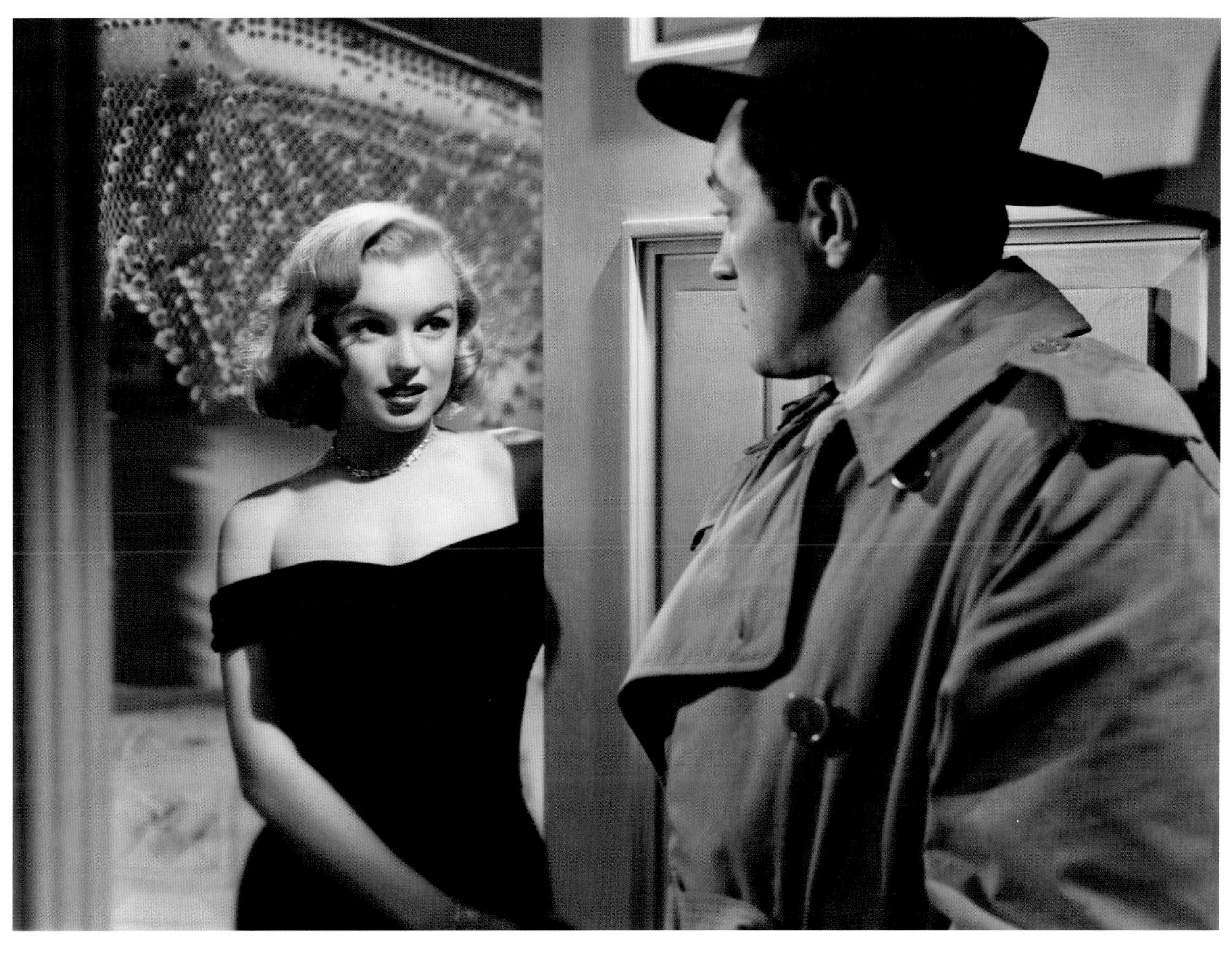

"I didn't recognize her star potential. . . . Darryl Zanuck signed Miss Monroe, and she became an extraordinary figure in movie history. For years I blushed in embarrassment every time her name was mentioned."

DORE SCHARY (President of MGM, 1951–1956)

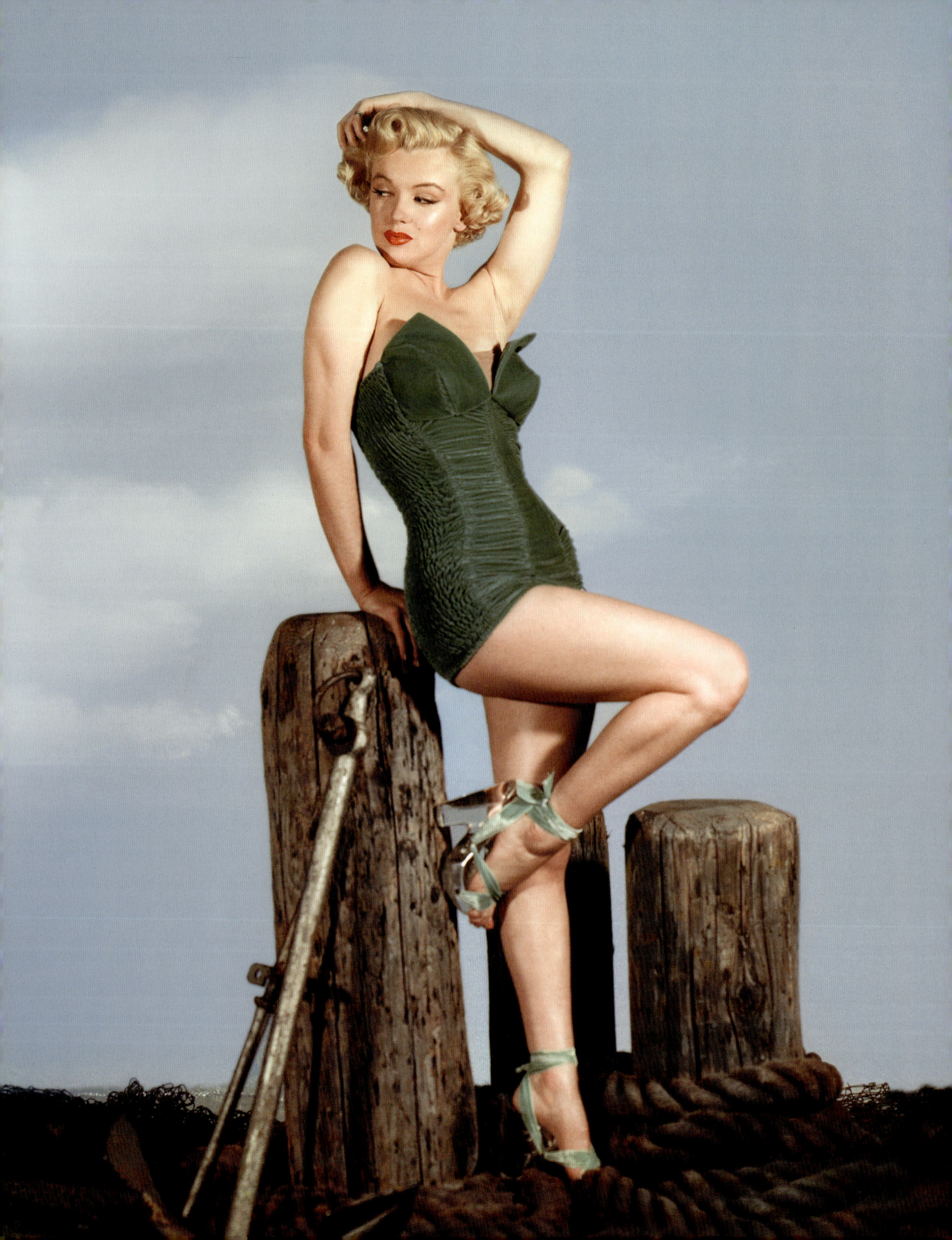

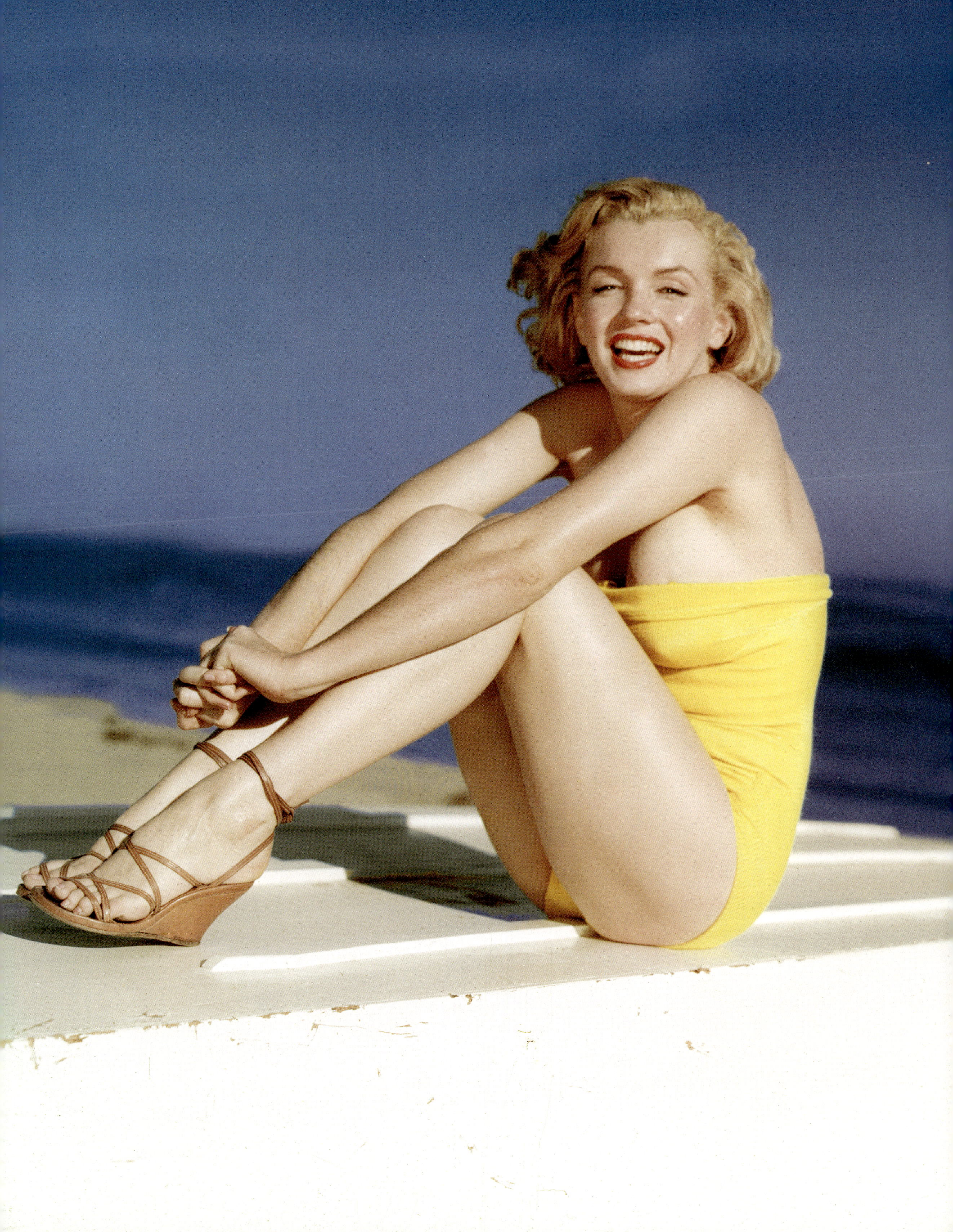

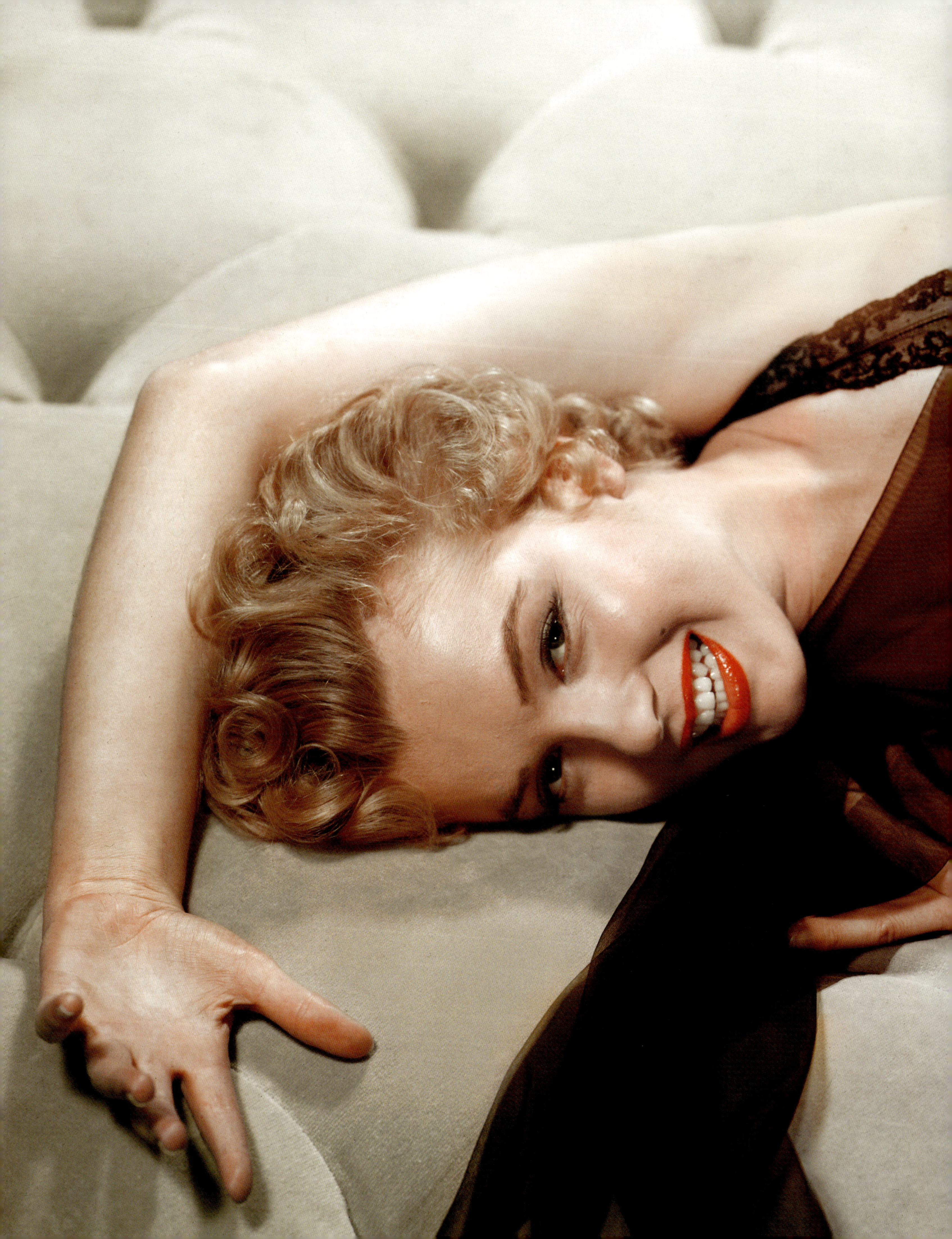

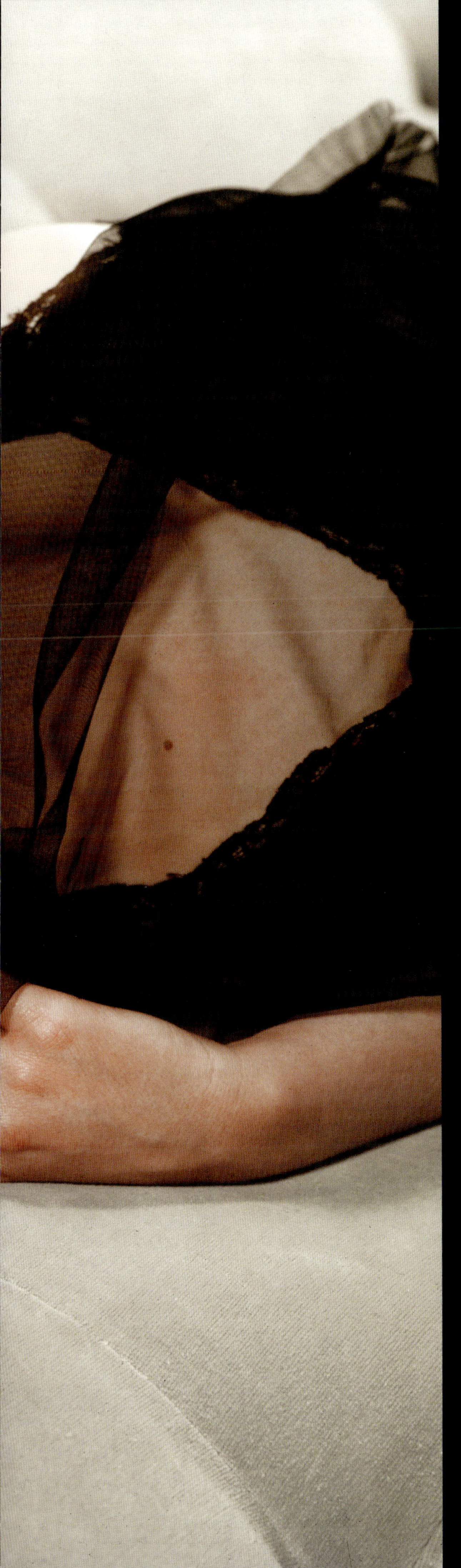

"Monroe was a wonderful person. I'd always hold her in esteem because she was gracious enough to accept a blind date with my brother, Ving. In the early fifties, Ving came out to the West Coast for a visit and asked me to fix him up for a night on the town. When Marilyn Monroe showed up, Ving's mouth dropped open."

SAMUEL FULLER (Director)

"She was so young and pretty, so shy and nervous on that picture, but I remember the scene where she was supposed to be sunning in the backyard of the apartment house we all live in. When Marilyn walked on the set in her bathing suit, the whole crew gasped, gaped, and seemed to turn to stone. They just stopped work and stared; Marilyn had that electric something—and mind you, movie crews are quite used to seeing us in brief costumes. But they just gasped and gaped at Marilyn as though they were stunned. In all my years at the studio, I'd never seen that happen before."

JUNE HAVER (Costar, *Love Nest*, 1951)

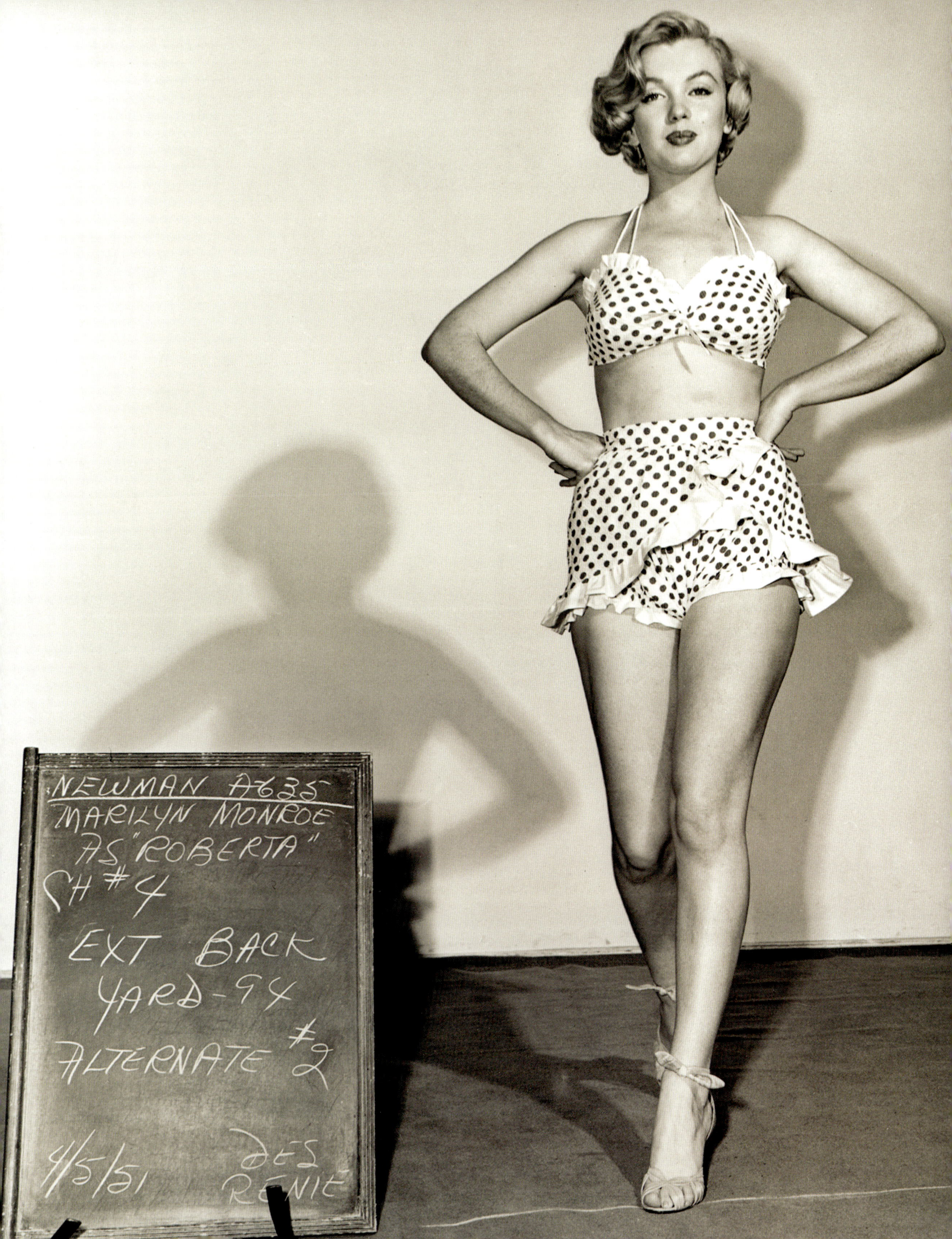
NEWMAN A635
MARILYN MONROE
AS "ROBERTA"
CH #4
EXT BACK
YARD-94
ALTERNATE #2
4/5/51
DES
RENIE

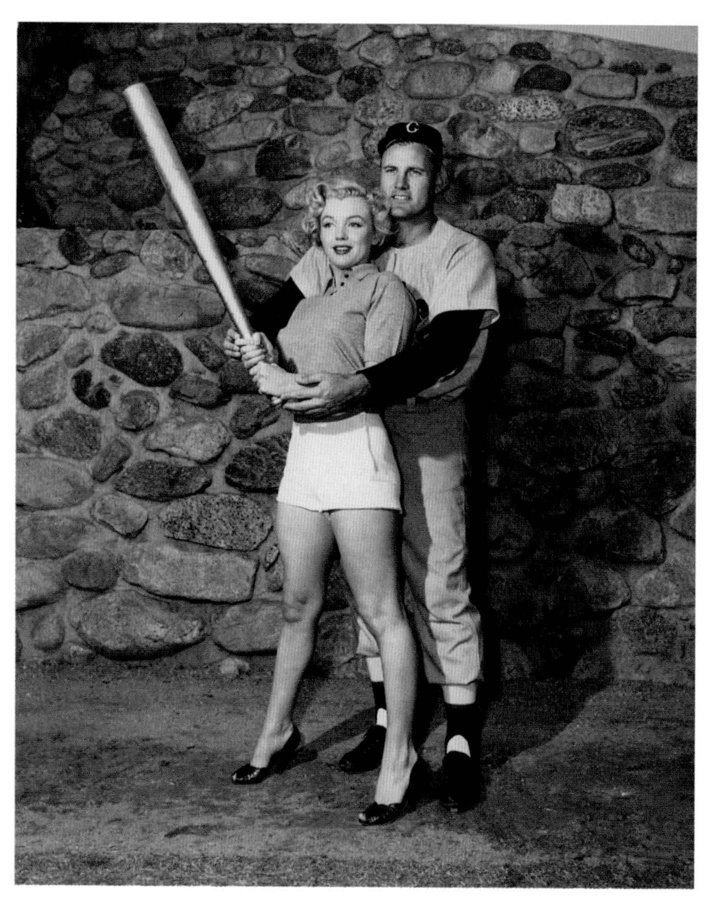

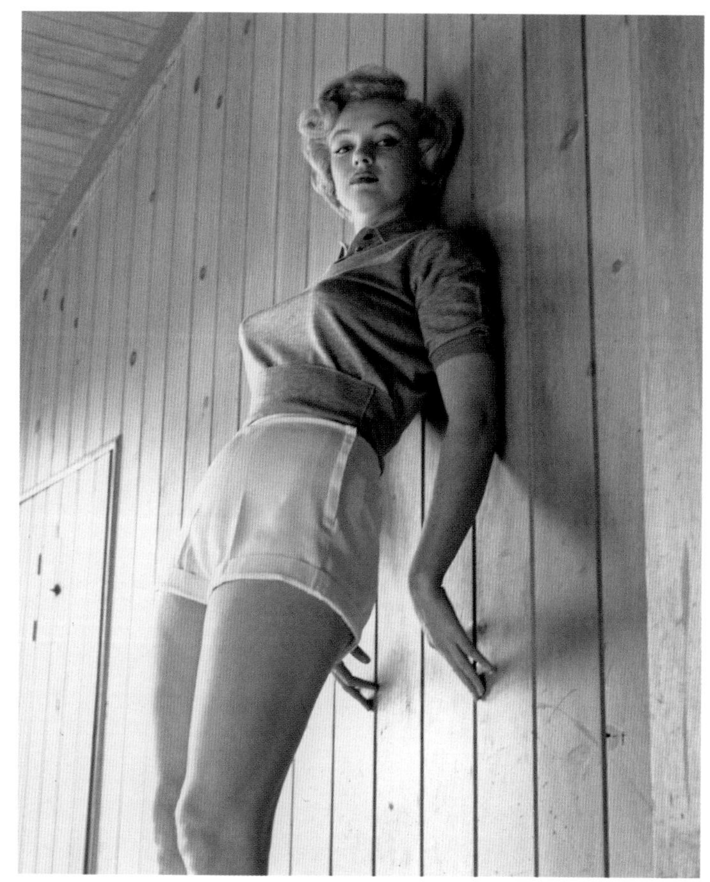

"She was awkward. She couldn't get out of her own way. She wasn't disciplined, and she was often late, and she drove Bob Ryan, Paul Douglas, and myself out of our minds . . . but she didn't do it viciously, and there was sort of a magic about her which we all recognized at once. Her phobias, or whatever they were, came later; she seemed just a carefree kid, and she owned the world."

BARBARA STANWYCK (Costar, *Clash by Night*, 1952)

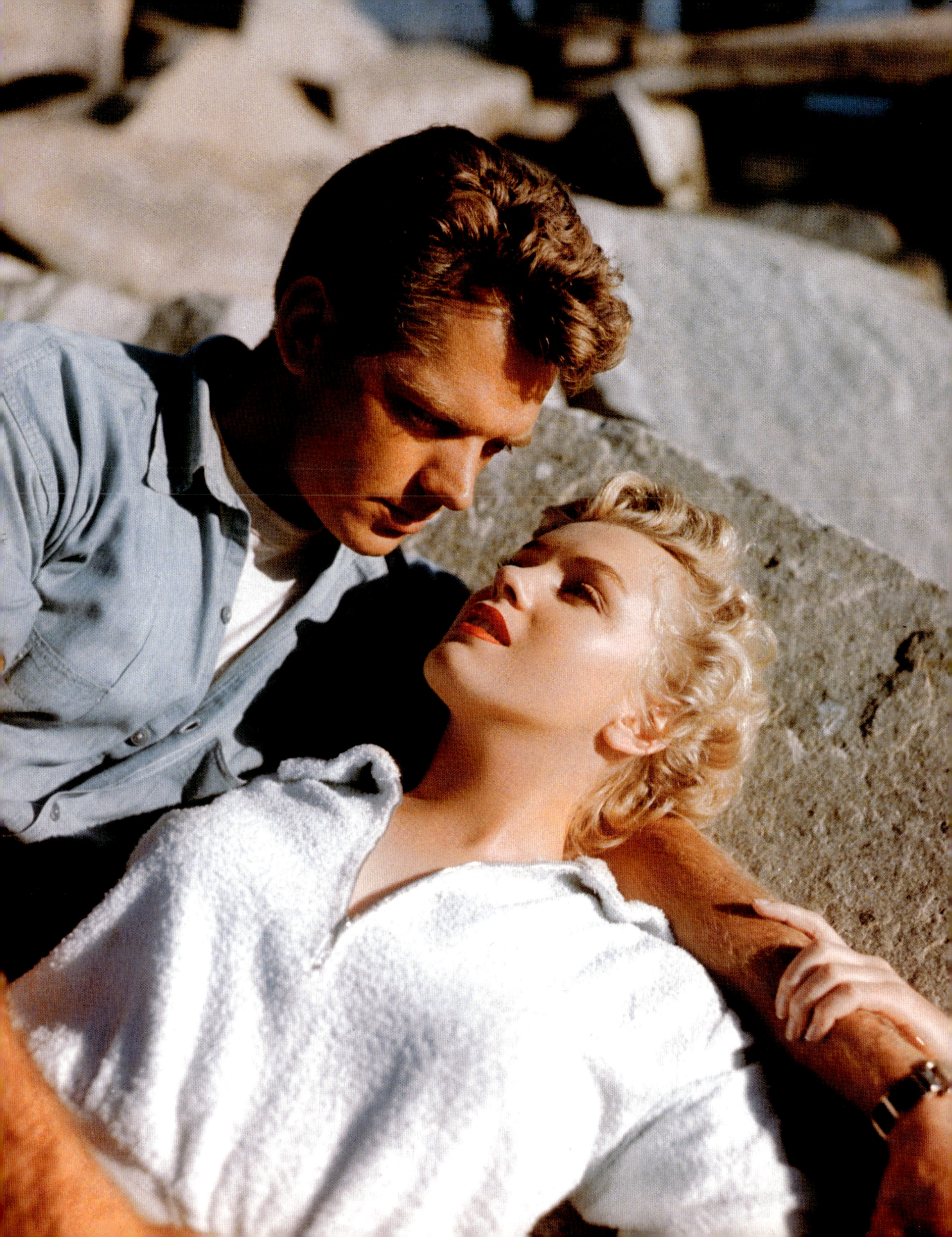

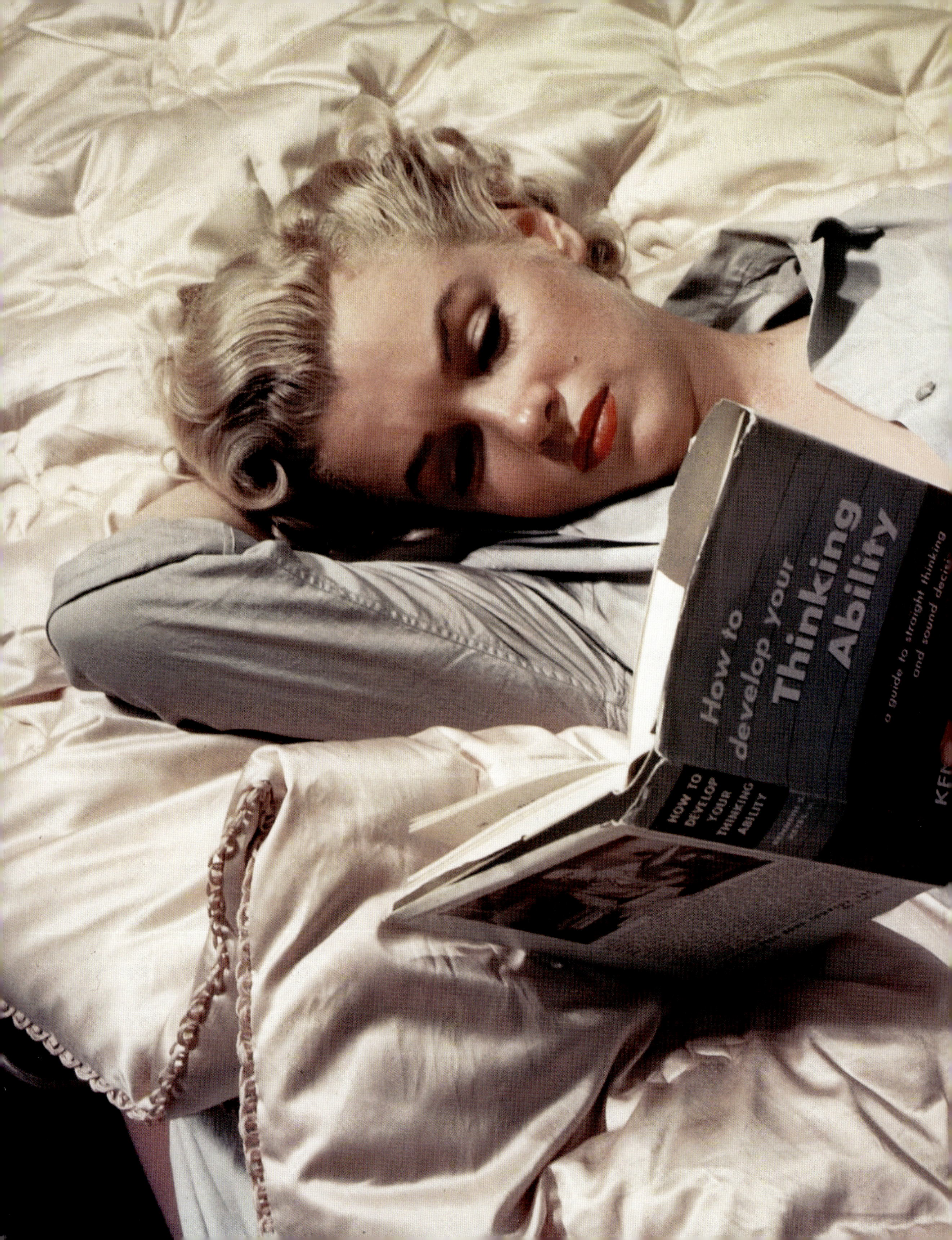
How to develop your
Thinking Ability
a guide to straight thinking
and sound
HOW TO DEVELOP YOUR THINKING ABILITY

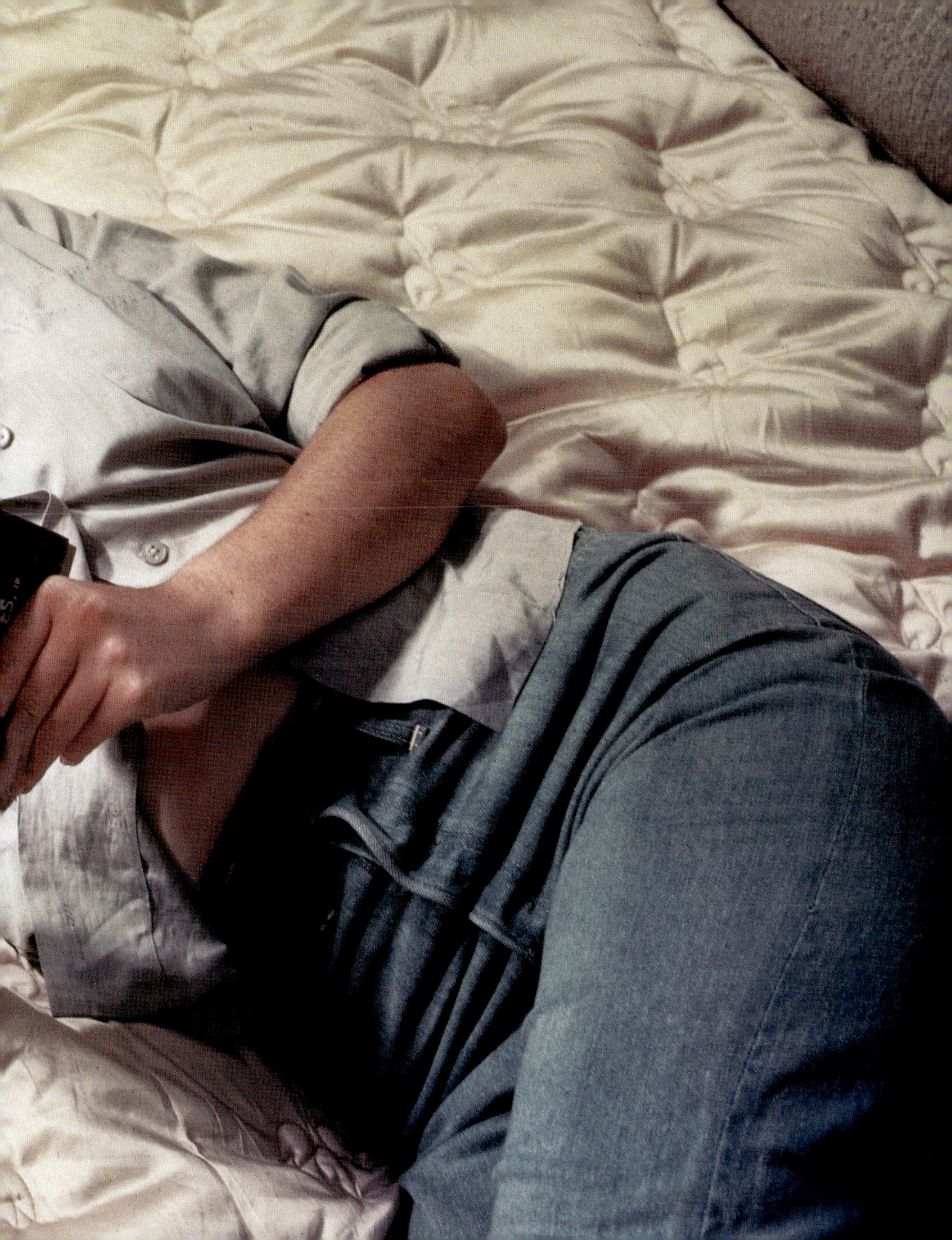

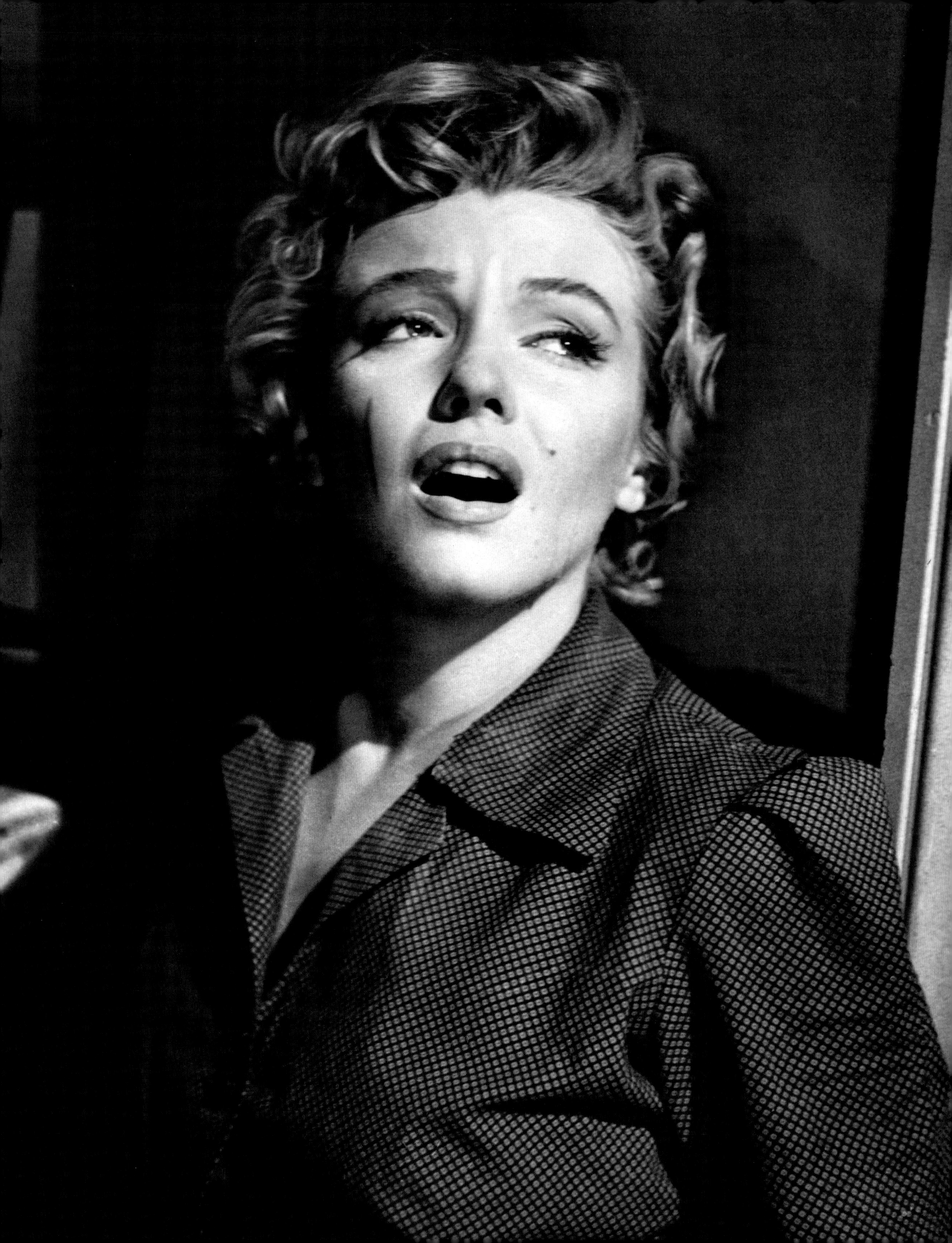

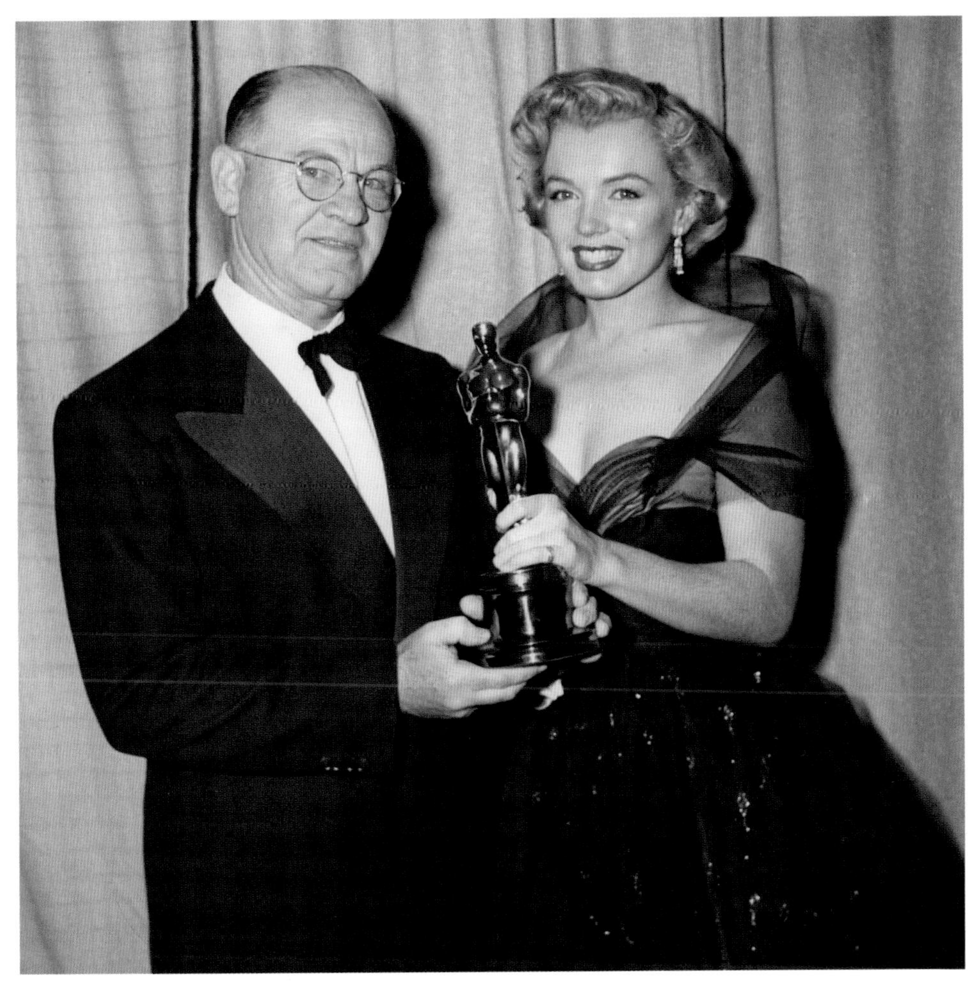

"It was a remarkable experience. Because it was one of those very few times in all my experiences in Hollywood, when I felt that give and take—that can only happen when you are working with good actors. There was just this scene of one woman seeing another woman who was helpless and in pain, and she was helpless and in pain. It was so real, I responded. I really reacted to her. She moved me so that tears came into my eyes."

ANNE BANCROFT (Costar, *Don't Bother to Knock*, 1952)

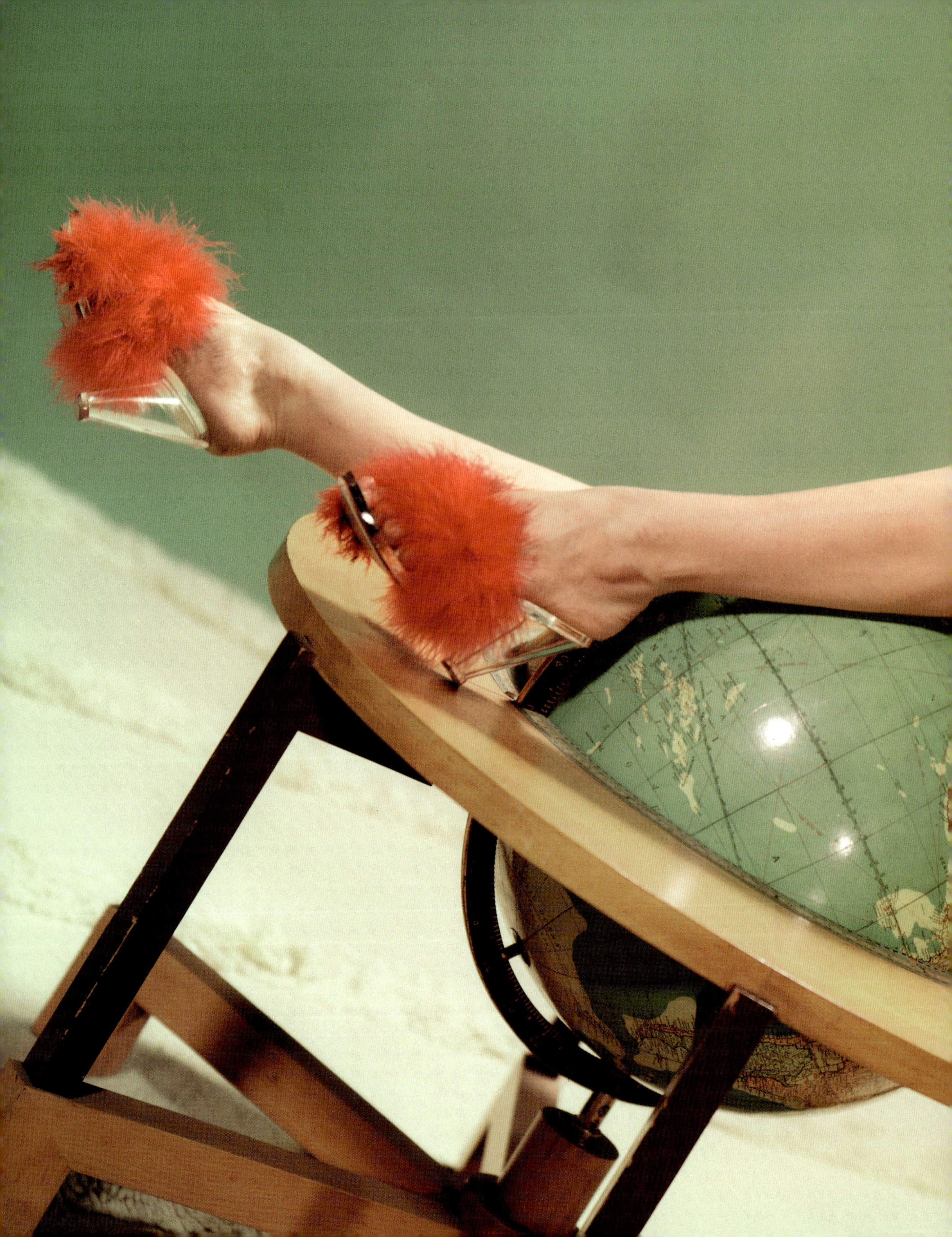

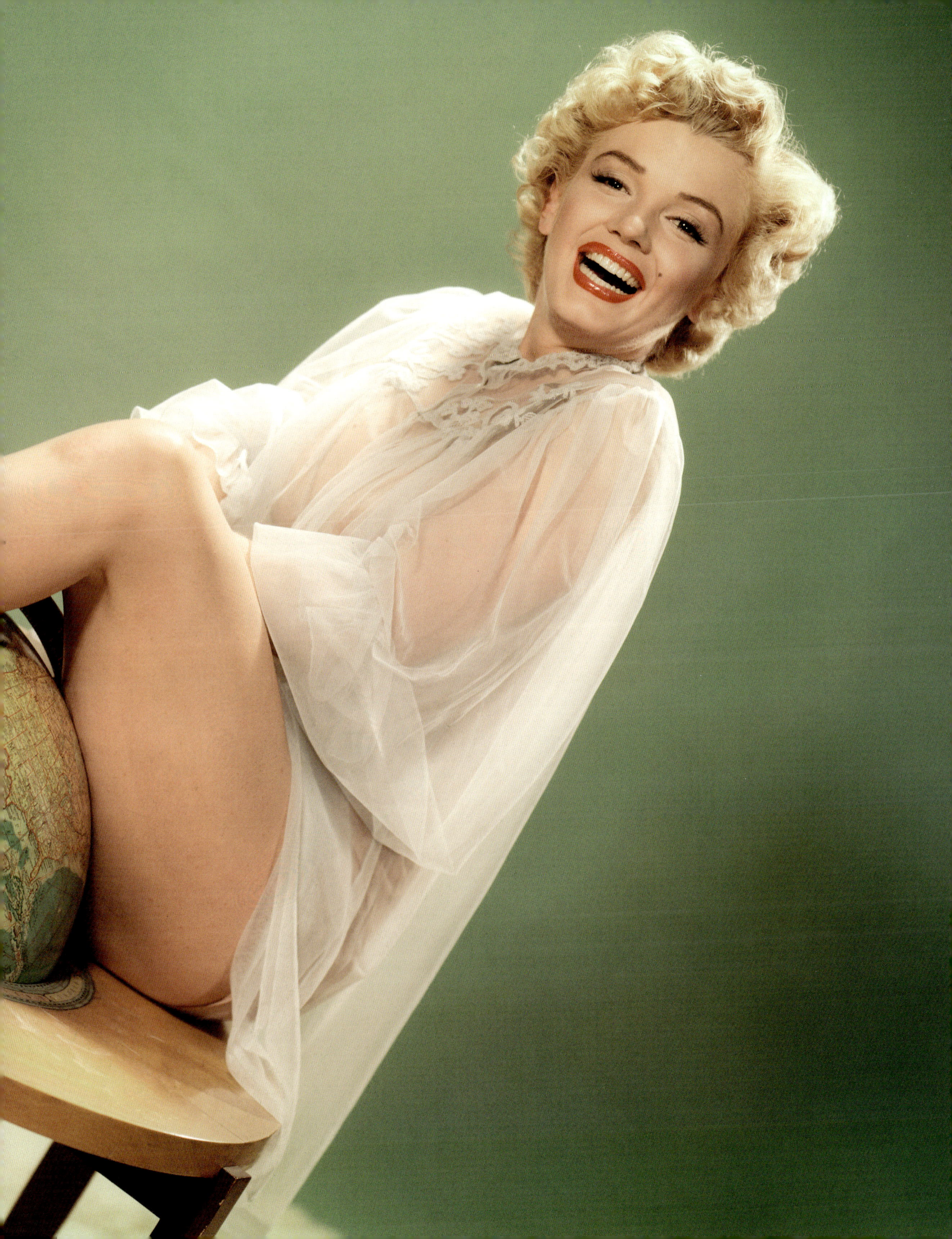

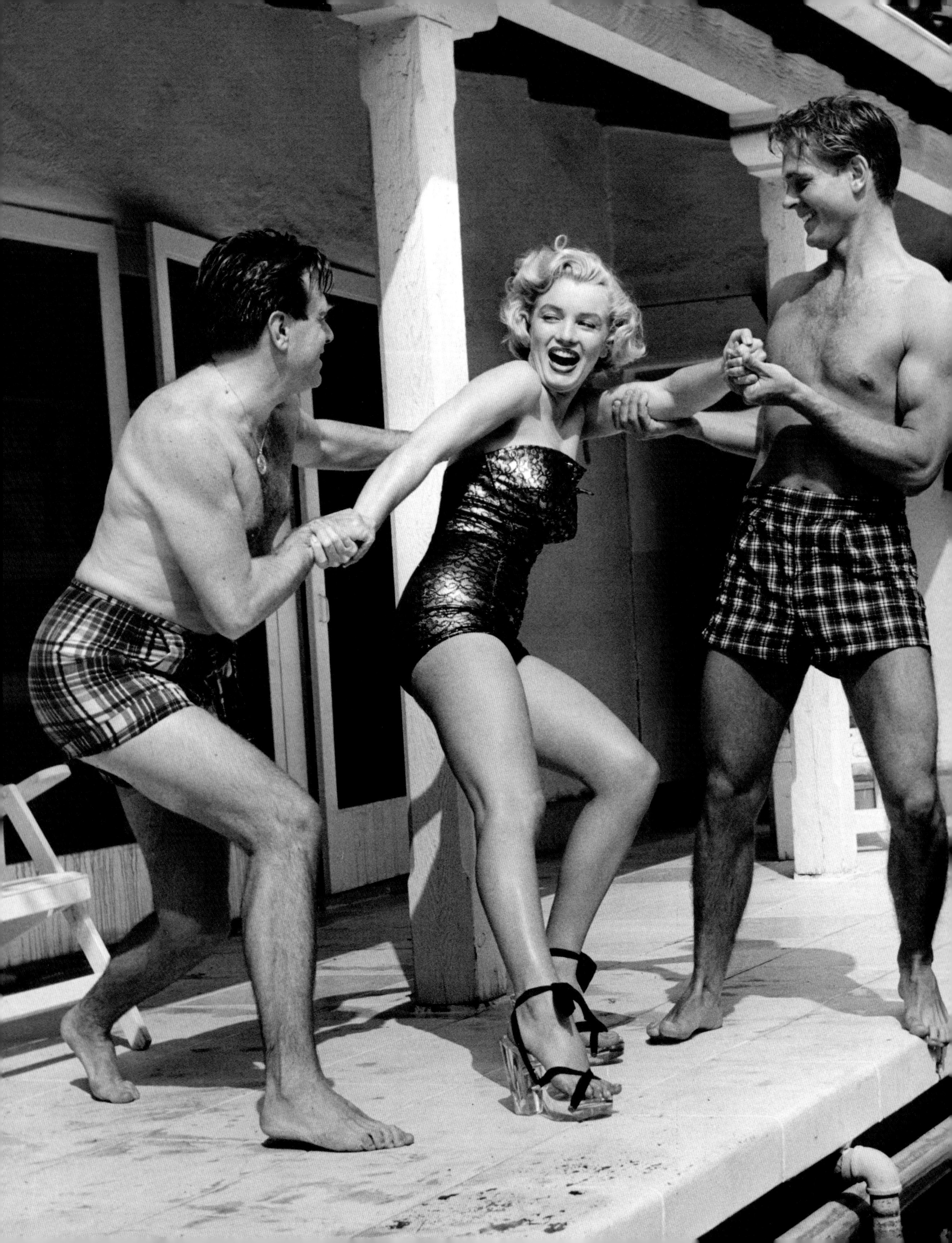

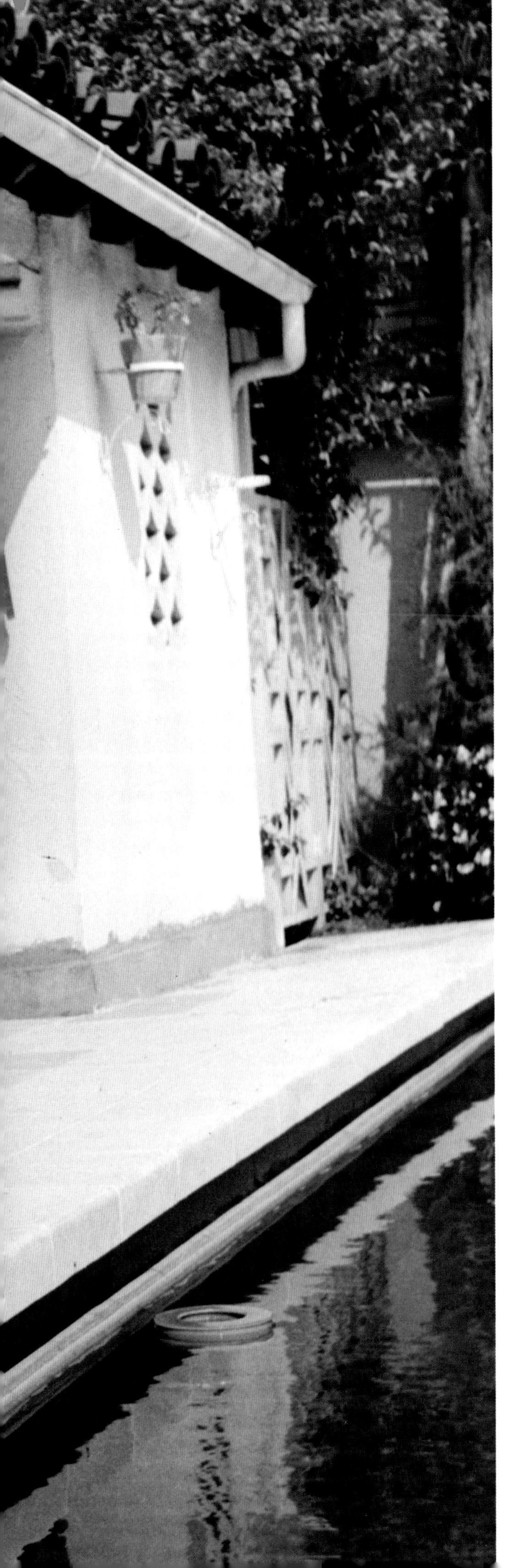

“She seemed very shy, and I remember that when the studio workers would whistle at her, it seemed to embarrass her.”

CARY GRANT (Costar, *Monkey Business*, 1952)

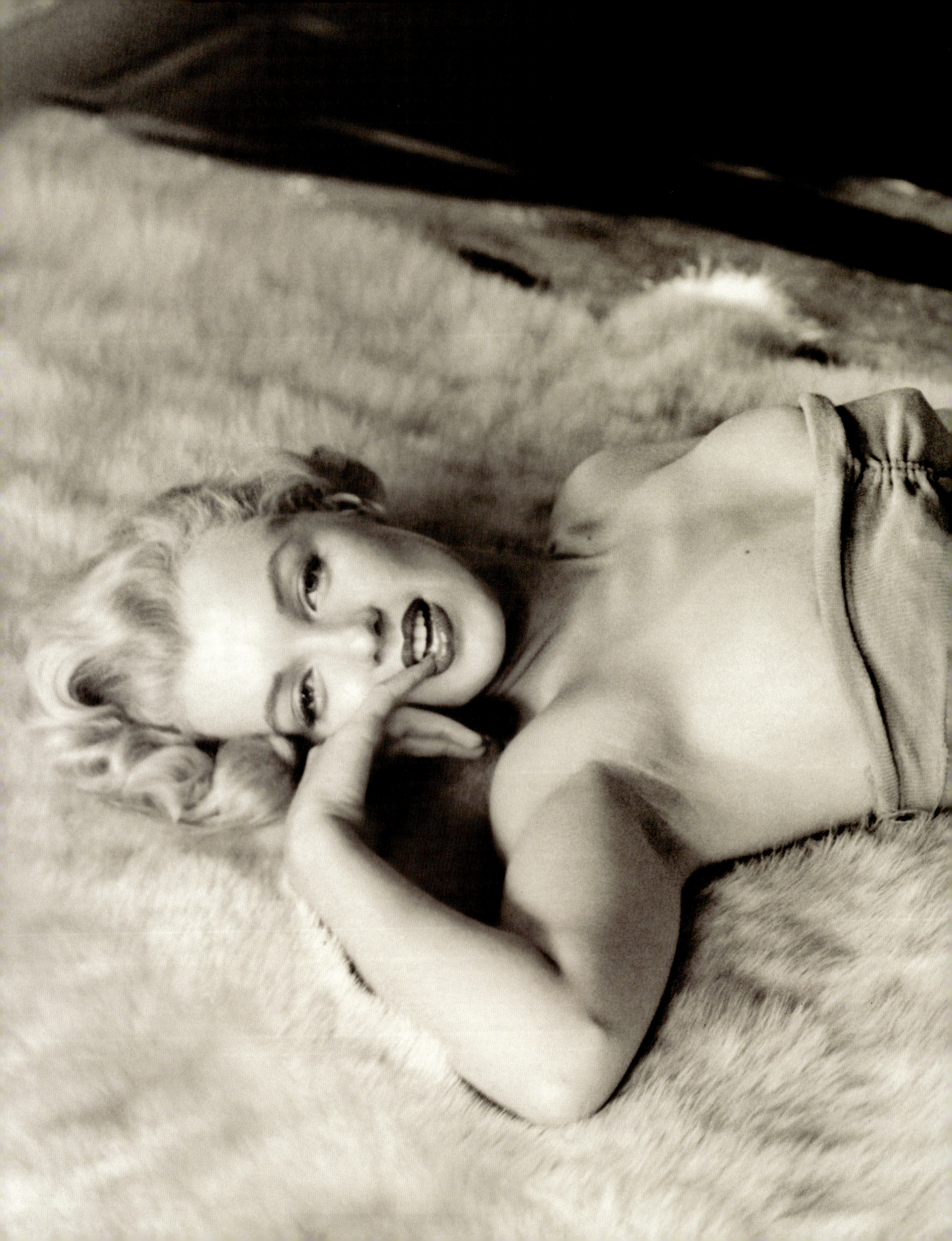

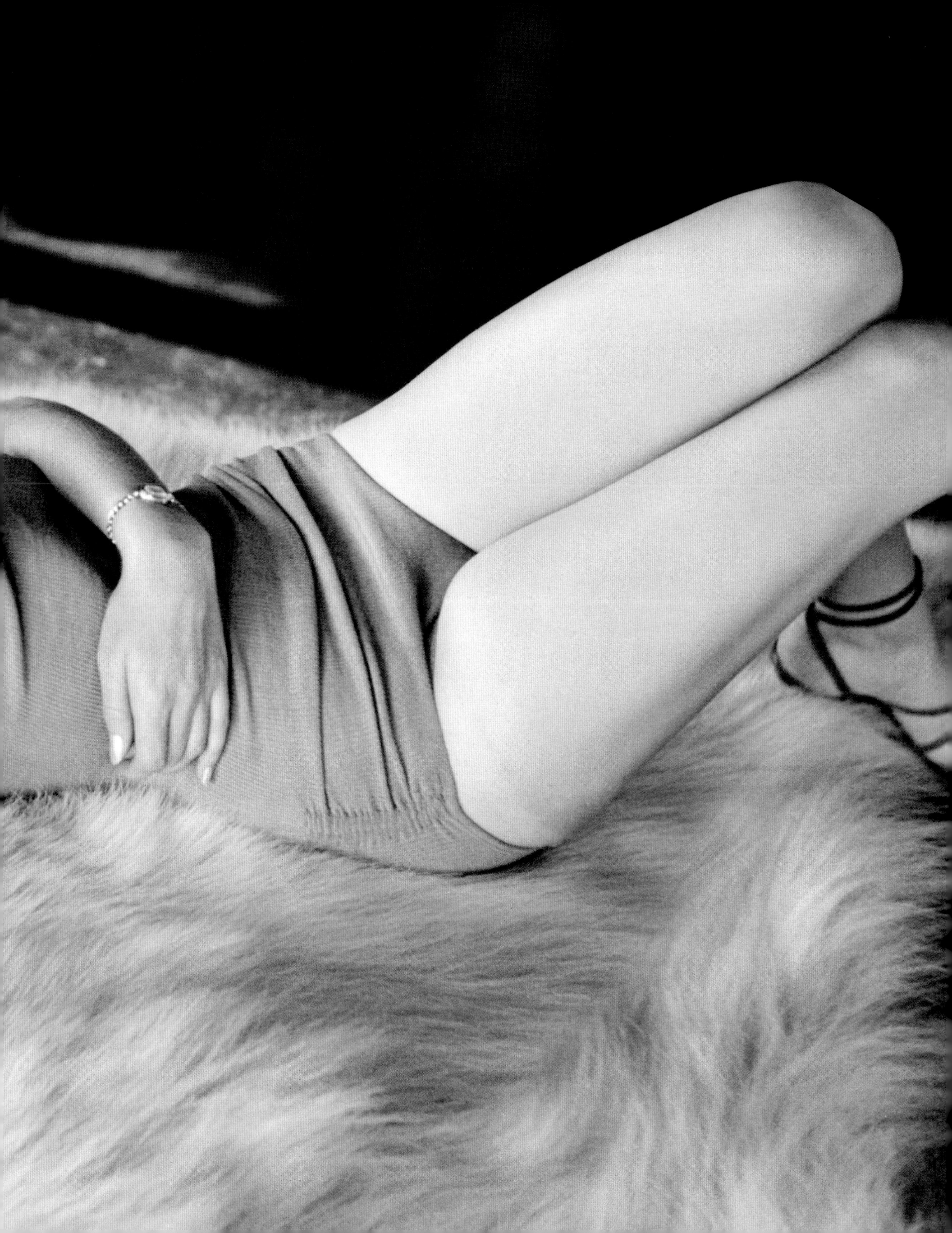

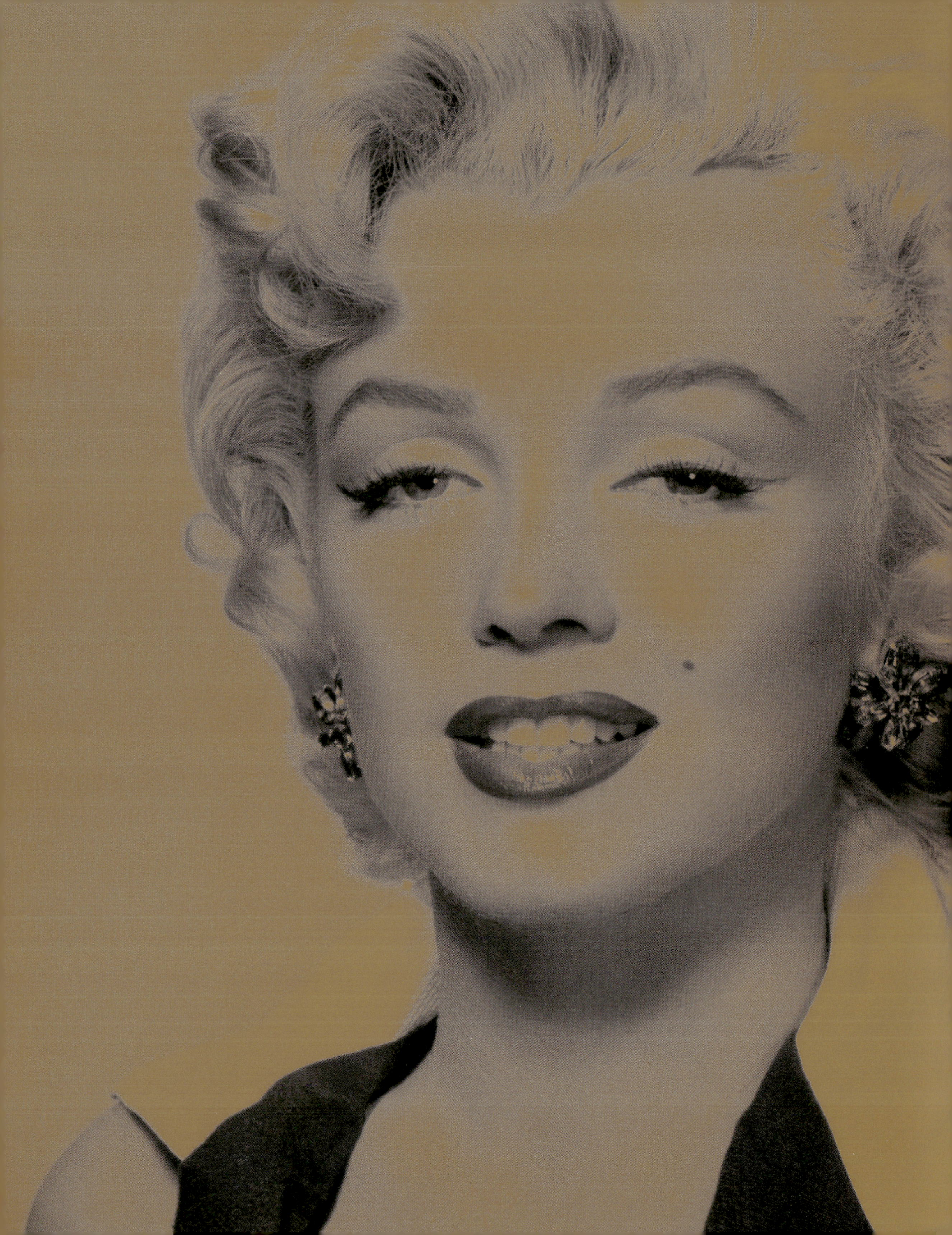

SIRIUS

Superstar 1952–1954

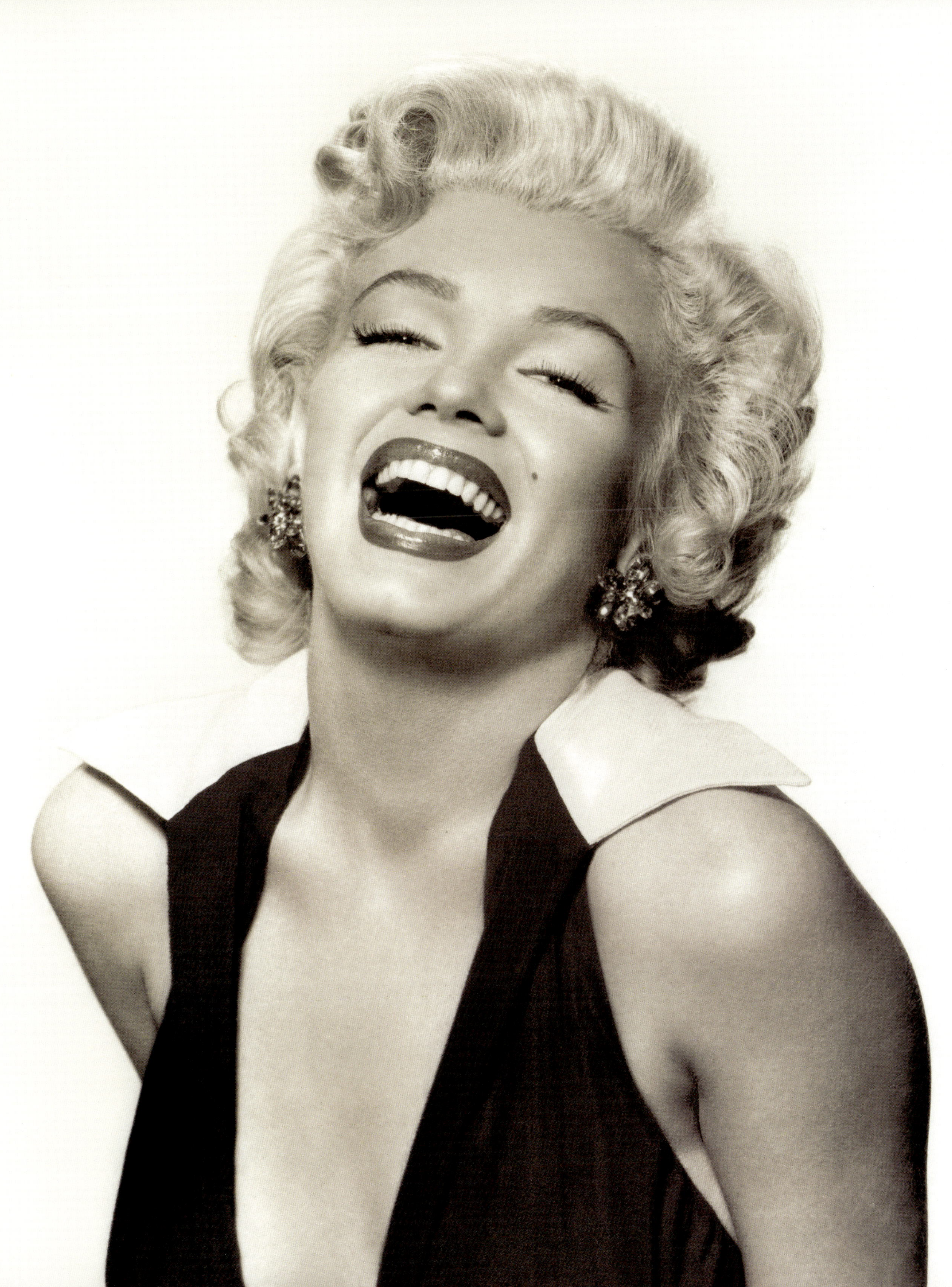

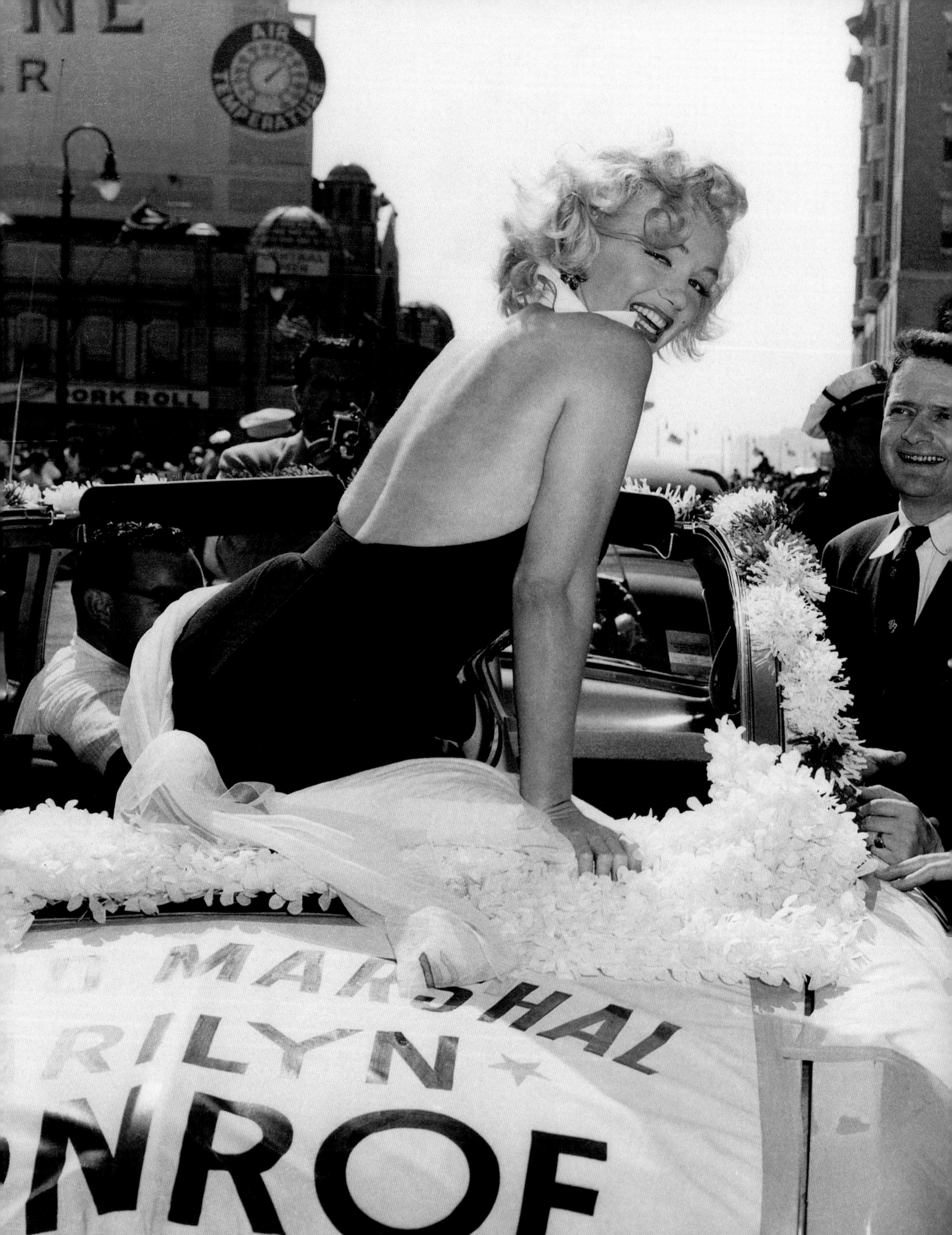
PORK ROLL
MARSHAL
RILYN

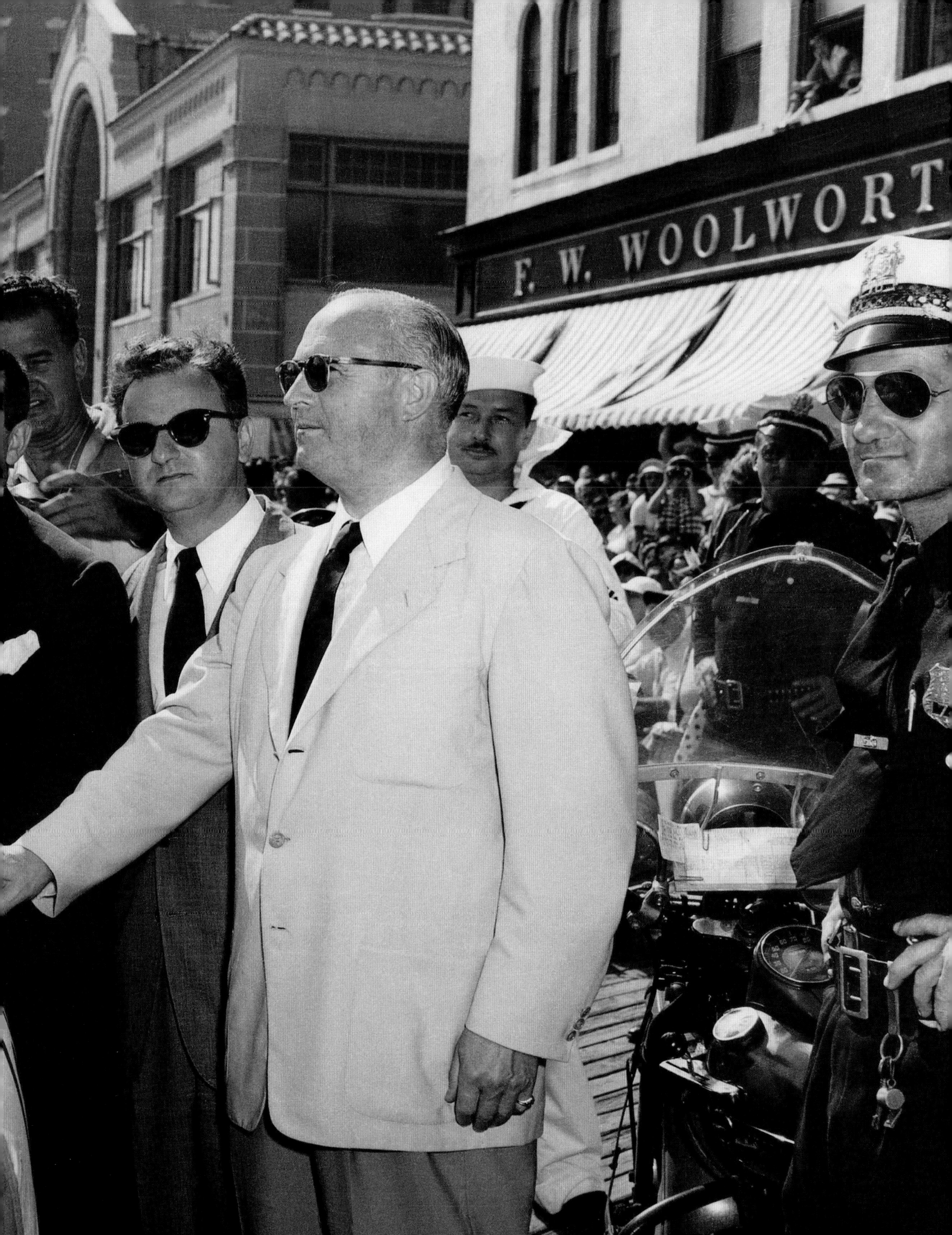
F. W. WOOLWORT

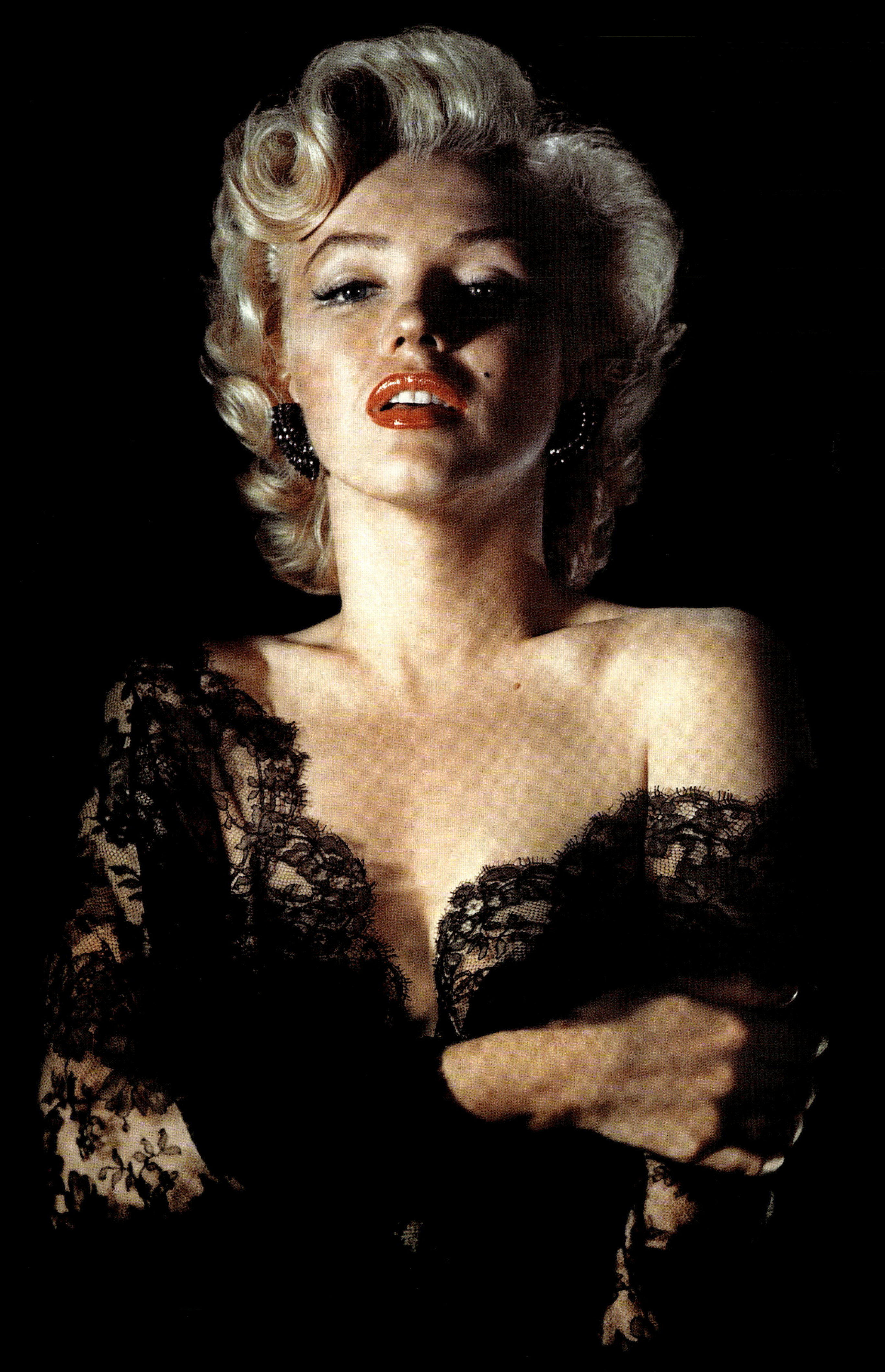

“On none is the grandeur and servitude of stardom visited more brutally than on the sex symbols. Owing their fame to their bodies, they seldom escape the indignity of being thought of as ‘a piece of flesh.’ The very way in which sex symbols are publicized brings out the latent sadism of a

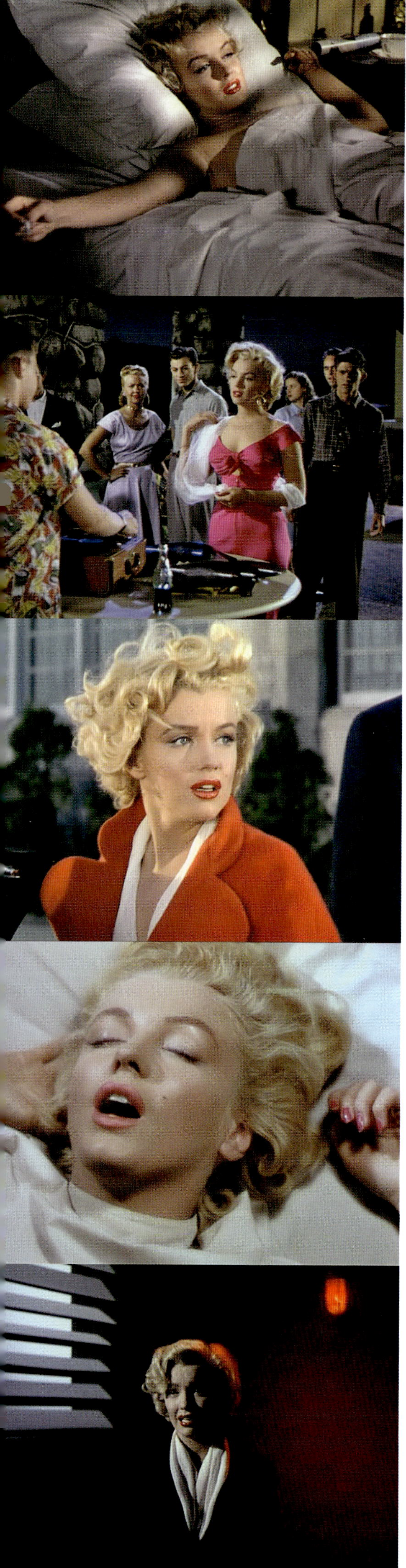

"She was outgiving and charming. If you wanted to talk about yourself, she listened. If you wanted to talk about her, she blushed. She gave the impression that she earnestly sought a specific definition, a practical and visible form of happiness, of satisfaction in achievement."

JOSEPH COTTEN (Costar, *Niagara*, 1953)

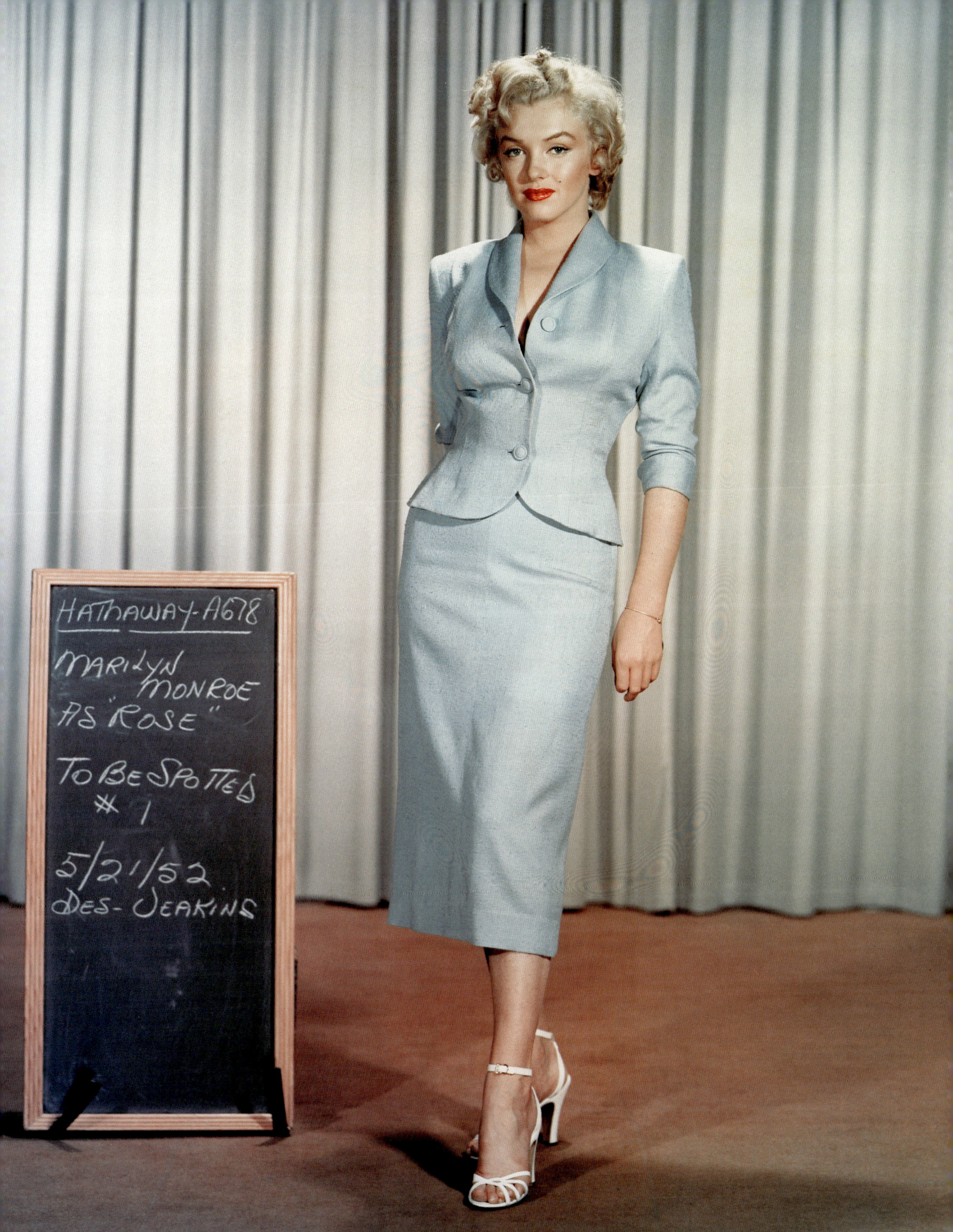
HATHAWAY-A678
MARILYN MONROE
AS "ROSE"
TO BE SPOTTED
#1
5/21/52
DES- JEAKINS

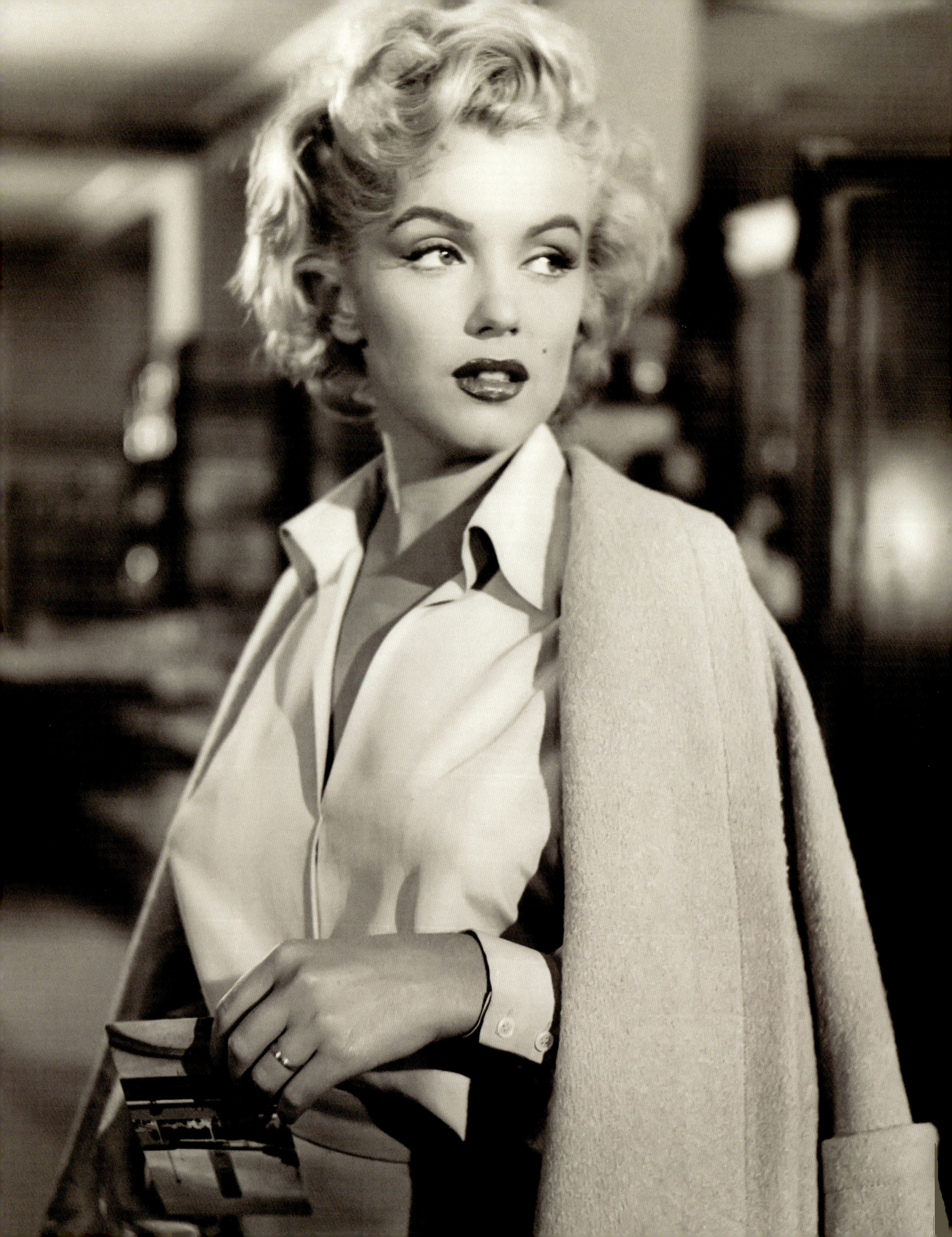

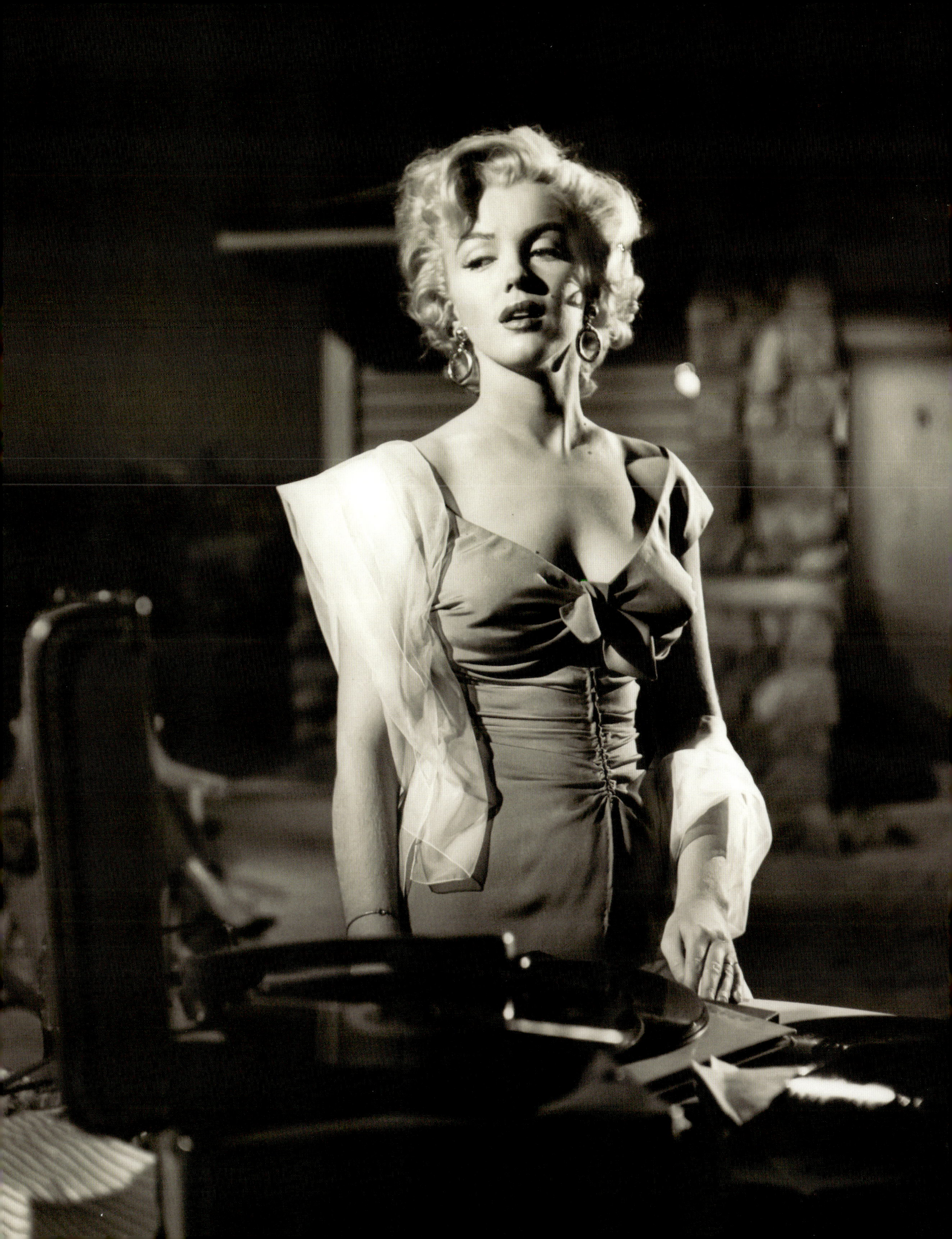

"People look the most kissable when they're not wearing makeup. Marilyn's lips weren't kissable, but they were very photographable."

ANDY WARHOL

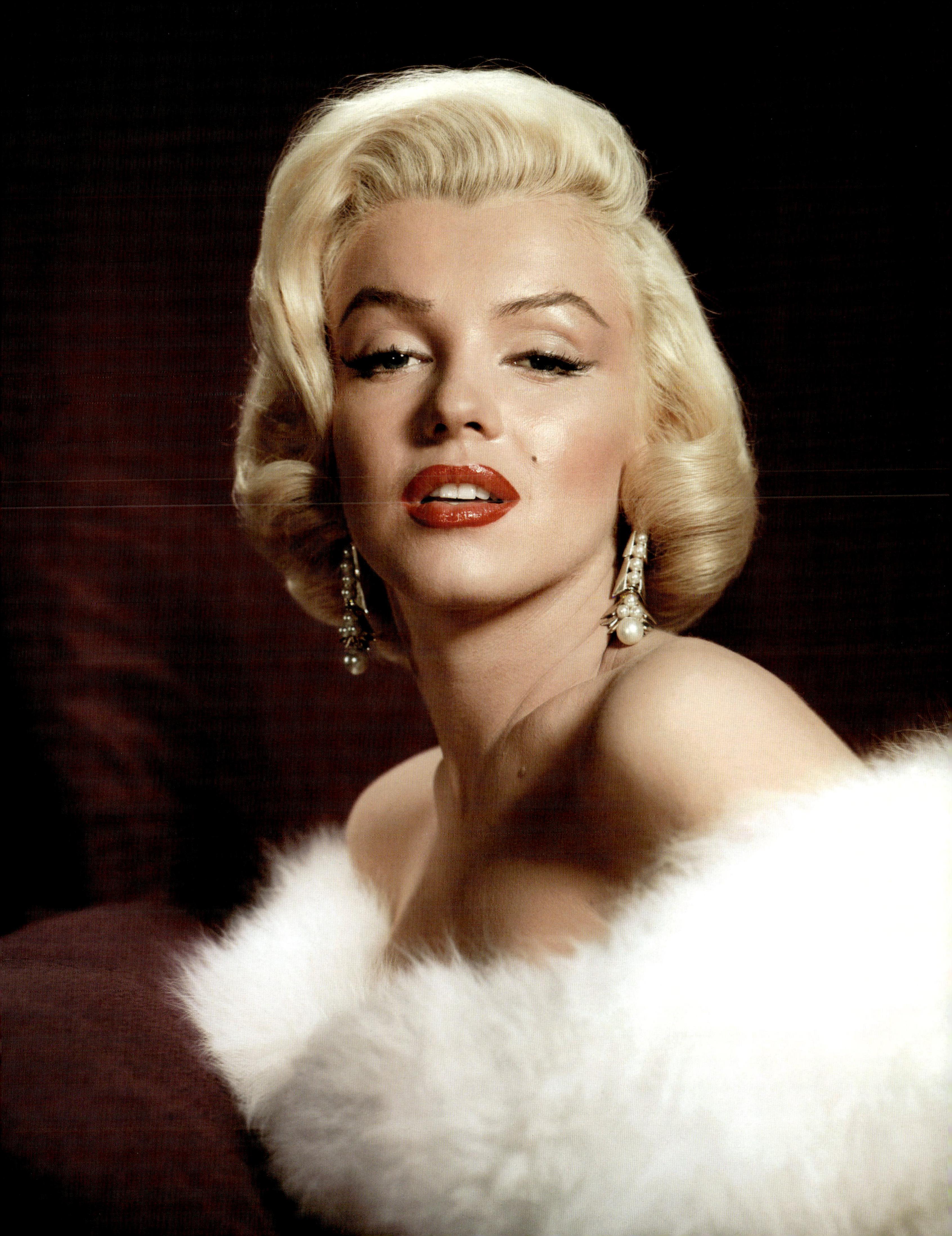

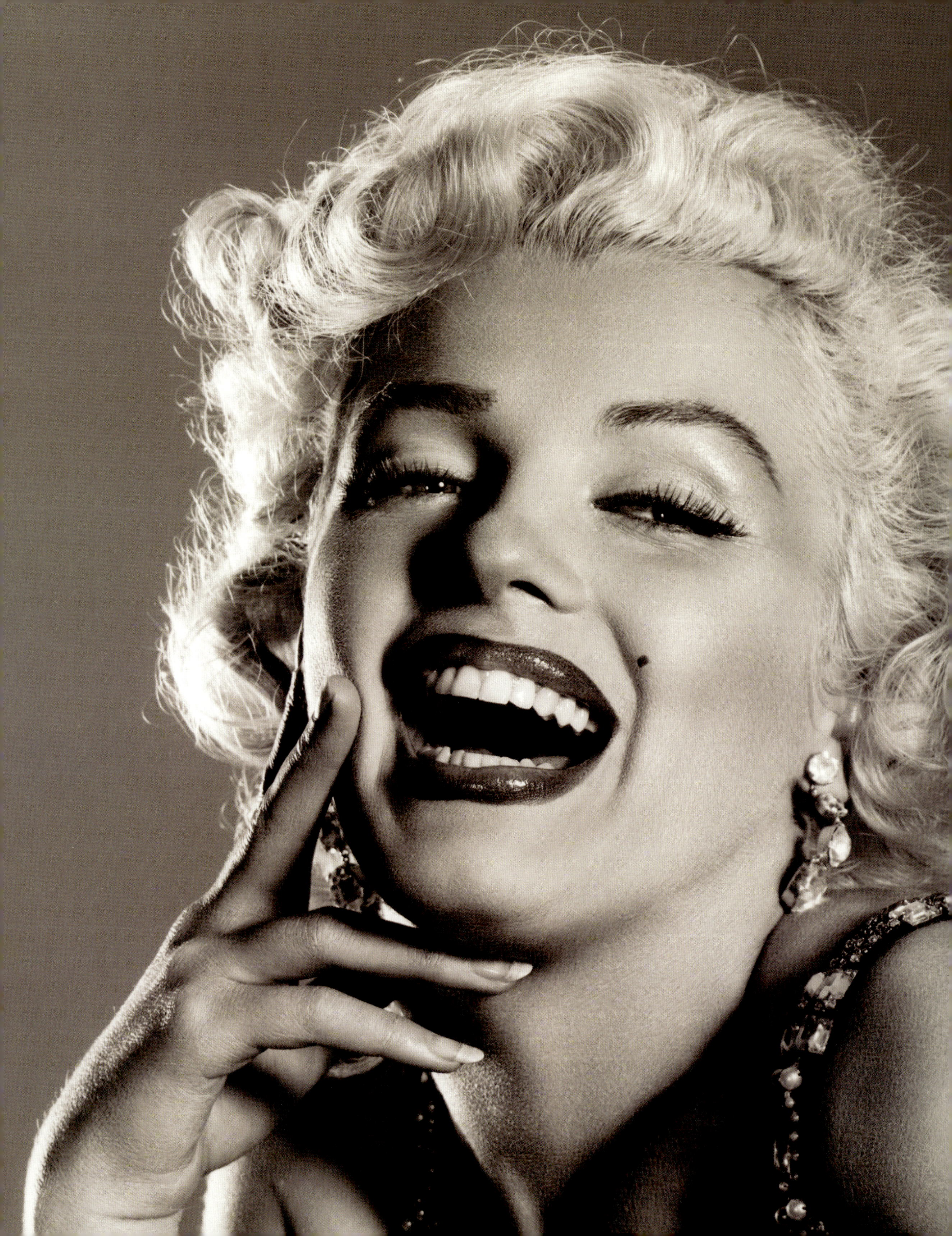

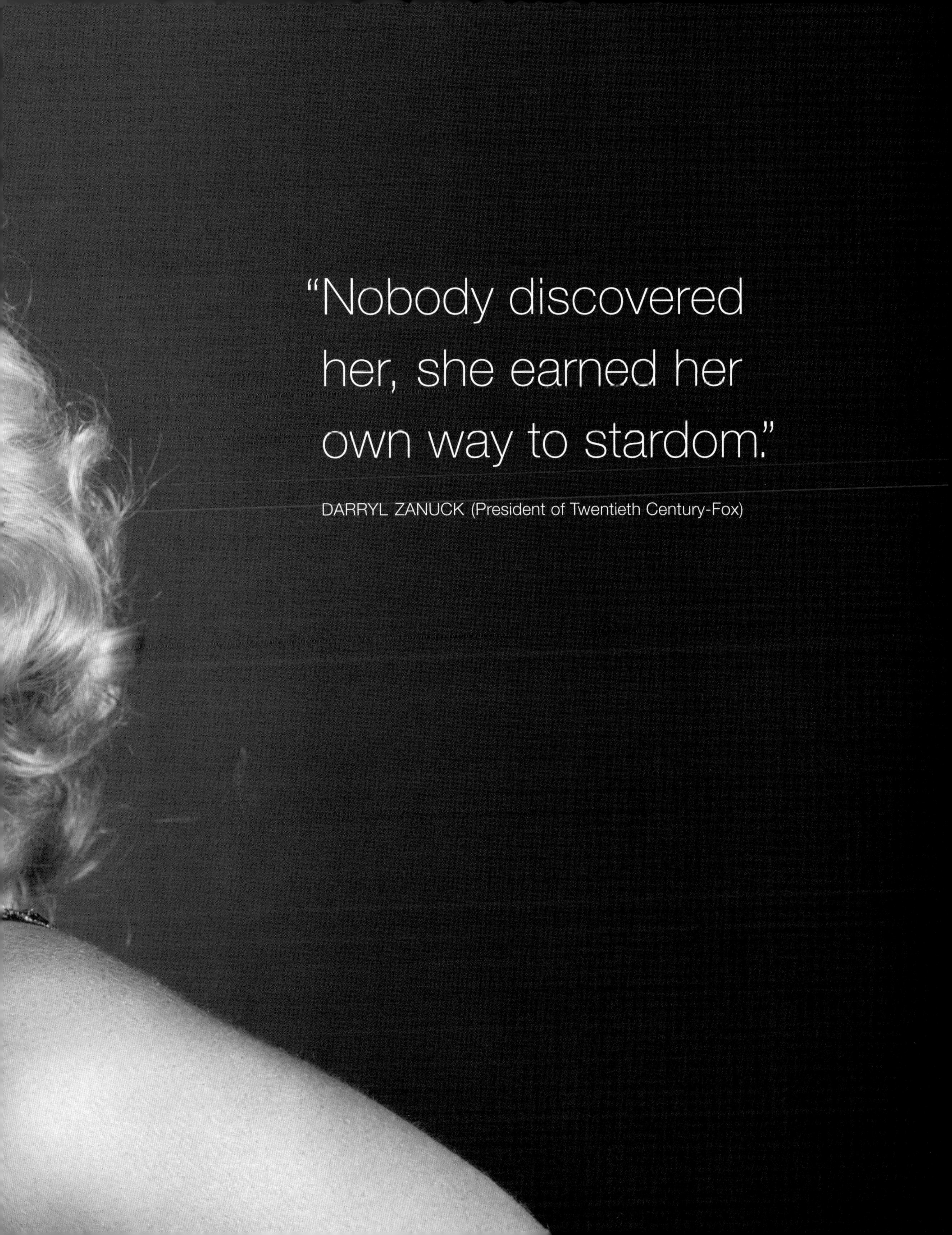

"Nobody discovered her, she earned her own way to stardom."

DARRYL ZANUCK (President of Twentieth Century-Fox)

"She had a delightful quality, being so beautiful, of wanting to show herself. Some people were offended by it—and of course she did it on purpose. She was so childlike she could do anything, and you would forgive as you would forgive a seven-year-old. She was both a woman and a baby, and both men and women adored her. She was not well educated, but an extremely bright woman, and she had the whims of a child. I think she wanted to love, but could only love herself. She was totally narcissistic. She adored her own face, constantly wanting to make it better and different. Everything she did in that regard, by the way, was right at the time. She once told me, 'I can make my face do anything, same as you can take a white board and build from that and make a painting.' But the only way she was highly sexed was the charge she got out of looking in the mirror and seeing that beautiful mouth that she'd painted with about five shades of lipstick, to get the right curves, the right shadows to bring out the lips, because her lips were really very flat."

WILLIAM TRAVILLA (Costume Designer)

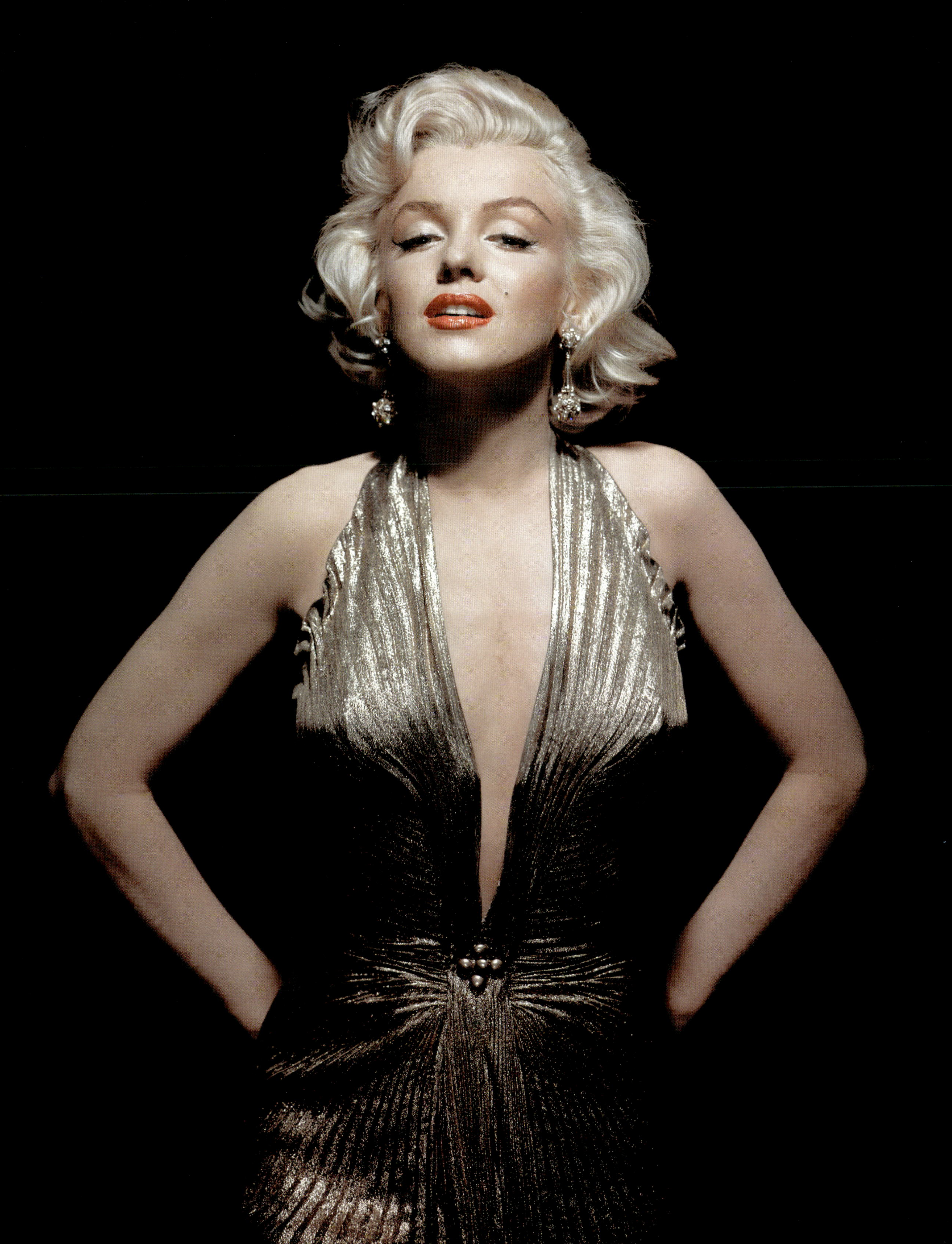

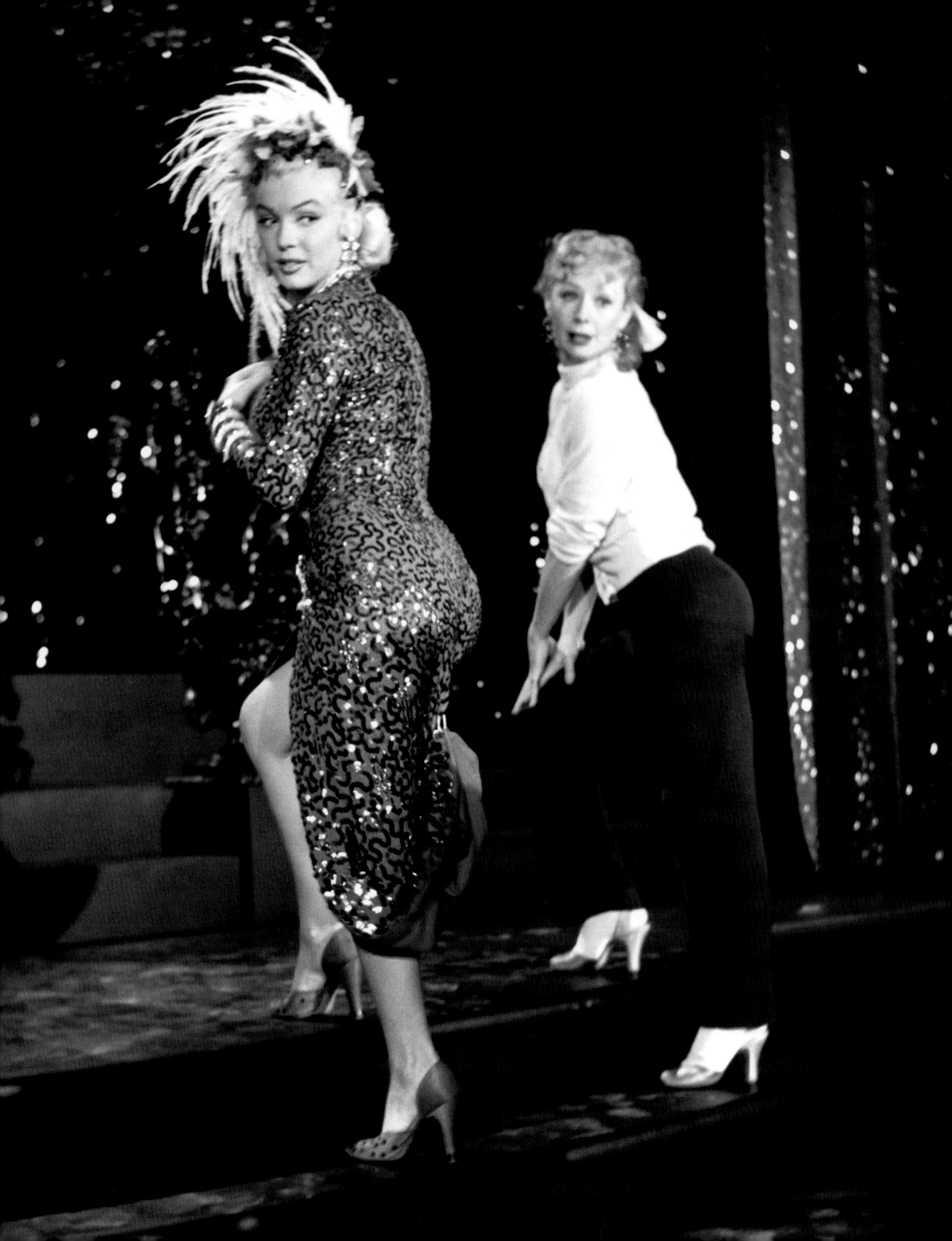

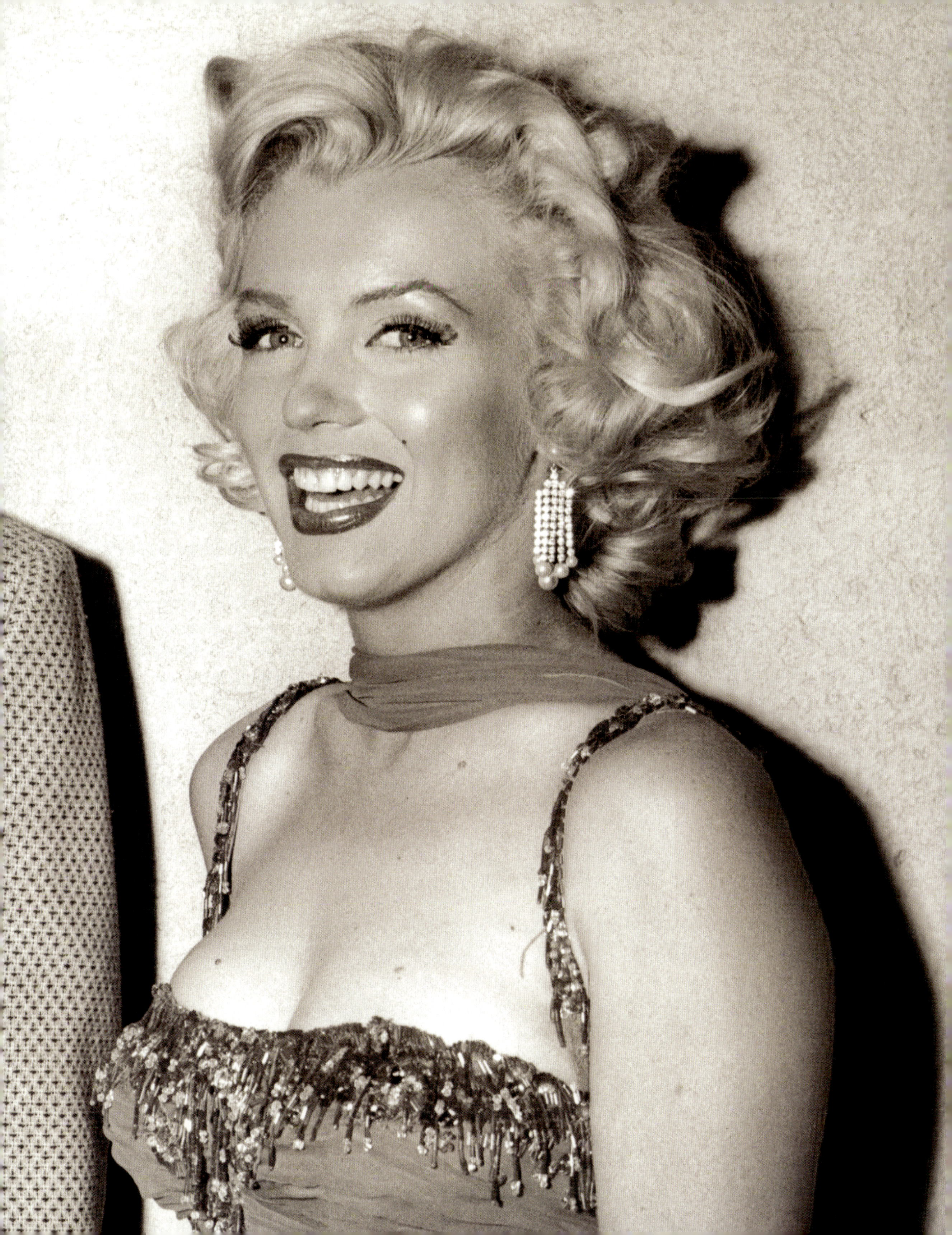

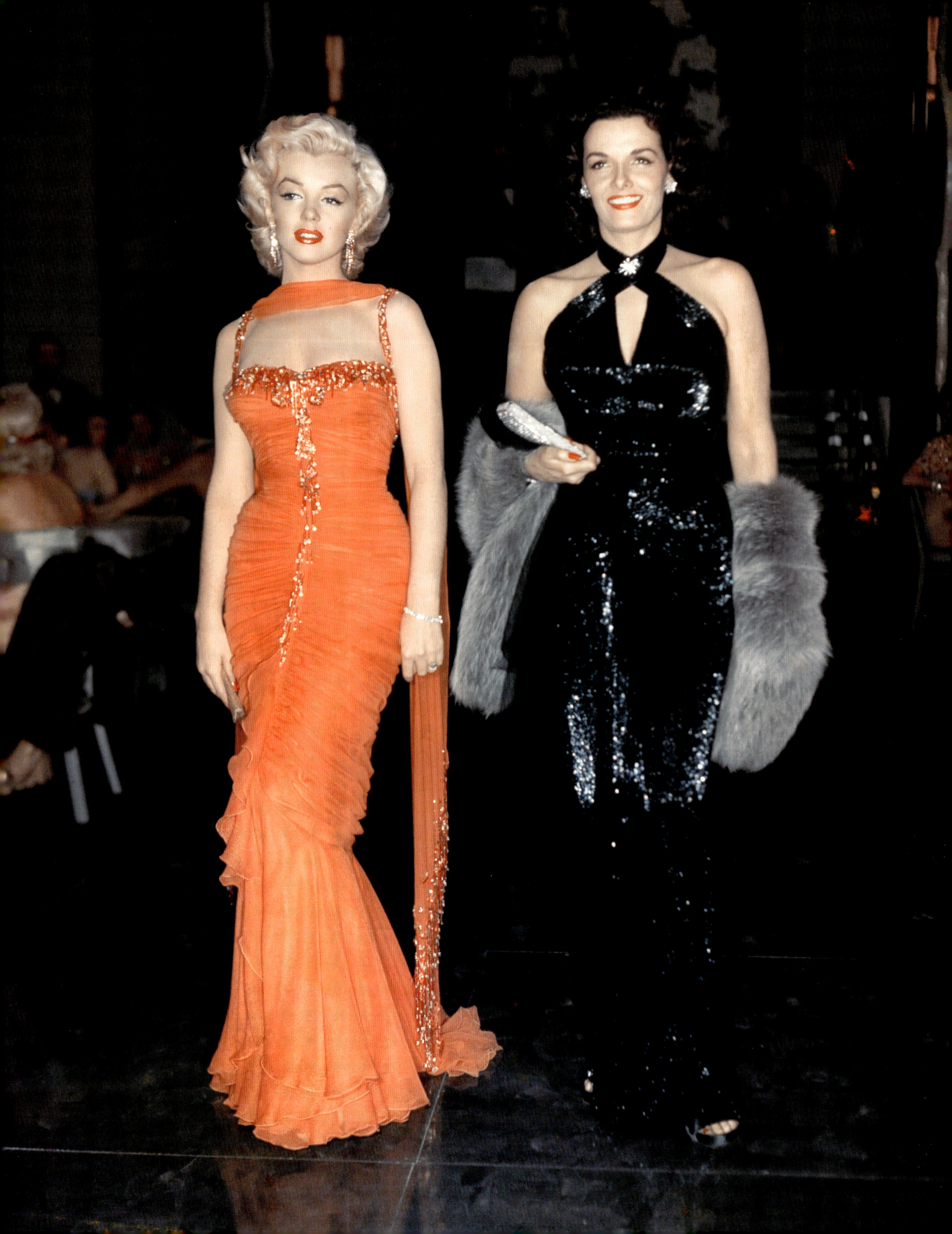

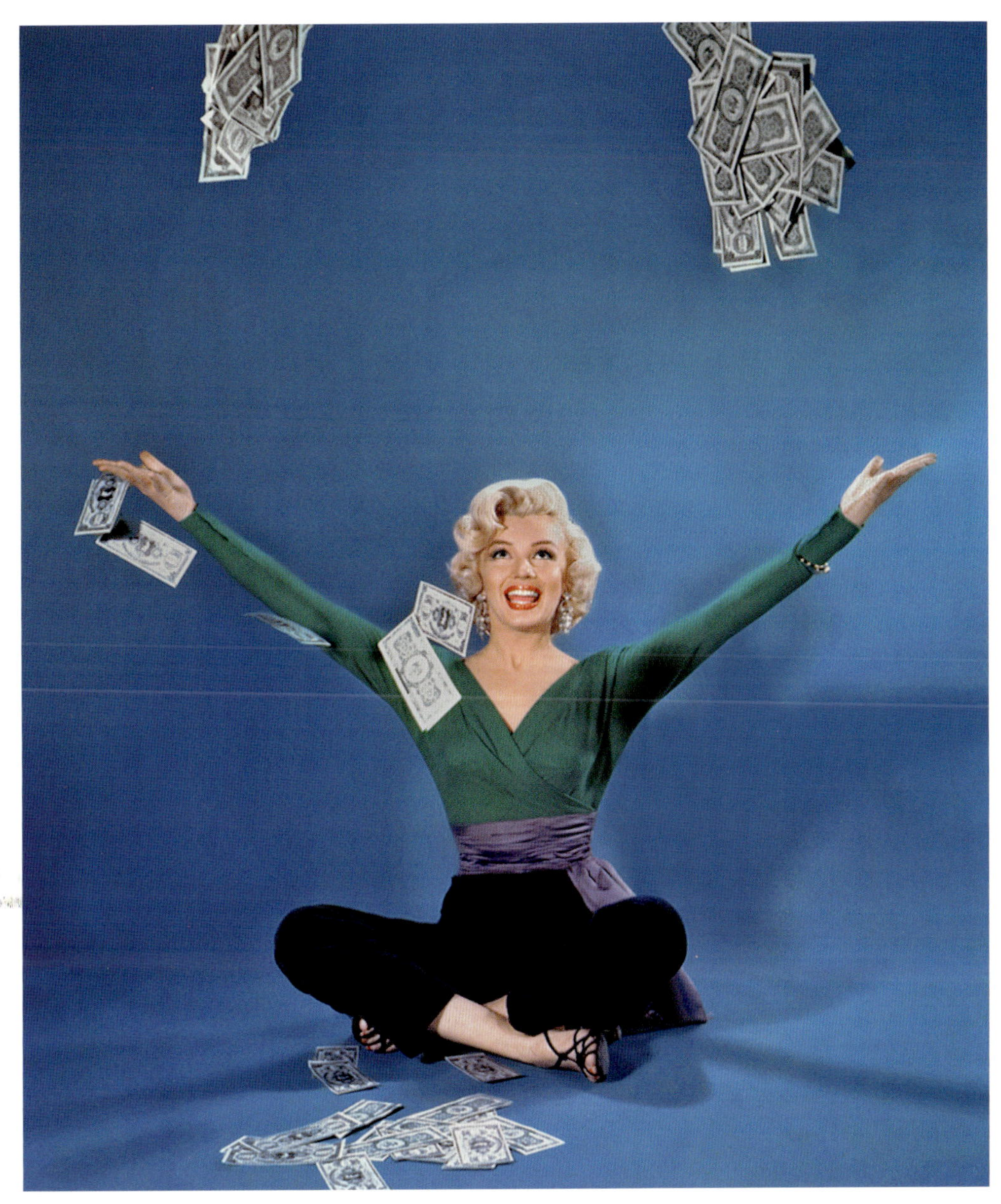

"She was terrified. She would come in way before me, and she'd have rehearsed. She'd be all ready, but too nervous to go out on the set. So I'd arrange it that when it was time to go I'd come and get her, and we'd walk out there together."

JANE RUSSELL (Costar, *Gentlemen Prefer Blondes*, 1953)

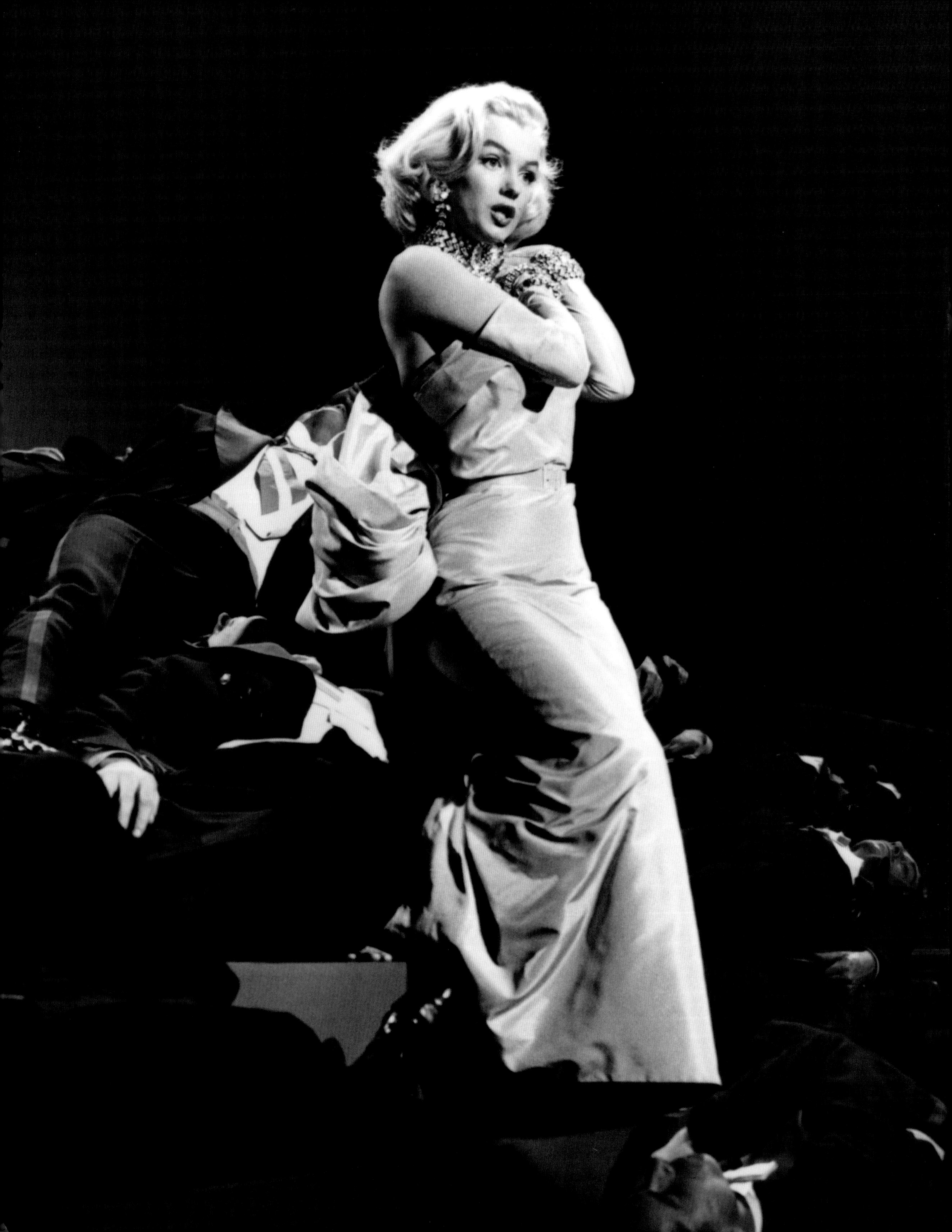

"As usual, Miss Monroe looks as though she would glow in the dark, and her version of the baby-faced blonde whose eyes open for diamonds and close for kisses is always amusing as well as alluring."

NEW YORK HERALD TRIBUNE

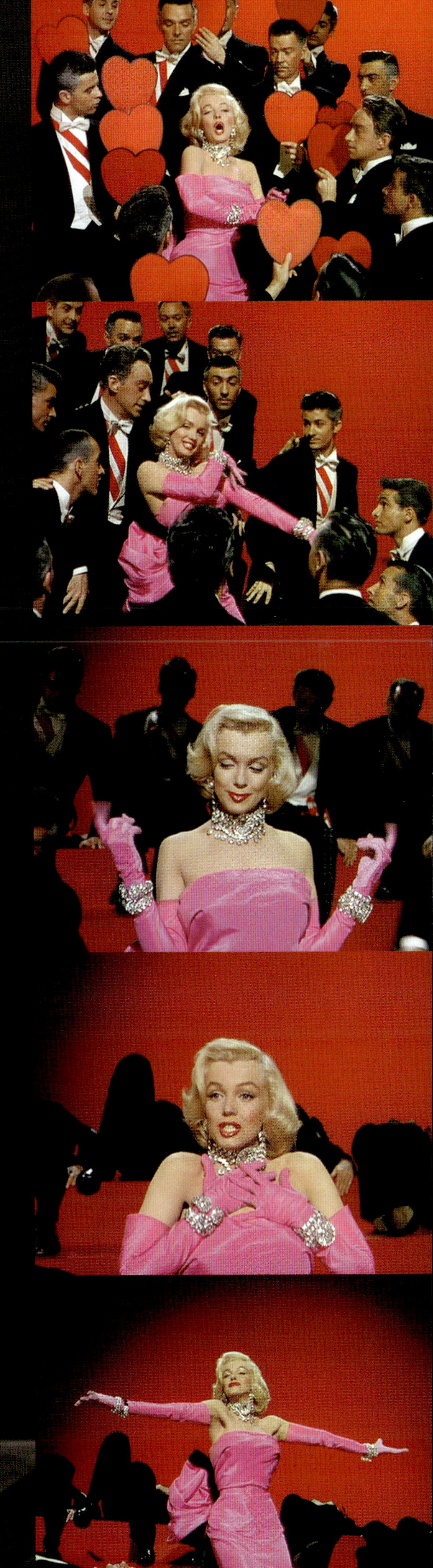

"I don't know if high society is different in other cities, but in Hollywood important people can't stand to be invited someplace that isn't full of other important people. They don't mind a few unfamous people being present because they make good listeners. But if a star or studio chief or any other great movie personages find themselves sitting among a lot of nobodies, they get frightened—as if somebody was trying to demote them."

MARILYN MONROE

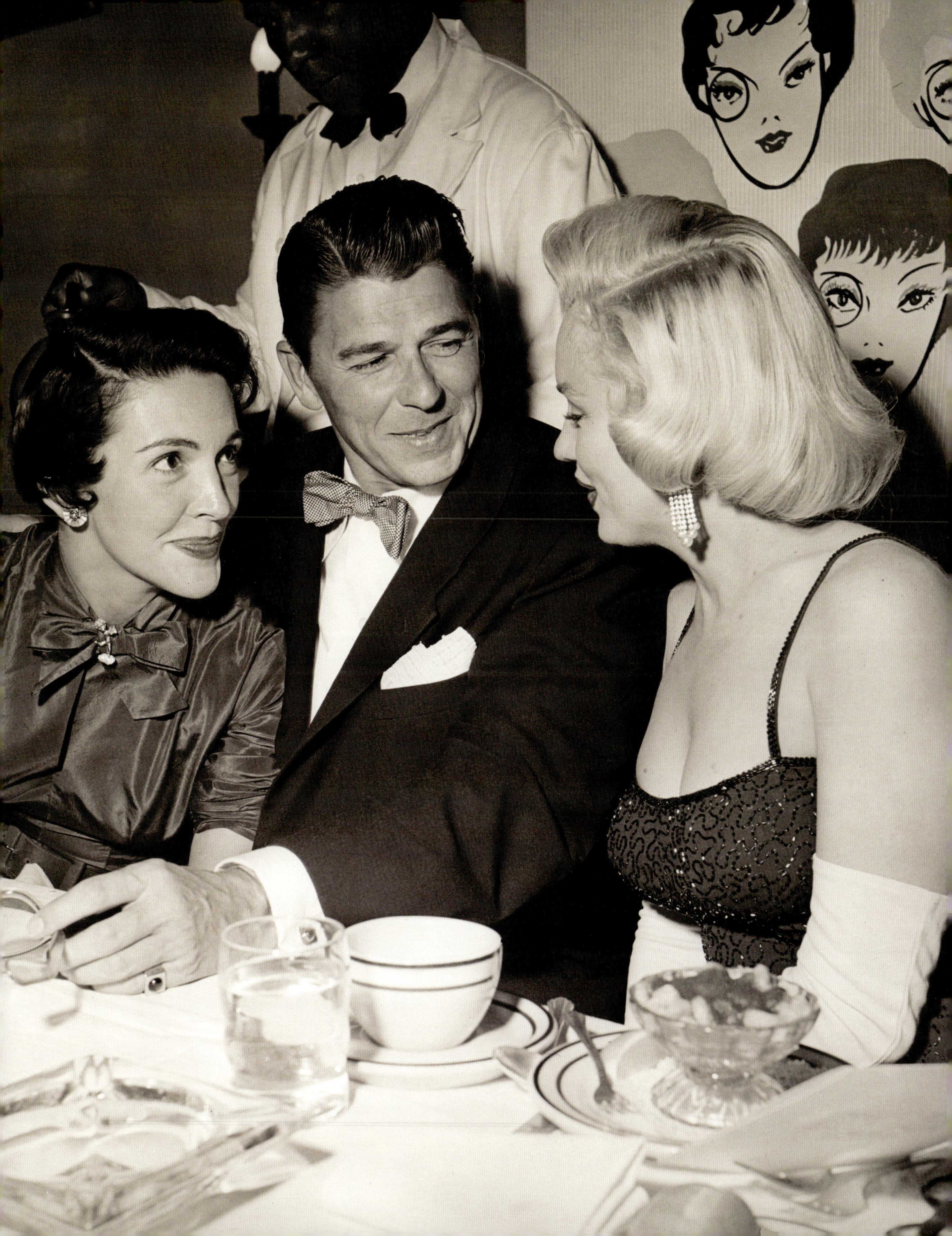

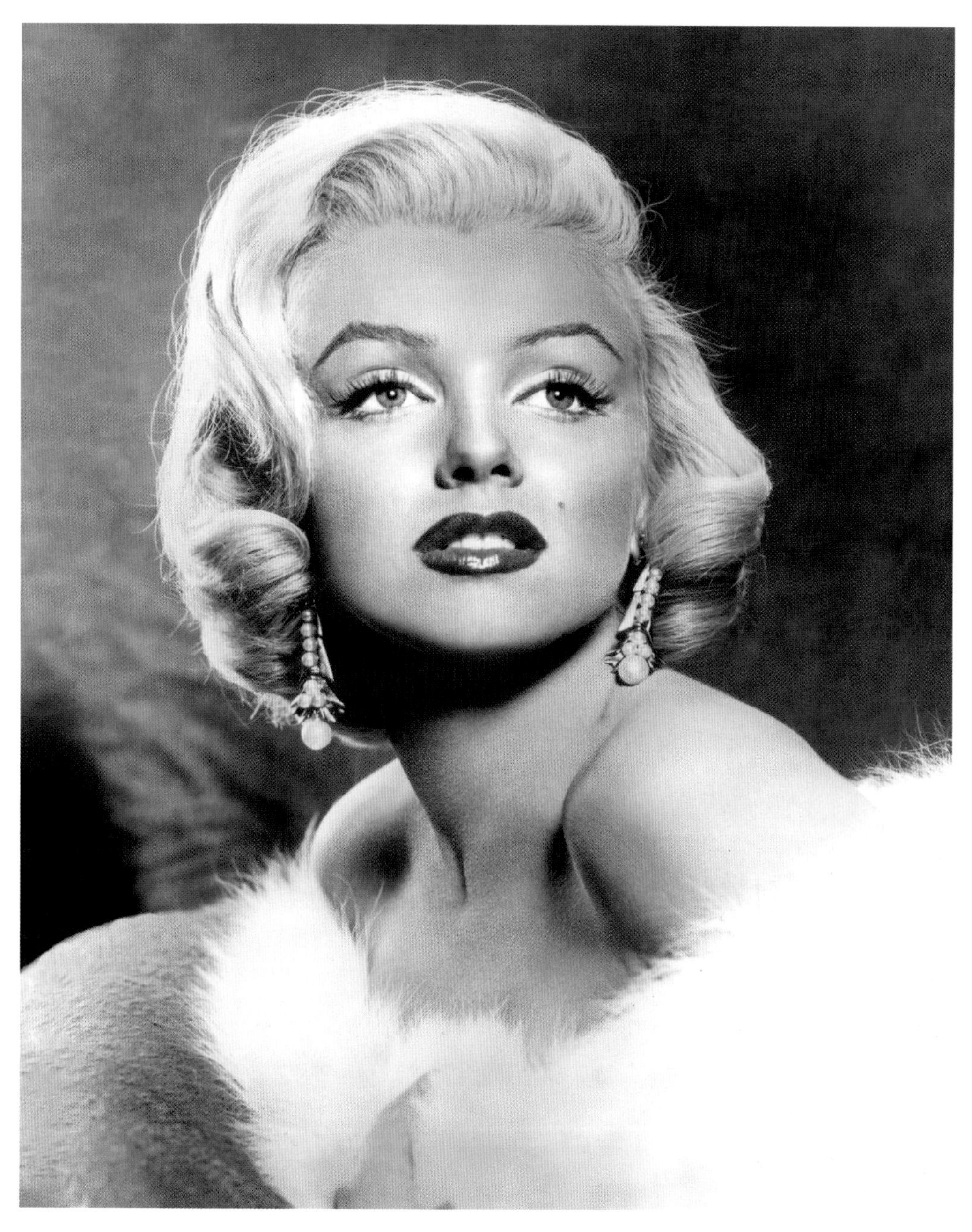

"When you look at Marilyn on the screen, you don't want anything bad to happen to her. You really care that she should be all right . . . happy."

NATALIE WOOD

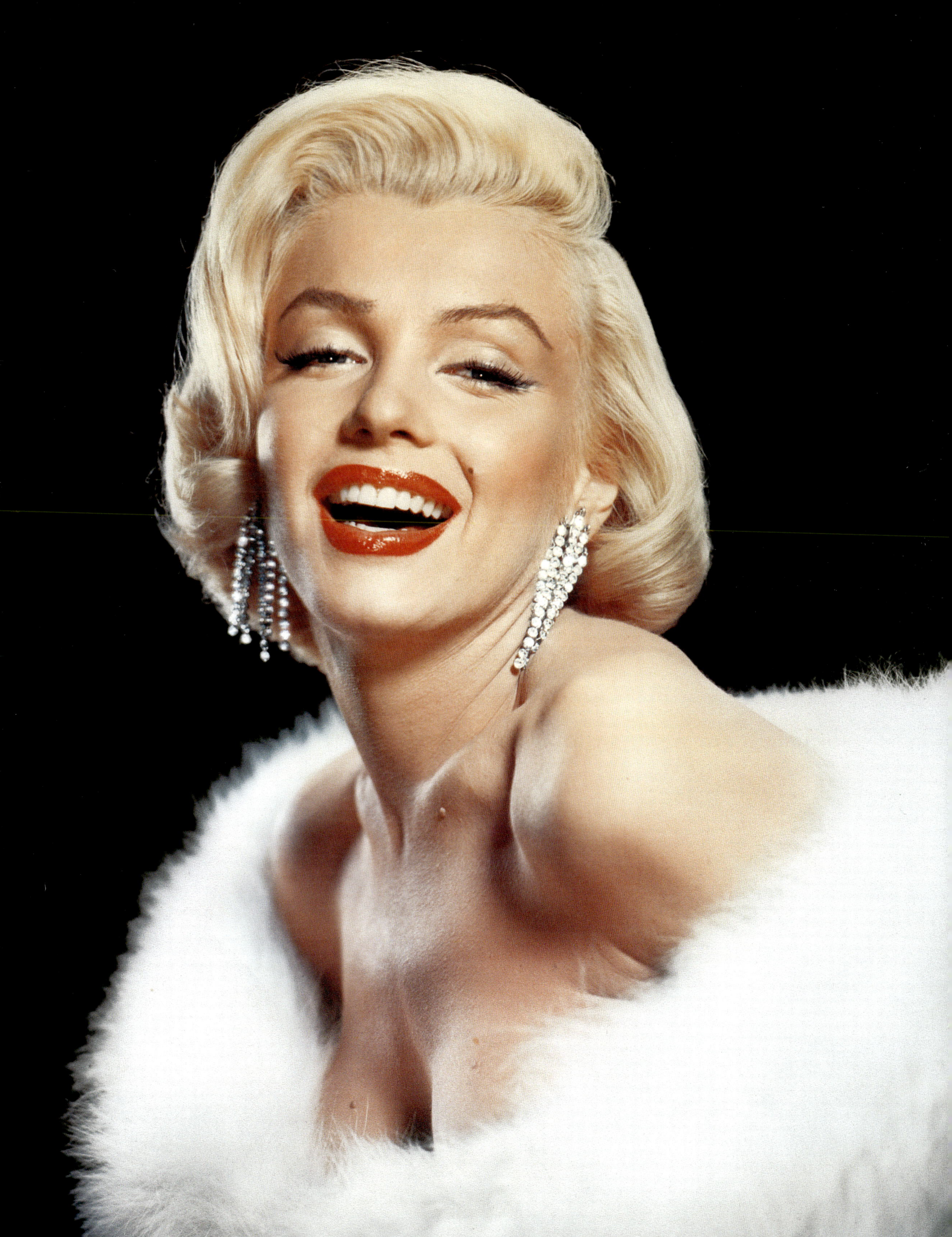

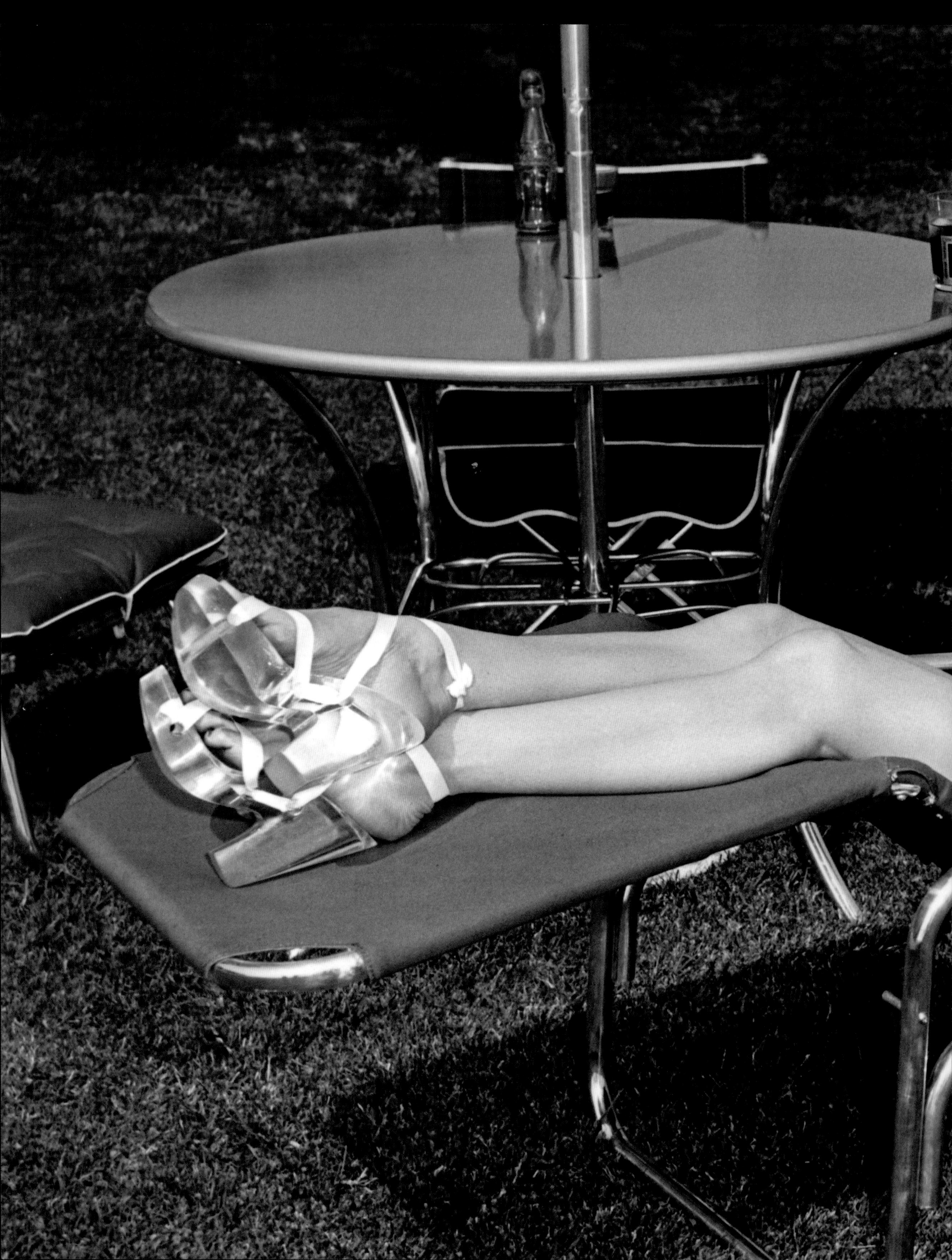

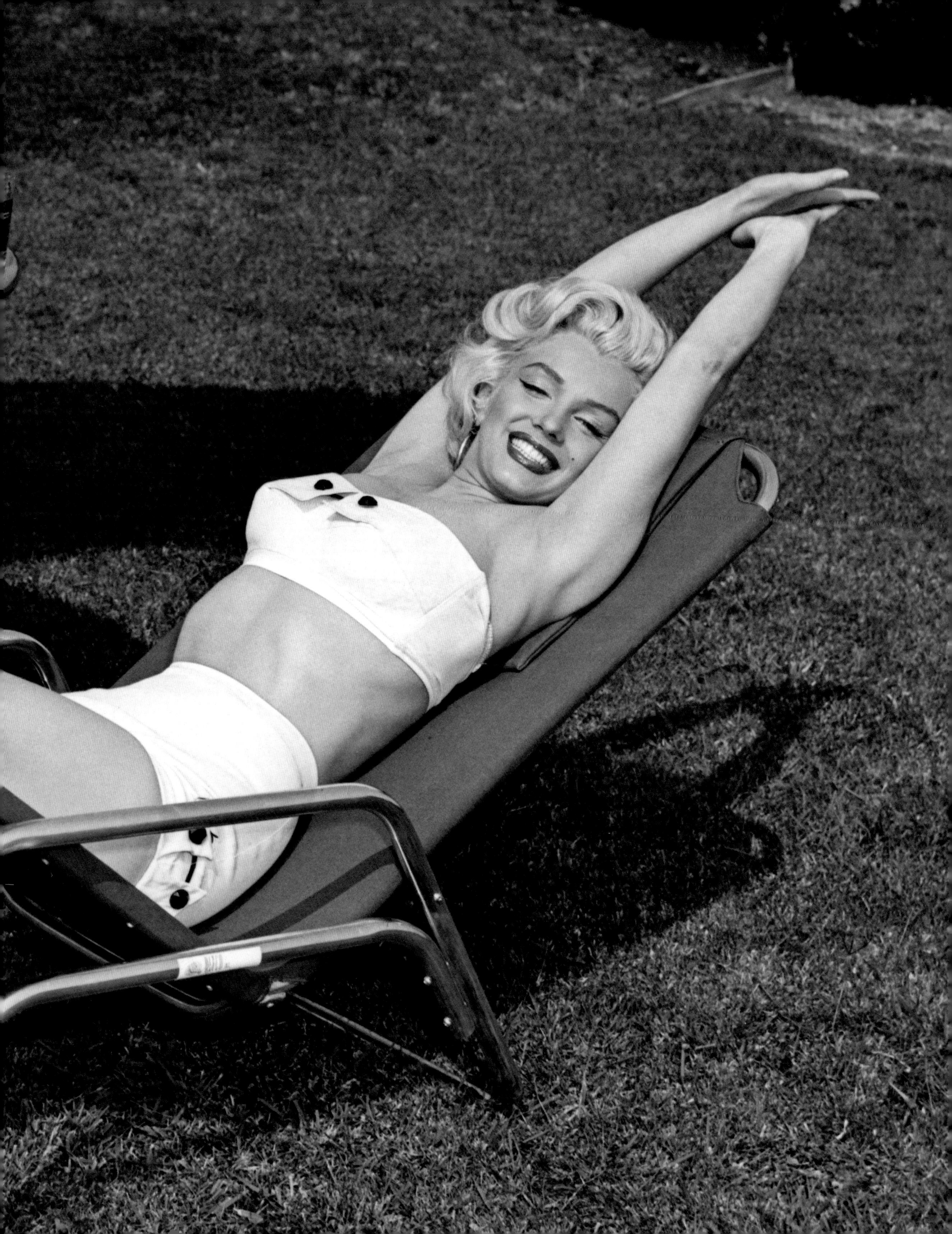

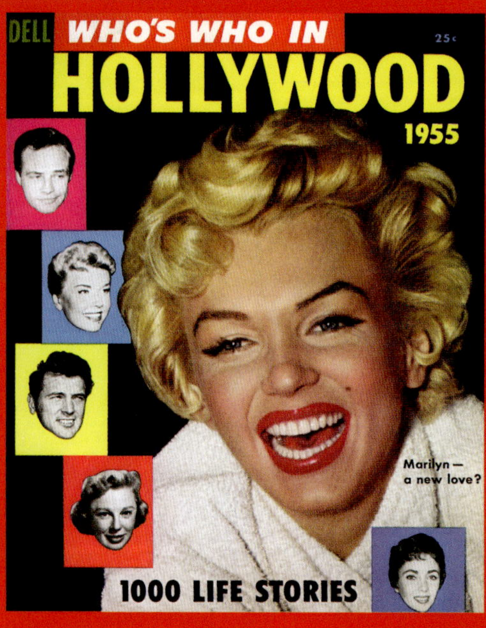
DELL
WHO'S WHO IN
HOLLYWOOD
1955
25¢
Marilyn—
a new love?
1000 LIFE STORIES

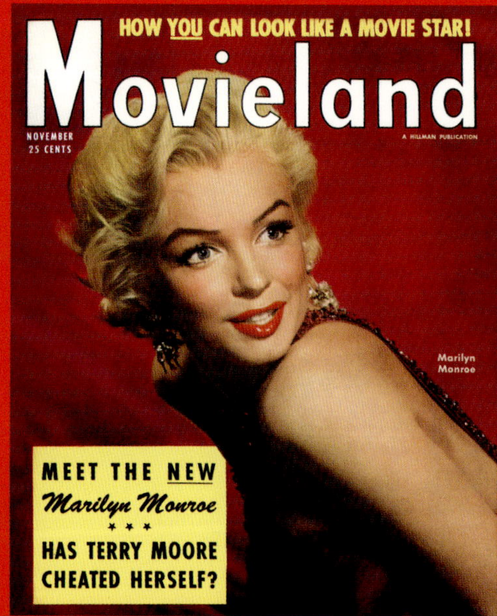
HOW YOU CAN LOOK LIKE A MOVIE STAR!
Movieland
NOVEMBER
25 CENTS
Marilyn
Monroe
MEET THE NEW
Marilyn Monroe
HAS TERRY MOORE
CHEATED HERSELF?

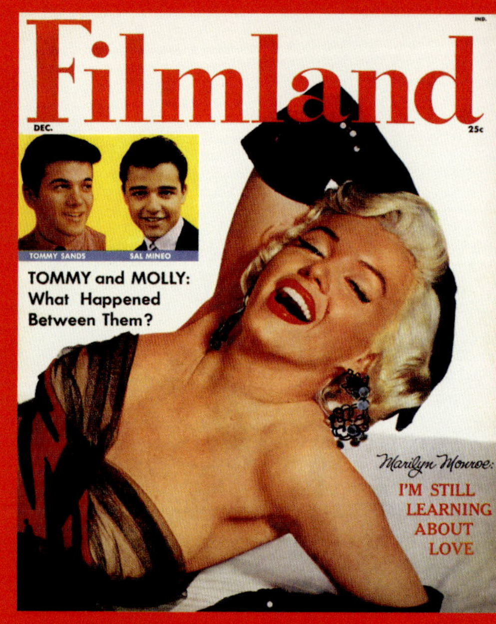
Filmland
DEC.
25¢
TOMMY SANDS
SAL MINEO
TOMMY and MOLLY:
What Happened
Between Them?
Marilyn Monroe:
I'M STILL
LEARNING
ABOUT
LOVE

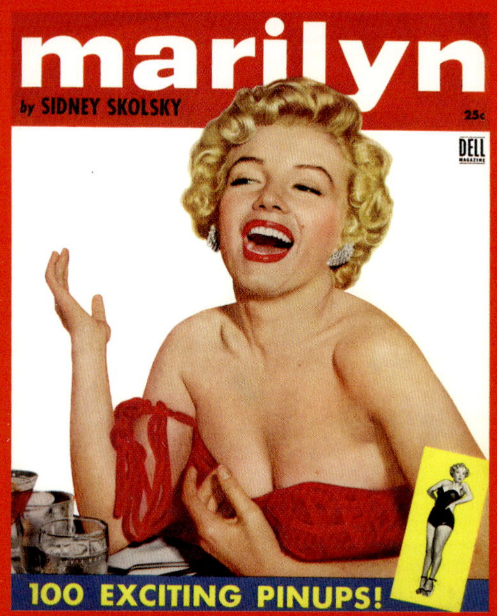
marilyn
by SIDNEY SKOLSKY
25¢
DELL
100 EXCITING PINUPS!

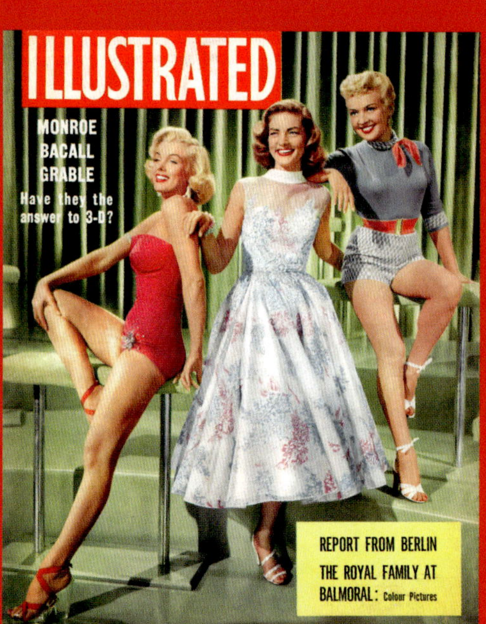
ILLUSTRATED
MONROE
BACALL
GRABLE
Have they the
answer to 3-D?
REPORT FROM BERLIN
THE ROYAL FAMILY AT
BALMORAL: Colour Pictures

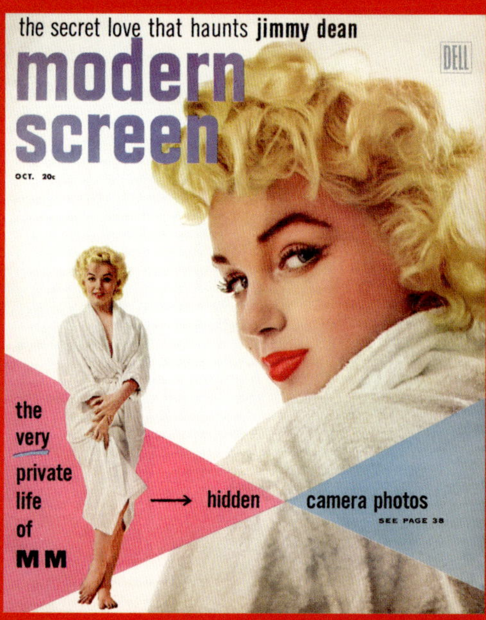
the secret love that haunts jimmy dean
modern
screen
DELL
OCT. 20¢
the
very
private
life
of
MM
→ hidden
camera photos
SEE PAGE 38

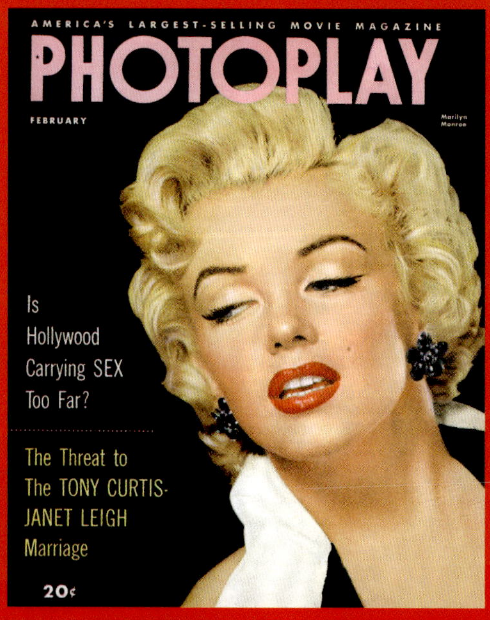
AMERICA'S LARGEST-SELLING MOVIE MAGAZINE
PHOTOPLAY
FEBRUARY
Is
Hollywood
Carrying SEX
Too Far?
The Threat to
The TONY CURTIS-
JANET LEIGH
Marriage
20¢

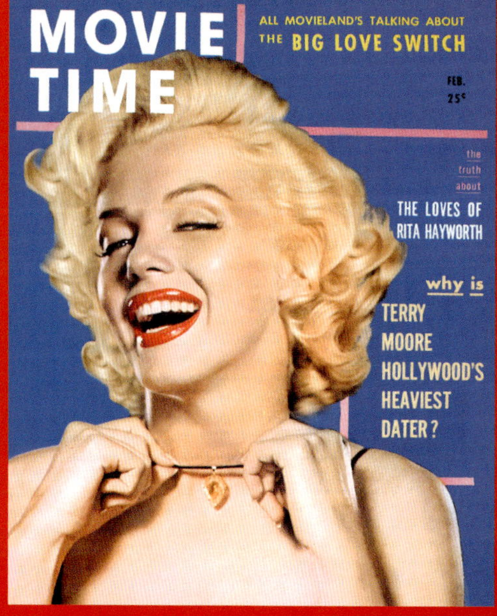
MOVIE
TIME
ALL MOVIELAND'S TALKING ABOUT
THE BIG LOVE SWITCH
FEB.
25¢
the
truth
about
THE LOVES OF
RITA HAYWORTH
why is
TERRY
MOORE
HOLLYWOOD'S
HEAVIEST
DATER?

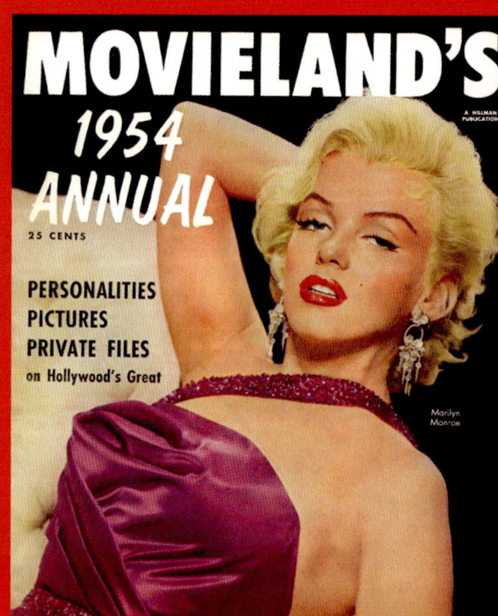
MOVIELAND'S
1954
ANNUAL
25 CENTS
PERSONALITIES
PICTURES
PRIVATE FILES
on Hollywood's Great

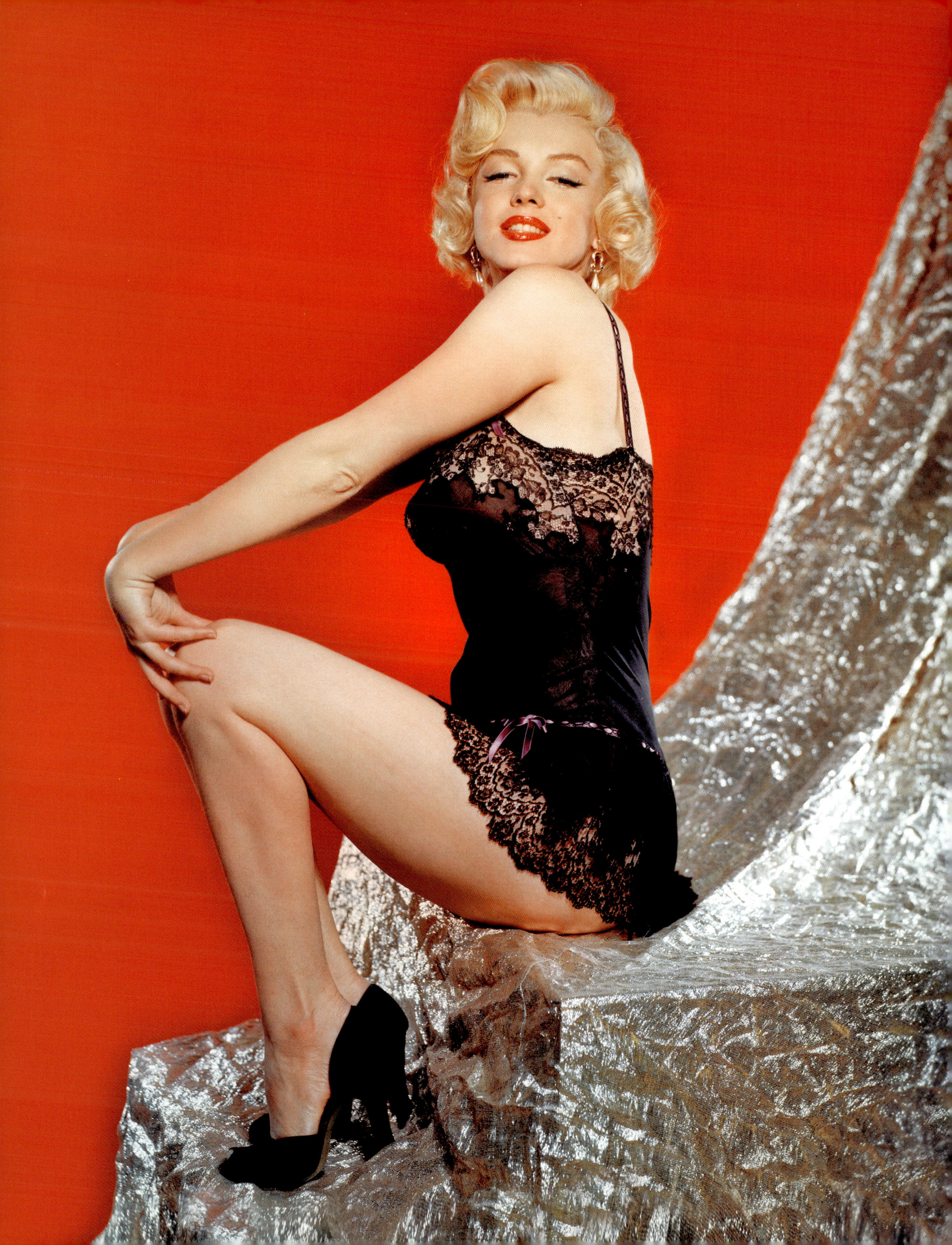

“She did the same routine Harlow did. She arrived wrapped in something and, all of a sudden let it fall. I presume the idea was to get you going. Well, they were exhibitionists.”

GEORGE HURRELL (Photographer)

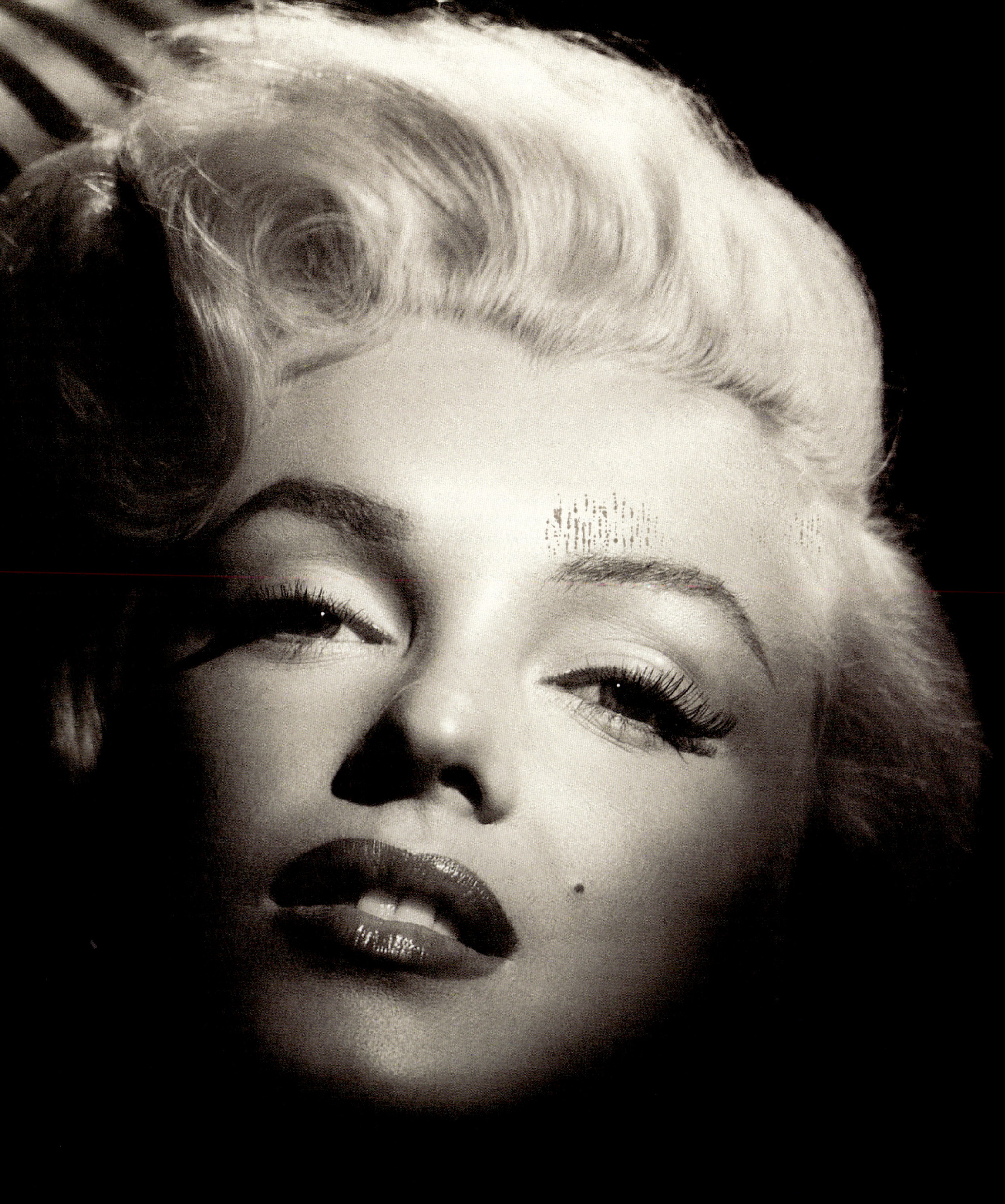

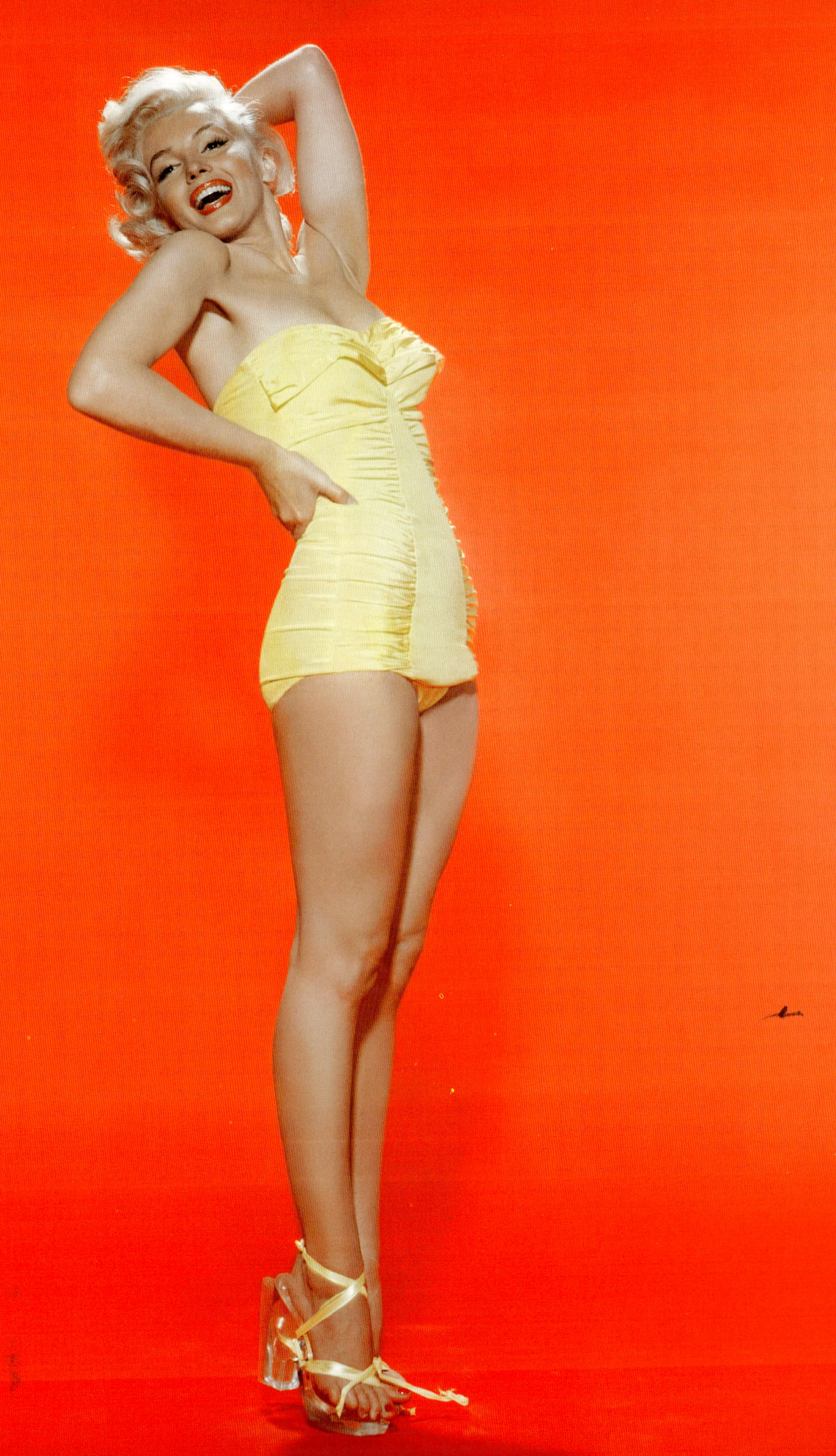

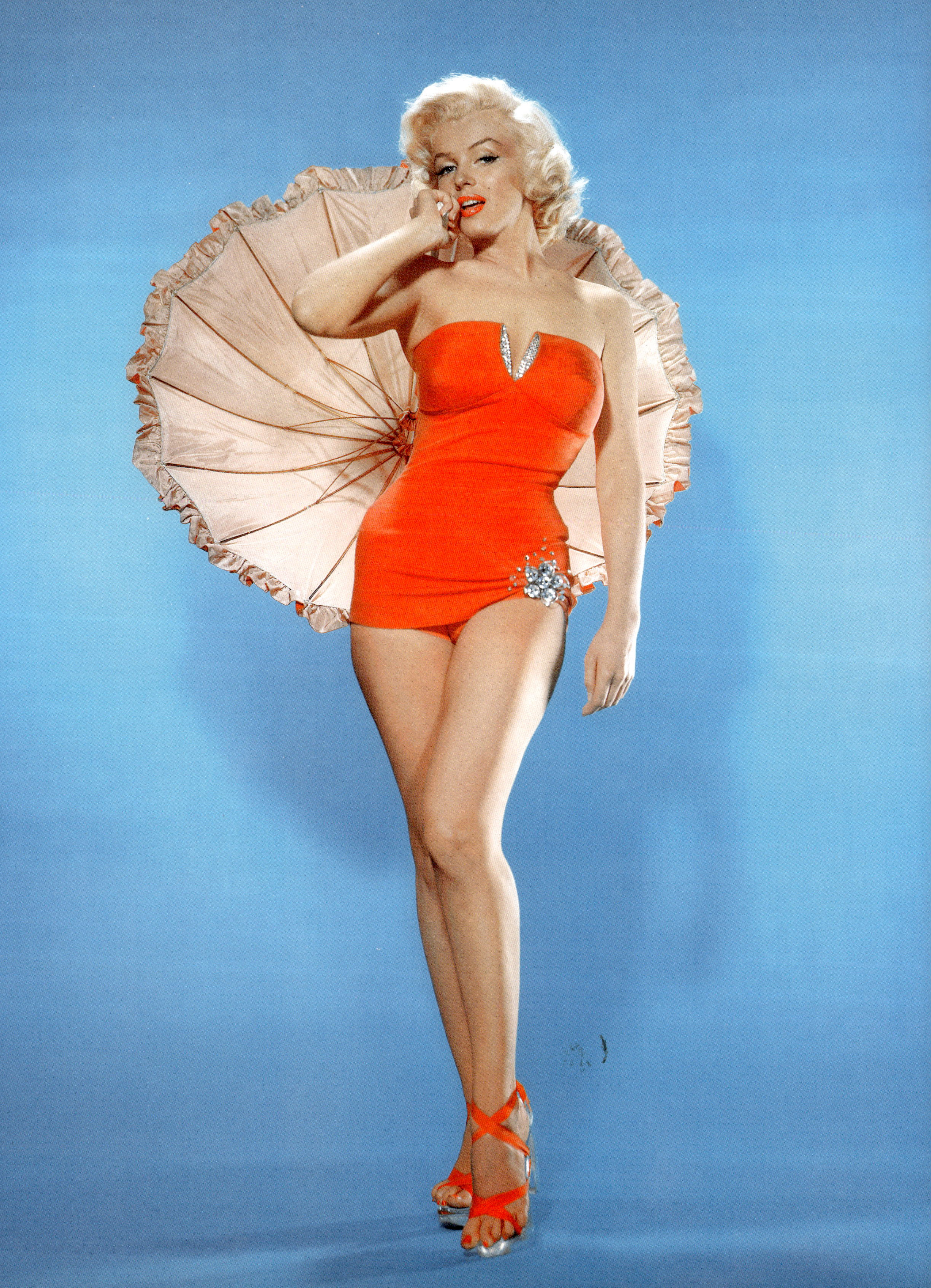

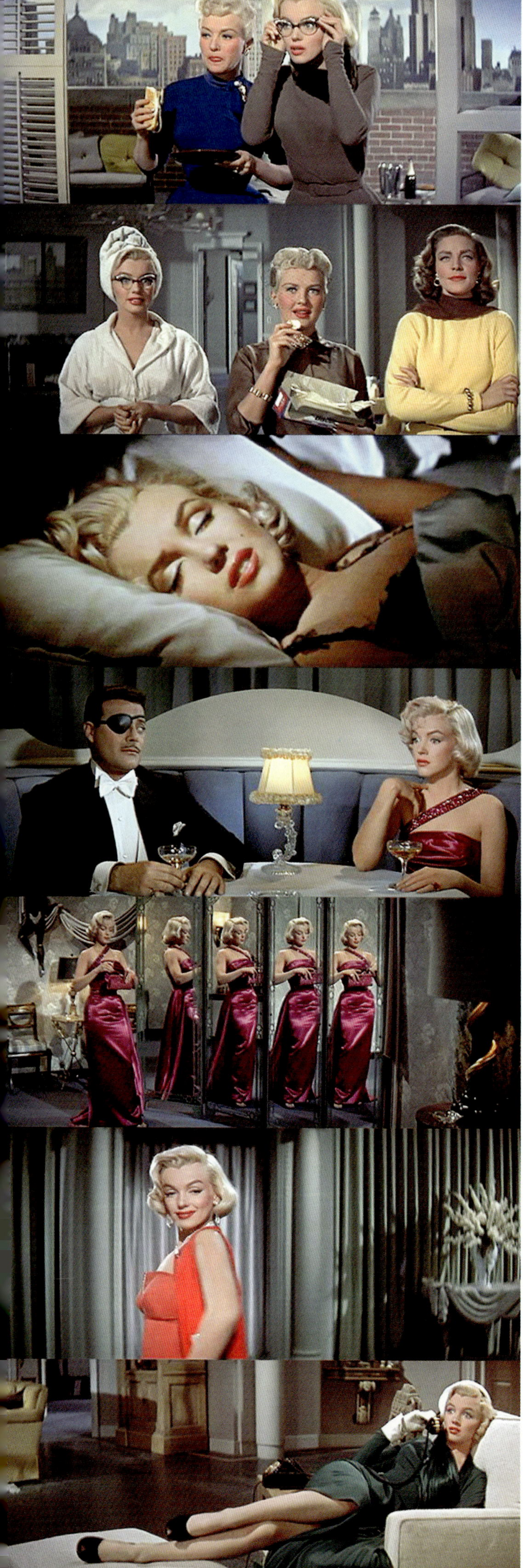

"We were very close. Once I got a call on the set: my younger daughter had had a fall. I ran home and the one person to call was Marilyn. She did an awful lot to boost things up for movies when everything was at a low state; there'll never be anyone like her for looks, for attitude, for all of it."

BETTY GRABLE

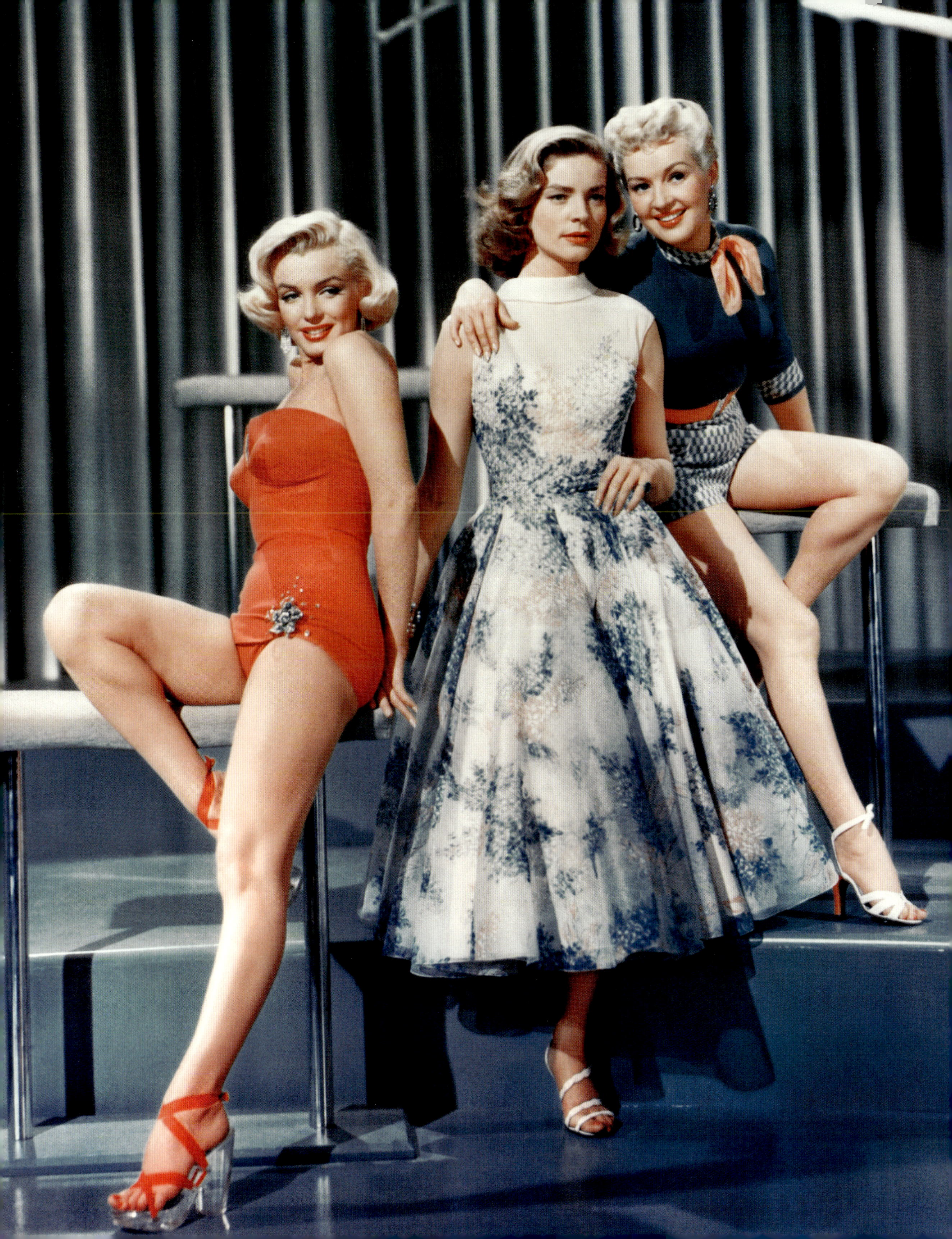

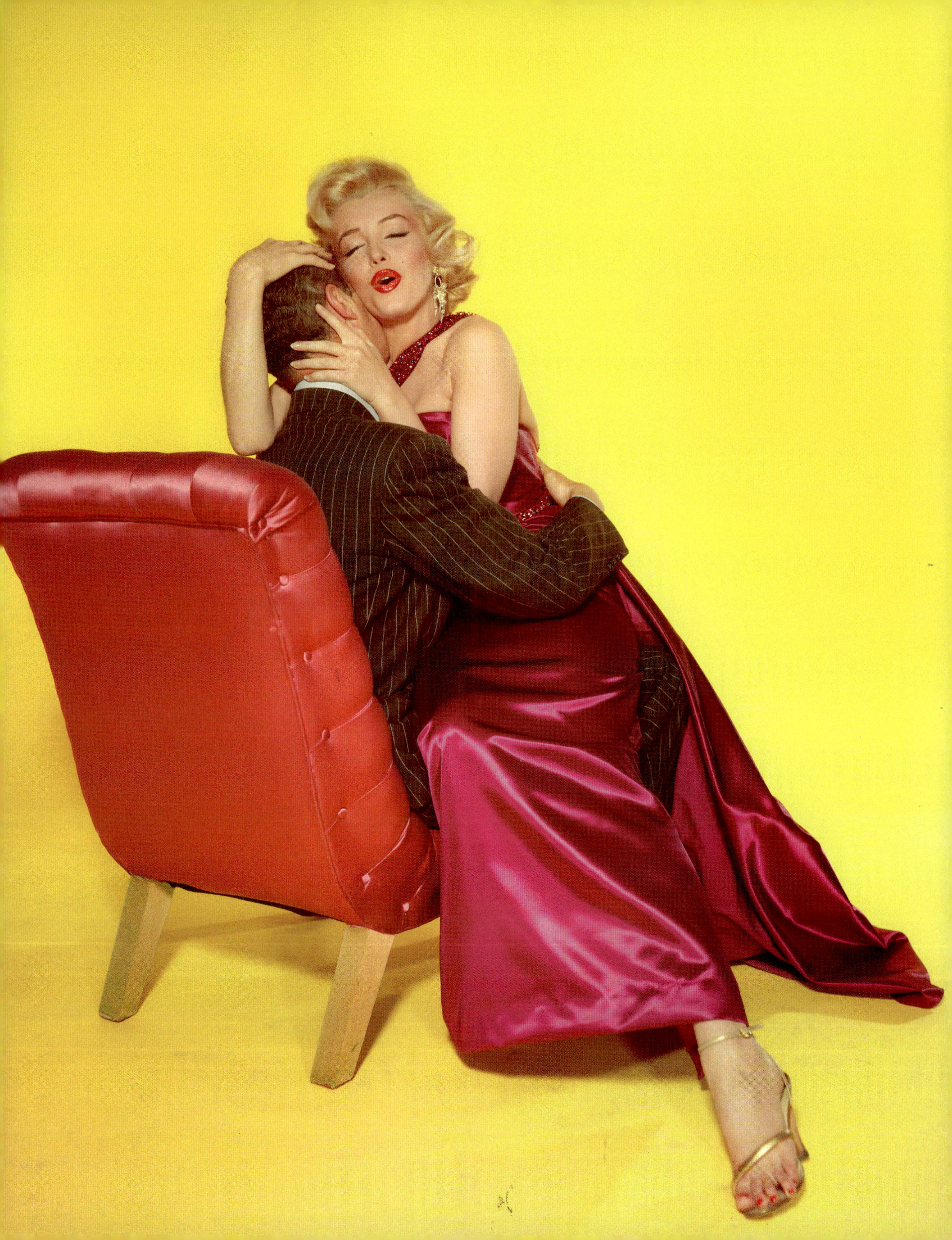

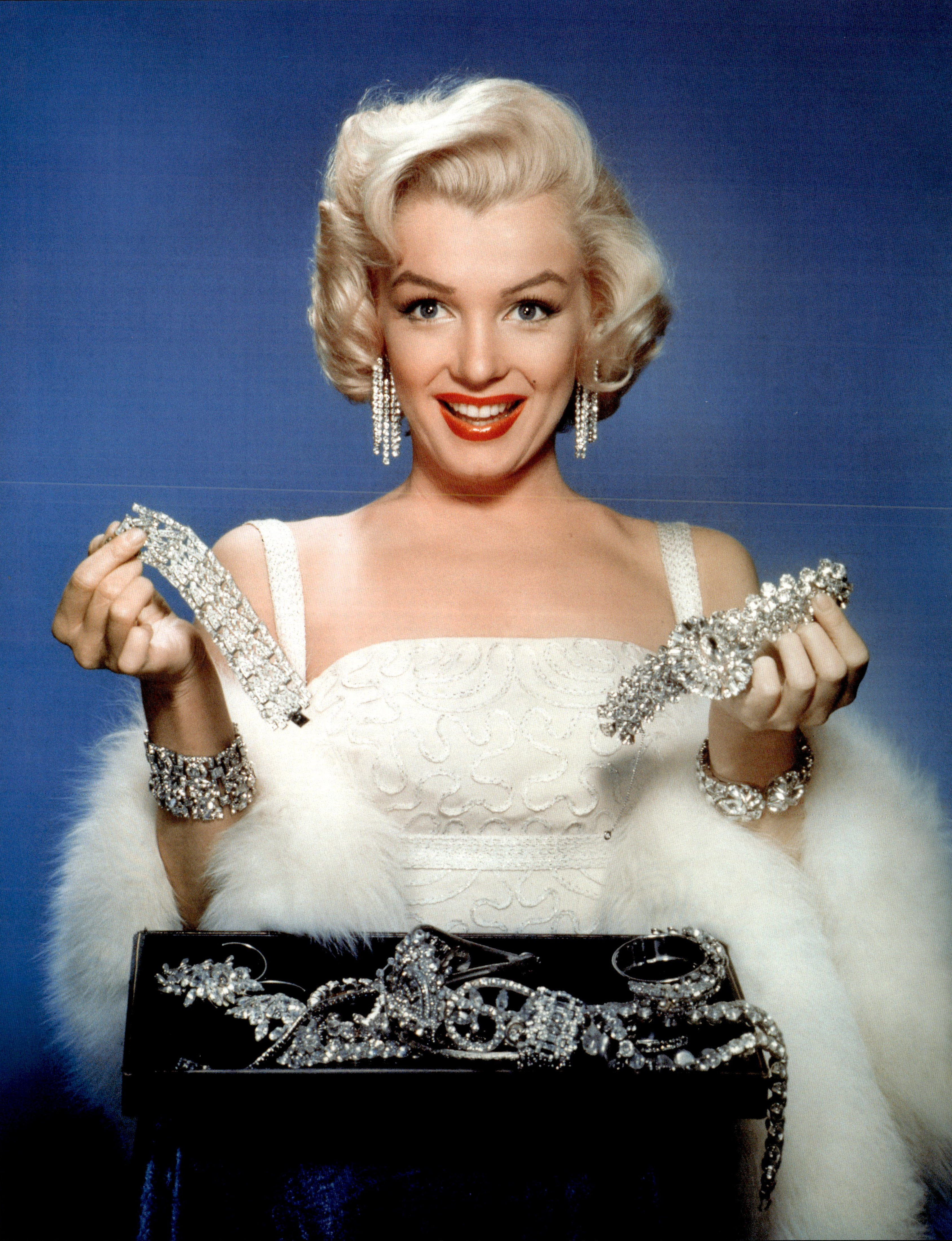

"I believe that the first time anyone genuinely liked Marilyn for herself in a picture, was in *Millionaire*. She herself diagnosed the reason for that very shrewdly. She said that this was the only picture she'd ever been in where she had a measure of modesty about her own attractiveness . . . she didn't think men would look at her twice because she wore glasses; she blundered into walls and stumbled into things and she was most disarming."

NUNNALLY JOHNSON
(Scriptwriter, *How to Marry a Millionaire*, 1953)

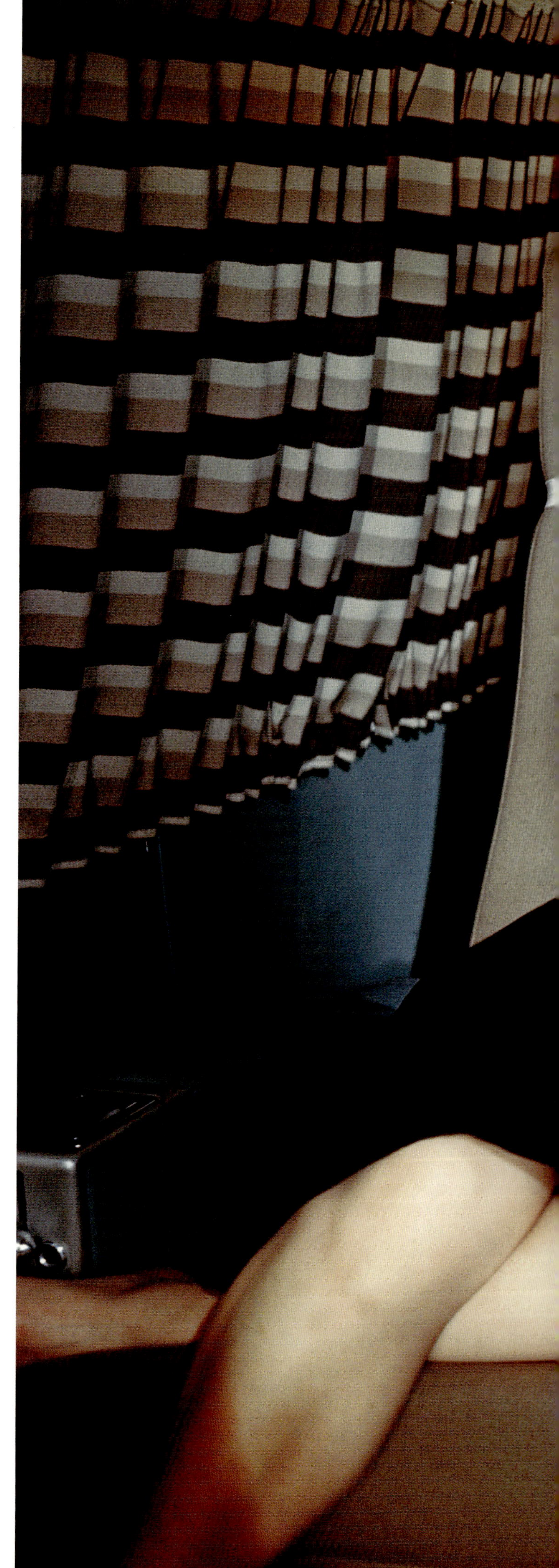

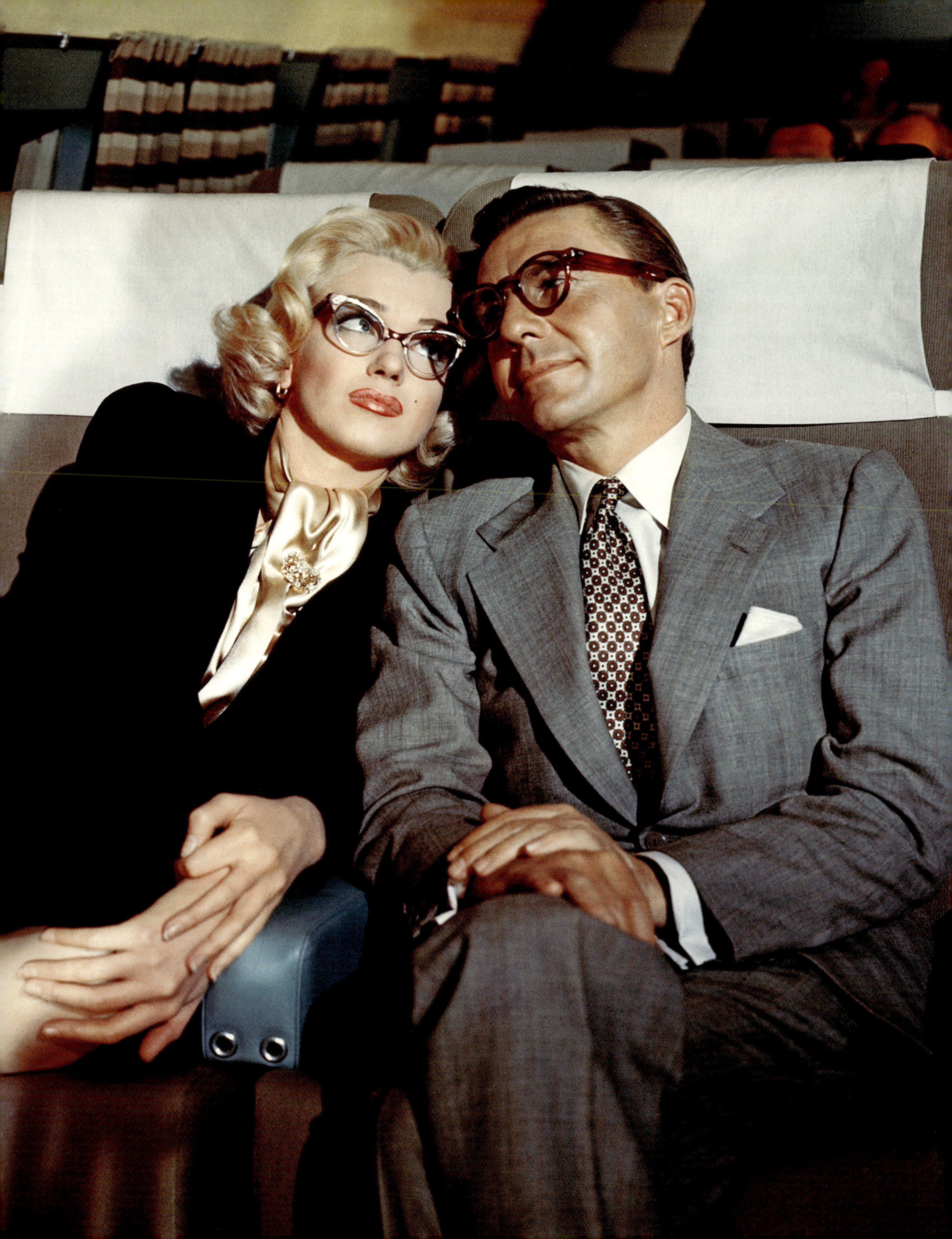

"Marilyn Monroe was a *real* sex symbol and so was the great Garbo. They didn't need to say things, they just were. They *photographed*. Name me a really true sex symbol in today's movies. She doesn't exist."

BETTE DAVIS

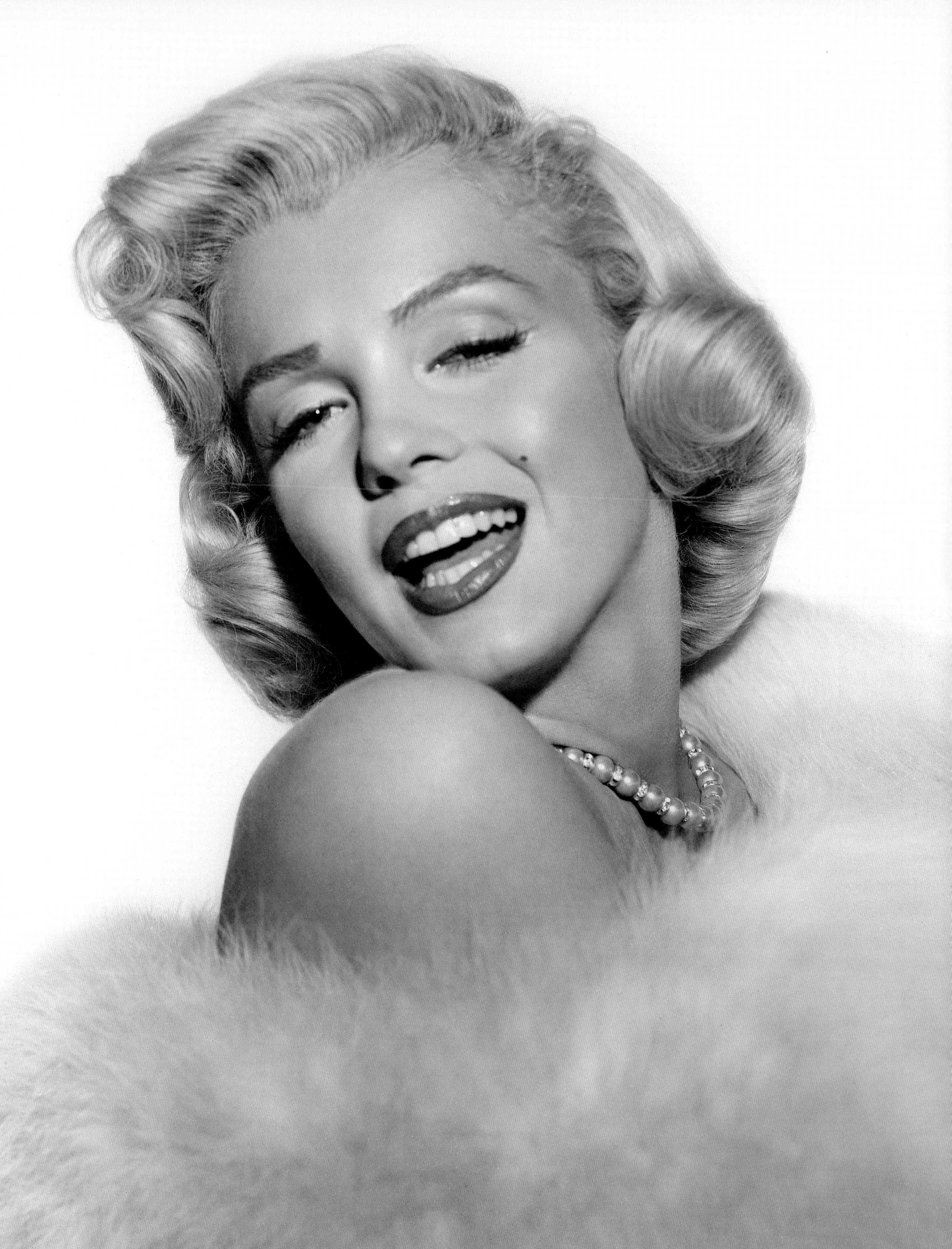

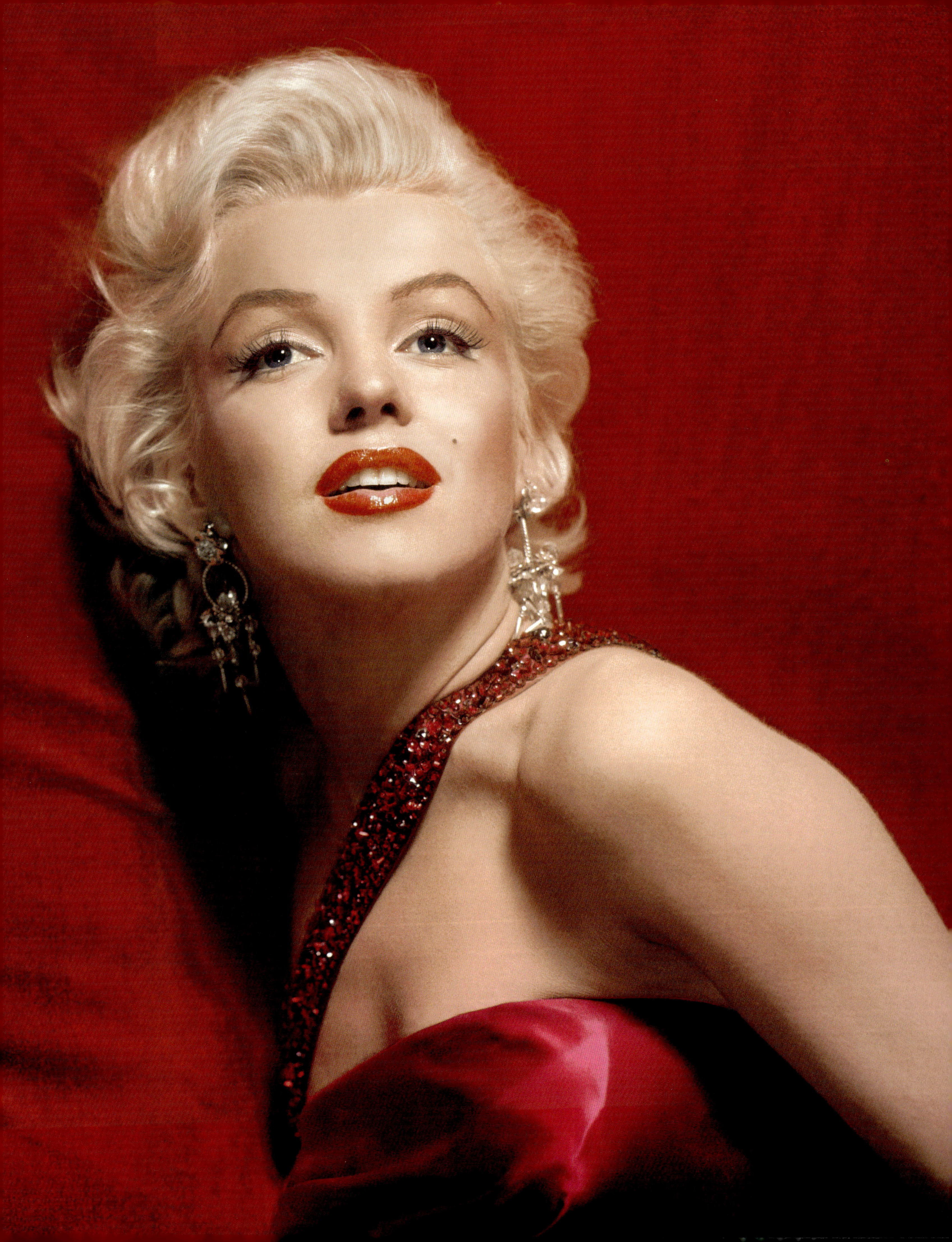

"I can sit here and do the whole thing in my sleep. Put the base all over, lightly. The formula we used that perfectly matched her natural flesh tone was to mix a quart of Max Factor's 'sun tan base,' a half cup of 'ivory' coloring, and an eyedropper of 'clown white.' Then, highlight under her eyes. Pull the highlight out over and across the cheekbones to widen. Highlight her chin. Eyeshadow was toned, and that also ran out to her hairline. Then the pencil on top. I'd outline her eyes very clearly with pencil, but I'd make a peak right up—say almost three-sixteenths of an inch—above the pupil of her eye, and then swing it out there. And from there on out was where we put eyelashes. Also, the bottom line was shaded in with a pencil to make her eyes stand out fully and good. Her eyebrows came out to a point as far as I could get them to widen her forehead. So I'd bring them to a peak just outside the center of her eyes and then sweep down to a good-looking eyebrow. You couldn't go out much farther than that or it would look phony. Shading broke the bones underneath her cheekbone. I just brought a little line down there, a little darker shadow, so that it helped her stand out. Lipstick, we used various colors. As the industry changed, we got down to normal colors. At first, we had a hell of a time with Cinemascope—no reds photographed anything but auburn. We had to go to light pink."

ALLAN "WHITEY" SNYDER (Marilyn's makeup artist)

Our father, John Florea, became very close to Marilyn during the early part of her career and his intimate photos captured both her sensuality and her thirst for knowledge and self-improvement. As her fame grew, she requested his expertise on the set of some her most famous films at Twentieth Century-Fox. Later, after he became a director, producer, and writer for more than 600 television shows, he always looked back at his brief years with Marilyn as one of the highlights of his career."

GWEN AND MELANIE FLOREA

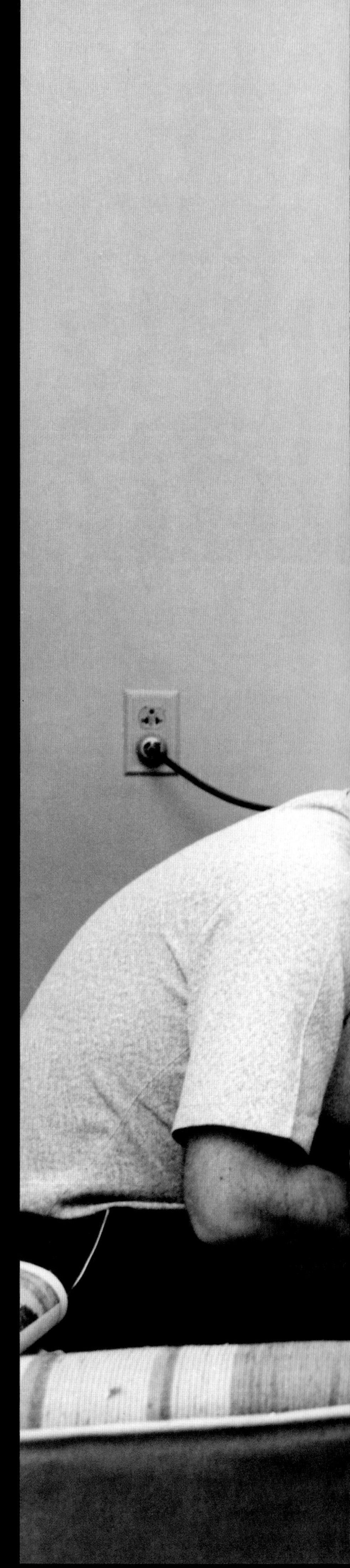

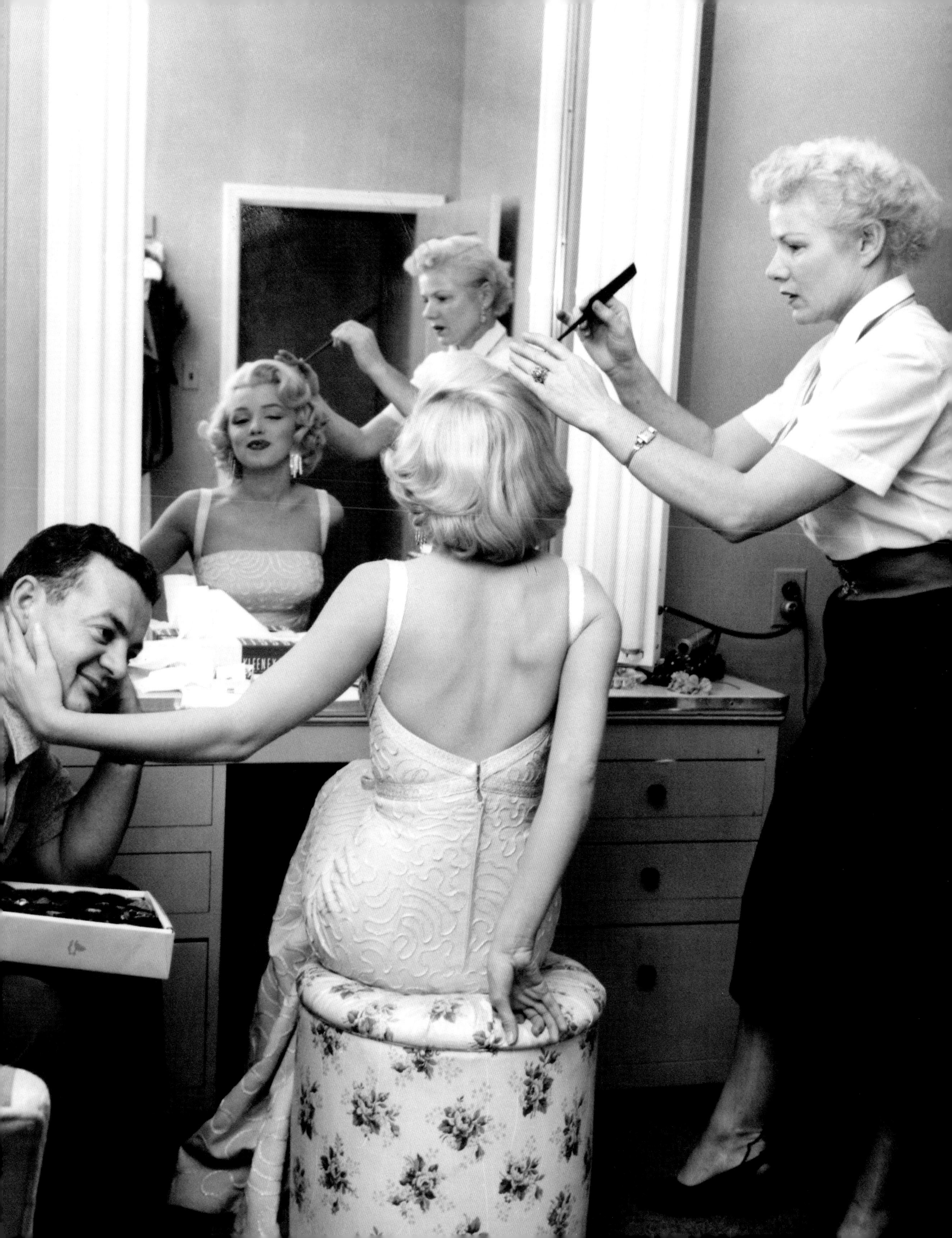

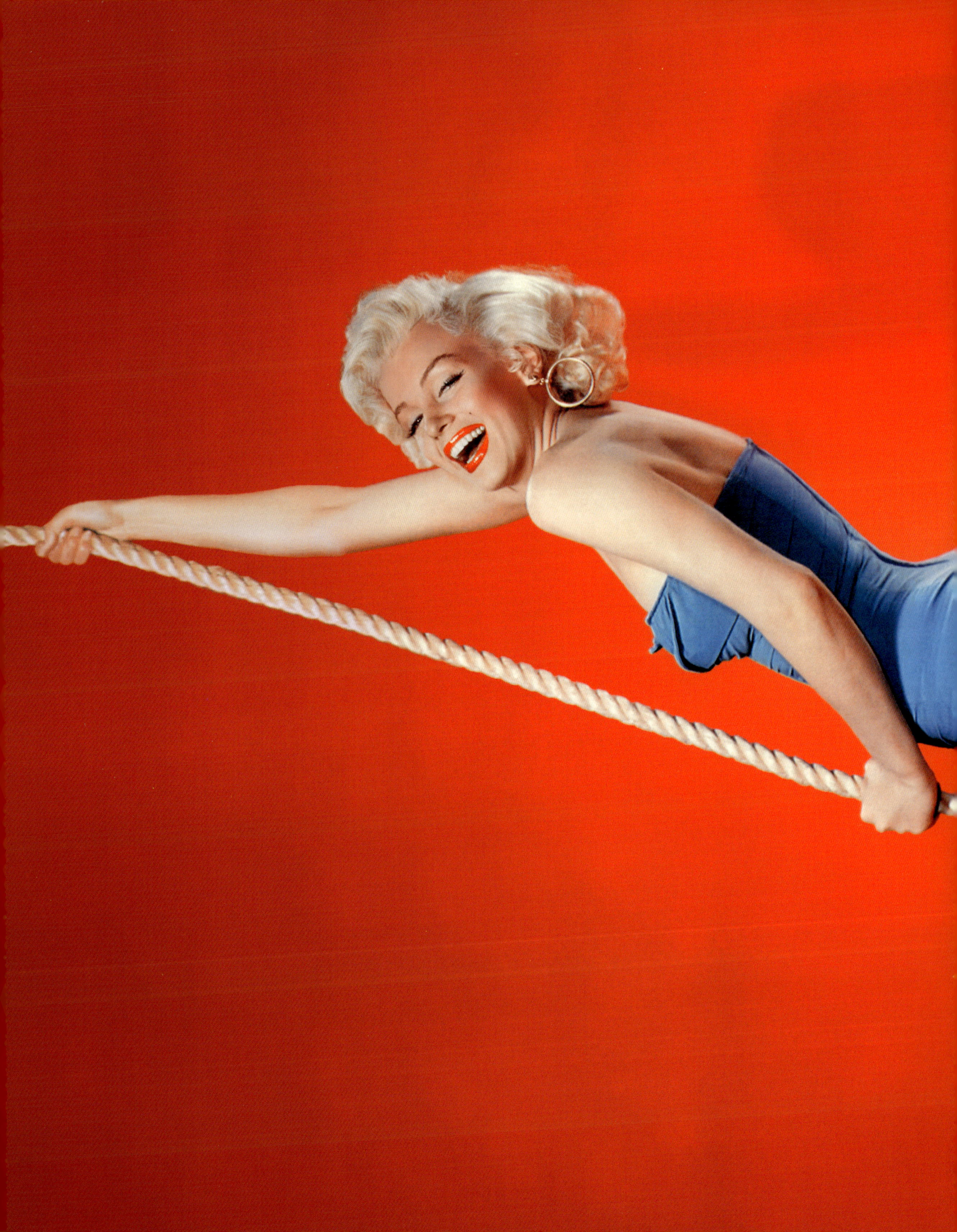

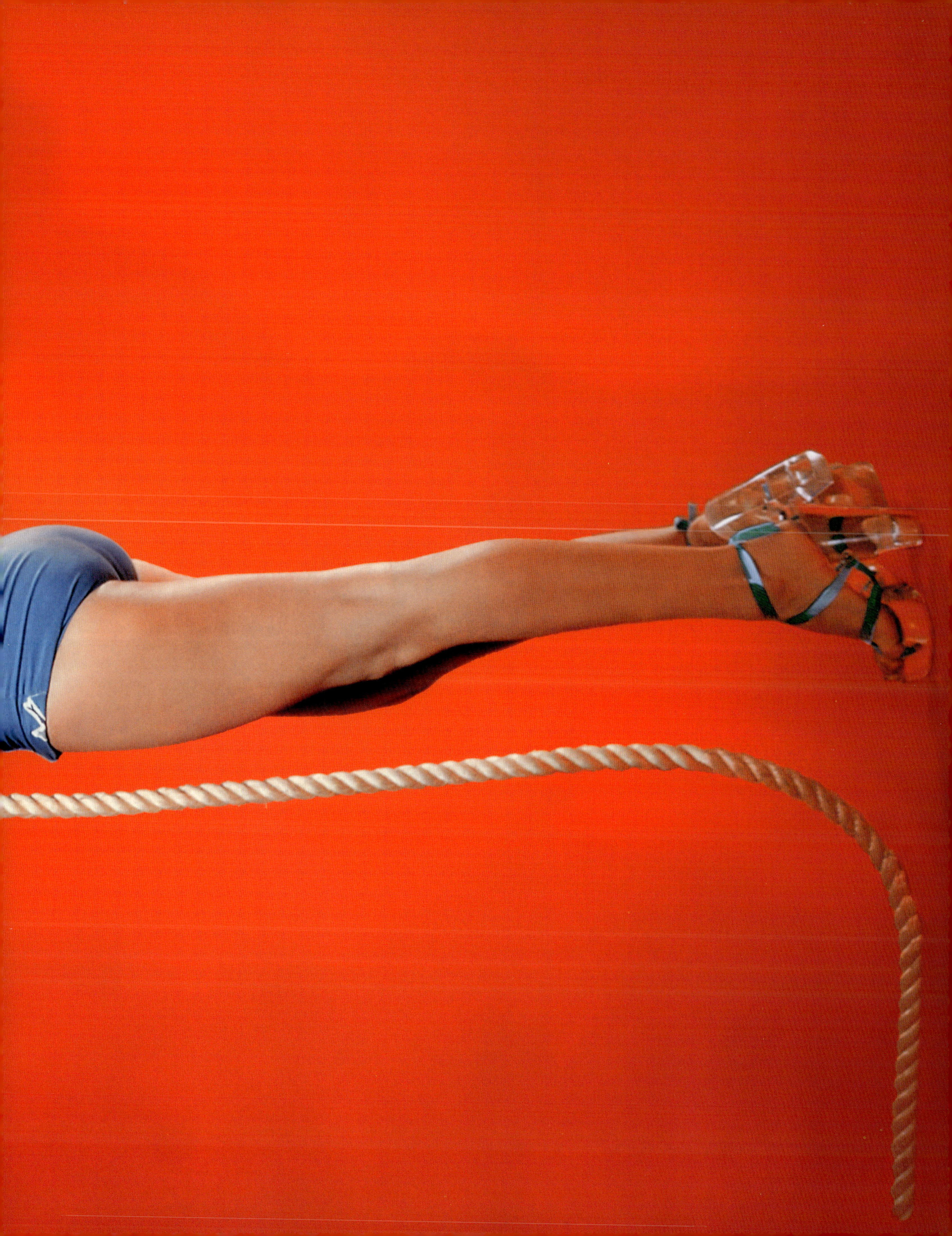

"I feel as though it's all happening to someone right next to me. I'm close, I can feel it, I can hear it, but it isn't really me."

MARILYN MONROE

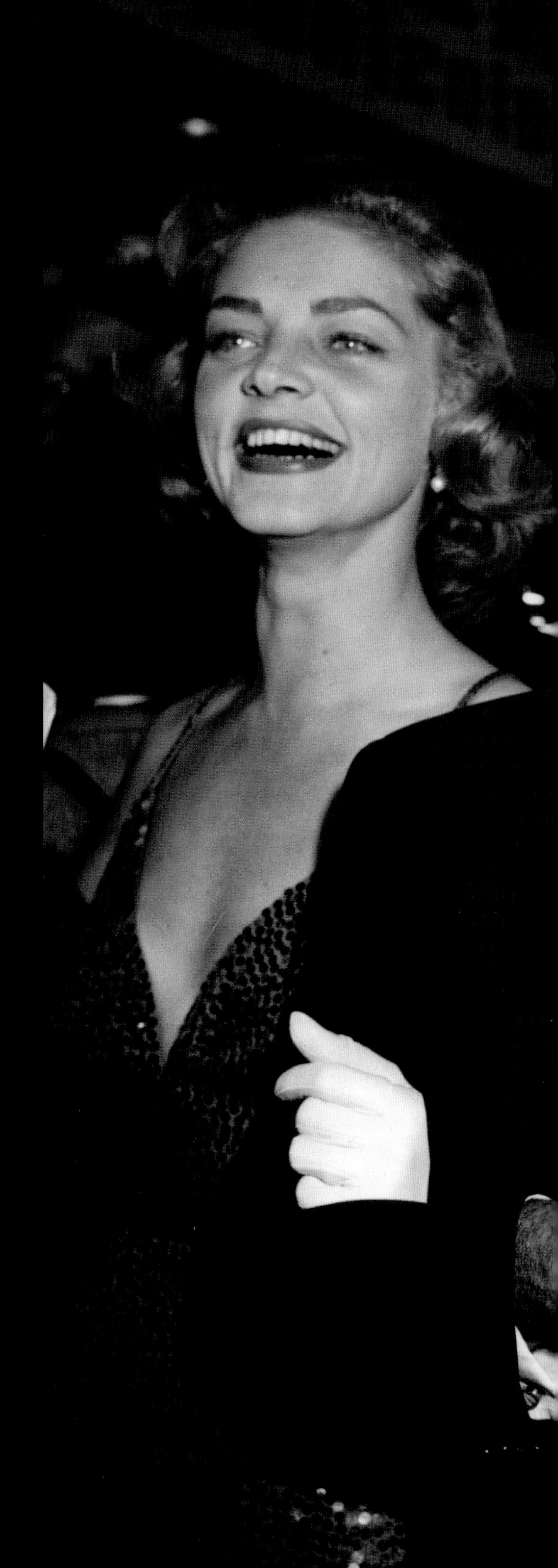

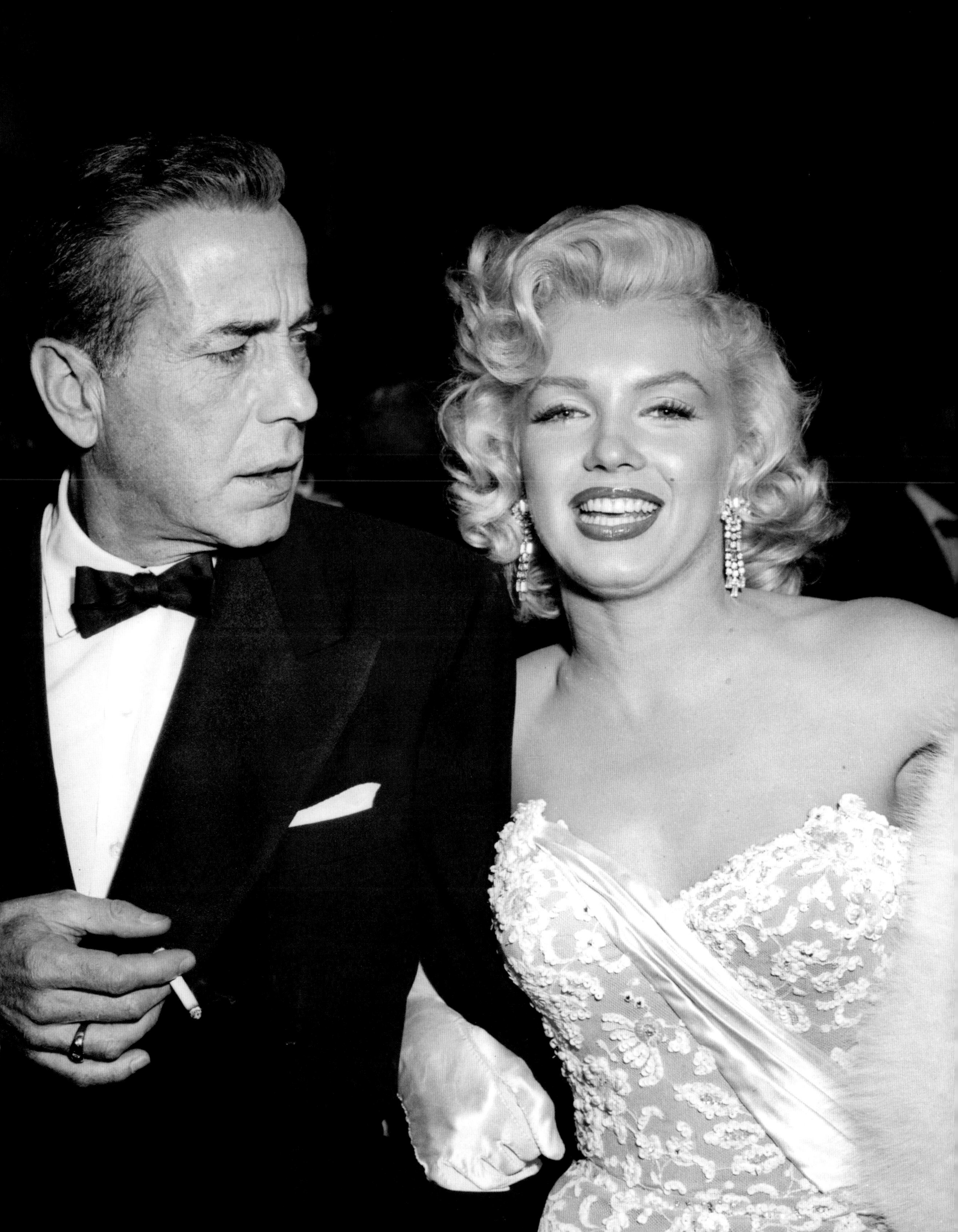

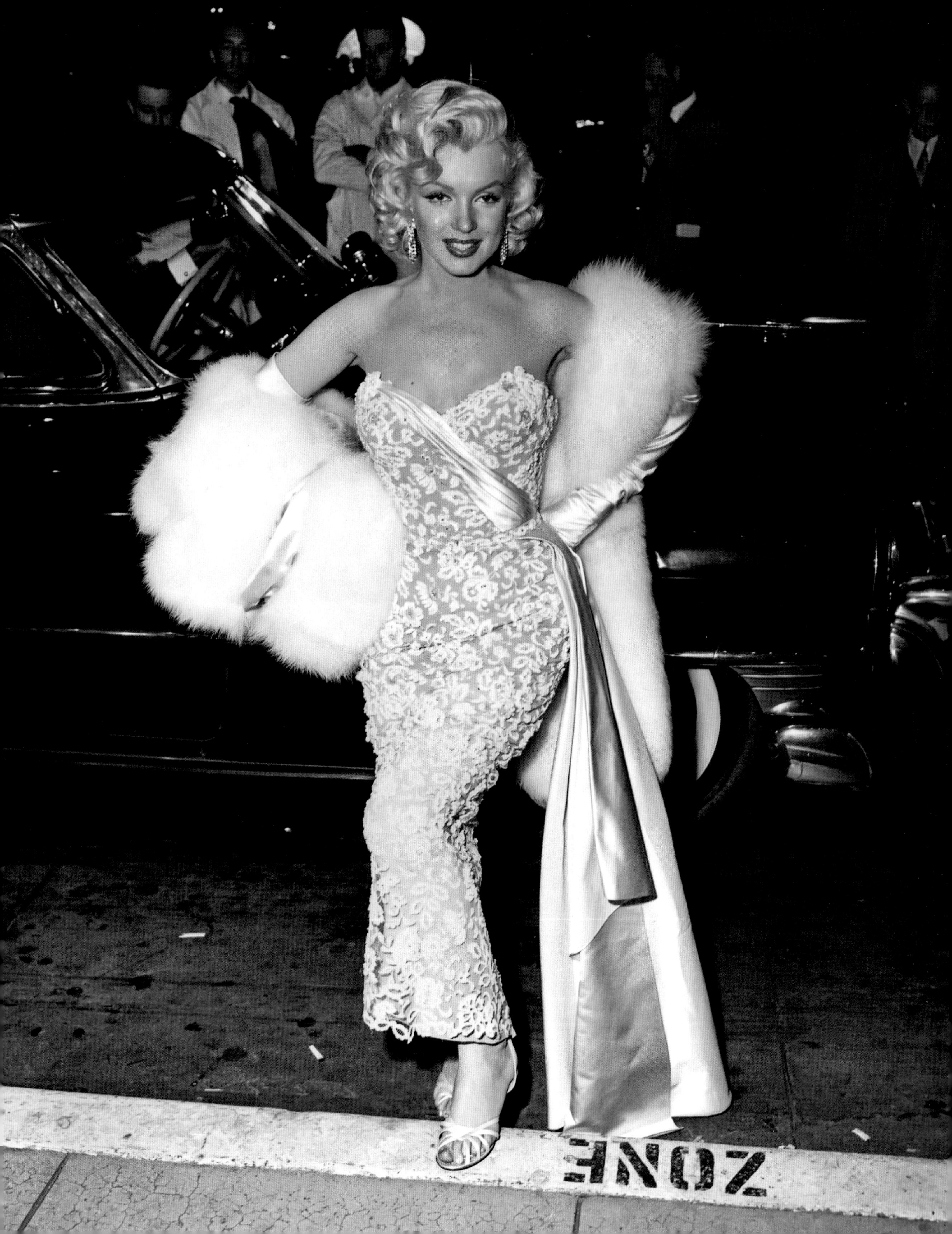
ZONE

"She sure registered on that screen. The minute the camera turned on her she became this incredible creature, and she was absolutely dazzling. She *was*—there's no question about that. . . . During our scenes she'd look at my forehead instead of my eyes. At the end of a take, she'd look to her coach for approval. If the headshake was no, she'd insist on another take. A scene often went to fifteen or more takes. Despite this I couldn't dislike Marilyn. She had no meanness in her—no bitchery. She just had to concentrate on herself and the people who were there only for her. . . . Fifty years on, we're still watching her movies and talking about her. That's not a dumb woman—trust me."

LAUREN BACALL

"We almost didn't meet. I'd heard of Joe DiMaggio but I didn't know much about him. I've never followed baseball. . . . I was very tired the night of the date and asked if I could get out of it. But I'd promised. I had visualized him as having slicked-back hair, wearing flashy sports clothes, with a New York line of patter. . . . He had no line at all. No jokes. He was shy and reserved but, at the same time, rather warm and friendly. I noticed that he wasn't eating the food in front of him, that he was looking at me. The next thing I noticed was that I wasn't tired any more. Joe asked me to have dinner with him the next night. I had dinner with him that night, the next night, and every night until he had to leave for New York."

MARILYN MONROE

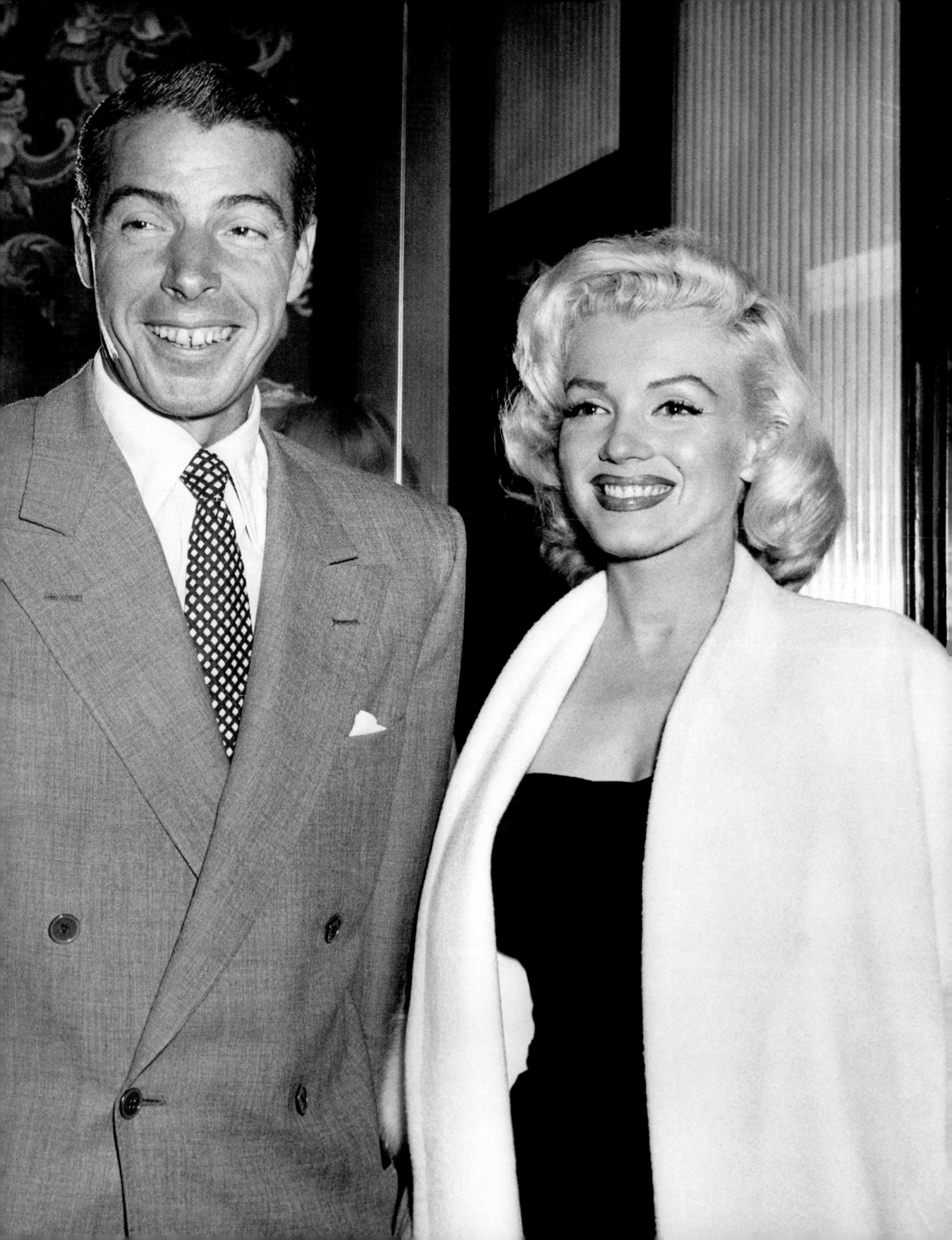

"She wasn't what she sold. You don't realize when you make these deals early in life—and she certainly did with publicity—that you have to live with them forever. And I don't think she was able to do it."

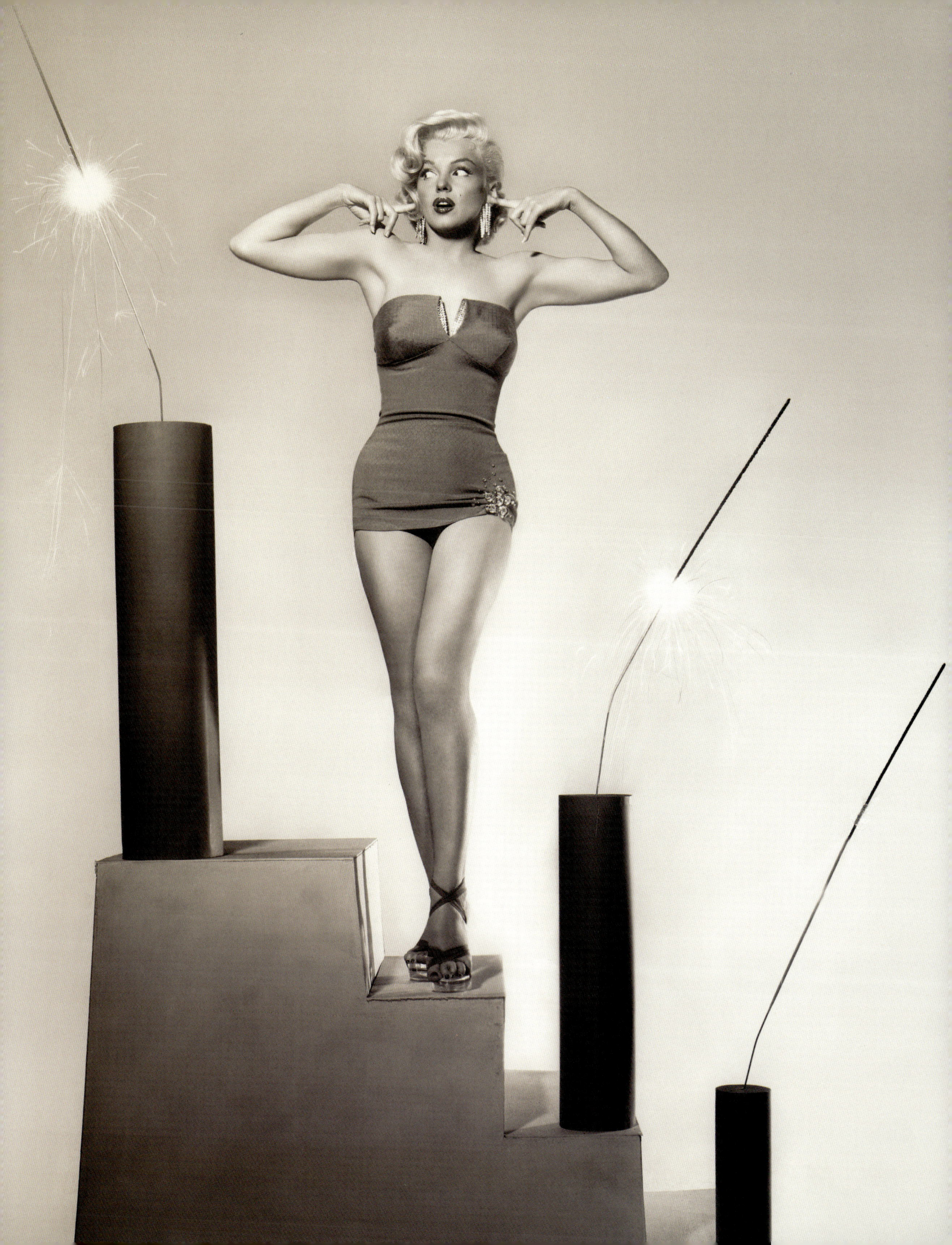

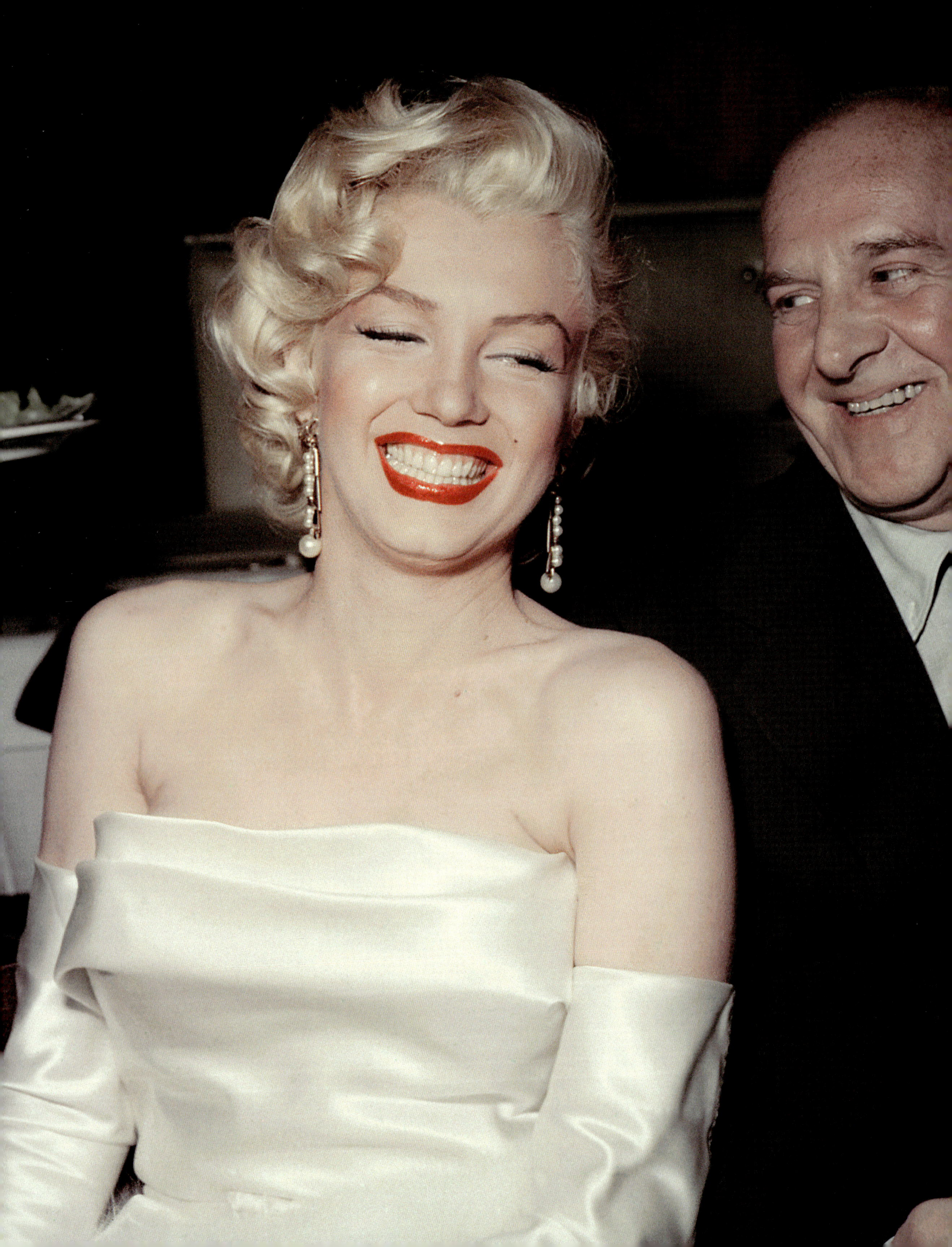

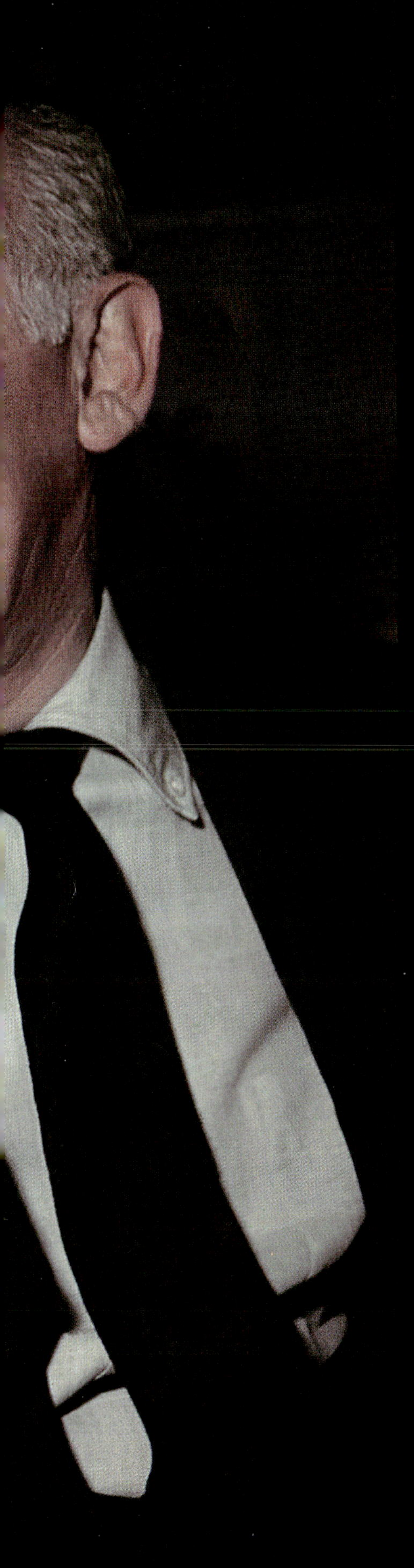

"She looked like, if you bit her, milk and honey would flow from her."

FRANZ KLINE (Artist)

"I owe Marilyn Monroe a real debt. It was because of her that I played Mocambo. She personally called the owner of the Mocambo, and told him she wanted me booked immediately, and if he would do it, she would take a front table every night. She told him—and it was true, due to Marilyn's superstar status—that the press would go wild. The owner said yes, and Marilyn was there, front table, every night. The press went overboard. . . . After that, I never had to play a small jazz club again. She was an unusual woman—a little ahead of her times. And she didn't know it."

ELLA FITZGERALD

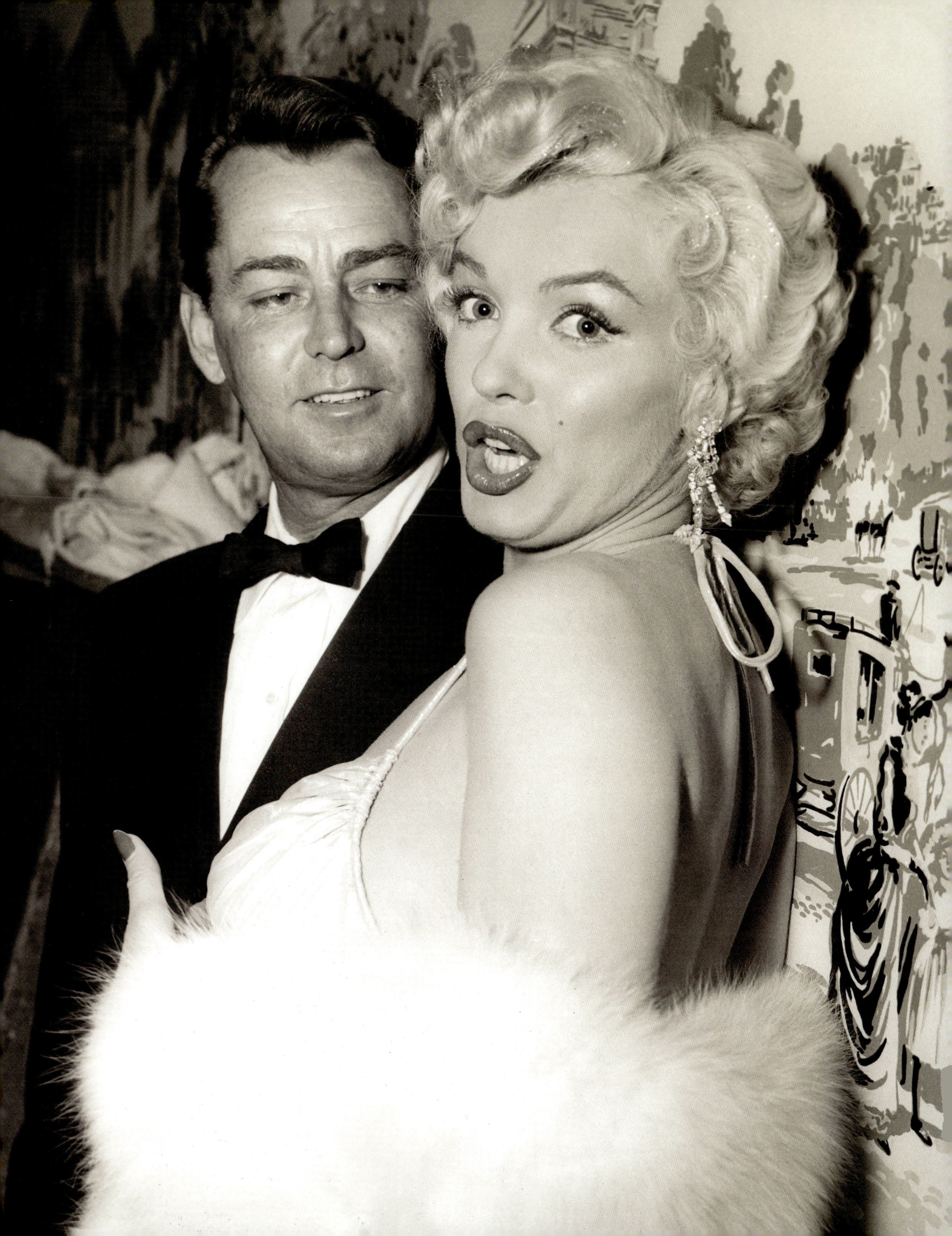

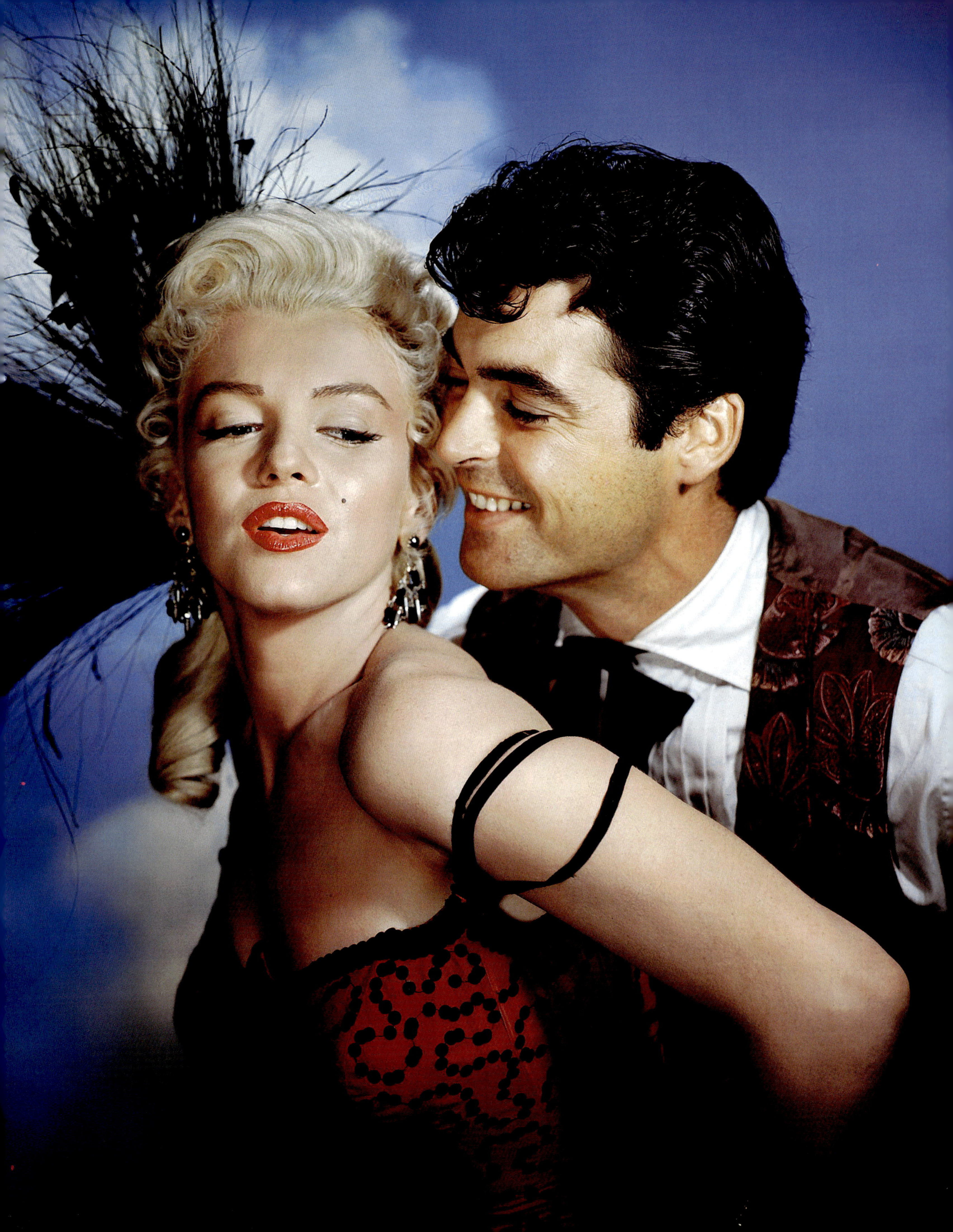

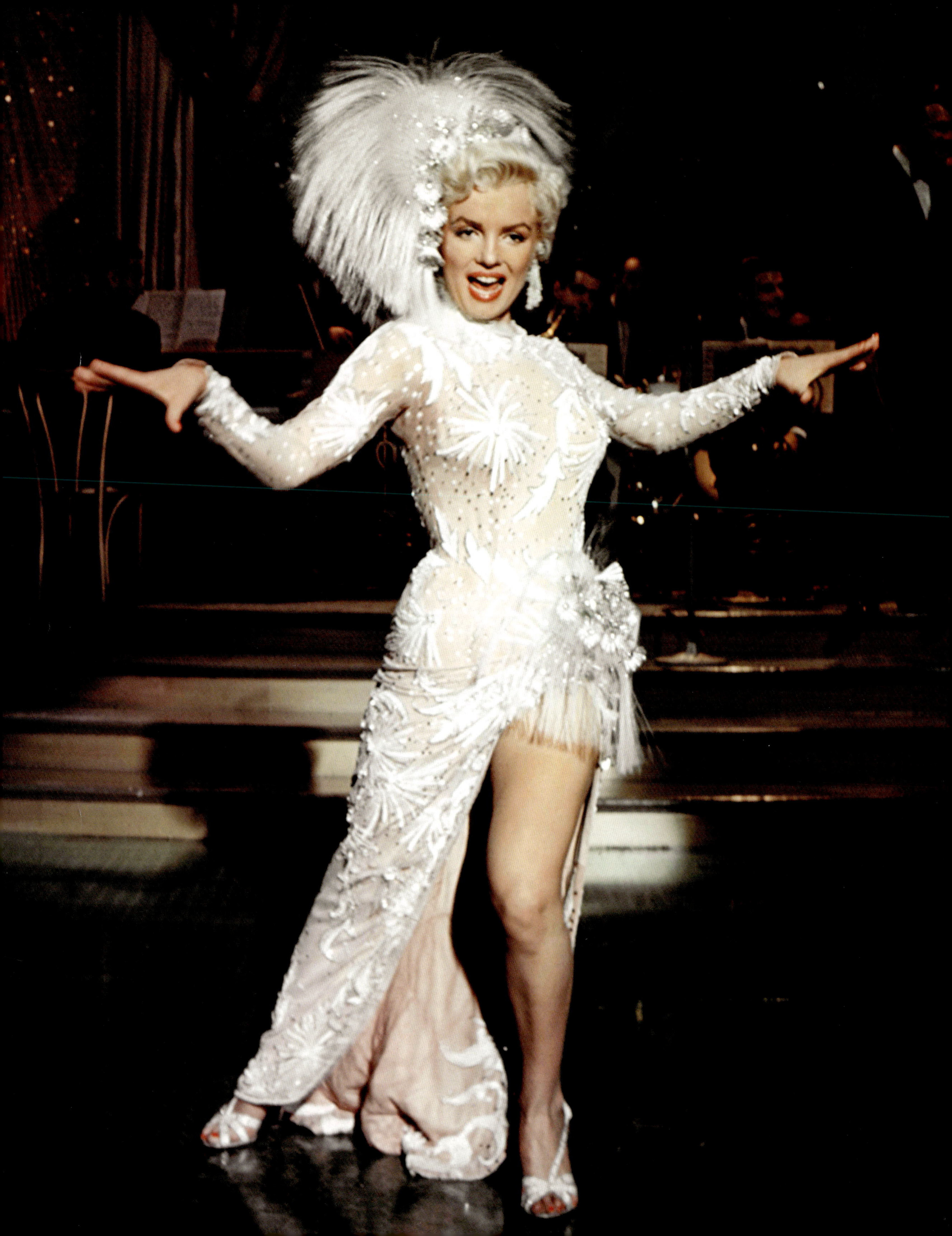

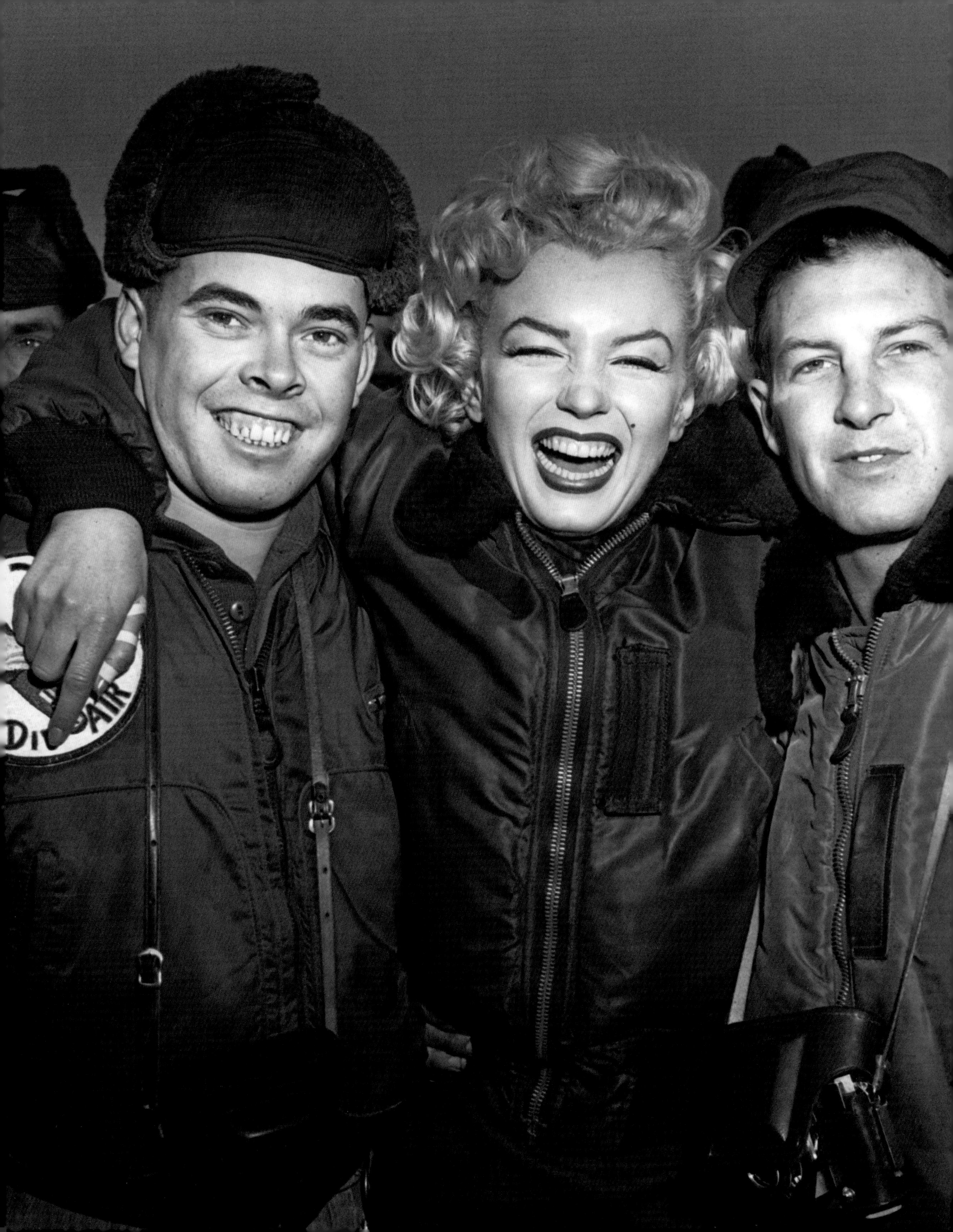

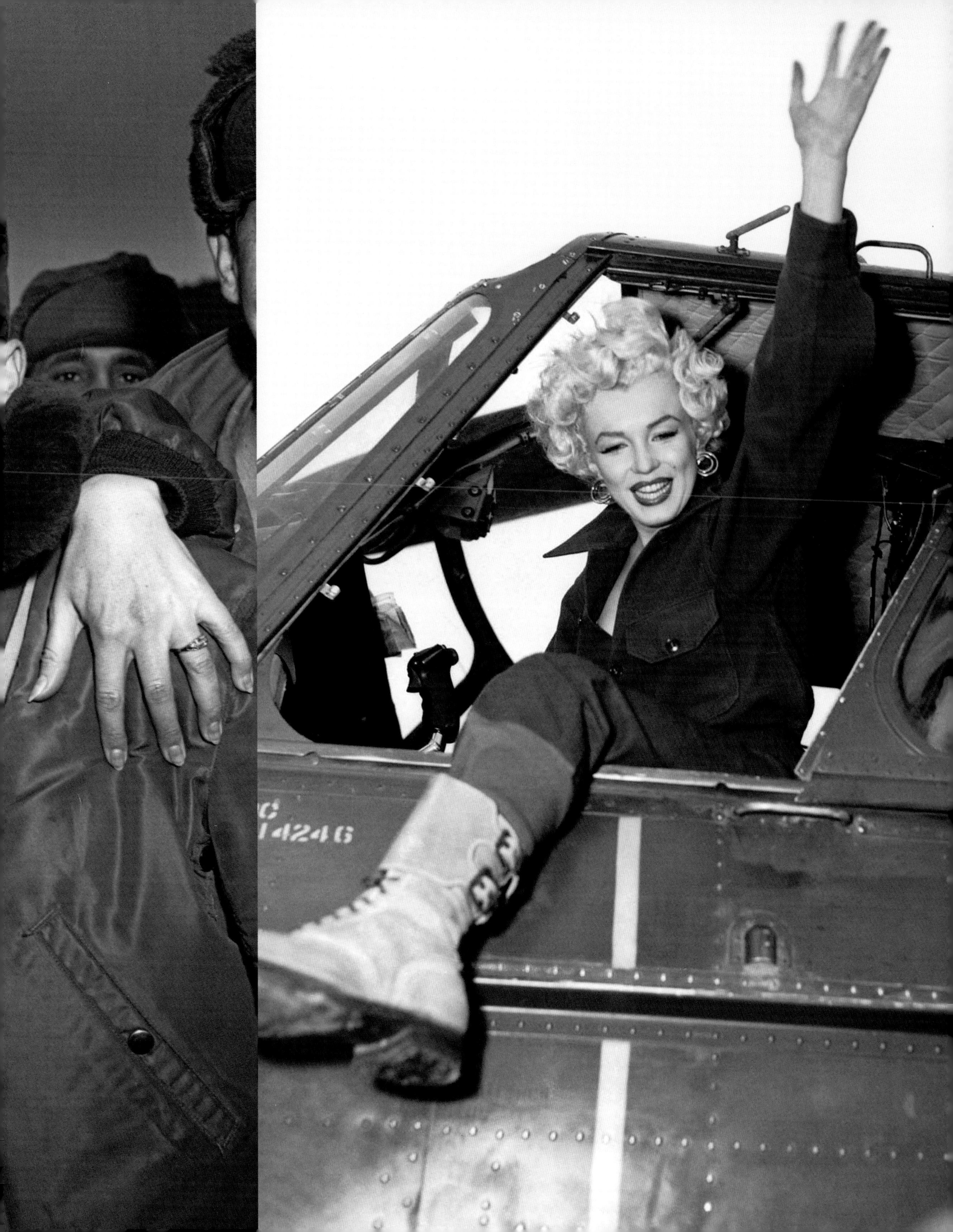
C
14246

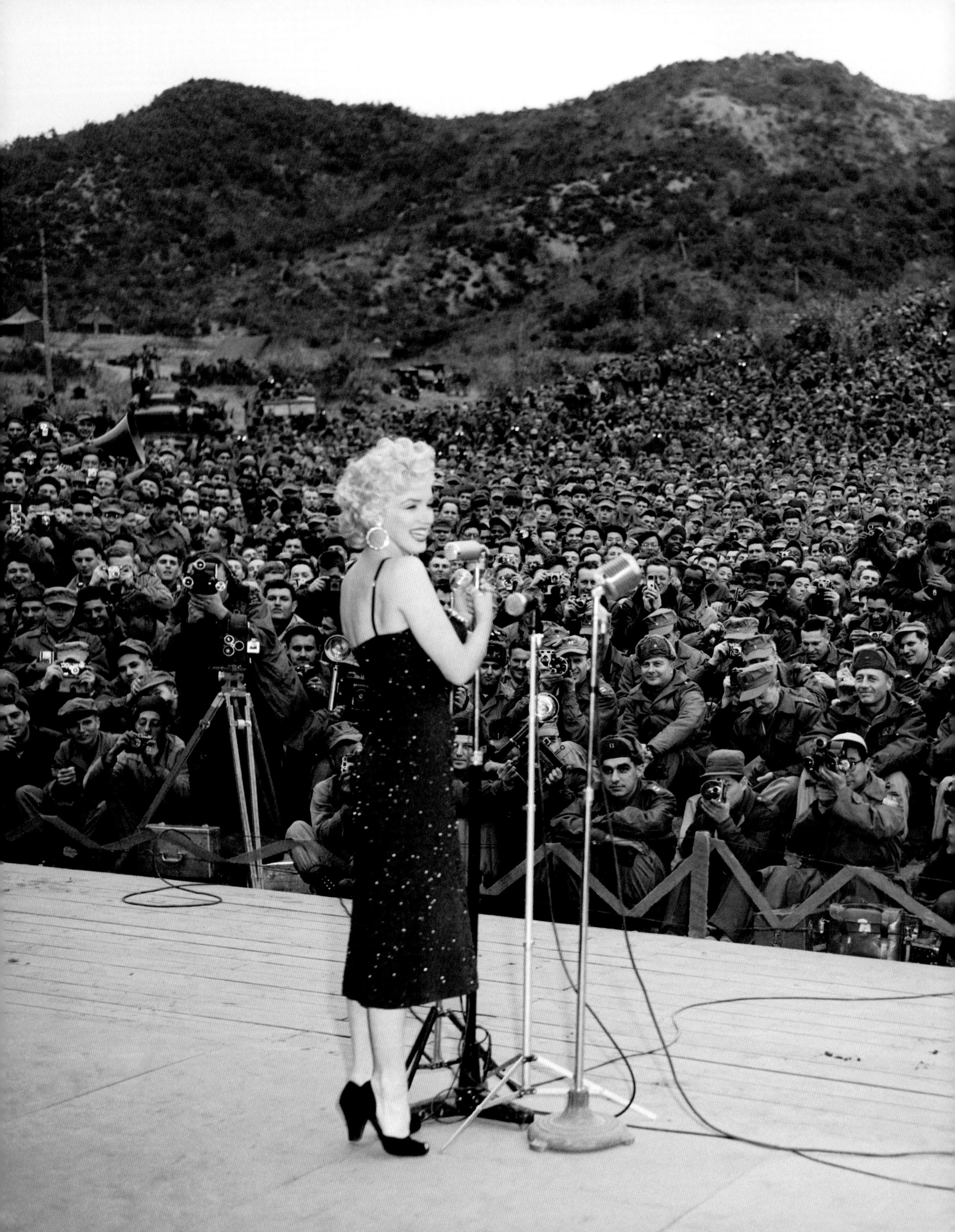

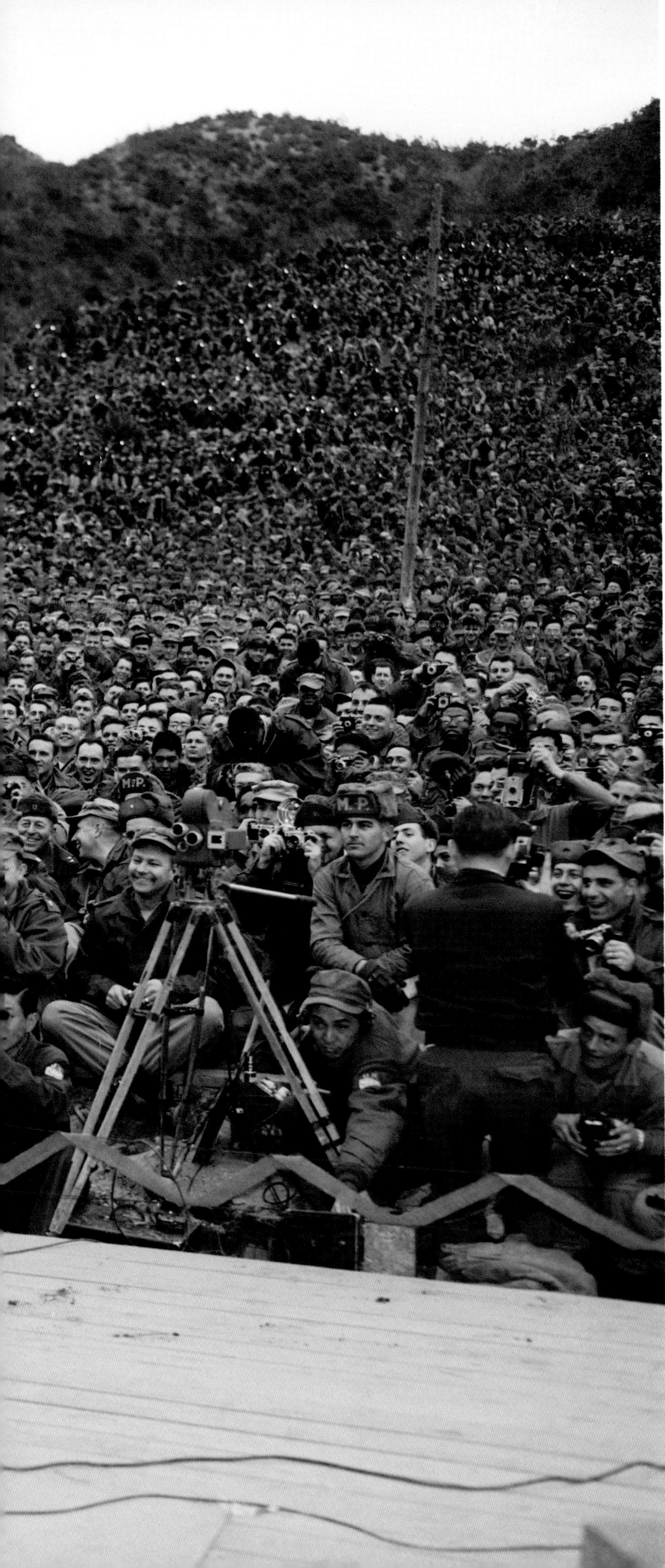

Marilyn:
"Joe, you never heard such cheering."

Joe:
"Yes, I have."

"There was something exceptional about Marilyn Monroe. Sometimes she could be ethereal and sometimes like a waitress in a coffee shop."

TRUMAN CAPOTE

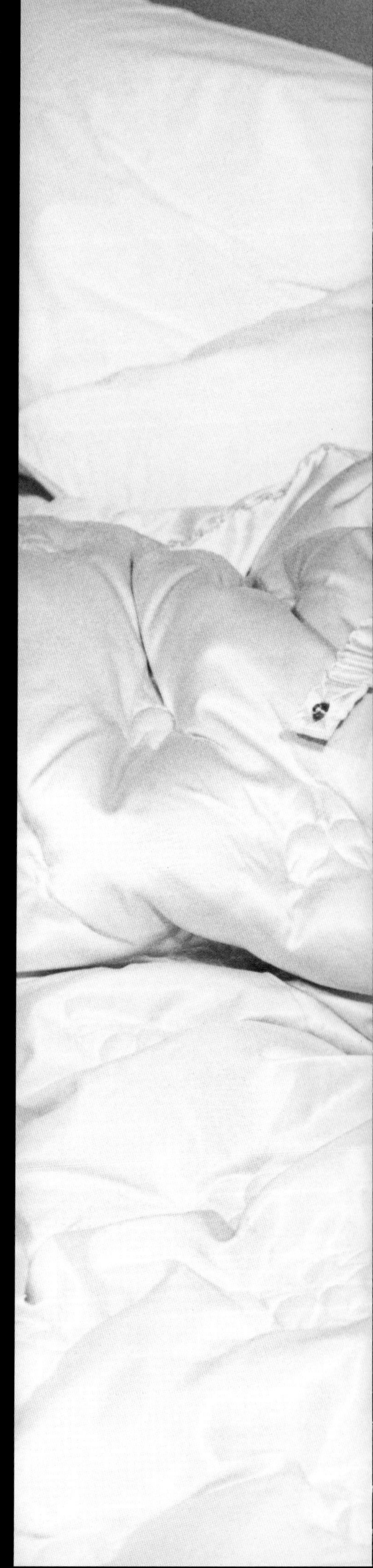

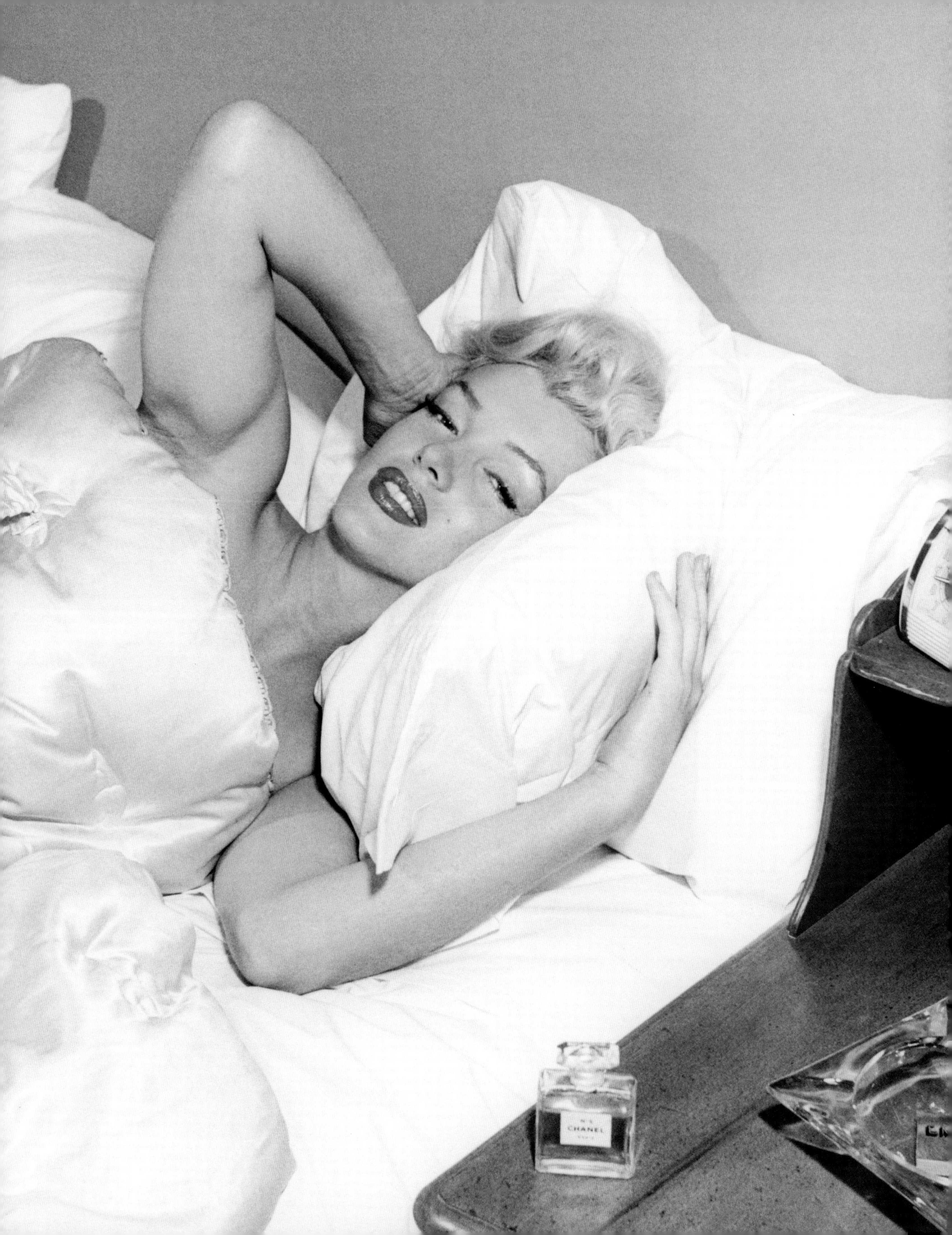
CHANEL

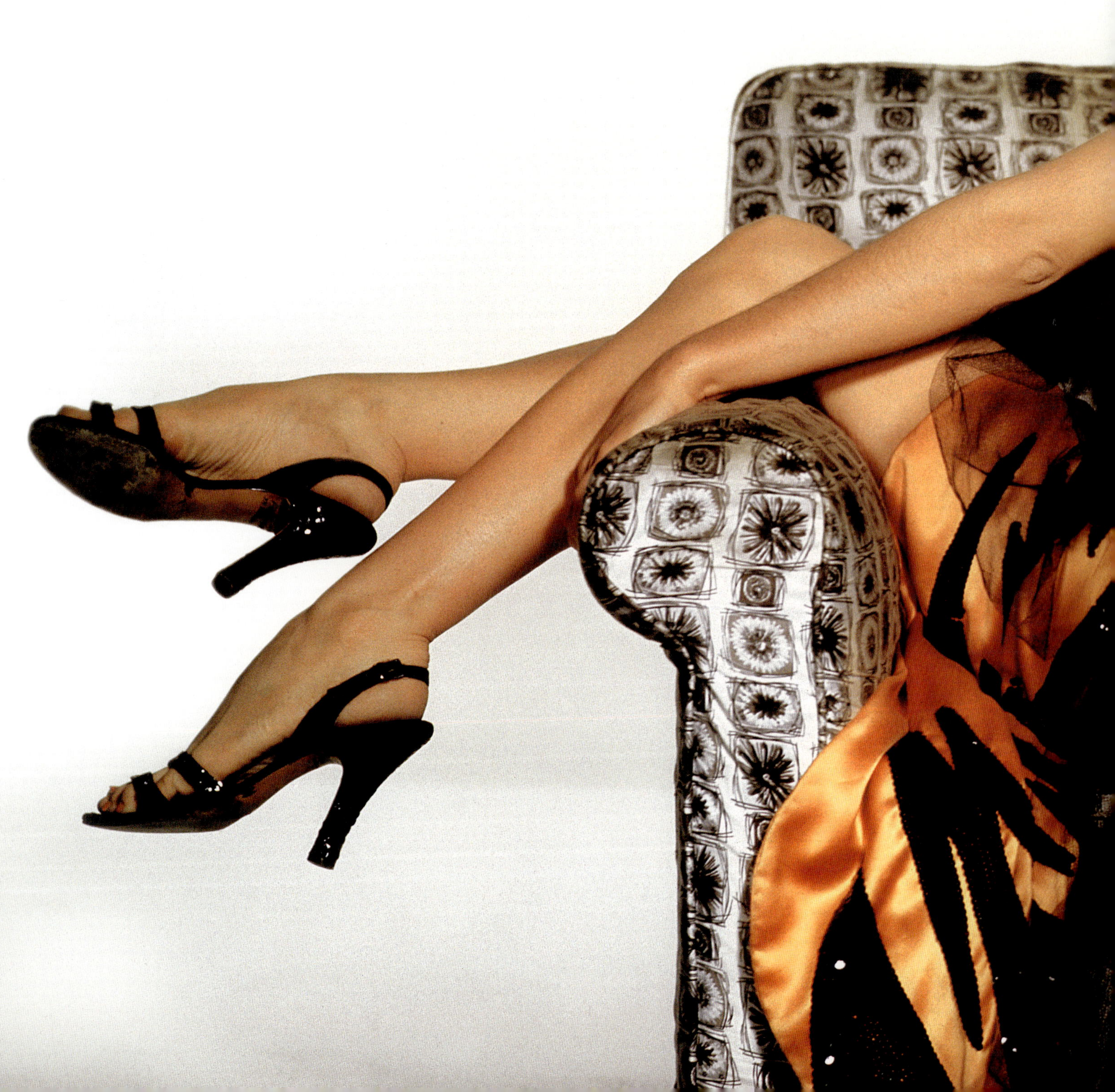

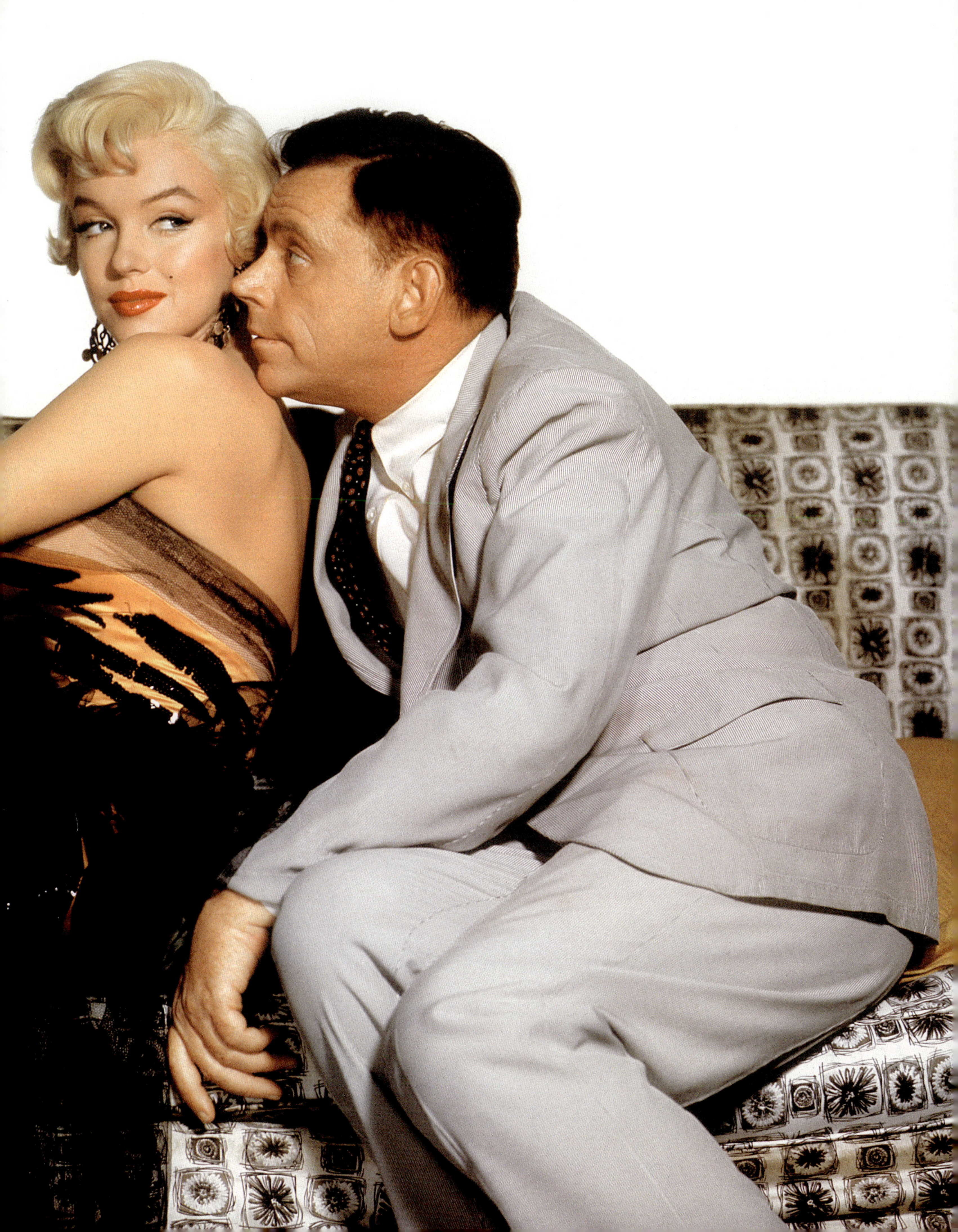

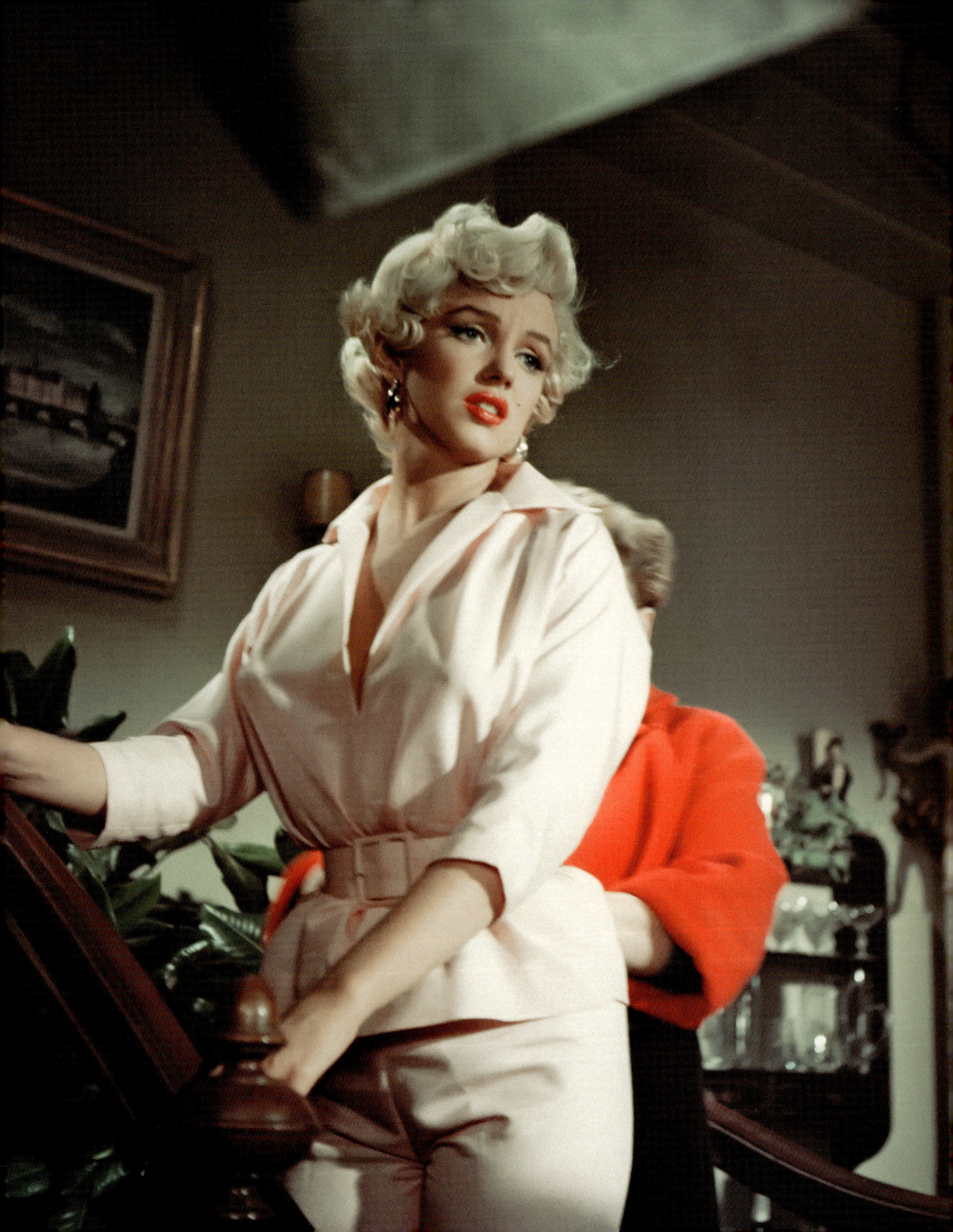

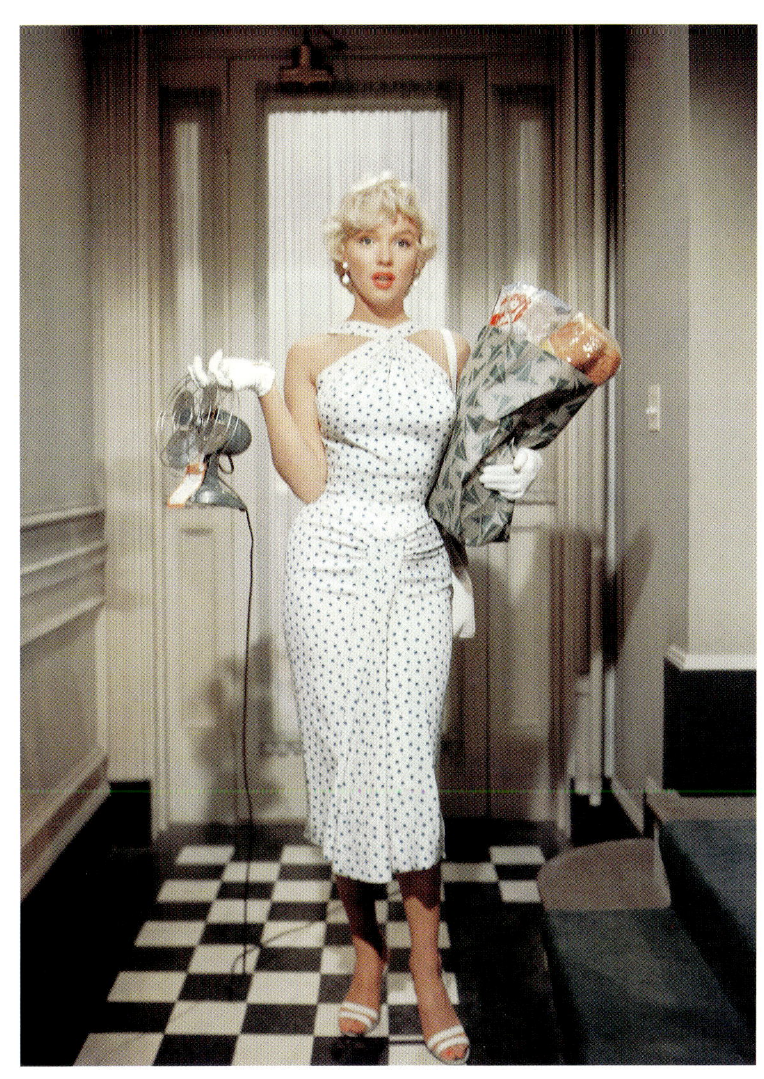

"From the moment she steps into the picture, in a garment that drapes her shapely form as though she had been skillfully poured into it, the famous screen star with the silver-blonde tresses and the ingenuously wide-eyed stare eminates one suggestion."

THE NEW YORK TIMES

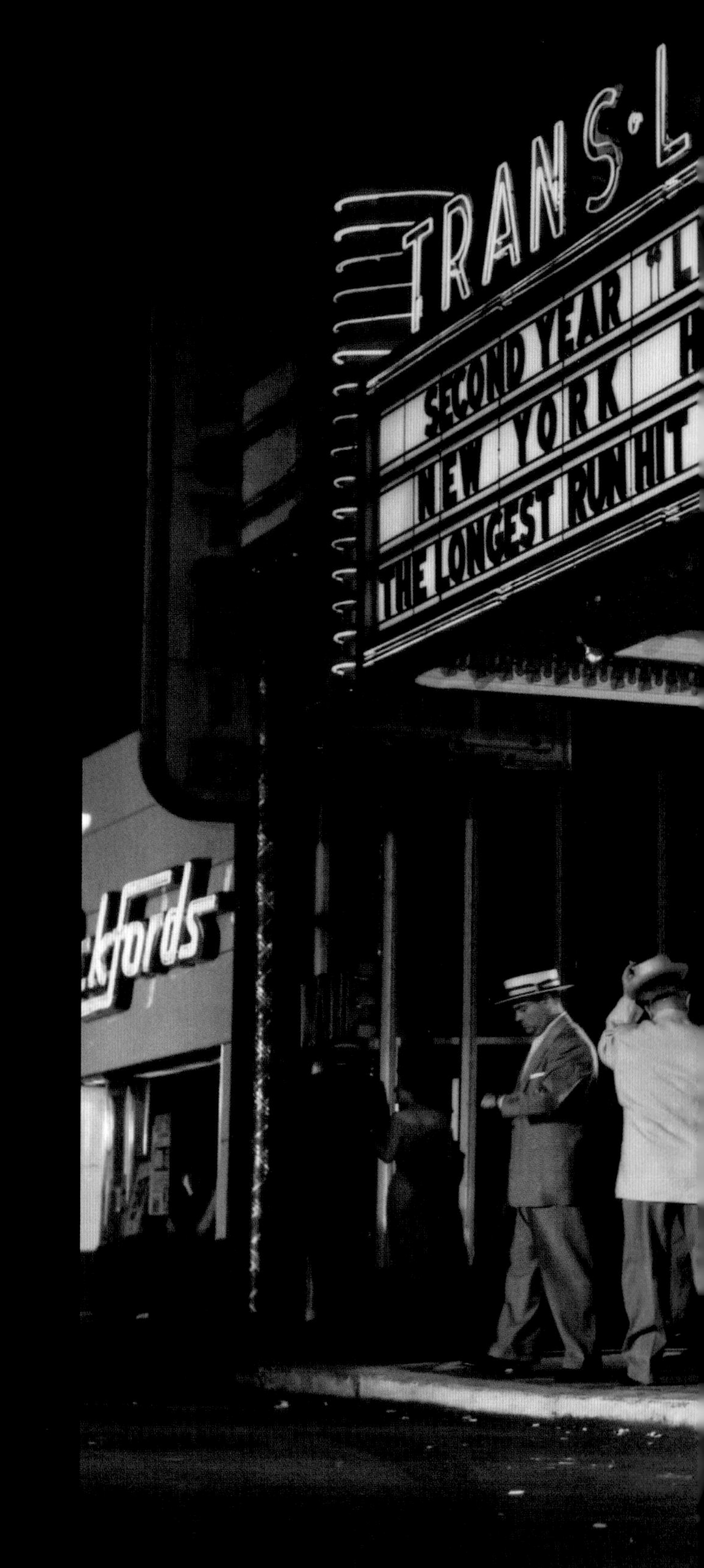
SECOND YEAR
NEW YORK
THE LONGEST RUN HIT

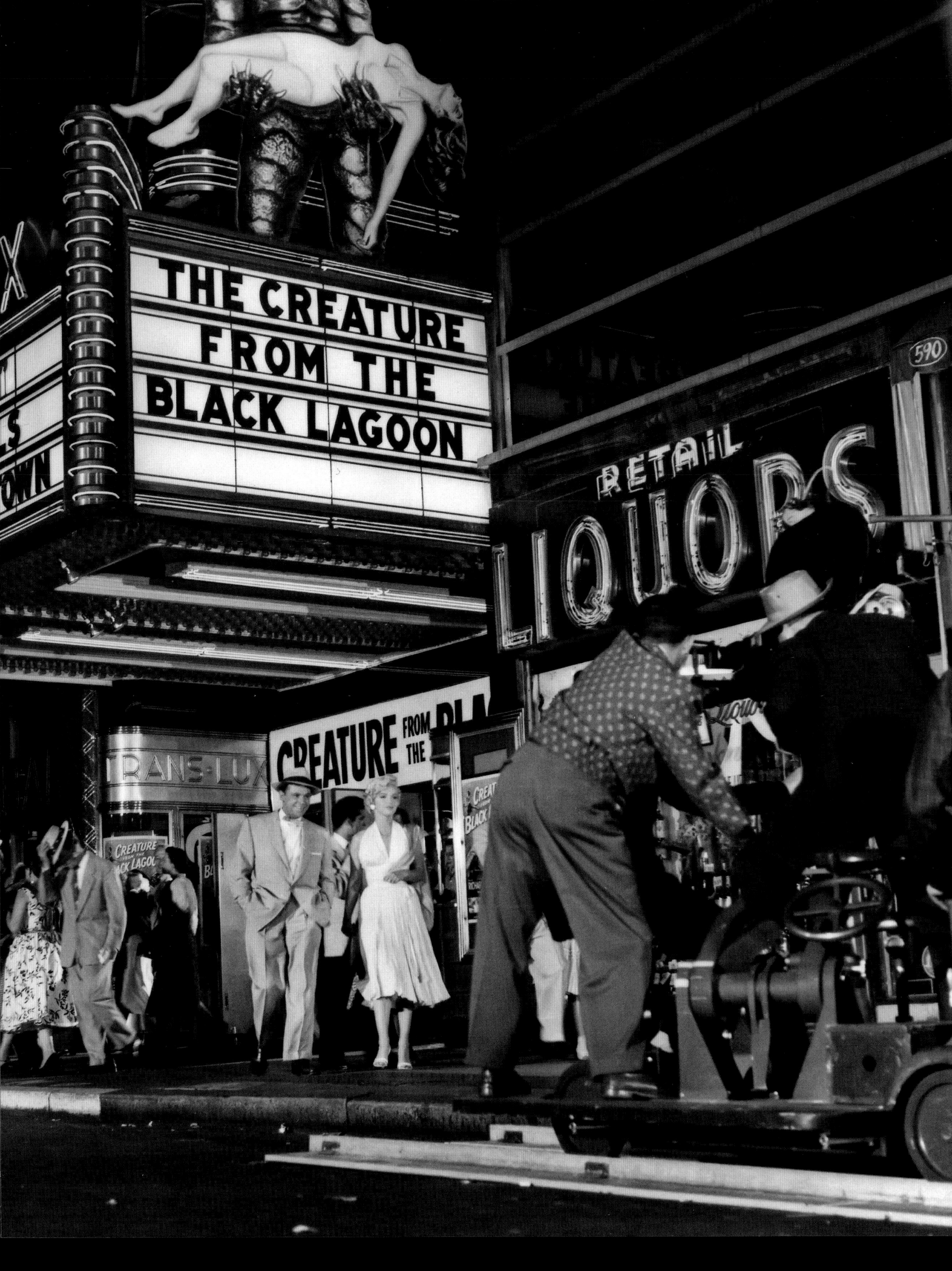
THE CREATURE
FROM THE
BLACK LAGOON
RETAIL
LIQUORS
590
CREATURE FROM THE
TRANS-LUX
CREATURE FROM THE BLACK LAGOON

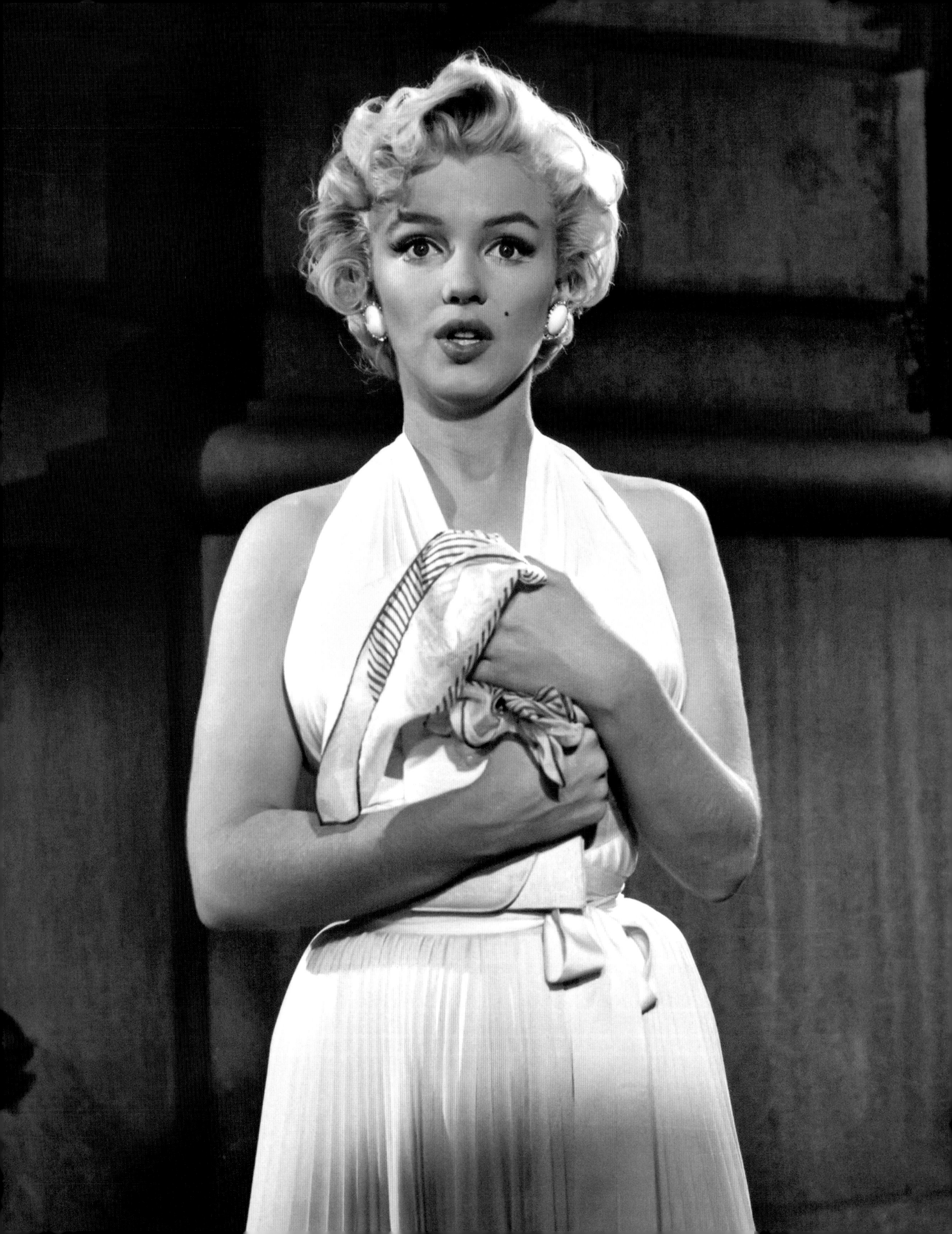

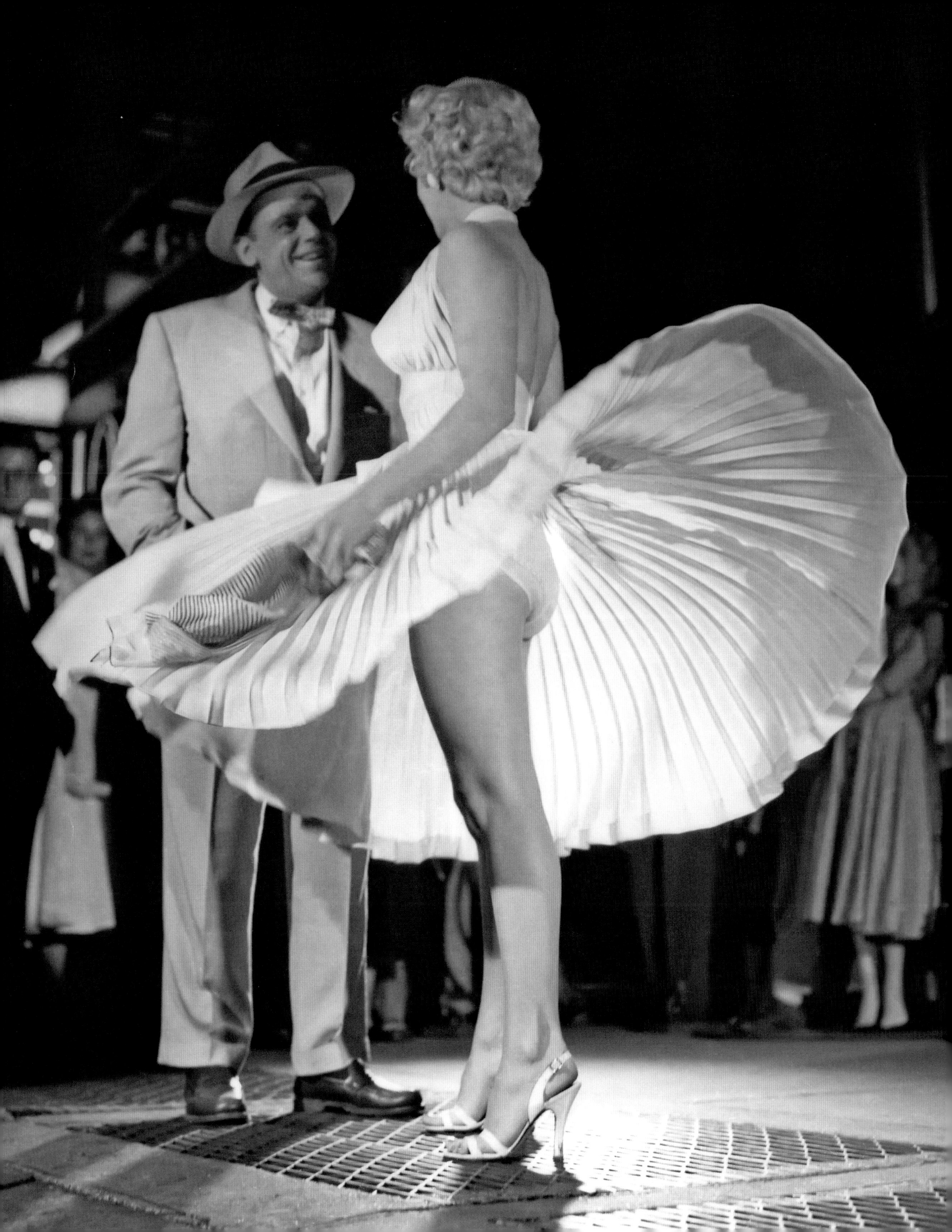

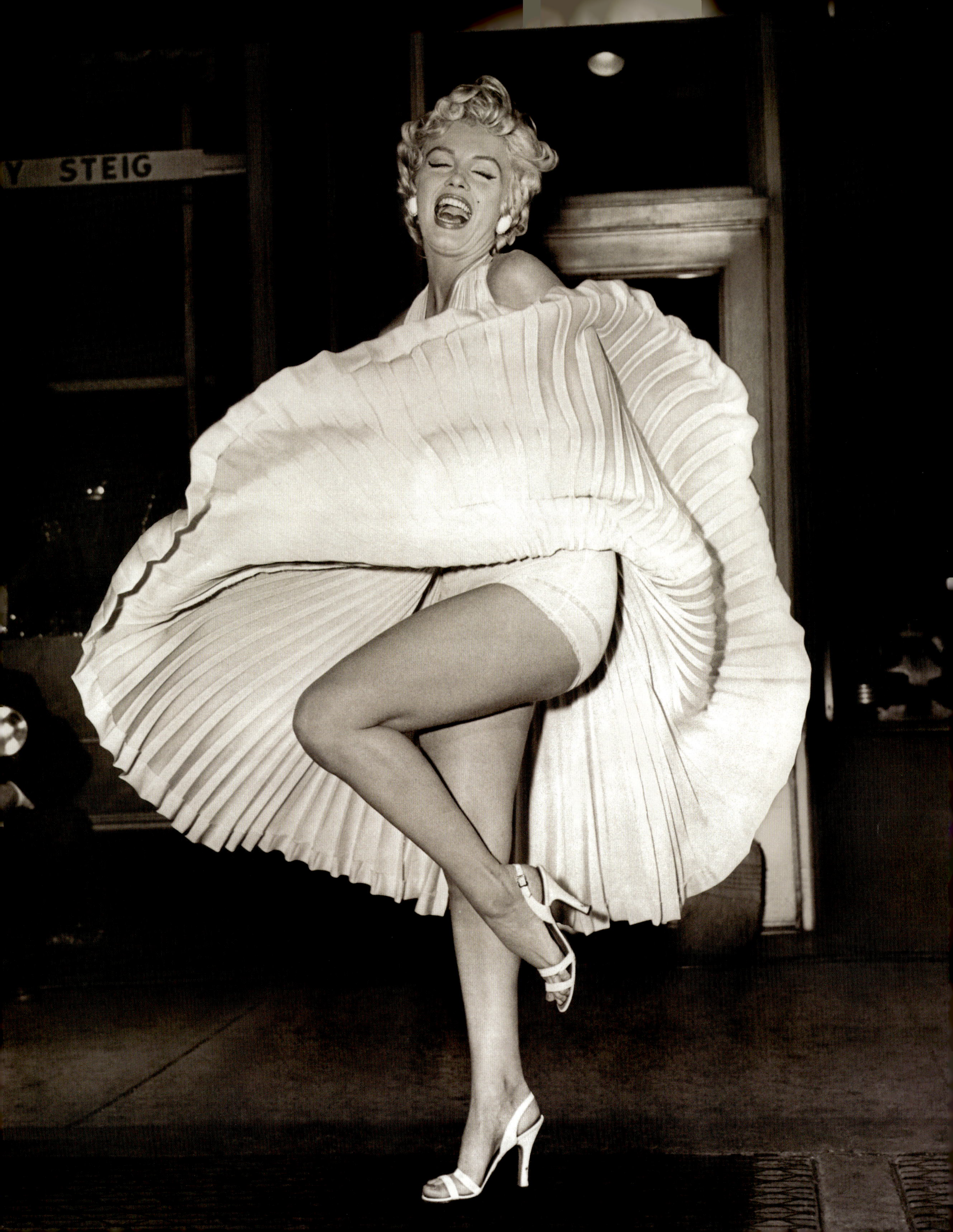
STEIG

"There was a police line separating the crowd from the photographers and film apparatus. There were quiet conversations between Marilyn and her drama coach [Natasha Lytess], and Marilyn and Billy Wilder. There were of course 'Hey, Marilyns' from the crowd, and she handled them with friendly waves. The warm-up over the subway grille served as a vehicle for the still photographers to get their work done. She played to the still photographers and she knew how to do it par excellence. Her dress was the perfect design for that scene, and it did wondrous things as she moved."

GEORGE ZIMBEL (Photographer)

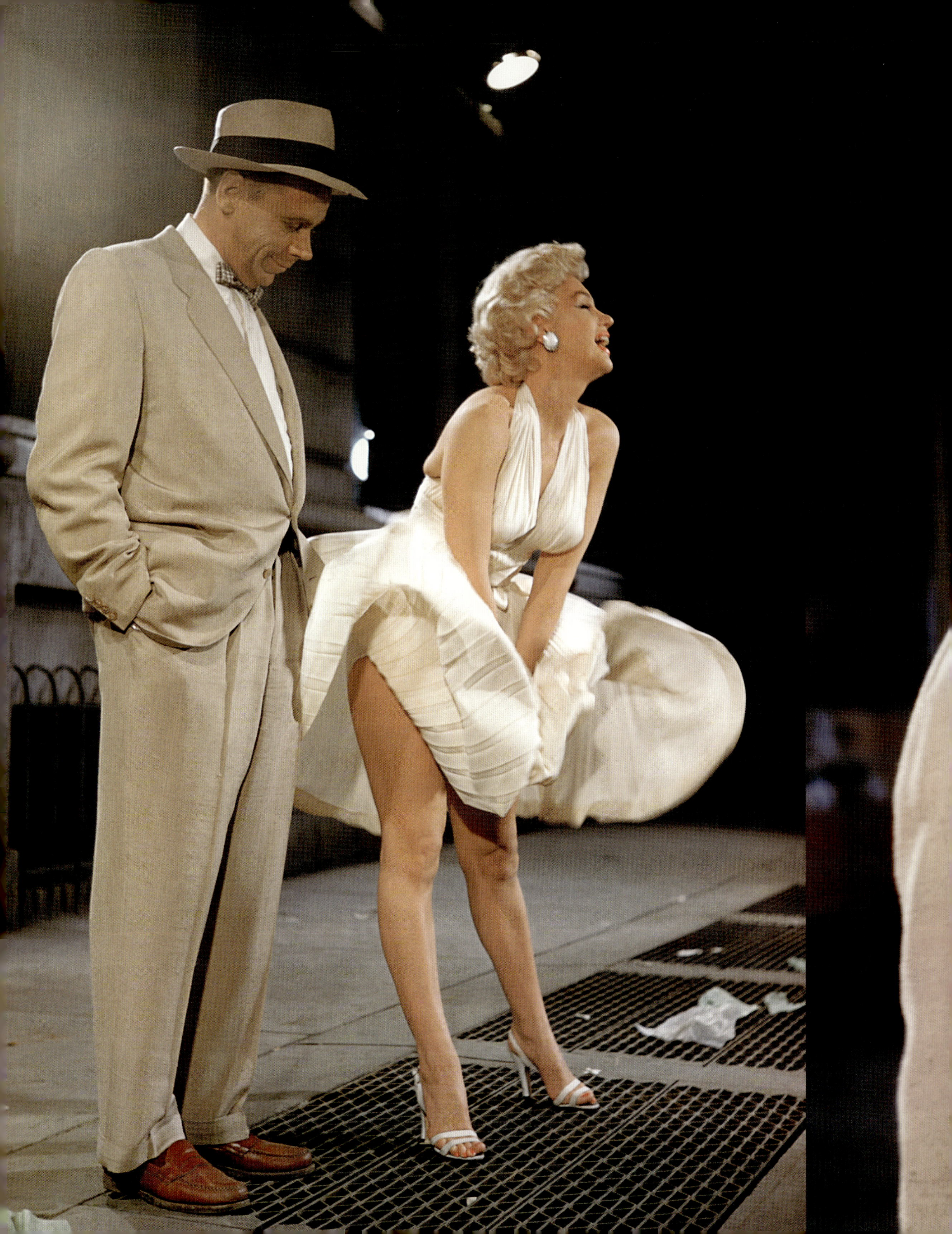

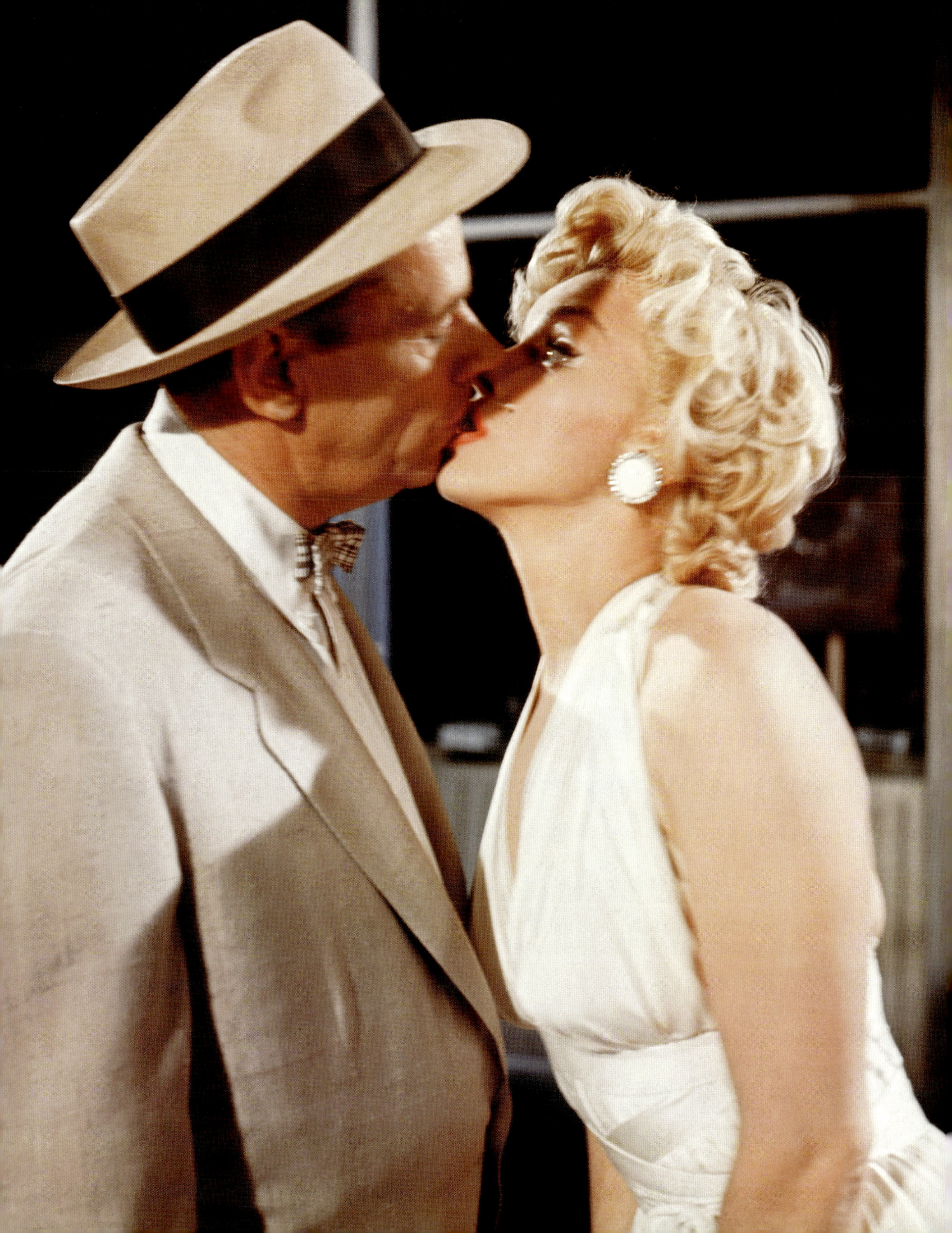

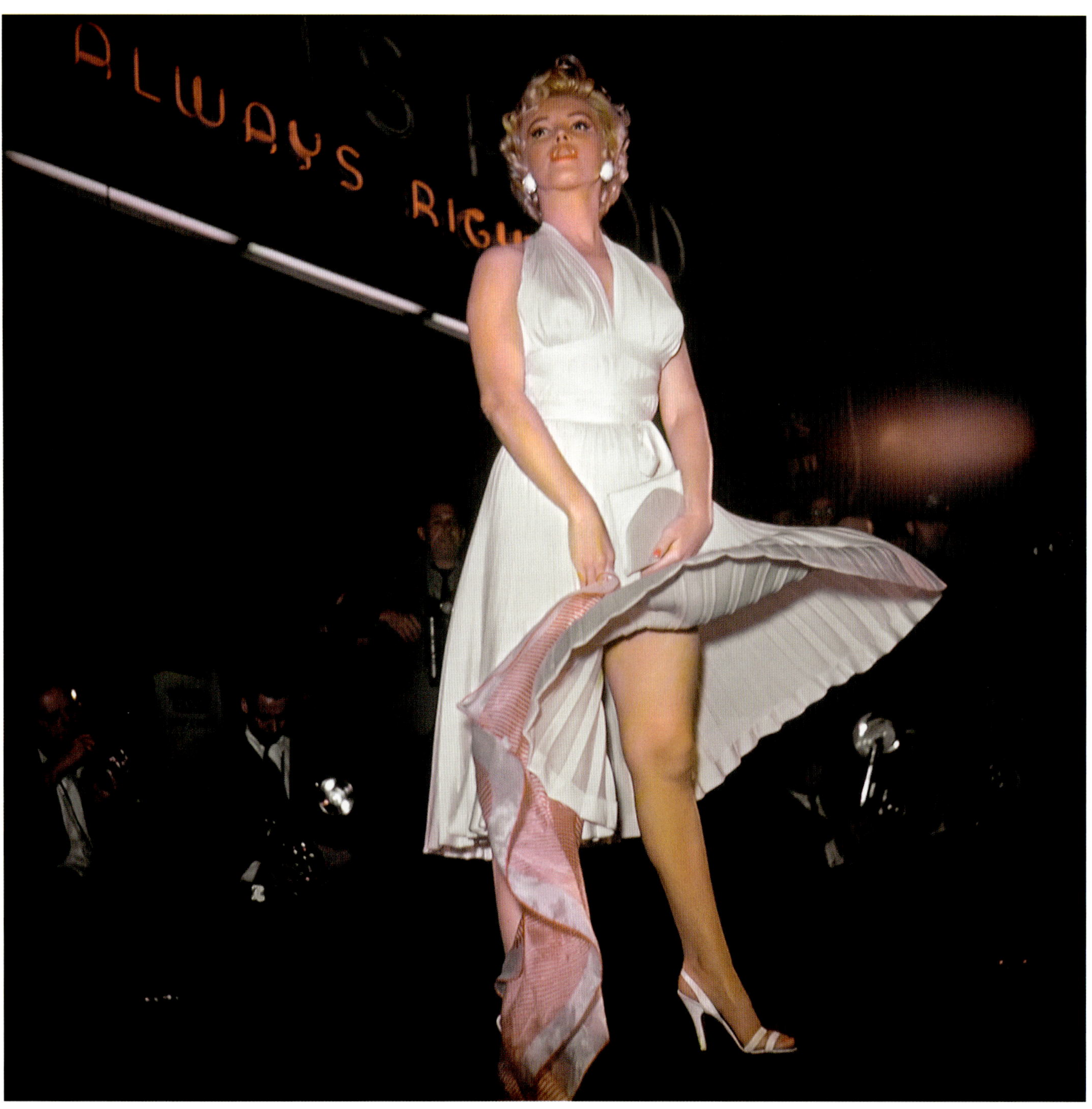
ALWAYS

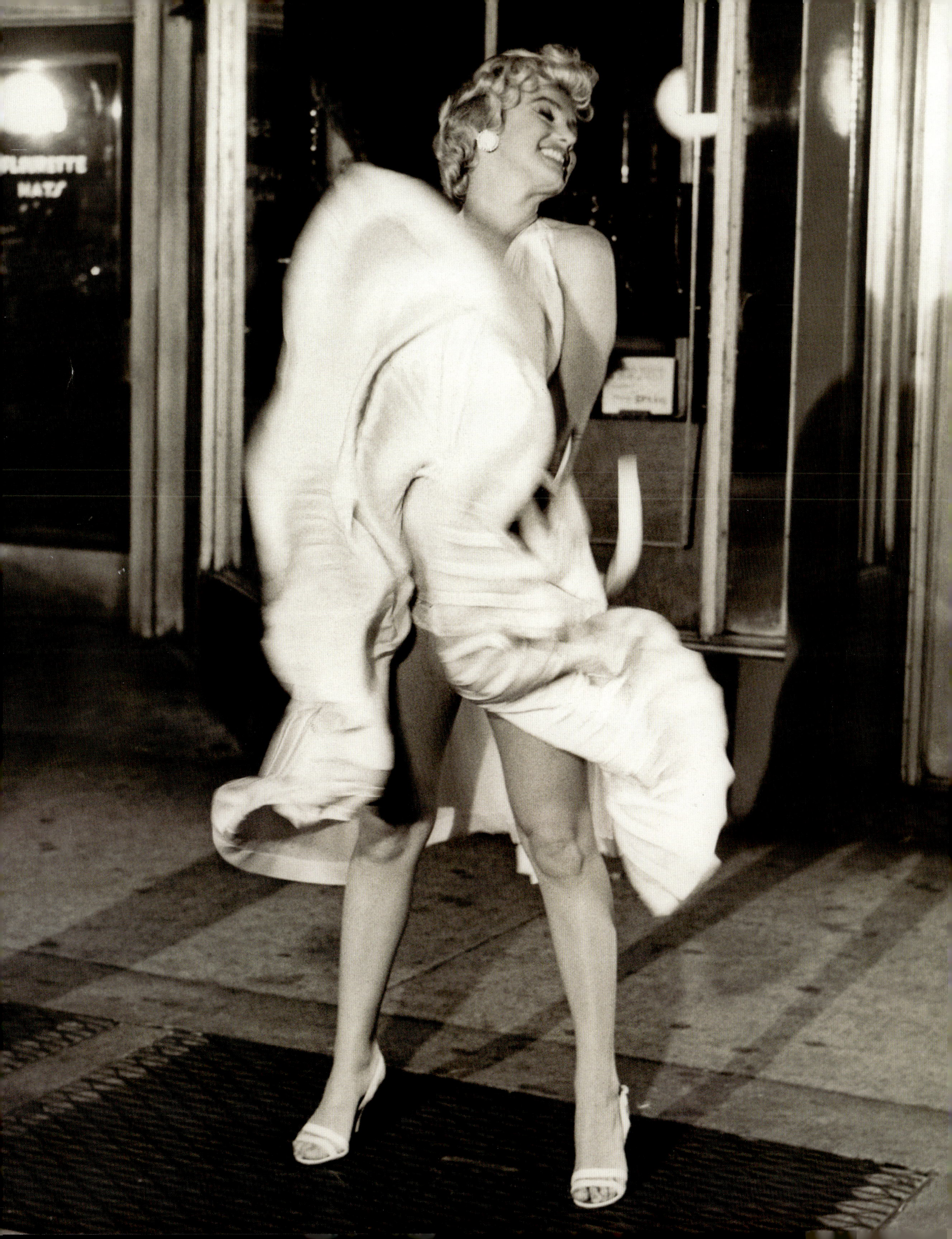

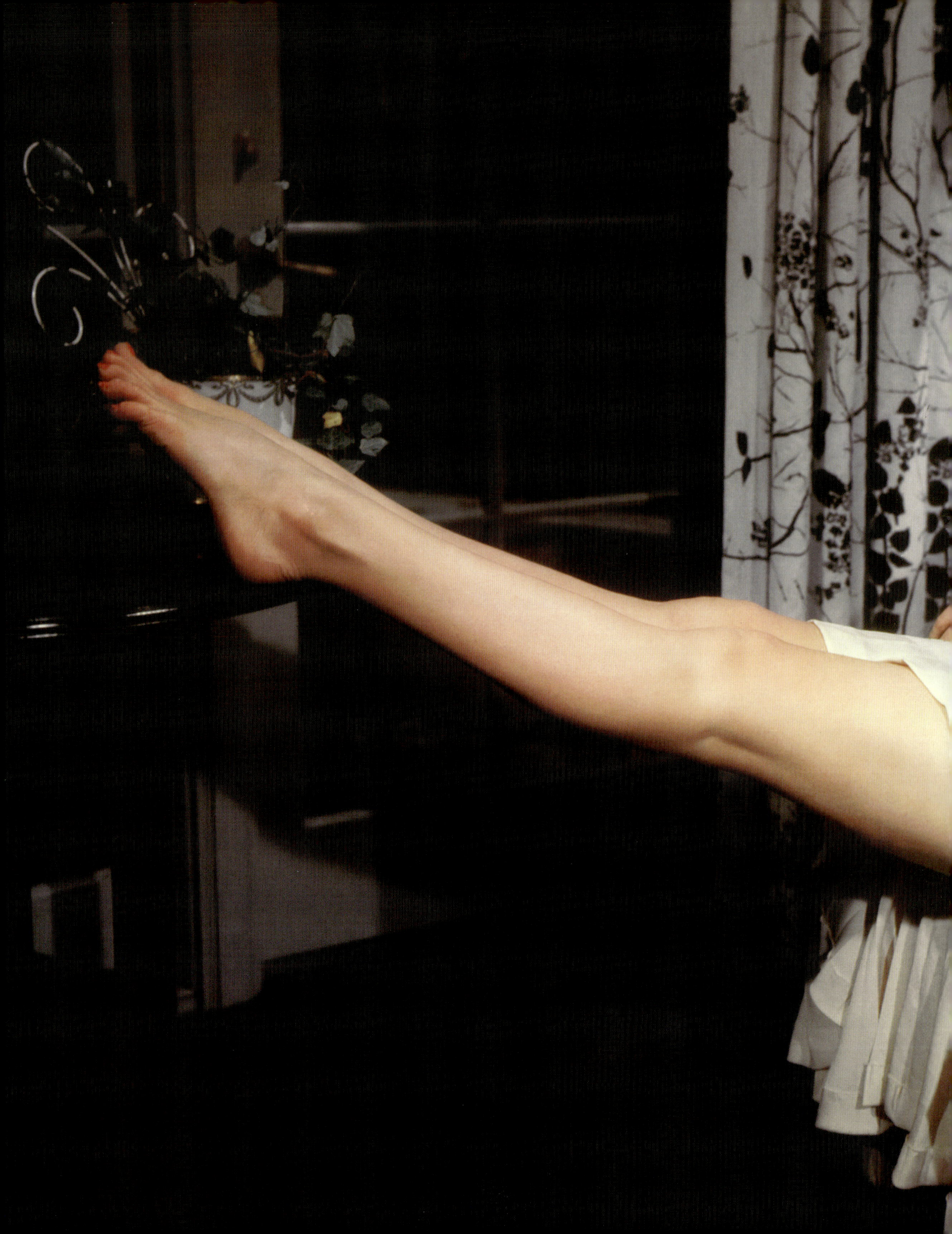

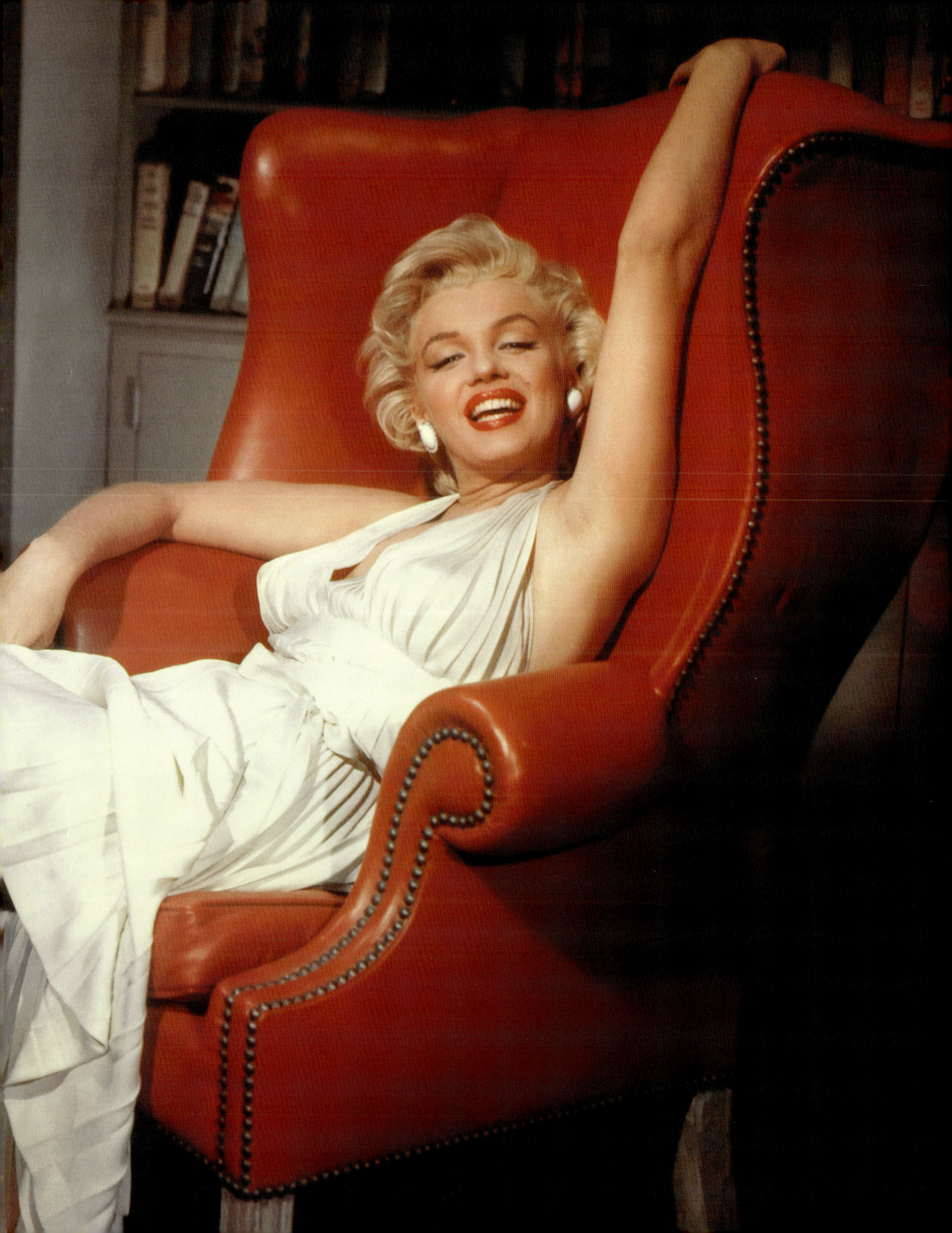

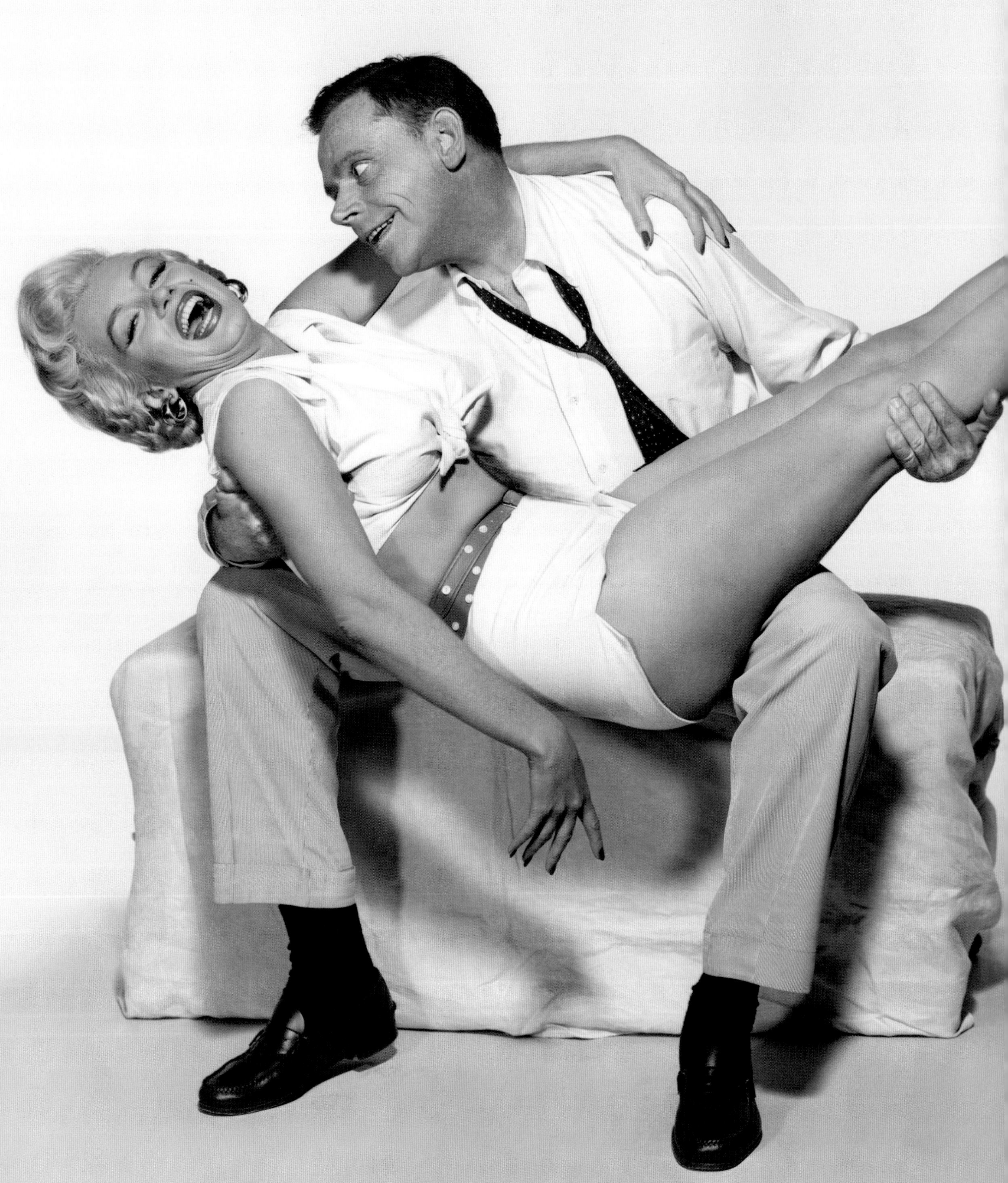

"She was an absolute genius as a comedic actress, with an extraordinary sense for comedic dialogue. It was a God-given gift. She had flesh which photographed like flesh. You feel you can reach out and touch it. *Unique* is an overworked word, but in her case it applies. There will never be another one like her."

BILLY WILDER (Director, *The Seven Year Itch*, 1955)

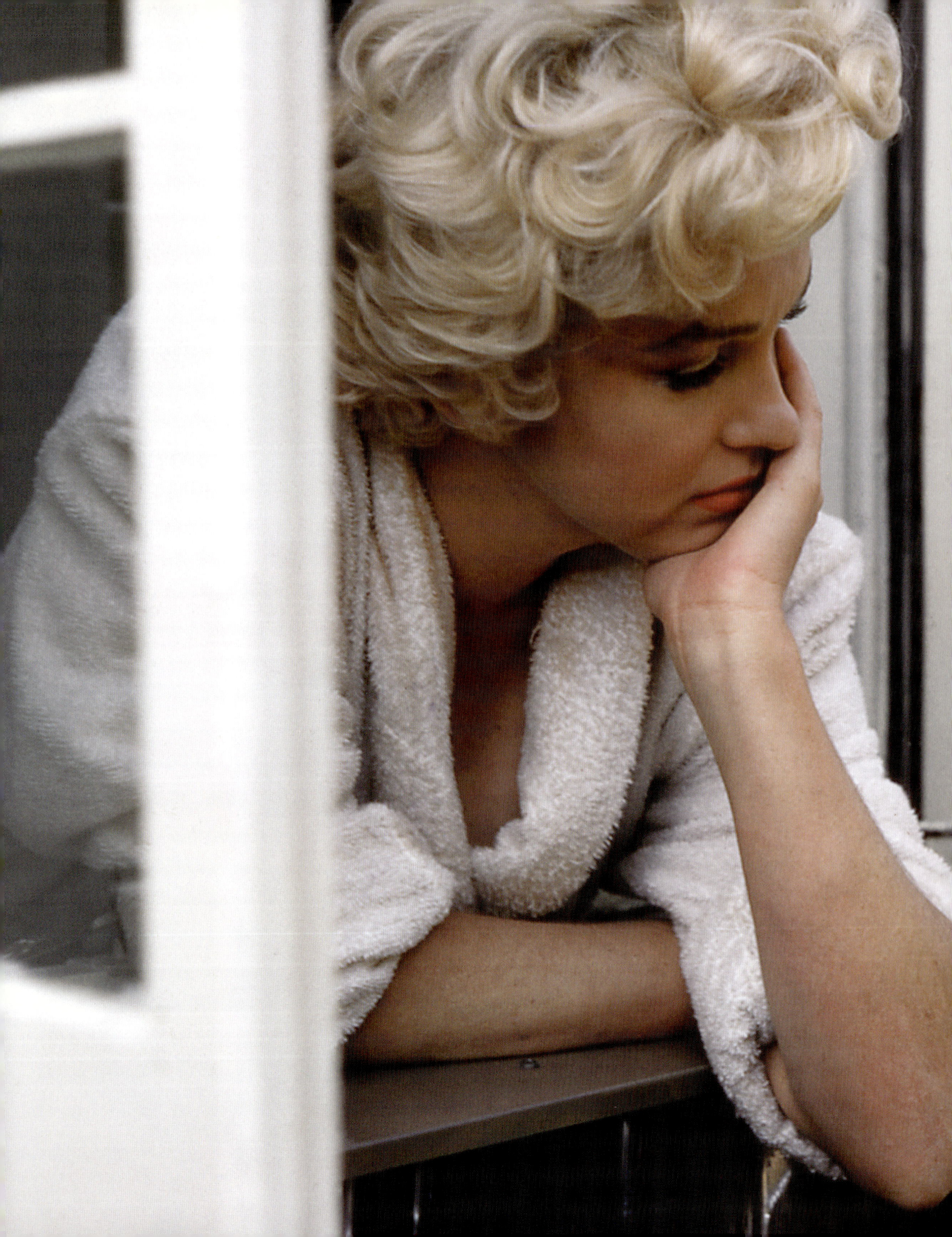

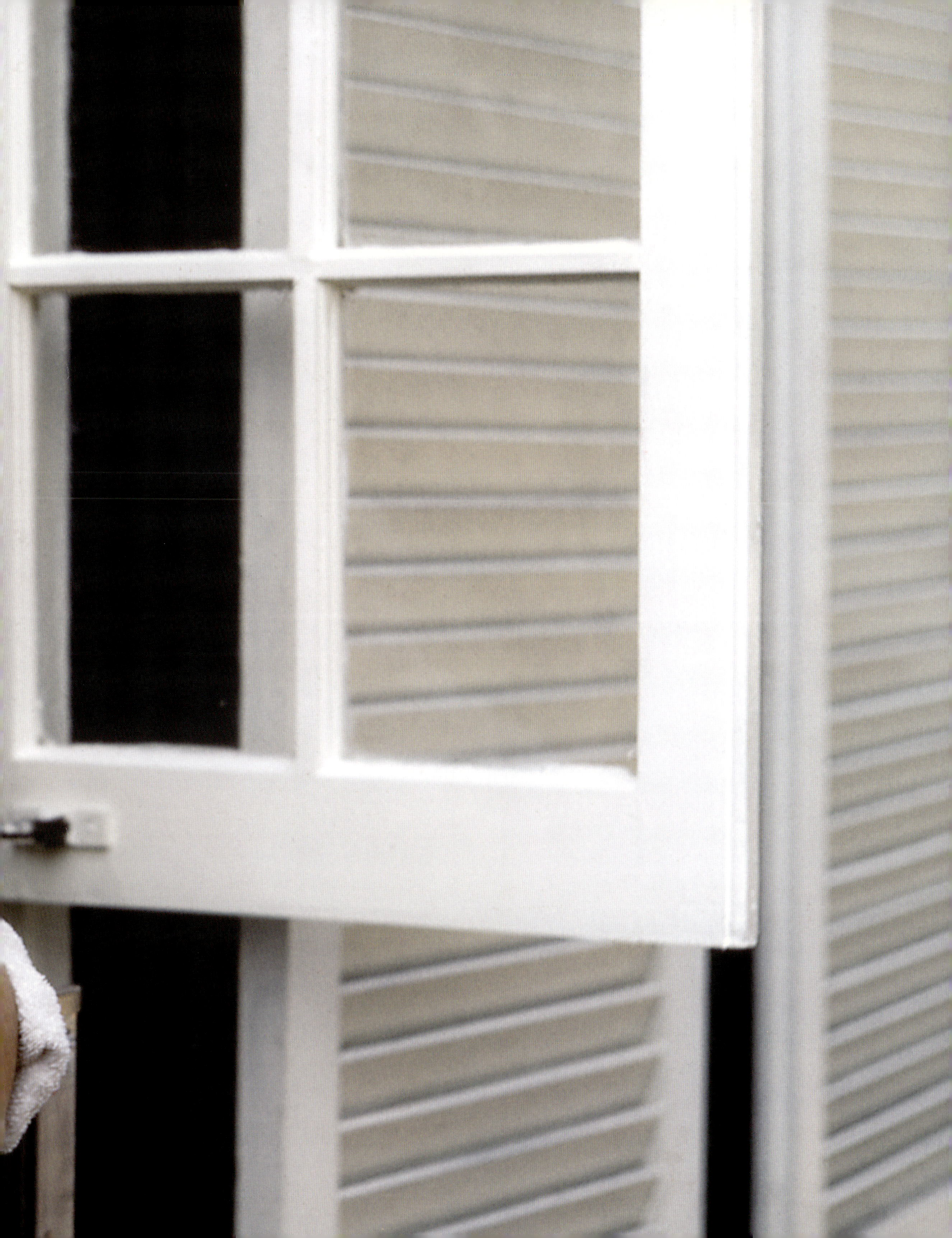

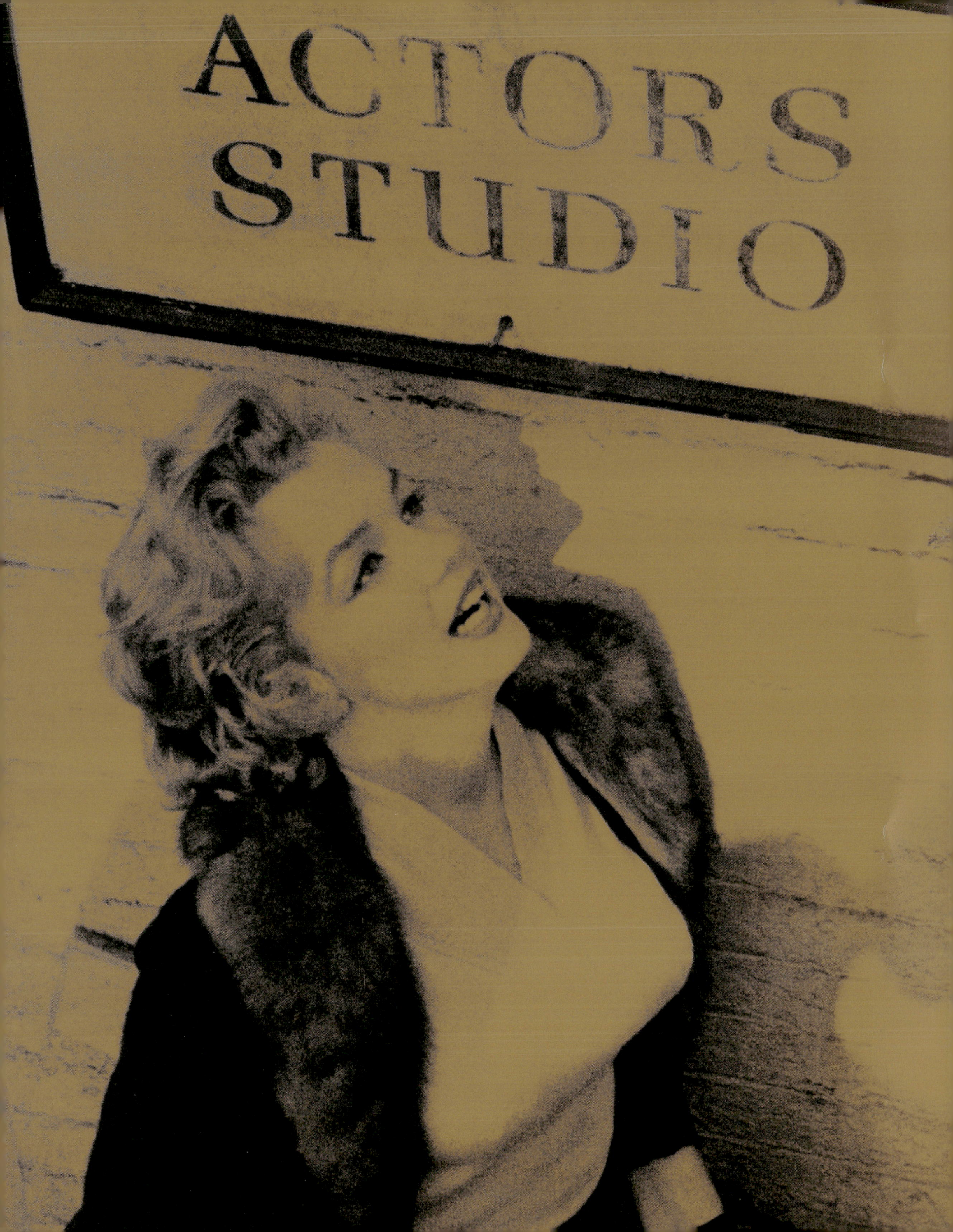
ACTORS
STUDIO

RENAISSANCE

The Independent Years 1955–1961

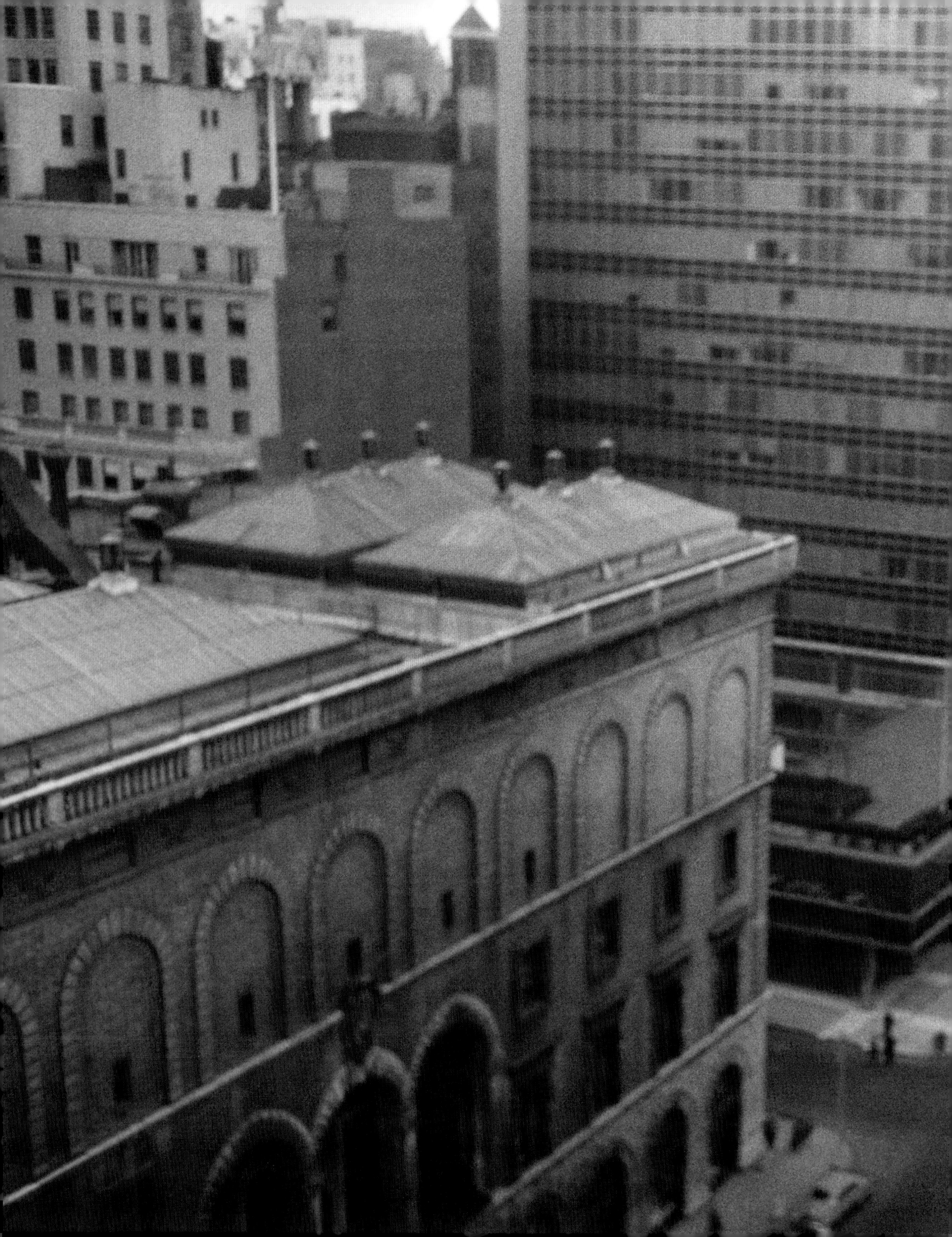

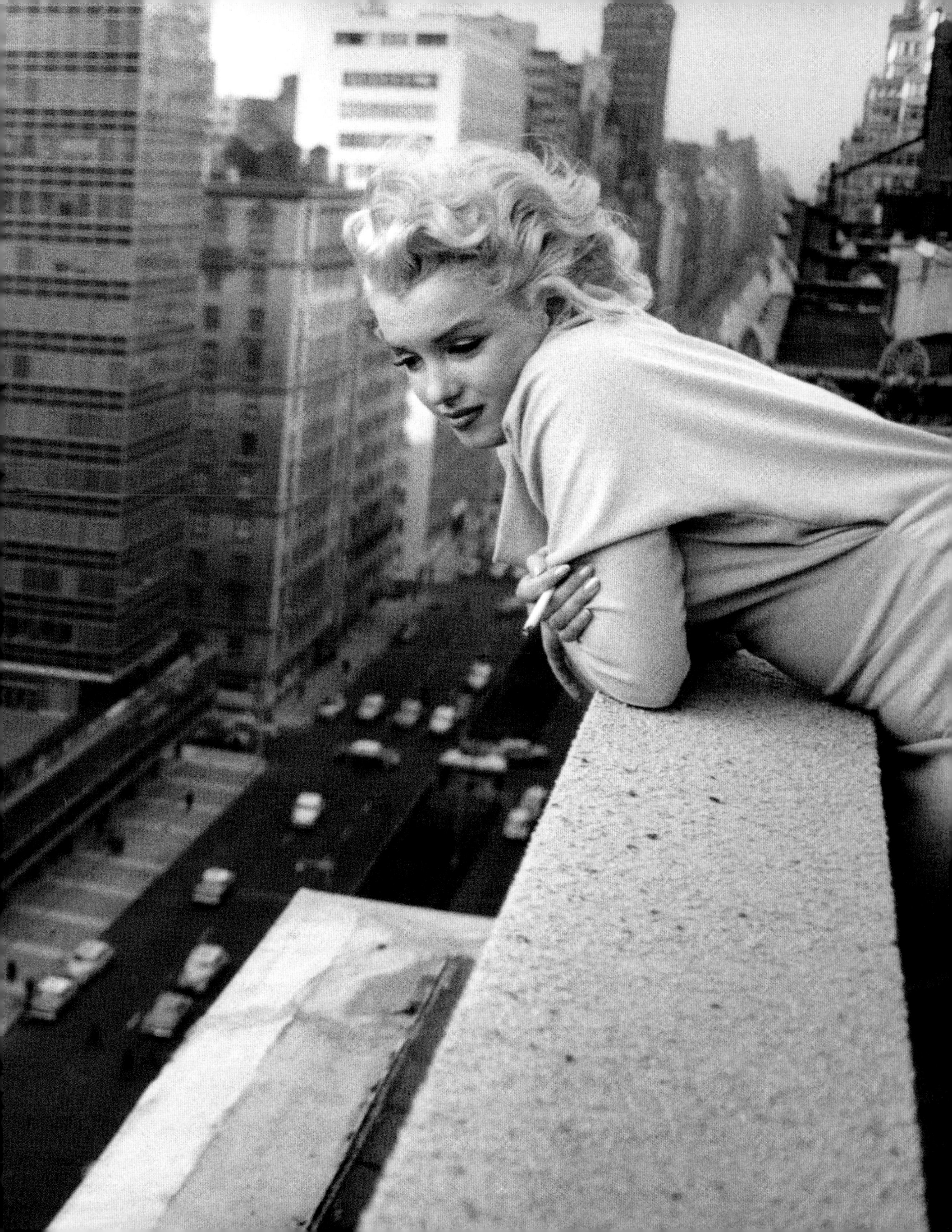

"The Actors Studio, the inner sanctum for working or aspiring actors, was suitably held in an old church with faulty plumbing and low ceilings. The day Marilyn did her famous scene from *Anna Christie*, the upstairs studio was packed to the rafters. It was just after 11:00 a.m. The atmosphere was hushed. Marilyn had elaborately set up and prepared the scene she does with Maureen Stapleton. She enters, she looks sick, worn, tired. Her hand is shaking as she picks up the drink at the bar, the same role that Garbo played in the film. The audience is in awe, realizing Marilyn *is* the character. All her fears and her life tragedies are in our face, she becomes stunningly real and moving on stage. She does what Lee Strasberg has always told us to do, 'Use your reality,' as if it were easy. She was simple, real, in the moment, not anticipating. Marilyn knew this revered place called The Studio was where she had to prove herself. And she did, brilliantly. She was the 'Golden Girl' in a sea of detractors and disbelievers. She didn't fail us, although later she was highly critical of herself. The audience members burst into applause, a rare phenomenon at The Studio. Lee, in his following comments, was restrained but generous. He loved three kinds of artists—the highly gifted; the injured, tortured souls; and the beauty queens. He adored Marilyn."

JULIE NEWMAR

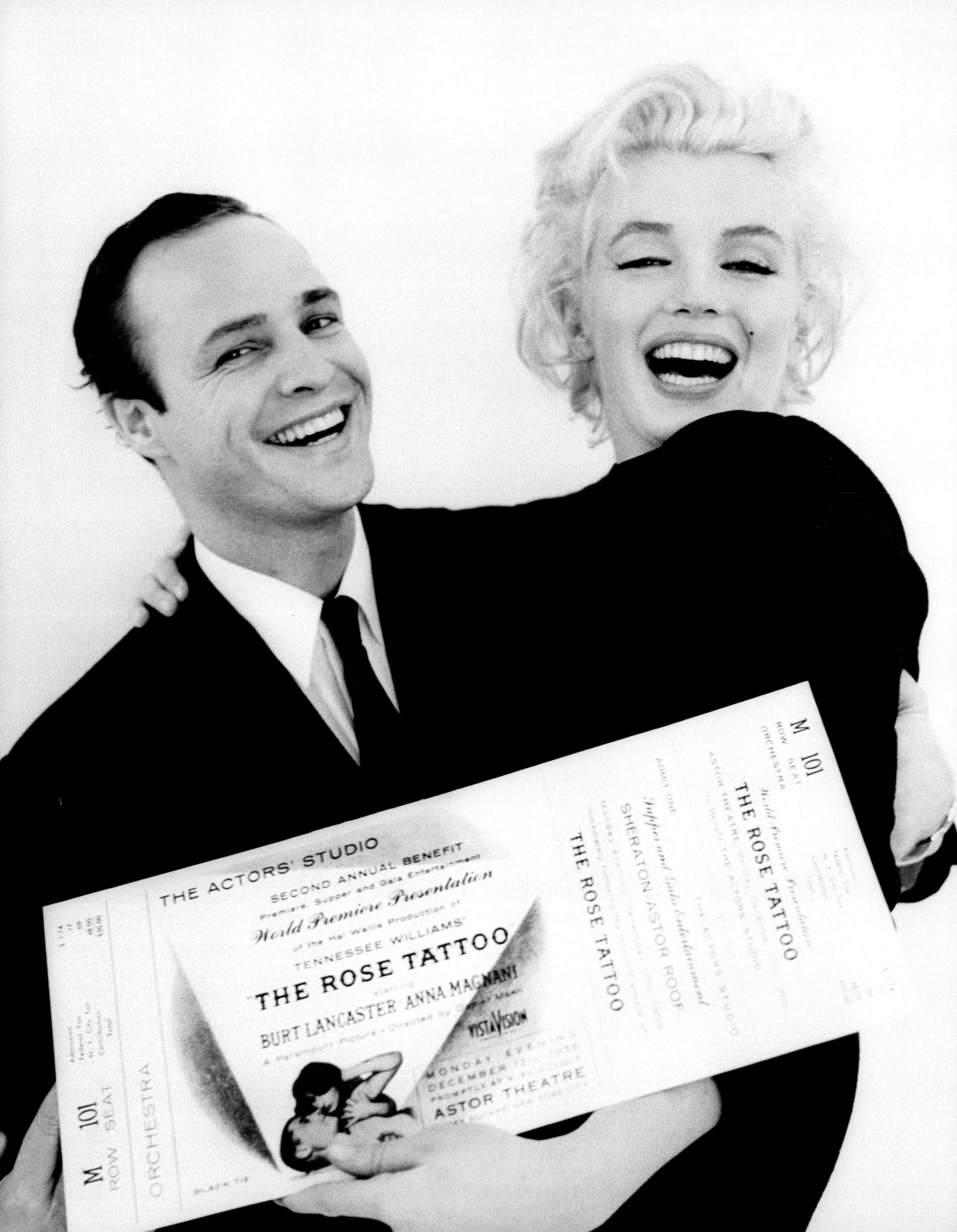
THE ACTORS' STUDIO
SECOND ANNUAL BENEFIT
Premiere, Supper and Gala Entertainment
World Premiere Presentation
of the Hal Wallis Production of
TENNESSEE WILLIAMS'
"THE ROSE TATTOO"
starring
BURT LANCASTER · ANNA MAGNANI
A Paramount Picture · Directed by
VISTAVISION
MONDAY EVENING
ASTOR THEATRE
M 101
ROW SEAT
ORCHESTRA
BLACK TIE
M 101
ROW SEAT
ORCHESTRA
World Premiere Presentation
THE ROSE TATTOO
THE ACTORS STUDIO
ADMIT ONE
Supper and Gala Entertainment
SHERATON-ASTOR ROOF
THE ROSE TATTOO

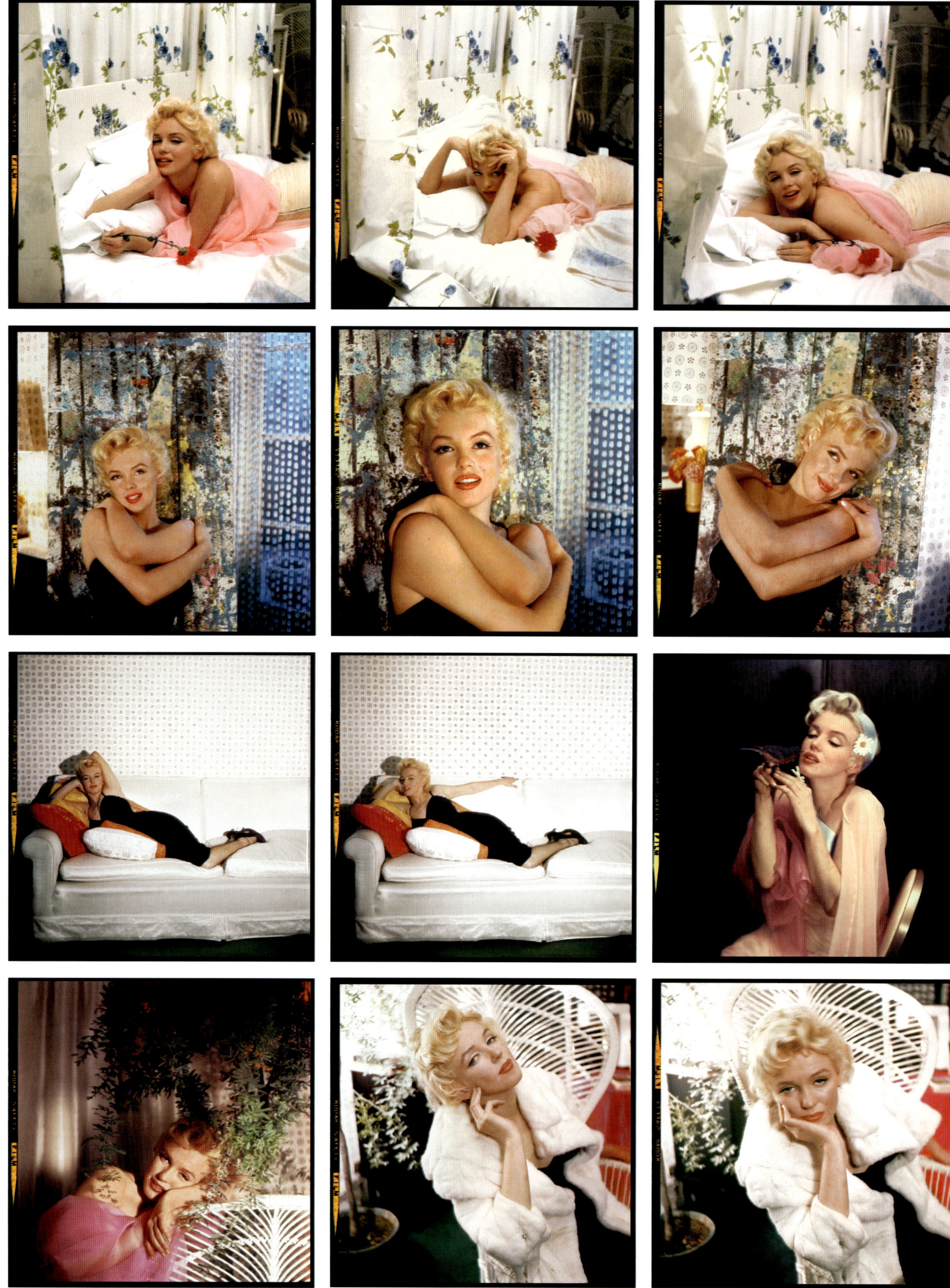

“Miss Monroe calls to mind the bouquet of a fireworks display. . . . She romps, she squeals with delight, she leaps onto the sofa. She puts a flower stem in her mouth, puffing on a daisy as though it was a cigarette. It is an artless, impromptu, high-spirited, infectiously gay performance. It will probably end in tears.”

CECIL BEATON (Photographer)

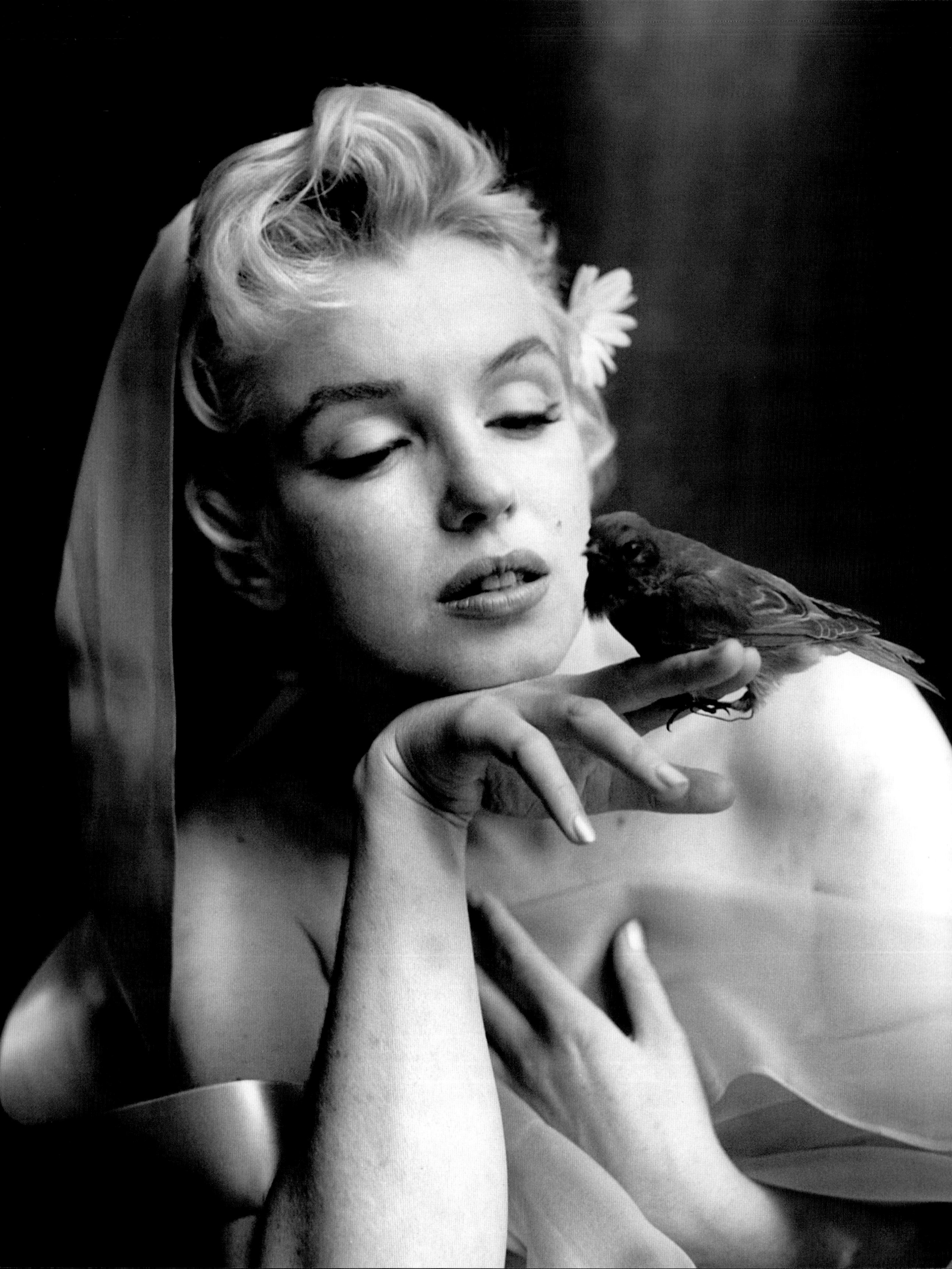

"Marilyn loved animals; she was drawn to all living things. She would spend hundreds of dollars to try to save a storm-damaged tree and would mourn its death. She welcomed birds, providing tree houses and food for the many species that visited her lawn; she worried about them in bad weather. She worried about dogs and cats. She once had a dog that was by nature contemplative, but she was convinced he was depressed. She did her best to make him play, and that depressed him even more; on the rare occasions when he did an antic pirouette, Marilyn would hug and kiss him, delirious with joy."

NORMAN ROSTEN (Poet)

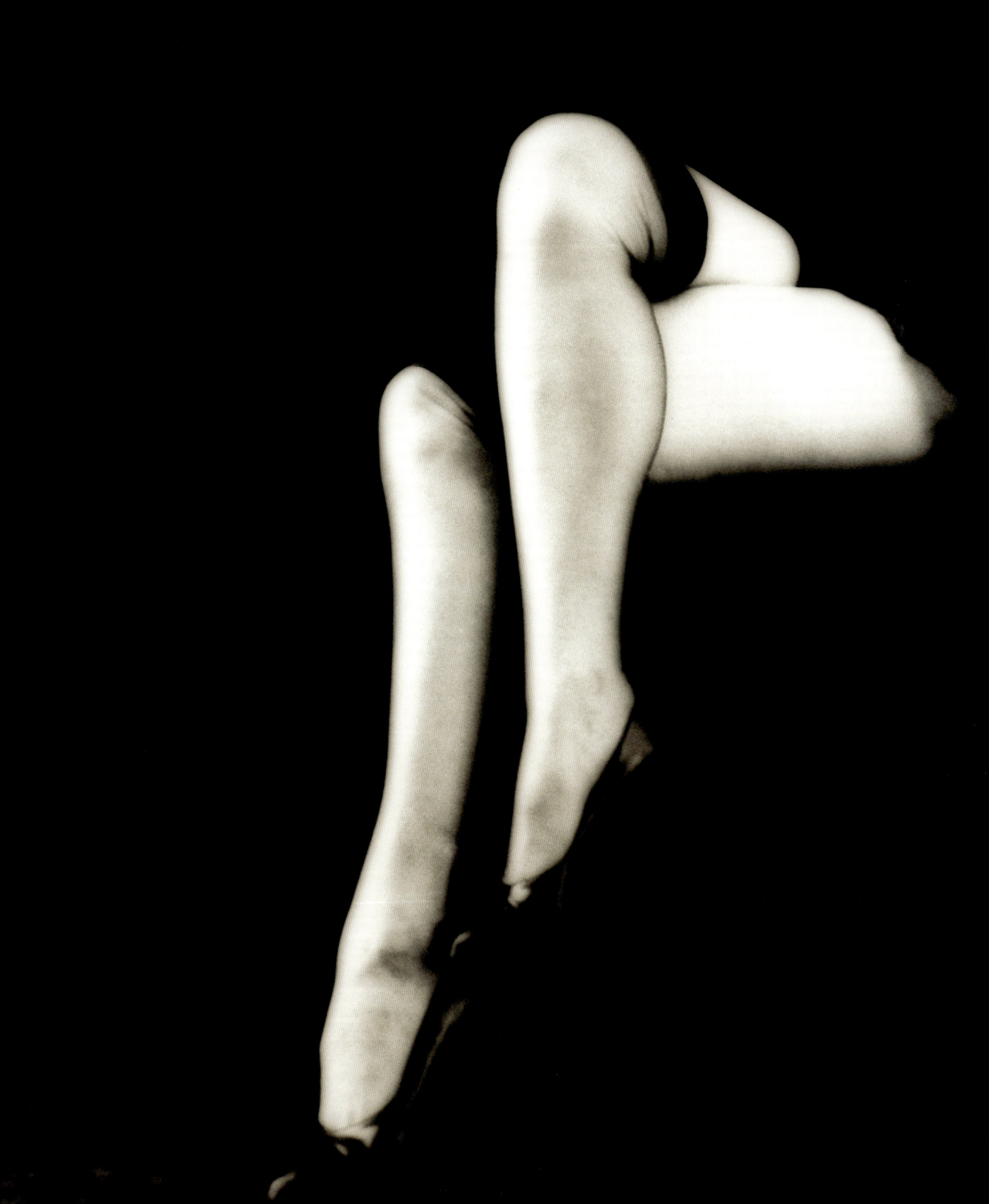

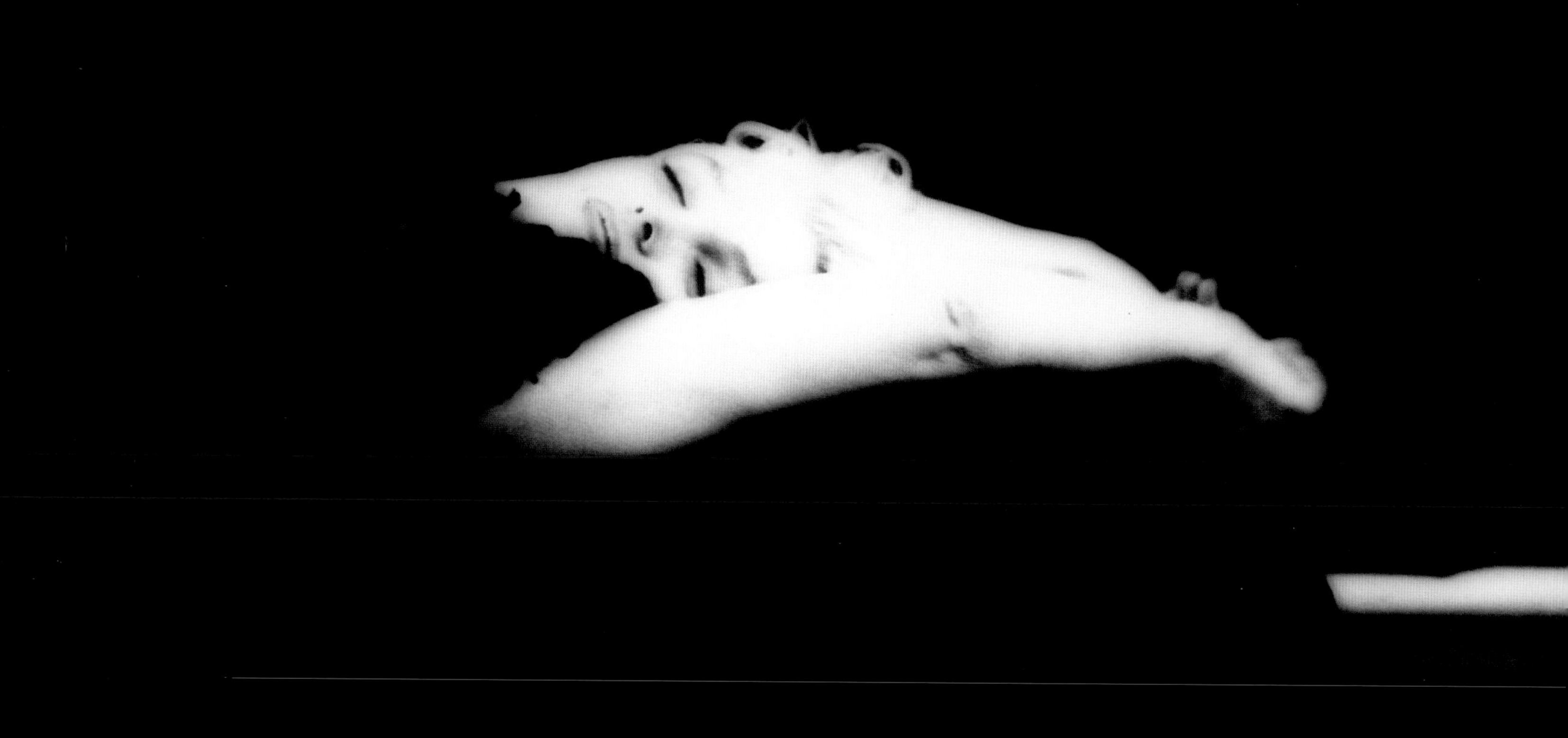

"In private life she was not in the least what her calumniators would have wished her to be. She was very quiet, had a great natural dignity, and was extremely intelligent. She was also exceedingly sensitive."

DAME EDITH SITWELL (Poet)

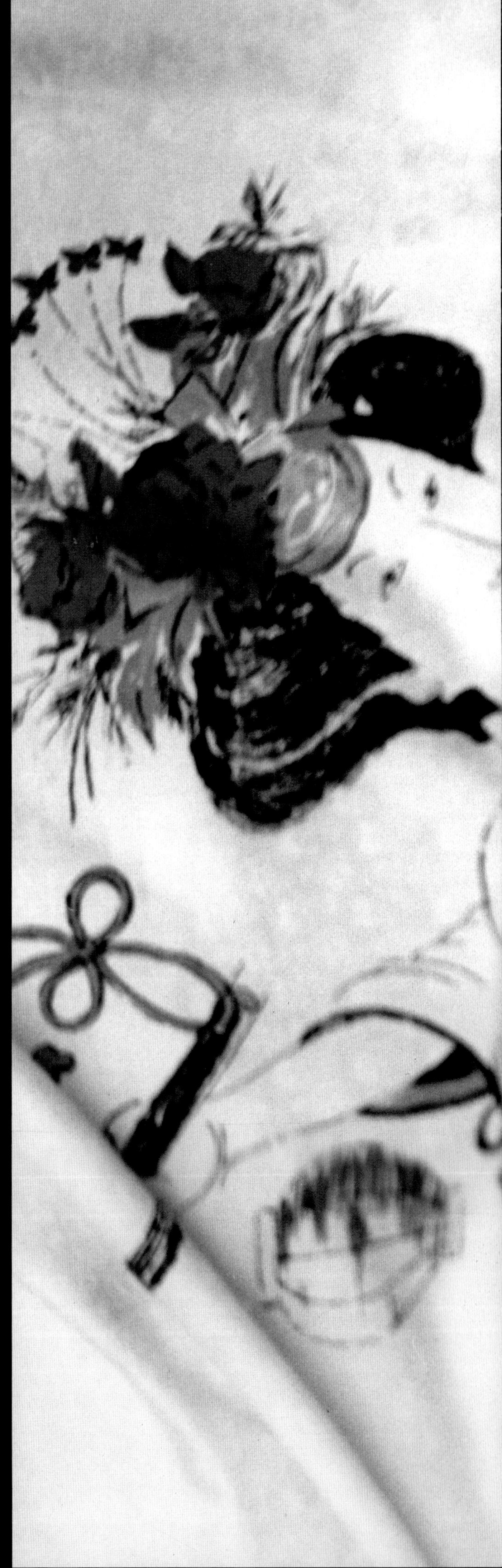

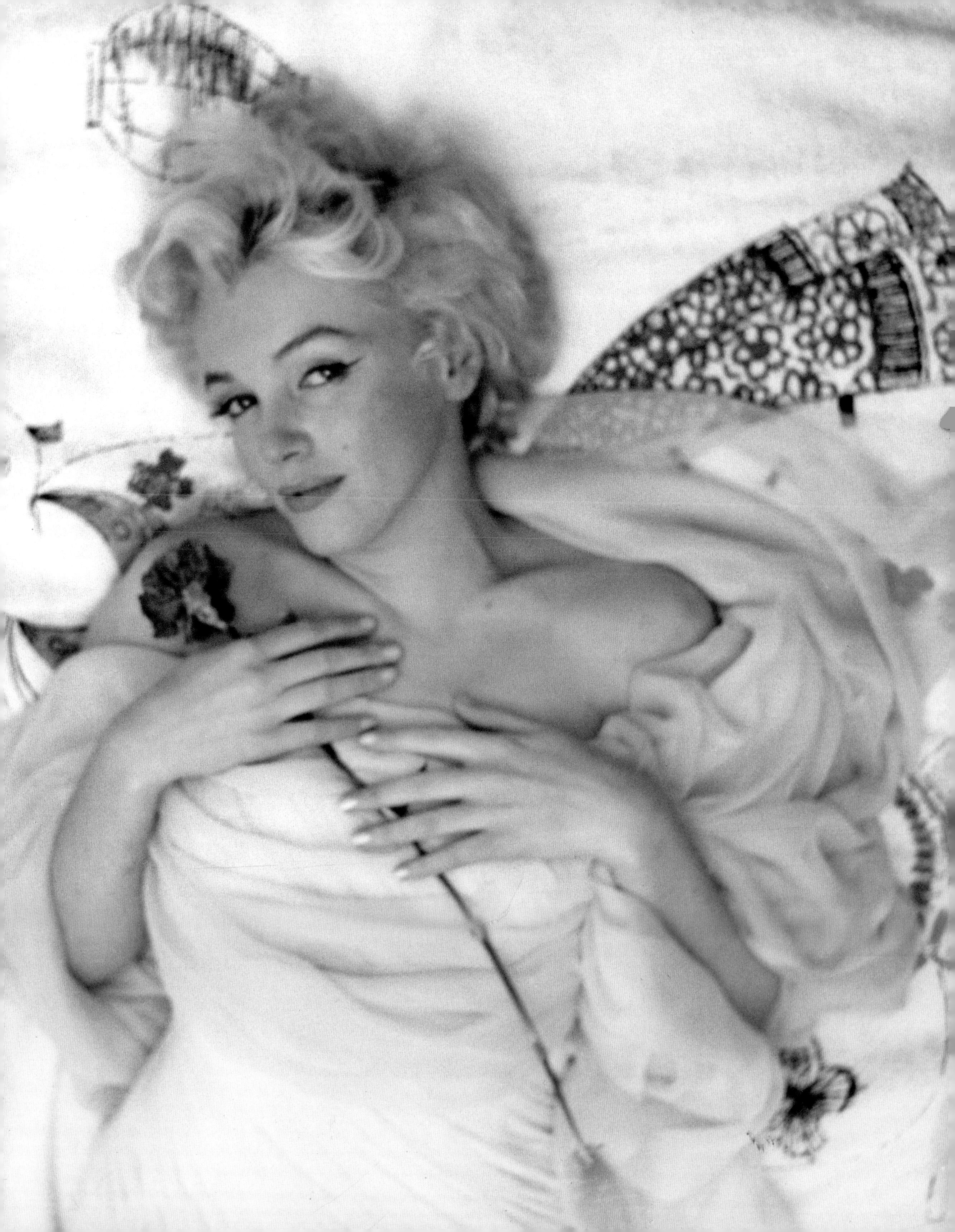

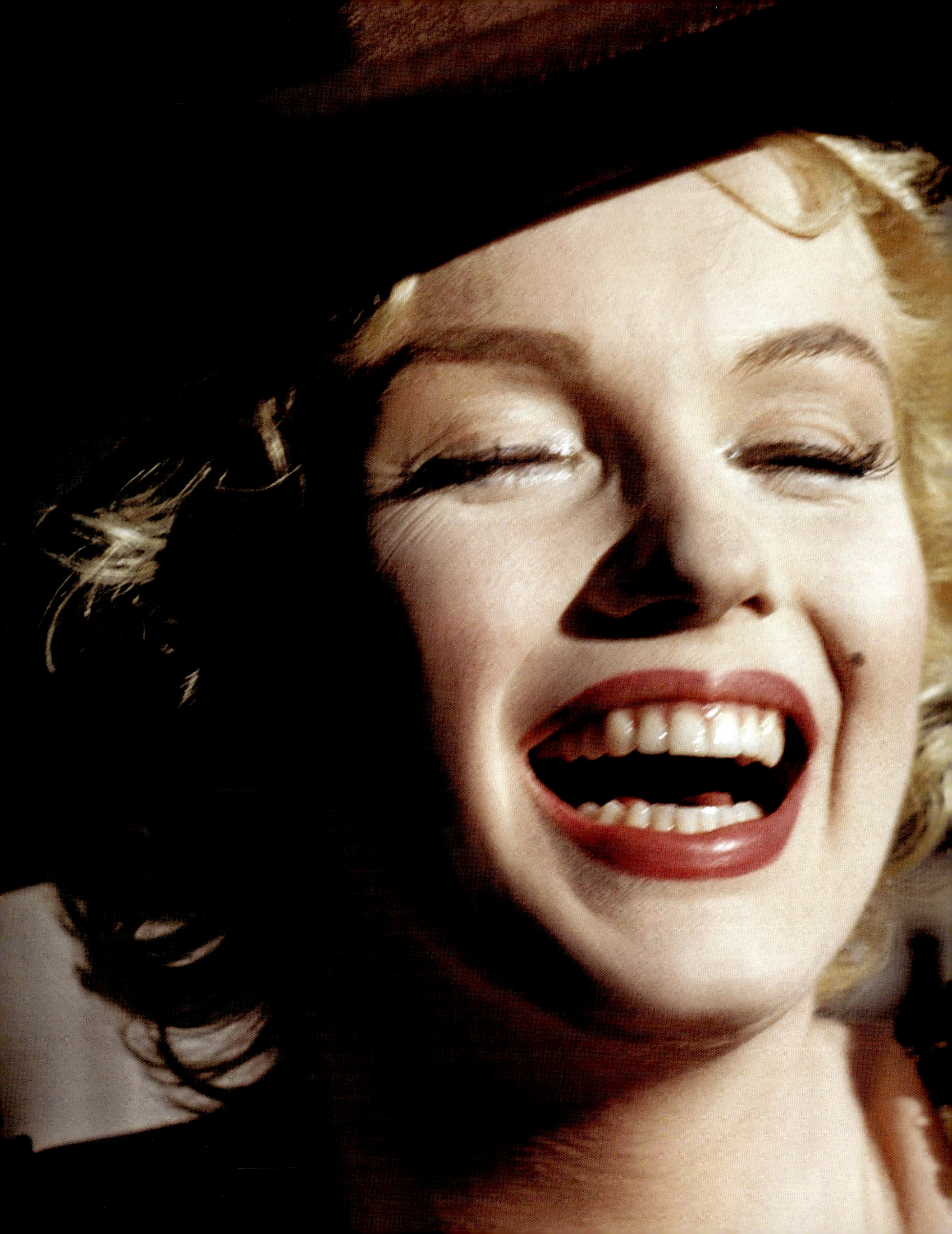

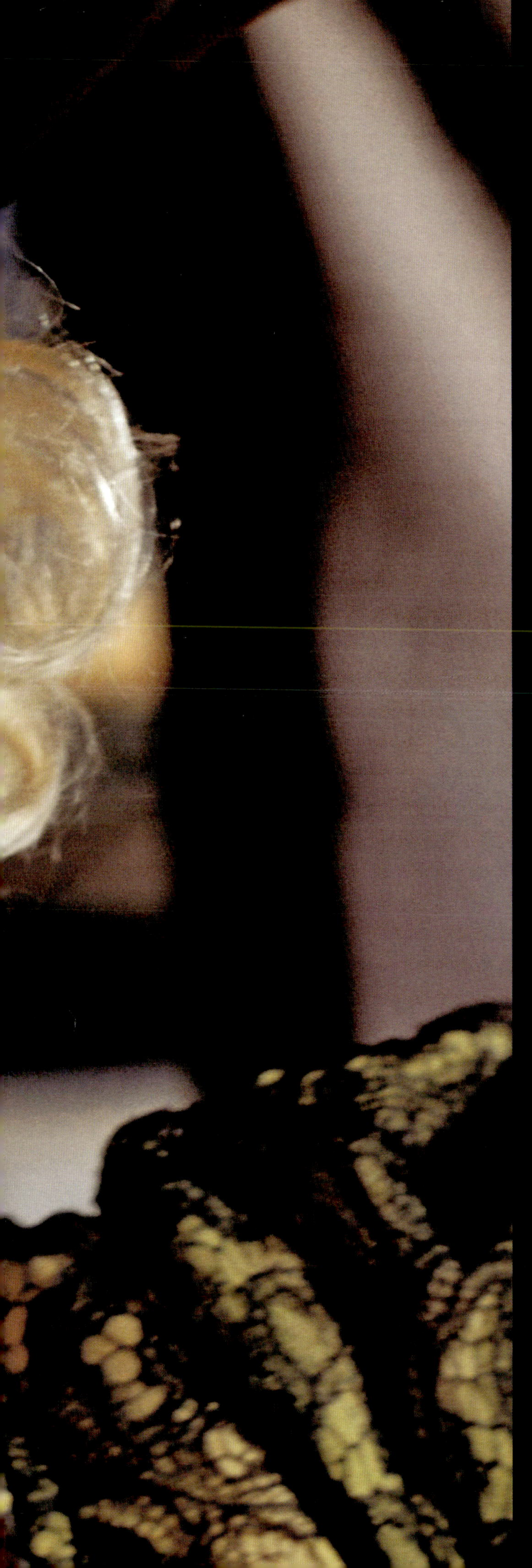

"Marilyn is as near genius as any actress I ever knew. . . . She is the most completely realized actress since Garbo. Watch her work. In any film. How rarely she has to use words. How much she does with her eyes, her lips, with slight, almost accidental gestures. . . . Monroe is pure cinema."

JOSHUA LOGAN (Director, *Bus Stop*, 1956)

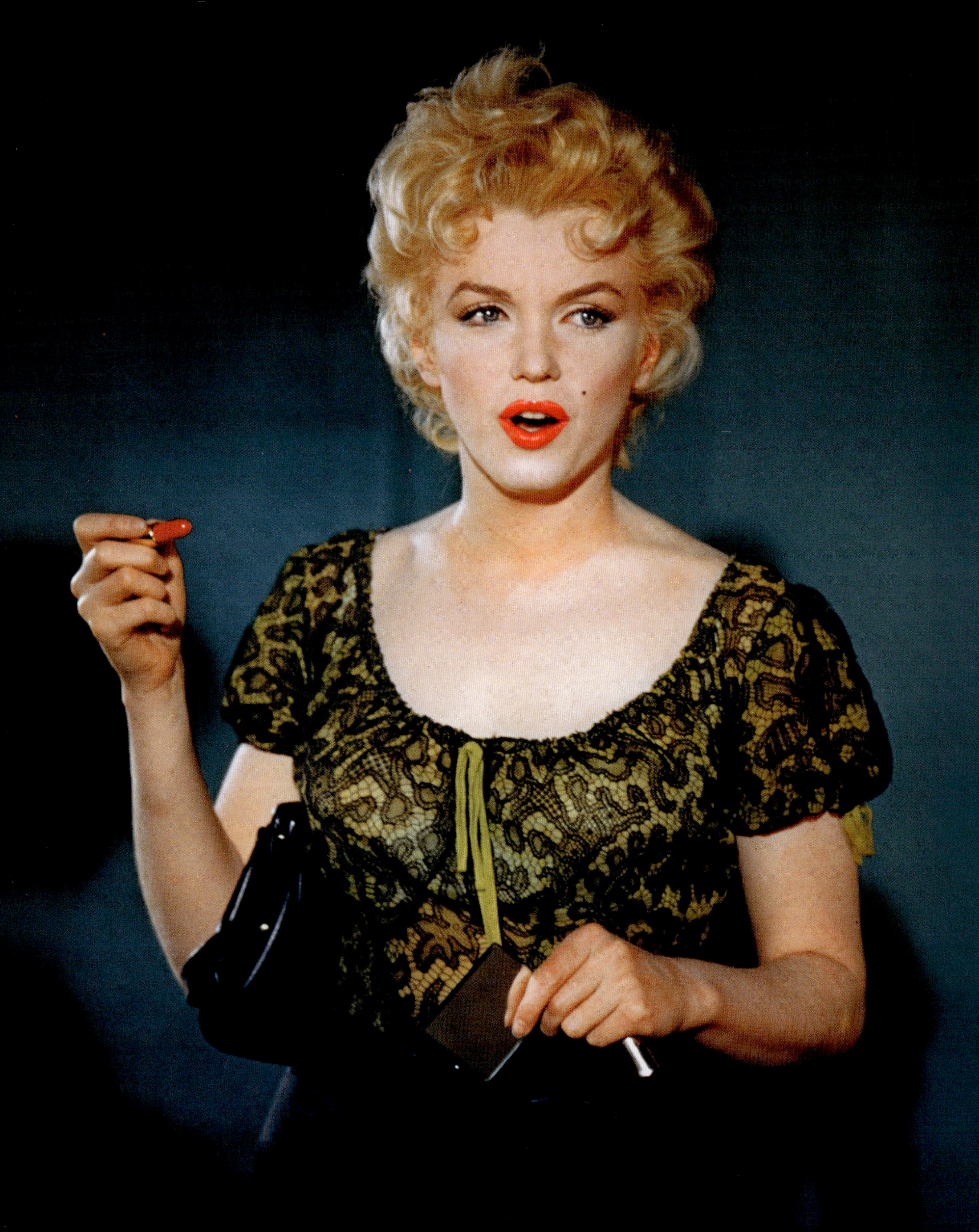

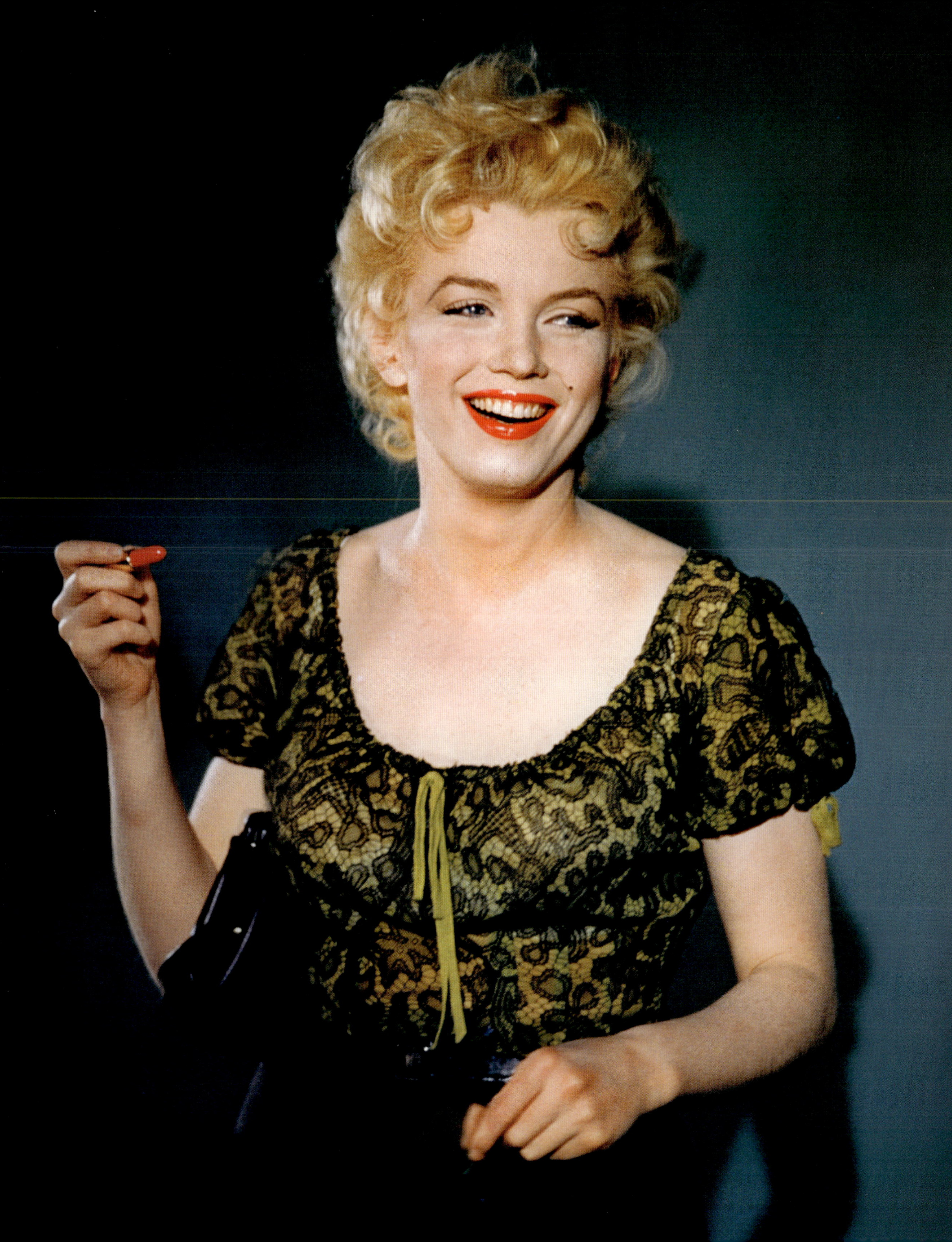

"To understand Marilyn best, you have to see her around children. They love her; her whole approach to life has their kind of simplicity and directness."

ARTHUR MILLER

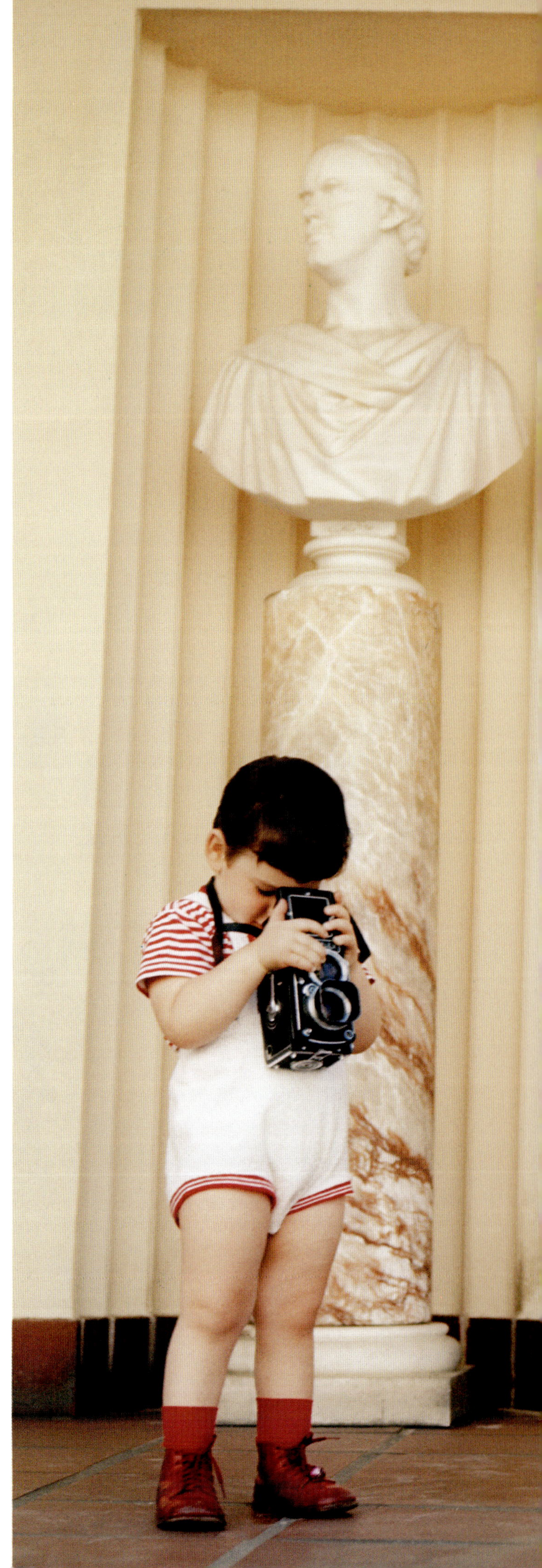

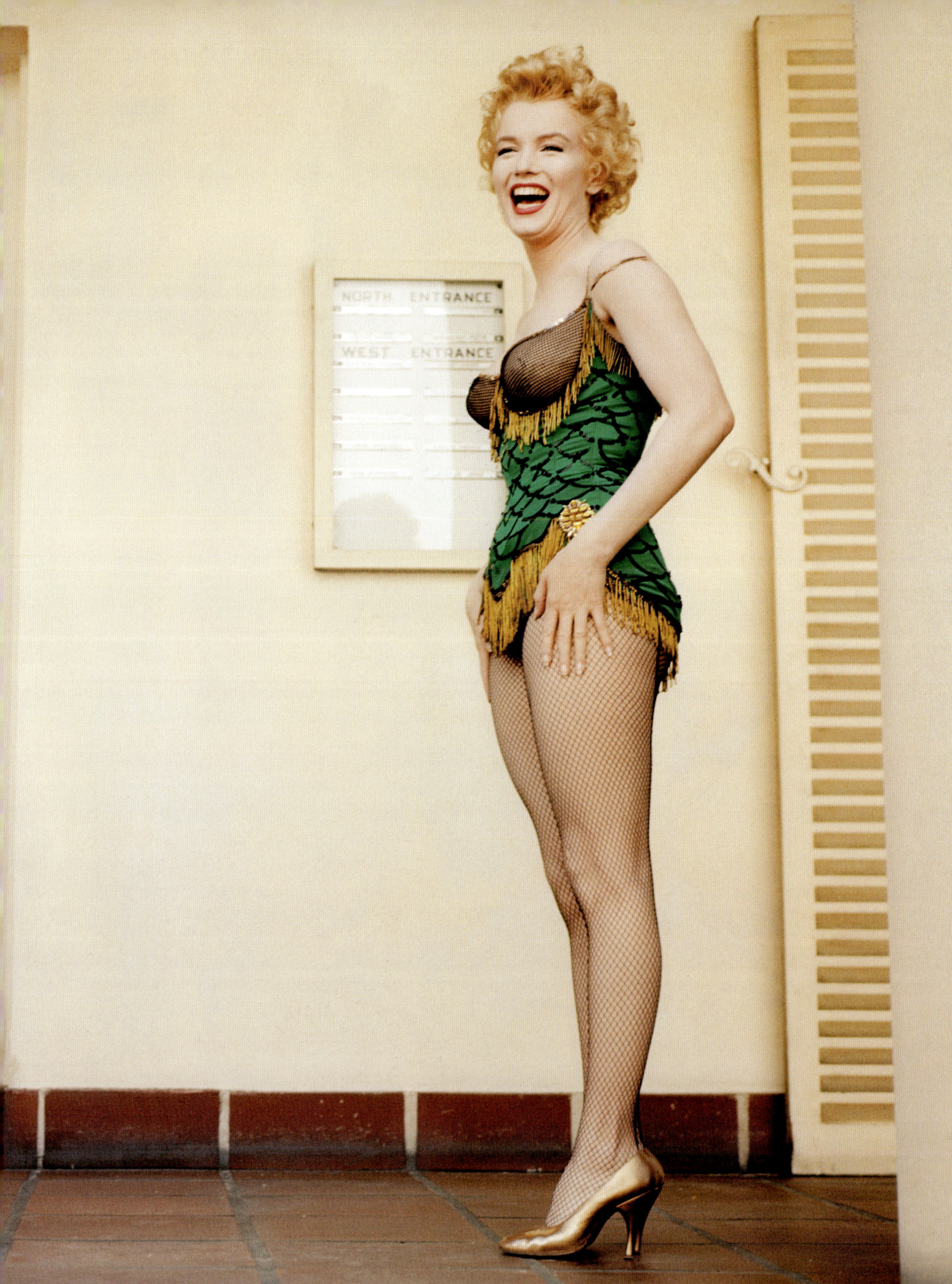
NORTH ENTRANCE
WEST ENTRANCE

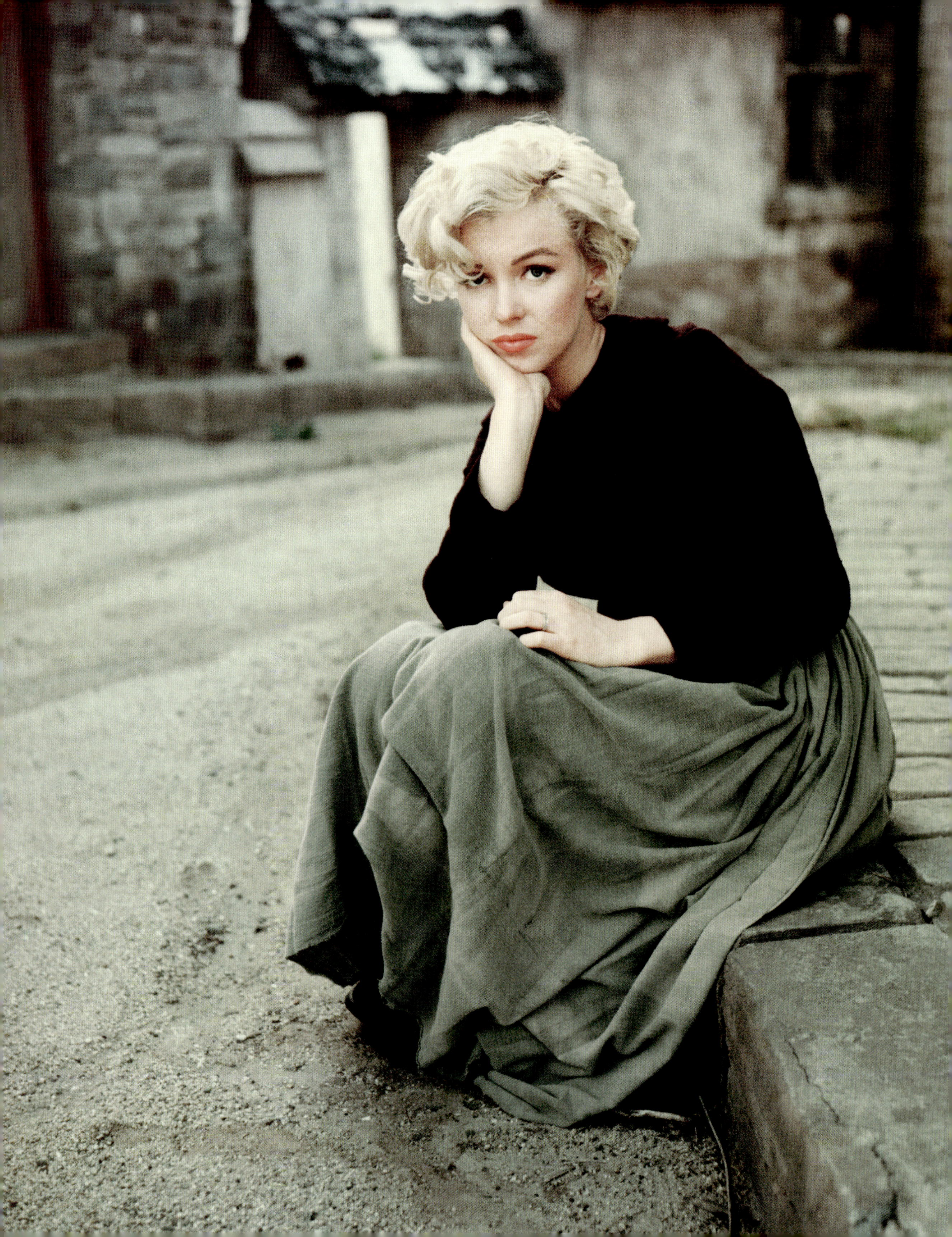

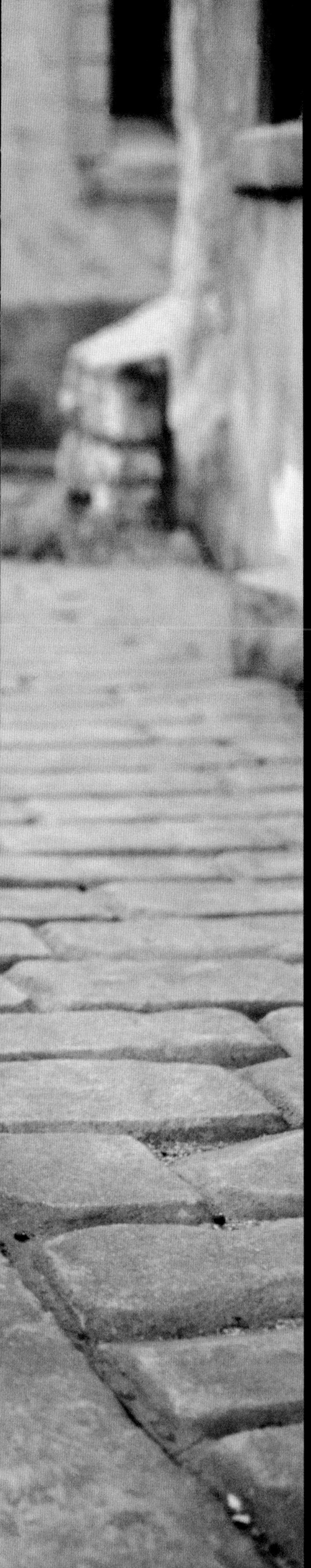

"She is a beautiful child. I don't think she's an actress at all, not in any traditional sense. What she has—this presence, this luminosity, this flickering intelligence—could never surface on the stage. It's so fragile and subtle, it can only be caught by the camera. I hope, I really pray, that she survives long enough to free the strange lovely talent that's wandering through her like a jailed spirit."

CONSTANCE COLLIER (Actress and acting coach)

“As we were about to meet the queen I rushed into the ladies’ dressing room to check if my makeup was all right. And who do I see? Marilyn. So there we were powdering our noses, looking at each other, saying ‘hello–hello.’ I really saw her close up. She was ravishing. It was the only time I saw Marilyn, and I will always remember it. She was so incredibly lovely, like a . . . baby. She was fresh, beautiful, and pure, and very touching with her vulnerability. . . . She always was for me what every woman, not only me, must dream to be. . . . I feel great affection for Marilyn Monroe.”

BRIGITTE BARDOT

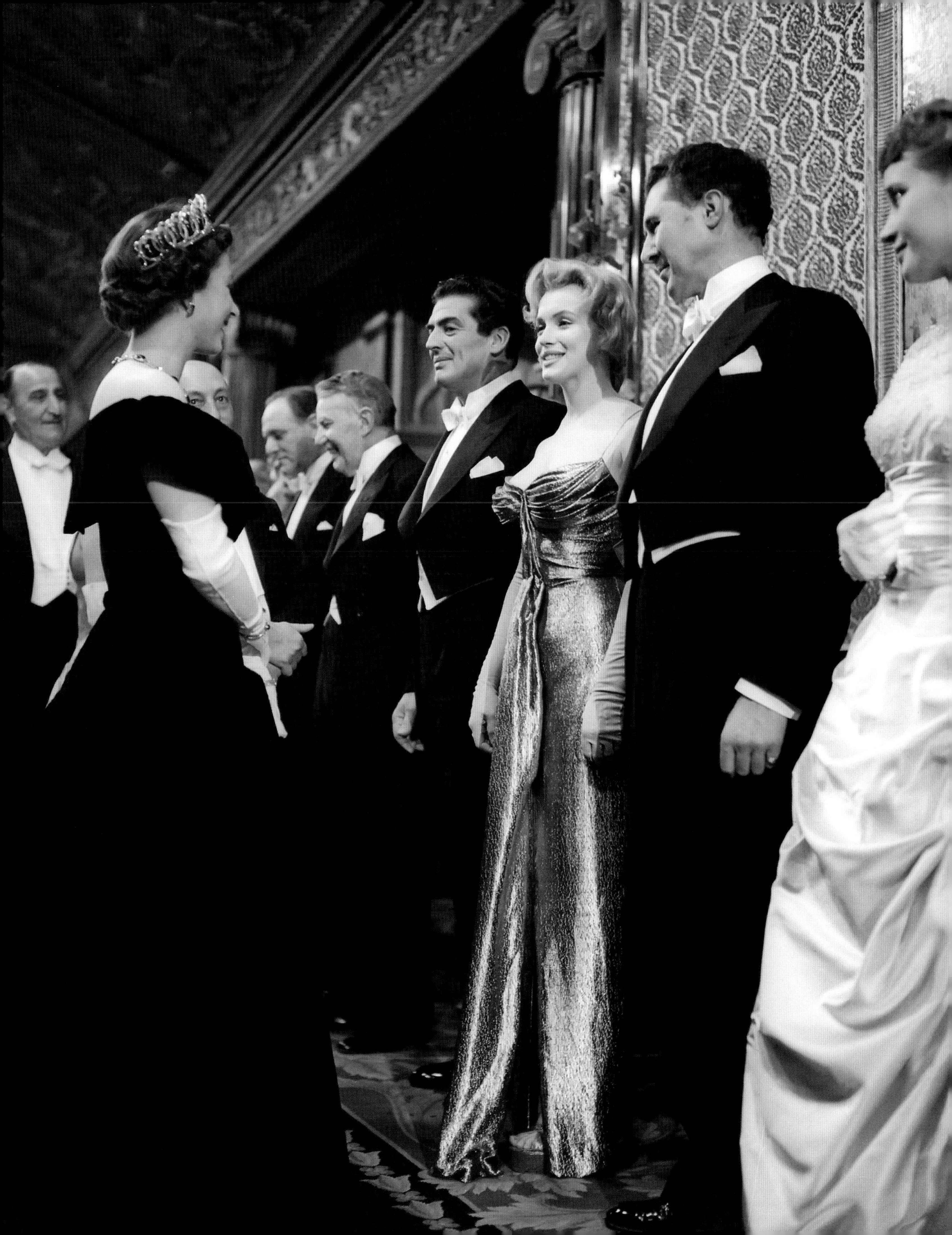

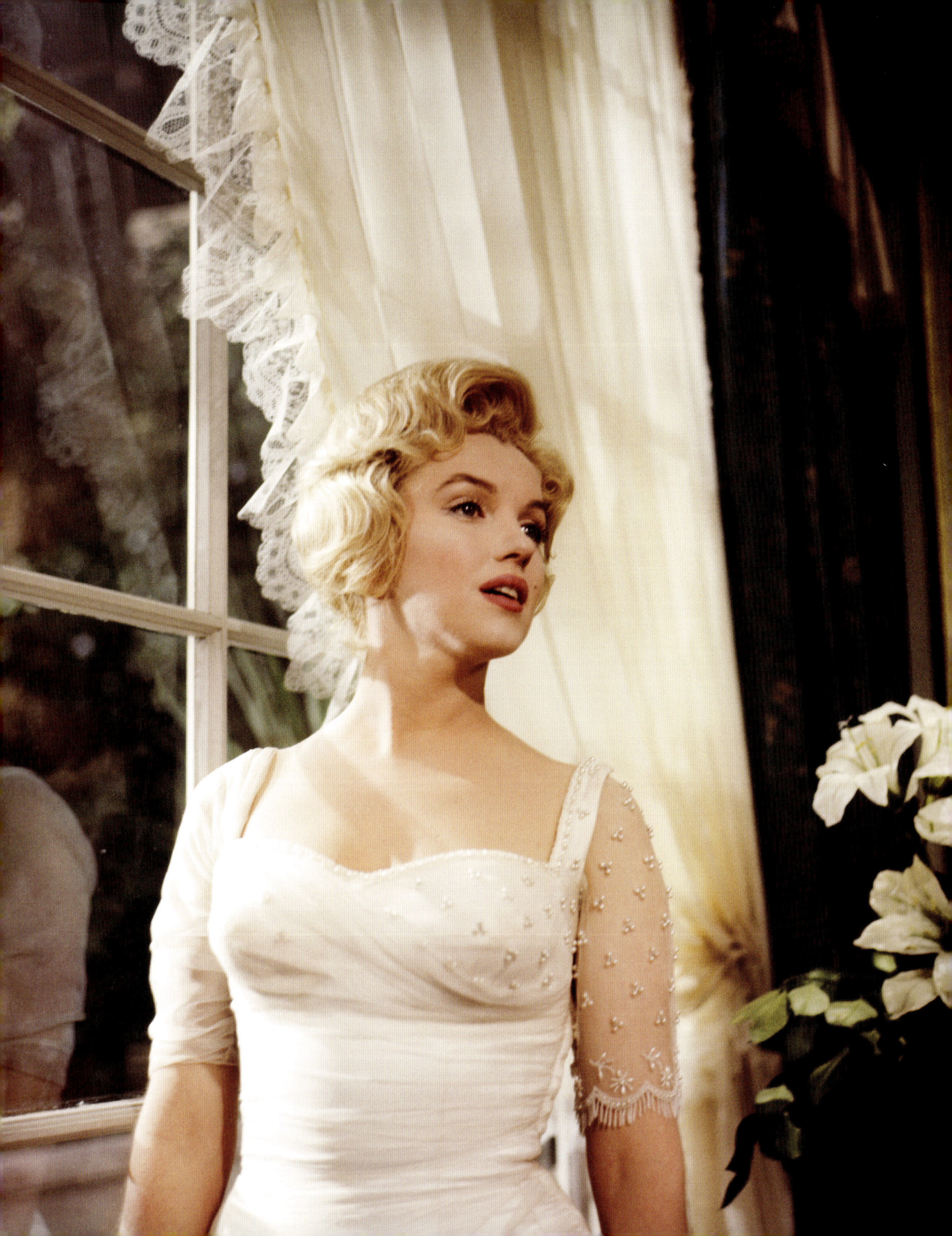

"It can be no news to anyone to say that she was difficult to work with. Her work frightened her, and although she had undoubted talent, I think she had a subconscious resistance to the exercise of being an actress. But she was intrigued by its mystique and happy as a child when being photographed; she managed all the business of stardom with uncanny, clever, apparent ease."

SIR LAURENCE OLIVIER
(Costar, *The Prince and the Showgirl*, 1957)

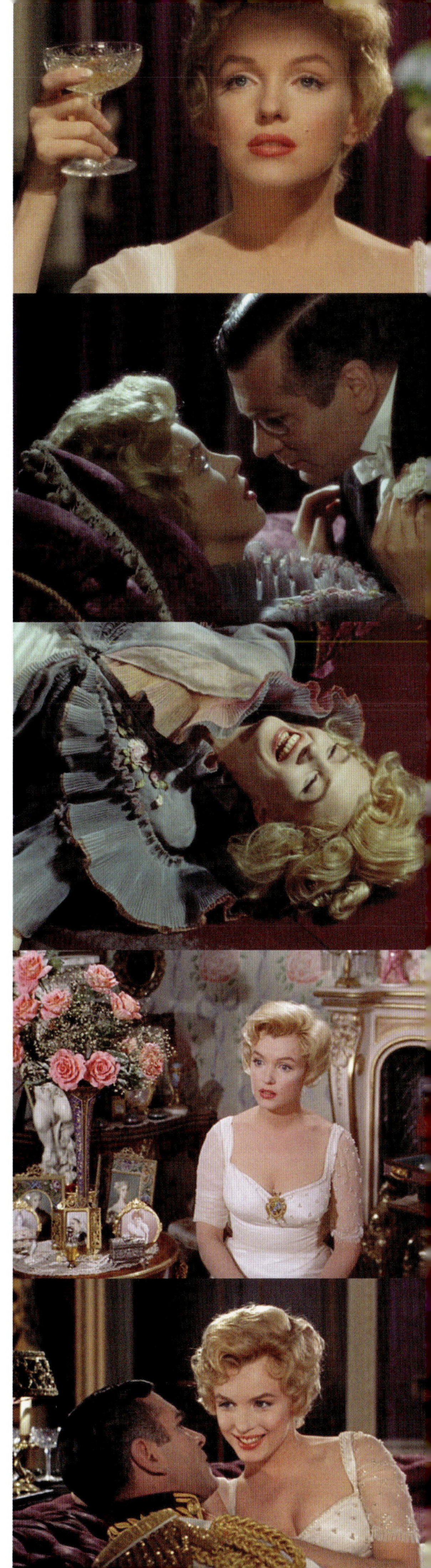

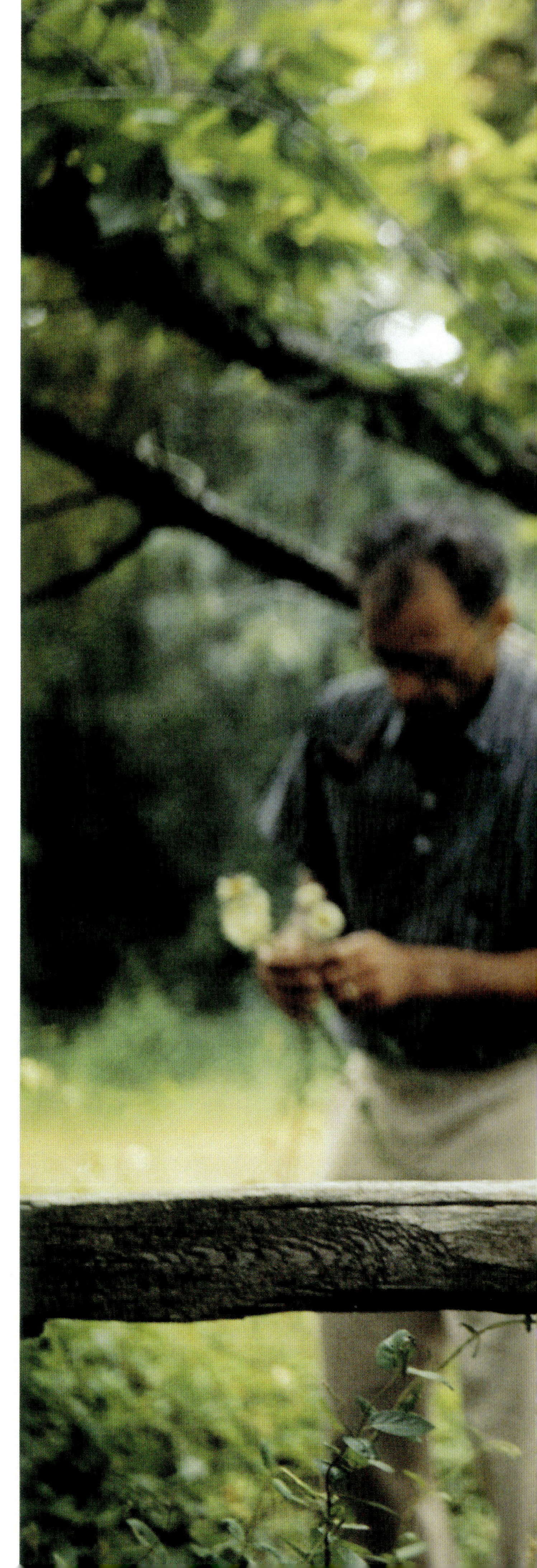

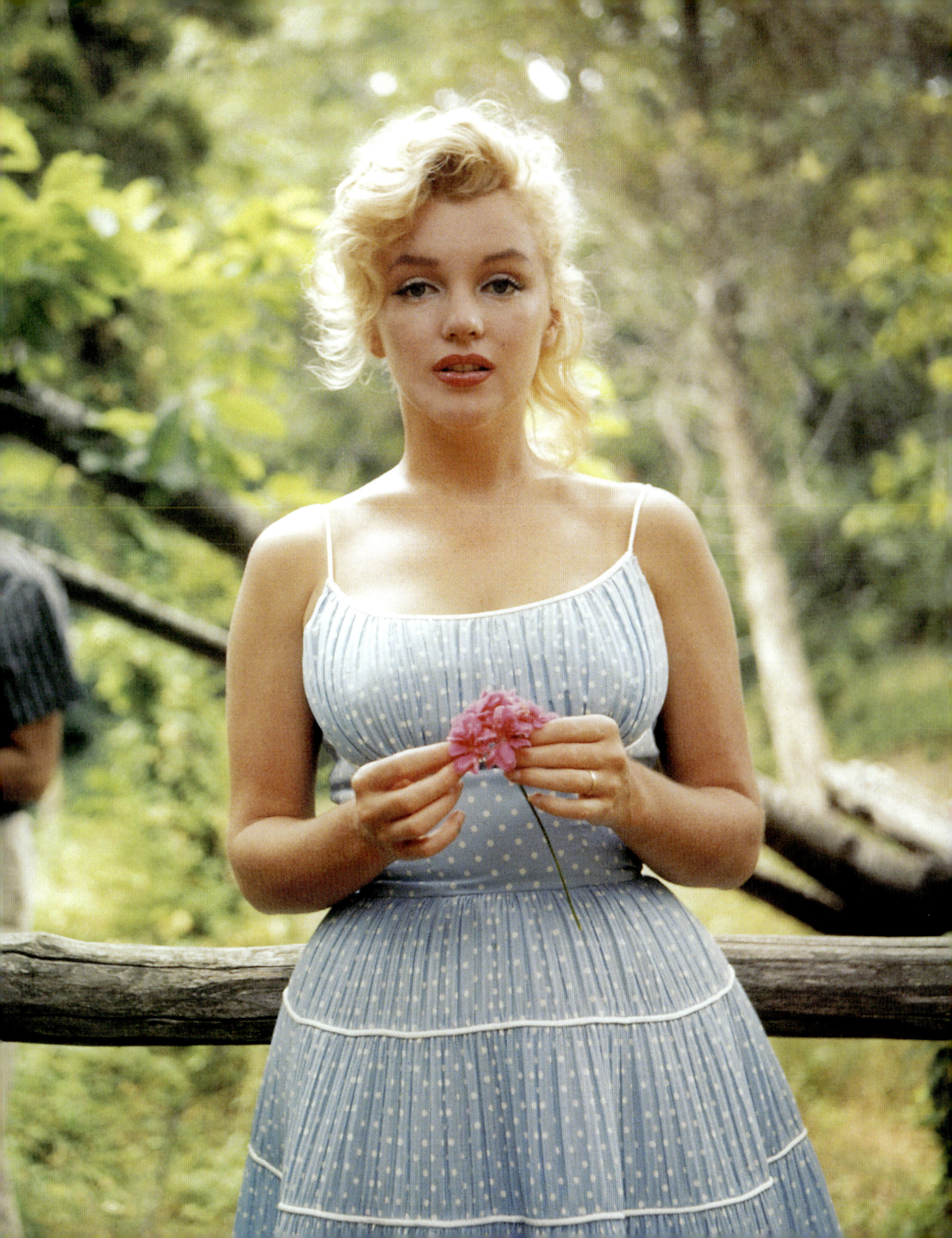

"There was no such person as Marilyn Monroe. Marilyn Monroe was an invention of hers. A genius invention that she created, like an author creates a character. ...She understood photography, and she also understood what makes a great photograph. She related to it as if she were giving a performance. She gave more to the still camera than any actress—any woman—I've ever photographed."

RICHARD AVEDON

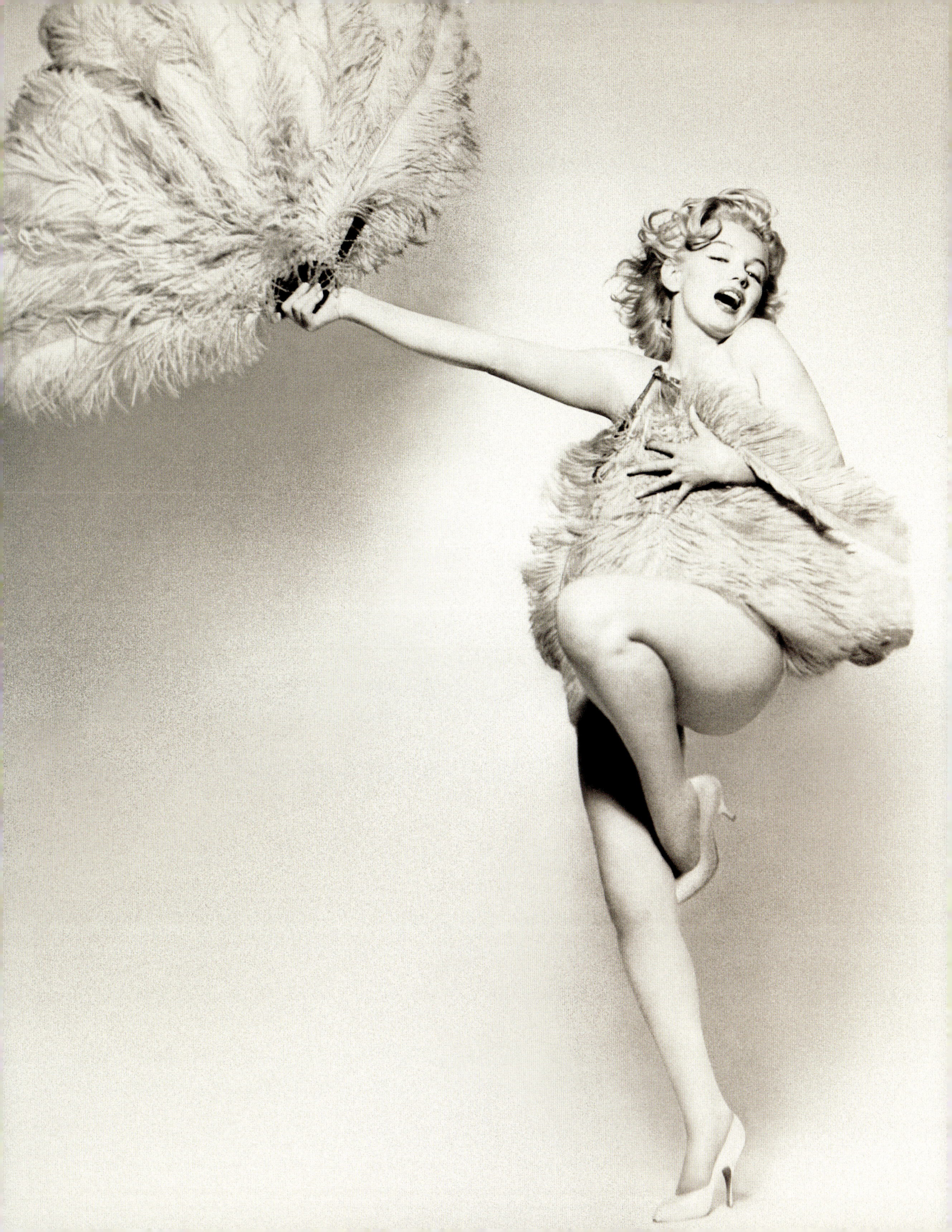

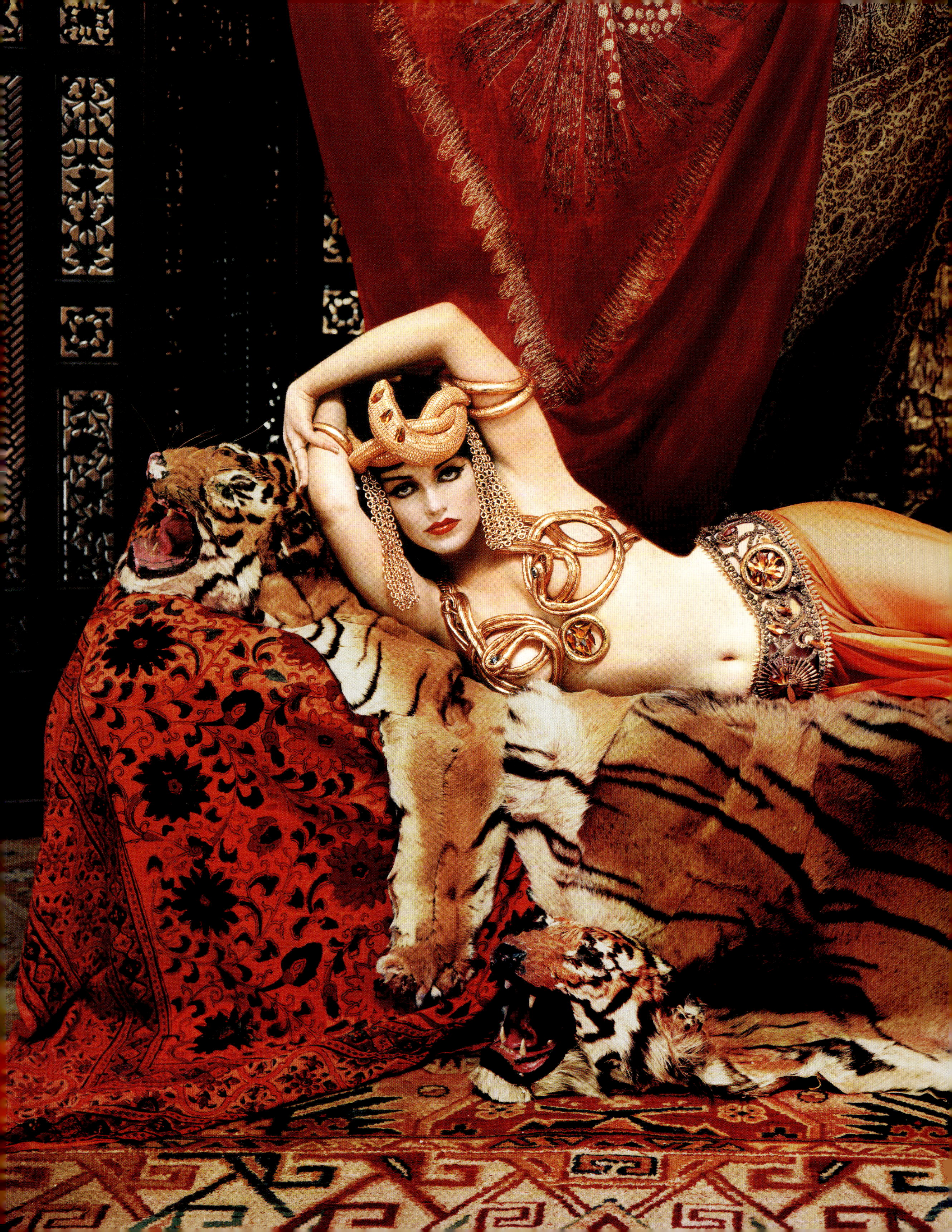

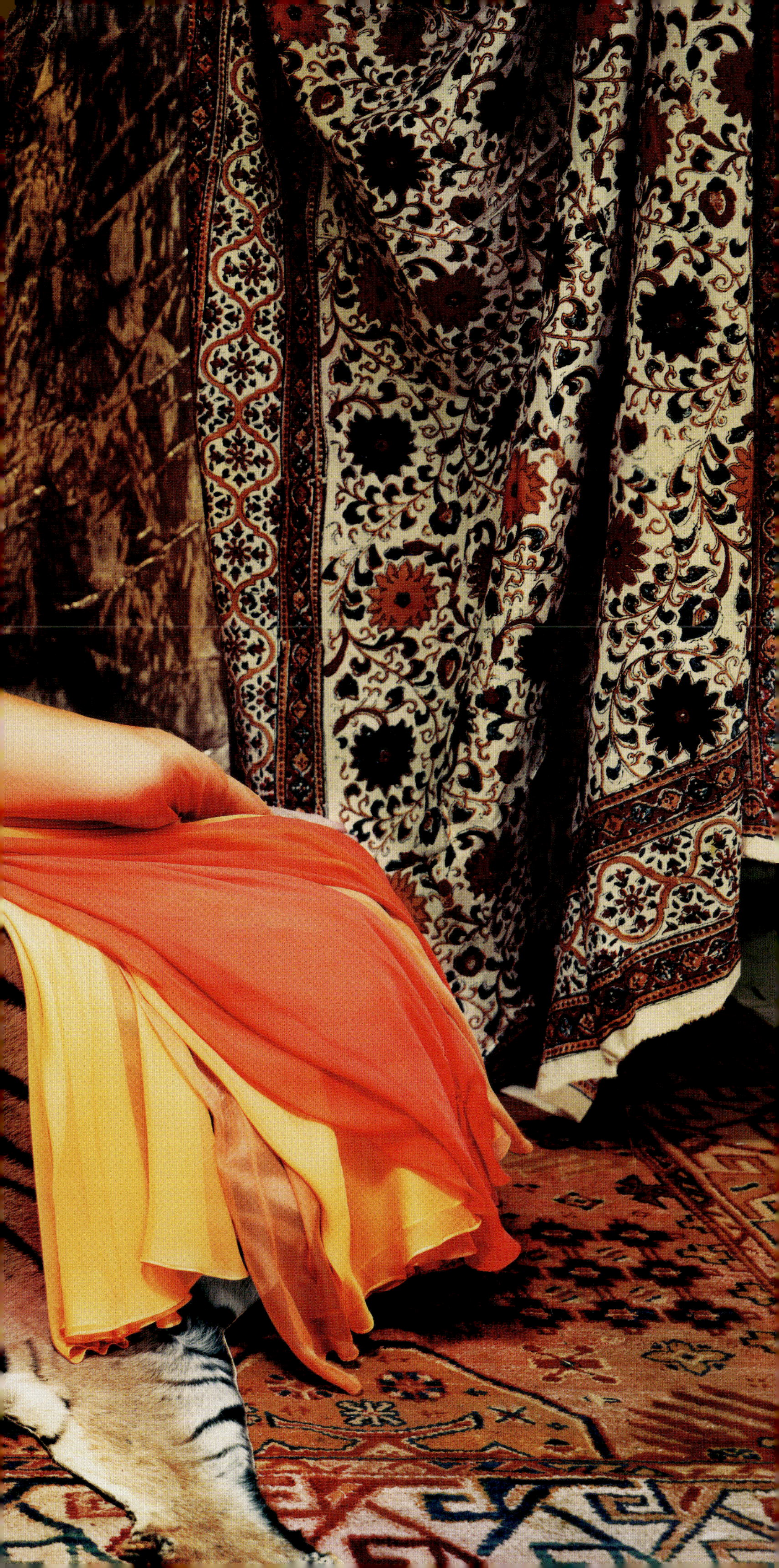

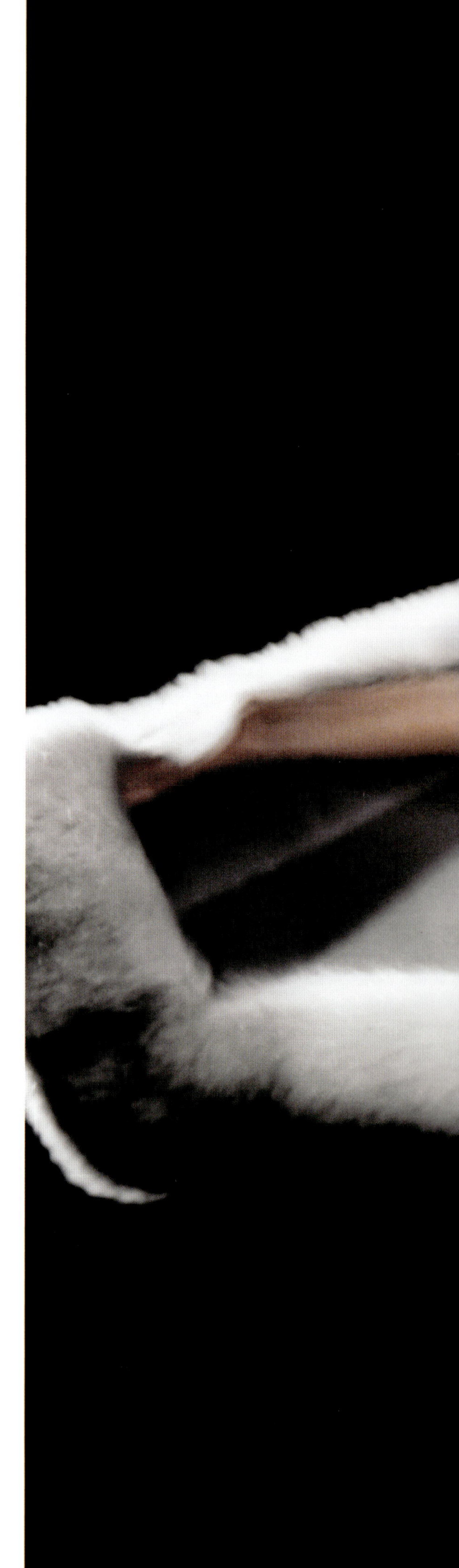

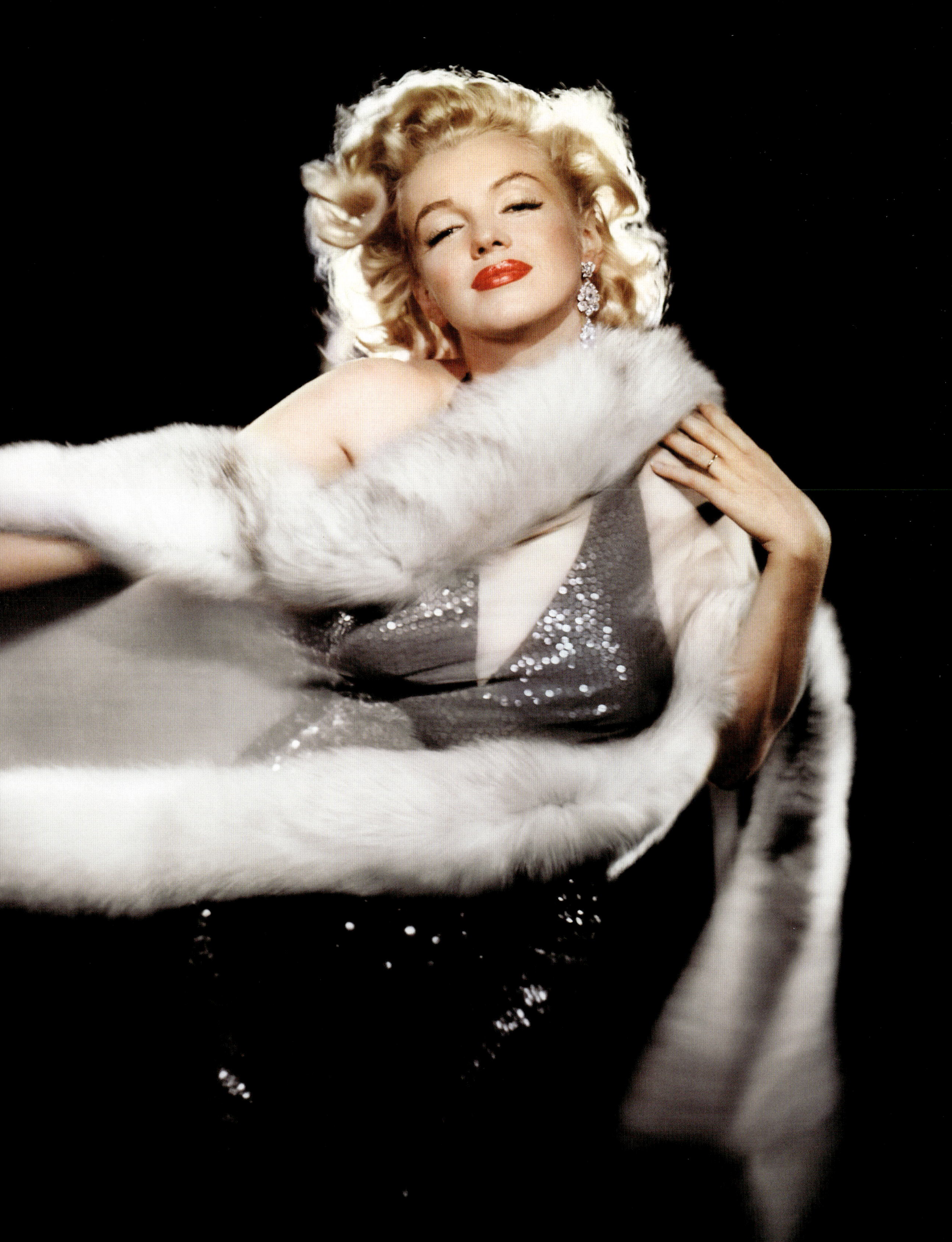

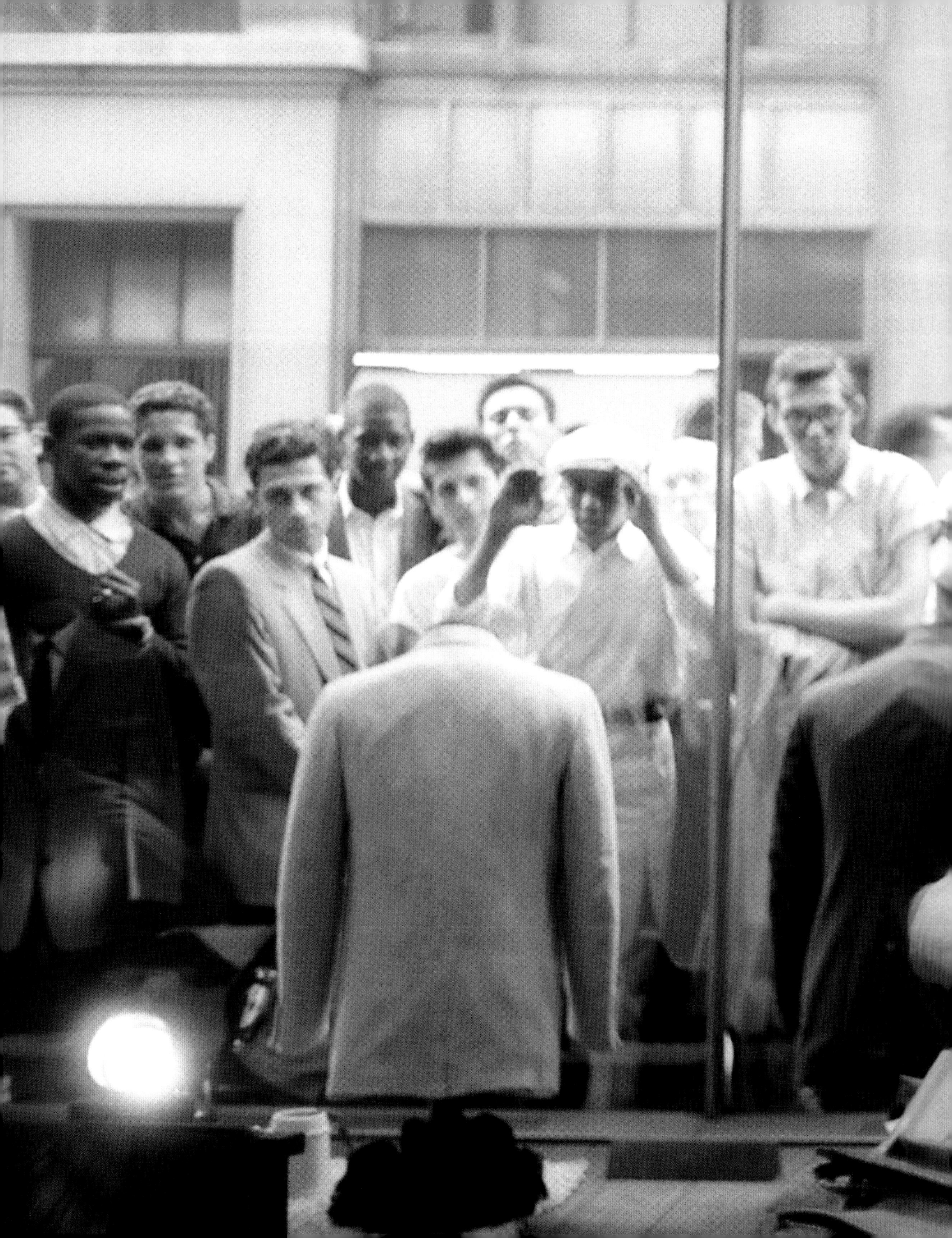

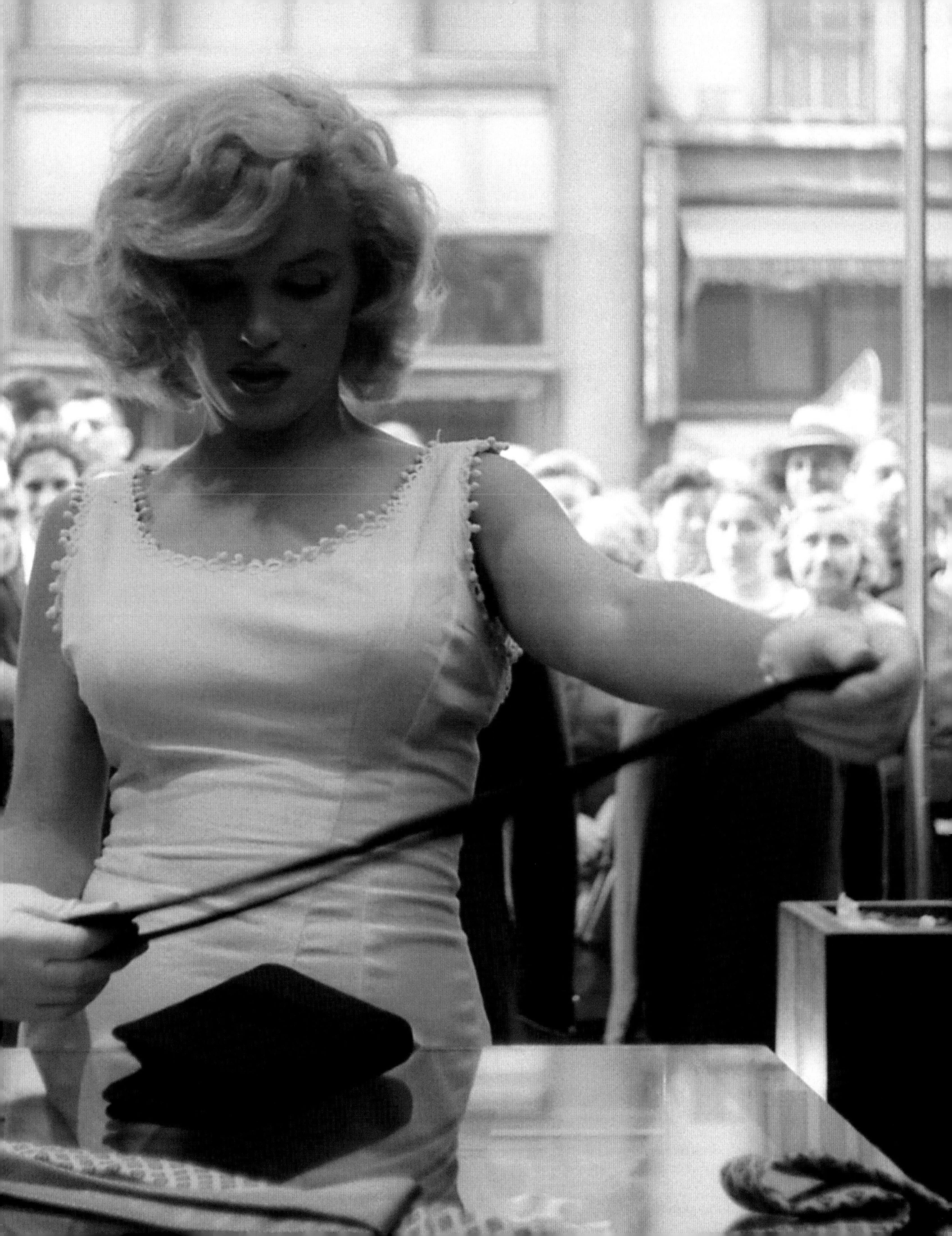

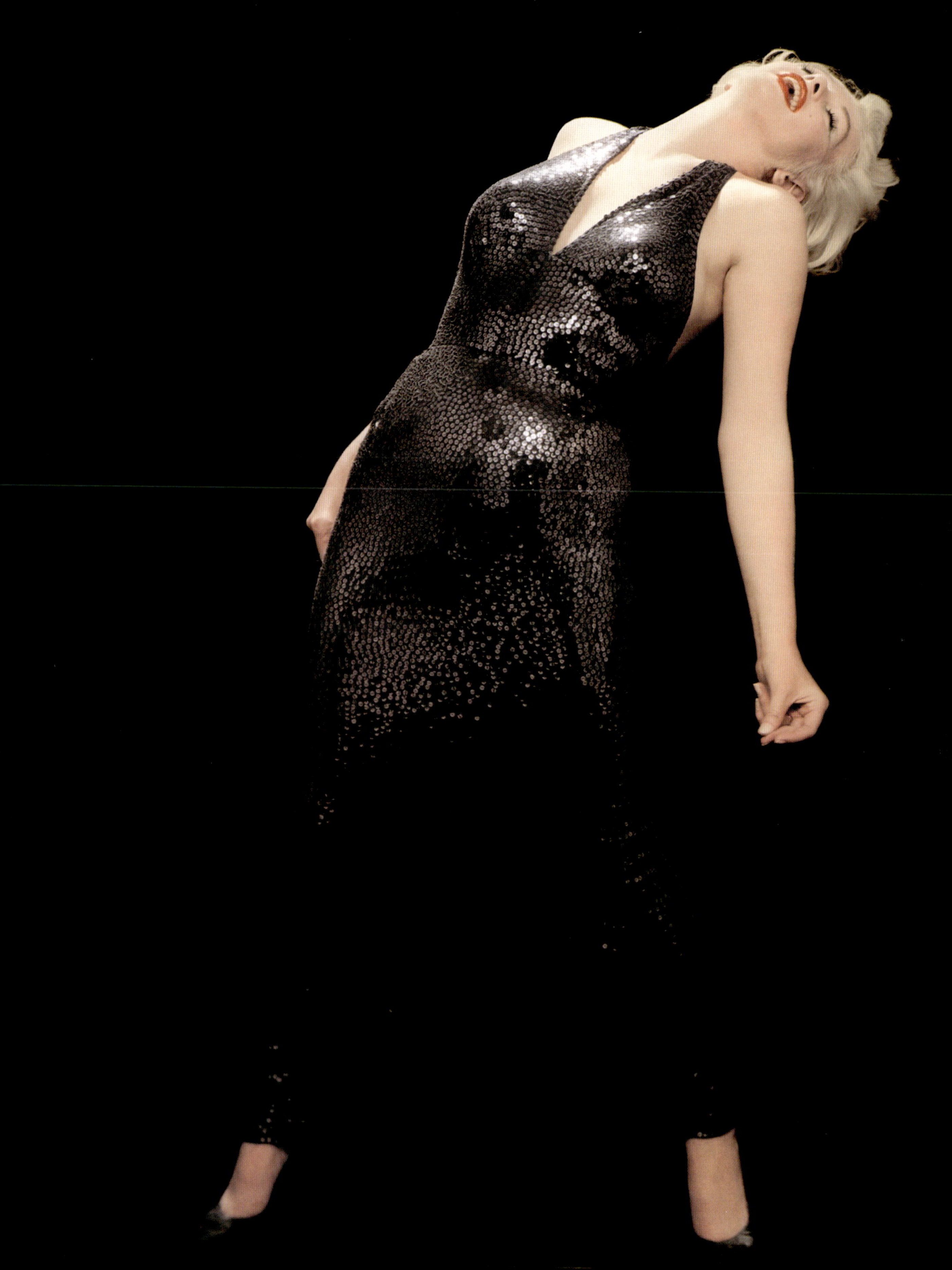

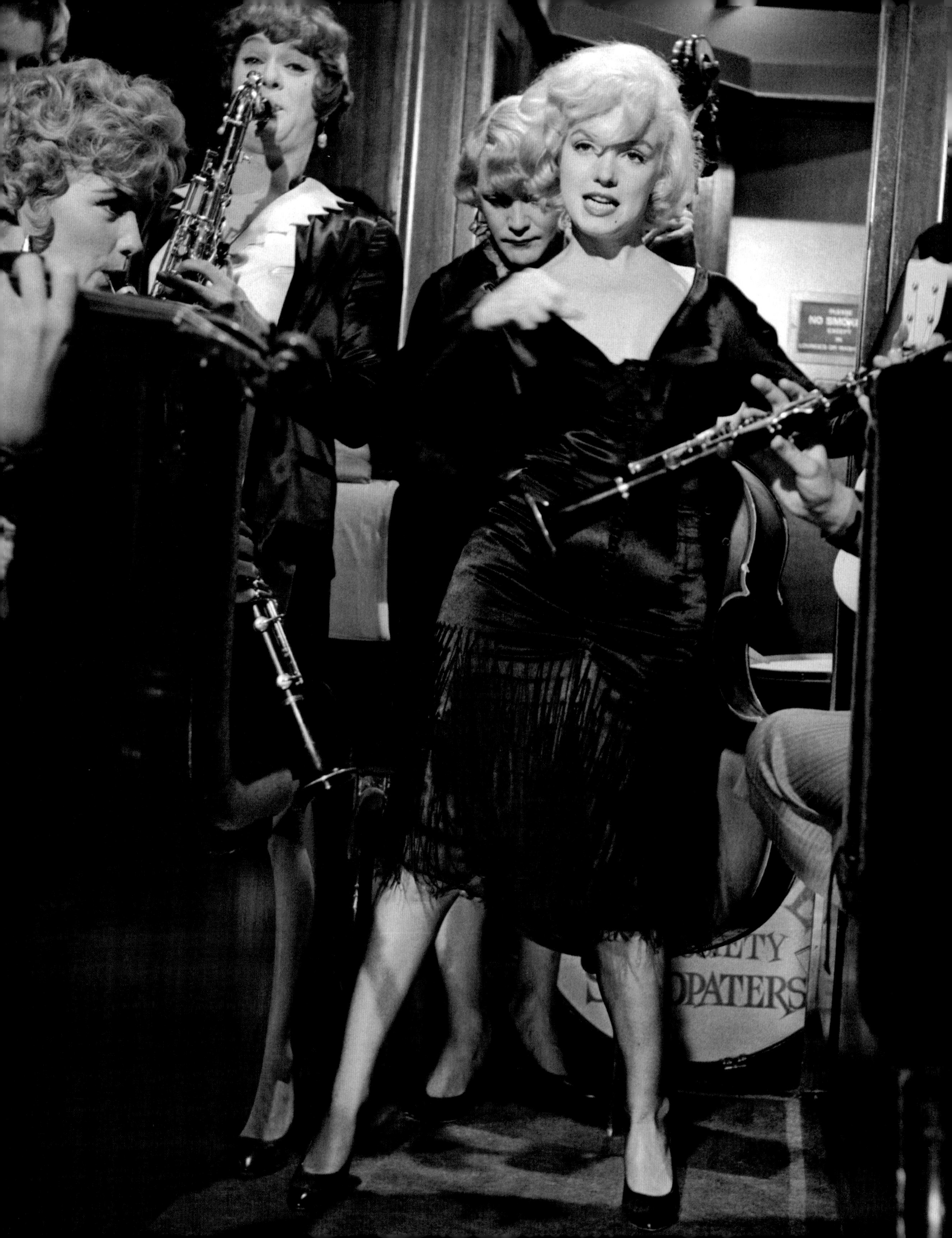

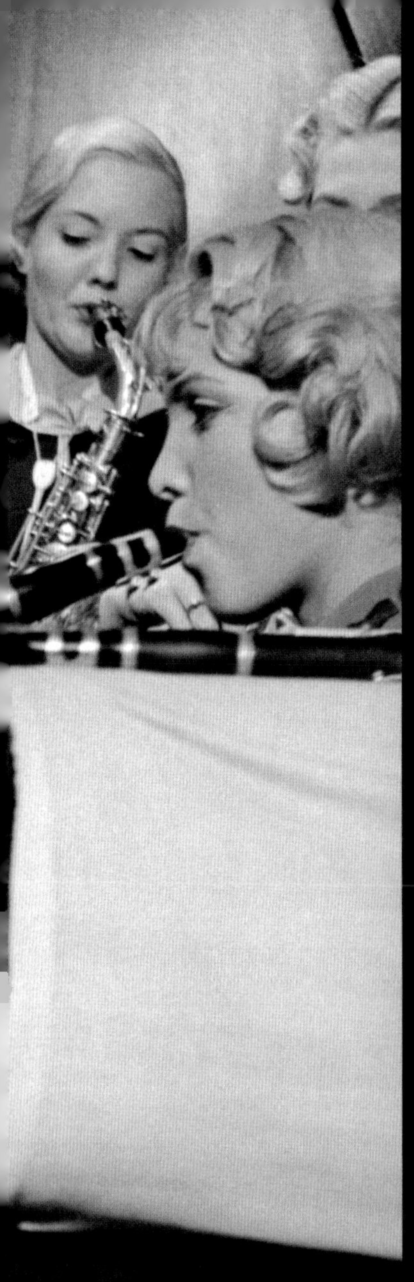

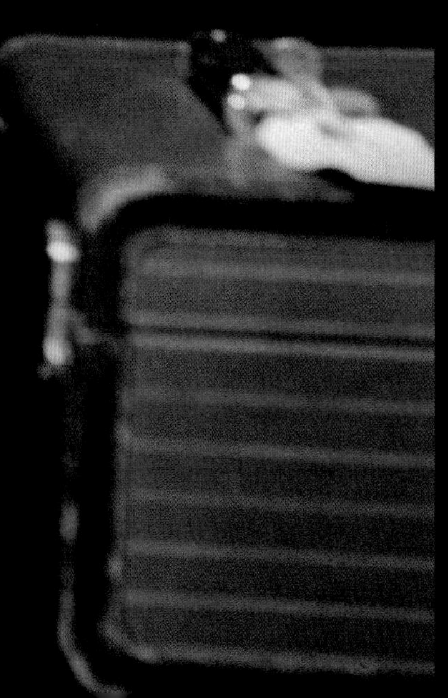

"Look at that! Look how she moves! That's just like Jell-O on springs. She must have some sort of built-in motor or something."

JACK LEMMON as "Josephine"
(Costar, *Some Like It Hot*, 1959)

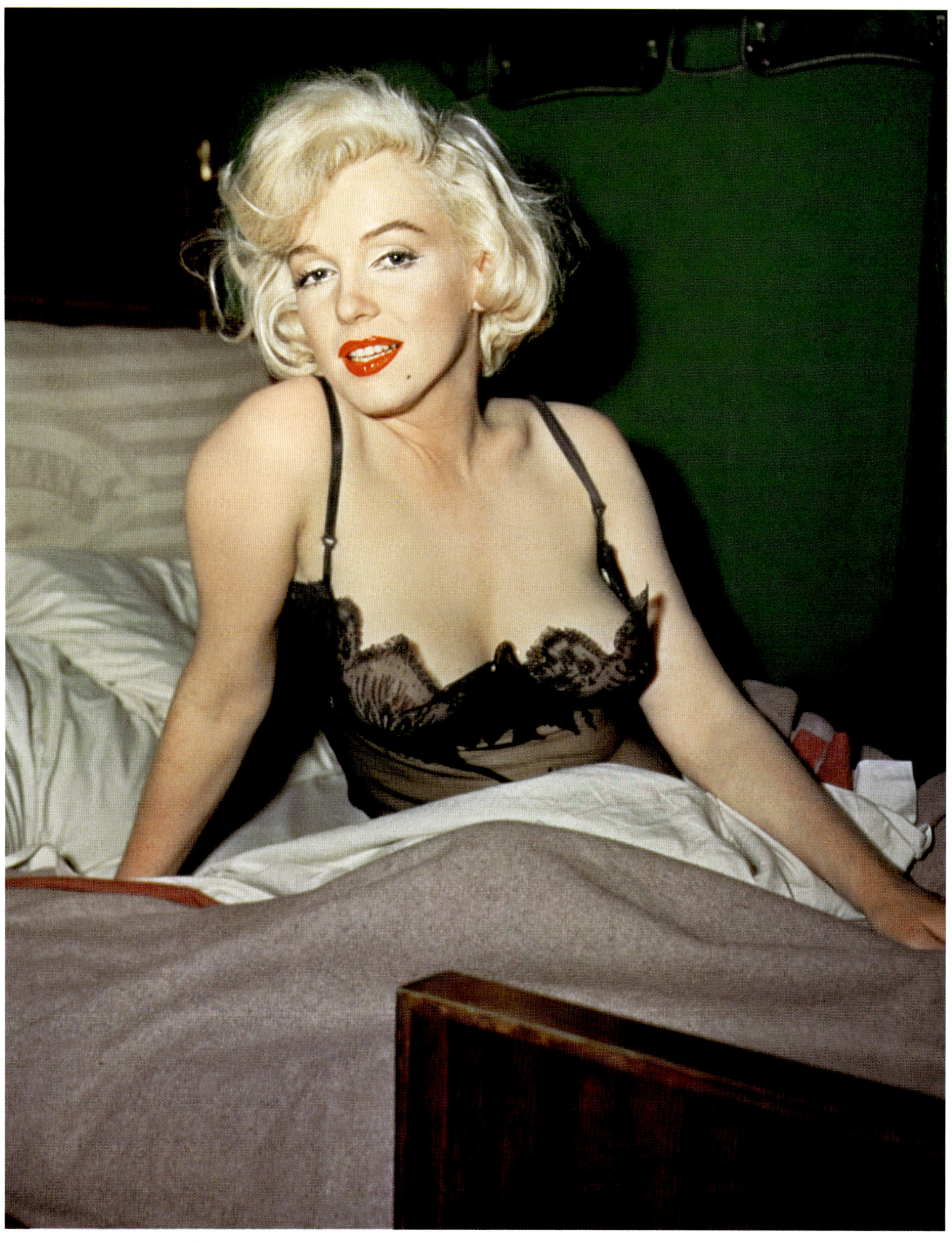

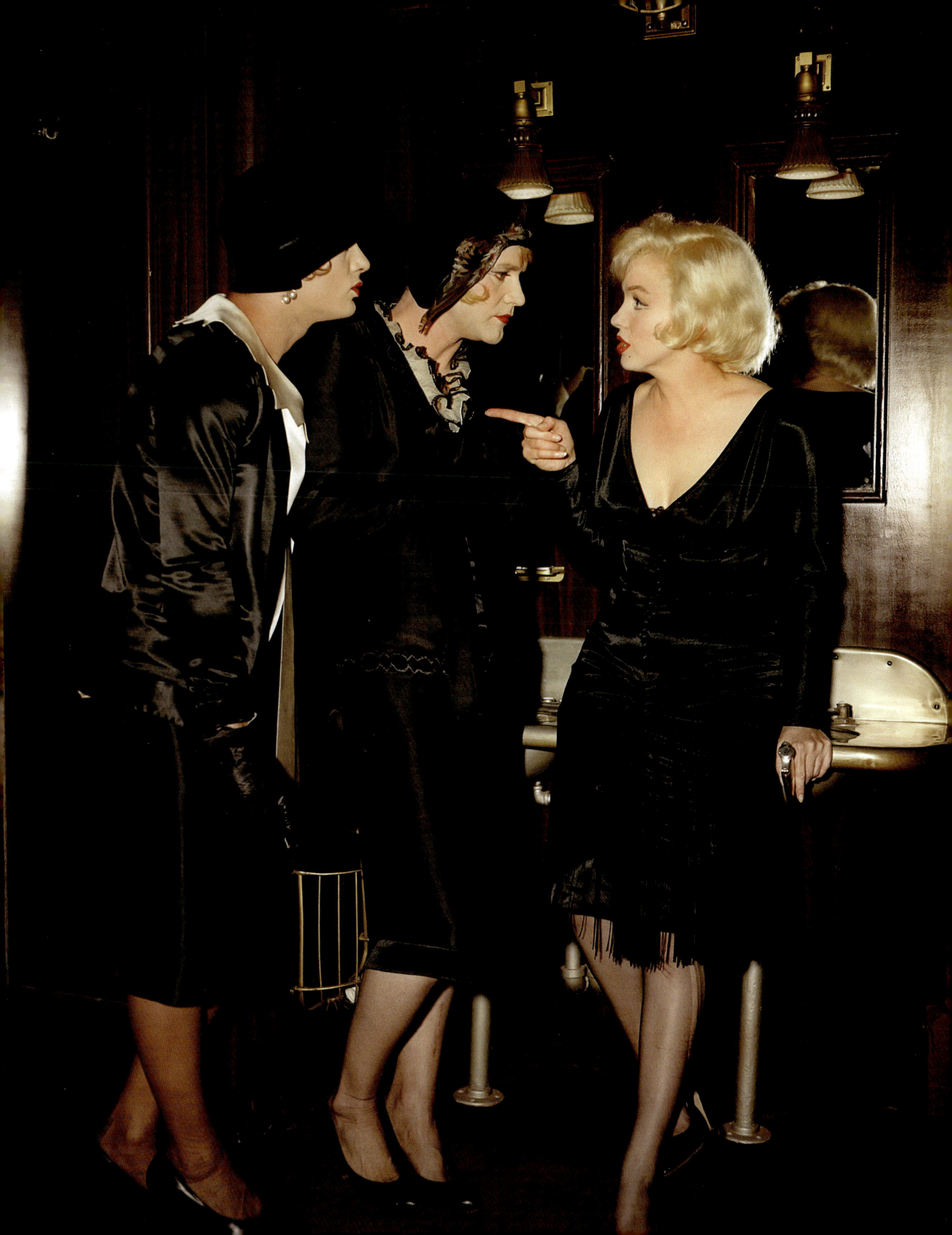

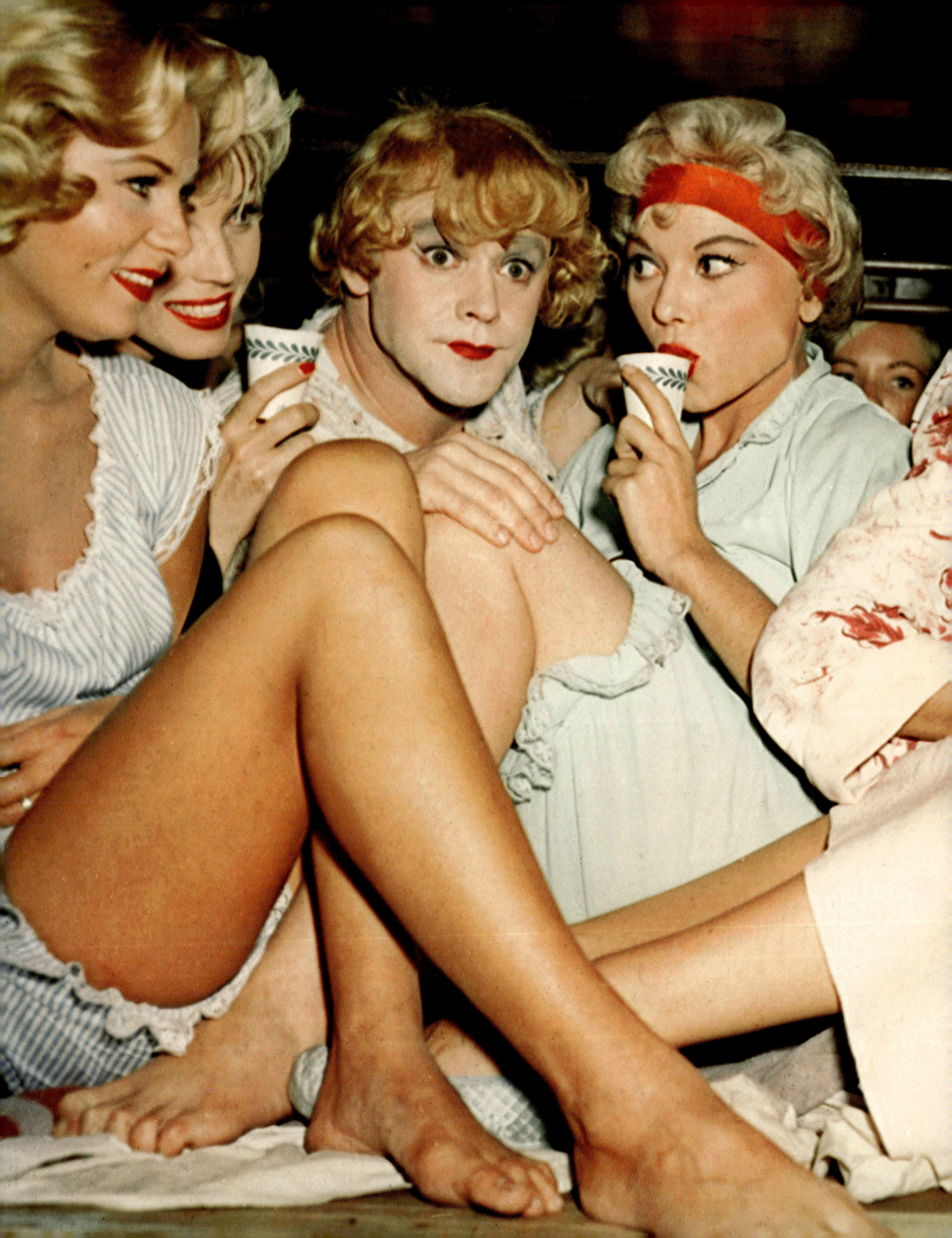

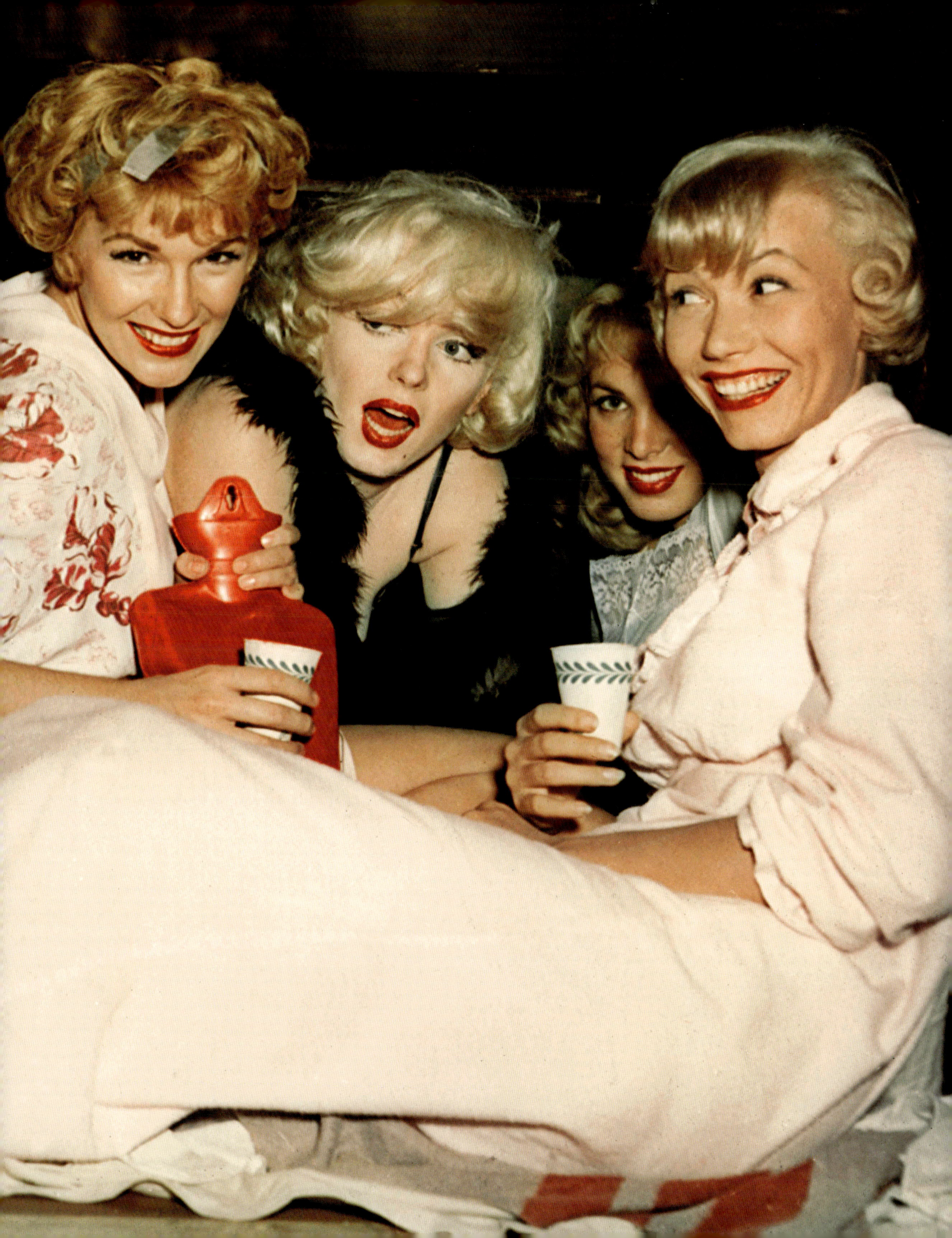

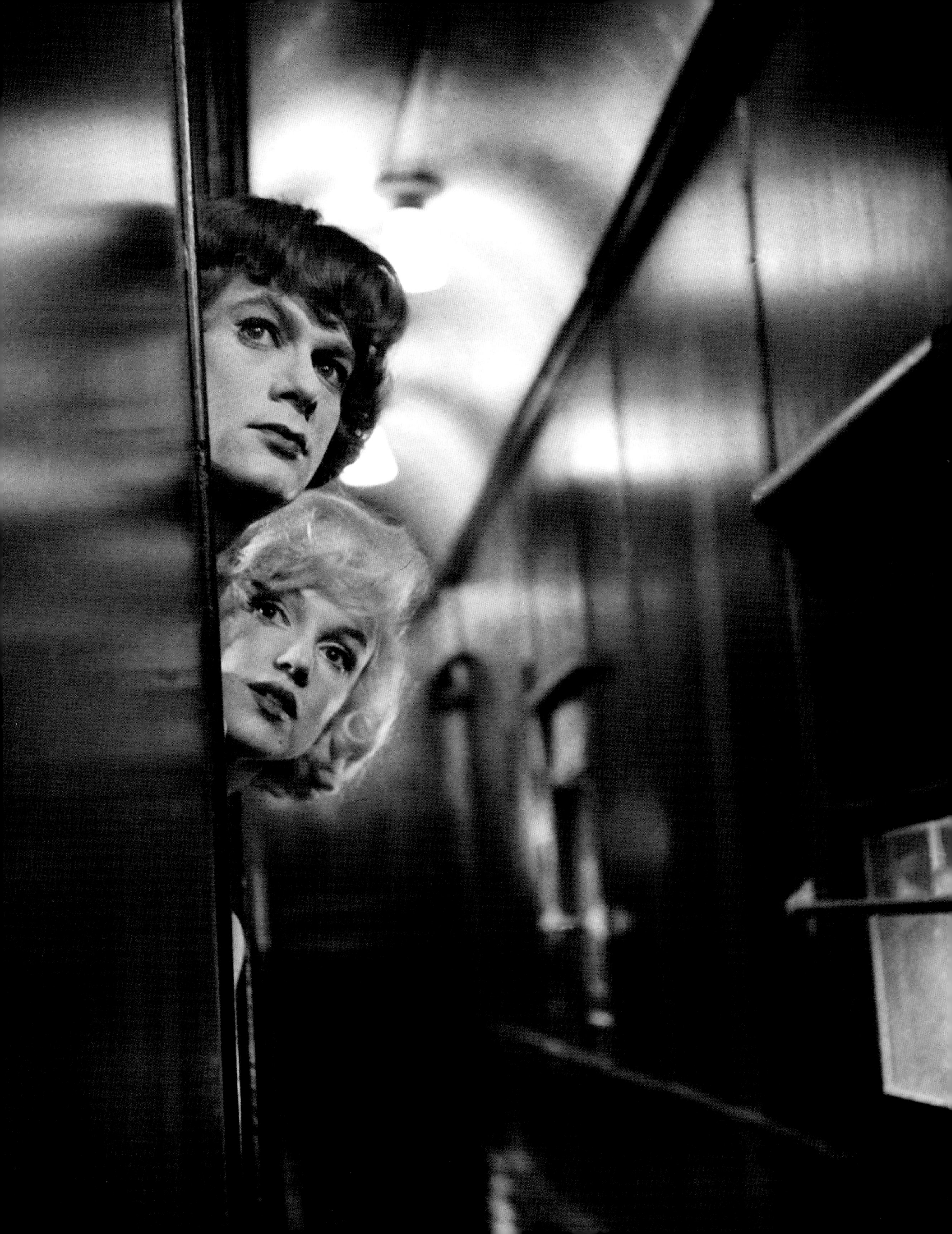

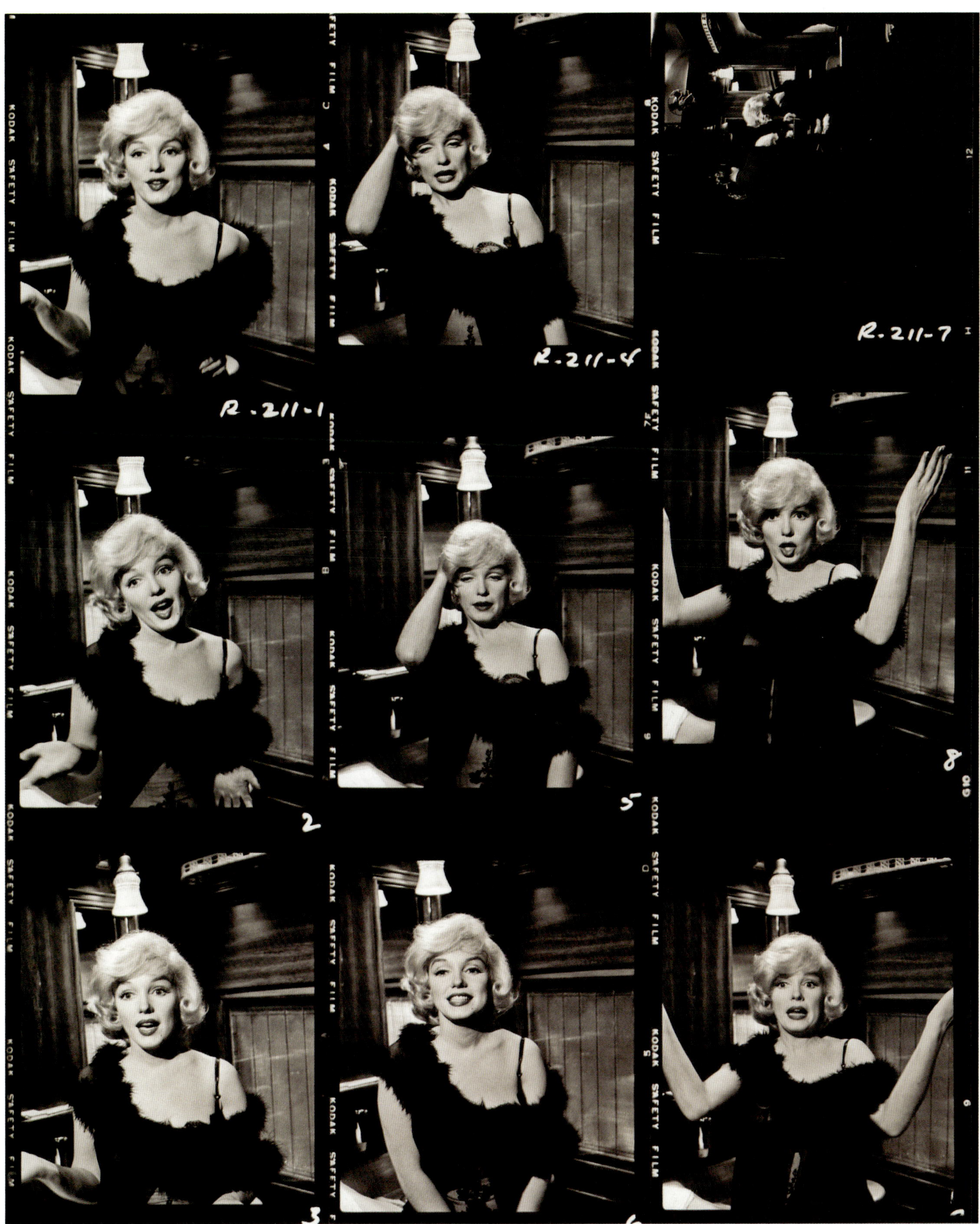
R-211-1
R-211-4
R-211-7
2
5
8
3

"She was a wonderful comedienne, and she had a charisma like no one before or since. . . . Marilyn had kind of a built-in alarm system. It would 'go off' in the middle of a scene if that scene was not right for her, and she would just stop everything. She would stand there with her eyes closed, biting her lip, and kind of wringing her hands until she had worked it out. Now this sounds like selfishness. . . . But she didn't mean to be selfish—it was the only way she could work. I didn't necessarily approve of that tactic; it was not easy working with her, but it was fascinating."

JACK LEMMON (Costar, *Some Like It Hot*, 1959)

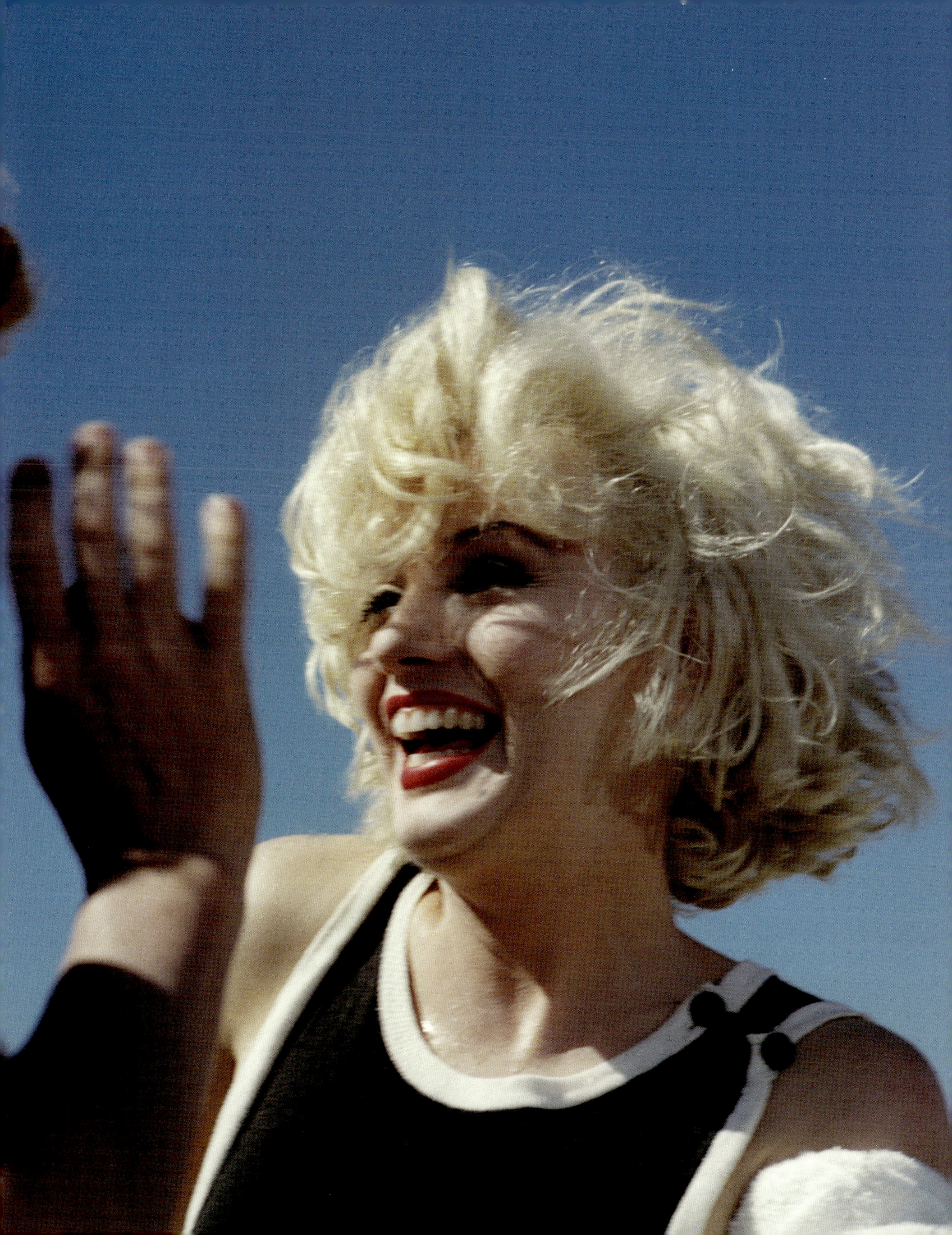

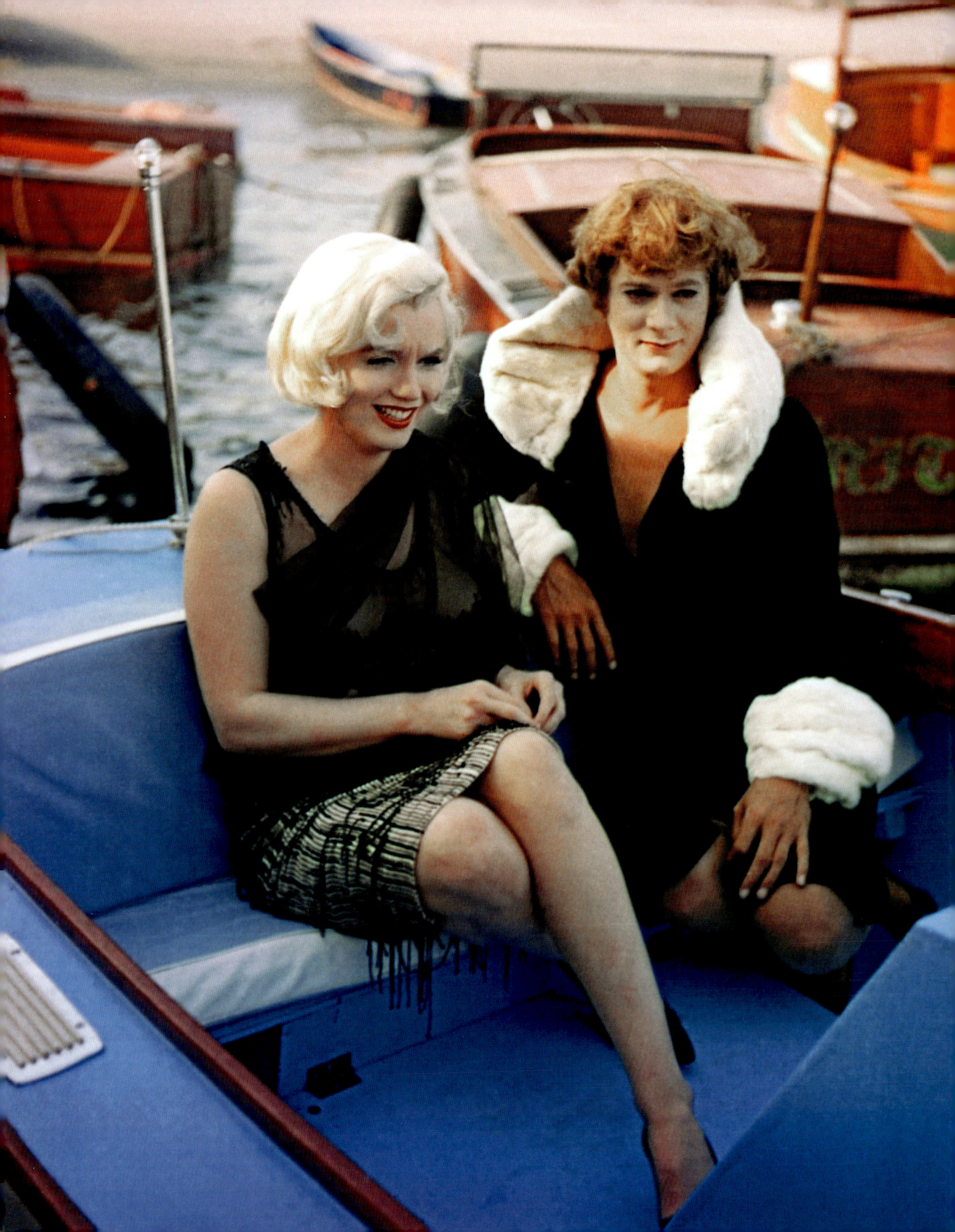

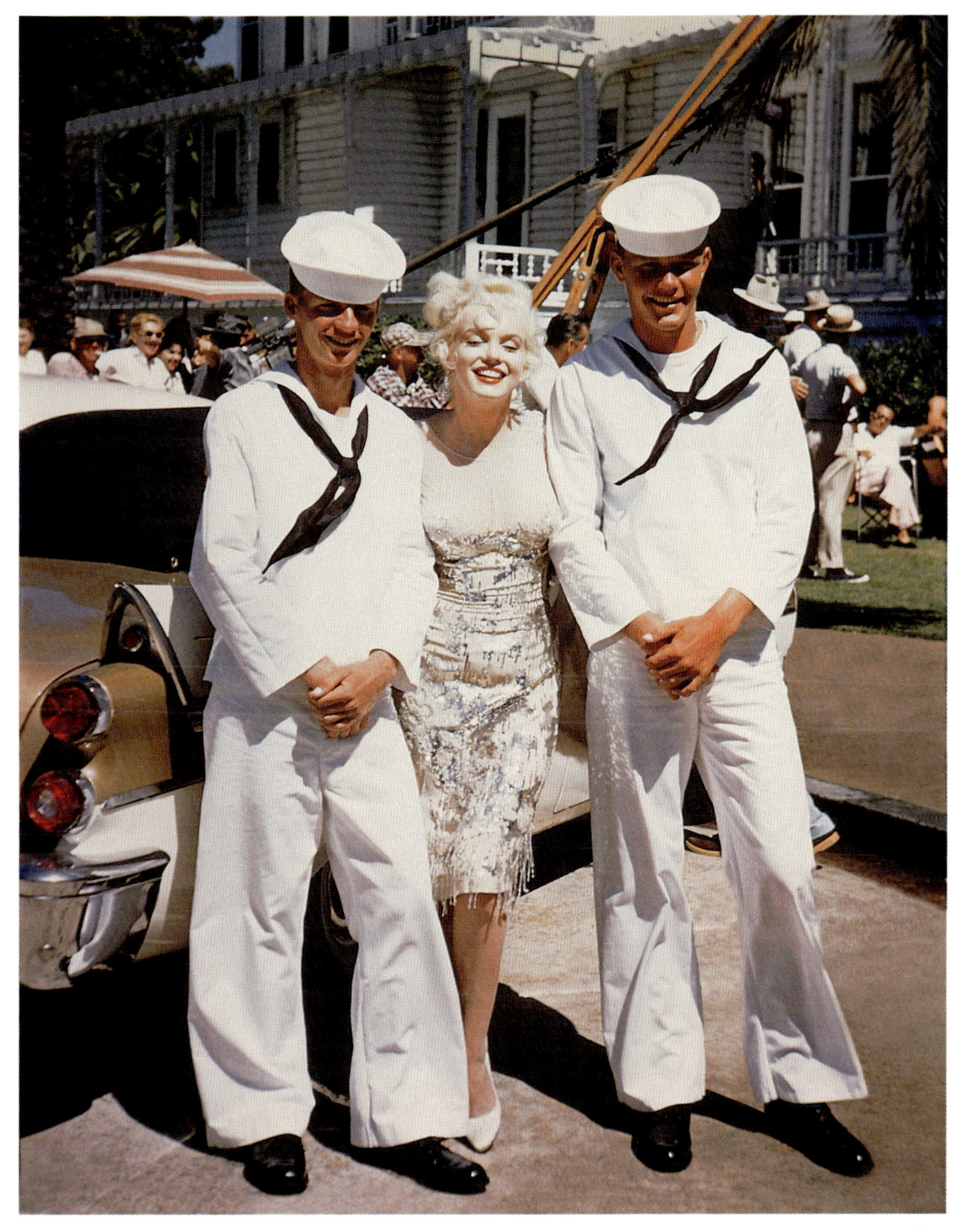

"To coin a phrase, Marilyn has never looked better. Her performance as 'Sugar,' the fuzzy blonde who likes saxophone players and men with glasses, has a deliciously naive quality. She's a comedienne with that combination of sex appeal and timing that just can't be beat."

VARIETY

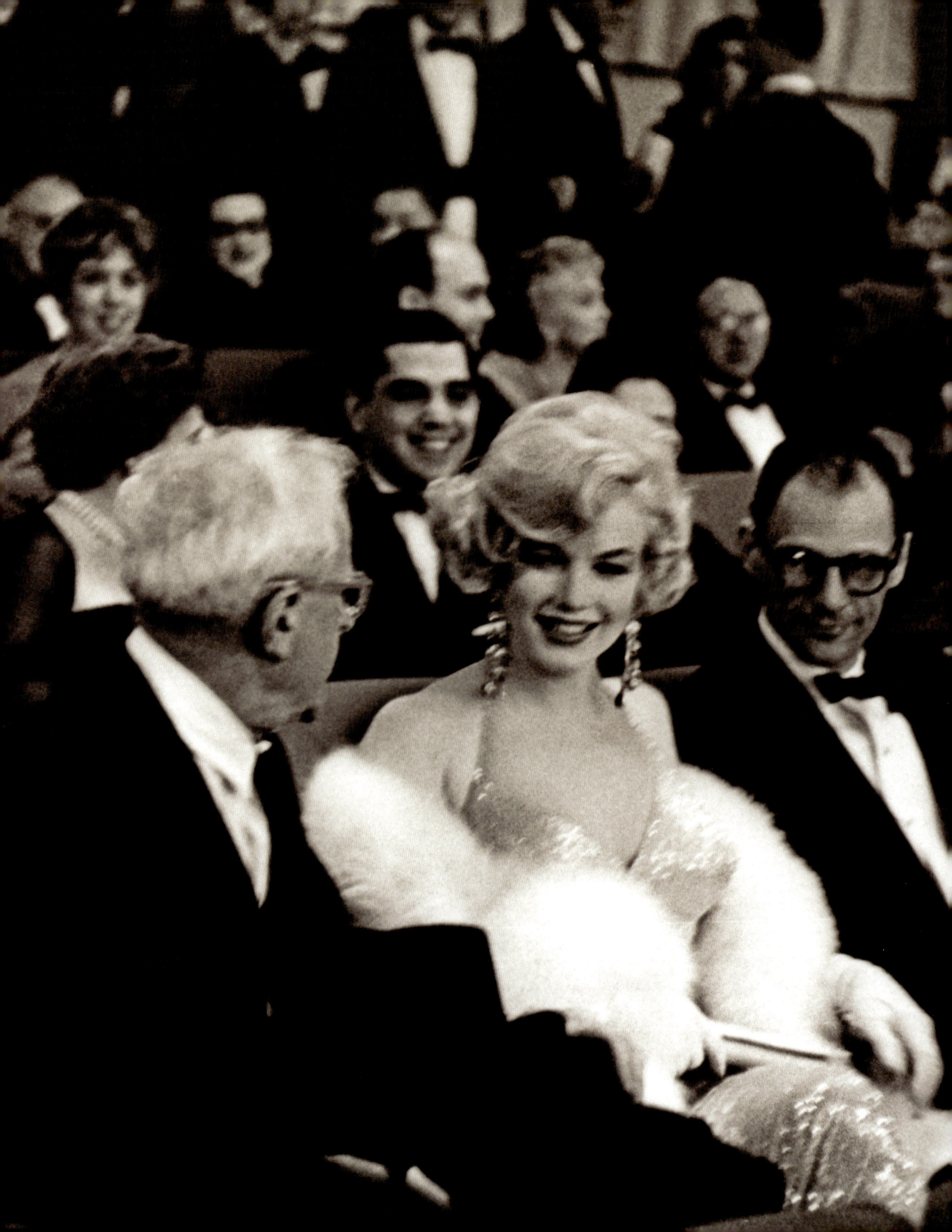

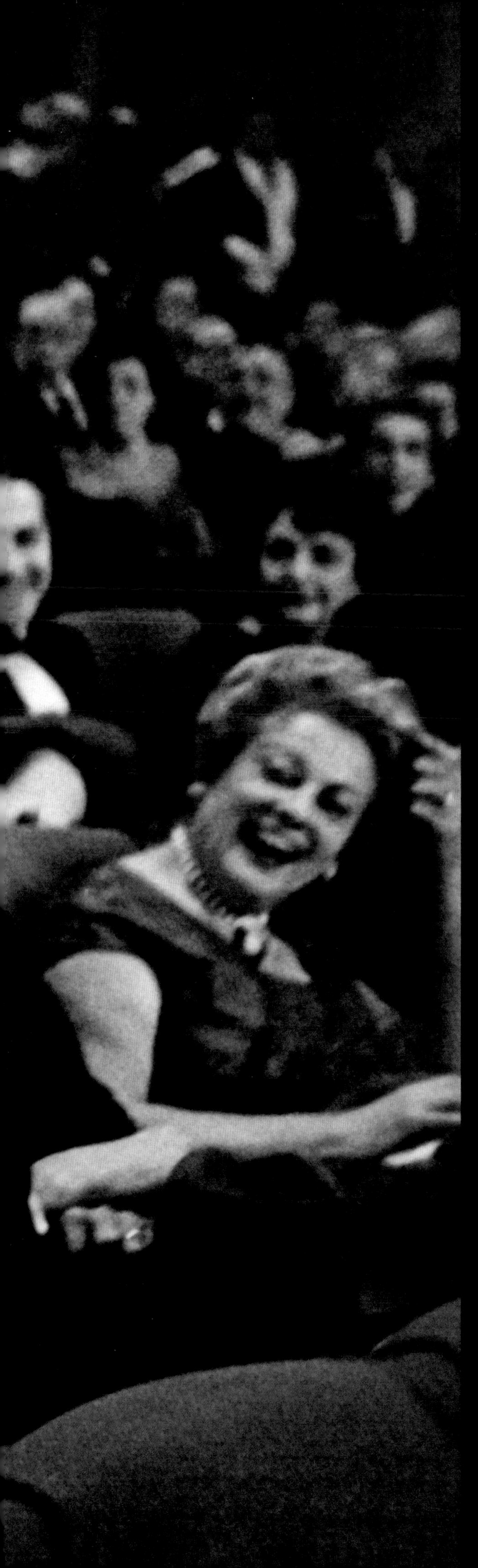

"It's a nice sensation to please an audience."

MARILYN MONROE

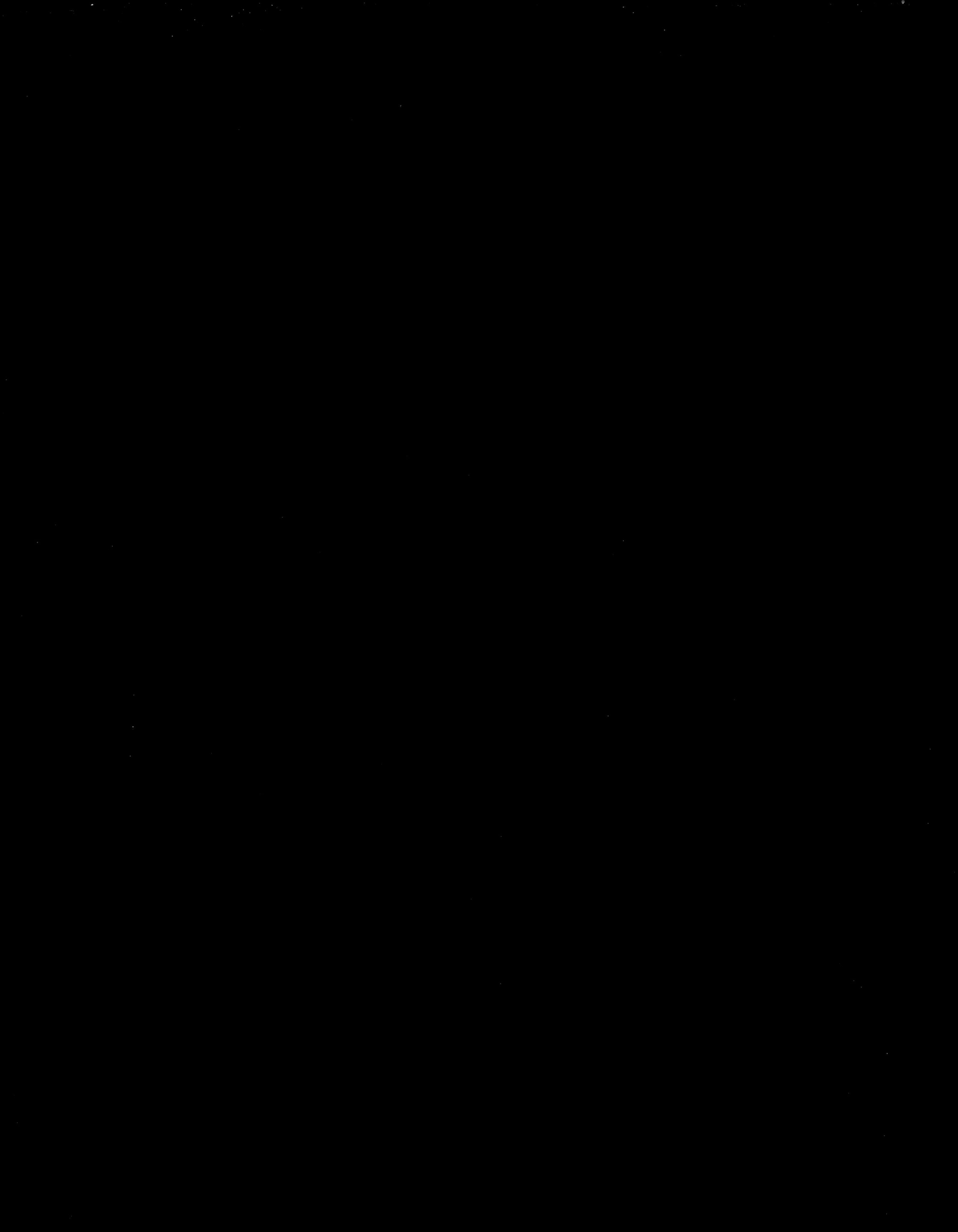

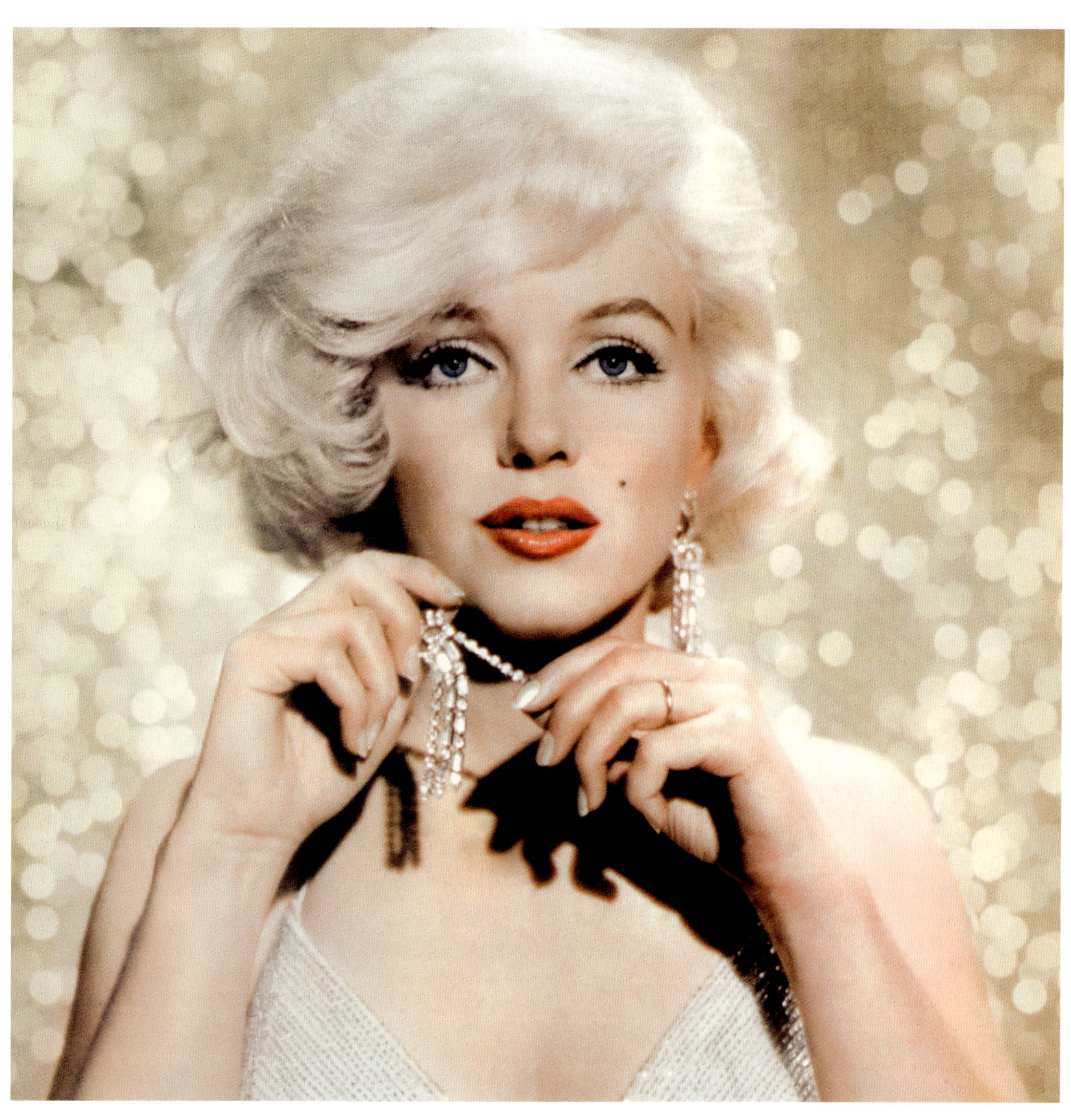

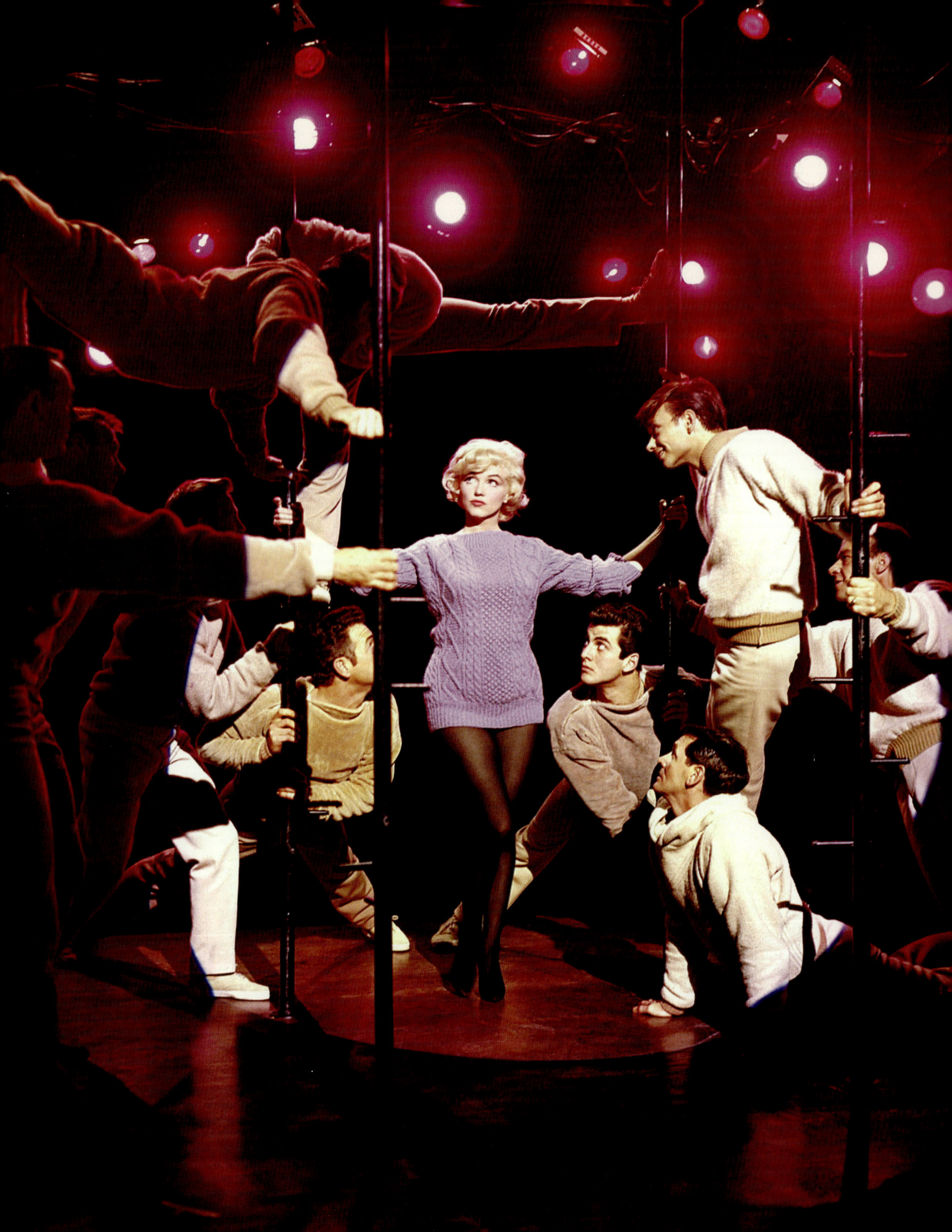

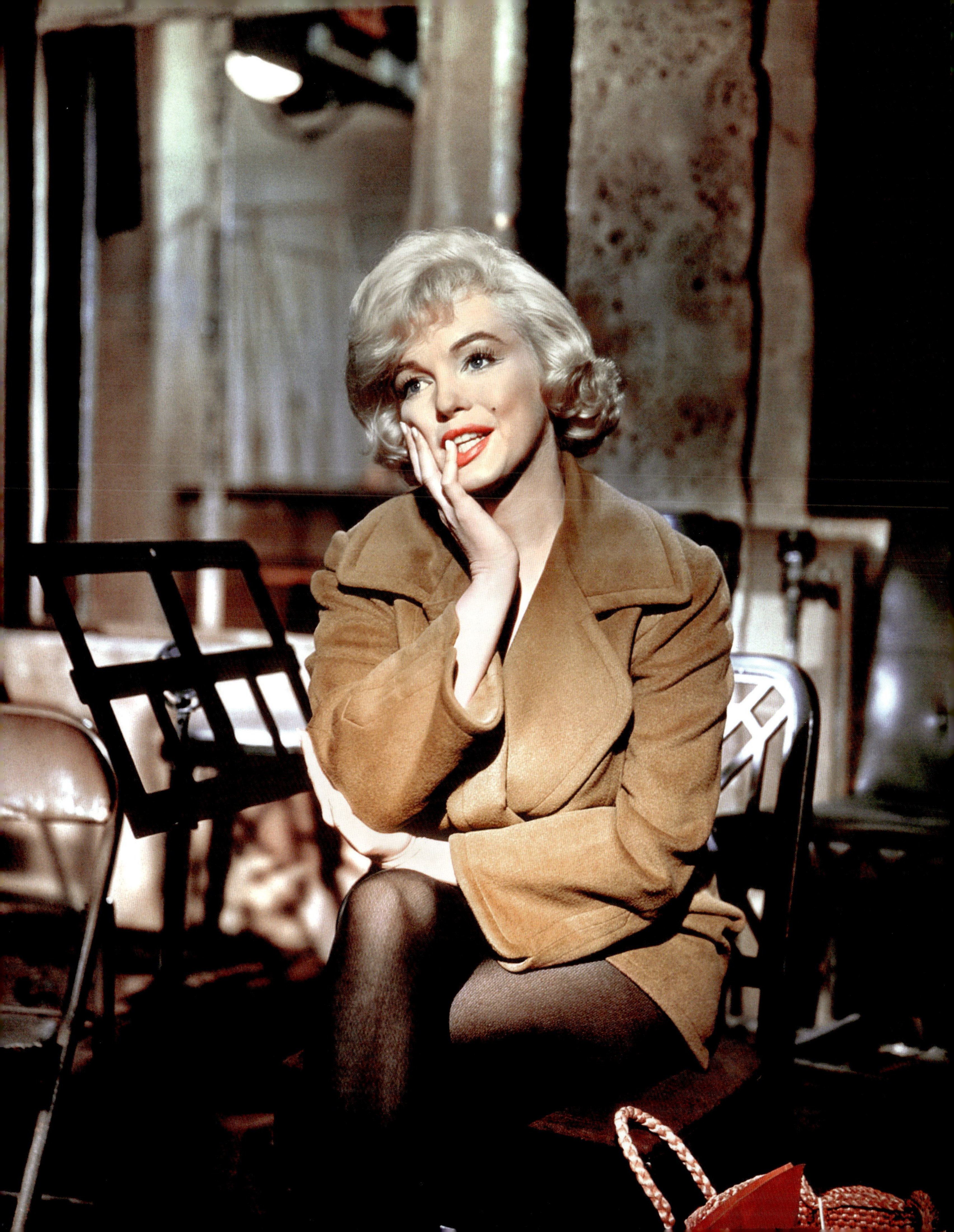

"She went right down into her own personal experience for everything, reached down and pulled something out of herself that was unique and extraordinary. She had no techniques. It was all the truth, it was only Marilyn."

JOHN HUSTON (Director, *The Misfits*, 1961)

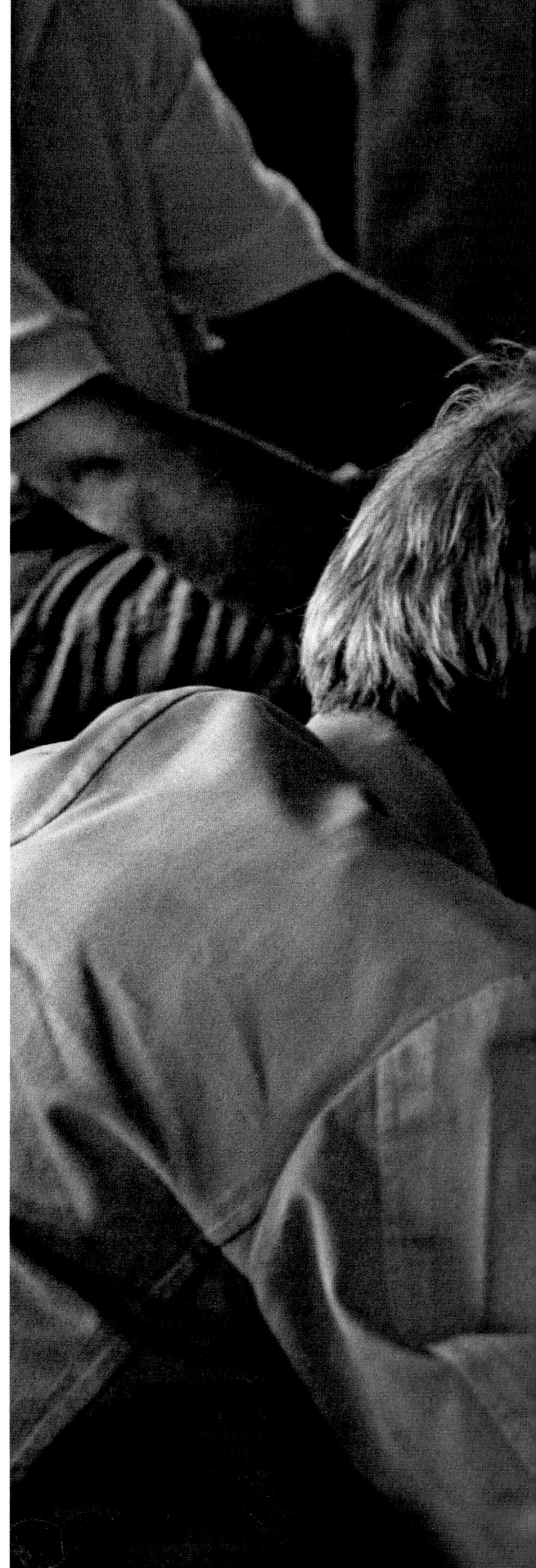

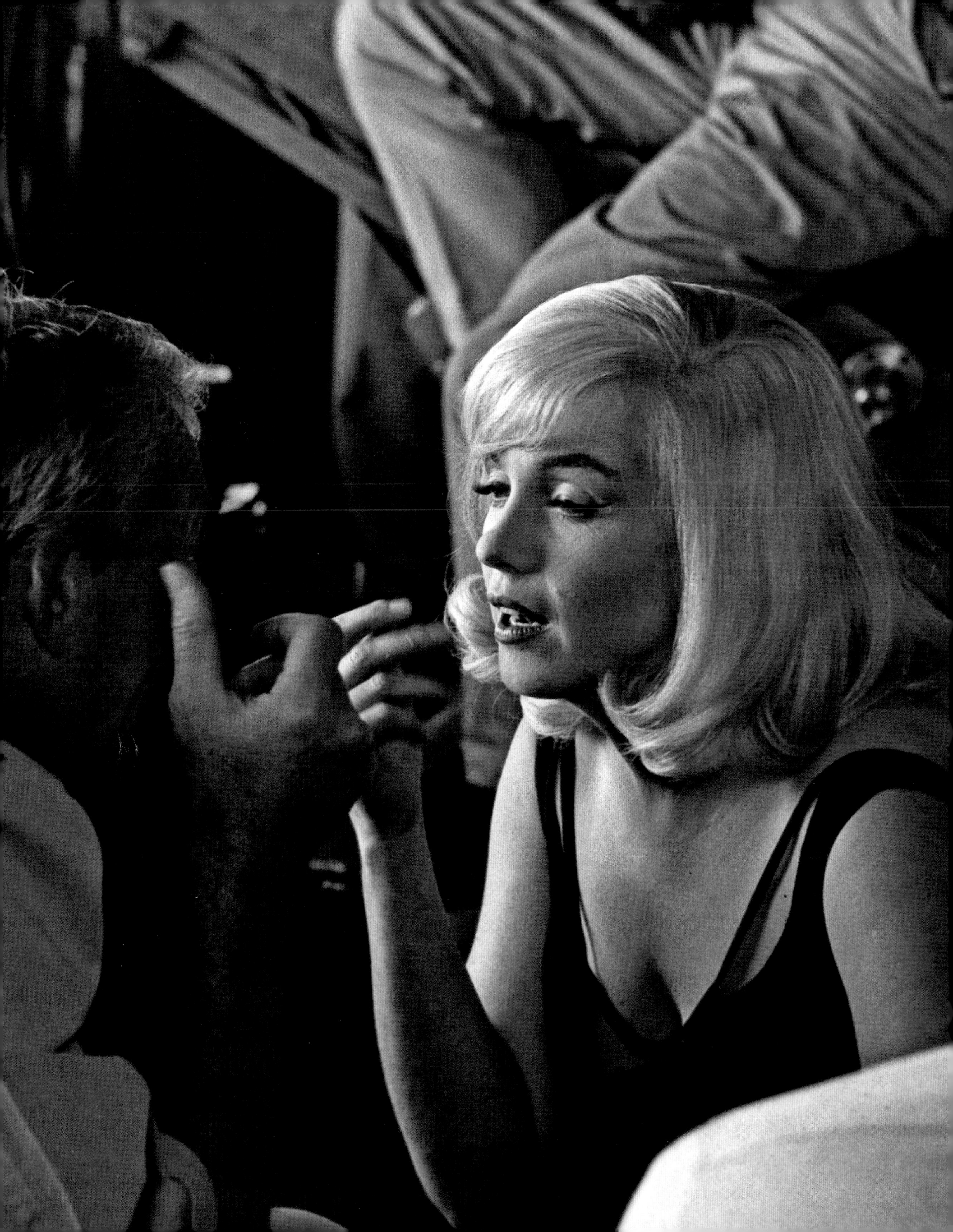

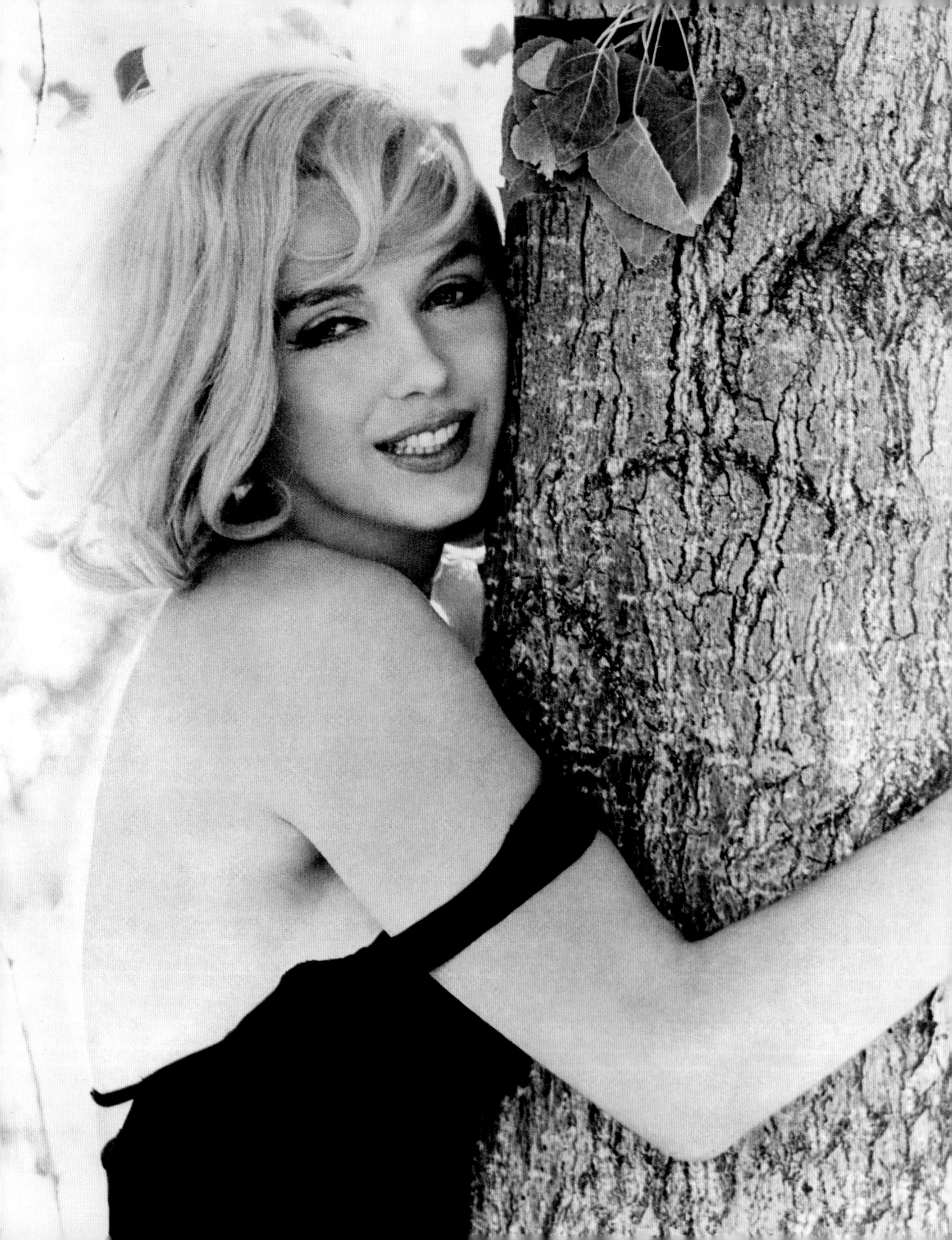

"I found myself in the privileged position of photographing somebody who I had first thought had a gift for the camera, but who turned out had a genius for it. She had a naive quality, but she also had a great sense of showmanship and self-promotion. She was very clever. She was able to assess each photographer. Even if it was only an amateur with a box camera, she worked with the same intensity and diligence that she would have if she were working with a top professional. She would photograph ten pounds lighter which is against every rule in the book. The smile was brilliant. Her skin was translucent, white, luminous. She was always sort of golden-looking, and because she had a down of just very fine golden hairs on her face it trapped the light and caused an aureole to form, giving her a faint glow. It was extraordinary. I've never seen it before. It was a nimbus, so that she looked almost angelic."

EVE ARNOLD (Photographer)

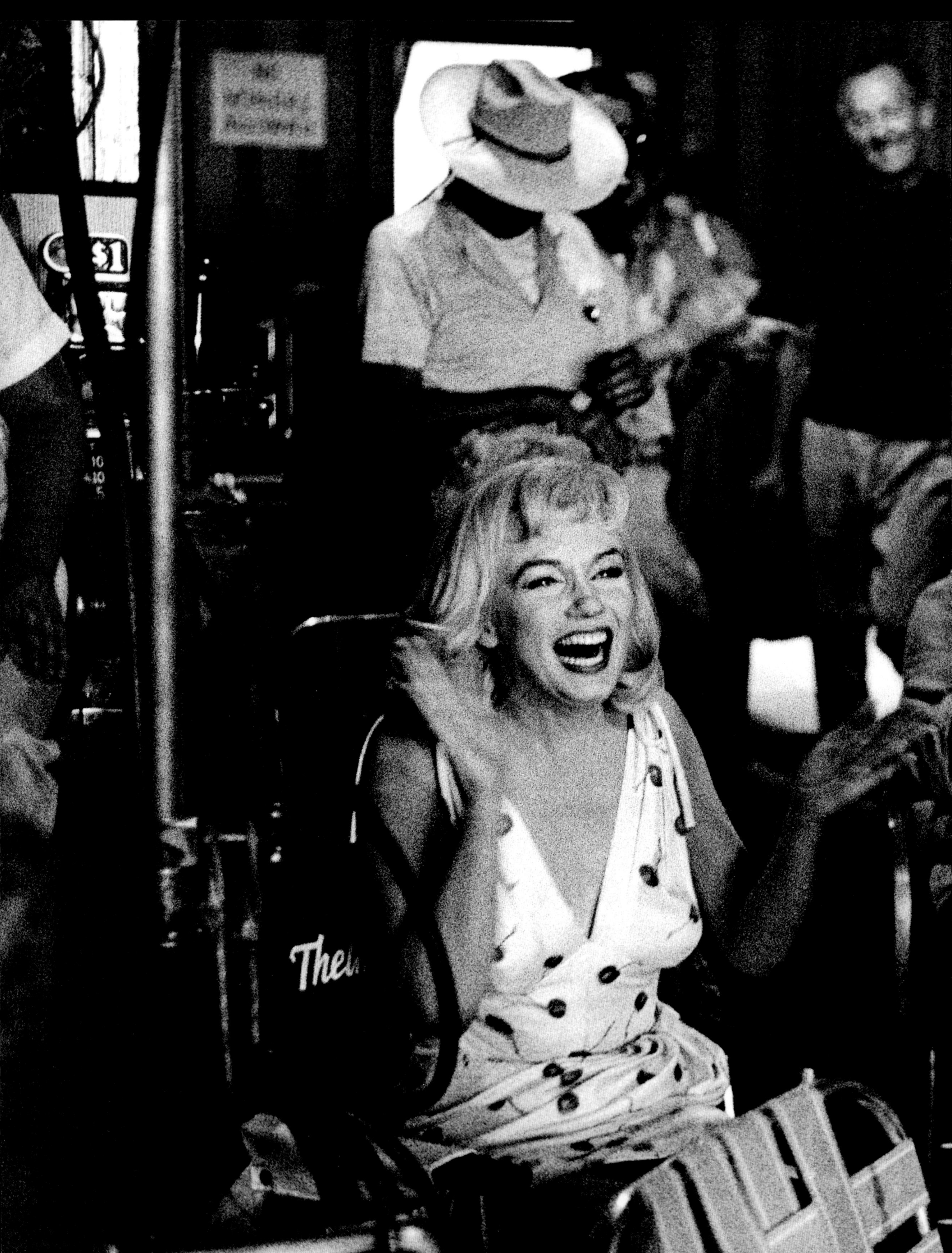
$1
Thel

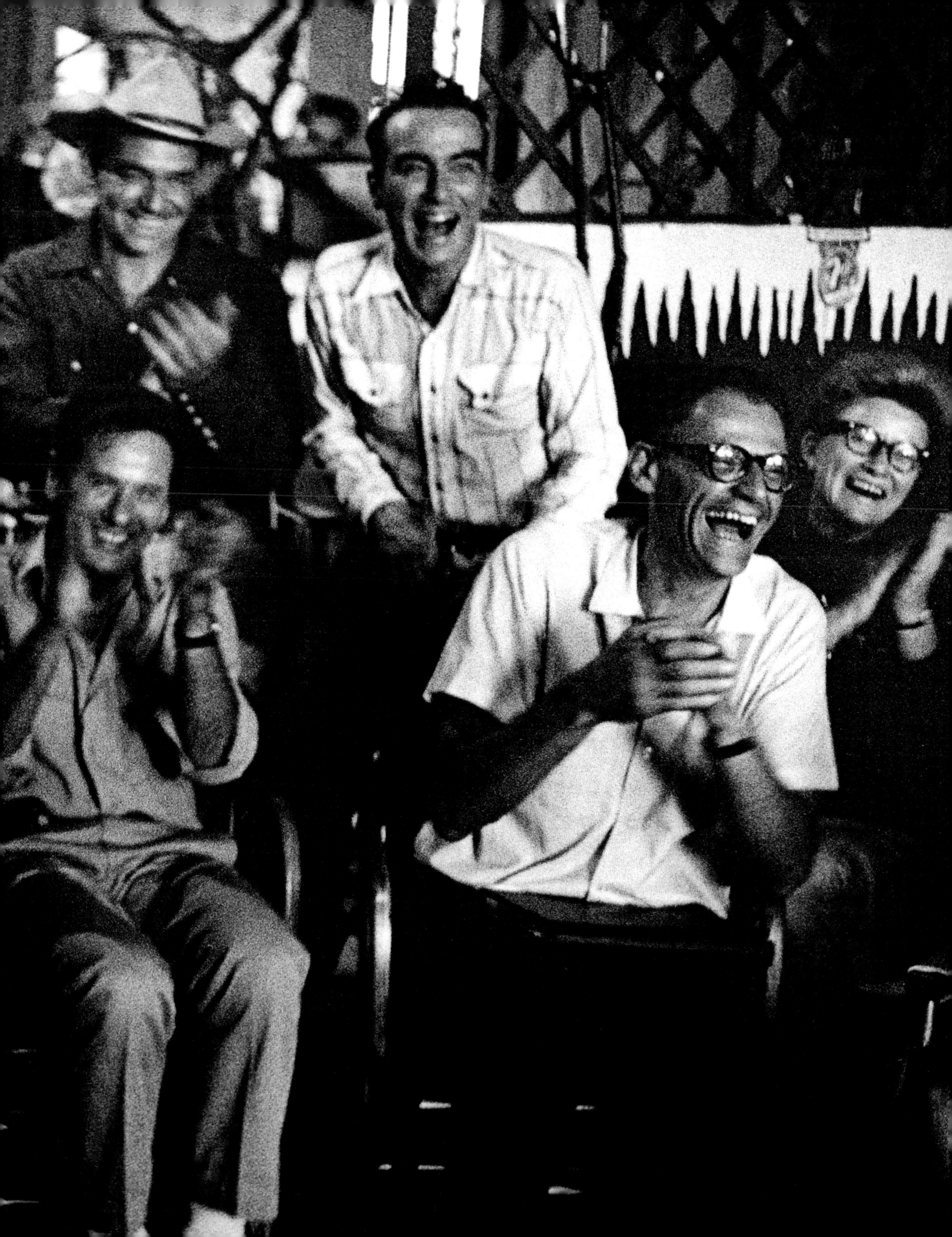

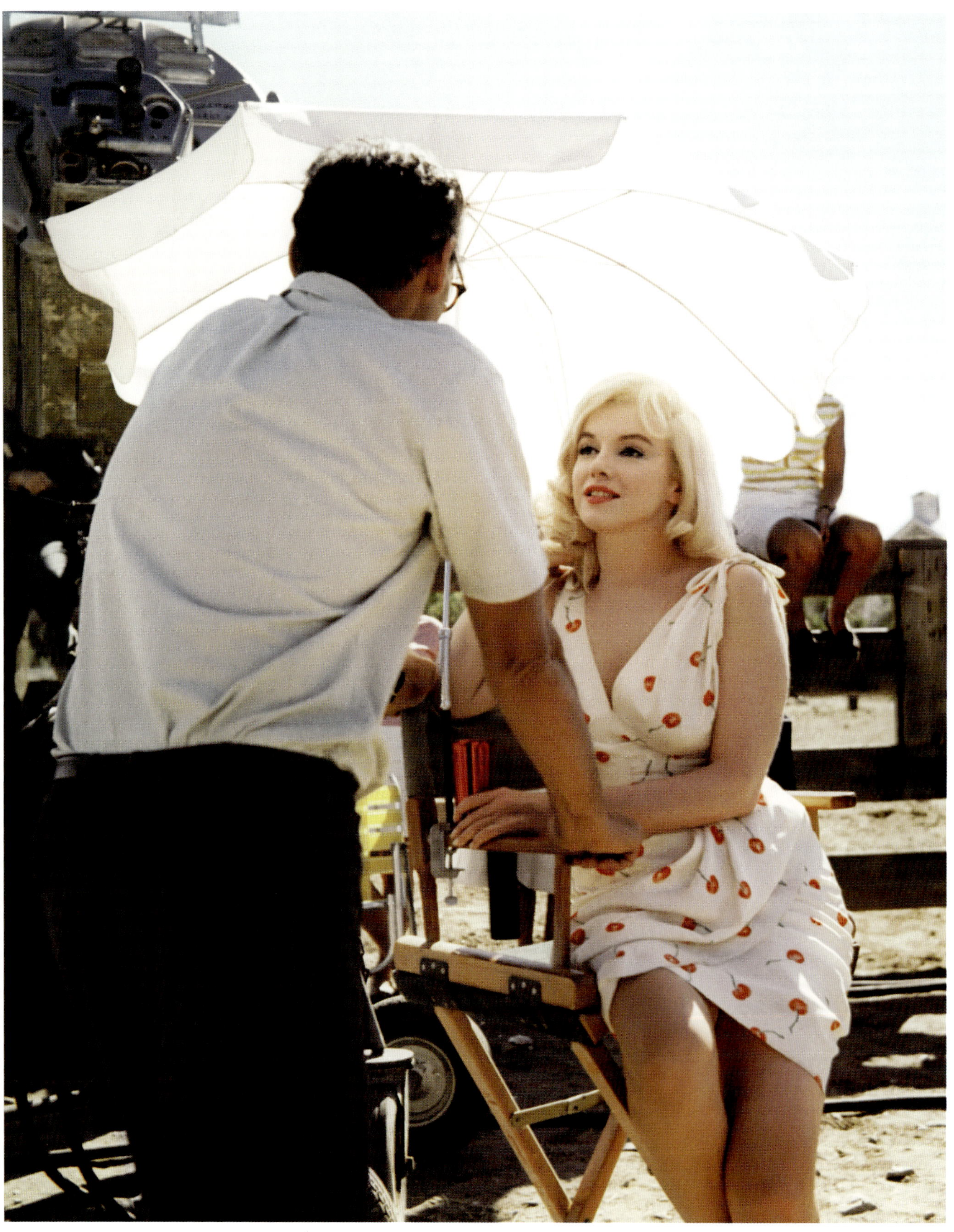

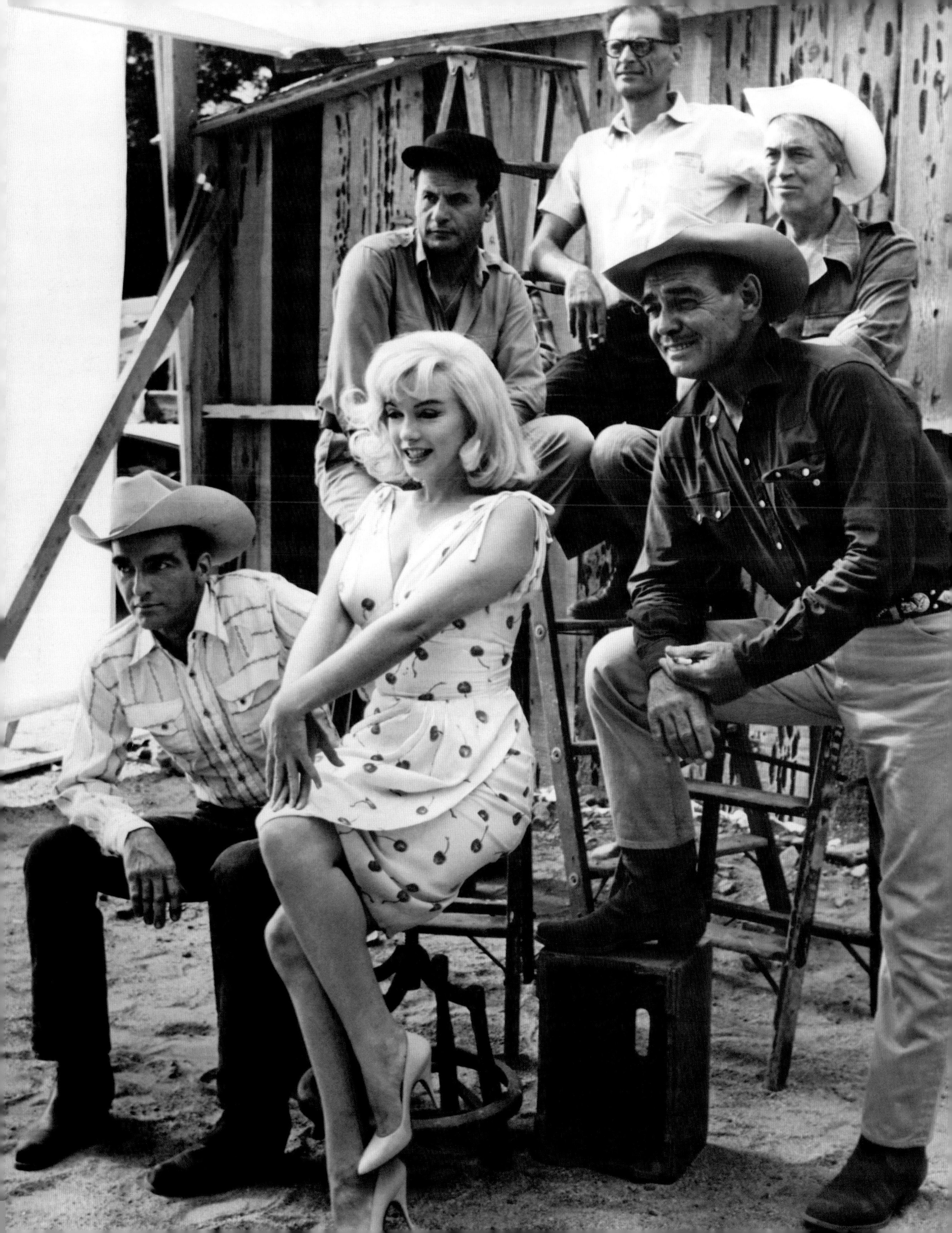

"What was so amazing about her was the thing she projected on the screen. She seemed so ordinary when doing a scene, and then you'd go to the rushes and see her up there, so different, like no one else . . . it was nearly incredible. The legend . . . suddenly made sense. I could understand why all the fuss had been made, why the crowds went out of their minds whenever they caught a glimpse of her. It's a kind of magic."

ANGELA ALLEN (Script supervisor, *The Misfits*, 1961)

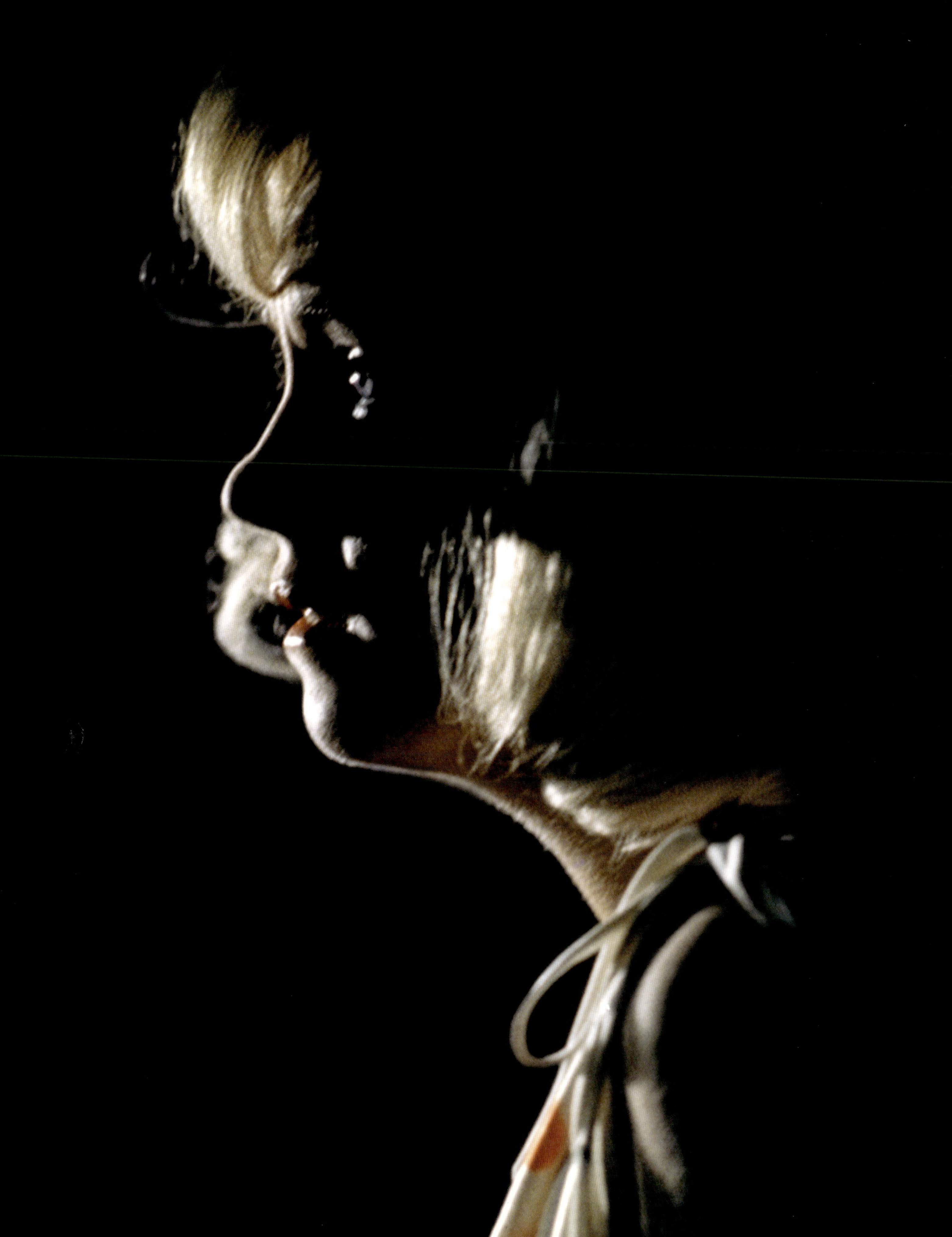

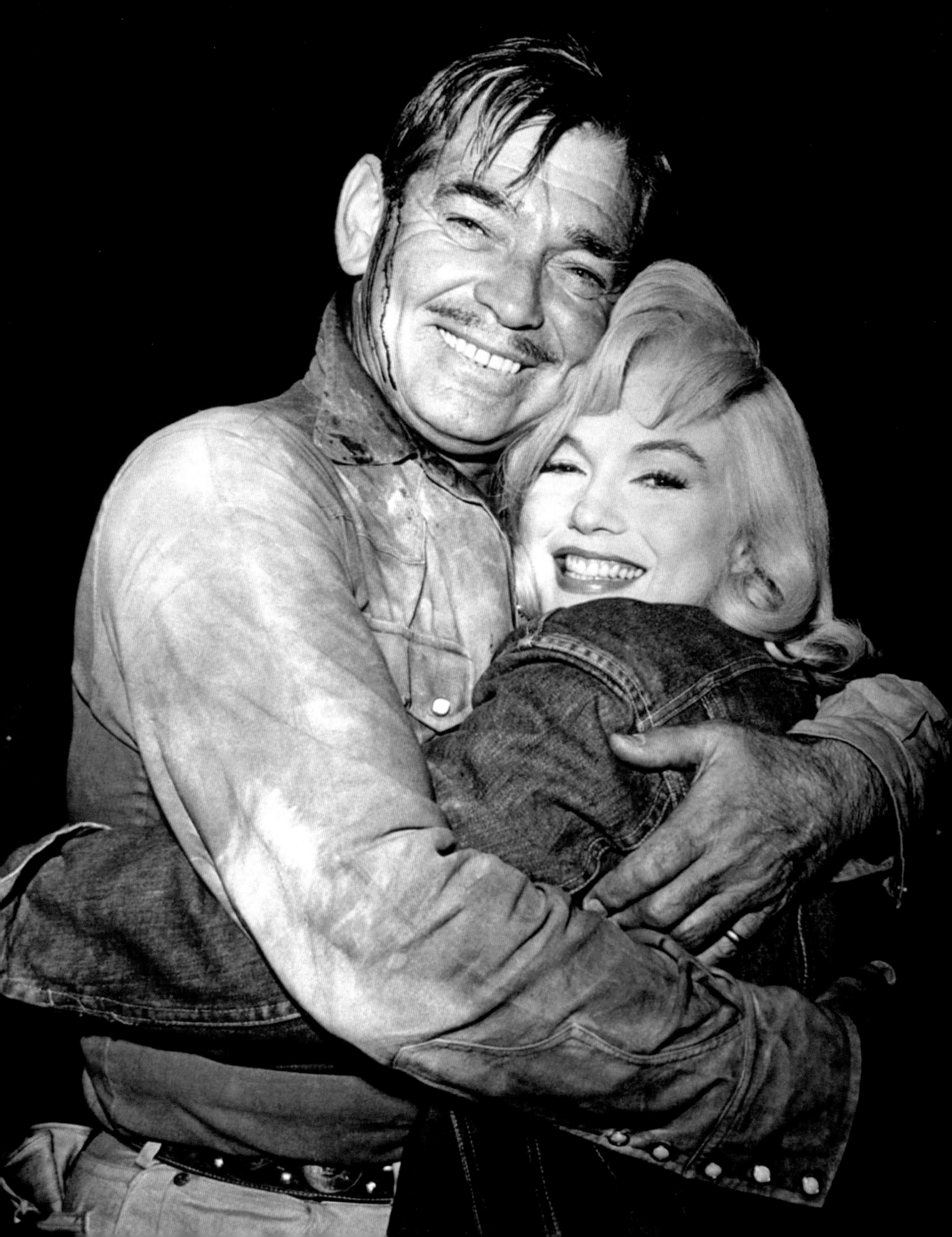

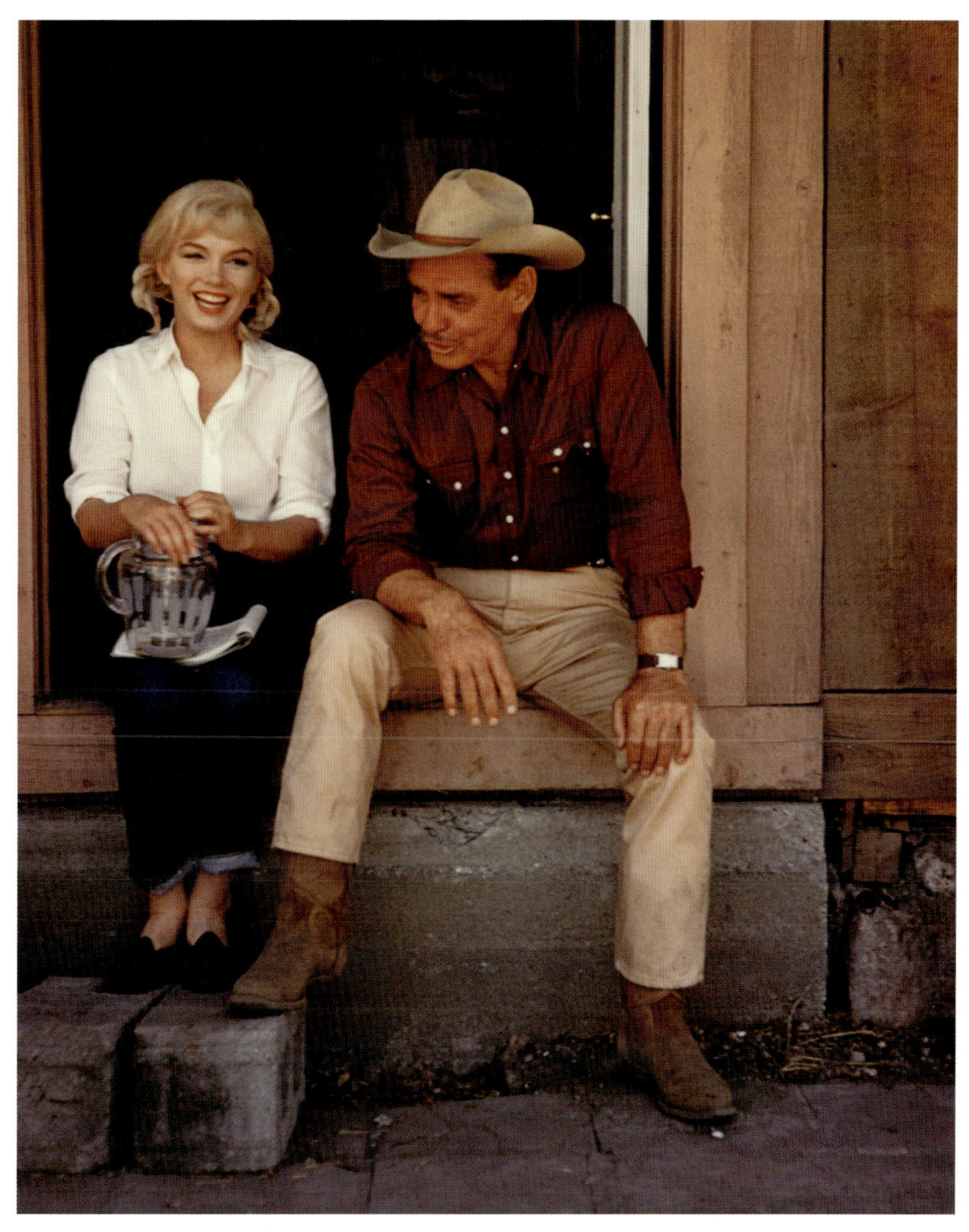

"Marilyn is a kind of ultimate. She is uniquely feminine. Everything she does is different, strange, and exciting, from the way she talks to the way she uses that magnificent torso. I think she's something different to each man, blending somehow the things he seems to require most."

CLARK GABLE (Costar, *The Misfits*, 1961)

"I have the same problem as Marilyn. We attract people the way honey does bees, but they're generally the wrong kind of people. People who want something from us—if only our energy. We need a period of being alone to become ourselves."

MONTGOMERY CLIFT (Costar, *The Misfits*, 1961)

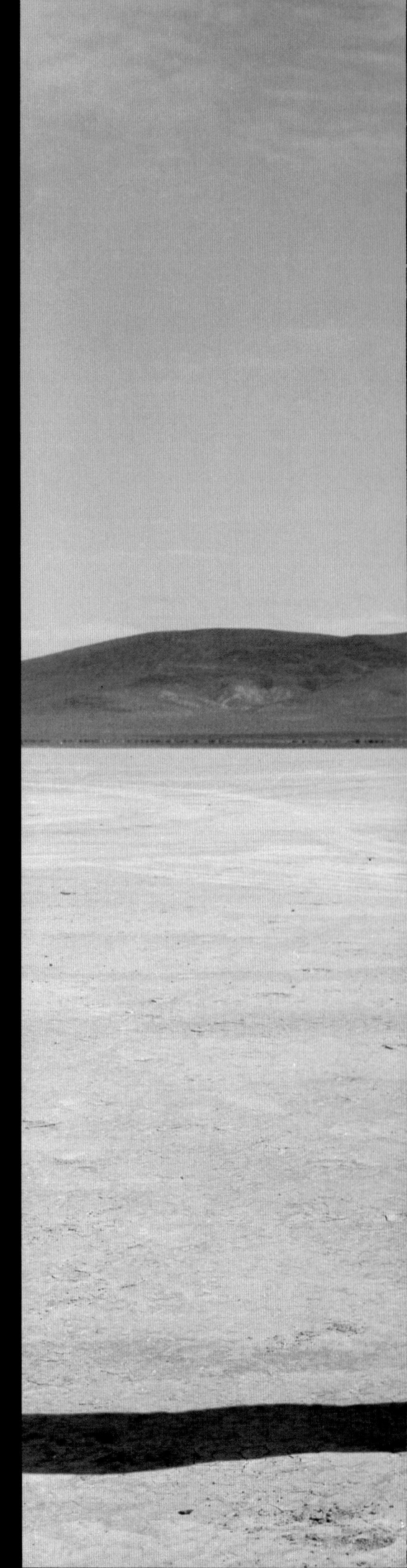

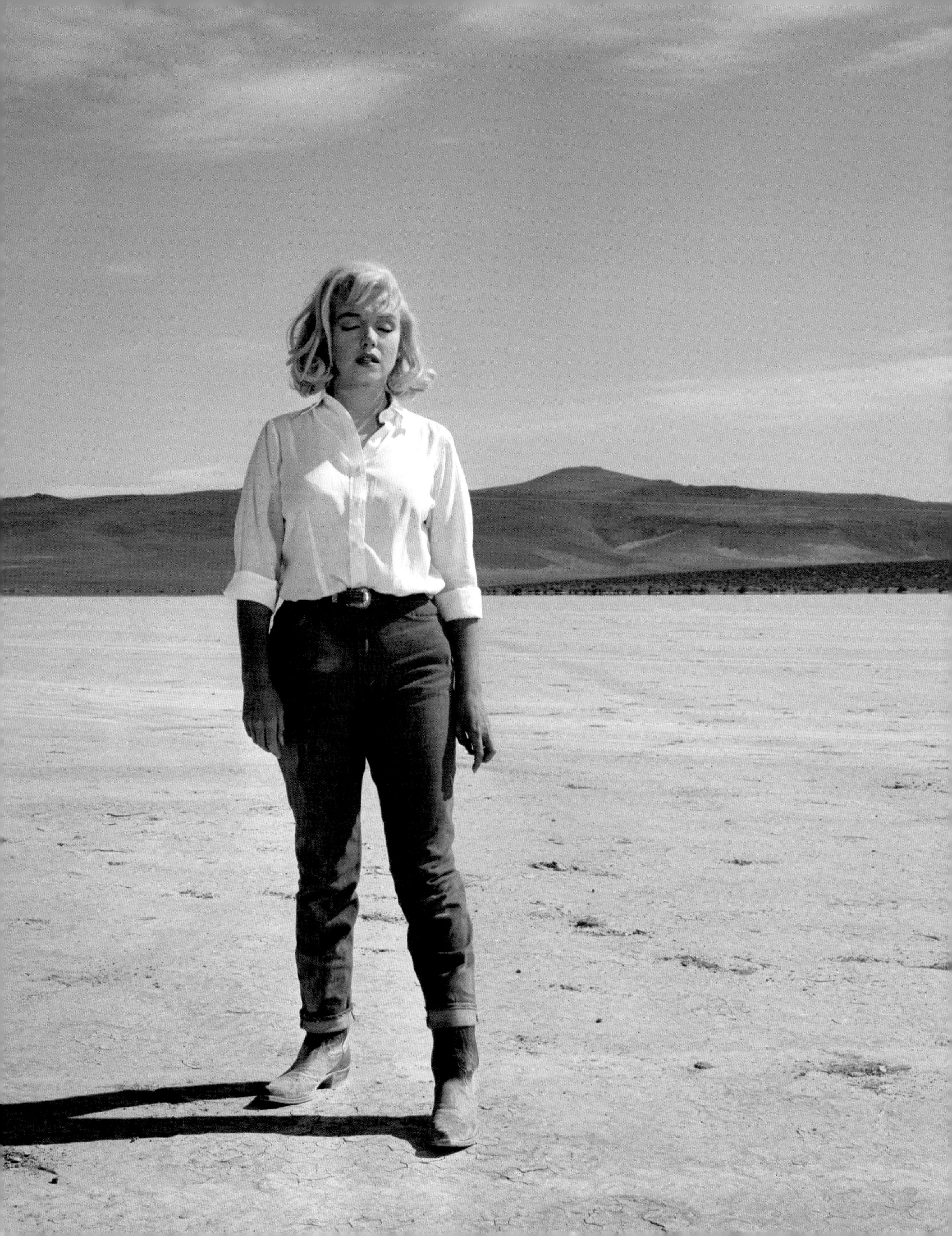

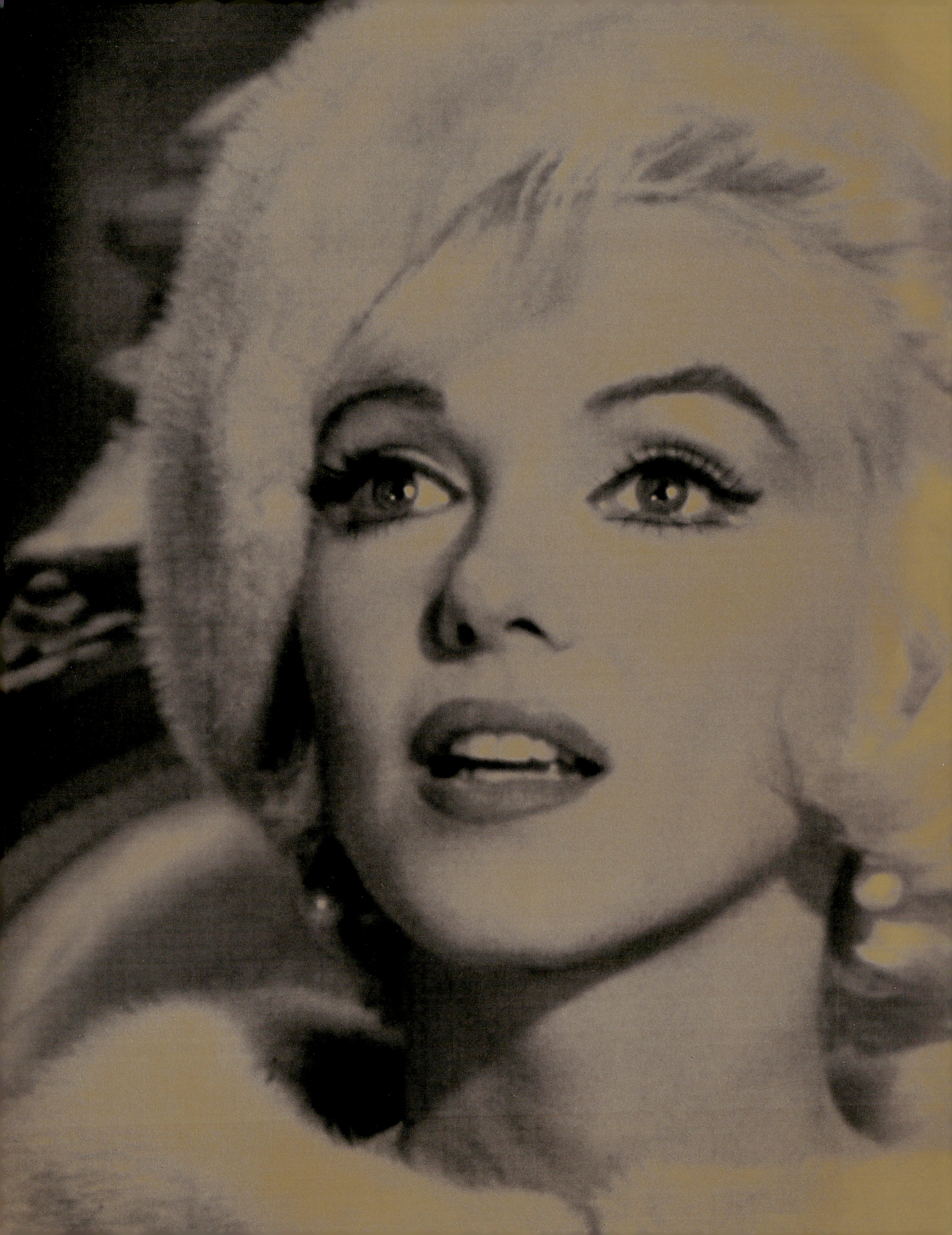

ICARUS

Goddess 1962

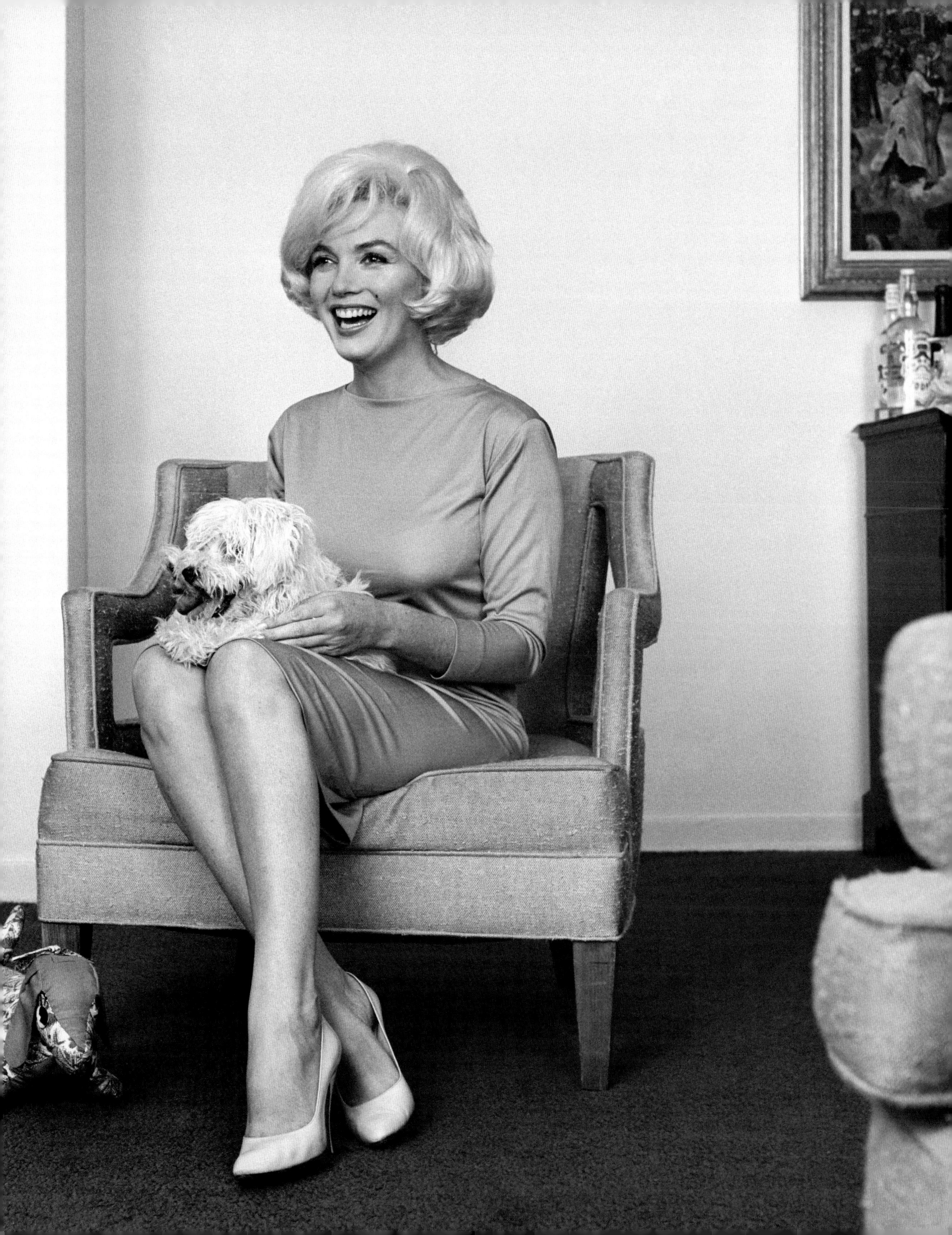

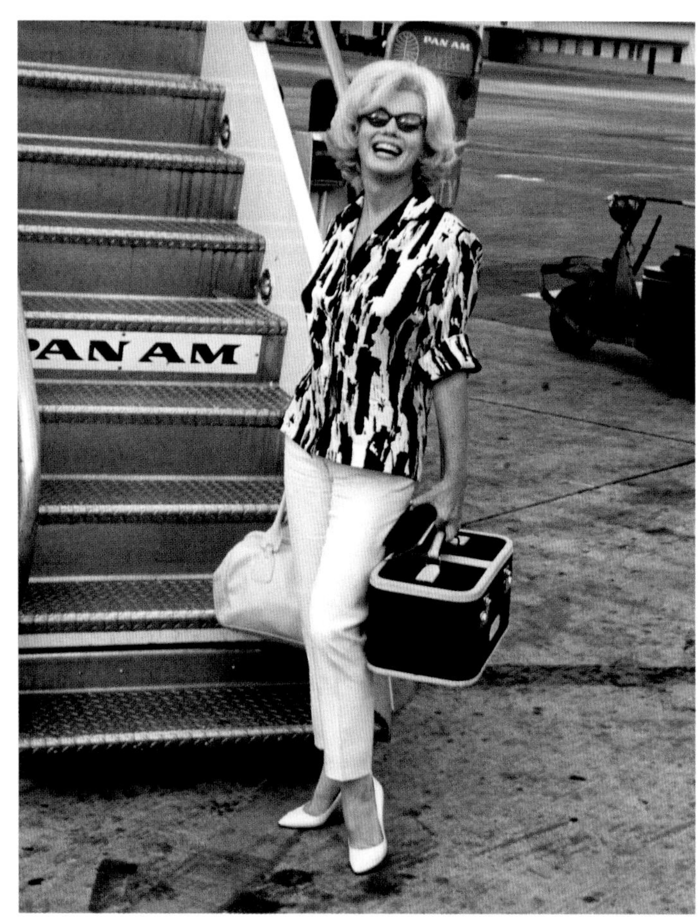

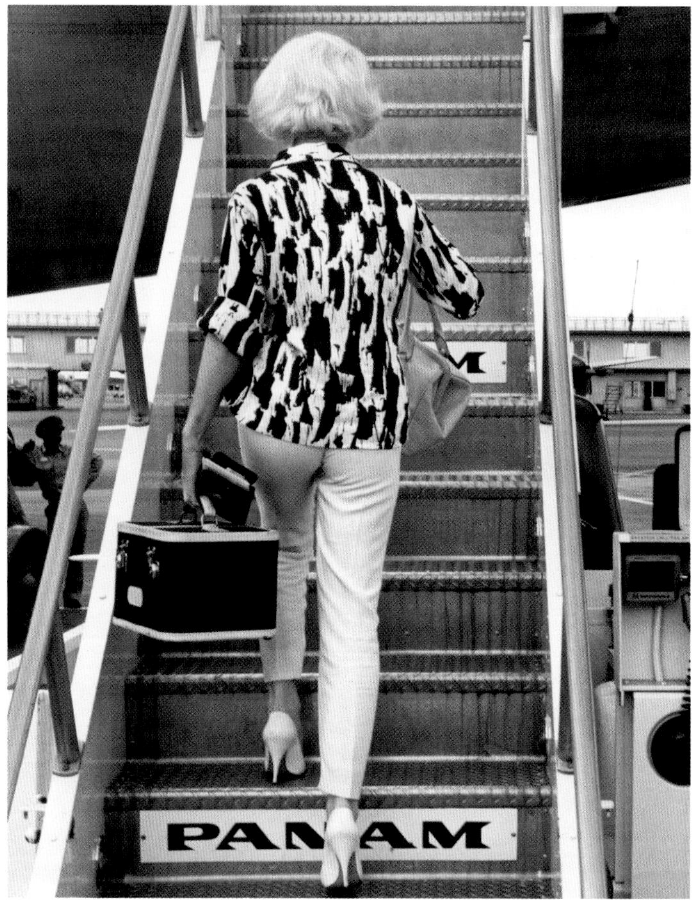

"Marilyn Monroe! She was a geisha. She was born to give pleasure, spent her whole life giving it—and knew no other way."

DIANA VREELAND

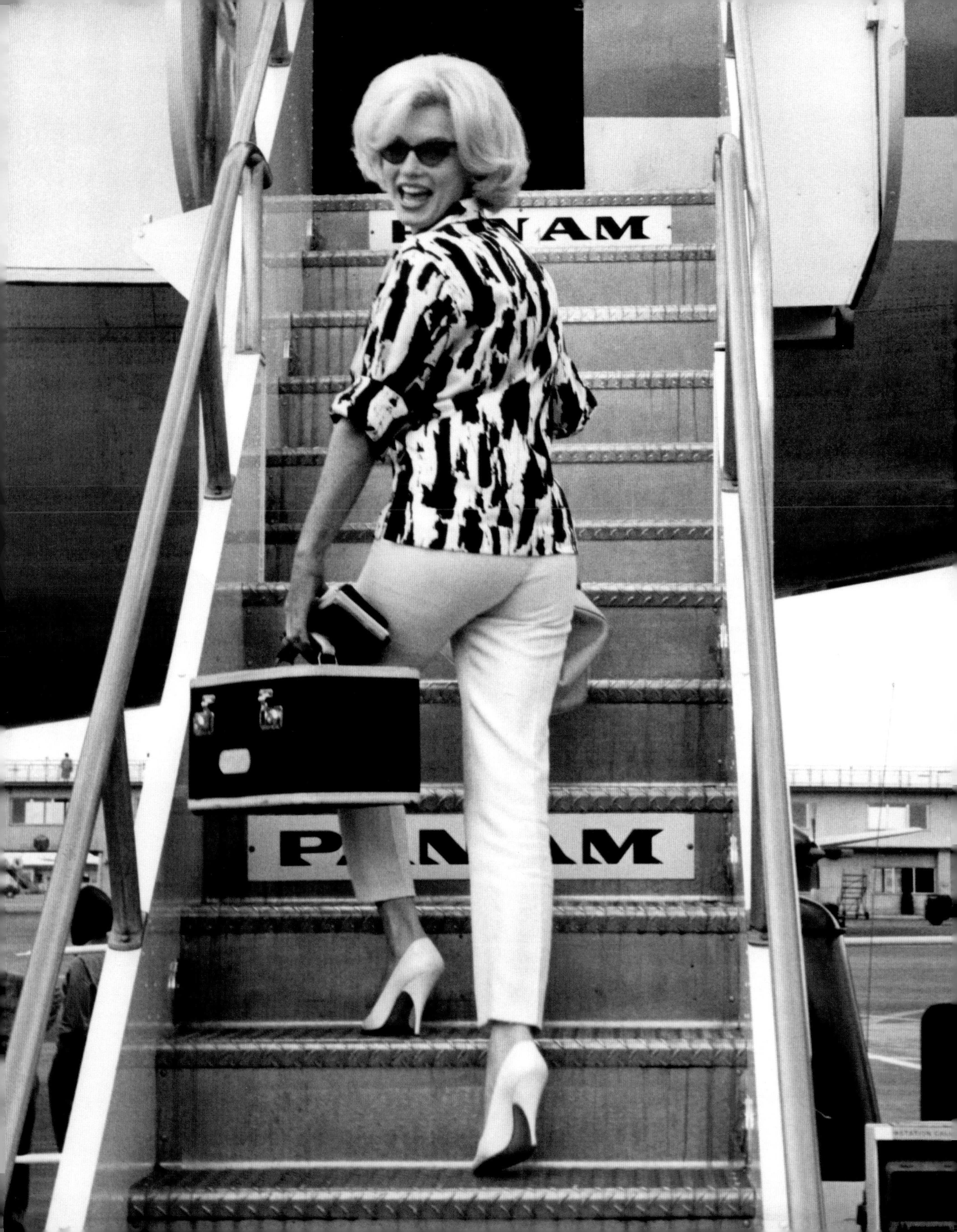

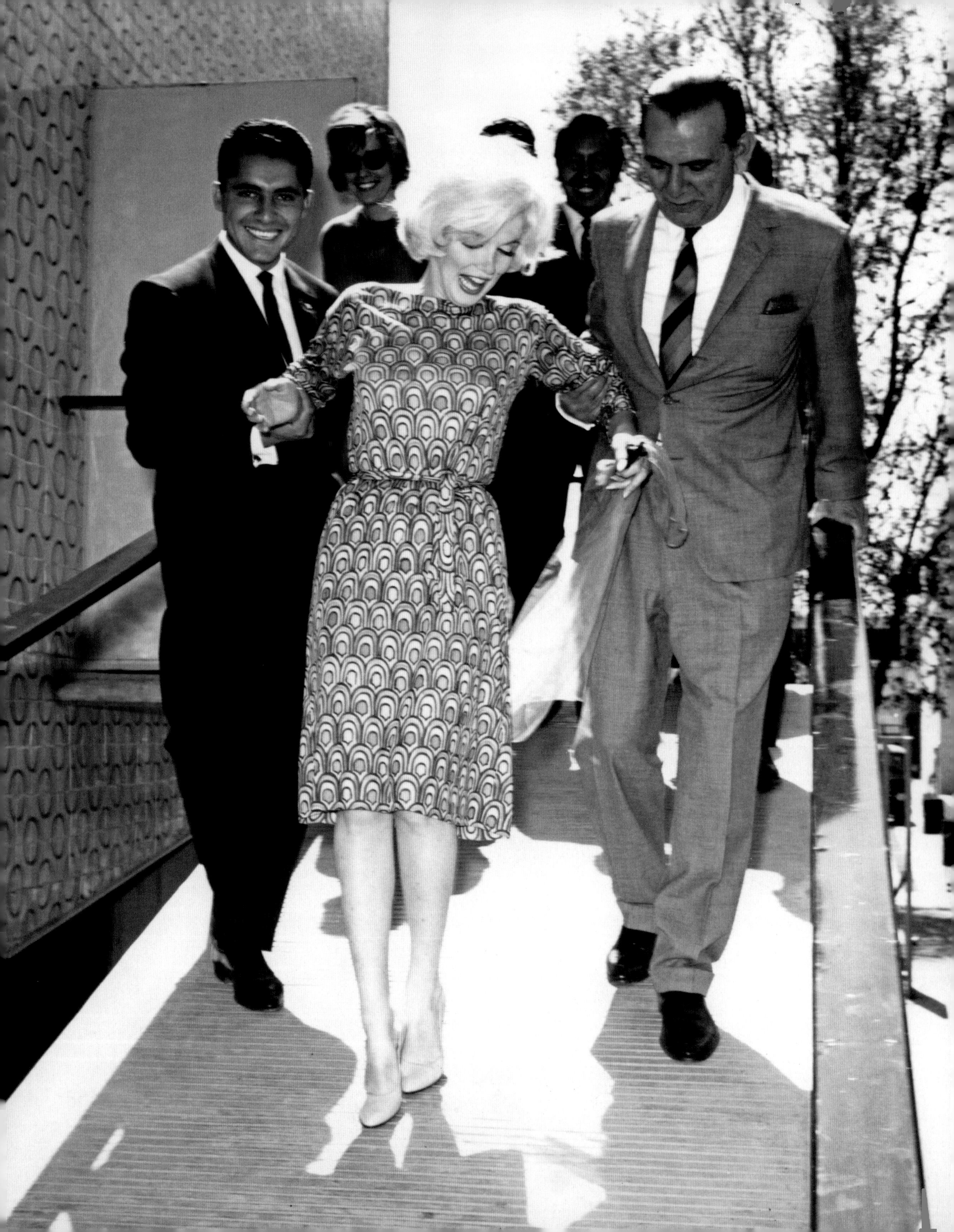

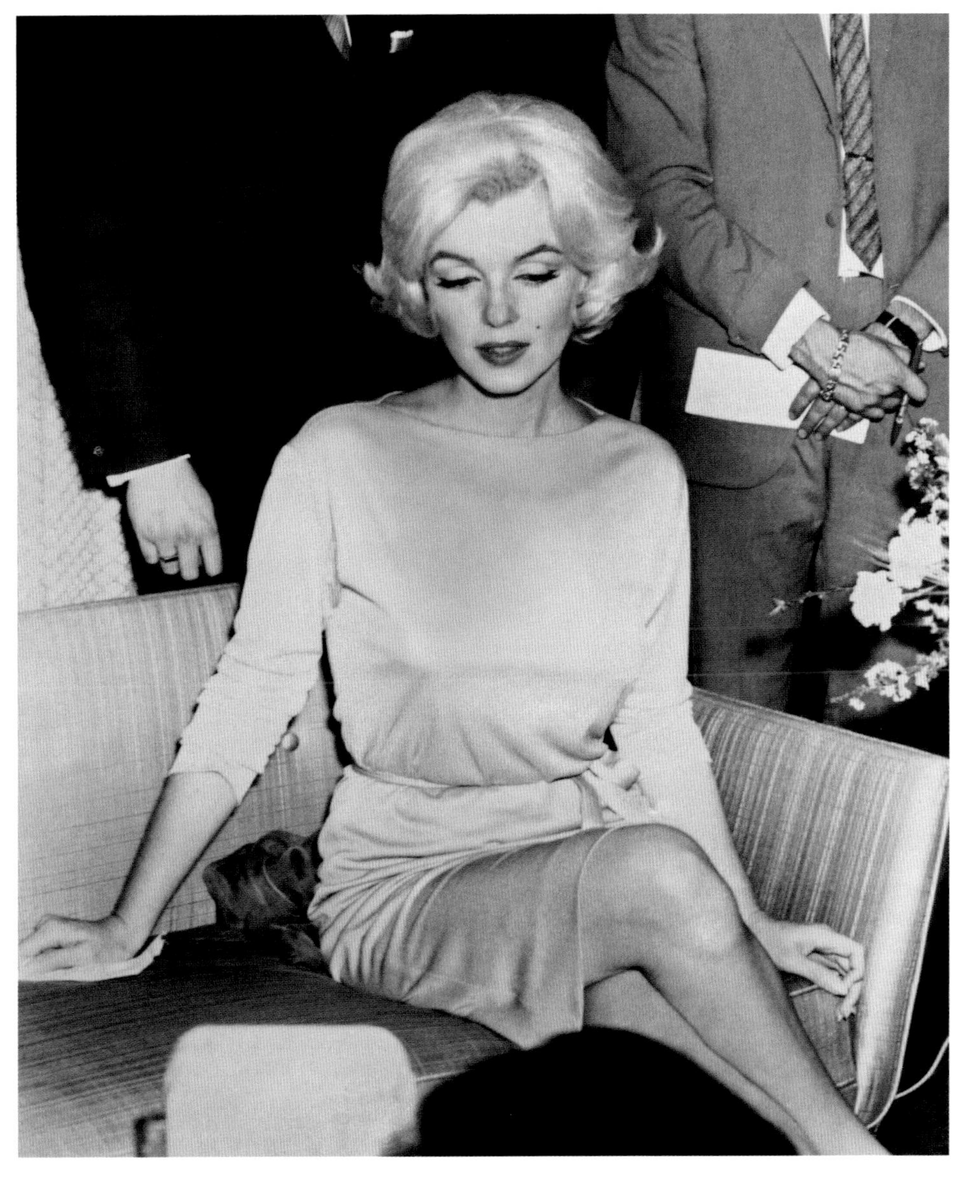

"She was not the usual movie idol. There was something democratic about her. She was the type who would join in and wash up the supper dishes even if you didn't ask her."

CARL SANDBURG (Writer and poet)

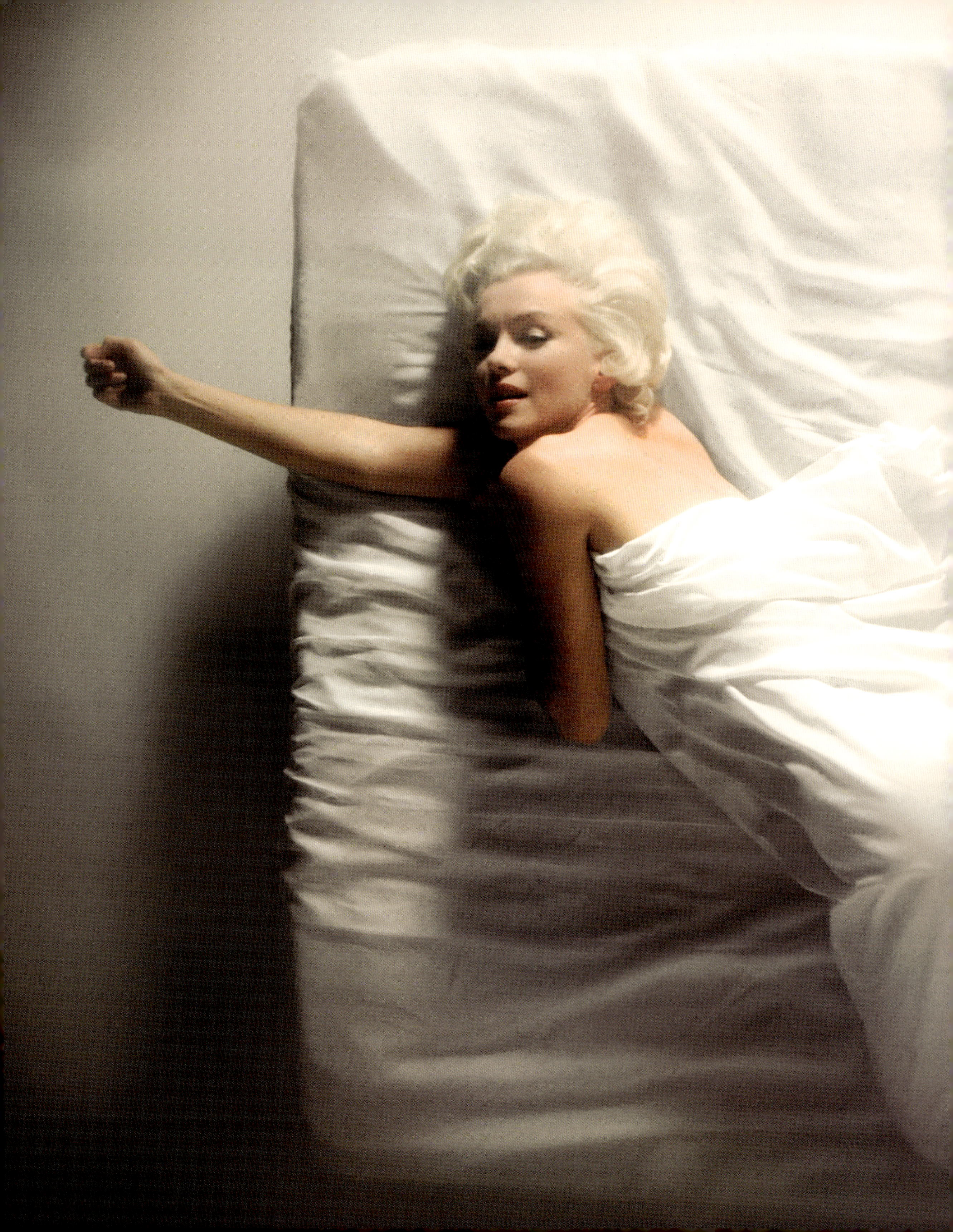

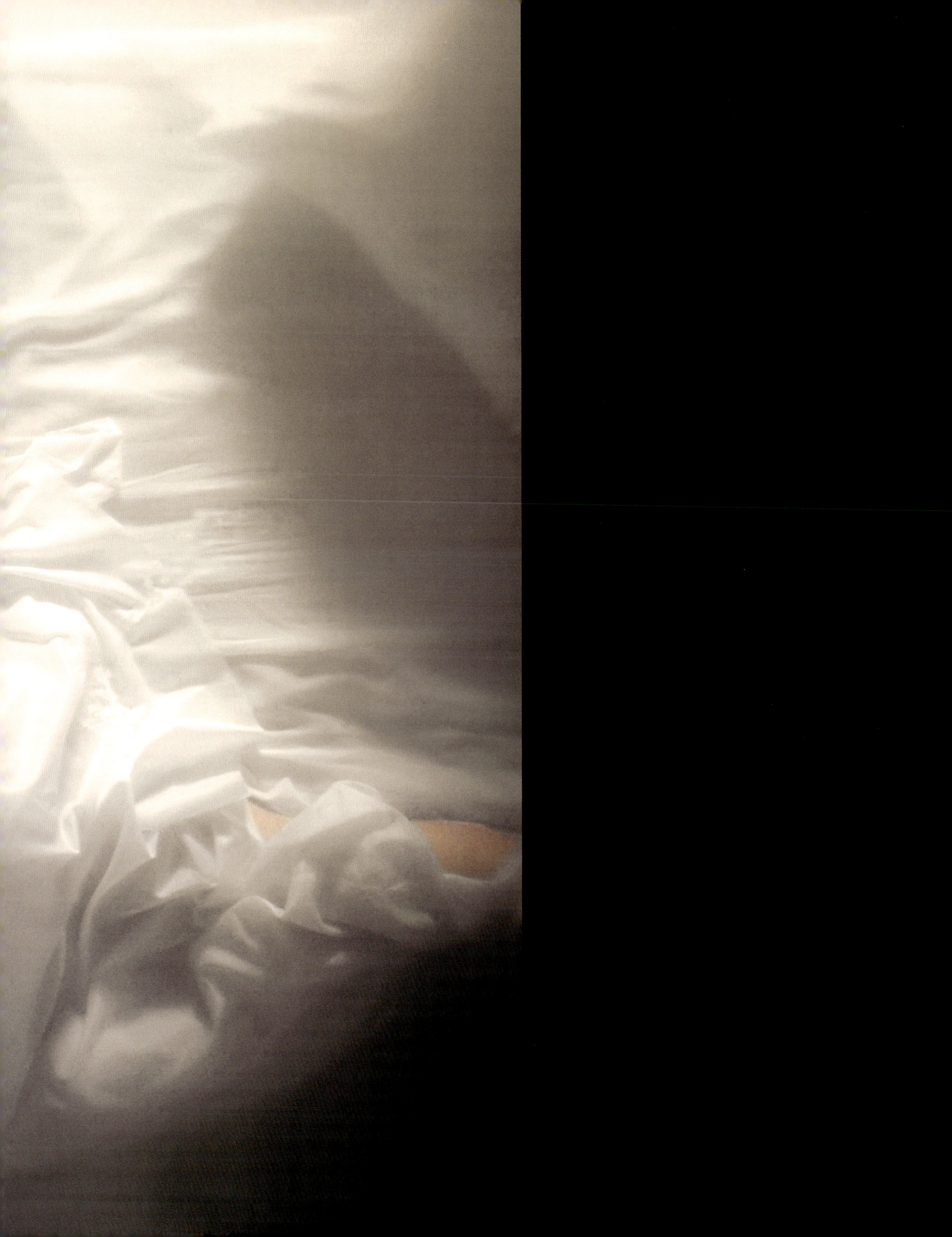

"I attended the Golden Globe Awards where the foreign press give their 'Oscars' for the year. Marilyn was receiving the World Film Favorite Award. When she made her entrance, something happened that knocked me out. There was a room full of the biggest stars in the world, and when Marilyn walked in and made her way slowly to the table, her dress was so tight she could hardly move; some people in the room stood on chairs, just to get a look at her, like kids. I'd never seen stars react to another star like that. . . . Marilyn seemed oblivious of them all; she was in one of her armored vapor clouds. . . . She mimicked her old Hollywood whispery voice in her thank-you speech. . . . Each time she caricatured herself, she chipped a piece out of her own dream."

SUSAN STRASBERG

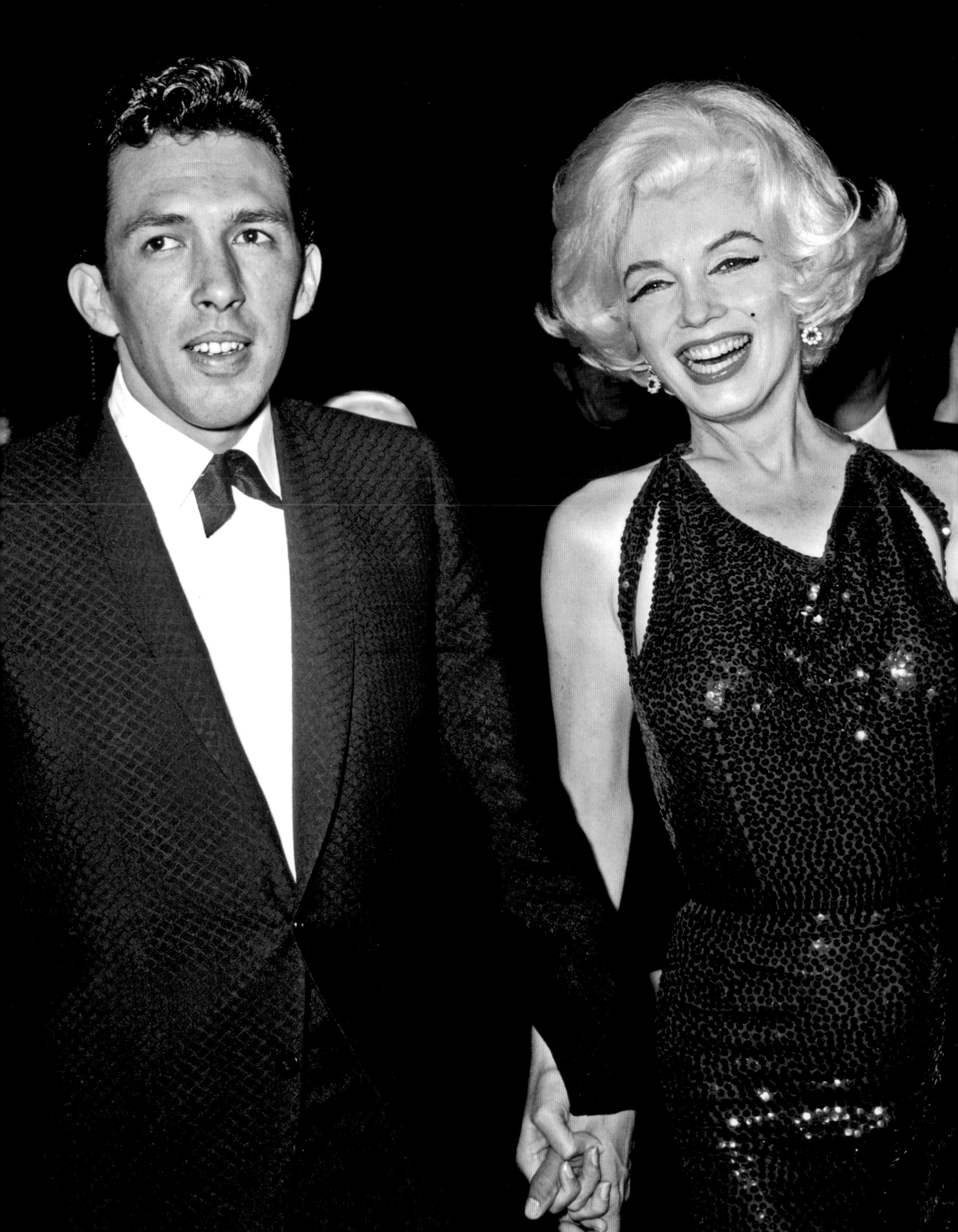

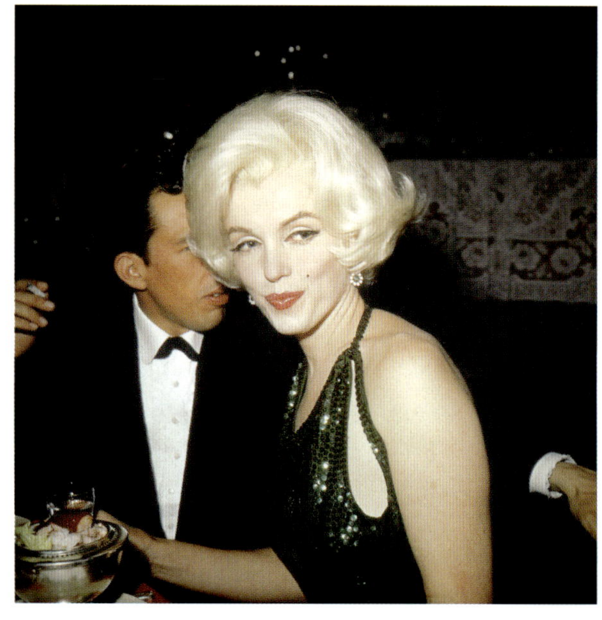

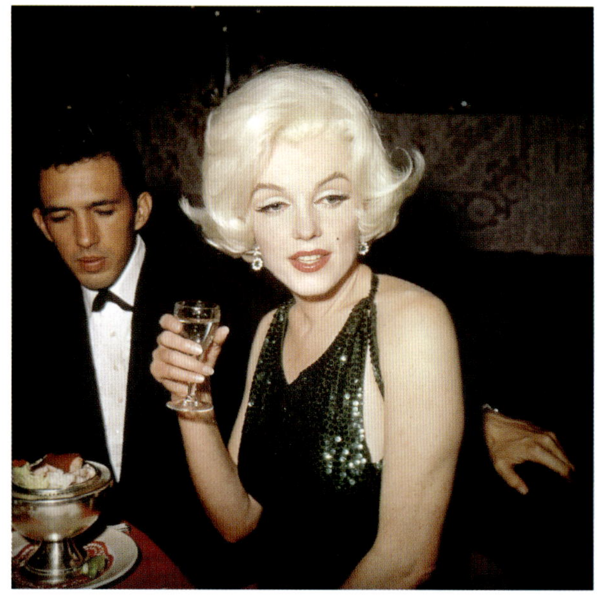

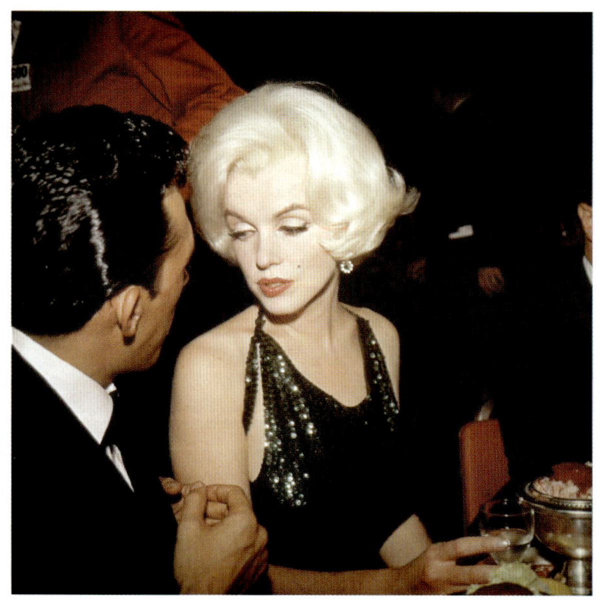

"Marilyn Monroe had the most beautiful mouth ever. No one has ever been able to convey so much sex appeal with just one feature. Whenever she was being made up some incredible change occurred and she *became* 'Marilyn Monroe.' Her voice changed, her hands and body motions altered. I'd never seen anything like this complete change of personality—a projection of sexuality and magnetism beyond belief. She was brilliant. She knew how to become what people expected."

GEORGE MASTERS (Hairstylist)

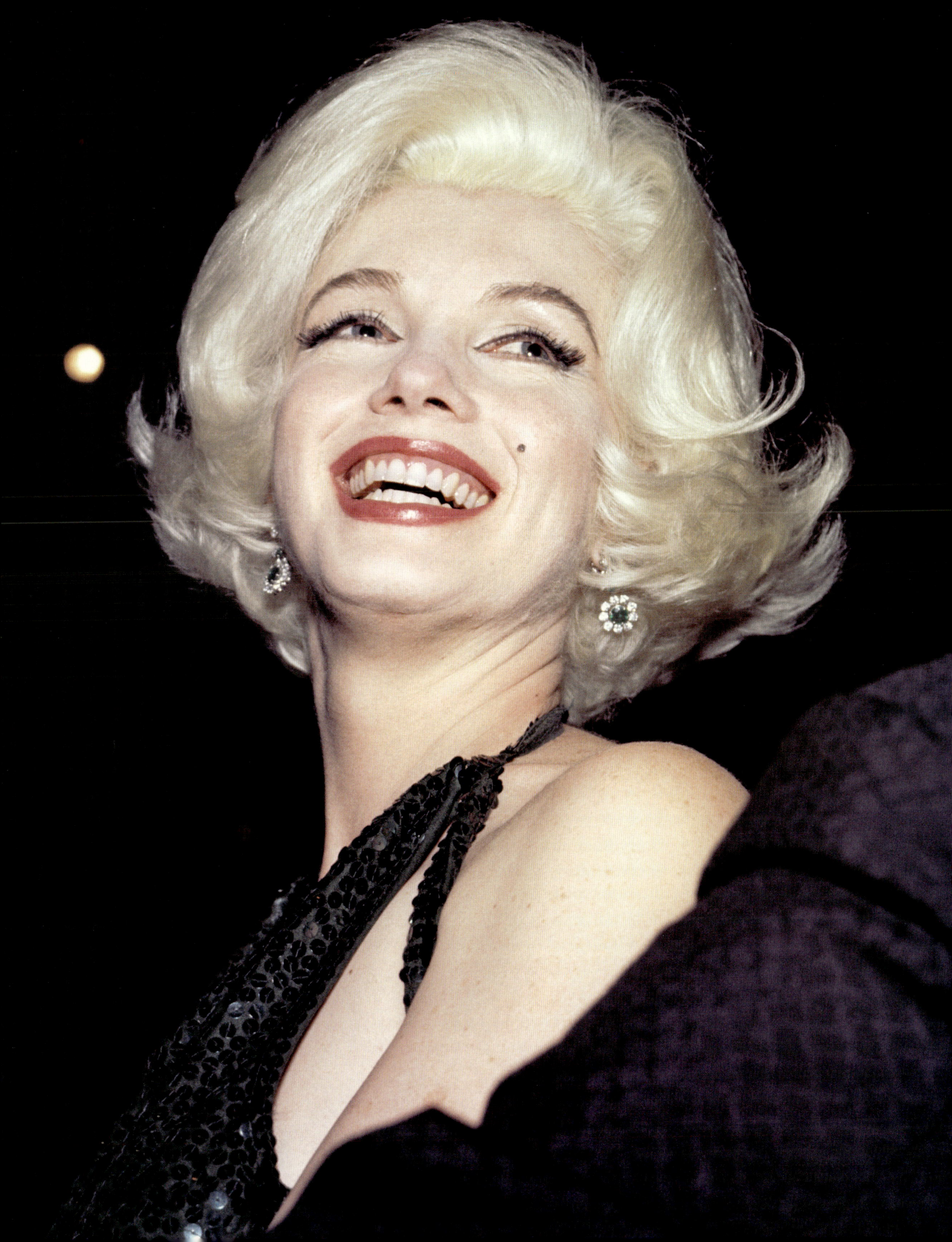

“Her quality when photographed is almost of a supernatural beauty.”

LEE STRASBERG

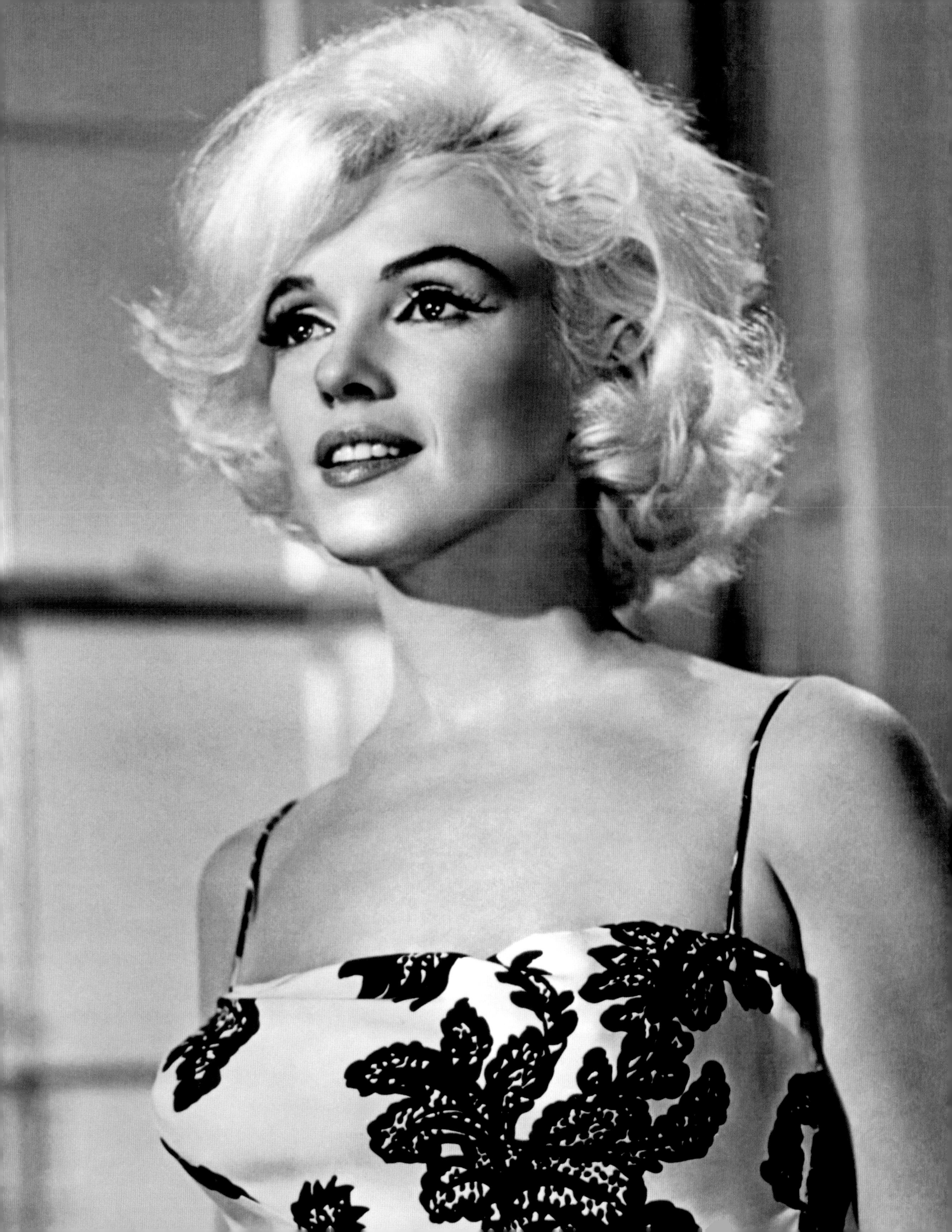

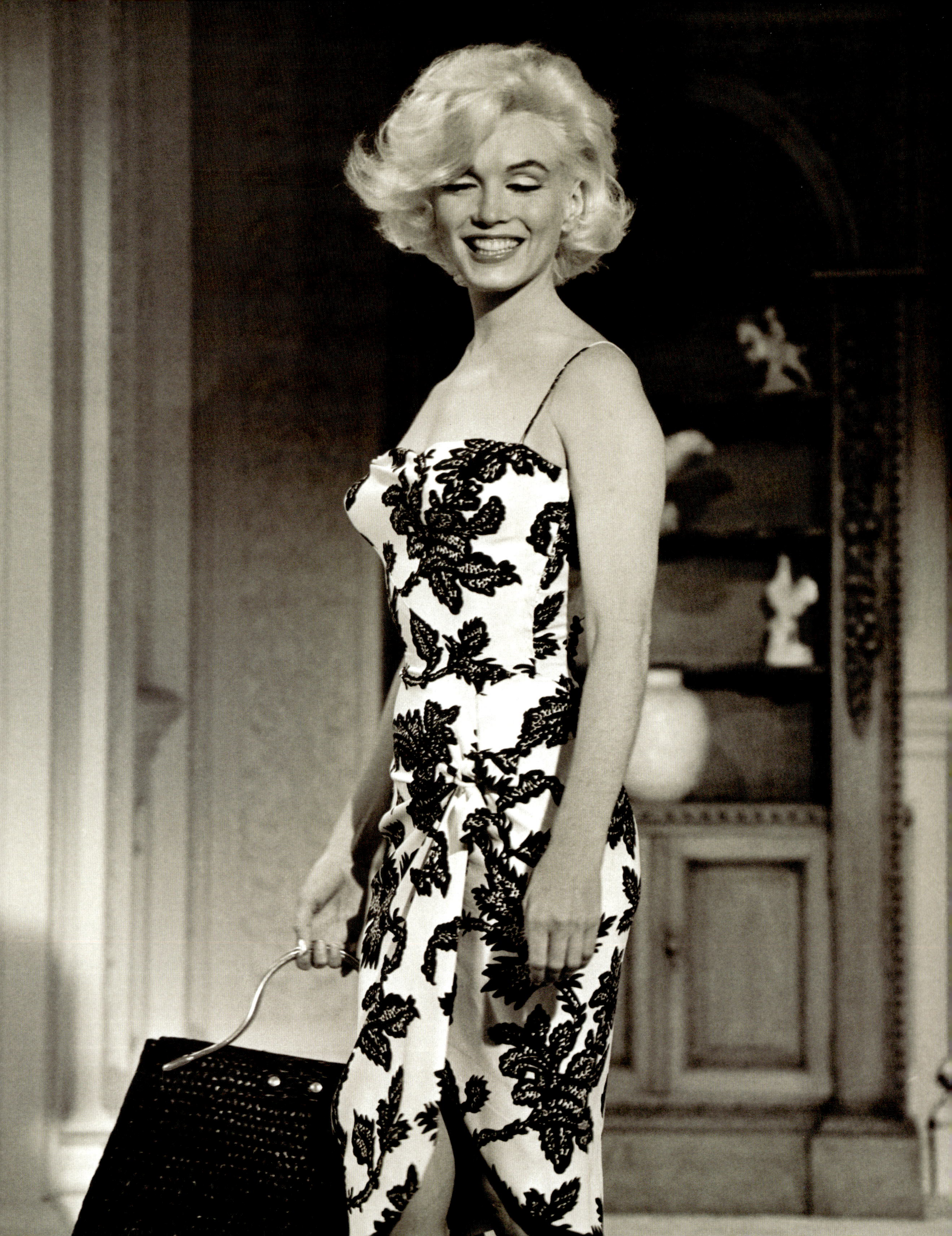

"I found her extremely intelligent—inarticulate, but extremely intelligent. And driven. In certain ways she was very shrewd. I once heard her talk in her ordinary voice, which was quite unattractive. So she invented this appealing baby voice. Also, you very seldom saw her with her mouth closed, because when it was closed she had a very determined chin, almost a different face. The face moved in a wonderful way. It was a wonderful movie face."

GEORGE CUKOR (Director, *Something's Got to Give*, 1962)

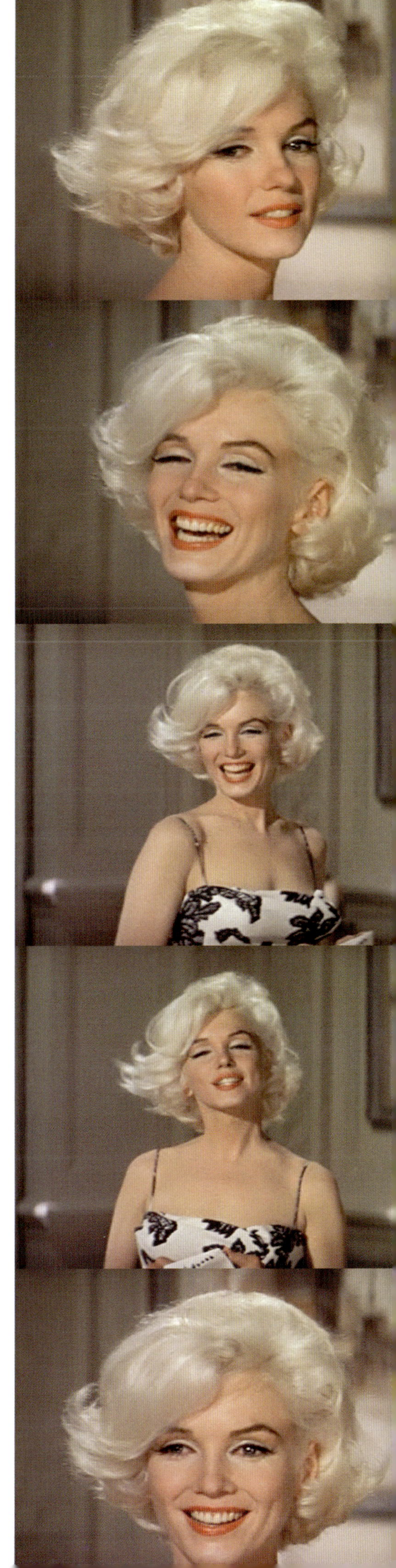

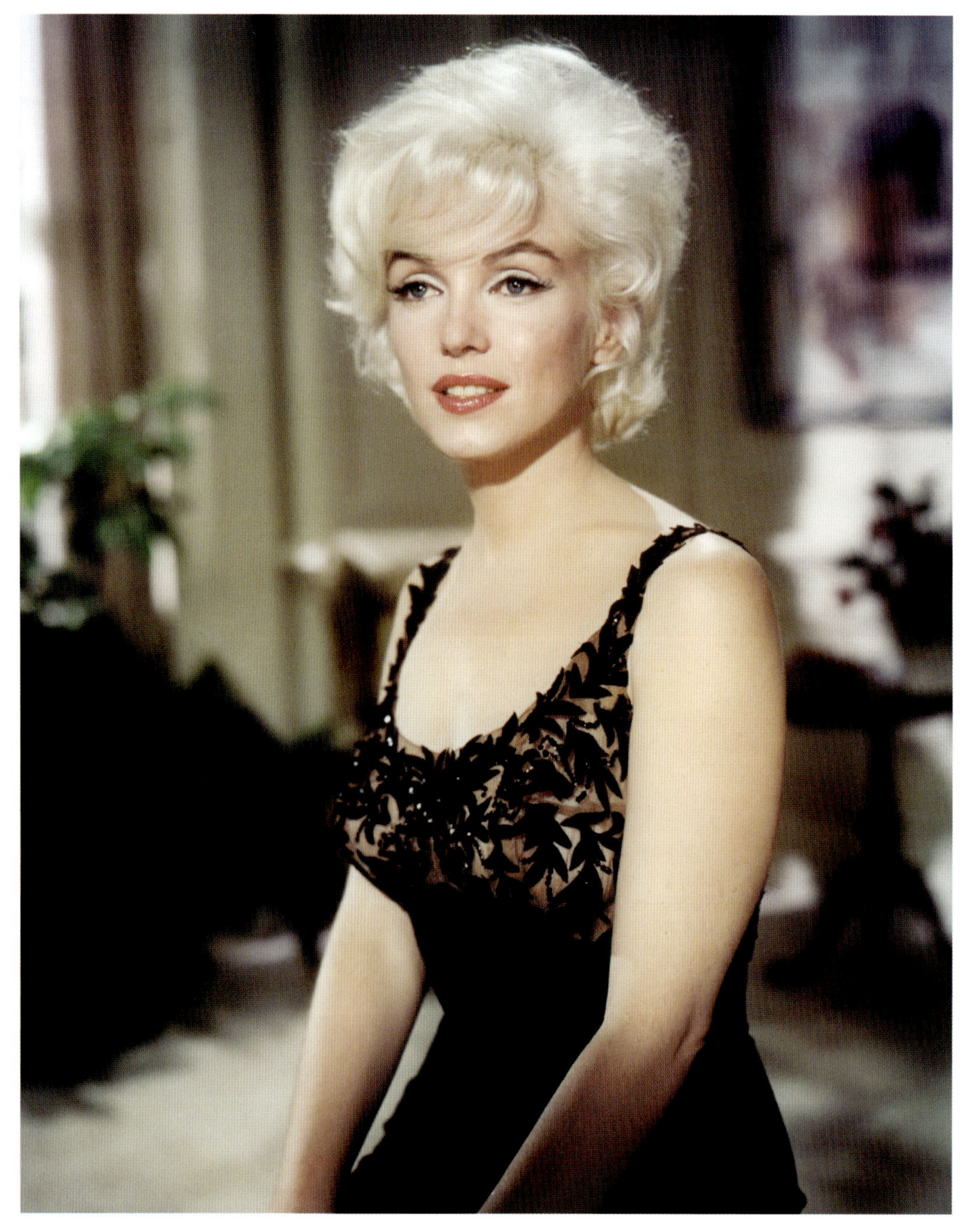

"The change in her was breathtaking. It was made even more startling because Marilyn had just lost twenty-five pounds. She had never been so slim and glowing."

JEAN LOUIS (Costume Designer, *Something's Got to Give*, 1962)

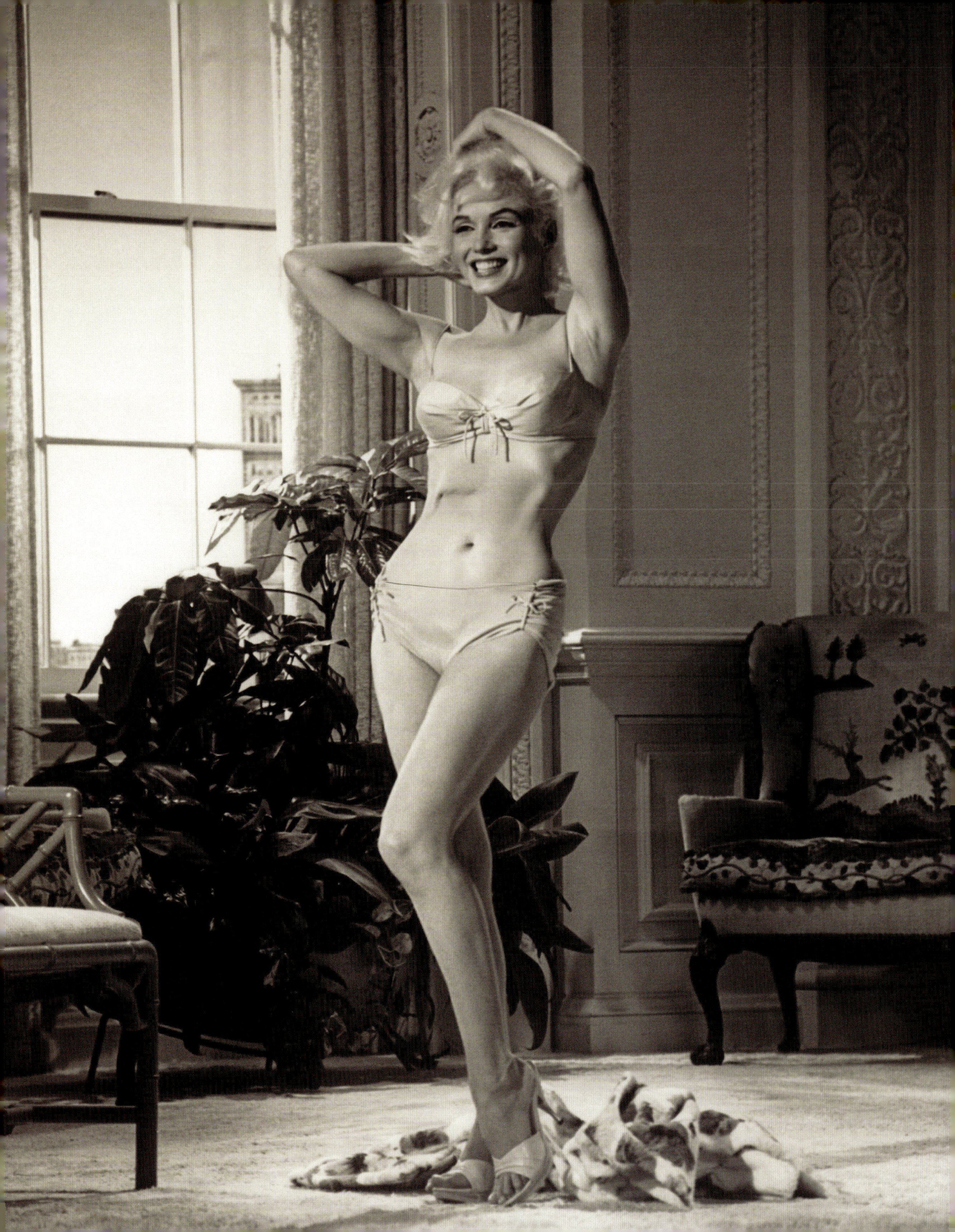

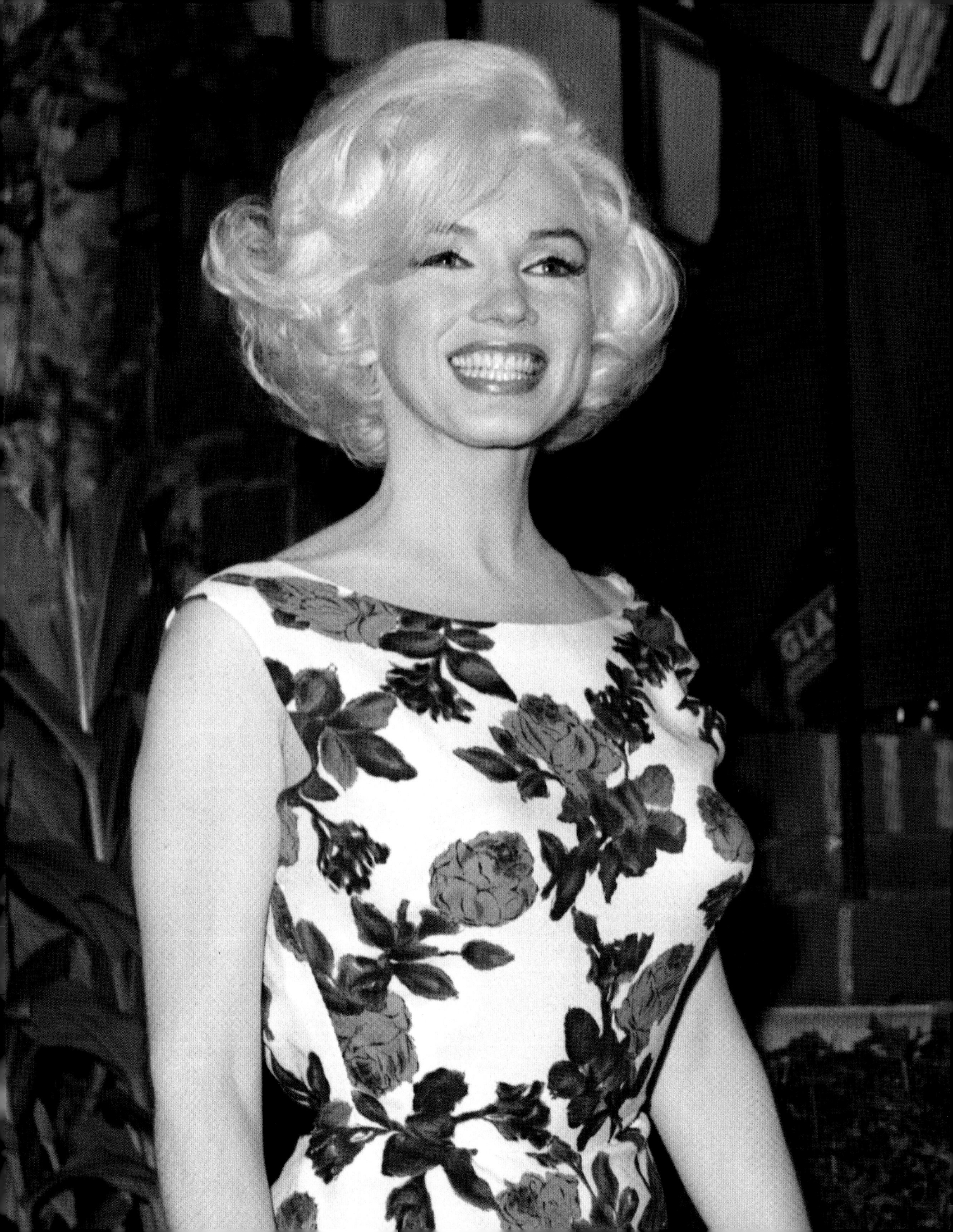

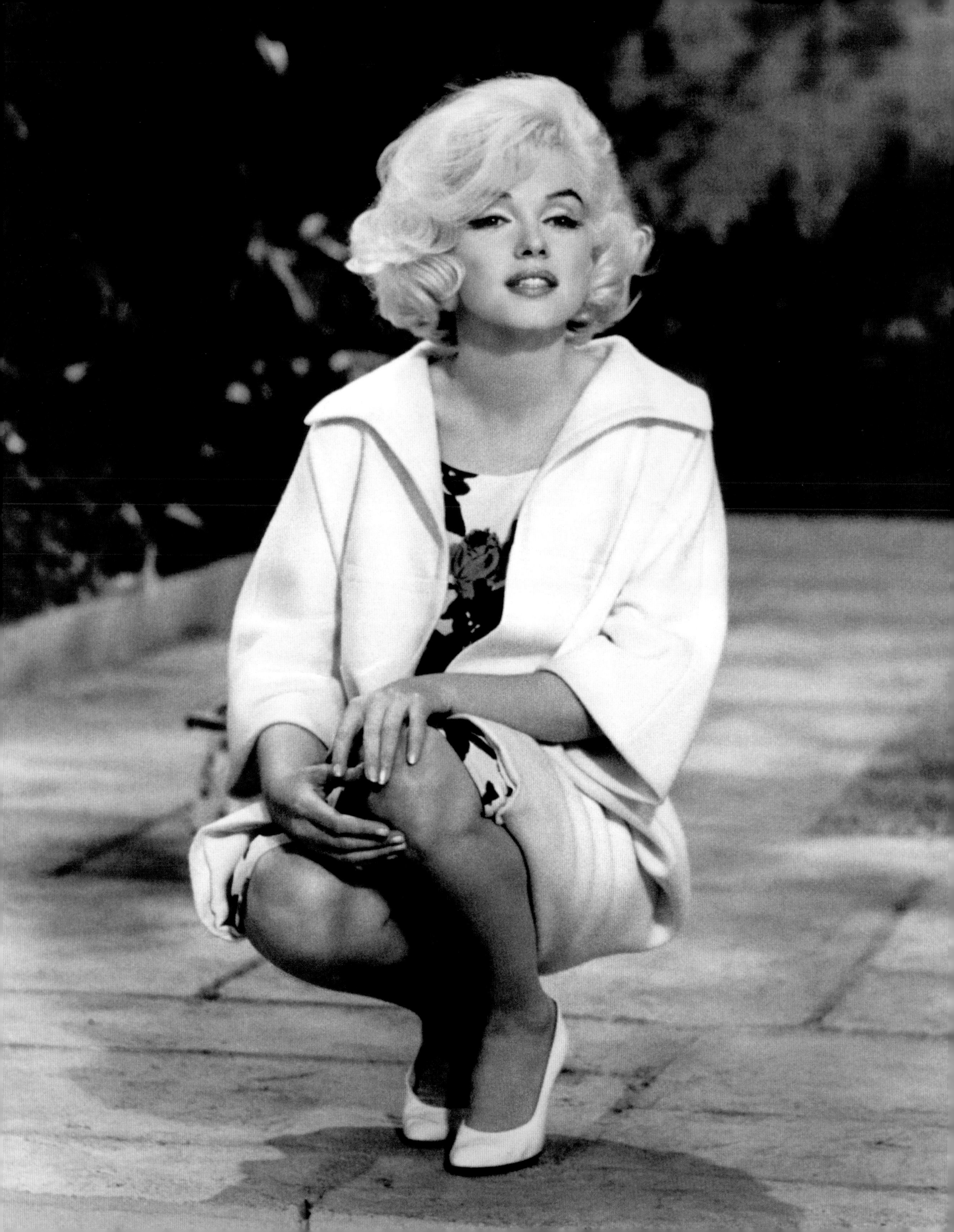

She was very shy about her own suggestions, as though she felt they were unworthy. But she had obviously been working very hard on her part and, like a good actor, had found insights that improved the character she played. On the other hand, also like an actor, many of her ideas were good for her and not so good for the story. But if I hinted at this, her face would go blank for a second, as though the current had been turned off, and when it was turned on again, she would continue as though I had said nothing at all, not disagreeing with me, not even referring to what I had said, simply going on with what followed. I had met this reaction before. It is the normal, uncomplicated self-involvement of the movie star. It stems from a splendid and incorruptible narcissism."

WALTER BERNSTEIN (Scriptwriter, *Something's Got to Give*, 1962)

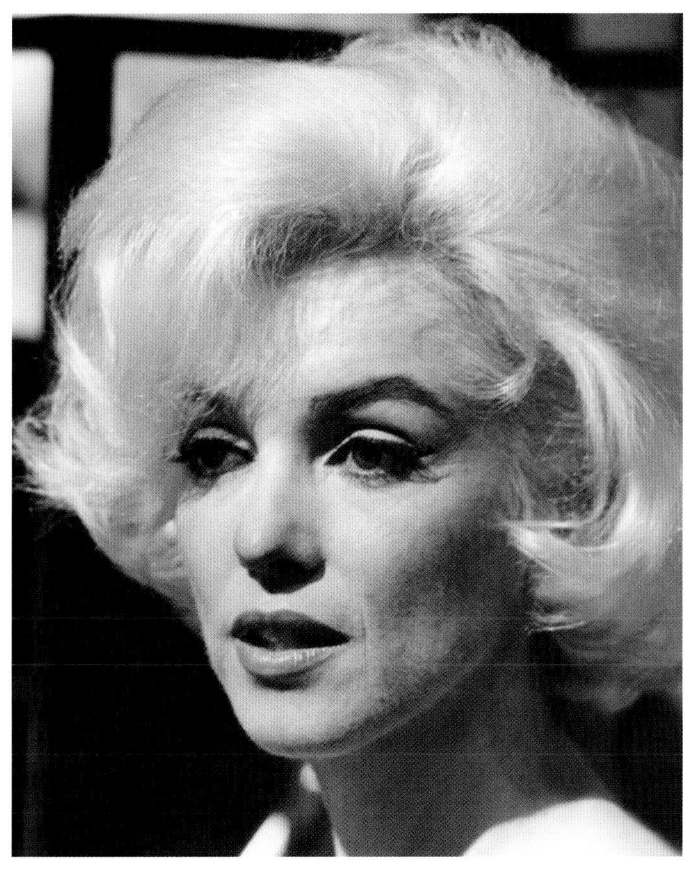

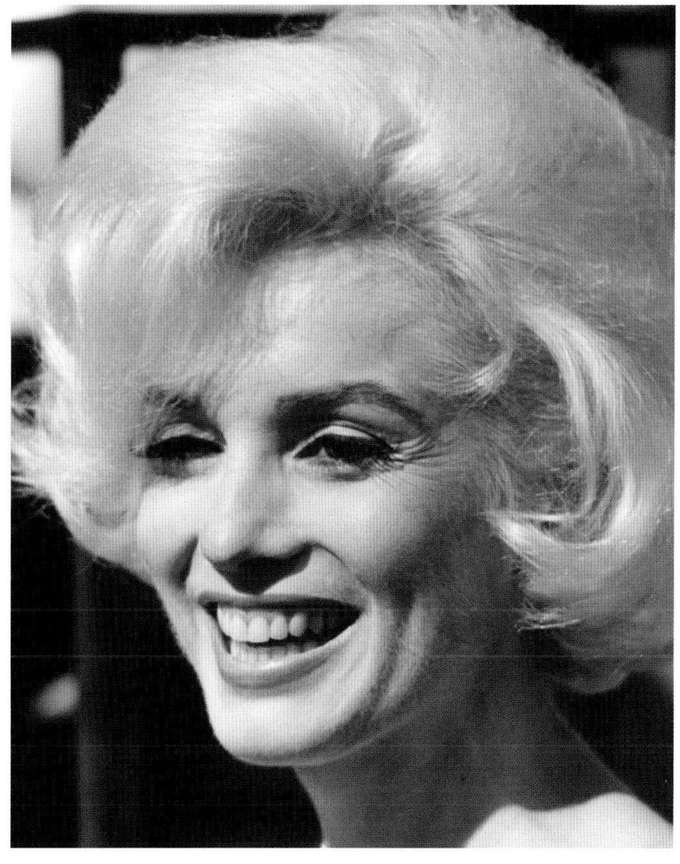

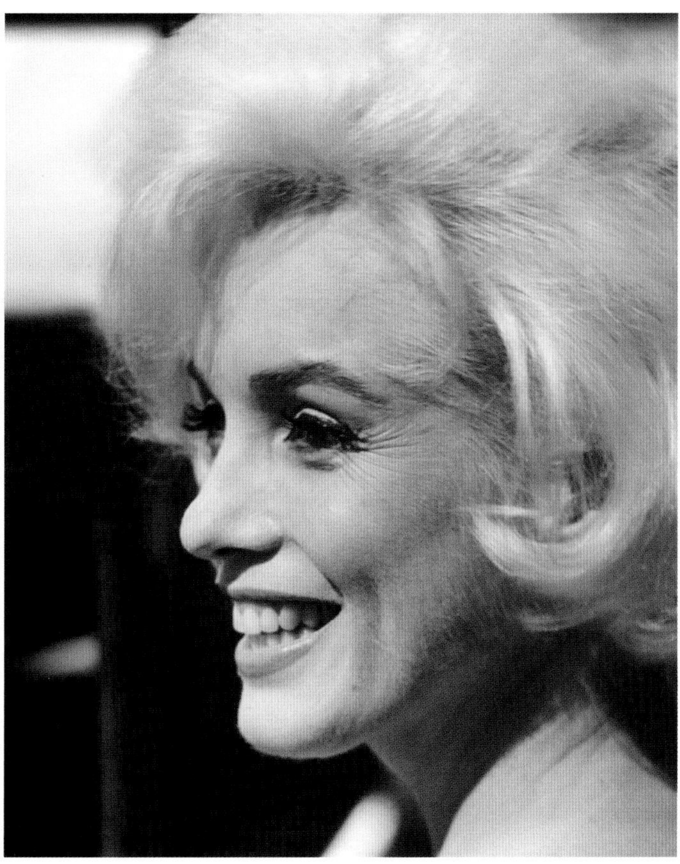

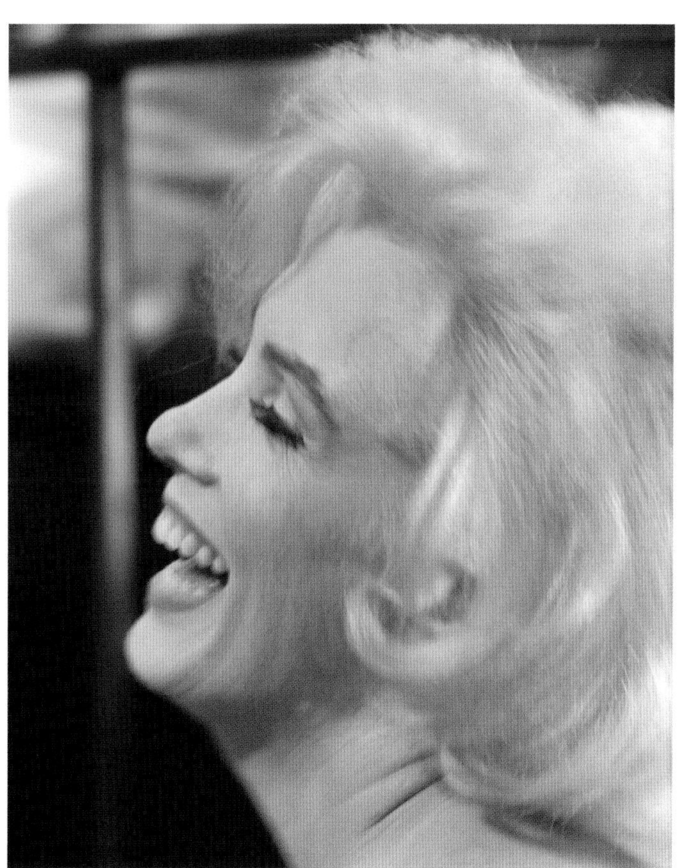

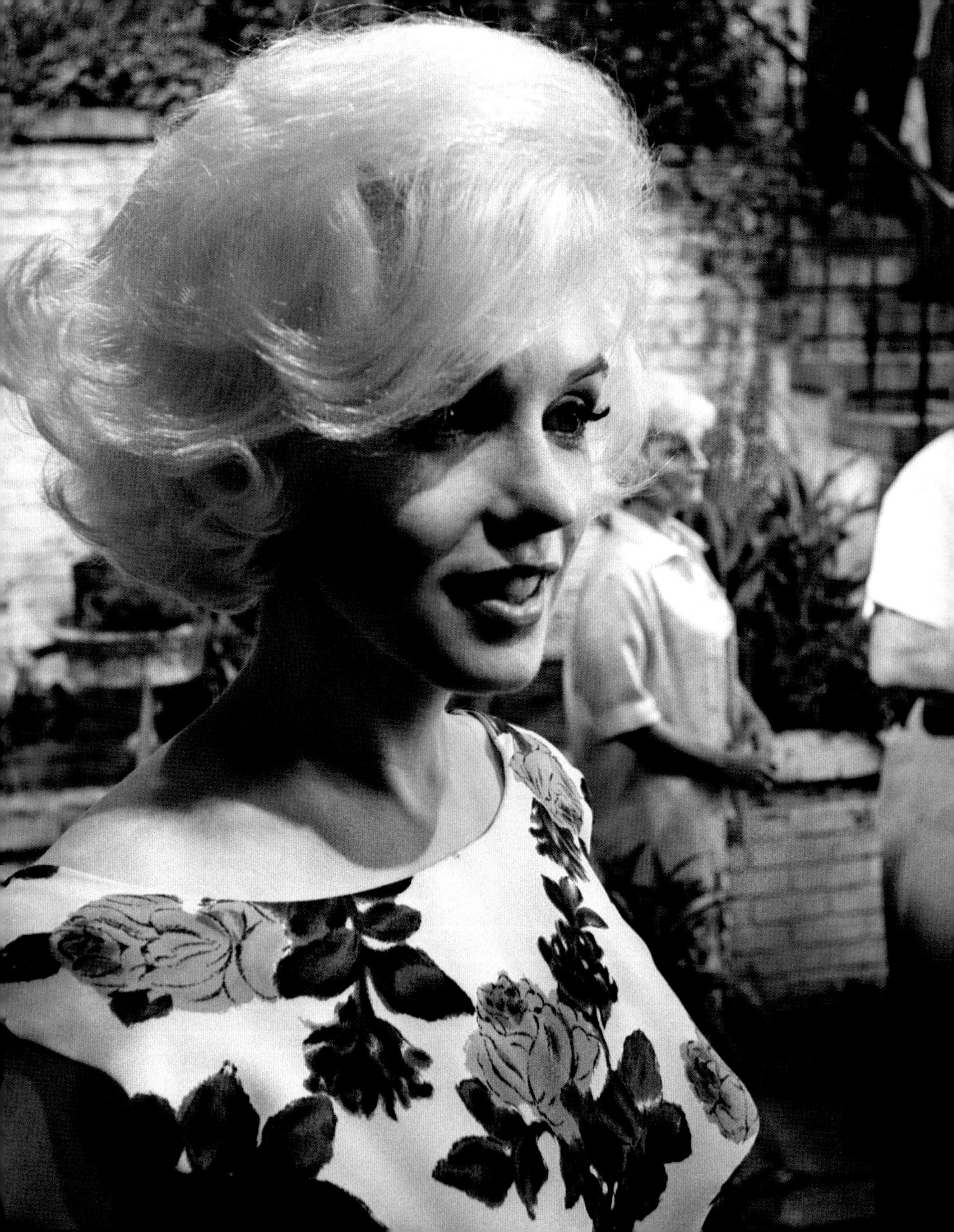

“Any little thing I did for her, she was so appreciative. She treated me more like a friend than a studio associate. Before I would go into a scene to stand in for her, she would come over and fix my hair and my clothes and she’d give me the motivation for the scene, so I would know what I was doing. She was my Paula Strasberg.”

EVELYN MORIARTY (Stand-in, *Something’s Got to Give*, 1962)

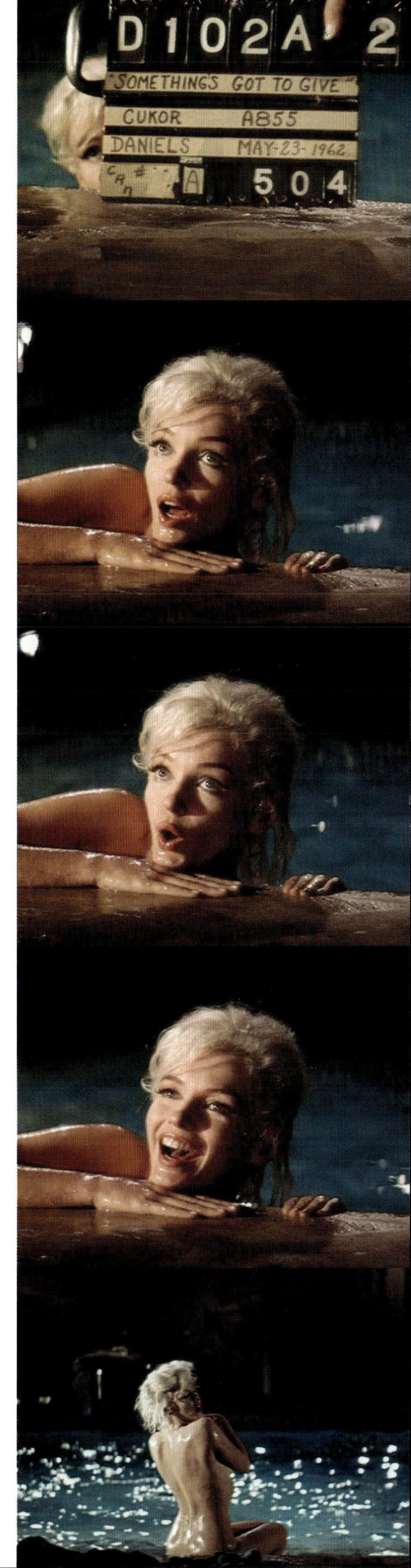

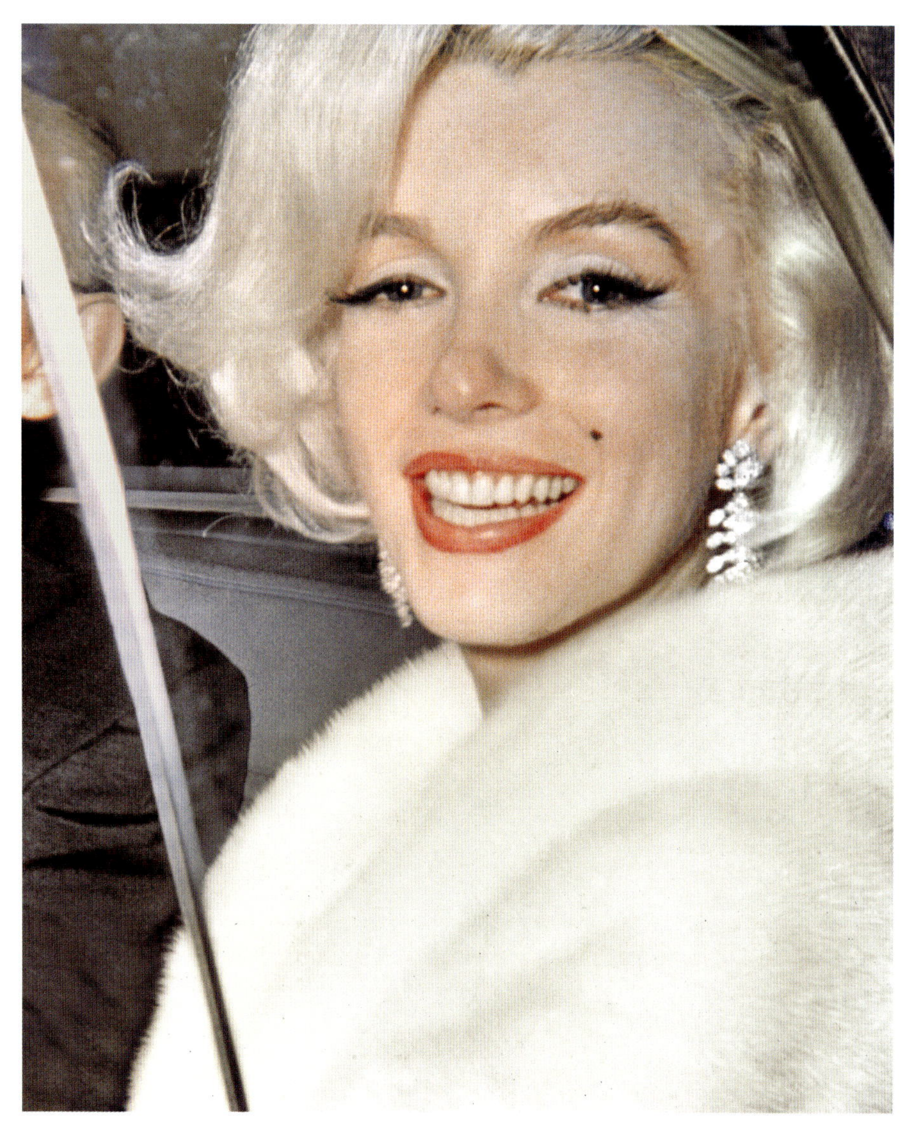

"Marilyn came dressed in a body stocking covered with sequins, which looked as if they were just stuck to her skin because the net was a flesh color. There was a softness to her that was very appealing. She was—well, just extraordinarily beautiful."

DR. MATHILDE KRIM (Scientist and founder of amfAR)

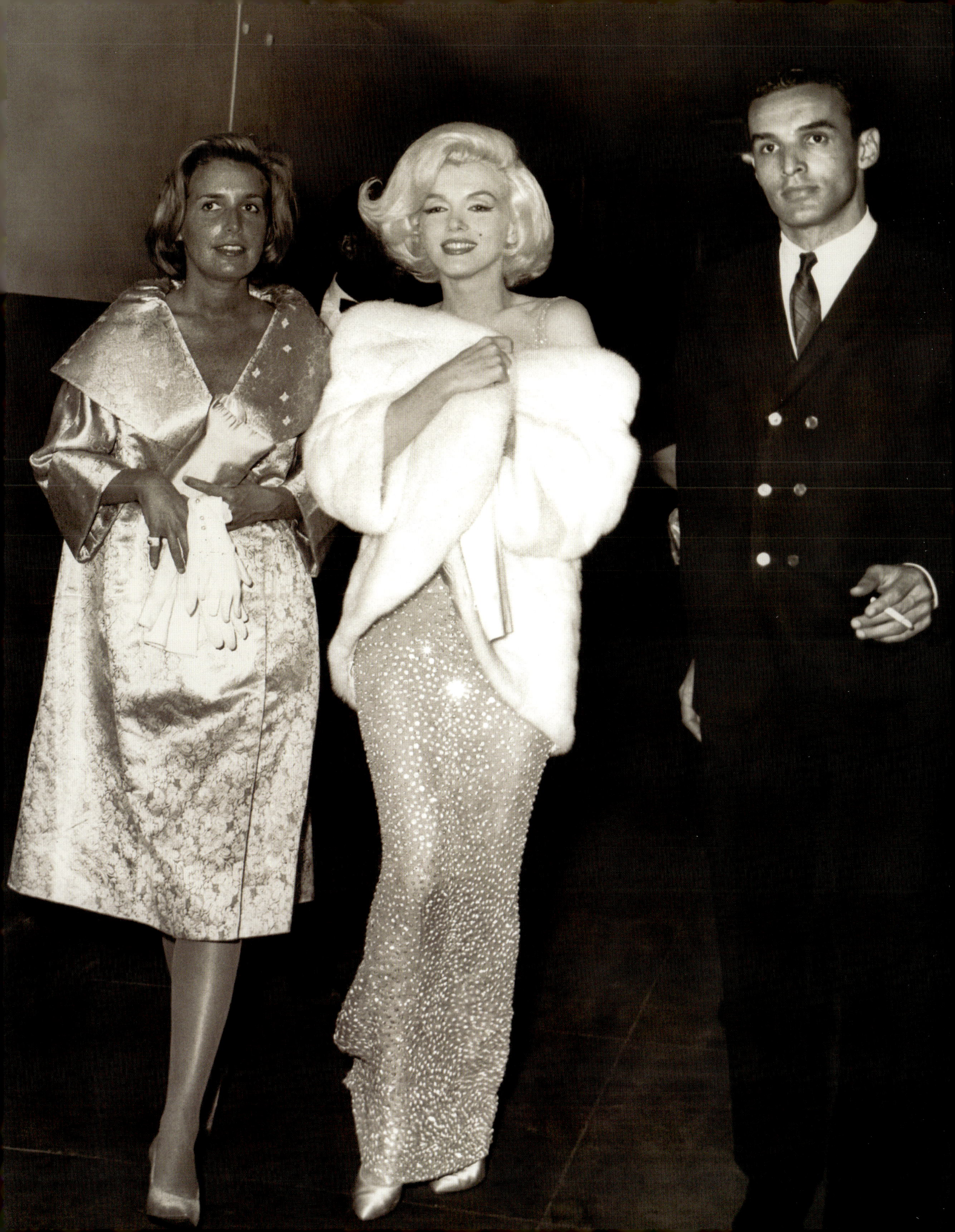

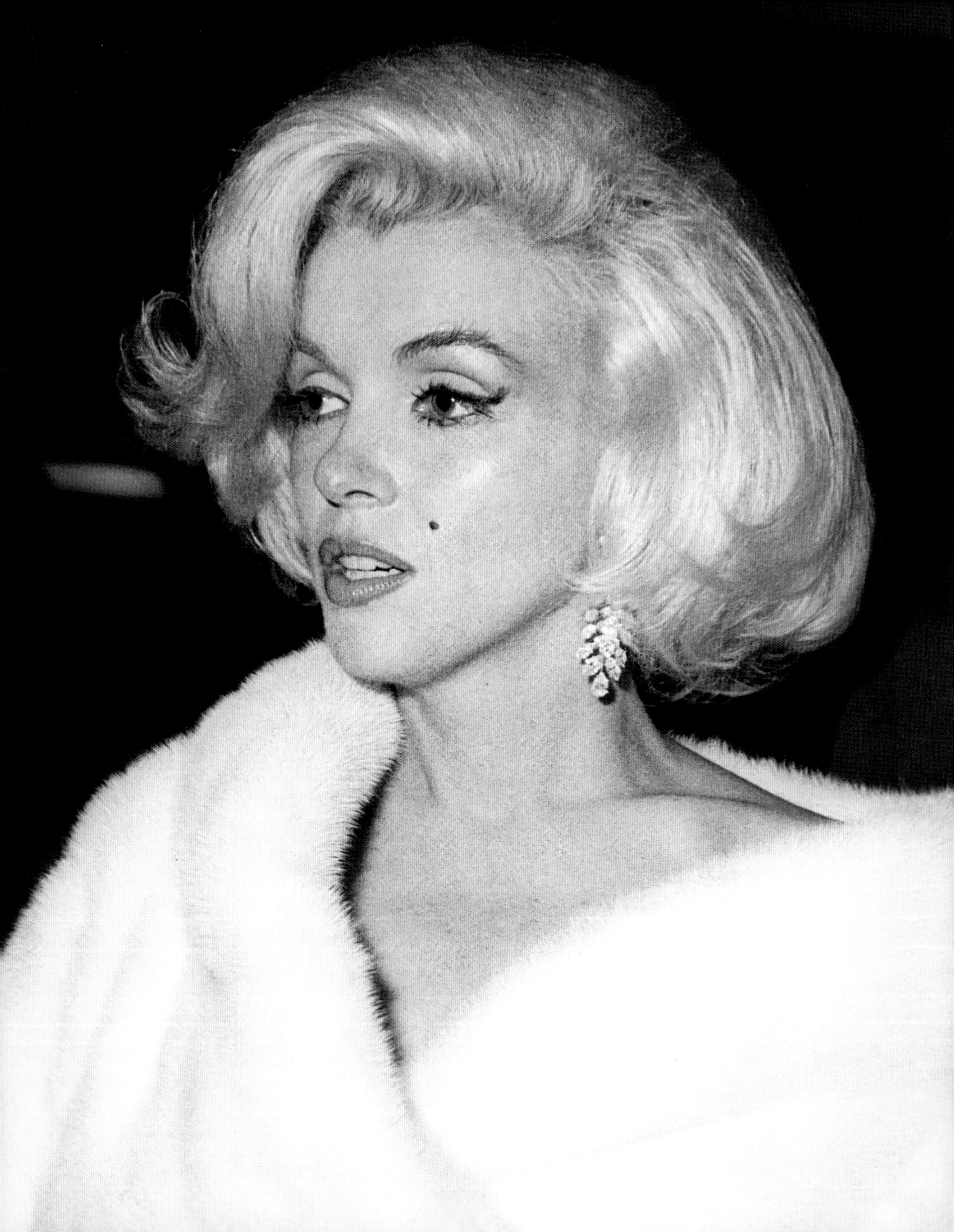

"I don't think I had ever seen anyone so beautiful as Marilyn Monroe that night."

ADLAI STEVENSON (Ambassador to the United Nations, 1961–1965)

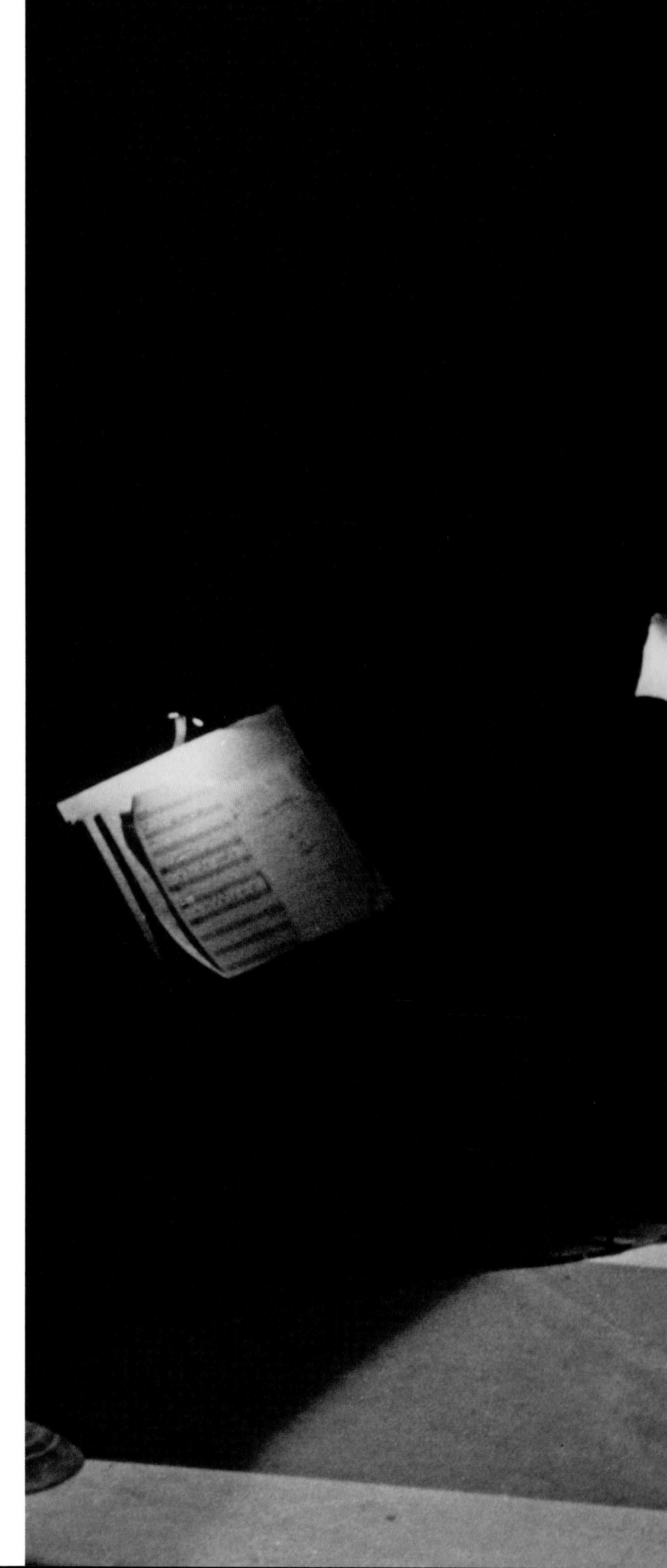

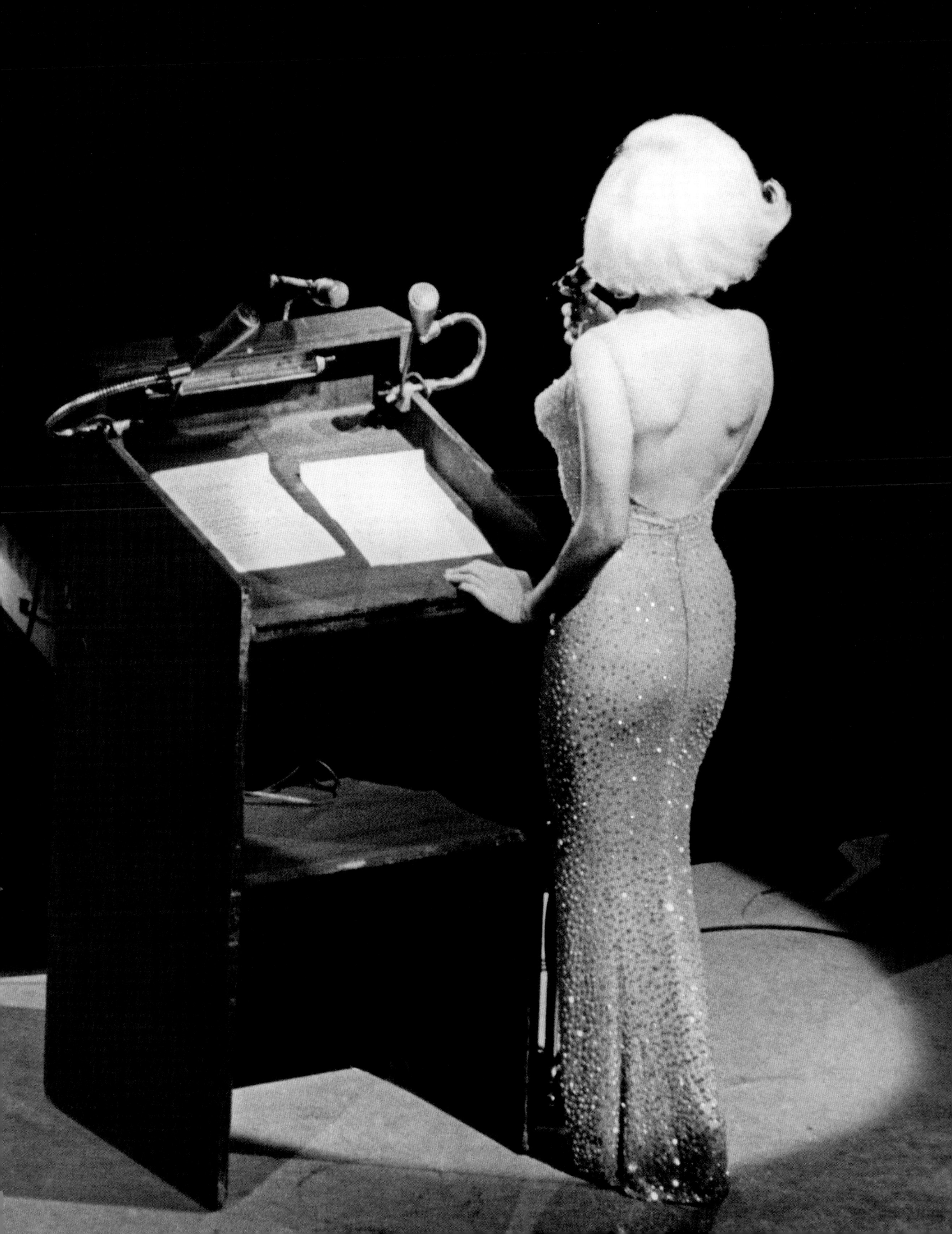

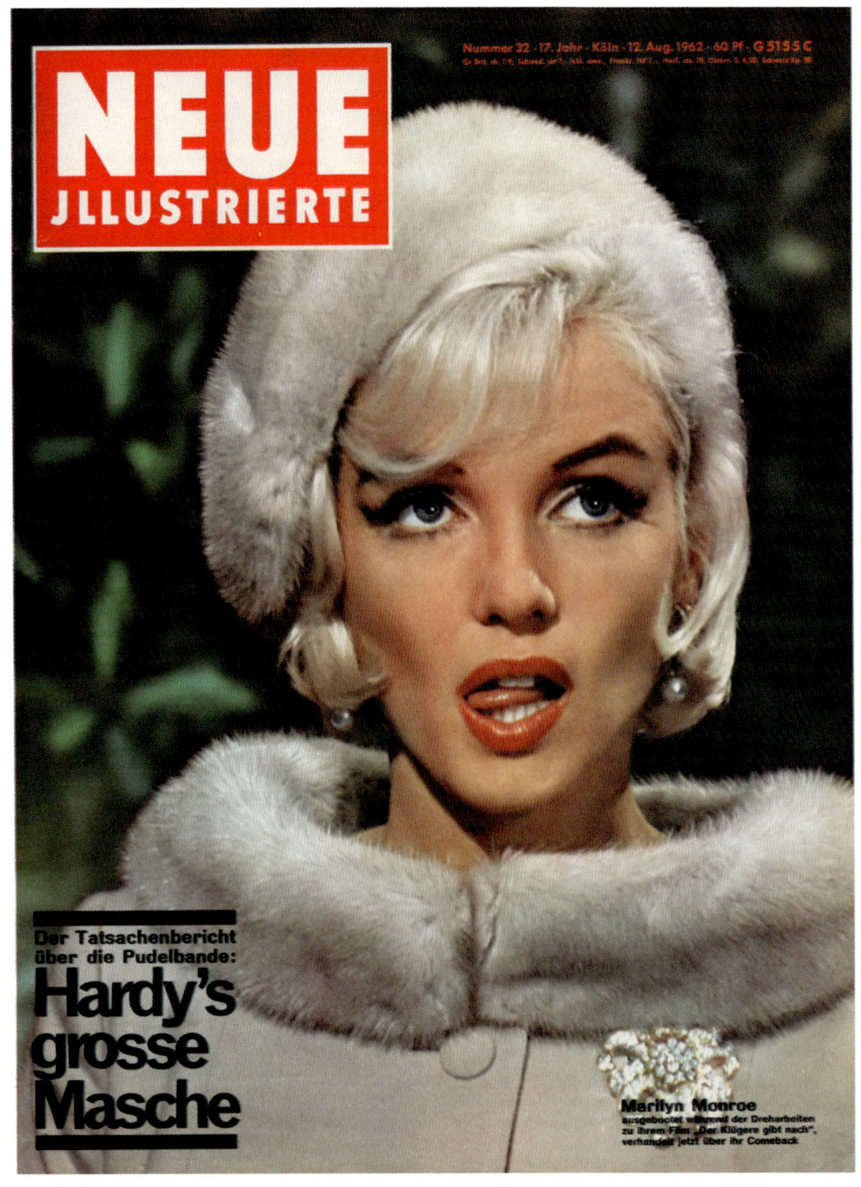

"I looked at the most famous, yet loneliest person I ever saw in my life. She was a beautiful shell. I was shocked. She played the part of America's sex symbol. She cooed. She posed for pictures. She shook hands, and walked off the field. Her smile, no longer required, immediately vanished."

ALBIE PEARSON (Baseball player, Los Angeles Angels, 1961–1966)

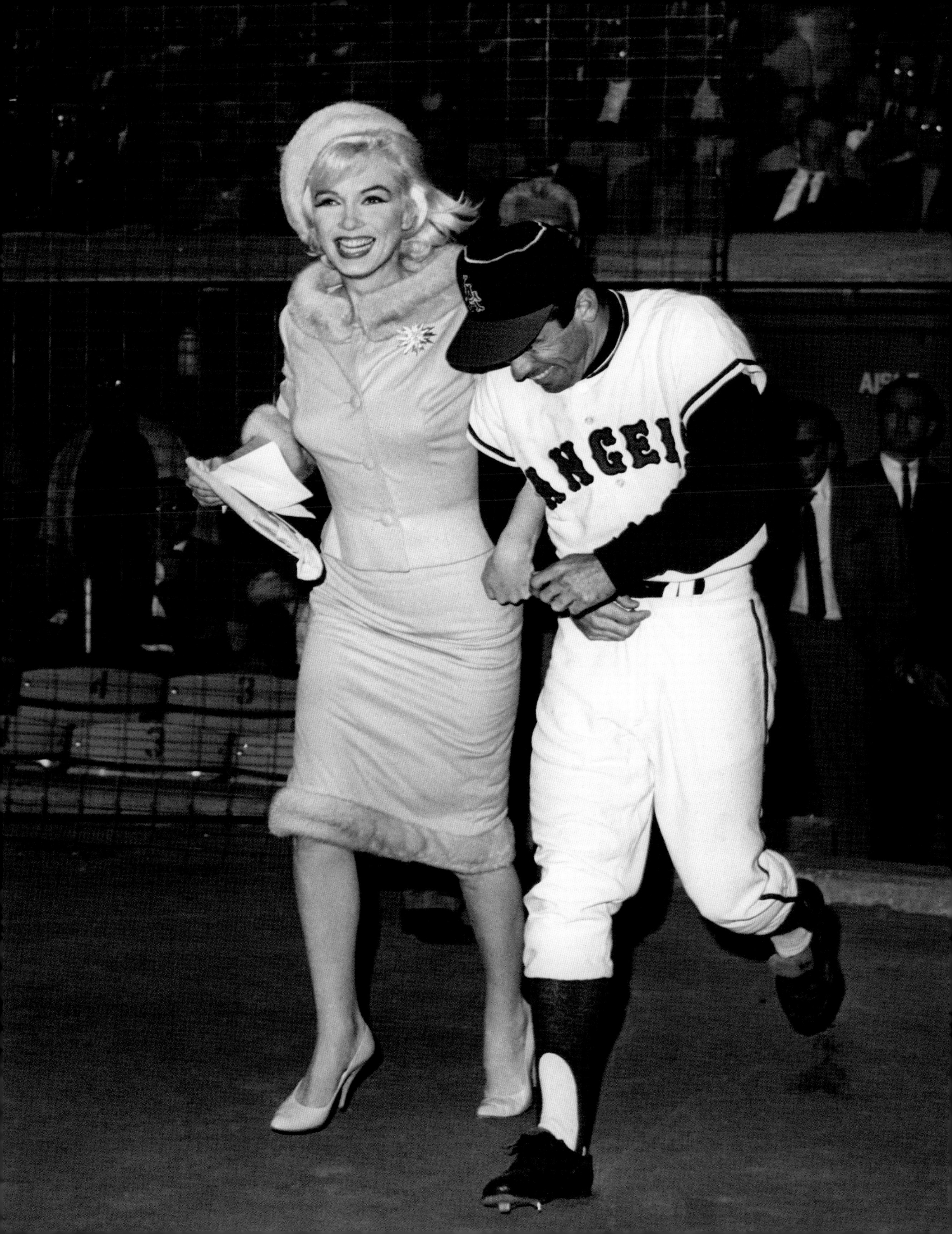

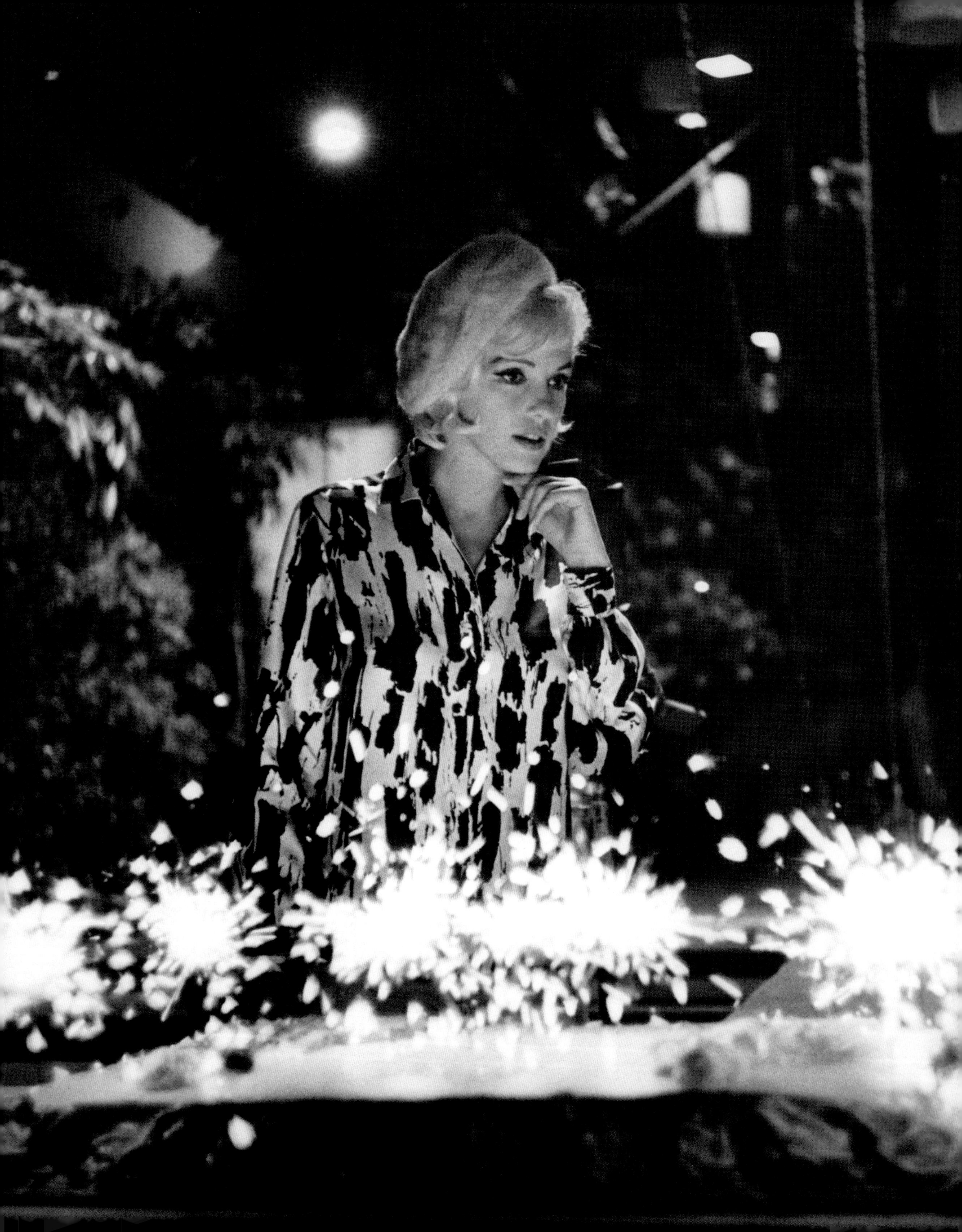

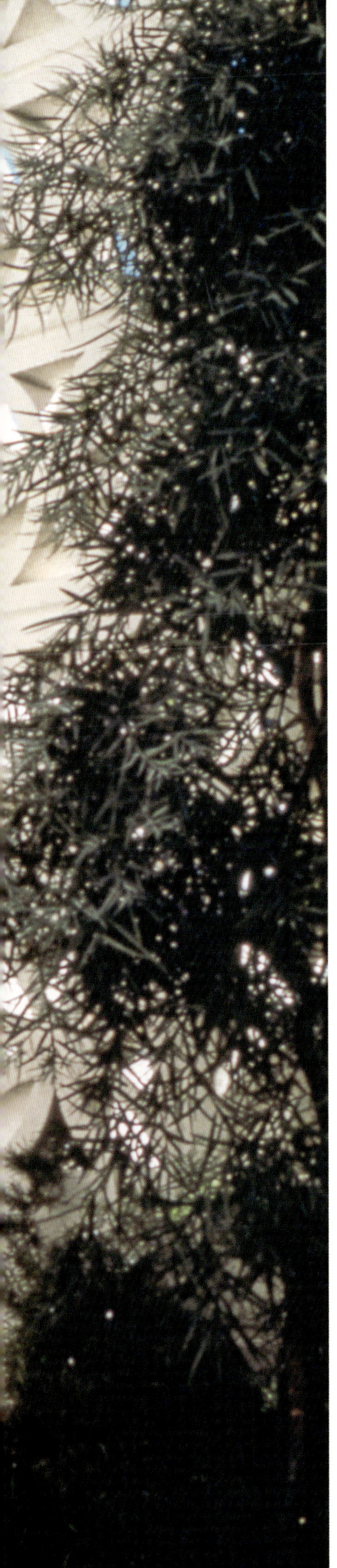

"At the core of her, she was really strong... and that was something we tended to forget, because she seemed so vulnerable, and one always felt it necessary to watch out for her."

PAT NEWCOMB (Marilyn's publicist, 1960–1962)

"Do you remember when Marilyn Monroe died? Everybody stopped work, and you could see all that day the same expressions on their faces, the same thought: 'How can a girl with success, fame, youth, money, beauty. . . how could she kill herself?' Nobody could understand it because those are the things that everybody wants, and they can't believe that life wasn't important to Marilyn Monroe, or that her life was elsewhere."

MARLON BRANDO

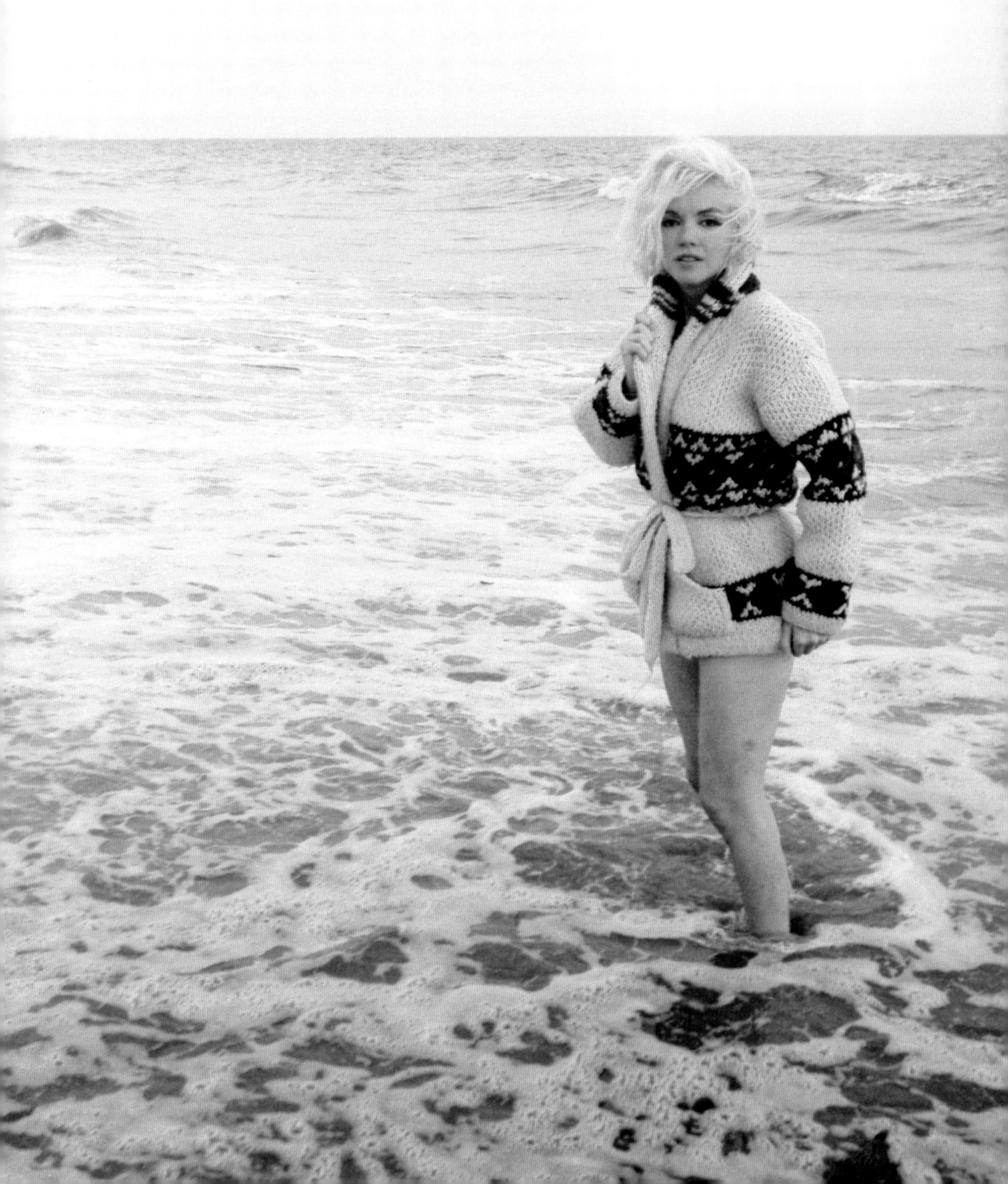

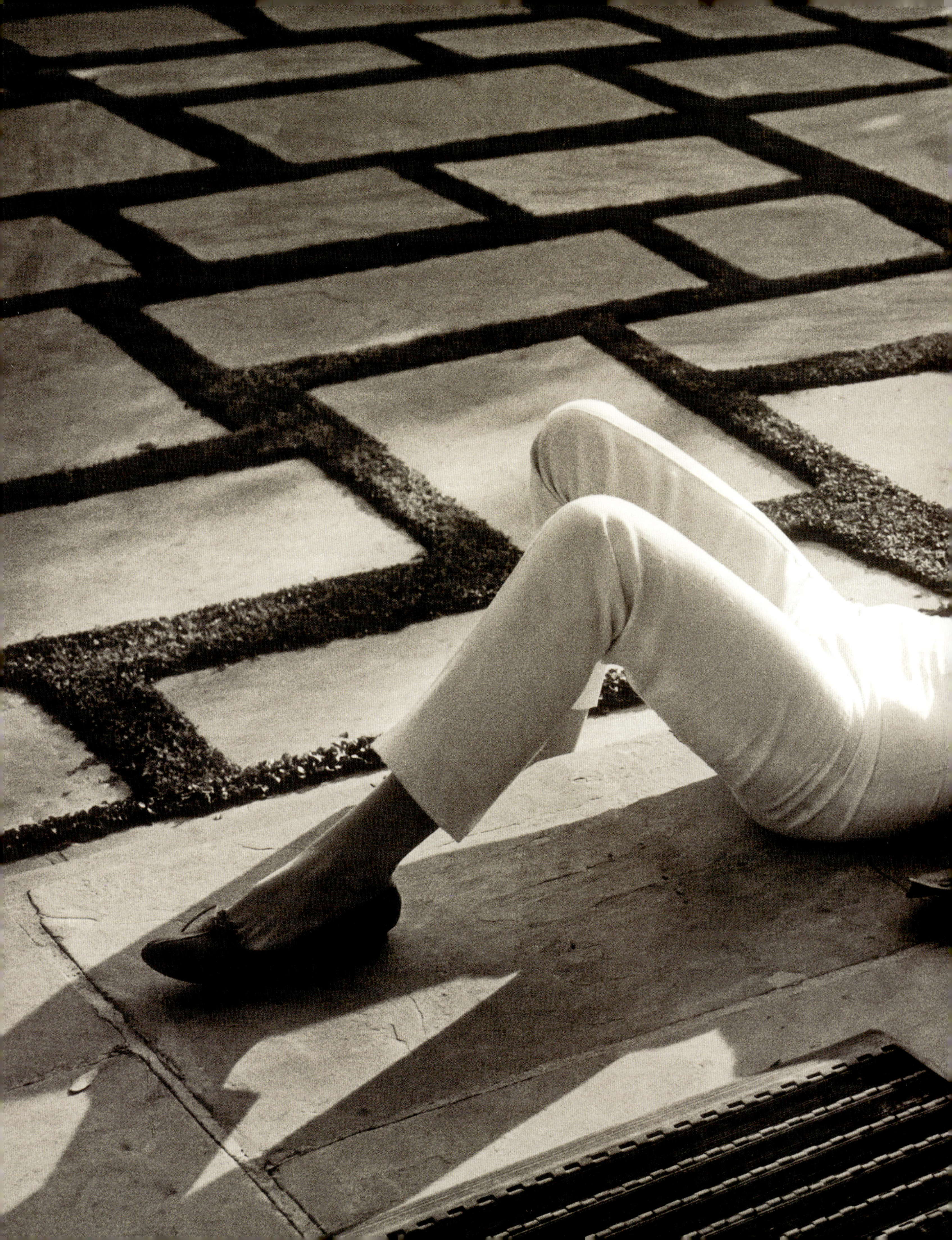

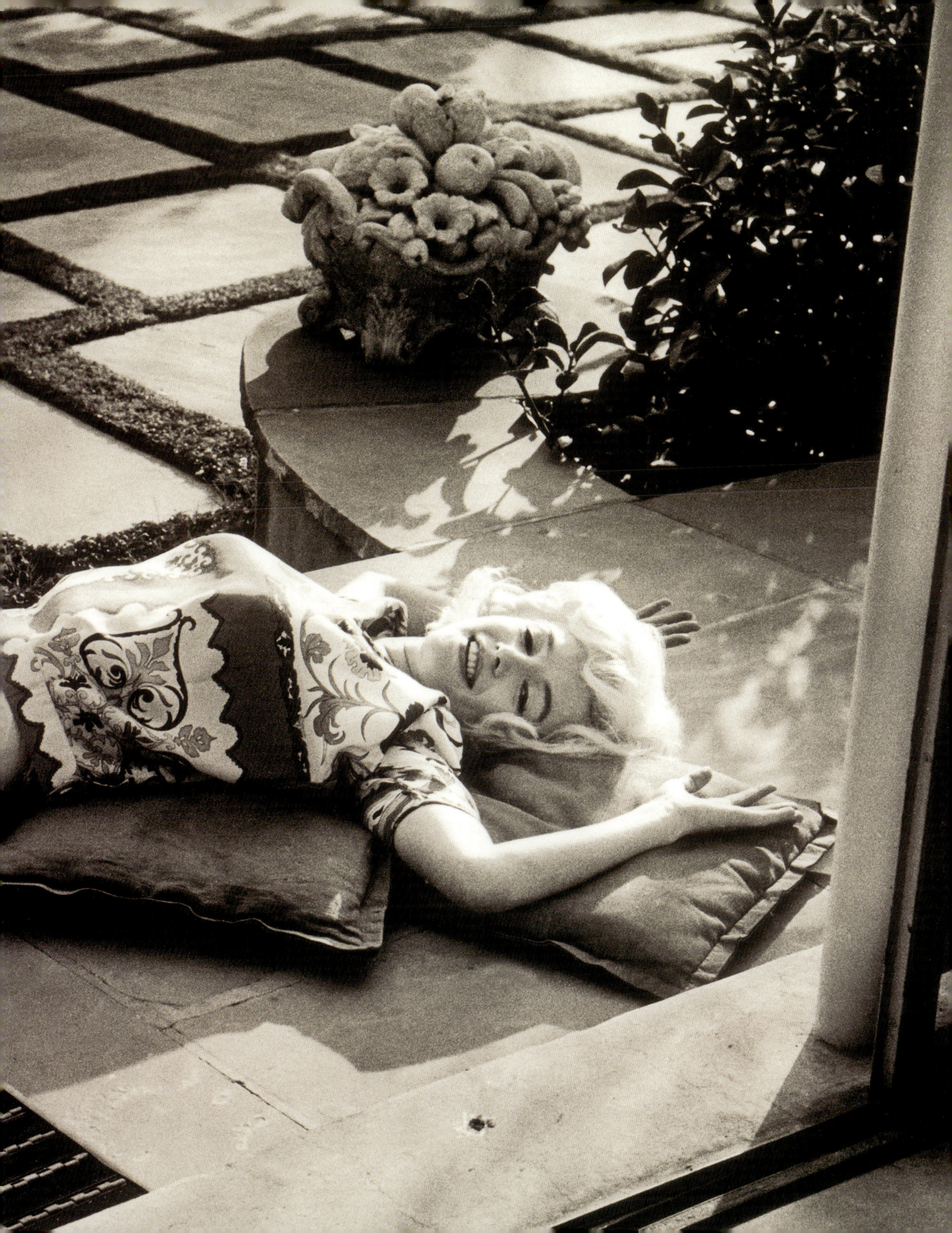

"She will go on eternally."

JACQUELINE KENNEDY ONASSIS

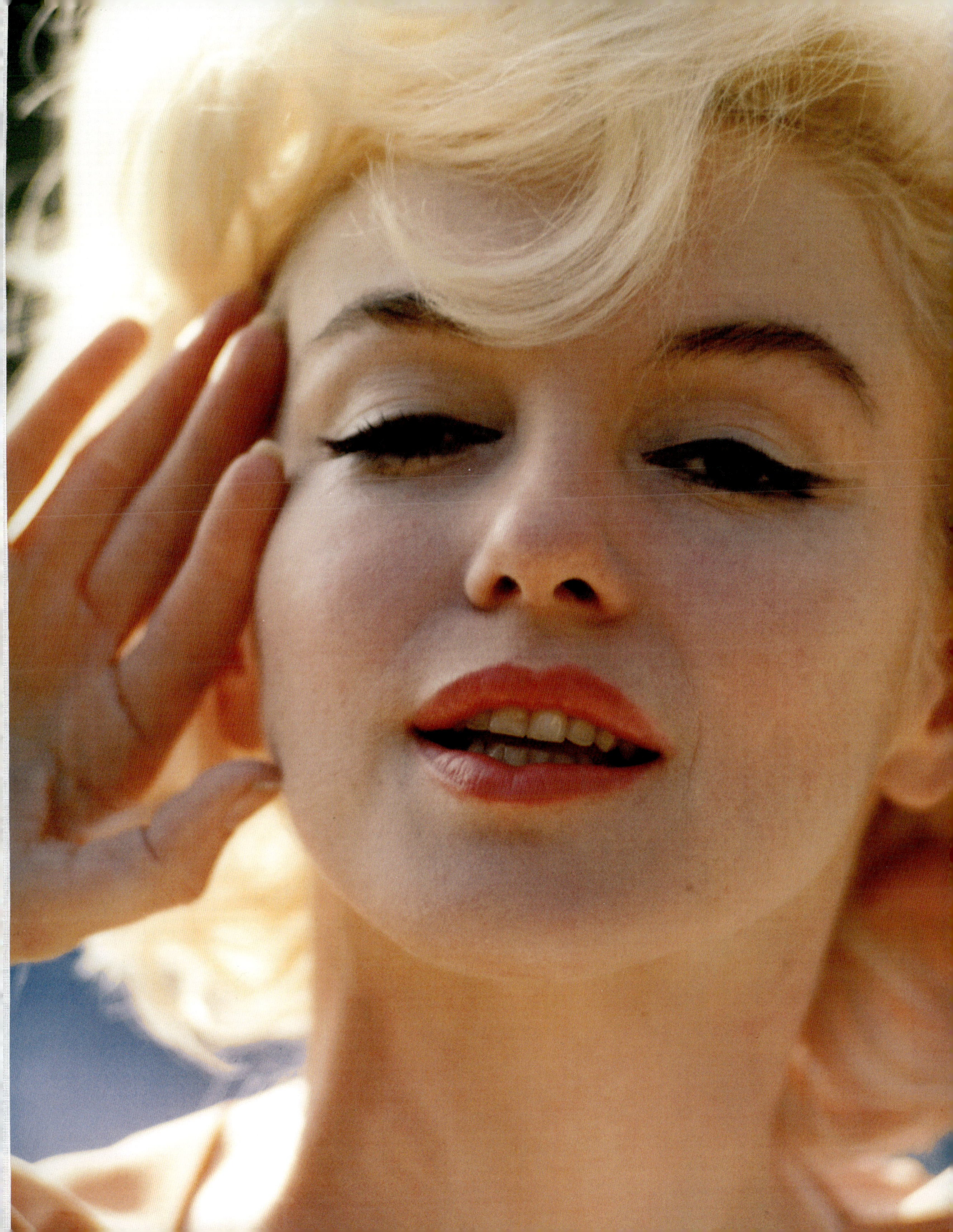

AFTERWORD

Interview by Richard Meryman. Originally published in the article *Marilyn Lets Her Hair Down About Being Famous*, *Life* magazine, August 3, 1962.

Sometimes wearing a scarf and a polo coat and no makeup and with a certain attitude of walking, I go shopping or just look at people living. But then you know, there will be a few teenagers who are kind of sharp and they'll say, "Hey, just a minute. You know who I think that is?" And they'll start tailing me. And I don't mind. I realize some people want to see if you're real. The teenagers, the little kids, their faces light up. They say, "Gee," and they can't wait to tell their friends. And old people come up and say, "Wait till I tell my wife." You've changed their whole day. In the morning, the garbage men that go by 57th Street when I come out the door say, "Marilyn, hi! How do you feel this morning?" To me, it's an honor, and I love them for it. The working men, I'll go by and they'll whistle. At first they whistle because they think, oh, it's a girl. She's got blonde hair and she's not out of shape, and then they say, "Gosh, it's Marilyn Monroe!" And that has its . . . you know, those are times it's nice. People knowing who you are and all of that, and feeling that you've meant something to them.

I don't know quite why, but somehow I feel they know that I mean what I do, both when I'm acting on the screen or when if I see them in person and greet them. That I really always do mean hello, and how are you? In their fantasies they feel "Gee, it can happen to me!" But when you're famous you kind of run into human nature in a raw kind of way. It stirs up envy, fame does. People you run into feel that, well, who is she who does she think she is, Marilyn Monroe? They feel fame gives them some kind of privilege to walk up to you and say anything to you, you know, of any kind of nature and it won't hurt your feelings. Like it's happening to your clothing. One time here I am looking for a home to buy and I stopped at this place. A man came out and was very pleasant and cheerful, and said, "Oh, just a moment, I want my wife to meet you." Well, she came out and said, "Will you please get off the premises?" You're always running into people's unconscious.

Let's take some actors or directors. Usually they don't say it to me, they say it to the newspapers because that's a bigger play. You know, if they're only insulting me to my face that doesn't make a big enough play because all I have to say is, "See you around, like never." But if it's in the newspapers, it's coast-to-coast and all around the world. I don't understand why people aren't a little more generous with each other. I don't like to say this, but I'm afraid there is a lot of envy in this business. The only thing I can do is stop and think, "I'm all right but I'm not so sure about them!" For instance, you've read there was some actor that once said that kissing me was like kissing Hitler. Well, I think that's his problem. If I have to do intimate love scenes with somebody who really has these kinds of feelings toward me, then my fantasy can come into play. In other words, out with him, in with my fantasy. He was never there.

It's nice to be included in people's fantasies, but you also like to be accepted for your own sake. I don't look at myself as a commodity, but I'm sure a lot of people have. Including, well, one corporation in particular, which shall be nameless. If I'm sounding picked on or something, I think I am. I'll think I have a few wonderful friends and all of a sudden, ooh, here it comes. They do a lot of things. They talk about you to the press, to their friends, tell stories, and you know, it's disappointing. These are the ones you aren't interested in seeing every day of your life.

Of course, it does depend on the people, but sometimes I'm invited places to kind of brighten up a dinner table like a musician who'll play the piano after dinner, and I know you're not really invited for yourself. You're just an ornament.

When I was five I think, that's when I started wanting to be an actress. I loved to play. I didn't like the world around me because it was kind of grim, but I loved to play house. It was like you could make your own boundaries. It goes beyond house; you could make your own situations and you could pretend, and even if the other kids were a little slow on the imagining part, you could say, "Hey, what about if you were such and such, and I were such and such, wouldn't that be fun?" And they'd say, "Oh, yes," and then I'd say, "Well, that will be a horse and this will be. . . ." It was play, playfulness. When I heard that this was acting, I said that's what I want to be. You can play. But then you grow up and find out about playing, that they make playing very difficult for you. Some of my foster families used to send me to the movies to get me out of the house and there I'd sit all day and way into the night. Up in front, there with the screen so big, a little kid all alone, and I loved it. I loved anything that moved up there and I didn't miss anything that happened and there was no popcorn either.

When I was eleven, the whole world was closed to me. I just felt I was on the outside of the world. Suddenly, everything opened up. Even the girls paid a little attention to me because they thought, "Hmmm, she's to be dealt with!" And I had this long walk to school, two and a half miles [there], two and a half miles back. It was just sheer pleasure. Every fellow honked his horn, you know, workers driving to work, waving, you know, and I'd wave back. The world became friendly. All the newspaper boys when they delivered the paper would come around to where I lived, and I used to hang from the limb of a tree, and I had sort of a sweatshirt on. I didn't realize the value of a sweatshirt in those days, and then I was sort of beginning to catch on, but I didn't quite get it, because I couldn't really afford sweaters. But here they come with their bicycles, you know, and I'd get these free papers and the family liked that, and they'd all pull their bicycles up around the tree and then I'd be hanging, looking kind of like a monkey, I guess. I was a little shy to come down. I did get down to the curb, kinda kicking the curb and kicking the leaves and talking, but mostly listening. And sometimes the family used to worry because I used to laugh so loud and so gay; I guess they felt it was hysterical. It was just this sudden freedom because I would ask the boys, "Can I ride your bike now?" and they'd say, "Sure." Then I'd go zooming, laughing in the wind, riding down the block, laughing, and they'd all stand around and wait till I came back. But I loved the wind. It caressed me. But it was kind of a double-edged thing. I did find, too, when the world opened up that people took a lot for granted, like not only could they be friendly, but they could suddenly get overly friendly and expect an awful lot for very little. When I was older, I used to go to Grauman's Chinese Theatre and try to fit my foot in the prints in the cement there. And I'd say, "Oh, oh, my foot's too big! I guess that's out." I did have a funny feeling later when I finally put my foot down into that wet cement. I sure knew what it really meant to me. Anything's possible, almost.

It was the creative part that kept me going, trying to be an actress. I enjoy acting when you really hit it right. And I guess I've always had too much fantasy to be only a housewife. Well, also, I had to eat. I was never kept, to be blunt about it; I always kept myself. I have always had a pride in the fact that I was my own. And Los Angeles was my home, too, so when they said, "Go home!" I said, "I am home." The time I sort of began to think I was famous, I was driving somebody to the airport, and as I came back there was this movie house and I saw my name in lights. I pulled the car up at a distance down the street; it was too much to take up close, you know, all of a sudden. And I said, "God, somebody's made a mistake." But there it was, in lights. And I sat there and said, "So that's the way it looks," and it was all very strange to me, and yet at the studio they had said, "Remember, you're not a star." Yet there it is up in lights. I really got the idea I must be a star or something from the newspapermen; I'm saying men, not the women who would interview me and they would be warm and friendly. By the way, that part of the press, you know, the men of the press, unless they have their own personal quirks against me, they were always very warm and friendly and they'd say, "You know, you're the only star," and I'd say, "Star?" and they'd look at me as if I were nuts. I think they, in their own kind of way, made me realize I was famous.

I remember when I got the part in *Gentlemen Prefer Blondes*. Jane Russell—she was the brunette in it and I was the blonde. She got $200,000 for it, and I got my $500 a week, but that to me was, you know, considerable. She, by the way, was quite wonderful to me. The only thing was I couldn't get a dressing room. Finally, I really got to this kind of level and I said, "Look, after all, I am the blonde, and it is *Gentlemen Prefer Blondes*!" Because still they always kept saying, "Remember, you're not a star." I said, "Well, whatever I am, I am the blonde!" And I want to say to the people, if I am a star, the people made me a star. No studio, no person, but the people did. There was a reaction that came to the studio, the fan mail, or when I went to a premiere, or the exhibitors wanted to meet me. I didn't know why. When they all rushed toward me I looked behind me to see who was there and I said, "My heavens!" I was scared to death. I used to get the feeling, and sometimes I still get it, that sometimes I was fooling somebody; I don't know who or what, maybe myself.

I've always felt toward the slightest scene, even if all I had to do in a scene was just to come in and say, "Hi," that the people ought to get their money's worth and that this is an obligation of mine, to give them the best you can get from me. I do have feelings some days when there are scenes with a lot of responsibility toward the meaning, and I'll wish, "Gee, if only I had been a cleaning woman." On the way to the studio I would see somebody cleaning and I'd say, "That's what I'd like to be. That's my ambition in life." But I think that all actors go through this. We not only want to be good, we have to be. You know, when they talk about nervousness, my teacher, Lee Strasberg, when I said to him, "I don't know what's wrong with me but I'm a little nervous," he said, "When you're not, give up, because nervousness indicates sensitivity." Also, a struggle with shyness is in every actor more than anyone can imagine. There is a censor inside us that says to what degree do we let go, like a child playing. I guess people think we just go out there, and you know, that's all we do. Just do it. But it's a real struggle. I'm one of the world's most self-conscious people. I really have to struggle.

An actor is not a machine, no matter how much they want to say you are. Creativity has got to start with humanity, and when you're a human being, you feel, you suffer. You're gay, you're sick, you're nervous or whatever. Like any creative human being, I would like a bit more control so that it would be a little easier for me when the director says, "One tear, right now," that one tear would pop out. But once there came two tears because I thought, "How dare he?" Goethe said, "Talent is developed in privacy," you know? And it's really true. There is a need for aloneness, which I don't think most people realize for an actor. It's almost having certain kinds of secrets for yourself that you'll let the whole world in on only for a moment, when you're acting. But everybody is always tugging at you. They'd all like sort of a chunk of you.

I think that when you are famous every weakness is exaggerated. This industry should behave like a mother whose child has just run out in front of a car. But instead of clasping the child to them, they start punishing the child. Like you don't dare get a cold. How dare you get a cold! I mean, the executives can get colds and stay home forever and phone it in, but how dare you, the actor, get a cold or a virus. You know, no one feels worse than the one who's sick. I sometimes wish, gee, I wish they had to act a comedy with a temperature and a virus infection. I am not an actress who appears at a studio just for the purpose of discipline. This doesn't have anything at all to do with art. I myself would like to become more disciplined within my work. But I'm there to give a performance and not to be disciplined by a studio! After all, I'm not in a military school. This is supposed to be an art form, not just a manufacturing establishment. The sensitivity that helps me to act, you see, also makes me react. An actor is supposed to be a sensitive instrument. Isaac Stern takes good care of his violin. What if everybody jumped on his violin?

You know a lot of people have, oh gee, real quirky problems that they wouldn't dare have anyone know. But one of my problems happens to show: I'm late. I guess people think that why I'm late is some kind of arrogance and I think it is the opposite of arrogance. I also feel that I'm not in this big American rush, you know, you got to go and you got to go fast but for no good reason. The main thing is, I want to be prepared when I get there to give a good performance or whatever to the best of my ability. A lot of people can be there on time and do nothing, which I have seen them do, and you know, all sit around sort of chitchatting and talking trivia about their social life. Gable said about me, "When she's there, she's there. All of her is there! She's there to work."

I was honored when they asked me to appear at the president's birthday rally in Madison Square Garden. There was like a hush over the whole place when I came on to sing "Happy Birthday," like if I had been wearing a slip, I would have thought it was showing or something. I thought, "Oh, my gosh, what if no sound comes out!"

A hush like that from the people warms me. It's sort of like an embrace. Then you think, by God, I'll sing this song if it's the last thing I ever do, and for all the people. Because I remember when I turned to the microphone, I looked all the way up and back, and I thought, "That's where I'd be, way up there under one of those rafters, close to the ceiling, after I paid my two dollars to come into the place." Afterwards they had some sort of reception. I was with my former father-in-law, Isadore Miller, so I think I did something wrong when I met the president. Instead of saying, "How do you do?" I just said "This is my former father-in-law, Isadore Miller." He came here an immigrant and I thought this would be one of the biggest things in his life. He's about seventy-five or eighty years old, and

I thought this would be something that he would be telling his grandchildren about and all that. I should have said, "How do you do, Mr. President," but I had already done the singing, so well you know. I guess nobody noticed it.

Fame has a special burden, which I might as well state here and now. I don't mind being burdened with being glamorous and sexual. But what goes with it can be a burden. I feel that beauty and femininity are ageless and can't be contrived, and glamour, although the manufacturers won't like this, cannot be manufactured. Not real glamour; it's based on femininity. I think that sexuality is only attractive when it's natural and spontaneous. This is where a lot of them miss the boat. And then something I'd just like to spout off on. We are all born sexual creatures, thank God, but it's a pity so many people despise and crush this natural gift. Art, real art, comes from it, everything.

I never quite understood it, this sex symbol. I always thought symbols were those things you clash together! That's the trouble, a sex symbol becomes a thing. I just hate to be a thing. But if I'm going to be a symbol of something I'd rather have it sex than some other things they've got symbols of! These girls who try to be me, I guess the studios put them up to it, or they get the ideas themselves. But gee, they haven't got it. You can make a lot of gags about it like they haven't got the foreground or else they haven't the background. But I mean the middle, where you live.

All my stepchildren carried the burden of my fame. Sometimes they would read terrible things about me, and I'd worry about whether it would hurt them. I would tell them: Don't hide these things from me. I'd rather you ask me these things straight out and I'll answer all your questions.

I wanted them to know of life other than their own. I used to tell them, for instance, that I worked for five cents a month and I washed one hundred dishes, and my stepkids would say, "One hundred dishes!" and I said, "Not only that, I scraped and cleaned them before I washed them." I washed them and rinsed them and put them in the draining place, but I said, "Thank God I didn't have to dry them."

I was never used to being happy, so that wasn't something I ever took for granted. You see, I was brought up differently from the average American child because the average child is brought up expecting to be happy. That's it: successful, happy, and on time. Yet because of fame I was able to meet and marry two of the nicest men I'd ever met up to that time.

I don't think people will turn against me, at least not by themselves. I like people. The "public" scares me, but people I trust. Maybe they can be impressed by the press or when a studio starts sending out all kinds of stories. But I think when people go to see a movie, they judge for themselves. We human beings are strange creatures and still reserve the right to think for ourselves.

Once I was supposed to be finished, that was the end of me. When Mr. Miller was on trial for contempt of Congress, a certain corporation executive said either he named names and I got him to name names, or I was finished. I said, "I'm proud of my husband's position, and I stand behind him all the way," and the court did, too. "Finished," they said. "You'll never be heard of."

It might be a kind of relief to be finished. You have to start all over again. But I believe you're always as good as your potential. I now live in my work and in a few relationships with the few people I can really count on. Fame will go by, and, so long, I've had you fame. If it goes by, I've always known it was fickle. So at least it's something I experienced, but that's not where I live.

PHOTO CREDITS

Cover

Marilyn Monroe, actor, New York, June 1958. Photograph by Richard Avedon. © The Richard Avedon Foundation.

Endpapers

Photo by Frank Powolny, 1953 (author's collection).

Opening

III: Photo by Andre de Dienes, 1945 (Reproduced with permission of Chuck Murphy. One West Publishing. www.1westpublishing.com).

IV: 1949 (author's collection).

VII: 1950 (author's collection).

VIII: Photo by Gene Kornman, 1952 (author's collection).

XI: Photo by Philippe Halsman, New York City, 1959 (Magnum Photos).

XII: *The Misfits*, Reno, Nevada, 1960 (United Artists / The Kobal Collection).

XV: *Something's Got to Give* costume test. April 10, 1962 (Kim Goodwin collection).

Introduction

XX: Marilyn Monroe, actor, New York, May 6, 1957. Photograph by Richard Avedon. © The Richard Avedon Foundation.

Chrysalis

XXX: 1942 (author's collection).

3: 1942 (author's collection).

4: Marriage to James Dougherty at the home of Mr. and Mrs. Chester Howell. West Los Angeles, June 19, 1942 (author's collection).

6: 1942 (author's collection).

7: 1943 (author's collection).

8: Radio Plane Company, 1944. Photo by David Conover (Kim Goodwin collection. Reproduced with permission of David Conover Jr. www.dconover.com).

10–11: Photos by Andre de Dienes. Highway 101, North Hollywood November 1945 (Reproduced with permission of Chuck Murphy. One West Publishing. www.1westpublishing.com).

12: Photo by Potter Hueth, 1945 (Kim Goodwin collection).

13: Photo by Potter Hueth, 1945 (Kim Goodwin collection).

14: Photo by Andre de Dienes, 1945 (Reproduced with permission of Chuck Murphy. One West Publishing. www.1westpublishing.com).

15: Photo by Andre de Dienes, 1945 (Reproduced with permission of Chuck Murphy. One West Publishing. www.1westpublishing.com).

16: Photo by Richard C. Miller, February 1946 (Reproduced with permission of Margaret Miller).

18: Photo by Andre de Dienes. Zuma Beach, CA, 1945 (Reproduced with permission of Chuck Murphy. One West Publishing. www.1westpublishing.com).

19: Photo by Andre de Dienes. Zuma Beach, CA, 1945 (Reproduced with permission of Chuck Murphy. One West Publishing. www.1westpublishing.com).

21: Photo by Bruno Bernard / Bernard of Hollywood, 1946 (Reproduced with permission of Susan Bernard. © Bernard of Hollywood Publishing / Renaissance Road Productions, Inc. www.bernardofhollywood.com).

22: Photo by Bruno Bernard / Bernard of Hollywood, 1946 (Reproduced with permission of Susan Bernard. © Bernard of Hollywood Publishing / Renaissance Road Productions, Inc. www.bernardofhollywood.com).

23: Miscellaneous magazine covers from the collections of the author and Clark Kidder.

24: Photo by Andre de Dienes. Zuma Beach, CA, 1945 (Reproduced with permission of Chuck Murphy. One West Publishing. www.1westpublishing.com).

25: Photo by Nat Dillinger, 1946 (author's collection).

27: Photo by Richard C. Miller, February 1946 (Reproduced with kind permission of Margaret Miller).

28: Photo by John Miehle, 1946 (author's collection).

Transfiguration

30: *Ladies of the Chorus*, 1948 (author's collection).

32–33: Photo by Andre de Dienes. San Juan Capistrano, 1947 (Reproduced with permission of Chuck Murphy. One West Publishing. www.1westpublishing.com).

34: Photo by Ed Cronenweth, 1948 (author's collection).

35: With Columbia Pictures hairstylist Helen Hunt, 1948. Photo by Ed Cronenweth (The Kobal Collection).

36: Photos by Ed Cronenweth, 1948 (author's collection).

37: Photo by Laszlo Willinger, 1948 (Kim Goodwin collection).

38–39: Photo by J.R. Eyerman, 1948 (Kim Goodwin collection).

40: Photo by J.R. Eyerman, 1948 (Kim Goodwin collection).

41: LA Press Club opening, June 11, 1947. Photo by R.O. Ritchie (author's collection).

42: Photo by Laszlo Willinger, 1948 (Kim Goodwin collection).

43: Photo by Laszlo Willinger, 1948 (Kim Goodwin collection).

44: *Ladies of the Chorus*, 1948 © Columbia Pictures (author's collection).

45: *Ladies of the Chorus*, 1948 (The Kobal Collection / Columbia Pictures).

46: Photo by Andre de Dienes. Tobay Beach, Long Island, NY, July 23, 1949 (Reproduced with permission of Chuck Murphy. One West Publishing. www.1westpublishing.com).

47: Photo by Andre de Dienes. Tobay Beach, Long Island, NY, July 23, 1949 (Reproduced with permission of Chuck Murphy. One West Publishing. www.1westpublishing.com).

49: Photo by Tom Kelley, May 28, 1949 (© Tom Kelley 1998. Reproduced with permission of Tom Kelley Jr. / Tom Kelley Studio).

50: Photo by Edward Clark, 1950 (author's collection).

51: *The Asphalt Jungle*, 1950 (author's collection).

52: Photo by Phil Burchman, 1951 (author's collection).

53: Photo by Joseph Hepner, 1950 (author's collection).

54–55: 1951 (author's collection).

57: *Love Nest*, 1951 (author's collection).

58 (left): With Chicago White Sox outfielder, Gus Zernial. Photo by Larry Barbier Jr., 1951 (author's collection).

58 (right): Photo by Larry Barbier Jr., 1951 (author's collection).

59: *Clash by Night*, 1952 with Keith Andes (The Kobal Collection / RKO Pictures).

60–61: Photo by John Florea, 1951 (Reproduced with permission of Melanie and Gwen Florea).

62: *Don't Bother to Knock*, 1952 (Kim Goodwin collection).

63: Presenting an Oscar to Thomas Moulton at the 1951 Academy Awards for Achievement in Sound Recording for *All About Eve*. Photo by Phil Burchman (Kim Goodwin collection).

64–65: Photo by Bruno Bernard / Bernard of Hollywood, 1951 (Reproduced with permission of Susan Bernard. © Bernard of Hollywood Publishing / Renaissance Road Productions, Inc. www.bernardofhollywood.com).

66–67: *Let's Make It Legal*, 1951 (author's collection).

68–69: Photo by John Florea, 1951 (Reproduced with permission of Melanie and Gwen Florea).

Sirius

70: Photo by Gene Kornman, 1952 (author's collection).

73: Photo by Gene Kornman, 1952 (author's collection).

74–75: Grand Marshal of the Miss America pageant. Atlantic City, New Jersey, September 2, 1952 (Sabin Gray collection).

76: Photo by Ernest Bachrach, 1952 (author's collection).

78: *Niagara*, 1953 © 20th Century Fox Film Corporation (author's collection).

79: *Niagara* costume test, 1953 (author's collection).

80: *Niagara*, 1953 (author's collection).

81: *Niagara*, 1953 (author's collection).

83: Photo by Frank Powolny, 1953 (The Kobal Collection).

84–85: 1952 (Sabin Gray collection).

87: *Gentlemen Prefer Blondes*, 1953. Photo by Frank Powolny (Kim Goodwin collection).

88: Rehearsing with Gwen Verdon. *Gentlemen Prefer Blondes*, 1953. Photo by Edward Clark (Time & Life Pictures / Getty Images).

89: Benefit for St. Jude Children's Research Hospital in Memphis, TN. Hollywood Bowl, July 1953. Photo by Darlene Hammond (Kim Goodwin collection).

90: With Jane Russell. *Gentlemen Prefer Blondes*, 1953 (author's collection).

91: *Gentlemen Prefer Blondes*, 1953 (author's collection).

92–93: "Diamonds Are a Girl's Best Friend," *Gentlemen Prefer Blondes*, 1953 (author's collection).

93: "Diamonds Are a Girl's Best Friend," *Gentlemen Prefer Blondes*, 1953 © 20th Century Fox Film Corporation (author's collection).

95: With Nancy and Ronald Reagan at Charles Coburn's birthday party. June 17, 1953 (author's collection).

96: Photo by Frank Powolny, 1953 (author's collection).

97: Photo by Frank Powolny, 1953 (Ernie Garcia collection).

98–99: Photograph by Mischa Pelz, courtesy of Andrew Strauss.

100: Miscellaneous magazine covers from the collections of the author and Clark Kidder.

101: Photo by John Florea, 1953 (Reproduced with permission of Melanie and Gwen Florea).

103: 1953 (author's collection).

104: Photo by Nick de Morgoli, 1953 (author's collection).

105: Photo by Bert Reisfeld, 1953 (Kim Goodwin collection).

106: *How to Marry a Millionaire*, 1953 © 20th Century Fox Film Corporation (author's collection).

107: With Lauren Bacall and Betty Grable in *How to Marry a Millionaire*, 1953 (author's collection).

108: *How to Marry a Millionaire*, 1953 (author's collection).

109: *How to Marry a Millionaire*, 1953 (author's collection).

110–111: With David Wayne in *How to Marry a Millionaire*, 1953 (The Kobal Collection / 20th Century Fox Film Corporation).

113: Photo by Gene Trindl, 1953 (author's collection).

114: Photo by Sam Shaw, 1953 (© Sam Shaw Inc., Licensed by Shaw Family Archives, Ltd.).

116–117: With John Florea and Gladys Rasmussen, 1953. Photo by Gene Trindl (Kim Goodwin collection).

118–119: Photo by Bert Reisfeld, 1953 (Kim Goodwin collection).

120–121: With Lauren Bacall and Humphrey Bogart at the premiere of *How to Marry a Millionaire*. Fox Wilshire Theatre, November 4, 1953 (author's collection).

122: Premiere of *How to Marry a Millionaire*. Fox Wilshire Theatre, November 4, 1953 (author's collection).

124–125: With Joe DiMaggio, 1953 (Kim Goodwin collection).

127: Photo by Bert Reisfeld, 1953 (The Kobal Collection).

128–129: With Walter Winchell at a benefit for the Damon Runyon Cancer Fund. Ciro's, October 1953 (author's collection).

131: With Alan Ladd at the Photoplay awards to receive "Best Actress" for her roles in *Gentlemen Prefer Blondes* and *How to Marry a Millionaire*. March 8, 1954 (author's collection).

132: With Rory Calhoun in *River of No Return*, 1954 (The Kobal Collection / 20th Century Fox Film Corporation).

133: "After You Get What You Want You Don't Want It", *There's No Business Like Show Business*, 1954 (The Kobal Collection / 20th Century Fox Film Corporation).

134: Korea, February 1954 (author's collection).

135: Korea, February 1954 (author's collection).

136–137: Korea, February 18, 1954 (author's collection).

138–139: Photo by Bob Beerman, 1953 (author's collection).

140–141: With Tom Ewell in *The Seven Year Itch*, 1955. Photo by Frank Powolny (Kim Goodwin collection).

142–143: With Tom Ewell in *The Seven Year Itch*, 1955. Photo by Sam Shaw (© Sam Shaw Inc., Licensed by Shaw Family Archives, Ltd.).

143: *The Seven Year Itch*, 1955. Photo by Sam Shaw (© Sam Shaw Inc., Licensed by Shaw Family Archives, Ltd.).

144–145: With Tom Ewell in *The Seven Year Itch*, 1955 (author's collection).

146: *The Seven Year Itch*, 1955. Photo by Sam Shaw (© Sam Shaw Inc., Licensed by Shaw Family Archives, Ltd.).

147: With Tom Ewell in *The Seven Year Itch*, 1955. Photo by Sam Shaw (© Sam Shaw Inc., Licensed by Shaw Family Archives, Ltd.).

148: *The Seven Year Itch*, 1955. Photo by Sam Shaw (© Sam Shaw Inc., Licensed by Shaw Family Archives, Ltd.).

150: With Tom Ewell in *The Seven Year Itch*, 1955. Photo by Sam Shaw (© Sam Shaw Inc., Licensed by Shaw Family Archives, Ltd.).

150–151: With Tom Ewell in *The Seven Year Itch*, 1955. Photo by Sam Shaw (The Kobal Collection / 20th Century Fox Film Corporation).

152: *The Seven Year Itch*, 1955 (Kim Goodwin collection).

153: *The Seven Year Itch*, 1955. Photo by Kas Heppner (author's collection).

154–155: *The Seven Year Itch*, 1955. Photo by Frank Powolny (Kim Goodwin collection).

156–157: With Tom Ewell in *The Seven Year Itch*, 1955. Photo by Frank Powolny (author's collection).

158–159: *The Seven Year Itch*, 1955. Photo by Sam Shaw (© Sam Shaw Inc., Licensed by Shaw Family Archives, Ltd.).

Renaissance

160: 1956 (author's collection).

162–163: Photo by Ed Feingersh. Ambassador Hotel, New York City, March 1955 (Getty Images).

165: With Marlon Brando prior to attending the premiere of *The Rose Tattoo*, a special screening to raise money for The Actors Studio. December 12, 1955. Photo by Milton H. Greene (© 2011 Joshua Greene. www.archiveimages.com).

166: Photos by Cecil Beaton, 1956 (Courtesy of the Cecil Beaton Studio Archive at Sotheby's).

168: Photo by Cecil Beaton, 1956 (Courtesy of the Cecil Beaton Studio Archive at Sotheby's).

170–171: 1956. Photo by Milton H. Greene (© 2011 Joshua Greene. www.archiveimages.com).

172–173: Photo by Cecil Beaton, 1956 (Courtesy of the Cecil Beaton Studio Archive at Sotheby's).

174–175: *Bus Stop*, 1956. Photo by Arthur Zinn (© Arthur Zinn / The Image Works).

176: *Bus Stop*, 1956 (author's collection).

177: *Bus Stop*, 1956 (author's collection).

178–179: With Joshua Greene on the set of *Bus Stop*, 1956. Photo by Milton H. Greene (© 2011 Joshua Greene. www.archiveimages.com).

180–181: 1956. Photo by Milton H. Greene (© 2011 Joshua Greene. www.archiveimages.com).

183: Meeting Queen Elizabeth II at The Royal Film Performance. The Empire Theatre, London, October 29, 1956 (author's collection).

184: *The Prince and the Showgirl*, 1957. Photo by Milton H. Greene (© 2011 Joshua Greene. www.archiveimages.com).

185: *The Prince and the Showgirl*, 1957 © Warner Bros. (author's collection).

186–187: With Arthur Miller. Connecticut, 1957. Photo by Sam Shaw (Reproduced with kind permission of Shaw Family Archives. www.samshaw.com).

189: Marilyn Monroe, actor, New York, May 6, 1957. Photograph by Richard Avedon. © The Richard Avedon Foundation.

190–191: Marilyn Monroe as Theda Bara, New York, May 27, 1958. Photograph by Richard Avedon. © The Richard Avedon Foundation.

192–193: Marilyn Monroe, actor, New York, May 6, 1957. Photograph by Richard Avedon. © The Richard Avedon Foundation.

194–195: New York City, June 12, 1957. Photo by Sam Shaw (Reproduced with kind permission of Shaw Family Archives. www.samshaw.com).

197: Marilyn Monroe, actor, New York, June 1958. Photograph by Richard Avedon. © The Richard Avedon Foundation.

198–199: *Some Like It Hot*, 1959 (author's collection).

200: *Some Like It Hot*, 1959 (author's collection).

201: With Tony Curtis and Jack Lemmon in *Some Like It Hot*, 1959 (The Kobal Collection / United Artists).

202–203: With Jack Lemmon in *Some Like It Hot*, 1959 (The Kobal Collection / United Artists).

204: With Tony Curtis in *Some Like It Hot*, 1959 (The Kobal Collection / United Artists).

205: *Some Like It Hot*, 1959 (The Kobal Collection / United Artists).

207: *Some Like It Hot*, 1959. Photo by Richard C. Miller (Reproduced with permission of Margaret Miller).

208: With Tony Curtis in *Some Like It Hot*, 1959 (author's collection).

209: *Some Like It Hot*, 1959 (© 2000 Marilyn by Moonlight).

210–211: Premiere of *Some Like It Hot*. Lowe's Capitol Theatre, Times Square, New York City, March 29, 1959 (author's collection).

213: Marilyn Monroe, actor, New York, April 2, 1959. Photograph by Richard Avedon. © The Richard Avedon Foundation.

214: "My Heart Belongs to Daddy", *Let's Make Love*, 1960 (author's collection).

215: *Let's Make Love*, 1960 (author's collection).

216–217: With John Huston on the set of *The Misfits*. Reno, NV, 1960 (author's collection).

218: *The Misfits*. Reno, NV, 1960. Photo by Inge Morath (author's collection).

220–221: With (l-r) Eli Wallach, Clark Gable, Montgomery Clift and Arthur Miller on the set of *The Misfits*. Reno, NV, 1960. Photo by Elliott Erwitt (© Elliott Erwitt / Magnum Photos).

222: With Arthur Miller on the set of *The Misfits*. Reno, NV, 1960 (The Kobal Collection / United Artists).

223: With (clockwise) Montgomery Clift, Eli Wallach, Arthur Miller, John Huston, and Clark Gable on the set of *The Misfits*. Reno, NV, 1960. Photo by Elliott Erwitt (The Kobal Collection / United Artists).

225: *The Misfits*. Reno, NV, 1960 (Kim Goodwin collection).

226: With Clark Gable on the set of *The Misfits*. Reno, NV, 1960 (author's collection).

227: With Clark Gable on the set of *The Misfits*. Reno, NV, 1960 (author's collection).

228–229: *The Misfits*. Reno, NV, 1960 (author's collection).

Icarus

230: *Something's Got to Give*, 1962 (author's collection).

232–233: Photo by Eric Skipsey. © 1978 Eric Skipsey (mptvimages.com).

234–235: Miami International Airport, February 21, 1962. Photos by Bob East (author's collection).

236: National Institute for the Protection of Children. Mexico City, February, 1962 (author's collection).

237: Press Conference. Continental Hilton Hotel, Mexico City, February 26, 1962 (author's collection).

238–239: Photo by Douglas Kirkland. © Douglas Kirkland 1961. Reproduced with permission.

241: With José Bolaños at Golden Globes to receive award for "Female World Film Favorite—1961." Beverly Hilton Hotel, March 4, 1962 (author's collection).

242: Golden Globe Awards, Beverly Hilton Hotel, March 4, 1962 (author's collection).

243: Golden Globe Awards, Beverly Hilton Hotel, March 4, 1962 © 1978 Bernie Abramson (mptvimages.com).

245: *Something's Got to Give* costume test, April 10, 1962 (author's collection).

246: *Something's Got to Give* costume test, April 10, 1962 (author's collection).

247: *Something's Got to Give* costume test, April 10, 1962 © 20th Century Fox Film Corporation (author's collection).

248: *Something's Got to Give* costume test, April 10, 1962 (author's collection).

249: *Something's Got to Give* costume test, April 10, 1962 (author's collection).

250: *Something's Got to Give*, 1962. Photo by James Mitchell (author's collection).

251: *Something's Got to Give*, 1962. Photos by James Mitchell (author's collection).

253: *Something's Got to Give*, 1962. Photo by James Mitchell (author's collection).

254: With Evelyn Moriarty on the set of *Something's Got to Give*, 1962. Photo by James Mitchell (author's collection).

255: *Something's Got to Give*, 1962 © 20th Century Fox Film Corporation (author's collection).

256: Arriving at Madison Square Garden to sing "Happy Birthday" to President Kennedy, New York City, May 19, 1962 (author's collection).

257: With press agent Pat Newcomb and unidentified man. Madison Square Garden, New York City, May 19, 1962 (author's collection).

258: Madison Square Garden, New York City, May 19, 1962. Photo by Irving Steinberg. Reproduced with permission (Copyright and collection of Keya Morgan—Lincolnimages.com).

260–261: Singing "Happy Birthday" to President Kennedy. New York City, May 19, 1962 (author's collection).

262: *Something's Got to Give*. June 1, 1962. Photo by Don Ornitz (author's collection).

263: With Albie Pearson at muscular dystrophy benefit. Dodger Stadium, Los Angeles, June 1, 1962 (author's collection).

264: Celebrating her thirty-sixth birthday on the set of *Something's Got to Give*. June 1, 1962. Photo by James Mitchell (author's collection).

266–267: *Something's Got to Give*. May 23, 1962. Photo by James Mitchell (Kim Goodwin collection).

268–269: Photo by George Barris, 1962 (Reproduced with permission of Chuck Murphy. One West Publishing. www.1westpublishing.com).

271: Photo by George Barris, 1962 (Reproduced with permission of Chuck Murphy. One West Publishing. www.1westpublishing.com).

272–273: Beverly Hills, 1962. Photo by Willy Rizzo. © 2011 Willy Rizzo.

275: Beverly Hills, 1962. Photo by Willy Rizzo. © 2011 Willy Rizzo.

Back Cover

Photo by Andre de Dienes. Highway 101, North Hollywood November 1945 (Reproduced with permission of Chuck Murphy. One West Publishing. www.1westpublishing.com).

Excerpt from "The Road" (1967) by J. R. R. Tolkien. Reprinted by permission of HarperCollins Publishers Ltd. © The J. R. R. Tolkien Estate, 2010.

Marilyn Lets Her Hair Down About Being Famous. Interview by Richard Meryman. Originally published in *Life* magazine, August 3, 1962. Copyright 1962 The Picture Collection Inc. Reprinted with permission. All rights reserved.

ACKNOWLEDGMENTS

Russell Adams, Jack Allen, George Barris, Charles Casillo, David Conover Jr., David Croland, Ernest Cunningham, Trevor Daley, Susan Davis, Shirley de Dienes, Lauretta Dives, Michael Epstein, Laura Ex, Paul Faherty, Gwen Florea, Melanie Florea, Jose Fuentes, Philippe Garner, Sabin Gray, Chris Green, Brittany Hamblin, James Haspiel, Moira Heffernan, Andrew Howick, Ron Hussey, Independent Visions, Jamie Kabler, Dave Kent, Clark Kidder, Glenn Kawahara, Tom Kelley Jr., Douglas Kirkland, Françoise Kirkland, Susan Kosko, Lisa Lavender, Gail Levin, Joanna Ling, Neeraja Lockart, Judy Lusk, Anna Macri, Howard Mandelbaum, Katherine Marshall, James Martin, Carmen Martinez, Jeffrey McCall, Margaret Miller, Keya Morgan, Christopher Nesbit, Julie Newmar, Mauricio Padilha, Roger Padilha, Francisco Platt, James Penrod, Dominique Rizzo, Willy Rizzo, Paul Roth, Lawrence Schiller, Greg Schreiner, Scott Schwimer, Edie Shaw Marcus, Meta Shaw Stevens, Peter Sherrott, Michael Shulman, Ramona Sliva, Deborah Spielman, Melissa Stevens, Suzette Toledano Becker, Victory Tischler-Blue, Adam Tolkien, Sabrina Tomasi, Isabel Torres, Miyuki Tsushima, Holman Turner, George Tyler, Jamie Vuignier, Veruschka, Trish Whittaker, Fay Wills, Ralph Wills, George Zimbel, George Zeno.

David Wills and Stephen Schmidt would like to give special thanks to Calvert Morgan and Carrie Kania at HarperCollins Publishers, Stan Corwin, Kim Goodwin, Danniel Rangel, Susan Bernard, Joshua Greene, Evan Macdonald, Chuck Murphy, and Michelle Franco at The Richard Avedon Foundation.

REFERENCES

All About Bette: Her Life From A To Z, Randall Riese. Contemporary Books, Inc. Chicago, 1993.
A Third Face, Samuel Fuller. Applause. New York, 2002.
Bernard of Hollywood's Marilyn, Susan Bernard. St. Martin's Press. New York, 1993.
Lemmon: A Biography, Don Widener. Macmillan Publishing Co., Inc. New York, 1975.
Marilyn and Me, Susan Strasberg. Warner Books. New York, 1992.
Marilyn at Twentieth Century-Fox, Lawrence Crown. Smithmark Publishers. New York, 1990.
The Marilyn Encyclopedia, Adam Victor. The Overlook Press. Woodstock, New York, 1999.
Marilyn Monroe: A Composite View, Edward Wagenknecht. Chilton Book Company. Philadelphia, 1969.
Marilyn Monroe: A Life of the Actress, Carl E. Rollyson Jr. New English Library. Hodder and Stoughton. London, 1990.
Marilyn Monroe: The Biography, Donald Spoto. Harper Collins Publishers. New York, 1993.
Marilyn Monroe Uncovers, Clark Kidder and Madison Daniels. Quon Editions. Edmonton, Alberta, Canada, 1994.
Marilyn: The Last Take, Peter Harry Brown and Patte B. Barham. Dutton. New York, 1992.
Norma Jeane: The Life and Death of Marilyn Monroe, Fred Lawrence Guiles. Grafton Books. London, 1986.
The Ultimate Marilyn, Ernest W. Cunningham. Renaissance Books. Los Angeles, 1998.
The Unabridged Marilyn: Her Life from A to Z, Randall Riese and Neal Hitchens. Congdon & Weed, Inc. New York, 1987.
Vanity Will Get You Somewhere, Joseph Cotten. Mercury House, Inc. San Francisco, 1987.
"A Long Last Talk with a Lonely Girl," Richard Meryman. *Life*. Time Inc. New York, August 17, 1962. Pages 32–33.
"Hit by a Bombshell," Bill Shaikin. Albie Pearson Interview. *Los Angeles Times*. www.articles.latimes.com. December 14, 1997.
"Marilyn Lets Her Hair Down about Being Famous." *Life*. Time Inc. New York, August 3, 1962. Pages 31–38.
"Marilyn Monroe's Last Picture Show," Walter Bernstein. *Esquire*. Hearst Corporation. New York, July 1973. Pages 104–108, 173–178.
"Tribute to Marilyn from a Friend," Carl Sandburg. *Life*. Time Inc. New York, September 11, 1962. Pages 90–94.
Eve and Marilyn. Eve Arnold Interview. BBC. London, 1991. 30 mins.
Making The Misfits. Great Performances. Producer: Gail Levin. PBS, 2002. 55 mins.
Marilyn Monroe: Still Life. American Masters. Producer: Gail Levin. PBS, 2006. 90 mins.
Private Screenings. Lauren Bacall interview. Turner Movie Classics. USA, 2005. 50 minutes.
Private Screenings. Robert Mitchum and Jane Russell interview. Turner Movie Classics. USA, 1996. 50 minutes.
"Brigitte Bardot about Marilyn Monroe." www.youtube.com. 2:28 mins.
"Brigitte Bardot Talks about Marilyn Monroe." www.youtube.com. 1:15 mins.

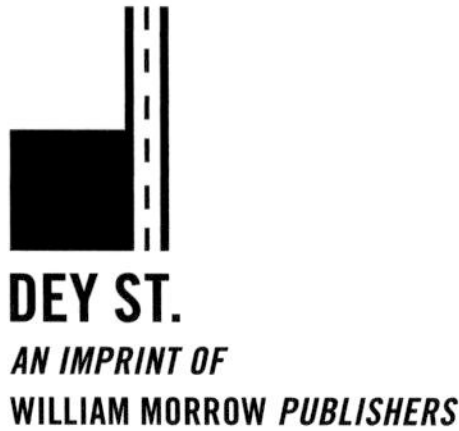

DEY ST.
AN IMPRINT OF
WILLIAM MORROW *PUBLISHERS*

HarperCollins books may be purchased for educational, business, or sales promotional use. For information please e-mail the Special Markets Department at SPsales@harpercollins.com.

Designed by Stephen Schmidt and David Wills

Library of Congress Cataloging-in-Publication Data has been applied for.

ISBN 978-0-06-203619-3

21 SCP 11

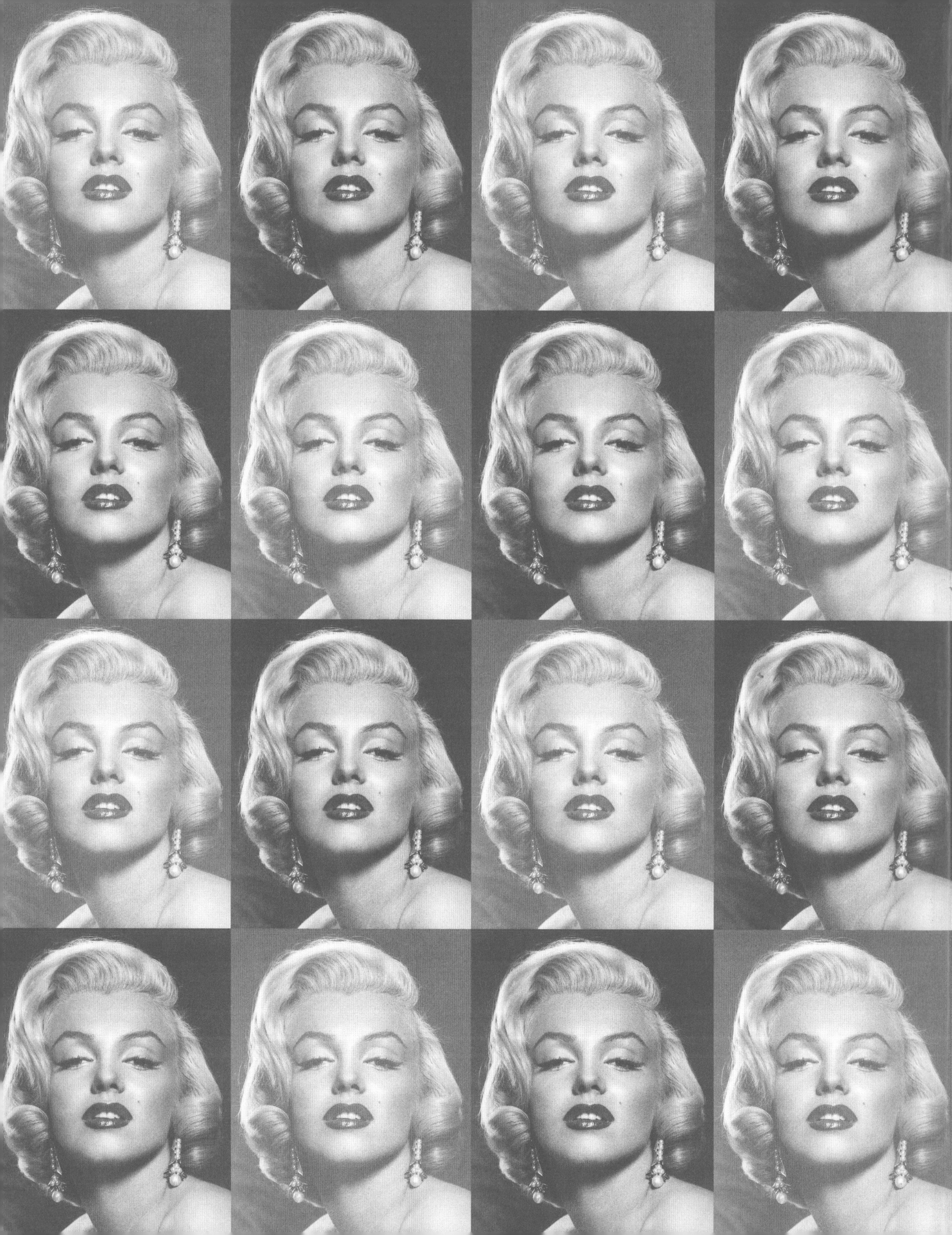